HyperTalk 2.0 The Book

HyperTalk 2.0 The Book

Dan Winkler and Scot Kamins

Foreword by Bill Atkinson

BANTAM BOOKS

NEW YORK · TORONTO · LONDON · SYDNEY · AUCKLAND

HYPERTALK 2.0: THE BOOK
A Bantam Book/August 1990

Bantam Books gratefully acknowledges Apple Computer, Inc.
for material included in Chapter 15, "Translators."

ISBN 0-553-34737-3

Bantam Books are published by Bantam Books, a division of Bantam
Doubleday Dell Publishing Group, Inc. Its trademark, consisting of the
words "Bantam Books" and the portrayal of a rooster, is Registered in U.S.
Patent and Trademark Office and in other countries. Marca Registrada,
Bantam Books, 666 Fifth Avenue, New York, New York 10103

PRINTED IN THE UNITED STATES OF AMERICA

0 9 8 7 6 5 4 3 2 1

———

The finer parts of this book are dedicated to

Bill Atkinson

Dan Winkler's friend and partner; and to

Ed Kammerer

Scot Kamins' friend and first computer mentor

———

Foreword

by Bill Atkinson

I have fond memories of the year that Dan Winkler spent six days a week, working very long hours over at my house to create the original HyperTalk language. In my mind I picture him hunched over and concentrating on the screen of a prototype Mac II, then known as a Reno, as our cat Sarah sat on his lap and drooled every time he pet her. Sometimes I picture him sitting in the big sofa chair in the corner, playing the guitar while he pondered a tough design problem, and sometimes I picture him discussing the syntax for a new command and how to present it in the simplest and clearest manner. I think of Dan with my daughter Laura and appreciate his warmth and playfulness. It was a fun and exciting time working together with Dan, and a privilege to share his company. I want to acknowledge Dan as a person with great sensitivity, passion, and determination.

I also want to acknowledge Dan for what he has accomplished with his work. Hundreds of thousands of people around the world who never used any other computer language before have found they can create useful scripts with HyperTalk, and customize their computers to do what they want them to. What Dan has created with HyperTalk has liberated programming from the priesthood of nerds and made it accessible to the lay person.

HyperTalk 2.0: The Book is the most complete and correct source of information on HyperTalk available anywhere. It contains valuable insights and details that only the author of the language could know. It's like having Dan's home phone number, except even better because Dan isn't always home. This book tells the truth, even when that means revealing bugs. It tells you what you need to know to get the job done.

This book is accessible. It makes it easy to find the information you need when you have a question. It's heavily cross-referenced, so you can jump in anywhere and quickly find all the related details. And it's written in Scot's clear, direct prose, which anyone can understand.

This book offers unusually well-written sample scripts that provide clean solutions to many common tasks, and also teach good programming style by example. Dan's scripts work well and are a pleasure to read. This is the book that any serious HyperTalk scripter will want to have by his side when he's at work.

This book comes out of Dan's passion and commitment to make tools that empower people to accomplish what they're up to, and let them have fun in the process. He has succeeded in a big way by putting a piece of himself into every HyperCard stack and into this book. I hope you enjoy it.

Bill Atkinson
Menlo Park, California
April 28, 1990

Acknowledgments

Besides the people whose names appear on the cover, nearly two dozen people contributed their time, effort, and creativity to the development of this book. Without their comments and suggestions, this book would have ended up in a lot worse shape. No kidding.

Alan Spragens, senior writer at Apple and author of Apple's *HyperTalk Script Language Guide*, was the real author of much of Chapter 15, "Translators"; we just edited his work a little. He also helped us straighten out the information about message passing.

Clay Nixon, Louisville's finest cinematographer, reviewed the manuscript from the point of view of the newer scripter. He managed to find several hundred ways to say "What are you people talking about?" without repeating himself once. His help was absolutely invaluable.

Gary ("XCMDs-R-Us") **Bond**, an engineer on the HyperCard Test Team and a fine writer to boot, wrote a bunch of creative examples for the book when we ran dry. In addition, he scrupulously read the manuscript from the point of view of the advanced scripter and already-expert on HyperTalk. While he found just one way to say "You call this quality work?," he repeated it enough times so that we finally started to listen to him. Anything in the text that's useful for advanced scripters was made more useful by his comments and suggestions.

Steven Smith, Real Live Developer and partner at San Francisco's CommuniTree Group, read the manuscript from the point of view of the developer. His suggestions for rearranging and adding material made the book three pounds heavier, and we've got a far better work for it.

Bennet Marks, another member of the HyperCard Development Team at Apple, read the manuscript from the point of view of a professional programmer who wanted to learn HyperTalk. He insisted on better examples; we hope we came through for him.

Scott Bongiorno, HyperCard testing engineer at Apple, made excellent suggestions for changing the way some of the material was phrased and spotted many areas that needed clarification.

Robin Shank, yet another HyperCard testing engineer and windoid washer at Apple, contributed a number of examples and gave us extremely valuable feedback on the major reference chapters.

Tim Pozar, resident C programmer and source of the most technical data imaginable at San Francisco's Late Night Software, provided the information we needed to see how buggy the Dial command really is.

James Francis Redfern, still another HyperCard testing engineer at Apple, provided arcane information about the file system and about some amusing HyperTalk anomalies, tried to crash our externals, and participated in a number of brainstorming sessions that formed the basis of the more advanced material in the book.

Dr. Jerome Coonen of Apple Computer, a member of the original Macintosh Development team, told us why midnight, January 1, 1904, was chosen as the Beginning of Time in the mind of the Macintosh.

Paul Finlayson, engineer with the SANE (Standard Apple Numerics Environment) Group at Apple Computer, showed us how LN1 and EXP1 are used to calculate compound interest.

Ed Kammerer, cosmic hacker of the Great NorthWest and the man most responsible for turning Scot Kamins into a computer nerd, reminded us to remember the art of Ralph Steadman.

Scott Knaster, whose name needs no comma-separated explanation, almost bought the pizza once.

Additional feedback, comments, encouragement, and suggestions also came from: Sedge Bekkala, Parry Forcier, Carol R. Frenier, Robert C. Frenier, Martin Gannholm, Dean Gengle, Amanda Goodenough, Chris Crawford, Sioux Lacy, David Leffler, Steve Maller, Michelle McCoskey, Ron Metzker, Doris Mitsch, Tim Oren, and Giovanni Paoletti.

Dan Winkler wants especially to thank the people who laid the foundation for HyperTalk before he even joined the HyperCard team. At Apple Computer, those folks include **Bill Atkinson, Ted Kaehler, Dan Ingalls,** and **Alan Kay.** And Outside of Apple, the major influencers were **Eric Roberts** and **Greg Nelson,** who invented the recursive descent operator precedence expression parser that HyperTalk uses to parse expressions. (Dan learned of this algorithm in Computer Science 163 taught by Eric Roberts at Harvard in the spring of 1985.)

And finally, to quote Dan's advisor at Harvard, Harry R. Lewis, from his book *An Introduction to Computer Programming and Data Structures Using MACRO-11* (Reston Publishing Company, 1981):

" ...to the others, not mentioned here by name, [we] apologize for [our] ignorance of their contributions."

Contents

CONTENTS

CONTENTS

Part One Elementary Material

Chapter 0

Rationales, Histories, and Guides

This chapter provides a frame of reference
for using this book. It tells why this book
was written, gives some historical perspectives on the development of the HyperTalk
language, tells what's where in the book,
and makes suggestions about how to get
the most out of your reading.

This book is the definitive reference guide to the HyperTalk programming language. It provides information unavailable elsewhere, even in the official
HyperCard publications designed and published by Apple Computer Inc.

We know the language better than anyone else because one of us (Dan
Winkler) designed and wrote it, and the other one of us (Scot Kamins) cajoled,
tormented, praised, beat up, and manipulated his partner until he (Winkler)
gave up all the secrets of the language — even the ones that hurt.

So this book tells what HyperTalk does. It also tells what it's supposed to do,
but it emphasizes what it *does*. And it reveals where the sore points are, the bugs
and glitches in the language — the anomalies that bite you on the backside when
you least expect it.

In short, it tells the truth.

HOW THIS BOOK CAME TO BE WRITTEN

We wrote this book because somebody had to. While books about HyperTalk
abound, none contains the whole truth. Most have factual errors; some miss the

point of how the language works; none gives a clear portrayal of where the holes are; and certainly, none is complete.

Apple's HyperCard Script Language Guide comes close to being complete for most early versions. Its unsung author, Alan Spragens, did a remarkable job collecting information for that book while HyperCard was nearing release — a period of turmoil that was frenetic even by Apple's hurricane standards. But even Spragens' incredible integrity and dedication to excellence couldn't totally overcome the obstacles of unavailable engineers and the madness of impossible schedules.

Then too, that book didn't have the advantage of time. HyperCard has been out for nearly three years as of this writing — enough time for both the opulence and the poverty of HyperTalk to emerge.

A Monastery of Scripters

Actually, in the early days preceding the release of HyperCard, few members of the HyperCard Development Team thought that extensive language documentation would be necessary. The primary purpose of HyperTalk was to allow stacks to contain intelligence in the form of scripts. The original idea was to allow non-programmers to move that intelligence around by cutting and pasting prescripted buttons. We (the members of the original HyperCard development team) thought that most people who wanted to create their own stacks would copy the models we gave them — either they'd modify the stacks that came with HyperCard, or they'd make new creations by raiding those stacks for prescripted buttons.

We also believed that, at the most, 25 percent of the people who used HyperCard would also want to write scripts for it.

We seriously underestimated the numbers.

THE INTENDED AUDIENCE FOR THIS BOOK

Time and the experience of 20-20 hindsight have shown that the original thinking about who would want to learn scripting was pretty far off. It's hard to come up with real numbers, but it looks like at least 40 percent of HyperCardiacs — nearly twice the original estimate — are doing their own scripting; and a sizable percentage of that group wants highly detailed information about every aspect of the language.

What happened to In-Box HyperTalk documentation?

Several powerful members of the HyperCard development team originally estimated that 50 percent of nonprogrammers would use the stacks as they came from Apple or from other developers, making only minor modifications; another 25 or 30 percent would create their own stacks from scratch doing just a little scripting; and the remaining 20 or 25 percent would venture shyly into scriptwriting.

(Several members of the team objected to these estimates, insisting that a far greater percentage of people would quickly move into scripting. These objections, however, were — umm — overcome.)

Because of these estimates, plus the rising cost of what was to be essentially a free product, little HyperTalk documentation was packaged with the product. The argument was that the small percentage of people who would want to learn scripting in detail could get the information they needed from the on-line documentation, from studying the scripts of included stacks, or from the purchase of outside documentation. Yeah, well....

This book is aimed at scripters with a variety of expertise. The lowest level we wrote for are those folks who have been scripting for at least a couple of months or who have extensive experience in at least one programming language (even BASIC); at the other end, we aim at hard-core programmers — those folks who write in Pascal, C, or assembler and who want to take HyperTalk far beyond its original limits.

We originally designed this book for advanced scripters who had already mastered the fundamentals of computer programming in general and HyperTalk in particular. But the paucity of good material available even at this late date for intermediate scripters, strong feedback from early reviewers, and the powerful urgings of newer scripters — especially from Clay Nixon, a remarkable cinematographer from the wilds of Louisville — convinced us to change the direction of this book to include a broader audience.

Still, even though HyperTalk has been designed to be the Language for The Rest of Us, this book is decidedly *not* a tutorial. If you're new to HyperCard, we suggest you read Danny Goodman's *The Complete HyperCard Handbook* from Bantam Books, an excellent preparation for this book and a fine introduction to HyperCard. New scripters might want to use *Cooking with HyperTalk 2.0* by Dan Winkler and Scott Knaster (Bantam, 1990) before tackling *The Book*.

WHAT'S WHERE IN THIS BOOK

This book is designed such that the farther you read in its main chapters, the more sophisticated the material becomes: material for newer scripters comes early on, with the most arcane material left for the later chapters.

The book is broken into four major sections. Part I, "Elementary Material," is made up of Chapters 1 and 2; you need to have these chapters down cold before you get serious about scripting. Part II, "Formal Reference," consists of Chapters 3 through 12; you'll refer to this material on a daily basis. Part III, "Advanced Material," is Chapters 13 through 15; it deals with everything you'll need to write externals, and translators, HyperTalk's most advanced features. Part IV, "Appendixes," is a collection of summaries (in the form of appendixes) that you're likely to thumb through often.

Here are the details on a chapter-by-chapter basis:

Chapter 0, "Rationales, Histories, and Guides," is the one you're reading now. It tells why this book was written, gives some historical perspectives on the development of the language, outlines the book, and makes suggestions about how to get the most out of your reading.

Part I: Elementary Material

Chapter 1, "Basics," deals with the three fundamental elements of HyperTalk — messages, handlers, and the message passing path. These three elements are intricately interwoven; it's impossible to understand any one of them completely without understanding the other two. Even if you think you know how HyperTalk works, read this chapter anyway. You'd be surprised...

Chapter 2, "Scripts and the Script Editor," describes the structure of a script as it appears in the script editor. It includes information on how to bring a script into the script editor, and what you can do to a script once the editor is operating. This chapter also covers how to break a long line into more manageable parts, how to enter and use comments, how to use automatic script formatting to get an indication of whether or not your scripts are syntactically correct, and how to use the various debugging tools new for version 2.0.

Part II: Formal Reference

Chapter 3, "Syntax," presents the syntax of HyperTalk. Everyone needs to read and understand the first section, "Syntax Symbols," to understand the syntax examples used throughout this book. The second section, "Formal Syntax," is especially valuable if you're an advanced scripter who wants a more formal and precise presentation of the syntax that appears within the context of individual vocabulary words, or if you're an experienced programmer who likes BNF fomats.

Chapter 4, "Referring to Objects," describes in precise detail the often misunderstood but vital process of how to name and refer to objects. (The amount of misinformation on this subject is staggering.)

Chapter 5, "Sources of Value," defines the basic elements from which all HyperTalk expressions are constructed. It describes the sources of value common to most languages (functions, literals, constants, and variables), plus the ones that are either unique to HyperCard or uniquely implemented (properties, fields, Message box, the Selection, and chunks).

Chapter 6, "Expressions," explains how to construct arithmetic, geometric, logical, and textual expressions using operators and sources of values. It describes how to use (and override) operator precedence and discusses the important difference between factors and expressions.

Chapter 7, "Keywords," is about the special HyperTalk words around which all handlers and control structures within handlers are built. This chapter shows you how to use keywords, and has several examples that show the proper and best use for each one.

Chapter 8, "Commands," lists all HyperCard commands alphabetically with detailed information (including bugs and performance oddities) and lots and lots of examples. You'll even find descriptions of commands that are documented here for the first time anywhere.

Chapter 9, "Functions," includes descriptions in alphabetic order for all of HyperCard's built-in functions. Each function description has complete syntax and examples that show how to use that function, plus any appropriate technical notes and comments about anomalies.

Chapter 10, "Properties," describes those native vocabulary words that reflect the current state of some object's or window's attribute. Every HyperTalk property is listed in this chapter, with complete syntax and appropriate examples for each one.

Chapter 11, "System Messages," covers every message that HyperCard sends. It tells what event triggers a particular message and the meaning of any parameters to the message. When a single event elicits more than one message, the event's description includes the order in which the messages are sent. The chapter takes particular note when the message-sending order is less than intuitive.

Chapter 12, "Speed and Style Issues," is divided into three sections. The first section concentrates on how to get the most speed from a script. The second section shows how you can write your scripts so that they're orderly and easy to read (and debug) without sacrificing speed. The final section deals with the placement of handlers in the message passing path and the order of handlers within a script.

Part III: Advanced Material

Chapter 13, "Overview of Externals," covers the basic elements of XCMDs and XFCNs — resources that contain executable machine language. These external commands and functions let you expand the language by creating new commands and functions. The chapter includes five or six complete external examples.

Chapter 14, "Glue Routine Reference," lists and describes external glue routines and callbacks. Most callback explanations include sample externals, using Pascal as the example language, that show how you'd use these routines to do useful work. (So you get a library of externals as a bonus.)

Chapter 15, "Translators," (the first half of which was essentially written by Alan Spragens) describes the poorly understood translator interface, the filter that sits between the disk and the script editor and that performs transformations on script editor text. While translators are most commonly used to translate scripts from English to non-English languages, you can also use them for other tasks; this chapter shows you how to do it.

Part IV: Appendixes

Appendix A, "ASCII Chart," is a representation of the American Standard Code for Information Interchange material for the Monaco font; you'll use this chart to encode and decode information for the `numToChar` and `charToNum` functions.

Appendix B, "1.2.# Error Messages," lists the contents of 1.2.# error dialogs, tells what condition(s) in your code might have produced the error, and makes suggestions for correcting the problem where such solutions aren't obvious.

Appendix C, "Summary of Tables," is a collection of the most useful tables in the book. Tables include Script Editing Tools, Operator Precedence, Result Strings, and many others.

Appendix D, "Boundaries and Limits," lists the extremes of HyperTalk — number of characters per field, overhead for each button, variable and object name lengths, and so on.

Appendix E, "Quick Dictionary," provides a summary definition of every HyperTalk native vocabulary word, plus a reference to a page where you can find more detailed information about that word. In some cases, this appendix is the only place you can find answers to such thorny riddles as legal uses of the article "the."

Appendix F, "Vocabulary Categories," divides HyperTalk's major native vocabulary words (commands, functions, properties) into basic categories — file manipulation, mouse simulation, keyboard, fields, and so on. Each word is followed by a pointer to that word's appearance in the formal reference section.

Appendix G, "Changes for 2.0," summarizes the changes to the language made for HyperTalk version 2.0. (This appendix is gleaned from the complete discussion of changes throughout the book.)

Appendix H, "1.2.# Syntax," describes the complete syntax of all the 1.2 versions of HyperTalk. (Some developers need to be sure that all their code works in both 1.2 and 2.0.)

Appendix I, "Late Breaking News," lists additions and changes to the language made at the last minute. These additions and changes happened so late in HyperTalk 2.0's development cycle that they couldn't be included in the main body of the book.

The glossary presents definitions for the specialized scripting terms used in this book. Whenever you run across a term you don't understand, turn to the glossary.

The index is an exhaustive cross-reference to every subject in the book. Use it to find quickly and easily whatever you're looking for.

CONVENTIONS AND ASSUMPTIONS

From time to time throughout this book, two different kinds of boxes appear.

The first type is for bugs and anomalies that are likely to be fixed in future versions of the product. Bug boxes look like this:

This command blows up computer

Take particular care when you use the **destroy machine** command. We've had several reports that Undo won't work in versions through 2.0 once this command is executed. Because we've chosen not to test this command with our own equipment, we can't be sure that these reports are unfounded.

The second type is for special features, historical notes, or bonus scripts, the descriptions of which don't exactly fit in with surrounding text but that belong in the current section anyway. A feature box follows:

Previously undocumented dial feature

The following previously undocumented `Dial with <modem>` form dials the home of Dan Winkler:

```
dial "415 555 1212" with modem "ATWinkler"
```

Dan likes to write code far into the night while most people are asleep, and enjoys answering HyperTalk questions to break up the work.

We assume that the **userLevel** property is set to 5, and that the Message box is visible and/or that the **blindTyping** property is set to true.

A reference to version 1.2.# means that whatever is the subject of the reference applies to all releases of 1.2 (1.2.0, 1.2.1, … 1.2.5). Information specific to version 2.0 (and higher) is clearly noted.

Chapter 1

Basics

This chapter deals with three fundamental elements of HyperTalk — messages, handlers, and the message passing path. These three elements are intricately interwoven; it's impossible to understand any one of them completely without understanding the other two.

Even if you think you know how HyperTalk works, please read this chapter anyway. If you're impatient to get on to the more referency and "how to" sections of the book, at least read the first section, "A Frame of Reference"; it's a summary of the main points in the chapter and ties the fundamental concepts together.

A FRAME OF REFERENCE

In order to understand how HyperCard works, you must first understand about messages, handlers, and the message passing path. The challenge is that it's difficult to understand any of these concepts without understanding all three. This section provides a quick overview of all three concepts for you to keep in mind as you read this chapter. Later in this chapter, each concept is discussed on its own in greater detail.

Handlers and Messages (Briefly)

A **script** is the collection of statements associated with a particular object. An **object** is any HyperCard unit capable of sending and receiving messages. Objects include buttons, fields, cards, backgrounds, stacks, and HyperCard itself. Within a script, statements are grouped into **handlers.** An object executes the statements within one of its handlers when it receives an instruction to do so. That instruction is called a **message** (see Figure 1-1).

Handlers and messages both have names. The handler executes when the object containing it receives a message of the same name.

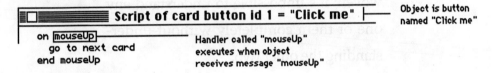

Figure 1-1 shows a handler from a script associated with a button. Statements in the handler execute in response to the message mouseUp.

Message Passing Path (Briefly)

A set of rules (or more accurately, the placement of objects) called the **message passing path** governs the order in which HyperCard objects are given the opportunity to respond to a message.

Each message has a target — the object on the message passing path that the message goes to first. If that object has a handler for the message, the statements in that handler execute. Unless explicitly passed back onto the message passing path, that message ceases to exist when that handler's statements have finished executing. If a message's target doesn't have a handler to respond to a message, the message goes to the next object down the message passing path to see if that object has a handler with a matching name, and so on.

If no handler catches it along the way, a message ends up at HyperCard itself. HyperCard sees if the message is a built-in command name: if it is, HyperCard executes that command. If the message isn't a built-in command name,

HyperCard sees if it's the name of another type of message that it knows about, called a **system message:** if so, HyperCard simply discards the message. (If a system message reaches HyperCard, it has no further use.) Finally, if the message is none of these, HyperCard assumes that it must be an error and so puts up an error dialog.

Using Message Passing (Briefly)

HyperCard provides ways to change the normal starting and ending points of the message passing path for specific messages. So a message can go on a normal path or can take a detour, depending on the situation. For example, a message caught by a handler usually dies when that handler finishes executing. But HyperCard adds life to a messsage by letting you pass that message further along the message passing path using the keyword **pass,** even though the message has been caught.

Once you become more familiar with how message passing works, you can make a single handler do the work of many handlers. For example, a mouseUp script on the card level can take you to one of any number of stacks, depending on the button you press. The key is to give each button the name of a different stack: while the scripts of those buttons are all empty, the card handler can tell the name of the button you clicked, and so bring you to the right place.

MESSAGES

A **message** is an instruction sent to an object. The sending and receiving of messages is fundamental to HyperCard. Without messages, nothing would ever happen.

Every statement in a HyperTalk script (except those that start with keywords, discussed in Chapter 7) is a message. A message is made up of the message name — always a single word — and an optional set of one or more **parameters** (a unit of data):

```
doMenu "Compact Stack" -- message name "doMenu" with parameter "Compact Stack"
mouseUp -- system message, meant to execute handler named "mouseUp"
doMyHandler -- user-defined message, looking for handler "doMyHandler"
```

(The double-dashes in each of the three lines above start **comments,** notes for people reading scripts; HyperCard ignores comments.) A message doesn't have to include parameters (as in the second and third examples); in that case, the message name alone is the message.

One message or another is always alive in the HyperCard environment. When a message is finished, the next one takes its place. A user generates messages by clicking the mouse, by moving the pointer over a button or field, or by typing something into the Message box and pressing Return (which, by the way, is why it's named the Message box). An object can generate messages in response to messages that it receives. HyperCard is always generating messages, even if the message is "nothing is happening" (the idle message).

HyperCard has four kinds of messages:

- System messages, sent by HyperCard when some event occurs in the HyperCard environment (`mouseUp` when the mouse button is released, `newCard` when a new card is created, and so on) or when nothing is happening (`idle`)

- Command messages, which are messages that HyperCard itself can respond to (`put`, `read`, `go`)

- User-defined messages, which ultimately send command messages to HyperCard (`myMessage`, `sendToDisk`, `foo`)

- Incomprehensible messages, typically misspellings or the names of messages for which responses have not yet been created. (These are the messages that make HyperCard display the dialog "Can't understand...".)

A Message's Audience

A message is in effect a general announcement to the HyperCard environment that something has happened or is about to happen. It's like a town crier, walking along town paths announcing the daily news: "The mouse button is down!" "A card is about to be deleted!" "Bring out your dead!"

All messages are at first sent to specific recipients. For example, when you click a button, you're sending a message to that button: "I just clicked you." You assume that your action will make something happen: you want the button to know that you clicked it, and you hope that the button will do something appropriate in return.

But the button — or any object — can respond to a message only if it has a set of instructions, called a **handler,** telling it what to do.

HANDLERS

A handler is a group of HyperTalk statements, and is the basic HyperTalk structure. Handlers look and act much like BASIC or assembly language subroutines, Pascal procedures, or C functions, and are designed to respond to a specific message. A message's name is the key that causes the statements in a handler to execute.

Message Handlers versus Function Handlers

HyperTalk has both message handlers and function handlers. Message handlers are meant to carry out a series of commands in order to get some larger job done. Function handlers (also called user-defined functions) are meant to return a specific value, perhaps carrying out a series of commands to calculate that value. In effect, function handlers live in service to message handlers.

The anatomies of message handlers and function handlers differ slightly: message handlers begin with the keyword **on,** while function handlers begin with the keyword **function.** In both types, the handler title (**on** or **function**) is followed by the message it responds to, plus a list of any parameters. Message handlers sometimes have parameters; function handlers often do.

Frame of reference here only

This section provides only enough information on handlers and parameter passing to provide you a frame of reference for understanding how HyperTalk works. For more details on this material, see **on** (page 142), **function** (page 128), and **parameter passing** (page 99).

Figure 1-2 shows a typical message handler. Its statements execute when an object receives the message `getTotals`.

And Figure 1-3 shows a typical function handler. It serves the message handler above, in that it returns a value for the function call `sum(field "Prices of Items")` in the third line of the message handler.

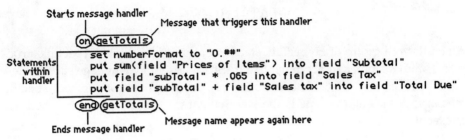

Figure 1-2   A typical message handler

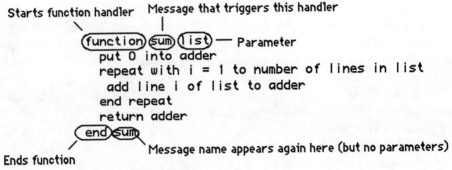

Figure 1-3   A typical function handler

In the above examples, a message handler and a function handler work together to produce a complete result — a sales report. The third line of the message handler getTotals calls the function handler sum to add up all the prices in field "Prices of items"; getTotals uses the value returned by sum to do the rest of the calculations.

When one handler invokes another handler, control returns to the calling handler when the statements in the called handler finish executing.

It's all the same to HyperCard

HyperCard uses the same internal code for function handlers and message handlers. The only real difference is the way you call them and the way that values are returned (details below). Thus you can pass parameters (also called arguments) to both kinds of handlers. For information on parameter passing, see Chapter 5, Sources of Value.

About message handlers: You invoke a handler to set off a series of events that ends up in a job getting done — going to another card, moving a graphic across the screen, locating the name and address of your dentist, and so on. You invoke a message handler by sending its name as a message, either through the Message box or through another handler:

```
on placeOrder
  getTheOrder
  getTotals -- this runs the message handler in figure 1-2
  askForMore
  showThankYou
  printReceipt
end placeOrder
```

Message handlers are discussed in detail on page 142.

About function handlers: Function handlers (discussed in detail on page 128) act in service to message handlers. The purpose of a call to a function handler is to get back a value — like you'd get an answer to a question. Function handler calls appear as expressions within a line, with their arguments within parentheses. (An **expression** is any value or any group of values, sources of value, and operators meant to be taken as a single whole.) This example is from the handler in Figure 1-2:

```
put sum(field "Prices of Items") into field "Subtotal"
```

The function handler returns a value to its caller through the **return** keyword. This example is from the function handler in Figure 1-3:

```
  return adder
```

The result of all this is that the value of `adder` ends up in field "Subtotal."

THE MESSAGE PASSING PATH

As noted earlier, the statements in a handler are executed when a message of the same name reaches the object whose script holds that handler. But HyperCard has to figure out where that handler is. The problem is that any handler can be in the script of any object. Further, several handlers with entirely different statement lists can have the same name. And depending on the object that receives a message, the same message can execute different handlers with totally different results.

So when HyperCard is trying to find a handler for a particular message, it needs a mechanism to decide (1) which object to look at first; (2) how to proceed if it can't find a handler in the first place it looks; and (3) what to do if more than one handler of the same name exists. That mechanism is the message passing path.

Getting the Message

Every message has a **target** — the object that gets the first chance to respond to that message. (The object responds by executing the statements within the handler whose name is the same as the message name, if the object has such a handler in its script.) This target object — or simply, the target — is a message's first, and perhaps only, stop on the message passing path.

For example, when you press the mouse with the pointer over a button, the target of the system message mouseDown is that button. Similarly, immediately after you create a new card, HyperCard sends the system message newCard to the newly created card — the new card is the target of the system message newCard. (Chapter 11, "System Messages", has tables that show the targets of all system messages.)

The examples in the last paragraph were both system messages — messages sent by HyperCard to announce that something had just happened. A message generated by a handler — either a command message or a user-defined message — also has a target. With the exception of messages sent with the **send** keyword (described later in this chapter), the target of a message that was sent from within an object's handler is that object itself. If the script of that object contains no handler for that message, then the message goes to the next object in the message passing path.

Passing Along the Message

The message passing path determines what happens when an object doesn't have a handler for a message it receives, or when an object's handler passes a message (using the statement pass <messageName>) — that is, hands the message to the next object on the message passing path. All messages travel through the message passing path looking for a handler to execute, starting with the script of the object that initiates the message.

A message can have both a static and a dynamic message passing path.

The static path

The static message passing path of any object is made up of the object itself plus the object(s) that contains it. A card contains fields and buttons, a background contains cards, a stack contains backgrounds, HyperCard contains stacks. The path goes in increasing order of containing unit (for example button to card, card to background, etc.) from the starting point through HyperCard, with the Home stack inserted between the current stack and HyperCard.

For example, HyperCard generates a mouseUp message (among other messages) when you click the mouse. Here's the static path for the mouseUp message if you click the mouse with the pointer over a button:

1. that button

2. the card it's on (even if it's a background button)

3. the background of that card

4. the stack of that background

5. any stacks named in the **stacksInUse** property (an advanced feature new in version 2.0, explained on page 615)

6. the Home stack

7. HyperCard itself

This doesn't mean that a message would have to go to all of these objects; rather, these are all the stops that a message would make looking for a matching handler. (And a message that starts out farther along the path — say, at the card level — wouldn't go back to a previous level; it would just go farther along.) As soon as it finds a matching handler the message stops its trip along the message passing path.

Using the mouse click as an example, here's what all that means in terms of what actually goes on:

1. HyperCard sends the message mouseUp to the button. The button checks its script to see if it has a handler called mouseUp: if it does, the handler is executed and, unless the handler contains the statement pass mouseUp, discussed later in this chapter, the message dies (and that's the end of the story); otherwise, the message goes on to #2.

2. The message mouseUp passes from the button to the current card, where HyperCard checks that card's script for a matching handler: if it's there, the statements execute (as in step 1); if not, the message goes on to step #3.

3. The message `mouseUp` passes from the card to the current background. HyperCard acts as in step 2; the message dies or moves on.

4. The message `mouseUp` passes from the background to the current stack. HyperCard acts as in step 3; the message goes the way of all flesh, or back on the trail to step 5.

5. The message `mouseUp` passes from the current stack through any stacks named by the **stacksInUse** property. Either the message is caught, or it goes on to step 6.

6. The message `mouseUp` passes to the Home stack. HyperCard acts as in step 5 and either disposes of the message or passes it to step 6.

7. The message `mouseUp` passes from the Home stack to HyperCard. HyperCard checks to see if it has a command called mouseUp: it doesn't, so the message dies. If there were a command called mouseUp, it would execute; then the message would (inevitably) die. If HyperCard doesn't recognize the message at all — as in the case of misspellings, user-defined messages that aren't caught by handlers, and other mistakes — HyperCard puts up an error dialog; and the message dies.

HyperCard's internal "send message" primitive

HyperCard has at its core a "send message" primitive. This primitive takes as its parameters a message and a starting object. In effect, it asks "What's the message, and where do I start looking for a handler to act on it?" (For example, the primitive might be `send mouseUp to button 1`.) Every message has an implied "send" before it and a "to object" after it. The destination is the target. If the target doesn't want it (that is, doesn't have a handler whose name matches the message name) the message goes to the next object in the message passing path to see if *it* wants the message ; and so it goes through the message passing path.

Points for techies: Actually, the message passing path is slightly more complex than stated earlier. It also includes the XCMDs and XFCNs of the current stack, Home stack, HyperCard, and system file (plus the XCMDs and XFCNs of any stacks that come into play if handlers go to other stacks). It looks like this:

1. button (or field)

2. the card it's on

3. the background of that card

4. the stack of that background

5. that stack's XCMDs and XFCNs

6. each stack (and accompanying XCMDs and XFCNs) named by the **stacksInUse** property.

7. the home stack

8. the home stack XCMDs and XFCNs

9. HyperCard XCMDs and XFCNs

10. system file XCMDs and XFCNs

11. HyperCard itself

XCMDs and XFCNs are explained in detail in Chapter 14.

The dynamic path

When a message goes to another card, HyperCard might check up to three additional objects for a handler that can handle subsequent message(s). These additional stops make up the dynamic path of the message — so called because the path of the message changes, depending on which card is the current one.

Here's a list of the objects on the path that such a message would follow if the message's handler were in a button (and take particular note of stops 5, 6, and 7):

1. that button

2. the card it's defined on

3. the background of that card

4. the stack of that background

5. the current card (that is, the card that was the destination of the go command)

6. the background of that card (the current background)

7. the stack of the current background (the current stack)

8. stacks in the **stacksInUse** property

9. the Home stack

10. HyperCard itself

Once again, HyperCard won't necessarily have to check every place in the path for a matching handler — if, for example, the card that the button is defined on is also the current card, HyperCard won't do steps 5, 6, and 7, because that would be redundant; the point is that this is the total path the message might have to follow.

(A stack can't pass a message to itself. So if the current stack is the stack of the object holding the currently running script and the message gets passed through the path, the current stack won't get the message again.)

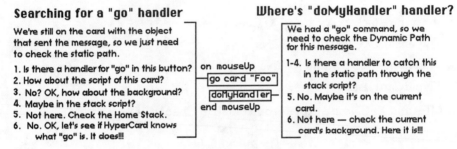

Searching for a "go" handler

We're still on the card with the object that sent the message, so we just need to check the static path.

1. Is there a handler for "go" in this button?
2. How about the script of this card?
3. No? OK, how about the background?
4. Maybe in the stack script?
5. Not here. Check the Home Stack.
6. No. OK, let's see if HyperCard knows what "go" is. It does!!!

```
on mouseUp
  go card "Foo"
  doMyHandler
end mouseUp
```

Where's "doMyHandler" handler?

We had a "go" command, so we need to check the Dynamic Path for this message.

1-4. Is there a handler to catch this in the static path through the stack script?
5. No. Maybe it's on the current card.
6. Not here — check the current card's background. Here it is!!!

Figure 1-4   Searching in the static and dynamic paths

In the example in Figure 1-4, the message go card "Foo" goes all the way to HyperCard through the static path; the message doMyHandler goes through part of the dynamic path but not all of it — its handler is in the background of the current card (different from the background of the card with the object that sent the message).

USING THE MESSAGE PASSING PATH

The basic premise of all HyperTalk programming is this: When a message is sent, a handler that you've written can catch it.

That statement goes for all kinds of messages — system, user-defined, or command. All types of messages are equal when they start out. A command message is treated no differently than is any other type of message.

For example, here's one of the most common handlers in HyperTalk:

```
on mouseUp
  go to next card
end mouseUp
```

This handler traps the message `mouseUp`, sent when the mouse button is released. When this handler is activated, it sends the command message `go`. If the `go` message gets to HyperCard, it activates the **go** command. But any object on the message passing path might have a handler for the `go` message, in which case the message never gets to HyperCard:

```
on go
   otherResponse -- sets off another handler
end go

on otherResponse
   global goTries
   add 1 to goTries
   if goTries = 1 then answer "I'm sorry — you can't do that."
   else if goTries = 2 then answer "I'm tired of talking to you about this."
   else
      answer "I warned you..."
      doMenu "Quit HyperCard"
   end if
end otherResponse
```

A hyperTechnicality: The Message box and message passing

The Message box is always available to get a message into the message passing path quickly and easily.

Here's how it works: When you press the return key or the enter key with the Selection in the Message box, the message `returnkey` or `enterKey` goes to the current card; if no object on the way to HyperCard has a handler that catches the `returnKey` or `enterKey` message, HyperCard invokes the **returnKey** or **enterKey** command — the job of which is to operate on the contents of the Message box.

Here's how the operations go: First, HyperCard tries to evaluate the contents of the Message box as an expression. If that works HyperCard puts the value of the expression into the Message box, replacing the original contents. (Thus you can type any expression directly into the Message box — `sqrt(65536)`, `pi * 75 ^2`, `the time && the date` — without having to preface it with the command word `put`.)

If HyperCard can't treat the contents of the Message box as an expression, it sends the contents as a message to the current card.

The first handler catches any **go** messages and sends a message of its own, the the user-defined message `otherResponses` which is itself caught by the second handler.

What's catchable? You can never catch a keyword (the subject of Chapter 7). Keywords are executed directly by HyperCard and don't go through the message passing path. You cannot catch properties either, although you can catch the **set** command message, thus changing a property before it gets to HyperCard. You cannot catch functions called with `the` and/or `of` (as in `the date` or `number of cards`); these go directly to HyperCard. But you can catch functions that use the parenthetical form (as in `sin (numExpr)`).

Thus you can have one of HyperCard's built-in functions called with `the` and/or `of`, plus your own function of the same name called with parentheses. This, however, is a dangerous practice in that it's easy to forget which function result is defined and which is built-in. Because naming is no problem in HyperCard, it makes sense to give unique names to all defined functions.

What happens to uncaught (or passed) messages?

Messages that get all the way to HyperCard receive different treatment, depending on their type:

System messages — Once they've had a chance to do their work, they serve no further use. So HyperCard casts system messages aside. (Who wants yesterday's news?)

Command messages — HyperCard has the equivalent of built-in handlers for commands (as well as for keywords, properties, and built-in functions); so it carries them out as specified in Chapters 7, 8, 9, and 10.

User-defined messages — HyperCard itself has no way of understanding user-defined messages. (That's the job of handlers.) If one of these gets all the way through the message passing path, either you forgot to write a handler for it, the handler is in the wrong part of the message passing path to catch the message, or you've made some other kind of error (probably spelling). HyperCard puts up a "Can't understand..." dialog box.

Changing caught commands is tricky: You can catch a command and easily do something other than what that command usually does. Typically, you might catch a "delete card" command and put up an announcement to the user:

```
on domenu which
    if which is not "delete card" then pass doMenu -- only stop card deletions
    answer "Sorry - card deletions not allowed." -- announcement to user
end domenu
```

But changing how a command operates and then sending it on to HyperCard is tricky at best. The syntax of parameters for handlers is different from the syntax of parameters for built-in commands, and the syntax for redefining commands isn't yet fully implemented. We leave it as an exercise to the highly expert scriptwriter....

Placing Handlers for Best Effect

Knowing how to use the message passing path can save lots of code. A card, background, or stack script can have code that defines the behavior for all the buttons, fields, cards, and/or backgrounds in that domain.

For example, assume you have a bunch of buttons, each of which goes to a different card in a stack when you click it. Also assume that each button has the same name as the card that is its destination. You might do things the long way and write a separate script for each button, as in Figure 1-5.

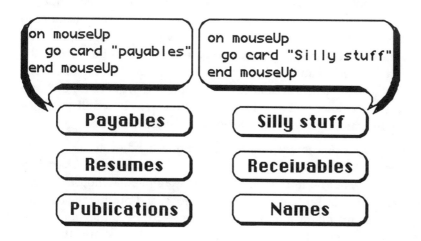

All these buttons have separate nearly identical scripts (Such a waste!)

Figure 1-5 Separate scripts

Or you might write a single handler, placed in the script of the current card, as in Figure 1-6.

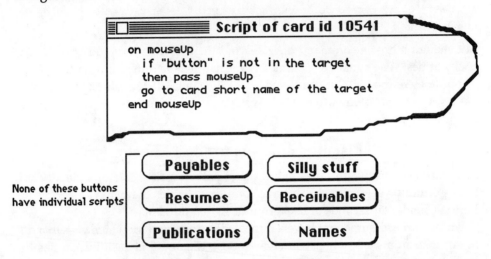

```
                          Script of card id 10541
on mouseUp
   if "button" is not in the target
   then pass mouseUp
   go to card short name of the target
end mouseUp
```

None of these buttons have individual scripts

Payables	Silly stuff
Resumes	Receivables
Publications	Names

Figure 1-6   All handled at once

When you use the method shown in Figure 1-6, clicking on one of these buttons goes to the intended card even though the button you click has no script.

Here's how it works: Because the button you click has no mouseUp handler to catch the `mouseUp` message, the message essentially goes through the button and farther along the message passing path. The next object in the path is the card, and it has a mouseUp handler that catches the message; that handler takes you to the card whose name is the same as the button you pressed. (The if construct in Figure 1-6's handler makes sure that a button was clicked; if you click any place else on the card, flow of control leaves the handler.)

The rule for the proper placement of a handler: Put a handler in the script of the object farthest along the message passing path required for it to be shared by everything that uses it, but no farther. In the above example, the mouseUp handler is in the card script: the buttons are all card buttons, and putting the handler in the background script might not be appropriate — for example, you might want a set of empty-scripted buttons on the next card (which shares the same background) to react differently than the buttons on this card.

Handlers in the script of the Home stack have impact throughout HyperCard. For example, HyperCard comes with the handler searchScript in the script of the Home stack. No matter what stack you're in, typing a message of the following form into the Message box (and pressing Return) makes HyperCard show you the scripts of all objects in that stack that contain a particular string:

```
searchScript <pattern>
```

For example, typing `searchScript "pass mouseUp"` would open the script of the card in Figure 1-6.

At the other end of the spectrum, a script in a button or field affects only that button or field: once a message is used up, it's used up.

Well, almost. You can always use the keywords `pass` and `send,` discussed in the next section, to get more mileage out of a message.

Default on mouseUp Skeleton

If you open the script of a newly created button, you see the skeleton of a mouseUp handler:

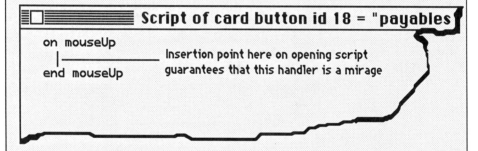

Figure 1-7 mirage lines

The lines you see aren't really part of a script yet. They're there to make writing button scripts quicker, because nearly all button scripts have a mouseUp handler. If you were to change the skeleton in any way, there *would* be a script in that button. HyperCard ignores such skeleton scripts until you change them in some way.

Pass and Send: Exploiting the Message Passing Path

Once a message is caught by a handler, the handler runs and the message ordinarily is discarded and has no further effect. The keywords **pass** and **send** let you take a message caught by the current handler and either put it back on the message passing path (**pass**) or send it directly to another object (**send**).

Pass *messageName* immediately transfers flow of control out of the current handler and passes *messageName* along the message passing path. You see a major use for this in Figure 1-6, where a message isn't appropriate for a particular handler — in this case, the message mouseUp gets passed back onto the message passing path because its original target wasn't a button. (It's passed so that it can be caught by a handler farther along the message passing path — either in the background script, the current stack script, one of the scripts of a stack named by the **stacksInUse** property, or the script of the Home stack.)

Send *message* **to** *object* sends a message and any accompanying parameters directly to the named object without traversing HyperCard's normal message passing path to get to that object. You can send a message to a point farther along the message passing path, earlier in the path, or to another object at the same level. For example, a card handler might send a message to a stack, to another card in the same stack, or to a button or a field. Once a message gets to its intended object, in terms of the message passing path it's as if that object were the first to receive the message: If that object has a handler for that message, the handler is executed; if that object has no handler for the message, or if a handler in that object's script passes the message, the message goes back on the message passing path at the point of that object.

Chapter 2

Scripts and the Script Editor

This chapter describes the structure of a
script as it appears in the script editor. It
includes information on how to bring a
script into the script editor, what you can
do to a script once the editor is operating,
and how to use HyperTalk's great
debugging tools.

This chapter also covers how to break a
long line into more manageable parts, how
to enter and use comments, and how to
use automatic script formatting to get an
indication of whether or not your scripts
are syntactically correct.

For information on how to organize a
script, see Chapter 12. For information on
which object's script should contain a
particular handler for best effectiveness,
see Chapter 1.

For features added to the script editor
and the Debugger so late in HyperTalk
2.0's development cycle that they couldn't
be included in the main body of this book,
see Appendix I.

Every object (except HyperCard itself) has a script you can look at. You look at a script with the **script editor**. The script appears as a collection of comments and handlers (see Figure 2-1).

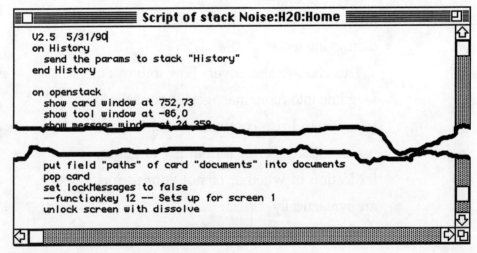

```
V2.5  5/31/90
on History
   send the params to stack "History"
end History

on openstack
   show card window at 752,73
   show tool window at -86,0
   show message wind    at 24,358
```

```
   put field "paths" of card "documents" into documents
   pop card
   set lockMessages to false
   --functionkey 12 -- Sets up for screen 1
   unlock screen with dissolve
```

Figure 2-1 Script with the editor open (2.0)

When more than one handler in a script has the same name, the earliest handler executes. HyperTalk ignores subsequent handlers in that script with the same name. This feature lets you write and test several variations of the same handler: just place earliest in the script the handler that you want to test.

Script limits and TextEdit: A script is limited to about 30,000 characters, or about 2,000 characters less than the limit of TextEdit. TextEdit is the simple (some would call it brain-damaged) word processor built into the Macintosh's operating system. It's the standard editing medium that lets programmers easily localize Macintosh applications so that they'll run in any country. HyperCard builds upon TextEdit to display text in fields and to edit scripts. HyperCard — and therefore HyperTalk — will always be based upon TextEdit. If TextEdit were to change, then HyperTalk's limits could change.

SUMMONING THE EDITOR

You can bring the script of an object into the script editor through any of several methods:

• Click the Script button in an object's Info box.

• Click the Script button in an error dialog box.

• Use one of the keyboard shortcuts (such as Command-Option-B).

• Type the Edit command into the Message box.

• Execute a handler that contains an Edit command.

• Click on a script that's currently under the control of the Debugger (page 40)

The Script Button

The Info box of every HyperCard object (except HyperCard itself, which lacks an Info box) has a script button (see Figure 2-2). With the user level set to 5, clicking that button brings up the script editor and shows the script of the object you've chosen. You get to an Info box by choosing the proper item from the Objects menu, described in detail in the *HyperCard User's Guide*.

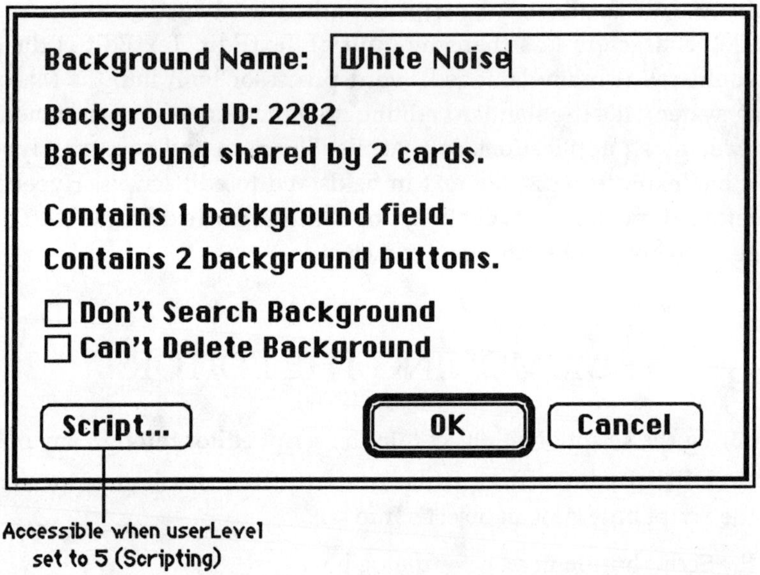

Background Name: |White Noise|

Background ID: 2282
Background shared by 2 cards.

Contains 1 background field.

Contains 2 background buttons.

☐ **Don't Search Background**
☐ **Can't Delete Background**

[Script...]   [[OK]]   [Cancel]

Accessible when userLevel
set to 5 (Scripting)

Figure 2-2   Getting to a script from an Info box

Obscure 1.2.# editor-access bug alert

Don't hold down the Control key (only available on keyboards for Mac SE and Mac II machines) when you choose any Info box from the Objects menu if you intend to edit an object's script. Doing so sets up a strange condition such that when you enter the editor by clicking on the Script button, you won't be able to press either the Return or Delete keys. (This bug is fixed in 2.0.)

Keyboard Shortcuts

HyperCard provides keyboard shortcuts for looking at scripts. What a shortcut gets you depends on the currently active tool (Table 2-1):

Table 2-1: Shortcuts to bring up script editor

Tool	Key press	Action
Browse	Command-Option	Displays outline of all visible buttons; click one to see its script.
	Shift-Command-Option	Displays outline of all visible buttons and fields; click one to see its script.
Field	Command-Option	Displays outline of all visible and invisible fields; click a visible field to see its script.
Button	Command-Option	Displays outline of all visible and invisible buttons; click a visible button to see its script.
Any	Command-Option-C	Displays script of current card.
	Command-Option-B	Displays script of current background.
	Command-Option-S	Displays script of current stack.

You can't use a keyboard shortcut to see the script of a hidden button or hidden field.

Edit in the Message Box

You can bring up the script editor by entering **edit** commands through the Message box. This is, in fact, the most common way to use the **edit** command (see Figure 2-3).

Figure 2-3 Summoning the script editor through the Message box

You can use the **Edit** command to edit the script of any button or field on the current card, of any background or card in the current stack, or of any stack:

```
edit script of button 3
edit script of bg fld "CD Titles"
edit script of cd 1
edit script of bg "Compact Disks"
edit script of stack "Accounts Receivable"
```

For details on the **Edit** command, see Chapter 8.

Edit in a Handler

You can use the **Edit** command in a handler to bring up any script. Most commonly, **edit** brings up the script of the handler that contains it:

```
edit script of me
```

When **edit** is called from within a handler, control returns to the executing handler when the script editor is closed.

THE 2.0 SCRIPT EDITOR

When you call for the script of any object, you open the script editor. The menus in Figure 2-4 temporarily replace all created and standard HyperCard menus. Although all the menu names except Script look familiar, the contents of these menus is in many ways different from what you might expect.

Figure 2-4 Script editor menu bar

1.2.# Users Take Note

To quote the Father of HyperTalk: "Editor functionality in version 1.2 could possibly benefit from some improvement in future versions."

The fact is, editor functionality in pre-2.0 HyperTalk is abysmal. You're limited to basic editing functions (cut, copy, paste) without undo, there is no find-and-replace, and you can't paste into the Find box's target field. Additionally, you can have only one script open at a time, and there is no debugger. (We could go on, but we're getting depressed.)

All of the material in this chapter applies to the 2.0 Editor and Debugger. For a table of keyboard editor shortcuts that includes the few available in HyperCard 1.2.#, see Table C-2 in Appendix C.

If you're going to do any real development work with HyperCard, we seriously recommend that you upgrade to HyperCard 2.# as soon as possible.

Really.

The editor's File, Edit, Go, and Script menus (described below) all act on the script with which you're currently working. You also have complete access to the Apple (Desk Accessories) menu.

The File Menu

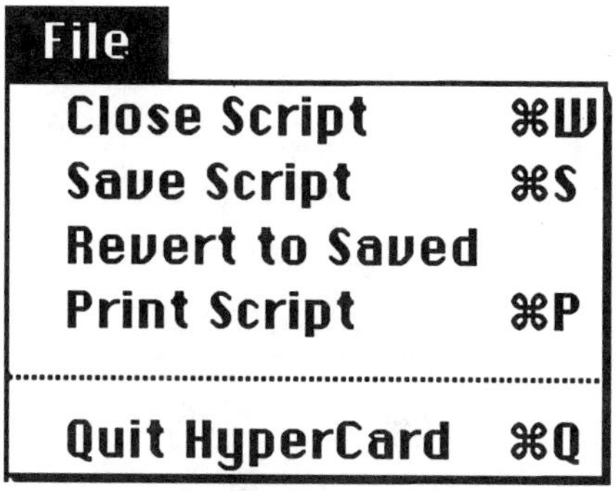

```
┌──────────────────────────────────┐
│ File                             │
├──────────────────────────────────┤
│ Close Script          ⌘W         │
│ Save Script           ⌘S         │
│ Revert to Saved                  │
│ Print Script          ⌘P         │
│ ································· │
│ Quit HyperCard        ⌘Q         │
└──────────────────────────────────┘
```

Figure 2-5   Script editor File menu

Close Script (Command-W) puts the script away and restores the menu bar to its previous state. If you've made any changes to the script, HyperCard produces a dialog asking if you want to save the changes.

Save Script (Command-S) saves any changes you've made to the script.

Revert to Saved tosses away the current version of the script and replaces it with the most recently saved version. A dialog appears asking if you really want to throw away the changes. You can't undo this command.

Print Script (Command-P) prints the script on the front layer. (You can have many scripts open at the same time starting in version 2.0.) The wording of this item changes to **Print Selection** if you've selected part of the script; in such a case, only the selection is printed. The date, time, script name, and page number appear at the top of each printed page.

Quit HyperCard (Command-Q) quits HyperCard. If you've made any unsaved changes to any open script, HyperCard asks if you want to save the changes on a script-by-script basis. To save and close the script in one operation (a combination of Command-S and Command-W), press the Enter key. To dismiss the script without saving anything and without having to deal with a dialog, press Command-period.

The Edit Menu

Edit	
Undo	**⌘Z**
Cut	**⌘X**
Copy	**⌘C**
Paste	**⌘U**
Clear	
Select All	**⌘A**

Figure 2-6   Script editor Edit menu

The commands on the Edit menu provide the Macintosh's basic text-editing functionality, as described in countless Macintosh books and product manuals. As this book already is heavy enough to flatten a Texas cockroach, we'll move right along.

The Go Menu

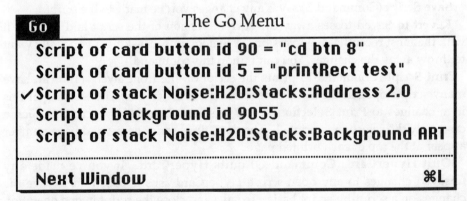

Go	
Script of card button id 90 = "cd btn 8"	
Script of card button id 5 = "printRect test"	
✓ Script of stack Noise:H20:Stacks:Address 2.0	
Script of background id 9055	
Script of stack Noise:H20:Stacks:Background ART	
Next Window	**⌘L**

Figure 2-7   Script editor Go menu

The Go menu lists all the open scripts, with the current one checkmarked. To bring a script to the front (thus making it current), choose its name.

Next Window (Command-L) cycles through the open windows (scripts, pictures, stacks, etc.), sending the frontmost window to the back of the card layer. Choosing this command with the shift key down brings the rearmost window of the card layer to the front.

The Script Menu

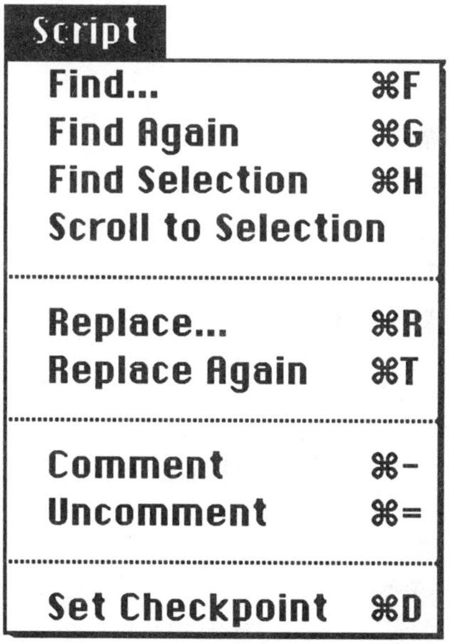

Script	
Find...	**⌘F**
Find Again	**⌘G**
Find Selection	**⌘H**
Scroll to Selection	
Replace...	**⌘R**
Replace Again	**⌘T**
Comment	**⌘-**
Uncomment	**⌘=**
Set Checkpoint	**⌘D**

Figure 2-8   Script editor Script menu

Find (Command-F) brings up the dialog in Figure 2-9.

Type the string you want to locate into the editable field. The string stays in the field until you change it or until you quit HyperCard. The field is initially blank. Set the options you want (as described immediately below); then click "Find" (or press Enter or Return) to put the dialog away and to search for the target string's first occurrence after the selection. To cancel, click "Cancel" or press Command-period.

If the script editor locates the target string, it highlights it; otherwise, it beeps and leaves the insertion point where it was before you started the search.

To search for the string with word boundaries respected, click the Whole Word button. (This finds "country" in "country side," but not in "countryside.")

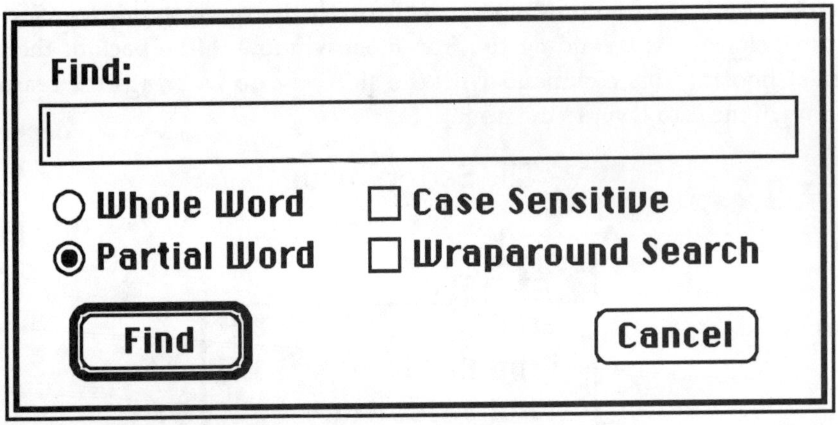

Figure 2-9 Script editor Find dialog

To search for the string as part of another string, click the Partial Word button, which is the default option. (This finds "mouse" in "the mouse button" and in "on mouseUp.")

To search for the string with uppercase and lowercase letters exactly as you've typed them, check the "Case Sensitive" box. (This finds "theHandler" in "theHandler" but not in "thehandler.")

To start searching from the top of the script after searching from the insertion point to the script's bottom, check the Wraparound Search box.

Find Again (Command-G) searches for the next occurrence of the string in the Find dialog, respecting the options set in that dialog.

Find Selection (Command-H) replaces the target string in the Find dialog with the current selection and looks for the next occurrence of the selection while respecting the options previously set in the dialog.

Scroll to Selection, if the line that the selection is on isn't visible, vertically scrolls the script window until the selection is in the approximate vertical center of the window. No horizontal scrolling is performed; if the selection is scrolled out of sight horizontally, it remains out of sight (but the position of the vertical scroll is correct).

Replace (command-R) brings up the dialog in Figure 2-10.

The options are the same as those listed for **Find**, above.

Click Replace to put away the dialog and to replace the next occurrence of the target Find string only; click Replace All to replace every instance of the Find string in the script. (If the "Replace with" field is empty, the target string is deleted.) Be careful with Replace All; you can't undo it.

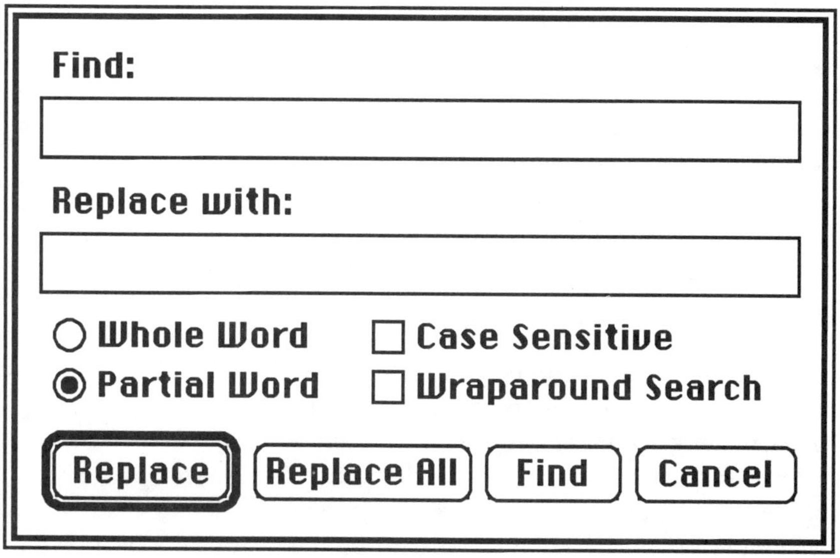

Find:

Replace with:

○ **Whole Word**   □ **Case Sensitive**
● **Partial Word**   □ **Wraparound Search**

[**Replace**] [**Replace All**] [**Find**] [**Cancel**]

Figure 2-10   Script editor Replace dialog

Replace Again (Command-T) locates the target string's next occurrence after the selection and replaces it with the contents of the "Replace with" field in the Replace dialog. (If the "Replace with" field is empty, the target string is deleted.)

Comment (Command-minus) inserts a double-dash (the comment marker) at the insertion point. When more than one line is in the selection, a double-dash is inserted at the start of each line in the selection. See the section on "Comments," later in this chapter.

Uncomment (Command-equals) removes the double-dash (the comment marker) to the immediate right of the insertion point. If no double-dash exists to the right of the insertion point, the double-dash to the immediate left of the insertion point is deleted. If no double-dash exists on either side of the insertion point, nothing happens. When more than one line is in the selection, a double-dash is deleted from the start of each line in the selection.

Set/Clear Checkpoint (Command-D) toggles a checkmark (✔) at the start of the line containing the insertion point. When a line with a checkmark next to it is about to execute, the Debugger is invoked with execution paused at that line. (See "The Debugger," below.) If the selection contains more than one line, the top line in the selection is marked. You can have up to 16 checkpoints per script, and up to 32 scripts with checkpoints in them. To toggle a checkpoint with the mouse, hold down the option key and click on a line.

THE DEBUGGER

Available starting in version 2.0, the Debugger lets you follow the progress of your handlers in a variety of ways. If you've done any serious scripting in 1.2.# HyperCard, you'll wonder how you ever got along without the Debugger after using it for just a few days.

You enter the Debugger when HyperTalk is about to execute a line of code that has a checkpoint set, when the command **debug checkPoint** executes, or when you press Command-Option-period while running a handler. (To set a checkpoint with the mouse, hold down the option key and click on a line of code.) Execution of the handler pauses, and the line of code that's about to execute has a box around it as shown in Figure 2-11.

The Debugger's actions are limited to the handler that has the checkpoint set, and to any handlers that the current handler calls or returns to.

While you're in the Debugger, the Debugger menu is the only one that you can use even though other menus might appear on the menu bar. The other menus are visible so that you can see what menus or items are created or deleted, enabled or disabled, and so on.

You can drag windows around and bring script windows to the front; but you can't work in any script window until you leave the Debugger.

You leave the Debugger by choosing Abort (Command-A) or Go (Command-G) from the Debugger menu, or by pressing Command-period.

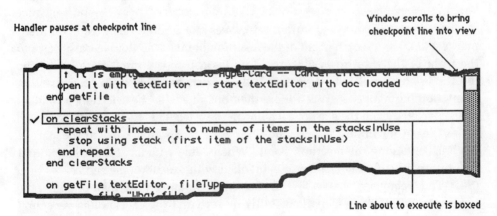

Handler pauses at checkpoint line

Window scrolls to bring checkpoint line into view

```
      t it is empty          to HyperCard -- cancel clicked or cmd Per
      open it with textEditor -- start textEditor with doc loaded
    end getFile

✓ on clearStacks
      repeat with index = 1 to number of items in the stacksInUse
        stop using stack (first item of the stacksInUse)
      end repeat
    end clearStacks

    on getFile textEditor, fileTyp
          file "What file
```

Line about to execute is boxed

Figure 2-11   Debugger is operating

The Debugger Menu

You control the actions of the Debugger through the Debugger menu (Figure 2-12).

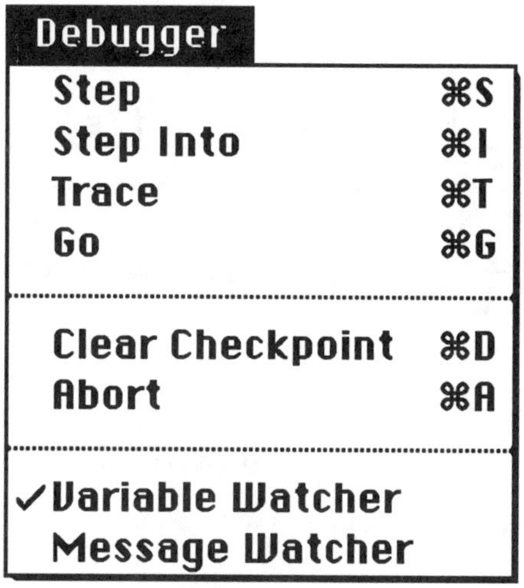

Debugger	
Step	⌘S
Step Into	⌘I
Trace	⌘T
Go	⌘G
Clear Checkpoint	⌘D
Abort	⌘A
✓**Variable Watcher**	
Message Watcher	

Figure 2-12 Debugger menu

Step (Command-S) single-steps through the lines in the current handler. (When you call for this command, the window of the script being debugged moves to the front if it isn't there already.) Each time you call **step**, another line executes. Just before the line executes, a box is drawn around it. Using the Variable Watcher and Message Watcher (both described below), you can trace the progression of your code on a line-by-line basis.

When the current handler calls another handler, the called handler runs at full speed with the box remaining around the calling line (as shown in Figure 2-13 — but see **Step Into**, immediately below); when execution returns to the calling handler, single-stepping resumes. The variable watcher shows the variables of the calling handler, but not the called handler. (The message watcher records all the messages all the time.)

Step Into (Command-I) acts like **step** (above), except that single-stepping continues into the called handler. The Variable Watcher (described below) switches to show the variables of whichever handler is current.

Trace (Command-T) acts like **step into** (above), except that you don't call **trace** after each line — stepping is automatic, and there's no pause after each line. To switch to single-stepping, issue the **step** or **step into** command at any time.

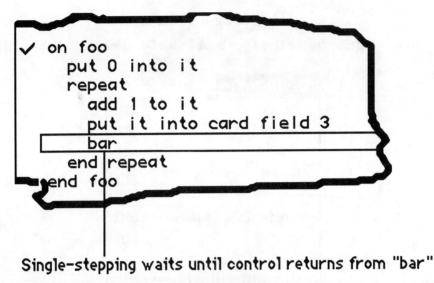

```
✓  on foo
       put 0 into it
       repeat
          add 1 to it
          put it into card field 3
          bar
       end repeat
   end foo
```

Single-stepping waits until control returns from "bar"

Figure 2-13   Single-stepping up to a calling line

Go (Command-G) exits the Debugger and resumes full-speed execution of the currently running handler with all variables intact.

Clear/Set Checkpoint (Command-D) clears the checkpoint at the current line if one exists, or puts one there if one doesn't already exist. You can have up to 16 checkpoints per script, and up to 32 scripts with checkpoints in them. To toggle a checkpoint manually: enter the editor, hold down the option key, and click on a line of code.

Abort (Command-A) exits the Debugger and stops the script. The script editor remains open, with the insertion point on the line that was about to execute.

Variable Watcher brings up a window that shows the current values of all variables in the currently executing handler. If no handler is executing, the window shows the current values of all globals (Figure 2-14).

Clicking on a variable puts its value into the editing field at the bottom of the window. If the value takes up more than one line, you can grow the field as appropriate. The field is editable; you can change the value of the variable and press Enter to update the system with the new value (Figure 2-15) — invaluable for testing limits and playing out "what if" scenarios!

Drag bar to increase
or shrink display areas

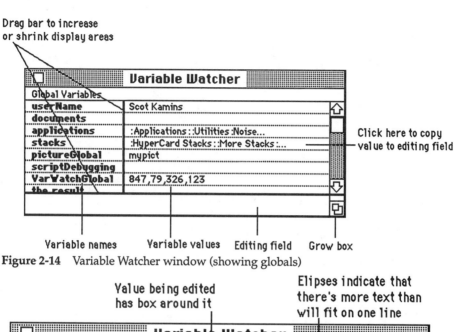

Variable names   Variable values   Editing field   Grow box

Figure 2-14   Variable Watcher window (showing globals)

Value being edited
has box around it

Elipses indicate that
there's more text than
will fit on one line

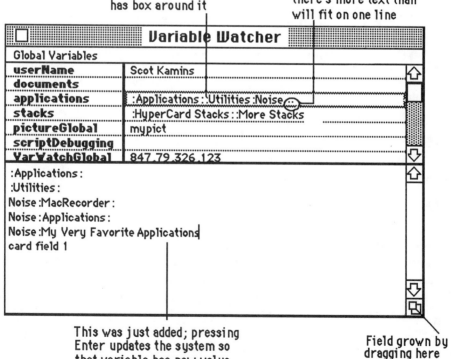

This was just added; pressing
Enter updates the system so
that variable has new value

Field grown by
dragging here

Figure 2-15   "Live" editing of variable values!

When the variable watcher is following a running script, it shows only those variables in the current handler (including any globals the handler might be using). When the current handler calls another handler, the variable watcher clears and then follows the values for the new handler (Figure 2-16).

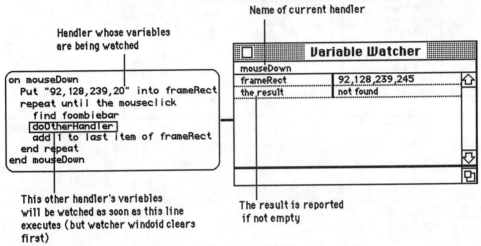

Figure 2-16   variableWatcher window for handlers

To show the Variable Watcher window at any time, use either of the following commands:

```
show the variable watcher
show window "Variable Watcher"
```

To hide the Variable Watcher window at any time, use either of the following commands:

```
hide the variable watcher
hide window "Variable Watcher"
```

Message Watcher brings up an editable window with a record of the last 150 messages sent, and shows through indentation what handler called which other handlers or sent which messages. If the "Hide unused messages" box is checked, only those messages that are caught by a handler (or, in the case of built-in commands, by HyperCard) are recorded. If the "Hide idle" box is checked, the Idle message is not recorded, even if there's a handler that catches it. Otherwise, all messages including all idle messages are recorded.

Messages are indented as appropriate to show called handlers and embedded subhandlers (Figure 2-17).

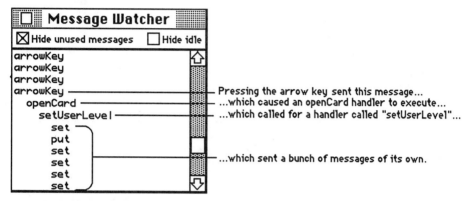

Figure 2-17   Message Watcher window

To show the Message Watcher window at any time, use either of the following commands:

```
show the message watcher
show window "Message Watcher"
```

To hide the Message Watcher window at any time, use either of the following commands:

```
hide the message watcher
hide window "Message Watcher"
```

Run-Time vs. Compile-Time

HyperTalk distinguishes between compile-time and run-time errors. Compile-time errors are errors that HyperCard can detect even before a handler starts running. These kinds of errors are errors in form (spelling errors, missing words, etc.).

HyperTalk 1.2.# was an interpreted language: when a handler caught a message, the words in the handler were turned into tokens, which HyperCard then interpreted. HyperCard knew about an error in a script only as the running handler reached the offending line.

HyperTalk 2.0, on the other hand, is a compiled language: when a handler catches a message, the words in that handler are again turned into tokens, which HyperCard then compiles into machine language. (The tokens are then discarded.) In the process of compiling the code HyperCard checks for errors in form and, when it finds them, announces them immediately; in such a case, the compilation fails, and the handler won't run.

Compile-time error dialogs have two buttons — one to enter the script editor, and one to cancel (Figure 2-18).

Run-time error dialogs have an extra button that lets you enter the Debugger. This button is missing from compile-time error dialogs because the Debugger can't display any information about a handler that isn't running (Figure 2-19).

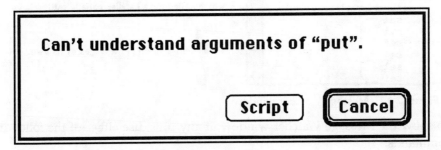

Figure 2-18   Compile-time error dialog

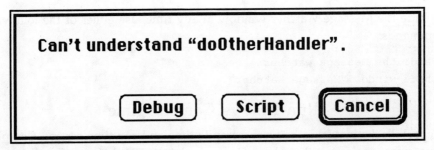

Figure 2-19   Run-time error dialog

FORMATTING

Formatting within handlers is handled automatically when you open a script, or when you press the Tab key after a script is already open and edited. (Pressing the Return key also reformats a script, but adds an extra line to it.)

The opening and closing lines in a handler are left-justified. Subsequent statements indent two spaces:

```
on makeNewPicture NewHorPos, NewVertPos
  set editBackgnd to true
  type "v" with commandkey, shiftkey
  drag from 256, 170 to newHorPos, newVertPos
  set editBackgnd to false
end makeNewPicture
```

Lines contained within If and Repeat structures are indented an additional two spaces. Nested structures are indented as appropriate:

```
on mouseUp
  -- compress multiple spaces in card field 1
  put 1 into charNum
  repeat while char charNum of card field 1 is not empty
    if char charNum of card field 1 is space then
      repeat while char charNum + 1 of card field 1 is space
        delete char charNum + 1 of card field 1
      end repeat
    end if
    add 1 to charNum
  end repeat
end mouseUp
```

All other leading spaces (ASCII 32, as opposed to option-space ASCII 202) are cleared to the first nonwhite character; all subsequent characters in a line appear as they were entered.

Don't subvert the formatting: Adding an option-space in front of any line within a handler always generates an error dialog because no valid line within a handler starts with that character.

Use Tab to check your work: To force formatting after you edit a script, press Tab. If indentation doesn't look right, something's probably wrong (see Figure 2-20).

Before Tab press

```
on mouseUp
  global a,b
  if a = b then edit script of me|
  end mouseUp
```

Improper indent here...

After Tab press

```
on mouseUp
  global a,b
    if a = b then edit script of me
end mouseUp
```

...is fixed here.

Figure 2-20 Tab forces formatting

BREAKING A LINE INTO VIEWABLE SEGMENTS

A single line of a script ends in a carriage return. There's no practical limit to the number of characters you can have on a single line of a script. (It can be up to 30,000 characters long!) But characters beyond the 80th or so go beyond the right edge of the screen, and in versions earlier than 2.0 there is no horizontal scrolling (see Figure 2-21).

```
≡≡≡≡≡≡≡≡≡≡≡≡ Script of card id 8001 ≡≡≡≡≡≡≡≡≡≡≡
on mouseUp
  if topLeft of card field 1 = botRight of background field foo and the h
    then put "It works great" into field 7
end mouseUp
```

Figure 2-21   You don't have to see a whole line for it to be legal...

The line continuation character lets you break up a long line into viewable segments. You produce a line continuation character (¬) by pressing option-return (see Figure 2-22).

```
≡≡≡≡≡≡≡≡≡≡≡≡ Script of card id 8001 ≡≡≡≡≡≡≡≡≡≡≡
on mouseUp
  if topLeft of card field 1 = botRight of background field foo¬
  and the hilite of card button 12 is true
    then put "It works great" into field 7
end mouseUp
```

Figure 2-22   ...but it sure is easier to read.

You can't use a line continuation character between open and close quotation marks. If you have a really long quotation in your code, break it up up and use ampersands, as in Figure 2-23. (The **ampersand** is the string concatenation operator.)

```
≡≡≡≡≡≡≡≡≡≡≡≡ Script of card id 2623 ≡≡≡≡≡≡≡≡≡≡≡
on fillTheField
  put "When I was a boy in Boston, I'd sometimes go to the Boston " &¬
  "Commons on weekends to watch Mrs. McGinty poisoning pigeons, " &¬
  "chipmonks, children, and other small undesirable wildlife." ¬
  into field "Charming Characters I Have Known"
end fillTheField
```

Figure 2-23   & and ¬ make life worth living

There's no limit to the number of line continuation characters in a single line of a script.

Formatting is sometimes buggy

In general, code that formats correctly works correctly; code that formats incorrectly usually won't work at all. But there are a few exceptions.

For example, a broken line sometimes throws formatting off:

```
on mouseUp
   global myVar
   if word 2 of myVar is "id" then put ¬ -- This breaks formatting
   "No Name" into backgndName
   else put it into backgndName
   end mouseUp
```

Comments before an **else** statement sometimes break formatting:

```
on mouseUp
   ask "Number" with empty
   if it is 3 then flash it
   -- my comment about the coming else
   else beep it
   end mouseUp
```

In all the above cases, the code runs fine even though the indentation is off. Additionally, a few cases have been reported where the editor indents a structure as such that it looks like the code will work — but it won't.

Formatting is an aid to writing code. In the last analysis, running the code is the only real way to tell if the code works.

Comments

Comments and their use is an area of hot controversy within the HyperTalk community. Many script writers have been bludgeoned into senselessness by textbook-wielding academicians over the subject.

Comments in a script provide explanations for whole handlers or for individual lines within a handler. Traditionally, the maxim has been "the more comments the better." This comes from a history of computer languages that restricted the programmer to very short variable and procedure names. The names were often far too short to be meaningful; comments became the only way to show what was going on.

HyperTalk, on the other hand, lets you write self-documenting code. With variable and object names up to 31 characters and handler names up to 254 characters, the code you write can describe itself:

```
on plotMonthlySalesFigures startDate,endDate
    put collectSalesData(startDate,endDate) into salesData
    drawAxes lowestSalesMonth(salesData),highestSalesMonth(salesData)
    plotLineChart salesData
end plotMonthlySalesFigures
```

So in HyperTalk the primary use of comments can shift. What it shifts to depends on whom you're writing for.

Who's the Audience?

Ultimately, the number and length of comments you use depend on your audience. Comments are a form of communication. Assuming you've written well-structured self-documenting code that only you will ever see, you can write handlers with just a few shorthand comments (or no comments at all). But you might need to spell out steps within a handler for a less knowledgeable audience.

The real question is this: six months after the code is written, will you or your intended audience be able to read and understand your scripts?

Dangerous code: No matter how clear your code is, use comments to call out dangerous code (for example, code that deletes data) or unusual code (code that is self-modifying or uses some really slick algorithm of which you're unusually proud):

```
on warning
   -- this handler uses a global named "warningCount"
   -- that must not be touched by other handlers (a dangerous
   -- practice, but the only way for handlers to have static data)
   global warningCount -- Global var inited to empty on creation...
   add 1 to warningCount -- ... and "empty" treated as zero for math
   if warningCount <= 3
   then answer "Please don't do that!"
   else
      answer "OK, I quit!"
      doMenu "Quit HyperCard"
   end if
end warning
```

Comment Mechanics

The comment delimiter is the double-dash (- -).

All comments within the body of a handler must be preceded by the comment delimiter:

```
on closeField
   -- update the last modified field for this card
   put the date into field "Last Modified"
   pass closeField
end closeField
```

HyperTalk ignores everything between a comment delimiter and the end of the line.

Entering comments outside handlers: Comment lines written outside of a handler don't need to start with the comment delimiter (although some people find it confusing when comments don't start with "- -").

But unmarked lines that begin with the handler-starting keywords on or function will mess up script formatting for the first handler following the comment, and might even catch a message (see Figure 2-24).

The handler shown in Figure 2-24 runs correctly; but if the unmarked comment line began with the name of an initiating message (for example, on mouseUp) you'd get an error dialog:

```
This will ─┐   These comments are made outside the body of a handler. But the
cause problems ─│function│ of a comment is to make things really clear. If you ignore
               │         this simple rule, you'll probably end up in trouble.

         │on mouseUp -- note the messed up indentation here.
See? ─│put "ok"
         │end mouseUp
```

Figure 2-24 Troublemaker comments

Comments and spaces: HyperTalk ordinarily truncates leading spaces. It leaves untouched all other spaces. To add leading spaces to comment lines outside of handlers, use Option-space.

Effect on Performance

Despite rampant rumors to the contrary, comments have zero impact on performance.

Scripts impact the size of a stack: each character in a comment adds one byte to the size of a stack. And because the size of a script is limited (32,000 characters), each character used in a comment is a character you can't use in a handler. But unless disk space is really critical or you write really big scripts, these facts seldom make any difference.

CLOSING THE EDITOR

To close the editor and keep any changes, press Enter.

To close the editor and throw away all changes since the editor was last opened, press Command-Period.

When you close the editor after editing the script of a noncurrent stack or background, or noncurrent card in the current stack, you go back to the card you were on when you summoned the editor.

1.2.# Users: "Changing Stacks" Bug

In 1.2.#, when you close the editor after editing the script of a non-current stack, that stack becomes current and you end up on the first card of that stack. (No open or close message are sent.)

This bug is fixed in version 2.0.

EDITOR KEYBOARD OPERATIONS

Table 2-2 summarizes editor operations in version 2.# you can perform from the keyboard:

Table 2-2: Shortcut editor operations

Operation	Keypress or Click
Enter line continuation char (¬)	Option-Return*
Select entire line	Triple-Click
Reformat script	Tab
Undo last edit	Command-Z
Cut selected text	Command-X
Copy selected text	Command-C
Paste text	Command-V
Select entire script	Command-A
Print selected/entire script	Command-P
Find text with dialog	Command-F
Find selected text	Command-H
Find again	Command-G
Replace	Command-R
Replace again	Command-T
Comment selected line(s)	Command-minus
Uncomment selected line(s)	Command-equals
Set/Clear Checkpoint	Command-D or Option-Click on line
Break into Debugger, running script	Command-Option-period
Close editor, keep changes	Enter or Command-W
Close editor, kill changes without warning	Command-period

*Option-return has the same effect as typing option-L and then pressing Return.

Table 2-3 summarizes Debugger operations you can perform from the keyboard (version 2.# only).

Table 2-3: Shortcut to Debugger operations

Operation	Keypress
Break into Debugger for running script	Command-Option-period
Step	Command-S
Step Into	Command-I
Trace	Command-T
Go	Command-G
Set/Clear Checkpoint	Command-D
Exit Debugger, Abort Handler	Command-A

Part Two Formal Reference

Chapter 3

Syntax

This chapter presents the syntax of HyperTalk. Everyone needs to read and understand the first section, "Syntax Symbols," to understand the syntax examples used throughout this book.

The later sections are concerned with the formal syntax of version 2.0. They're especially valuable if you're an advanced scripter who wants a more formal and precise presentation of the syntax than appears within the context of individual vocabulary words, or if you're an experienced programmer who likes BNF formats.

For the complete syntax of all the 1.2 versions of HyperTalk, see Appendix H. (Some developers need to be sure that all their code works in both 1.2 and 2.0.)

For the syntax and use of words and operators added so late in HyperTalk 2.0's development cycle that they couldn't be included in the main body of this book, see Appendix I, "Late Breaking News."

SYNTAX SYMBOLS

The following is a list of syntactic symbols and terms you must know for the rest of this book to make sense.

Special Symbols

< > Angle brackets enclose an italicized general term (as in *<card>*). This **nonterminal** (as the general term is formally called) is meant to be replaced by a specific instance of that term. For example, in the syntactic statement go *<card>*, you can replace *<card>* with any valid form of a card reference — go card 7, go card "Terry", and so on. The next section, "Syntactic Terms," is a complete list of all the nonobvious terms that might appear within angle brackets.

| A vertical bar separates mutually exclusive options. For example, the syntactic statement

```
go [ help | home | back ]
```

means that it's legal to say go help or go home or go back (but you can't say go help home or go home back).

{ } Curly braces enclose optional elements that you can use or ignore. For example, the syntactic statement

```
go {to} <card>
```

means that legal forms for the **go** command include go *<card>* and go to *<card>*.

[ ] Square brackets enclose a group of related terms. Square brackets are often used to indicate precedence of consideration. For example, part of the syntax for backgrounds is:

```
background [id <unsigned> | <endLine> | <expr>]
```

The brackets indicate that HyperCard first looks for the word ID (to indicate an ID number); if it can't find one, it looks to see if the next character after the word background is an end-of-line marker; and so it goes.

Table 3-1 presents a synopses of the special syntactic symbols described above:

Table 3-1: Syntactic symbols

Symbol	Meaning
< >	Enclose generic term meant to be substituted by a specific form (that is, enclose nonterminal)
|	Separates mutually exclusive alternatives indicating left-to-right precedence
{ }	Enclose optional elements
[ ]	Enclose group of terms, indicating left-to-right precedence

Syntactic Terms

<bkgnd> is any valid background reference.
<button> is any valid button reference.
<card> is any valid card reference.
<empty> is the null string.
<endLine> is the end of line character (which is ASCII 13).
<expr> is any expression — value, source of value, or group(s) of values —meant to be resolved and taken as a single value. Expressions are covered in detail in Chapter 6.
<factor> is the first fully resolvable portion of an expression. Factors are covered in detail in Chapter 6.
<field> is any valid field reference.
<line> is everything remaining in a line up to the end of the line or a comment.
<numericFactor> is a factor that can be converted to a number.
<object> is any object.
<ordinal> is one of the ordinal numbers first through tenth, plus the special ordinals last, middle, and any. (If the something that middle is in has an even number of units, then middle moves toward the high end. So the middle of 6 is 4.)
<return> is the return character, entered by pressing the Return key or appended

within a script by the vocabulary word `return` or the expression `numToChar(13)`.

<stack> is any valid stack reference.

<token> is a single word without quotation marks meant to be taken literally.

<unsigned> is any expression that can be converted to an integer whose value is zero or greater.

The adjectives `this`, `prev`, and `next` refer only to cards and backgrounds in the current stack.

All words that are not within angle brackets must appear in a reference exactly as they appear in the given syntax examples. So in the phrase `<ordinal>` card the word *ordinal* is replaced with one of the ordinal numbers (first, second, third...), but the word `card` (or its legal synonym `cd`) must appear as in the example.

At times throughout this book you'll see other nonterminals enclosed within angle brackets or in italicized type; in all such cases, the meanings of the terms will be self-evident.

About synonyms: Here's a list of legal synonyms for objects, tools, and containers:

bg	bkgnd	background
bgs	bkgnds	backgrounds
button	btn	
buttons	btns	
card	cd	
cards	cds	
char	character	
chars	characters	
commandChar	cmdChar	(new in 2.0)
fields	flds	
fld	field	
gray	grey	
menuMessage	menuMsg	(new in 2.0)
msg	message	
pict	picture	
poly	polygon	
prev	previous	
reg	regular	

So, for example, wherever you see syntax that uses the word `bg` you could also use either `background` or `bkgnd` and get the same results.

FORMAL SYNTAX: 2.0

HyperTalk 2.0 syntax is much simpler than the syntax of earlier versions, making it closer to natural language.

In 1.2.#, HyperTalk had a mechanism called "automatic expansion" (expressed in the formal syntax of 1.2.# with the symbol "@"). It gave broader lattitude to the grammar of the language by letting you use certain expressions in certain situations to go beyond what the grammar specified. But 2.0 gives "automatic expansion" throughout the language: HyperTalk now accepts an expression in place of any nonterminal (items enclosed in "<" and ">" in this chapter) or any sublist (items enclosed in "{" and "}" or "[" and "]").

Unquoted tokens are now allowed everywhere in HyperTalk. So the nonterminals *<factorOrToken>* and *<exprOrToken>* aren't used anymore.

And the use of the ancillary "the" is now allowed in more cases.

These new freedoms have a minor cost. In previous versions of HyperTalk, "in" and "of" were lexically equivalent — where you could use one, you could use the other. In HyperCard 2.0, there are two places where they're not equivalent: first, when you use `find expr in field`, you can use only "in" (indicated in this syntax by the nonterminal *<inOnly>*). And when you refer to properties (as in the **set** command, with expressions such as `name of card 1`), you can only use "of" (indicated by the nonterminal *<ofOnly>*). This restriction became necessary so that the HyperTalk compiler could distinguish statements such as `find name` *in* `field 1` from `find name` *of* `field 1`. The HyperTalk interpreter used in previous versions could do this using runtime information not available to a compiler.

Seems like a small price to pay, however, for the simplicity and flexibility brought to the language.

For a summary of all changes made for HyperTalk 2.0, see Appendix G, "Changes for 2.0."

For additions made to the syntax of the language too late to be included in this chapter, see Appendix I, "Late Breaking News."

2.0 Scripts

```
<script> = <script> <handler> | <handler>

<handler> =
  on <messageKey> <return>
```

```
    <stmntList>
  end <messageKey> <return>
```

`<stmntList>` = `<stmnt>` | `<stmntList>` `<stmnt>`

`<stmnt>` = [`<messageSend>` | `<keywordStmnt>` | `<empty>`] `<return>`

`<keywordStmnt>` =
```
  do <expr> |
  exit repeat | exit <messageKey> | exit to HyperCard |
  global <identList> |
  next repeat |
  pass <messageKey> |
  return <expr> |
  send <expr> { to [<object> | window <expr>]}|
  <ifBlock> | <repeatBlock>
```

`<ifBlock>` =
```
  if <logical> { <return> } then [<singleThen> | <return> <multiThen>]
```

`<singleThen>` = `<stmnt>` { {`<return>`} `<elseBlock>` }

`<multiThen>` = `<stmntList>` [end if | `<elseBlock>`]

`<elseBlock>` = else [`<stmnt>` | `<return>` `<stmntList>` end if]

`<repeatBlock>` =
```
  repeat {forever | <duration> | <count> | with <identifier> = <range>} <return>
    <stmntList>
  end repeat
```
`<duration>` = until `<logical>` | while `<logical>`
`<count>` = { for } `<unsigned>` { times }
`<range>` = `<integer>` { down } to `<integer>`

2.0 Expressions

`<expr>` = `<source>` | - `<expr>` | not `<expr>` | `<expr>` `<op>` `<expr>` |
  (`<expr>`) | `<chunk>` `<expr>`

`<op>` =
```
  + | - | * | / | & | && | ^ | = | < | > | <> | ≠ |
  <= | >= | ≤ | ≥ | and | or | contains | div | mod |
  is | is not | is in | is not in | is within | is not within
```

```
<source> =
  <literal> | <constant> | <simpleContainer> |
  { <adjective> } <function> |
  { <adjective> } <property> of [<object> | <window> |
    { <menuItem> of } <menu> | <chunk> <field>]

<literal> = "quoted string" | unquoted token

<constant> =
  down | empty | false | formFeed | lineFeed |
  pi | quote | space | tab | true | up |
  zero | one | two | three | four | five |
  six | seven | eight | nine | ten

<adjective> = long | short | abbrev | abbr | abbreviated

<window> =  {the} [ card | pattern | tool | scroll ] window |
  <messageBox>

<menuItem> = <ordinal> menuItem | menuItem <expr>
<menu> = <ordinal> menu | menu <expr>

<function> = the <theFunc> | { the } <theFunc> of <oneFuncArg> |
<identifier> ( <funcArgs> )

<theFunc> =
    abs | annuity | atan | average | charToNum | clickChunk |
    clickH | clickLine | clickLoc | clickText | clickV | commandKey |
    compound | cos | date | diskSpace | exp | exp1 | exp2 |
    foundChunk | foundField | foundLine | foundText | heapSpace |
    length | ln | ln1 | log2 | max | menus | min | mouse |
    mouseClick | mouseH | mouseLoc | mouseV | number | numToChar |
    offset | optionKey | param | paramCount | params | random |
    result | round | screenRect | seconds | selectedChunk |
    selectedField | selectedLine | selectedText | shiftKey | sin |
    sound | sqrt | stackSpace | tan | target | ticks | time | tool |
    trunc | value
```

Syntax for each individual function appears later in the Functions section.

```
<property> =
  autoHilite | autoTab | blindTyping | botRight | bottom |
  bottomRight | brush | cantAbort | cantDelete | cantModify |
```

```
cantPeek | centered | checkMark | cmdChar | commandChar | cursor |
dontSearch | dontWrap | dragSpeed | editBkgnd | enabled | filled |
fixedLineHeight | freeSize | grid | height | highlight |
highlite | hilight | hilite | icon | id | language | left |
lineSize | loc | location | lockMessages | lockRecent |
lockScreen | lockText | markChar | marked | menuMessage |
menuMsg | messageWatcher | multiple | multiSpace | name |
numberFormat | pattern | polySides | powerKeys | rect | rectangle |
right | script | scriptEditor | scroll | sharedHilite |
sharedText | showLines | showName | showPict | size |
stacksInUse | style | suspended | textAlign | textArrows |
textFont | textHeight | textSize | textStyle | top | topLeft |
userLevel | userModify | variableWatcher | version | visible |
wideMargins | width
```

Syntax for each individual property appears at the end of the Commands section, in the notes about the **set** command.

2.0 Objects

<object> =
HyperCard | me | { the } target | *<button>* | *<field>* | *<card>* |
<bkgnd>| *<stack>*
Note: "card field 1" is a field and "card (field 1)" is a card.

<button> =
{card | bkgnd} [button id *<unsignedFactor>* | button *<factor>* |
<ordinal> button] { of *<card>*}

<field> =
  {card | bkgnd} [field id *<unsignedFactor>* | field *<factor>* |
  <ordinal> field] { of *<card>* }

<part> = *<button>* | *<field>*

<ordinal> = {the}
  last | mid | middle | any |
  first | second | third | fourth | fifth |
  sixth | seventh | eigth | ninth | tenth

<card> =
 recent card | back | forth |

```
[card id <unsigned> | card <expr> | card <endLine> | <ordinal>
card | <position> card] { of <bkgnd> } |
<ordinal> marked card | <position> marked card |
marked card <expr>
```

`<position>` = this | {the} prev | {the} next

`<bkgnd>` =
  bkgnd id `<unsigned>` | bkgnd `<expr>`| bkgnd `<endLine>` |
  `<ordinal>` bkgnd | `<position>` bkgnd

`<stack>` = this stack | stack `<expr>` | stack `<endLine>`

2.0 Containers

`<simpleContainer>` =
`<variable>` | `<field>` | `<messageBox>` | { the } selection

`<container>` = `<chunk>` `<simpleContainer>` | `<simpleContainer>`

`<messageBox>` = { the } msg { box | window }

`<chunk>` =
  {[`<ordinal>` char | char `<expr>` { to `<expr>` }] of}
  {[`<ordinal>` word | word `<expr>` { to `<expr>` }] of}
  {[`<ordinal>` item | item `<expr>` { to `<expr>` }] of}
  {[`<ordinal>` line | line `<expr>` { to `<expr>` }] of}

2.0 Commands

Command Nonterminals

These nonterminals appear in the **command** syntax (which follows immediately).

`<dateItems>` =
  `<unsigned>`,`<unsigned>`,`<unsigned>`,`<unsigned>`,
  `<unsigned>`,`<unsigned>`,`<unsigned>`

`<date>` =
  `<unsigned>` | `<dateItems>` |
  `<humanDate>` { `<humanTime>` } |
  `<humanTime>` { `<humanDate>` }

`<dateFormat>` = { `<adjective>` } [seconds | dateItems | date | time]

`<dayOfWeek>` =

Sunday | Sun | Monday | Mon | Tuesday | Tue | Wednesday |
Wed | Thursday | Thu | Friday | Fri | Saturday | Sat

<dest> =
  [*<card>* | *<bkgnd>*] { of *<stack>* } | *<stack>* |
  [*<card>* | *<bkgnd>*] of { stack } *<exprOrLine>*

<duration> = until *<logical>* | while *<logical>*

<humanDate> =
  { *<dayOfWeek>* , } *<month>* *<unsigned>* , *<unsigned>* |
  <unsignedFactor> [/ | -] *<unsignedFactor>* [/ | -]
  <unsignedFactor>

<humanTime> =
  <unsigned> : *<unsigned>* { : *<unsigned>* } { am | pm }

<month> =
  January | Jan | February | Feb | March | Mar |
  April | Apr | May | June | Jun | July | Jul |
  August | Aug | September | Sep | October | Oct |
  November | Nov | December | Dec

<point> = *<integer>* , *<integer>*

<preposition> = before | after | into

<rect> = *<integer>*, *<integer>*, integer>, *<integer>*

<springKeys> = *<springKeys>* , *<springKey>* | *<springKey>*

<springKey> = shiftKey | optionKey | commandKey

<style> =
  transparent | opaque | rectangle | roundrect | shadow | checkBox |
    radioButton | scrolling | plain |diagonal| zoom

<textAlign> = right | left | center

<textStyleList> = *<textStyleList>*,*<textStyle>* | *<textStyle>*

<textStyle> =
  plain | bold | italic | underline | outline |
  shadow |condense | extend | group

<visEffect> = *<visKind>* { { very } [slow | slowly | fast] }
  { to *<visSrc>* }

<visKind> =

```
    barn door [open | close] |
    cut | plain | dissolve | venetian blinds | checkerboard |
    iris [open | close] |
    scroll [left | right | up | down] |
    shrink to [ top | center | bottom ] |
    stretch from [ top | center | bottom ] |
    wipe [left | right | up | down] |
    zoom [open | out | close | in ]
<visSrc> = card | black | white | gray | inverse

<window> = {the} [card | pattern | scroll | tool] window | <messageBox>
```

Commands

```
add
  <arith> to <container>
answer
  <expr> {with <factor> {or <factor> {or <factor> }}} |
  file <expr> { of type <factor> {or <factor> {or <factor>}}}
arrowkey
  left | right | up | down
ask
  {password | file} <expr> { with [<expr> | <line>] }
beep
  {<unsigned>}
choose
  tool <unsigned> |
  [browse | button | field | select | lasso | pencil |
  brush | eraser | line | spray { can } | rect |
  round rect | bucket | oval | curve | text |
  reg poly | poly] tool
click
  at <point> { with <springKeys> }
close
  file <exprOrLine> | printing
controlkey
  <unsigned>
convert
  [<container> | <date>] to <dateFormat> { and <dateFormat> }
```

```
create
   [stack <expr> { with <bkgnd> } { in { a } new window }
   | menu <expr> ]
debug
   hintBits | pureQuickDraw [ true | false ] | checkPoint
delete
   <chunk> <simpleContainer> | {<menuItem> [of | from]} <menu>
dial
   <expr> { with modem | with { modem } <expr> }
disable
   { <menuItem> of } <menu>
divide
   <container> by <float>
doMenu
   <exprOrLine> | <expr> {, <expr>}{without dialog}
drag
   from <point> to <point> { with <springKeys> }
edit
   { the } script of <object>
enable
   { <menuItem> of } <menu>
enterInField
enterkey
export
   paint to file <expr>
find
   { whole | string | words | word | chars | normal }
   <expr> { in <field> }
functionkey
   <unsigned>
get
   <expr> |
   { the } <property>
   { <ofOnly> [<window> | <object> | {<menuItem> of} <menu> |
     <chunk> <field>]}
go
   {to} [[<ordinal> | <position>] <endLine> | <dest>]
   {in {a} new window}{without dialog}
```

```
help
hide
  menuBar | picture of <object> |
  [ card | bkgnd ] picture | <window> | <part>
import
    paint from file <expr>
lock
  screen
mark
  all cards | <card> | cards where <expr>
multiply
  <container> by <arith>
open
  printing { with dialog } |
  file <exprOrLine> |
  <expr> { with <exprOrLine> }|
  <exprOrLine>
play
  stop | <expr> { { tempo <unsigned> } <exprOrline> }
pop
  card { <preposition> <container> }
print
  <expr>  with <exprOrLine> |
  <unsigned> cards | all cards | marked cards | <card> |
  <field> |  <expr>
push
  <dest>
put
  <expr> { <preposition> [<container> | {<menuItem> of }
    <menu> { with menuMessage{s} <expr> } ] }
read
  from file <expr> [until <expr> | for <unsigned>]
reset
  paint | menuBar
returnInField
returnkey
save
  [{ this } stack | stack <expr> ] as { stack } <expr>
```

```
select
  { before | after } [text of | <chunk> ] [ <field> | <message>] |
  <part> | <emptyExpr>
set
  { the } <property>
  { <ofOnly> [<window> | <object> | {<menuItem> of} <menu> |
  <chunk> | <field>] }
  to <propVal>
```

(See "Notes on Set," below.)

```
show
  menuBar | picture of <object> |
  [ card | bkgnd ] picture |
  [<window> | <part>] { at <point> } |
  { all | marked | <unsigned> } cards
sort
  { ascending | descending }
  { text | numeric | international | dateTime }
  by <expr>
start
  using <stack>
stop
  using <stack>
subtract
  <arith> from <container>
tabkey
type
  <expr> { with <springKeys> }
unlock
  screen { with { visual { effect }} <visEffect> }
unmark
  all cards | <card> | cards where <expr>
visual
  { effect } <visEffect>
wait
  <duration> | <count> { ticks | tick | seconds | second | sec }
write
  <expr> to file <exprOrLine>
```

Notes on Set

The following syntax refers only to the **set** command.

```
<propVal> =
  <exprOrLine>] | <integer> | <unsigned> | <logical> |
  <point> | <rect> | <style> | <textAlign> | <textStyleList>
```

   Set has a different syntax for different groups of properties. The following list shows which nonterminals apply to which properties:

exprOrLine:
   cmdChar, cursor, icon, language, markChar, menuMsg,
   messageWatcher, name, numberFormat, script, scriptEditor,
   scriptWatcher, text, textFont, variableWatcher

integer:
   bottom, height, left, right, top, width

unsigned:
   brush, dragSpeed, lineSize, multiSpace, pattern, polySides,
   scroll, textHeight, textSize, userLevel

logical:
   autoHilite, autoTab, blindTyping, cantAbort, cantDelete,
   cantModify, cantPeek, centered, checkMark, dontSearch, dontWrap,
   editBkgnd, enabled, filled, fixedLineHeight, freeSize, grid,
   hilite, lockMessages, lockRecent, lockScreen, lockText, marked,
   multiple, powerKeys, sharedHilite, sharedText, showName,
   showPict, textArrows, userModify, visible, wideMargins

point:
   botRight, loc, scroll, topLeft

rect: rect

style: style

textAlign: textAlign

textStyleList: textStyle

2.0 Functions

Note that `<funcArith>`, `<funcFloat>`, `<funcExpr>`, and `<funcUnsigned>` all take expressions when they're called with parentheses, but they all take factors when they're called with "of."

abs
  <funcArith>
annuity
  <float> , *<float>*
atan
  <funcFloat>
average
  <arithList>
charToNum
  <funcExpr>
clickChunk
clickH
clickLine
clickLoc
clickText
clickV
commandKey
compound
  <float>, *<float>*
cos
  <funcFloat>
date
diskSpace
exp
  <funcFloat>
exp1
  <funcFloat>
exp2
  <funcFloat>
foundChunk
foundField
foundLine
foundText
heapSpace
length
  <funcExpr>
ln
  <funcFloat>

```
ln1
   <funcFloat>
log2
   <funcFloat>
max
   <arithList>
menus
min
   <arithList>
mouse
mouseClick
mouseH
mouseLoc
mouseV
number
   cards { in <bkgnd> } |  bkgnds |
   { card | bkgnd } [buttons | fields] |
   [chars | words | items | lines] in <funcExpr> |
   <object> |
   menus | menuItems in <menu> | marked cards
numToChar
   <funcUnsigned>
offset
   <string> , <string>
optionkey
param
   <funcUnsigned>
paramcount
params
random
   <funcUnsigned>
result
round
   <funcFloat>
screenRect
seconds
selectedChunk
selectedField
```

```
selectedLine
selectedText
shiftKey
sin
  <funcFloat>
sound
sqrt
  <funcFloat>
stackspace
tan
  <funcFloat>
target
ticks
time
tool
trunc
  <funcFloat>
value
  <funcExpr>
```

2.0 Messages

closeBackground	mouseWithin
closeCard	newBackground
closeField	newButton
closeStack	newCard
deleteBackground	newField
deleteButton	newStack
deleteCard	openBackground
deleteField	openCard
deleteStack	openField
exitField	openStack
idle	quit
mouseDown	resume
mouseEnter	resumeStack
mouseLeave	startup
mouseStillDown	suspend
mouseUp	suspendStack

Chapter 4

Referring to Objects

The HyperCard environment is composed mainly of objects. Nearly all scripting deals with one object or another; this chapter describes in precise detail the process of referring to them.

For a definition of the complete HyperTalk formal syntax, see Chapter 3.

SPECIFYING OBJECTS

You can specify any object by giving its name, and you can specify any object smaller than a stack by ID or by positional number.

Names

Every stack must have a name. All objects smaller than a stack can, but don't have to, have names. You can change the name of any object (except HyperCard) by setting its name property:

```
set the name of stack "My favorite stack" to "Fave Rave"
```

A name can have up to 31 characters. It can include letters, numbers, and special characters (that is $,#,@, and so on) but the name of a stack can't include a colon (:).

A name can have any number of spaces within it. Except in the case of a stack name appearing at the end of a line, you must enclose names that contain spaces within quotation marks.

You can put the name of any object into a variable and refer to the object by referring to the variable:

```
put "Fave Rave" into myFavoriteStack
go to stack myFavoriteStack
```

Name forms: You refer to an object using one of three forms of the object's name property — the short name, the name, or the long name:

The form `short name` is just the name of the object:

```
myButton
myField
myBackground
```

If the object doesn't have a name, the short name is the object's type and ID:

```
card button id 4
card id 3745
bkgnd id 5170
```

The form `name` is the object's type plus its `short name`:

```
card button "myButton"
bkgnd field "myField"
stack "myStack"
```

The form `long name` is the object's name preceded by its full path:

```
stack "myHardDisk:myFolder:myStack"
bkgnd "myBackground" of stack "myHardDisk:myFolder:myStack"
card "myCard" of stack "myHardDisk:myFolder:myStack"
```

No matter what form you use for the object HyperCard, you always get HyperCard.

Also see the **name of object** property (page 579) for a list of naming oddities.

IDs

All objects within a stack (but not the stack itself) have IDs. When a background, card, field, or button is created, HyperCard assigns it a permanent ID. While several objects of the same type might have the same name, they'll never have the same ID in places where such a similarity might cause confusion. For example, no two buttons on the same card will have the same ID, although all buttons can have the same name.

Name bug alert

If you're using any HyperCard version earlier than 2.0, keep the names of objects other than stacks to 29 or fewer characters. A bug in all HyperCard versions through 1.2.# lets HyperCard match only the first 29 characters of a name when you reference that object. If the real name has 30 or more characters in it, a reference to that object by name will fail all the time (but a reference to it by ID or number will succeed).

You can change the name of an object, but you can't change its ID.

The ID is a property of an object. For more information on IDs, including how to use them, see the **ID** property (page 548).

Numbers

An object's number is that object's position in its domain. All objects within a stack (but not the stack itself) have numbers:

- A button's number is its layer from back to front among all buttons in its background or on its card (higher numbers closer to the front).

- A field's number is its layer from back to front among all fields in its background or on its card (higher numbers closer to the front).

- A card's number is the card's position in a stack.

- A background's number reflects the order in which it was created in the family of backgrounds for that stack.

The positional number is a property of an object. For more information on numbers, see the **Number** function (page 438).

HOW TO REFER TO OBJECTS

This section shows the complete and exact syntax for referring to all HyperCard objects. All exceptions and anomalies are noted.

The reference description for each object starts with a list of all allowable syntactic forms for referring to that object. After that come a series of one-line examples showing how to apply the syntactic forms. Finally a list of notes appears, as applicable.

Referring to HyperCard

```
HyperCard
```

There is no other syntax for HyperCard. The word has few uses, except to bypass the message passing path:

```
send "Find" && thisString to HyperCard
```

Referring to Stacks

```
this stack | stack <endLine> | stack <expr>
```

A stack always has a name, first assigned when the stack is created but which you can change at any time:

```
freesize of stack -- current stack
short name of this stack
set name of this stack to "My Stack"
go stack Some Other One -- likely to be some other stack
go stack "Some Other One" -- quotation marks always allowed with literals
go stack notThisStack -- a variable
```

The word "stack" used by itself (meaning the current stack) can appear only at the end of a line:

```
put name of stack
```

but

```
put name of this stack into oldStack
```

Unknown stack: When you refer to a stack that HyperCard doesn't know about, HyperCard puts up a dialog (technically called the standard file dialog box) listing all the folders and stacks and asks you where the stack is (see Figure 4-1). HyperTalk assumes that whatever stack name you click is the stack you want, whether or not that stack has the same name as the one the code asks for.

HyperCard adds this pathname to the Stack Searchpath card in the Home stack if it's not there already. But if the stack is misnamed, its name isn't added; each time you ask for that stack, you'll have to tell HyperTalk where to find it.

Stack name is the file name: The name of a stack is the name of that file as it appears in the Finder. So no two stacks in the same folder can have the same name.

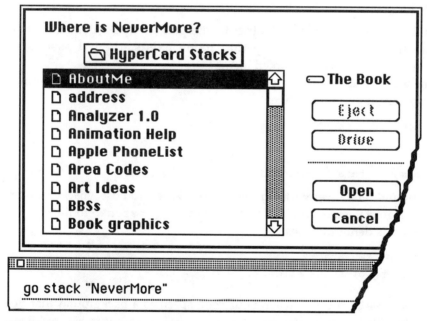

Figure 4-1 "Stack? What stack?"

Referring to Backgrounds

```
background [id <unsigned> | <endLine> | <expr> ]
```

or

```
<ordinal> background | [this|prev|next] background
```

```
bkgnd id 5
number of cards in background -- the current background
bg 3
fifth background -- of this stack
background "theBackground" -- name is "theBackground"
background theBackground -- could be either variable or literal
this bg
next bg
```

In the last example, HyperTalk tries to interpret theBackground as a variable name first; if no variable by that name exists, then it assumes that theBackground is an unquoted literal.

The word "background" used by itself (meaning the current background) can appear only at the end of a line:

```
put name of background
```

but

```
put name of this background into oldBackground
```

Background references with Go command: When you use a background reference in a **go** statement, you can add the syntax of <stack> to the end of both of the syntax definition lines:

```
go bg 3 of "My Stack"
go third bg of stack myStack.
```

Unknown background: When your code specifies a background that doesn't exist, HyperTalk puts up the error dialog "No such card," as in Figure 4-2.

Figure 4-2 "No background 13 in this stack."

Referring to Cards

```
card [id <unsigned> | <endLine> |  <expr> ] { of <bkgnd> }
```

or

```
<ordinal> card { of <bkgnd> }
```

or

```
[ this | next | previous] {marked} card
```

or

```
<ordinal> marked card
```

or

```
recent card
```

or

```
back
```

or

```
forth

card id 2
ID of card
id of card 3 of bg 4
card thisNumber + thatNumber
fifth card
name of this card is not "foo"
```

```
recent card
button 3 of back
next marked card
```

Note that the syntax calls for an expression, not a factor. So the expresssion

```
get field 1 of card 2 + 1
```

gets field 1 of card 3, and *not* 1 added to the contents of field 1 which resides on card 2. To get the latter, you'd use this form:

```
get (field 1 of card 2) + 1
```

Card references with Go command: When you use a card reference in a **go** statement, you can add the syntax {of <stack>} to the end of the first two syntax definition lines:

```
go cd 3 of stack myStack
go third cd of stack myStack

card <endLine> -- means this card
card 3 + 4 -- means card 7
field 1 of card 3 + 4 -- means first field of 7th card
(field 1 of card 3) + 4 -- 4 + numeric value of first field of third card
```

Unknown card: When you try to go to a card that doesn't exist from the Message box, HyperTalk puts up the error dialog "no such card." When you try to go to a nonexistent card from a script, HyperTalk sets the value of the **result** function (described on page 454) but doesn't put up a dialog.

For the causes and cures of some common errors with cards, see "Object References and the Parsing of Expressions" at the end of this chapter.

Referring to Fields

```
{card|bkgnd} field [id <numericFactor> | <factor> ] { of <card> }
```

or

```
<ordinal> {card|bkgnd} field { of <card> }

fld id thisNumber
card field 12 of card 18
```

```
field "Counties"
field "data" of card 1
any card field
fifth field of card 325
field fred
```

Note that the syntax calls for a factor, not an expression. So the phrase

```
put field 1 + 7
```

adds 7 to the contents of field 1 and puts the total into the Message box; it does *not* put the contents of field 8 into the Message box.

A field reference must always be to a field in the current stack. If you don't say what card the field is on, HyperTalk assumes that it's on the current card. If you don't specify whether you're referring to a card or to a background field, HyperCard assumes you're referring to a background field.

Unknown field: When your code specifies a field that doesn't exist, HyperTalk puts up an error dialog saying that "there is no" such field, as in Figure 4-3.

For the causes and cures of some common errors with fields, see "Object References and the Parsing of Expressions" at the end of this chapter.

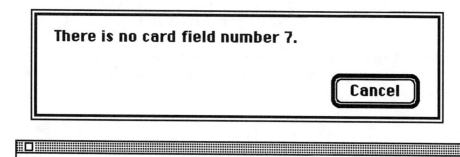

Figure 4-3   Nonexistetr field reference

Referring to Buttons

```
{card|bkgnd} button [id <numericFactor>| <factor> ] {of <card>}
```

or

```
<ordinal> {card|bkgnd} button {of <card>}
btn ID thisNumber
bg btn 12 of card 18
button myButton
button "Additional Info" of card 1
any background button
fifth button of card 325
```

A button reference must always be to a button in the current stack. If you don't say what card the button is on, HyperTalk assumes that it's on the current card. If you don't specify whether you're referring to a card or to a background button, HyperCard assumes you're referring to a card button.

Unknown button: When your code specifies a button that doesn't exist, HyperTalk puts up an error dialog saying that "there is no" such button.

ME AND THE TARGET

Me and the Target are special synonyms for objects. Me is the object containing the currently running script; the target is the object that the current message was first sent to.

Me

When you use the script editor to look at a script that has the word me in it, you can immediately tell who me is — it's the object whose name is the title of the script editor window.

In Figure 4-4, me refers to card button "Book Graphics."

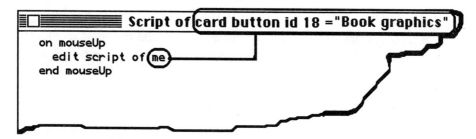

Figure 4-4 Who's me?

A button might have a handler that alternately changes its name to reflect a current condition:

```
on setName
  if visible of field "Extra Information" is true
  then set name of me to "Hide Info"
  else set name of me to "Show Info"
end setName
```

The following statements all work as you'd expect if you'd specified the object by name:

```
put short name of me
put name of me
put long name of me
```

When me is a field: The field is the only object that is also a container. So HyperTalk gives me special consideration when me refers to a field. The statement

```
put me into thisVar
```

copies the *contents* of me into thisVar. Similarly, the statement

```
put thisVar into me
```

copies the contents of the variable thisVar into whatever field me represents.

But statements like put name of me work for fields as they do for any other object.

The Target

The target is the object that gets the first chance to respond to a message. The target never changes while a handler is running, and there's no way you can change the target from within a handler. The target was set up before the handler started running.

For example, assume that a card script has this handler in it:

```
on mouseUp
   if "card button" is not in the target then pass mouseUp
   beep
   put the target
end mouseUp
```

(The terms `the target` and `the name of the target` are synonymous.) Whenever you click on a button on the card in the example, if that button has an empty script (that is, a script with no code in it) HyperCard beeps and puts the name of that button into the Message box. The button you clicked was the first recipient of the mouseUp message — that is, it was `the target` of the message.

By the way, if the third line of that handler were this:

```
put the target & " of " & the name of me
```

you'd get the name of the button and the name of the card that holds the handler (as in `card button "New Button" of card "Home"`).

"Target" versus "the target": Fields get special treatment with `the target`, as with `me`. When a field is `the target`, you can use the term `target` — that is, `the target` without `the` — to refer to the contents of the field in question. (**Target** is both an object that optionally can have "the" before it, and a function called with "the.")

For example, assume that card field id 3 has this script in it:

```
on differences
   put the target & return & target into card field "Recipient"
end differences
```

Further assume that card field id 3 has this text typed into it: "The contents of the target field."

You enter this into the Message box and press return:

```
send "differences" to card field id 3
```

86

Figure 4-5 shows what happens.

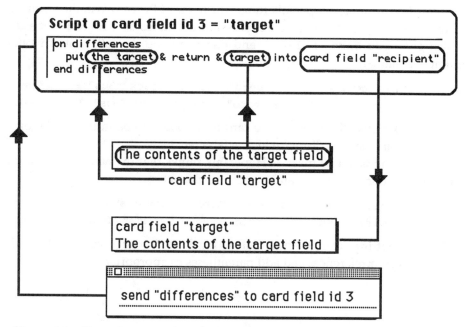

Figure 4-5 "Target" versus "the target"

This is the only case where using the word "the" changes the meaning of a phrase.

OBJECT REFERENCES AND
THE PARSING OF EXPRESSIONS

You need to be sure that you religiously follow the rules outlined in this chapter when you refer to objects. Some constructions can look tricky at first, but are all explainable (he said, with a wise expression) in terms of these rules.

For example, the syntax for referring to cards says that HyperTalk looks for a factor after the word "field" and for an expression after the word "card." Here's the tricky part: when HyperTalk evaluates an expression, it goes as far as it can. And an expression often includes an operand, an operator, and another operand:

```
if short name of card 3 is "foo" then beep 3 -- fails with "no such card"
if (short name of card 3) is "foo" then beep 3 -- succeeds
```

In this first example, HyperTalk thinks the name of the card is in the resolution of the expression *3 is "foo"*; that expression evaluates as a logical to `false`, which gives you `card false` — and `card false` doesn't exist. This next example is similar:

```
if field 1 of cd i contains "bozo" then go stack "Bus" -- fails
if (field 1 of cd i) contains "bozo" then go stack "Bus" -- succeeds
```

HyperTalk thinks the name of the card is supposed to be in the resolution of the expression *i contains "bozo,"* which is false (etc.):

Example 3 adds a new twist — HyperTalk thinks that the name of the card is the concatenation between `i` and a `return` character:

```
put fld 1 of cd i & return after cd fld "Table of Contents" of cd 1 -- fails
put (fld 1 of cd i) & return after cd fld "Table of Contents" of cd 1 -- succeeds
```

If you're getting strange error dialogs (such as "no such card"), check the phrasing of your references and add parentheses as appropriate.

Chapter 5

Sources of Value

This chapter defines the basic elements
from which all HyperTalk expressions are
constructed. It holds a description of
sources of value common to most languages (functions, literals, constants, and
variables), plus the ones that are either
unique to HyperCard or uniquely implemented (properties, fields, Message box,
the Selection, and chunks).

You can use all of these sources of values — or simply, sources — interchange-
ably to construct expressions, the details of
which appear in Chapter 6.

HyperTalk has five basic categories for sources of value: functions, properties,
literals, constants, and containers. This chapter describes each of these in turn,
with special emphasis on containers.

FUNCTIONS AND PROPERTIES

These sources of value each have their own chapters. They're included here
briefly for completeness.

Functions

A function returns a value, usually based on one or more arguments (that is, values passed to the function and upon which the function operates). Certain system functions such as **the date** and **the time** require no argument; these functions return a value reflecting the current state of the system. In either case, the value of a function is changeable, and is calculated at the time that it's called:

```
put the long date
put random(500) into field 12
put average(field 3, field 4, field 5) into averageAge
```

Properties

A property is an attribute of an object, window, menu, menu item, or chunk of text. Properties return a logical, numeric, geometric, or string value, depending on the specific attribute. Many properties can be set by the scripter:

```
put the hilite of button "Click me" into onOff
put the freeSize of stack "Home"
put the multiSpace after line 3 of field "System State"
```

Literals

A literal is a string whose value is the string itself. HyperTalk has three types of literals: quoted, unquoted, and numeric.

Quoted

A quoted literal is a string that appears within double quotation marks ("):

```
put "What - me worry?" into field "Quotations" -- Two quoted literals
```

Unquoted

An unquoted literal is one that doesn't have quotation marks around it:

```
put the freeSize of stack Home -- "Home" is an unquoted literal
```

Unquoted literals not recommended: The ability to use unquoted literals is an ability you should use infrequently, if at all. You reduce your chances for error substantially if you enclose all literals within quotation marks. A common error is creating an unquoted literal early in the development process and later using that same word as the name of a variable. When HyperCard comes across an ambiguous situation where that literal/variable pops up, you're liable to get unwanted results.

Unquoted literals and objects

You can use a single-word unquoted literal when you refer to any object name:

```
put 0 into field Payment -- Payment is an unquoted literal
```

Only a stack name can be a multiple-word unquoted literal:

```
go to stack All The World's a Stage
```

You're guaranteed to get an error when you use multiple-word unquoted literals for any nonstack object:

```
put field All My Wives into field Soaps -- Looks for field "All"
```

See Chapter 4 for details on how to refer to all objects.

Numeric

A numeric literal is a digit (0,1,2,3,4,5,6,7,8,9) or a combination of digits (42, 65536, 98.6, 3.14159). Digits require no quotation marks:

```
add 3 to totals
```

Because HyperTalk is a string-oriented language, even numbers are treated as strings. Thus you can have a form such as

```
answer "What number?" with char 2 of 45673 -- yields 5
```

CONSTANTS

A constant is a source whose value never changes. Because you refer to constants by name, they look like variables with permanent values.

Here's a list of all the constants in the language with their values (Table 5-1). Notes appear after the table for items followed by a dagger (†).

Table 5-1: Constants

Constant	Value/comment
up†	The name *is* the value
	as in: if the shiftKey is up
down†	
true	The logical value
false	The name *is* the value
empty	"" (ASCII 0)†
space	" " (ASCII 32)
pi†	3.14159265358979323846
zero	0
one	1
two	2
three	3
four	4
five	5
six	6
seven	7
eight	8
nine	9
ten	10
tab†	ASCII 9
formfeed†	ASCII 12
linefeed†	ASCII 10
quote†	ASCII 34
return†	ASCII 13

About up and down: While up and down are constants, in versions through 1.2.# "left" and "right" are not. Thus when you specify a direction for arrowKeys you can use a form like `if it is up`, but in versions through 1.2.# you must use the form `if it is "left"`. Because HyperCard 2.0 allows unquoted literals everywhere, all self-evaluating constants are now obsolete.

About ASCII: ASCII is an acronym for American Standard Code for Information Interchange, a system whereby a specific integer represents a text character or special code. See Appendix A for a list of these codes.

About pi: Pi is a string constant. Doing math on it forces its conversion to a binary number. Putting the result of that math into a field converts the result back to a string; that string is displayed using the current setting of **numberFormat**. For example, the default value for **numberFormat** is 0.###### — which means that pi + 0 would yield the string 3.141593, and not 3.14159265358979323846. (But all internal calculations are carried out to 19 digits of accuracy.) See the **numberFormat** property for details.

About tab, formfeed, etc: These constants exist because the characters that they represent are not typeable in a script:

```
set the script of button 2 to ¬
"on upDate" & return &¬ -- Return character isn't typeable
"set visible of button " & quote & "Text Arrows" & quote & ¬ --embeds quotes
" to the userLevel >= 2" & return & ¬
"end upDate"
```

CONTAINERS

A container holds information that you supply. HyperTalk has four kinds of containers: fields, variables, the Selection, and the Message box. Additionally HyperTalk lets you specify a **chunk**, defined as a portion of a container; that portion is itself a container.

From a script you always have complete control over the contents of any container. So you can create, edit, or delete the text in any container at any time, and you can at any time copy all or some of the contents of any container into any part of any other container.

Fields

A field has the following characteristics (see Figure 5-1):

- It's also an object (you can send a message to it).

- You can destroy it (using `select field` foo and `doMenu "Clear Field"`
  — but see "Local Variables," below).

- It has a limit on the number of characters it can contain (30,000) other than
  available memory.

- It has its contents regularly stored to disk (and thus its contents are not lost
  when you quit HyperCard).

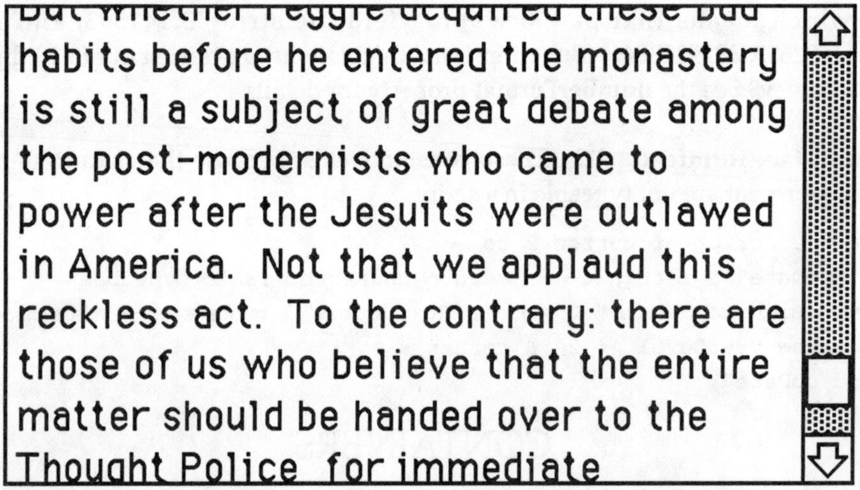

habits before he entered the monastery
is still a subject of great debate among
the post-modernists who came to
power after the Jesuits were outlawed
in America. Not that we applaud this
reckless act. To the contrary: there are
those of us who believe that the entire
matter should be handed over to the
Thought Police for immediate

Figure 5-1   A field

To create a field from within a script, you can do any of the following:

- copy an existing field by peeling off a copy:

```
on copy_Field choice, hor, vert
  choose field tool
  drag from the loc of card field choice to hor, vert with optionKey
  choose browse tool
end copy_Field
```

• drag out a field from scratch:

```
on drag_Field left,top,right,bottom -- you set these values
  choose field tool
  drag from left,top to right,bottom with commandKey
  choose browse tool
end drag_Field
```

• create a field based on the menu command "New Field":

```
on menu_Field left,top,right,bottom
  domenu "new field"
  set the rect of last card field to left,top,right,bottom
  choose browse tool -- "New Field" chooses field tool
end menu_Field
```

Compact stack after field deletions

When you delete an entire field (including all its text), you're actually just resetting pointers. The disk space that the field and its text take up in a stack is still allocated. To free up this trapped disk space, use the Compact Stack menu item.

The contents of a field is written to disk at idle time (that is, when no handler is running) if it has changed.

Variables

A variable is a container that you create. You can create a variable any time you need one; and there's no limit (beyond available RAM) to the number of variables you can create or to the size of the number or the length of the string they can hold.

HyperTalk has two types of variables — **global** and **local.** Both types reside in RAM, and are never stored to disk. The value of a global variable is accessible throughout HyperCard for the current session (that is, until you quit HyperCard); the value of a local variable is accessible only in the handler that created it, and only as long as the handler in which it is created continues to run (that is, until the handler's **end** line executes or an **exit, return,** or **pass** statement executes, or until some error condition occurs — whichever comes first).

Global variables

You create a global variable (or gain access to one that's already been created) by using the form `global  <variableName>` within a handler, or by assigning a value to a variable through the message box. The following handler creates a global variable called theRealName

```
on create_Global
  global theRealName -- theRealName created here as global
  ask "What's your name?" with "John Scribblemonger"
  put it into theRealName
end create_Global
```

Once a global is created, its value is available in the Message box (because all variables in the Message Box are global) and throughout HyperCard to any handler that asks for it. Assuming that the above handler has already run, the following handler uses the value of the global variable `theRealName` defined above:

```
on use_Global
  global theRealName -- theRealName has a value already
  put "Have a great day, " & theRealName into the message box
end use_Global
```

For more details about the **global** keyword , see "Global" in Chapter 7, Keywords.

Local variables

You create a local variable by putting a value into it from within a handler:

```
put the time into currentTime
pop card into top_Of_Stack
```

Local variables go out of existence as soon as the handler in which they're created finishes running. In the next handler, the variables named "hours" and "minutes" have life spans limited to that of the running handler:

```
on local_Vars
  put round(the ticks/60/60) div 60 into hours
  put round(the ticks/60/60) mod 60 into minutes
  put "System on for " & hours & " hours and " & minutes & " minutes"
end local_Vars -- "hours" and "minutes" now gone
```

The variable "It"

The variable named "it" is special in that the commands **ask, answer, read,** and **get** automatically put their values into it (and only into it), automatically creating it as a local variable. (**Convert** also uses it to hold conversion results when another container isn't specified.) This dates back to the time when "it" was the only variable allowed in HyperTalk.

When one handler invokes another, and they both use local variables with the same name, the values of the variables are still local to their own handlers :

```
on firstHandler
  put 10 into localVar
  put localVar -- puts 10 into Message box
  secondHandler -- calls other handler
  put " " & localVar after msg -- localVar still has value 10
end firstHandler

on secondHandler
  put 5 into localVar
  put " " & localVar after msg -- puts " 5" at end of Message box
end secondHandler
```

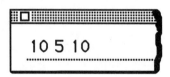

10 5 10

Figure 5-2 localVar's values in the Message box

Variable rules

Here are all the restrictions on variables:

• You can't have global and local variables of the same name in the same handler.

• A variable must already exist before you can operate on its contents (that is, you can't say `add 3 to adder` if `adder` hasn't already been created).

• A variable name can be up to 31 characters long.

• A variable must start with a letter, and can contain letters, digits, and the underscore character (_). Underscore is considered a letter, so a variable name can start with one (as in _Weird_Looking_Variable).

• No other characters are allowed in a variable name (for example: $,%, ?, ¥).

• A variable name cannot be a keyword or either of the special words target or me. Here's a complete list:

```
do    end    exit   function  global  if      then   else
me    next   on     pass      repeat  return  send   target
```

The content of a variable is limited only by RAM. It can contain any text characters, including invisible ones:

```
put charToNum(4) after invisible -- ASCII 4 (non-printable character)
```

Variables always in memory

All variables are always in memory and never on disk. The implications of this are as follows:

• Variables are far faster than fields for storing and retrieving values.

• You can create as many variables as you want.

• To free up memory, clear the value of unneeded globals by putting empty into them.

• To preserve the value of a variable between runs, store its value in a field.

Parameters and Parameter Passing

Parameters are values that can be passed from handler to handler. The following statement sends the message `updatePhoneNumber` with two parameter values:

```
updatePhoneNumber "(617) 555-1212", "(503) 555-1212"
```

The capturing handler accepts the values into parameter variables (called **formal parameters**) in the linear order that they're passed:

```
on updatePhoneNumber oldPhone,newPhone -- parameters captured here
   find oldPhone in field "telephone number" -- (617) 555-1212
   do "put newPhone into" && the foundLine -- (503) 555-1212
end updatePhoneNumber
```

Because they're local variables, parameters are only accessible to the handler that created them, and they go out of existence as soon as the handler in which they were created stops running.

A receiving handler can have a different number of formal parameters than the number of parameter values actually passed. If more formal parameters exist than the number of values passed, HyperTalk puts empty into the extra parameter variables:

```
-- update just two fields
updateAddress "John Scribblemonger", "123 Alcott Lane"

on updateAddress name,street,city,state,zip
   -- update only fields that have been changed
   if name is not empty then put name into field "name"
   if street is not empty then put street into field "street"
   if city is not empty then put city into field "city"
   if state is not empty then put state into field "state"
   if zip is not empty then put zip into field "zip"
end updateAddress
```

If more parameters are passed than there are formal parameters to receive them, the parameter values are still available through the **param** function:

```
put product (12, 24, 36, 48)
function product x,y,z
  put X * Y * Z into total
  repeat with i = 4 to the paramCount -- use up all the parameters
    multiply total by param(i)
  end repeat
  return total
end product
```

For more information about parameters, see the keywords **on** (page 142) and **function**.

How many parameters? Parameters are separated by commas, but a list of comma-separated items that appears either within quotation marks or in any other expression is taken as a single parameter:

```
product (12, 24, 36) -- 3 parameters
product ("12", "24", "36") -- 3 parameters
product ("12, 24, 36") -- 1 parameter
product (field 1) -- 1 parameter (even if its contents has commas)
```

When you refer to a container, the entire contents of the container is considered to be a single parameter. To have each item in a container of items appear as such, use the **value** function:

```
value ("product (" & field 1 & ")")
-- each item in field 1 is separate parameter
```

The Selection

The Selection is any selected text taken as a whole. When no text is selected but the insertion point is present, the Selection is the insertion point (see Figure 5-3). The Selection is always associated with text, and never with graphics or objects.

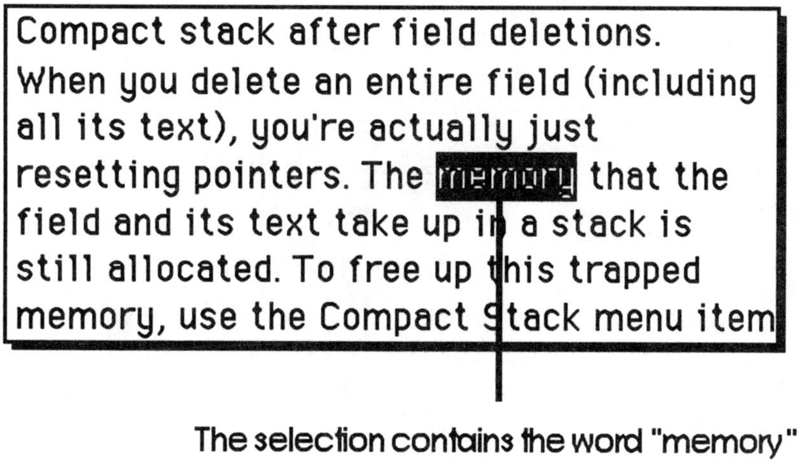

Compact stack after field deletions.
When you delete an entire field (including all its text), you're actually just resetting pointers. The `memory` that the field and its text take up in a stack is still allocated. To free up this trapped memory, use the Compact Stack menu item

The selection contains the word "memory"

Figure 5-3   A Selection

When you say

```
put the selection into field 1
```

a copy of the selected text goes into field 1 (replacing the old contents of field 1). When you say

```
put field 1 into the selection
```

a copy of the text in field 1 replaces the currently selected text; if no text is selected but an insertion point is present, then a copy of the text in field 1 appears at the insertion point.

You can put the insertion point wherever you want it:

```
click at <point>
select [before|after] [text of|<chunk> of] [<field> | msg box]
```

You can't always count on the Selection: The Selection is quite fragile; lots of things can deselect it, including (but not limited to) the following:

- A **find, enterInField, enterKey, returnInField, returnKey, tabKey,** or **sort** command executes.

- The **hilite** of any button or **cantModify** property changes.

- A new tool is chosen.

- HyperCard moves from one card to another.

- The Enter key or the Return key is pressed (the latter of which replaces the selected text with a return character).

- Something else is selected.

The wise scripter acts upon the Selection as soon as is practicable after the Selection appears.

Message Box

The Message box is a one-line container. Only the first line of what you put into the Message box is used; any lines beyond the first are discarded. (All containers except the Message box can hold multiple lines.) The line can be of any length, and so can extend off the display (see Figure 5-4).

How much wood would a woodchuck chuck if a woodchuck could chuck...

Figure 5-4   Message box

You can refer to the Message box in a number of ways. Here's the syntax:

```
{the} [msg | message] {box | window}
put line 3 of field "My favorite candidates" into msg
put total_Taxes after the message window
```

Chunks

A chunk is a portion of the text of any source of value. A chunk can be a character, word, item, line, or a range of any one of these.

A chunk of any container is itself a container in that you can put text into it:

```
pop card before line nextLine of field "My Favorite Cards"
put char 85 of field 1 into word 5 to 12 of the Selection
put field 3 into word 6 of field "Running Text"
```

SOURCES OF VALUE

You refer to a chunk using one of these forms:

```
[ char{acter} | word | item | line ] <integer> {to <integer>} of <factor>
```

or

```
<ordinal> [ char{acter} | word | item | line ] of <factor>
```

A chunk specification always moves from the smallest unit to the largest containing unit. The last designation in a chunk specification is always the source itself:

```
character 8 of exp2(32)
word 6 of line 3 of namesList
line 7 to 12 of field "CD collection"
```

Character

Character (or char) is the designator for the smallest possible unit of any source:

```
character 3 of "wonderful" -- yields n
character 3 of pi -- yields 1 (1 is 3rd char of 3.1415...)
char 12 of line 6 of field myField
fifth char of line 6 of the Selection
```

Note that a space is considered a character.

Word

Word is the designator for text separated by ASCII 32 space characters (that is, space characters produced by pressing the space bar).

At the start of an expression, a word includes all text up to the first space. (Leading spaces are ignored.) At the end of an expression, a word includes all text between a final space and the end of the expression. (If the final character(s) in an expression is a space, it's ignored.)

Anywhere within a container, all characters within quotation marks make up a single word. For example, the following phrase contains three words:

```
this "brief example contains three" words
```

A word can contain any other characters, including punctuation marks, hyphens, and ASCII 202 space characters (option-space):

```
word 4 of "at this petty pace, from day"-- yields pace,
word seven of line foo of the Selection
any word of field 12
```

Item

Item is the designator for text separated by commas:

```
item 3 of "bell, book, candle, myrrh and gypsum" -- yields candle
middle item of field "List"
item 2 of the mouseLoc
number of items in the rect of field 5
```

At the start of an expression, an item includes all text up to the first comma. At the end of an expression, an item includes all text from the last comma to the end of an expression, including return characters. If an expression contains no commas, then it's composed of a single item. An item does *not* include its comma.

Empty items don't always work correctly

Commas are meant to separate items. So it is the intent of the language that a source with a single comma has two items in it, even through there might be nothing either before or after the comma. But in HyperCard versions through 2.0, if the last nonspace character of a source is a comma, that comma is *not* considered to be an item delimiter and the source contains one less item than you'd expect. To work around this bug, put "" after a final comma that otherwise would be followed by nothing.

Line

Line is the designator for text terminated by carriage returns:

```
line 6 of field whatEver
last line of my_Most_Favorite_Variable
```

At the start of an expression, a line is all text up to (but not including) the first return character in that expression. At the end of an expression, a line is all text from (but not including) the last return character to the end of the expression. If the expression contains no return characters, it's comprised of a single line.

If the last character is not a carriage return, adding a carriage return doesn't change the line count; otherwise adding one does (see Figure 5-5).

An empty field has 0 lines. A field with any single character, even if that character is a carriage return, has one line.

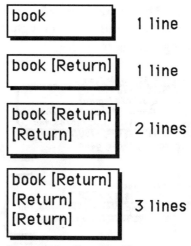

Figure 5-5 Counting lines

Range of a chunk

You can specify a range using the form

```
<chunkName> <integer> to <integer> of <factor>
```

```
character 12 to 15 of Msg
word 5 to 12 of the Selection
item 3 to 6 of line 15 of myVariable
char start to finish of item this to that of line 6 to 10 of theSource
char 2 of (9 * field 1) -- if field 1 contains 3, this yields 7
```

If you ask for an item that's out of range or that doesn't exist, you get nothing. If you ask for a range that is partially out of range, you get as much as is within range:

```
put char 5 to 7 of "word" -- gets EMPTY
put char 3 to 5 of "word" -- gets rd
```

Chunk range within chunk range within...: When you specify a chunk range within a chunk range, evaluation happens from largest to smallest. So in the example

```
char 13 to 18 of word 3 to 5 of item 7 to 8 of line 2 to 5 of theSource
```

HyperTalk first separates lines 2 through 5 from the rest of the variable theSource. Next it culls out items 7 through 8 from this new, 4-line string. Then it pulls out words 3 through 5 of the still shorter 2-item string composed of items 7 and 8. Finally, it ends up with the thirteenth through the eighteenth characters of the resulting 3-word string (see Figure 5-6).

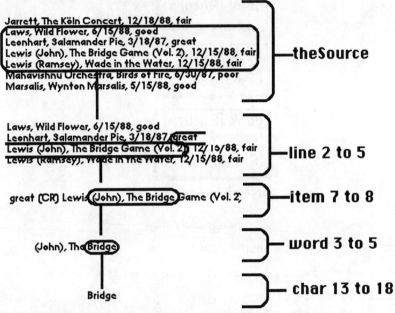

Figure 5-6 Specifying a range within a range

Out-of-range chunks: Sometimes you'll assign text to a chunk with a specification so high that it doesn't exist in the named container. For example, your code says

```
pop card into line 5 of field 8
```

when field 8 only has 3 lines in it. What happens in such a situation depends on the kind of chunk you've specified:

• **Character** or **word** puts the value of that character or word at the end of the container without filling extra spaces. (This is actually a bug that will likely be fixed.)

• **Item** adds sufficient commas (each one defining a null item) to bring that item into existence.

• **Line** adds sufficient return characters to bring that line into existence.

(These out-of-range actions might change in versions after version 2.0.)

How HyperCard counts chunk characters

Consider a variable called source whose contents looks like this (ignoring the quotation marks):

```
"first     last"
```

Assume that five ASCII 32 spaces occur between the words first and last:

```
put length of word 1 of source -- yields 5
put length of word 2 of source -- yields 4
```
But:
```
put length of word 1 to 2 of source -- yields 14
```

Word 1, word 2, and word 1 to 2 are measured as three separate strings. The range word 1 to 2 designates a string that starts at the beginning of word 1 and goes through the end of word 2 — and thus includes the intervening spaces. What applies to words also applies to lines: unless a line has only one word in it, *the length of a line will be greater than the length of the sum of its words* (because a word doesn't include its spaces) *or the sum of its items* (because an item doesn't include its commas).

Expanded text: In the example put field 3 into word 6 of field "Running Text", word 6 of field "Running Text" is replaced and expanded to a series of words to accommodate all the text from field 3; any text after word 6 of field "Running Text" is pushed ahead to accommodate the inserted text (see Figure 5-7).

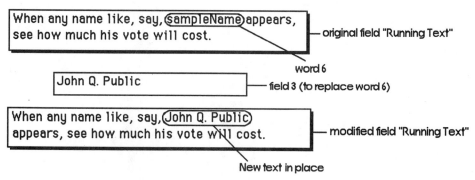

Figure 5-7 Inserting text via chuck expressions

A Minor Inconsistency

Sometimes how HyperTalk deals with nonexistent chunks can be unusual. ("Yeah. Unusual. That's the ticket.") For example, assume the existence of field 1, which is empty:

```
put "x" into item 4 of line 3 of field 1
```

produces

```
(blank line)
(blank line)
 x
```

as opposed to the expected

```
(blank line)
(blank line)
,,,x
```

but if you issue the example statement a second time, you get the expected results.

Chapter 6

Expressions

This chapter explains how to construct arithmetic, geometric, logical, and textual expressions using operators and sources of values. It describes how to use (and override) operator precedence and discusses the important difference between factors and expressions.

For information on the sources of values that constitute expression operands, see "Sources of Value," Chapter 5.

For a host of examples that show expressions in relation to objects, see "Referring to Objects," Chapter 4.

SOME BASIC DEFINITIONS

An **expression** is any source of value, or group(s) of values meant to be combined and taken as a single value.

A **factor** is the linearly first fully resolvable portion of an expression. Elements that appear within parentheses, when combined, are considered to be factors.

The following comparative lists illustrate the differences:

Expression	Factor
3 + 4	3
(3 + 4)	(3 + 4)
(3 + 4)/field 4	(3 + 4)
field 6 * pi	field 6
sin of pi / 4	sin of pi
sin(pi/4)	sin(pi/4)
sin(pi/4) * exp2(12)	sin(pi/4)
whole world	whole
"whole world"	"whole world"

Who cares?   You need to know the difference between expressions and factors because of the differences among the syntaxes of HyperTalk vocabulary words. For example, when you call a function using the form `functionName of param,` `param` must be a factor. So in the expression `round of pi / 4,` it would first find `the round of pi` (which is 3) and divide the results by 4 (3/4), ending up with .75. What you really wanted might have been `round of (pi/4)` which yields 1.

The syntaxes of objects also differ. Field references, for example, are always by factor. A reference to `field 7 + 1` doesn't deal with field 8; rather, the syntax combines the value of field 7 (assumed here to be a numeric value) and adds 1 to it. But card references are by expression: a reference to `card 2 + 3` gets you card 5, and `field 1 of card 2 + 3` gets you field 1 of card 5.

All elements within a single set of parentheses are assumed to represent a single factor:

```
put card field 1 of card 3 + 4  -- gets field 1 of card 7.
put (card field 1 of card 3) + 4 -- gets value of field 1 on card 3,
                                 -- then adds 4 to that value
```

TYPES OF VALUES

All values in HyperTalk are strings. But HyperTalk converts strings to logical or numeric values as such values are needed. For example, the functions `sin` and `cos` take numeric arguments, `charToNum` and `length` take string arguments, and comparisons return logical results.

Logical Values

Logical values are always represented by the words true or false, and represent the outcome of some comparison:

```
10 > 7 -- true, because 10 is greater than 7
A = 12 -- true if the value of variable A is 12,
       -- false in all other cases
field 2 is EMPTY -- true if field 2 is empty, false if not empty
7 < 3 = field 7 -- true if field 7 holds the string value "false"
```

Strings

String values are groups of ASCII characters meant to be taken literally as a list of characters:

```
put charToNum("Q")
put "Nuclear war is unthinkable" into field 12
```

Numerics

Numeric values are groups of characters that represent numbers. As such, these values consist of the digits 0 through 9, with the period (.) representing the decimal point.

International Hyperdecimals

Even though many countries use the comma (,) to represent the decimal point, all versions of HyperTalk use the period. When you localize your stack, you might want to use commas as decimal points in order to be sensitive to local custom. The following handler does it for you:

```
function localize numToChange
   put "," into char offset(".", numToChange) of numToChange
   return numToChange
end localize
```

Operators

Operators act upon the value of expressions. HyperTalk has a variety of operators, defined in this section (but also see "Operators" in Appendix I).

Relationals

A relational operator compares the relationship between two sources and produces a logical (true or false) result (see Table 6-1).

Table 6-1: Relational operators

Operator	Relationship
is, =	equal to
is not, <>, ≠	not equal to
>	greater than
<	less than
>=, ≥	greater than or equal to
<=, ≤	less than or equal to
contains	presence of
is in	presence of
is not in	absence of

Here are some examples:

```
x = y -- x and y have the same value
x is not y -- x and y do not evaluate to the same value
x > y -- value of x is greater than the value of y
x < y -- value of x is less than the value of y
"rats" contains "at" -- true because the string "at" is in "rats"
"at" is in "rats" -- true because the string "at" is in "rats"
foo is in field 3 -- true if the contents of foo is in field 3
joy is not in wealth -- true if the contents of joy is not
                     -- an exact match for a pattern of characters
                     -- in the contents of wealth
```

Most relational comparisons happen within the context of if...then...else constructs (discussed on page 135). But you can test relationships within the Message box:

```
userName = "John Scribblemonger" -- returns true or false
field 12 = 17 -- ditto
```

Point for techies: When you compare two floating–point numbers for equality, in order to compensate for low bit error HyperTalk automatically checks if the numbers are really close rather than exactly equal. Here's what the code looks like internally:

```
floatThresh = 0.00000000001;
EQ := ABS(num1 - num2) < floatThresh;
NE := ABS(num1 - num2) > floatThresh;
```

Concatenation

The concatenation operator ties separate strings together, as shown in Table 6-2.

Table 6-2:   Concatenation operator

Operator	Effect	Result
&	concatenates operands	single string
&&	concatenates operands, adding a space between them	single string

Here are some examples using string operators:

```
"a" & "b" -- yields "ab"
"a" && "b" -- yields "a b"
foo & bar -- yields contents of foo concatenated with contents of bar
```

Arithmetic

Arithmetic operators combine two arithmetic values to produce an arithmetic result, as shown in Table 6-3.

About div and mod: The div operator divides the second operand into the first and returns an integer result. The mod operator divides the second operand into the first and returns the remainder. Both operators take integer operands.

The second operand for div must not be the value 0, or you'll get the value INF. (Under certain circumstances, you'll get an error dialog.)

Table 6-3: Arithmetic operators

Operator	Operation	Example	Yield
^	exponentiation	13 ^ 3	2197
*	multiplication	13 * 3	39
/	floating-point division	13 / 3	4.333333
div	integer division	13 div 3	4
		-13 div 3	-4
mod	modulo division	13 mod 3	1
		-13 mod 3	-1
+	addition	13 + 3	16
-	subtraction	13 - 3	10

Logical Operators

Logical operators combine logical (true or false) values and produce a logical result:

```
if Val > Cost and this = that then doSomeHandler
```

HyperTalk has two logical operators for combining logical results: **and** and **or**. When you combine two values using **and**, both operands must be true to get a true result. When you combine two values using **or**, either value (or both values) must be true to get a true result.

In the above example, HyperTalk performs the following steps:

1. The contents of Val is compared to the contents of Cost. The comparison is numeric if possible, alphabetic if not. If Val is greater than Cost, then the result is true — else the result is false.

2. The contents of this is compared to the contents of that. The comparison is numeric if possible, alphabetic if not. If the values are the same, then the result is true — else it is false.

3. The result of comparison 1 is logically combined (that is, ANDed) with the result of comparison 2. If both results are true, then the handler doSomeHandler is called.

Table 6-4 shows how HyperTalk combines the results of relational operations using the **and** and **or** logical operators:

Table 6-4: Truth table

Operator	1st Operand	2nd Operand	Yield
and	true	true	true
	true	false	false
	false	false	false
	false	true	false
or	true	true	true
	true	false	true
	false	false	false
	true	false	true

Assume that the expression "a = b" is true, and that the expression "c = d" is also true:

a = b and c = d yields true   a = b or c = d yields true
a = b and c ≠ d yields false   a = b or c ≠ d yields true
a ≠ b and c ≠ d yields false   a ≠ b or c ≠ d yields false
a ≠ b and c = d yields false   a ≠ b or c = d yields true

Not: The **not** modifier (technically called a unary or prefix logical operator) negates the value of the factor immediately following it:

not (a = b) and c = d yields false   not (a = b or c = d) yields false
a = b and not (c ≠ d) yields true   not (a = b) or c ≠ d yields false
not (a ≠ b and c ≠ d) yields true   not (a ≠ b) or c ≠ d yields true
not (a ≠ b) and c = d yields true   a ≠ b or not (c = d) yields false

The expression not (a = b) is the same as a ≠ b.

Not takes a factor. So if a and b both contain false, then:

not a and b yields false
but
not (a and b) yields true

You can chain logical operations to any length; the order of precedence in logical operations from highest to lowest is **parentheses, not, and, or:**

not (a = b) and c = d or not (a = b or c = d) yields false
a = b and c = d or not (a = b or c = d) yields true

Geometric

HyperTalk's geometric operators **is within** and **is not within** report whether a point is within a rectangle (true or false). A point is two integer items; a rectangle is four integer items (an **integer** is any whole number):

```
the mouseLoc is within "10,10,100,100"
rect of field 2 is within rect of field 1
this is within that
"20,30" is within "10,10,100,100"
topLeft of field 6 is not within field 7
bottomRight of button 7 is not within "20,30,50,100"
```

You must use expressions or quoted coordinates for geometric operands.

Precedence

Precedence determines the order in which calculations are carried out upon expressions. Table 6-5 shows the precedence of operators in HyperTalk.

Table 6-5 is ordered from highest precedence to lowest precedence. Operators whose precedence numbers are the same have the same level of precedence; when two or more such operators appear in the same expression, HyperTalk evaluates the expression from left to right (except for exponentiation, which is evaluated right to left):

Table 6-5: Precedence

Precedence	Operator
9	unary -, not
8	^
7	*, /, mod, div
6	+, -
5	&, &&
4	contains, >=, >, is in, is not in, is within, is not within, <=, <
3	=, <>
2	and
1	or

Parentheses change the way expressions are interpreted, such that everything within parentheses is combined before anything else happens.

Here are some examples of precedence in the evaluation of numeric expressions. Each example shows the intermediate steps that Hypertalk takes to evaluate the expression; the portion of the expression currently being evaluated is underlined. Expressions on the same line begin with similar operators and values, but the ones on the right demonstrate how parentheses change evaluation:

5 * 3 + 20 div 3 ^ 2	5 ((3 + 20) div 3) ^ 2
5 * 3 + 20 div 9	5 * (23 div 3) ^ 2
15 + 2	5 * 7 ^ 2
17	5 * 49
	245

2 ^ 3 ^ .5	(2 ^ 3) ^ .5
2 ^ 1.732051	8 ^ .5
3.321997	2.828427

12.5 mod 5 * 4 div 3	12.5 mod 5 * (4 div 3)
2.5 * 4 div 3	12.5 mod 5 * 1
10 div 3	2.5 * 1
3	2.5

String Comparisons, ASCII, and Non-English Alphabets

HyperTalk uses dictionary ordering for equality string comparisons, without regard to capitalization; but it uses ASCII (American Standard Code for Information Interchange) ordering for nonequality comparisons. So "Peace" = "peace" yields true (dictionary ordering); but "Peace" < "peace" also yields true because uppercase letters precede lowercase ones in ASCII ordering.

Characters from non-English alphabets (for example å, ë, œ, æ) also follow this secondary ordering in non-equality comparisons. So `"a"` = `"å"` and `"åø"` = `"ao"` because the base characters are the same ("a" and "o"); but `"a"` < `"å"` because the secondary ordering is different.

If you intend to write stacks that need to compare non-English characters, see the chapter on International utilities in *Inside Macintosh* (Volume 1).

Chapter 7

Keywords

Keywords form the skeleton that all handlers and control structures within handlers are built around.

Statements containing keywords aren't sent as messages — which means that they don't go through the message passing path. Rather, they're executed directly. So keywords can't be caught and redefined as can messages.

This chapter lists each keyword in alphabetic order (but then and else are with if), with a detailed definition and examples for each one. For a summary listing of all HyperTalk vocabulary words with brief definitions, see Appendix E.

DO

Forms

```
do expr

do line 5 of var_with_statements_in_it
do field "Command"
do "go card" && line 5 of cardList
do it
```

Action

The **do** keyword execute any sequence of statements.

The following handler sends each of the items in the variable jobList as messages:

```
on doJobs
  put "push card,go to next card,beep 2,pop card" into jobList
  repeat with count = 1 to the number of items in jobList
    do item count of jobList
  end repeat
end doJobs
```

Comments

expr is any expression that yields one or more HyperTalk statements. If *expr* has more than one line (where a line is everything up to the first return character), HyperTalk executes each line as a separate statement.

Do is especially useful for forcing another level of evaluation. The following handler locates and deletes a line of text by forcing an evaluation of the function **the foundLine:**

```
on findAndDelete string
  find string
  if the result is empty -- find succeeded
  then do "put empty into" && the foundLine
end findAndDelete
```

Only first line sent in version 1.2.#:   In versions through 1.2.#, **do** sends only one line. So if you say `do field 6`, HyperTalk sends line 1 of field 6 and ignores all other lines in the field.   (This is true even if that line ends in the line continuation character,¬.)   Similarly, `do line 7 of thisVar` sends only line 7 of the contents of the variable `thisVar`.

Send and Do are nearly identical: The keywords **do** and **send** perform nearly the same actions. The only difference is that you can direct the message that **Send** delivers to a particular object, whereas **do** always delivers its message to the object containing the currently running script. "Do *message*" is identical to "send *message* to me".

Also See:

RESULT function, page 454
SEND keyword, page 155

END

Forms

```
end [handlerName|if|repeat]

end myDefinedFunction
end mouseUp
end repeat
end if
```

Action

The **end** keyword starts the final line of every multiline structure:

```
on mouseUp
  repeat 3 times
    play "boing"
  end repeat -- end of repeat structure
  if the shiftKey is down then
    play "harpsichord"
    flash 2
  end if -- end of if structure
  play "boing"
end mouseUp -- end of handler structure
```

Comments

The words `end repeat` (plus an optional comment) make up the whole last line of every **repeat** structure.

The words `end if` (plus an optional comment) make up the whole last line of multiline **if** structures that don't end with single-line `else` statements.

The words `end handlerName` (plus an optional comment) make up the whole last line of every handler, where `handlerName` is the name of the handler.

Also See:
FUNCTION keyword, page 128
IF keyword, page 135
ON keyword, page 142
REPEAT keyword, page 147

EXIT

Forms

```
exit [repeat | handlerName]
exit to HyperCard

exit myHandler
exit mouseWithin
exit repeat
exit to HyperCard
if total <> expectedTotal then exit thisHandler
```

Action

The **exit** keyword immediately transfers flow of control out of the current handler or repeat structure. (Where flow of control goes next depends on the structure being exited.)

```
on openTheDoor
  ask "Who wants the door open?"
  if it is "Dave" then
    answer "I'm sorry, Dave. I'm afraid I can't do that."
    exit openTheDoor
  end if
  answer "Come on in." -- Does this if Dave ain't knockin'
end openTheDoor
```

Comments

The form `exit repeat` immediately transfers flow of control to the line following the next `end repeat` line. No further statements in the current repeat structure are executed (but statements in other repeat blocks in the handler are unaffected).

Exit repeat is the only way you can guarantee that a loop executes at least once.

The following handler (which also demonstrates a technique called binary search) guesses your weight in the most efficient way by zeroing in on it: each time through the loop it guesses a value that's midway between the highest number it knows is too low and the lowest number it knows is too high:

```
on guessYourWeight
  put 0 into tooLow
  put 500 into tooHigh
  put 0 into guessCount
  repeat
    add 1 to guessCount
    put tooLow + (tooHigh - tooLow) div 2 into guess
    answer "Do you weigh " & guess & "?" ¬
    with "Higher" or "Lower" or "Yes"
    if it is "Yes" then exit repeat
    if it is "Lower" then put guess into tooHigh
    if it is "Higher" then put guess into tooLow
  end repeat
  play "Boing"
  answer "I got it in only " & guessCount & " guesses!"
end guessYourWeight
```

Exit repeat is extremely useful when you want to guarantee that a user is providing valid information to **answer** and **ask** requests. The following handler, assumed to be part of a "catalogue-ordering" stack, makes sure that an item a user wants to order is in the catalogue:

```
on orderMerchandise
  repeat
    ask "What item do you want to order?"
    find it
    if the result is empty then exit repeat -- it's a valid item
    answer "We don't have that.  Want to try again?" with "No" or "Yes"
    if it is "No" then exit orderMerchandise -- give up
  end repeat
  put it into itemToOrder
  -- now we have a valid item to order and continue
  answer "How would you like to pay for that?" with ¬
  "Cash" or "Check" or "Charge"
  put it into payMethod -- can't get bad input from answer
  placeOrder itemToOrder,payMethod -- handler (not here) places order
end orderMerchandise
```

Exit *handlerName* immediately transfers flow of control out of the current handler. No further commands in the current handler are executed. *handlerName* must be the name of the currently executing handler.

The following handler hides several of HyperCard's windows (unless a large screen is in use, in which case it will do nothing):

```
on hideWindows
  if rect of card window is not the screenRect
  then exit hideWindows -- don't do anything on large screen
  hide tool window
  hide pattern window
  hide message window
end hideWindows
```

The following handler (an example of generalized binary search) uses both **exit** *handlerName* and **exit repeat** to find a card with a given field holding a value between a given lower and upper limit. It assumes that the stack is sorted by the field that it's searching on. The example finds a value between 25 and 30 in a field called "Retail price":

```
locate 25,30,"Retail Price"
on locate low,high,whichField
  put 1 into tooLowCard
  put the number of cards into tooHighCard
  repeat
    put tooLowCard + (tooHighCard - tooLowCard) div 2 into guessCard
    get field whichField of card guessCard
    if it >= low and it <= high then
      go to card guessCard
      select text of field whichField -- found
      exit locate
    end if
    if it < low then
      if guessCard is tooLowCard then exit repeat -- failure
      put guessCard into tooLowCard
    end if
    if it > high then
      if guessCard is tooHighCard then exit repeat -- failure
      put guessCard into tooHighCard
```

```
    end if
  end repeat
  answer "Can't find anything between " & low & " and " & high
end locate
```

To exit or to pass...

In actual practice, it's usually better to use `pass` *handlerName* for system messages than `exit` *handlerName* so that *handlerName* can continue through the message passing path as a message (unless, of course, you specifically intend for the message to stop here).

Exit to HyperCard immediately closes any open files and transfers flow of control directly back to the user. No further commands in the current repeat structure, handler, or any pending handlers are executed. Its effect is exactly the same as pressing Command-Period.

How Exit to HyperCard came to be: The form `exit to HyperCard` was brought into the language to abort multi-handler operations in case of errors. In fact, it's implemented internally the same way that Command-period is implemented. The following example reads a given file into a given field but aborts if the file is empty or too big for a field:

```
fileToField "Fred", "Forms" -- how you might call this handler

on fileToField fileName,fieldName
  open file fileName
  put empty into fileContents
  repeat
    read from file fileName for 16384
    if it is empty then exit repeat
    put it after fileContents
  end repeat
  close file fileName
  if length(fileContents) is zero
  then abort "There's nothing in file " & fileName & "."
  if length(fileContents) > 32000
  then abort "File " & fileName & " is too big for a field."
```

```
   put fileContents into field fieldName
end fileToField

 on abort why
  answer why
  exit to HyperCard
end abort
```

Obscure external/exit to HyperCard bug alert

The **exit to HyperCard** statement works by signalling a quiet
error condition — it stops the handler that it's in, and all pending handlers, without putting up any error dialog. But because
of a HyperTalk bug in all versions through 2.0, an external can't
be stopped by a handler that the external itself calls (or any handler that that handler calls). When control returns to the external, the error condition is cleared so that the external continues
to run.

Also See:

FUNCTION keyword, page 128
HANDLERS, page 15
OVERVIEW OF EXTERNALS, Chapter 13
PASS keyword, page 145
REPEAT keyword, page 147

FUNCTION

Forms

```
function definedFunctionName {paramList}

function convertTemp someNumber
function totalThese
function midPoint x1,y1,x2,y2
```

Action

The **function** keyword is the first word in a handler that defines a function. The word just after it is the name of the function that the handler defines. Any words after the name of the function are parameter variables.

The keyword **return**, explained in detail on page 151, is the mechanism that gets a value computed by a defined function back to the calling statement.

The following function takes a string and returns an exploded version of it (that is, with spaces between all the characters):

```
put explode("IMPORTANT MESSAGE") into field "Forms"

function explode string
  repeat with i = length(string) - 1 down to 1
    put " " after char i of string
  end repeat
  return string
end explode
```

Comments

definedFunctionName is the name of the function being defined. *ParamList* is an optional comma-separated list of parameters. The parameter list can hold up to 50 separate parameters.

Once a function is defined, you use the function as you would any other HyperTalk function.

Parentheses required: Unlike built-in functions that have two or three forms (the *functionName, functionName ()*, and sometimes {the} *functionName of factor*), user-defined function handlers always take the form *functionName ()*.

This is because function calls with parentheses are sent as messages, where they can be caught by handlers. Function calls without parentheses, on the other hand, go directly to HyperCard: if the function isn't built into HyperCard, HyperCard won't recognize the function as its own and will complain with an error message.

The following function removes trailing return characters from a string (which can be the contents of any container). Note that the function returns a copy of the string, modified; the function doesn't affect the original string:

```
function stripReturns string
  repeat while last char of string is return
    delete last char of string
  end repeat
  return string
end stripReturns
```

The statement that calls for this function might look like this:

```
put stripReturns(field "Dirty File") into field "Clean File"
```

About function and message names

Names for defined functions are the same as the message names that invoke them, so both follow the same naming rules: names must begin with a letter, and can contain letters or digits (with the underscore character (_) treated as a letter). You can't use special characters (*,%,@,?,¢, etc.) in a defined function's name. There's no practical limit to the number of characters in a defined function's name.

Commenting out handlers: Commenting out the **function** line effectively comments out everything between it and the start of the next handler. To see this, comment out the first line of any handler in the script editor and then press Tab — all the normal handler indentation goes away:

```
--function product x,y,z -- Whole handler commented out.
put x * y * z into total
if the paramcount > 3 then
repeat with i = 4 to the paramCount
```

```
multiply total by param(i)
end repeat
end if
return total
end product

on readMyLips -- normal indentation starts with next handler
  answer "I TOLD you to vote, Dummy!" with "Hrumph."
end readMyLips
```

About parameters: The parameter variables in a defined function get their values from the statement that calls the function. The first value passed goes into the first parameter, the second value goes to the second parameter, and so on. (These parameters are all local variables.) So if the calling statement is this:

```
put substring (5,8, "How goes it?")
```

and the first line of the function is this:

```
function substring start, finish, source
```

then `start` gets the value 5, `finish` gets the value 8, and `source` gets the value "How goes it?".

If the parameter list in the defined function has more variables than there are parameters passed to fill them, the extra variables hold empty. If there are more parameters passed than there are variables to receive them, the extra parameters are still available through the **param** function even though these extra parameters are unnamed.

How many parameters?

The maximum number of parameter values depends upon the amount of space available at any given time to HyperTalk's internal stack. But at any time, you can have at least 50 parameter values.

The following handler shows how to mix named and unnamed parameters. It replaces one word with another in each of the named fields. For example,

```
replace "Fred","Martha","Forms","Action"
```

would replace every occurrence of "Fred" with "Martha" in fields "Forms" and "Action":

```
on replace oldWord,newWord
  repeat with fieldNum = 3 to the paramCount
    put param(fieldNum) into fieldName
    get field fieldName
    repeat until offset(oldWord,it) is 0
      put offset(oldWord,it) into startChar
      put newWord into ¬
      char startChar to startChar+length(oldWord)- 1 of it
    end repeat
    put it into field fieldName
  end repeat
end replace
```

Also See:

HANDLERS, page 15
PARAM function, page 445
Parameter Passing, page 99
RETURN keyword, page 151
SYSTEM MESSAGES, Chapter 11

GLOBAL

Forms

```
global variableList

global theVariableName
global this,that,theOther
global customerNames, customerAddresses, customerPhoneNumbers
```

Action

The **global** keyword declares the variable(s) whose name(s) follow it as global. A global variable continues to exist and hold its value until you quit HyperCard.

If the global variable whose name appears after **global** doesn't already exist, HyperTalk creates it and sets its value to empty. If the global variable already exists, it becomes available to the current handler with its most recent value intact.

The following handler declares two variables as global and initializes them (in case they already contain values):

```
on initGame
  global theHighScore, theWinners
  put 0 into theHighScore -- sets up for numbers
  put empty into theWinners -- sets up for strings
end initGame
```

Comments

variableList is a comma-separated list of variable names. The list can be of any length.

You can have any number of **global** statements in the same handler.

When you name more than one variable using the same **global** keyword, separate the variable names with a comma. You can name any number of global variables in the list (but you can't use this method to assign values):

```
global this, that, theOther, yetAnother, stillAnother, andSoOn
```

The **global** statement can appear anywhere in a handler, but you must declare a variable as global in any handler where you want to use it.

You must declare a variable as global *before* you use that variable in a handler or HyperTalk assumes that the variable is local. If you try to declare a variable as global *after* you've used that variable, you'll get an error dialog box. The following handler is an example of this error:

```
on initializeOops
  put 5 into oops -- Oops is initialized as a local variable
  global oops -- This'll never fly.
end initializeOops
```

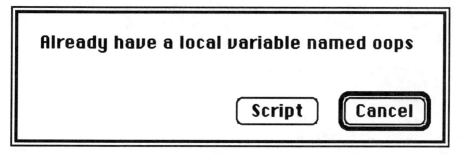

Figure 7-1   Local variable defined as global

You can use **global** from the Message box, but it has no effect. Variables created in the message box are by definition global, and any variables that you examine from the message box must already be globals (see Figure 7-1).

About a global's value: Changing the value of a global variable in one handler or in the Message box changes its value to all handlers (or to a call for its value from the Message box):

```
on newGlobal
  global itemCount -- creates global variable if it didn't already exist
  put 5 into itemCount
  nextHandler -- leaves this handler with 5 in itemCount
  put itemCount -- comes back with 8 in itemCount
end newGlobal

on nextHandler
  global itemCount -- declares itemCount as global
```

```
    put itemCount -- puts 5 into Message (got value in newGlobal handler)
    add 3 to itemCount -- new value is 8
end nextHandler
```

The value of a global variable is maintained throughout HyperCard until you
quit HyperCard. It continues to be maintained while HyperCard is suspended
under MultiFinder (either by using the **Open Application** command or by
directly opening or making active another application). But all global values
are lost when you quit HyperCard or when you open another application
with MultiFinder turned off. (To preserve a value, put it into a field or write it
to a text file before you quit HyperCard.)

Globals can get large: Because globals hold their values throughout an entire
HyperCard session, and because all variables live in RAM, it's a good idea to
clear out the values of globals that no longer have any use:

```
on if_I_Were_Prez
  global pershingSites,cruiseSites,mxSites
  put empty into pershingSites
  put empty into cruiseSites
  put empty into mxSites
end if_I_Were_Prez
```

Also See:

SOURCES OF VALUE, Chapter 5

IF...THEN...ELSE

Forms

```
if condition then statement {else statement}
```

```
if condition then statement
{else statement}
```

```
if condition
then statement
{else statement}
```

```
if condition then
   statementList
{else
   statementList}
end if
```

```
if condition then
   statementList
else statement
```

```
if condition then -- this form not preferred because hard to read
statement else statement
```

```
if condition then statement else
 -- this form not preferred because it's hard to read
   statementList
end if
```

Action

If...then...else determines what statement(s) to execute, based on the outcome of some comparison.

When *condition* is true, the statement(s) after **then** execute (but not the statement(s) after **else**). When *condition* is false, the statement(s) after **else** (and only the statement(s) after **else**) execute.

```
on guessTheAnimal
   put any item of "dog,bear,horse,cat,mule,lion,goldfish" into animal
   ask "What animal am I thinking of?"-- only 1 of next 2 lines executed
```

```
   if it is animal then answer "Nice going!"
   else answer "No, I was thinking of a" && animal
end guessTheAnimal
```

Comments

Condition is any expression that evaluates to true or false, *statement* is any single valid HyperTalk command line, and *statementList* is any group of valid HyperTalk statements separated by returns:

```
on functionKey whichKey
   if whichKey is 1 or whichKey is 2 or whichKey is 3 or whichKey is 4
   then pass whichKey
   if whichKey is 5 then doMenu "Card Info…"
   if whichKey is 6 then doMenu "Bkgnd Info…"
   if whichKey is 7 then doMenu "Stack Info…"
end functionKey
```

Each **if** can have only one **else**.

Choosing among forms: Always use the simplest form possible for your operation. In general, the simpler the form, the easier it is to follow and in many cases (in versions prior to 2.0) the faster will it run. All the suggestions that follow are aimed at making your code as efficient (fast, clean, easy to debug) as possible.

• If it fits on one line, put it on one line:

```
if condition then statement else statement
```

• Avoid the line continuation character (¬) if possible; it makes reading more difficult. So if it fits on two lines, put it on two lines:

```
if condition then veryLongStatement
else veryLongStatement
```

• If necessary, go to three lines:

```
if veryLongCondition
then veryLongStatement
else veryLongStatement
```

• If you can avoid using **else** by exiting the handler after an **if**, then do it:

```
if condition then [exit [handler | repeat] | pass handler]
```

A guide to ending multiline IF forms

A return after `then` starts a multiline `then` form: this form must end
with the statement `end if`, or with a single line `else` statement.
A return after `else` starts a multiline `else` form: this form must end
with the statement `end if`.

Nested if structures: You can nest any form(s) of the **if** structure up to any
necessary level:

```
on matchEnds
  global a,b,c
  if a = 1 then
    if b = 1 then
      if c = 1 then
        put c
      end if
    end if
  end if
end matchEnds
```

In actual practice, you seldom have to nest very deeply if you're writing code
that takes full advantage of the language. Stylistically, deep nesting isn't a
great idea because it gets complex and hard to read. The entire example
above, for instance, can more elegantly be written as

```
if a = 1 and b = 1 and c = 1 then put c
```

The way you reduce nesting determines how much work HyperTalk must do
(and consequently governs how fast your code runs):

```
if myfunc1() and myfunc2() -- calls both even if first is false
if myfunc1() then if myfunc2() -- only calls both if first is true
```

Emulated case statements

The script editor indenter doesn't indent certain forms of nested **if-then-else** so that they can emulate case statements in other languages. (Case statements let you select among several choices.)

For example, the following handler changes the meanings of the **first, prev, next,** and **last** menu choices so that they apply to the current background rather than the whole stack (useful if you were using multiple backgrounds to contain multiple sections of your stack and you wanted to restrict movement to within a single section at a time):

```
on doMenu what
  if what is "First" then go to first card of this bkgnd
  else if what is "Prev" then go to prev card of this bkgnd
  else if what is "Next" then go to next card of this bkgnd
  else if what is "Last" then go to last card of this bkgnd
  else pass doMenu
end doMenu
```

The following dice game (such as it is) avoids deep indentation by using a series of **else** clauses:

```
on dice
  answer "Click the mouse to get each number!"
  put "0 0 0" into rolls
  repeat with roll = 1 to 3
    repeat until the mouseClick
      put random(6) into word roll of rolls
      put rolls
    end repeat
  end repeat
  put 0 into matchCount
  if word 1 of rolls = word 2 of rolls then add 1 to matchCount
  if word 2 of rolls = word 3 of rolls then add 1 to matchCount
  if word 3 of rolls = word 1 of rolls then add 1 to matchCount
  if matchCount is 0 then -- nothing
    play "boing"
```

```
   answer "You lose!" with "Crud.".
 else if matchCount is 1 then -- doubles
   play "harpsichord" c c
   answer "Doubles!" with "Great!"
 else if matchCount is 3 then -- triples
   beep 5
   answer "Triples!" with "Unbelievable!"
 end if
end dice
```

But how deep can nesting *really* be?   There's no specific limit to the depth you can nest **if** structures. But in versions through 1.2.#, the maximum number of nested blocks pending across all handlers is 128. A nested block is essentially anything that causes a script to indent. So a running handler is one block; a handler it calls is another block; an executing **repeat** loop is another block, as is each executing level of a nested **repeat**; and an executing **if** structure is another block, as is each executing level of a nested **if**. (The nested **if** example above accounts for four blocks.) There are no reported cases of anybody running out of block space.

If and the Message box: In versions through 1.2.#, you can't use **if** structures from the Message box (not even single line ones), but you can evaluate logical expressions there. So you can't say

```
 if A = B then put true else put false
```

but (assuming that A and B are globals) you can say

```
 A = B
```

and get the same results. This limitation has been removed in version 2.0.

Also See:

LOGICAL OPERATORS, page 114

NEXT REPEAT

Forms

```
next repeat

next repeat
if this > that then next repeat
if skipFlag then next repeat
```

Action

Next repeat ends the current execution of a **repeat** loop and sends control to the **repeat** statement at the top of the loop:

```
on brainSurgery
  global oops, cut_Along_Dotted_Line
  repeat until cut_Along_Dotted_Line = 0
    subtract 1 from cut_Along_Dotted_Line
    nextIncision
    if oops then next repeat -- if oops is true, go to top of loop
    send "addAnotherOne" to card "Billing" -- no charge for errors
  end repeat
end brainSurgery
```

Comments

When **next repeat** executes, any statements between it and the bottom of the loop are ignored for the current pass through the loop.

Next repeat works with all forms of the **repeat** structure, and can appear anywhere within a structure.

In the following example, you give the handler two numbers as parameters through the Message box (as in `factors 15, 3`) and it tells you all the numbers (up to the product of the two parameters) that are divisible by both of them (see Figure 7-2):

```
on factors num1,num2
  if the msg box contains " --"
  then put return into char offset(" --",the msg box) of the msg box
```

```
put " -- " after the msg box
repeat with i = max(num1,num2) to num1*num2
  set cursor to busy
  if i mod num1 <> 0 then next repeat -- not divisible by num1
  if i mod num2 <> 0 then next repeat -- not divisible by num2
  put i & " " after the msg box
end repeat
beep 2
end factors
```

```
factors 35, 7 -- 35 70 105 140 175 210 245
```

Figure 7-2   Figuring factors through the Message box

Also See:

REPEAT keyword, page 147

ON

Forms

```
on handlerName {paramList}

on mouseUp
on myHandlerName
on addTheseUp num1, num2, num3
```

Action

The **on** keyword is the first word in all message handlers. It comes just before the name of the handler, which is the same as the name of the message to which the handler responds.

The following handler displays how long the computer has been turned on in hours, minutes, and seconds:

```
on upTime
  get the ticks
  put it div 60 mod 60 into seconds
  put it div 60 div 60 mod 60 into minutes
  put it div 60 div 60 div 60 into hours
  put "The computer has been on for " & hours & ¬
  " hours, " & minutes & " minutes, and " & seconds & " seconds."
end upTime
```

Comments

HandlerName is the name of the current handler. It's also the name of the message (either a system message, command message, or one you've created yourself) that starts the execution of this handler. *ParamList* is an optional comma-separated list of variables.

Each message handler contains one and only one **on** keyword (unless the word "on" is part of a quoted string):

```
on getOffIt -- Only the first line can hold an active "on" keyword
  put "Are you still on it?" -- "on" can be in quoted string
end getOffIt
```

Once you've defined a handler, you can use its name as you would any HyperTalk message or command.

About handler and message names: Handler names are the same as the message names that invoke them, so both follow the same naming rules: names must begin with a letter, and can contain letters or digits (with the underscore character (_) treated as a letter). There's no practical limit to the number of characters in a handler name.

Commenting out handlers: Commenting out the **on** line effectively comments out everything between it and the start of the next handler, and makes the commented-out handler nonfunctional. To see this, comment out the first line of any handler in the script editor and then press Tab — all the normal handler indentation goes away:

```
--on vertAlign -- All normal indentation canceled
repeat with i = 2 to the number of buttons -- This handler won't run
set bottom of button i to bottom of button 1
end repeat
end vertAlign

on enterInField -- normal indentation returns to the script here
   tabkey
end enterInField
```

About parameters: The optional variables after *messageName* accept parameters passed with the message name. The first parameter passed goes into the first variable, the second parameter goes to the second variable, and so on.

If *paramList* has more variables than there are parameters to fill them, the extra variables hold empty. If there are more parameters passed than there are variables to receive them, the extra parameters are still accessible through the **param** function (page 445).

In the following trivial example, the message addEmUp gets sent — either from a handler or from the Message box — along with the parameter values 6, 13, and 47. (HyperTalk evaluates expressions before sending them.)

```
addEmUp 3*2, 5+8, 50 - trunc(pi)
```

The message gets grabbed by the on addEmUp handler, and the values are assigned to the variables in order: num1 gets 6, num2 gets 13, and num3 gets 47. (num4 gets empty.)

```
on addEmUp num1, num2, num3, num4
```

What happens to the parameter values after that depends on the rest of the statements in the handler:

```
on addEmUp num1, num2, num3, num4
  add num1 + num2 to field "Running total"
  subtract num3 from field "Taxes"
  put num4 * field "Employee benefits deduction" into field "Outgo"
  -- num4 is empty; empty treated as zero in numeric calculations.
end addEmUp
```

In this next example, the handler gets two parameters, amount and account; account holds the identifier of a card, which might be the complete record for a particular customer. The handler performs some arithmetic:

```
on debit amount, account
  subtract amount from field "balance" of card account
end debit
```

Also See:

HANDLERS, page 15
MESSAGES, page 13
PARAM function, page 445
Parameter Passing, page 99
RETURN keyword, page 151

PASS

Forms

```
pass messageName

pass mouseUp
pass myFunction
```

Action

The **pass** keyword immediately stops execution of the current handler and passes *messageName* along the message passing path.

The following handler captures menu commands, checks for a particular one, and passes the menu command along. If no other handler intercepts it, it eventually gets to HyperCard itself:

```
on doMenu what
  if what is "help" then go to card "help"
  else pass doMenu
end doMenu
```

Comments

messageName must be the same as the name of the handler that contains the **pass** statement.

Essentially, **pass** changes the end of the message passing path for a given message. Ordinarily a message stops once it's been caught; but **pass** puts the message back onto the message passing path.

If a handler named *messageName* is between the passing handler and HyperCard, that handler executes. So the same message can set off a number of same-named handlers in different locations along the message passing path. (But HyperTalk won't let a stack pass to itself, so **pass** can't make the same handler execute twice.)

The message passed must be the same as the message that invoked the current handler:

```
on sort
  answer "Are you sure you want to sort this stack?" with "OK" or "Cancel"
  -- If we don't pass the message, the command won't execute
  if it is "OK" then pass sort
end sort
```

Pass pretends message never caught: When you pass a message, you're effectively saying to HyperTalk "pretend that this message wasn't caught by the current handler;" the message and any parameters are put back on the message passing path, just as they appeared before they entered the current handler. Any changes your code made to a message's parameters are ignored. (But changes that were made to any nonparameter values — global variables, contents of fields, values of properties, and so on — remain in effect.)

Passing changed parameters: If you want to send along the message with changed parameters, don't use pass. Instead, use something like this in the card script:

```
on myMessage var1
  put var1 * 3 into var1
  send "myMessage" && var1 to this background
end myMessage
```

Also See:

EXIT keyword, page 123
Message Passing, page 13

REPEAT

Forms

```
repeat repeatForm
   statementList
end repeat
```

where *repeatForm* is one of the following:

- {forever}
- {for} *integerExpr* {times}
- until *condition*
- while *condition*
- with *variable* = *start* [to|down to] *finish*

Action

The **Repeat** structure repeats execution of the statements in *statementList* until some condition is met or until an **exit, pass,** or **return** statement executes. How many times the statements are executed depends upon the *repeatForm* used. (See the box labeled "Forms of Repeat" later in this description.)

The following example checks each character of a string to make sure it contains only digits:

```
put justDigits (field "total") -- passes field "total" to the function

function justDigits string
   repeat with i = 1 to the length of string
      if char i of string is not in "0123456789"
      then return false
   end repeat
   return true
end justDigits
```

For an example that uses each of these forms, see the box entitled "Form of Repeat," later in this section.

Comments

StatementList is any number of valid HyperTalk statements.

To terminate the current iteration of any **repeat** loop and go on to the next iteration, use the statement `next repeat` (described in more detail on page 140).

To leave the **repeat** loop entirely and go to the statement following `end repeat`, use the statement `exit repeat` (described in more detail on page 123).

Repeat checks the truth of the given condition (if it has a condition) at the top of the loop; so if a condition evaluates to false before the first time through the loop, the loop won't execute even once:

```
on mouseUp
  repeat until the shiftKey is down
    beep -- could be done 0 times
  end repeat
end mouseUp

on mouseUp
  repeat forever
    beep  -- done at least once, no matter what
    if the shiftKey is down then exit repeat
  end repeat
end mouseUp
```

Forms of repeat

The **repeat** form you use depends on the situation you're in. One's no better than another, but in HyperCard versions through 1.2.# there's a very slight difference in their relative speed of execution. They're listed here in decreasing order of speed (fastest first), with **repeat until** and **repeat while** about equally fast.

Repeat: All the statements repeat while HyperCard has breath in its body, until an **exit, pass,** or **return** statement executes, or you press Command-Period:

```
repeat
  beep
  if the mouseclick then exit repeat -- Shut up already!
end repeat
```

Repeat *integerExpr:*   All the statements repeat *integerExpr* times, after which flow of control goes to the first statement after end repeat:

```
put 0 into adder -- creates variable necessary for add statement
repeat 5 times
   add 12 to adder -- this happens 5 times
end repeat
put adder -- displays 60
```

Repeat until *condition:*   All the statements repeat until some condition evaluates to true, after which flow of control goes to the first statement after end repeat:

```
repeat until the sound is done -- Yo! Disco!
   set hilite of button "Flash" to not hilite of button "Flash"
end repeat
```

Repeat while *condition:*   All the statements repeat while some condition remains true, after which flow of control goes to the first statement after end repeat:

```
repeat while the mouse is down
   put the long time -- keeps updating until mouse released
end repeat
```

Repeat with *variable* = *start* [to | down to] *finish:* All the statements repeat once for each value of *variable. Variable's* value increases by 1 (or, in the case of **down to**, decreases by 1) each time the last statement in the list finishes executing. As soon as *variable's* value equals *finish's* value, flow of control goes to the first statement after end repeat:

```
repeat with counter = 3 to 6 -- increasing order
   put empty into field counter -- clears fields 3, 4, 5, and 6
end repeat
repeat with counter = 6 down to 3 -- decreasing order
   put empty into field counter -- clears fields 6, 5, 4, and 3
end repeat
```

HyperTalk compares the value of *variable* to the value of *finish* at the top of the loop, so **repeat** structures with contradictory starting forms (such as loopCounter = 1 to 0 **or** loopCounter = 0 down to 1) don't execute even once.

Repeats are nestable: You can nest any form(s) of the **repeat** structure up to 32 levels; but in versions through 1.2.#, the total number of all running repeats — including calls to other handlers that might themselves have repeats — is 32:

```
on tune
  put "cdedc" into notes
  repeat with i = 1 to the length of notes
    play "harpsichord" char i of notes
    repeat with j = the length of notes down to i
      play "harpsichord" char j of notes
    end repeat
  end repeat
end tune
```

Also See:

EXIT keyword, page 123
NEXT REPEAT keyword, page 140
PASS keyword, page 145
RETURN keyword, page 151

RETURN

Forms

```
return value

return total
return calculation - corrections
```

Action

The **return** keyword has two actions: it assigns a value to a defined function when you use **return** in a function handler, or it assigns a value to the function **the result** when you use **return** in a message handler. In either case, its execution immediately returns control to the caller.

The following function shows **return** used in a defined function. It converts between the Fahrenheit and Centigrade scales. (Every computer book has a Fahrenheit-to-Centigrade converter — it's traditional.) This function takes a temperature as its first parameter and a scale indicator (either f or c) as its second parameter, such that change (32, f) yields 0 and change (0, c) yields 32:

```
function change temperature, scale
  if scale is "f"
  then return (temperature - 32) * 5/9 -- Does this and ends...
  if scale is "c"
  then return (9/5 * temperature) + 32 -- ...or does this and ends...
  answer "Can't convert that scale" -- ... or discovers an invalid scale...
  exit to HyperCard -- ...and so ends all handlers.
end change
```

The following example shows **return** used in a message handler. The second handler compacts the stack and passes the amount of space that was saved back to the first handler:

```
on mouseUp
  compactStack
  answer the result && " bytes recovered."
end mouseUp
```

```
on compactStack
   get size of this stack
   doMenu "Compact Stack"
   return it - size of this stack
end compactStack
```

Comments

When the **Return** statement executes, control leaves the current handler; any commands remaining in the handler are ignored.

Return with defined functions: **Return** is the mechanism that gets a value computed by a defined function back to the calling statement. (Defined functions are covered in detail on page 128).

The following example returns true if its argument is odd, otherwise it returns false:

```
put odd(87) -- returns true
function odd integer
   return integer mod 2 <> 0
end odd
```

The following function, which uses the odd() function just defined, finds the rectangle at a given location, given the center, width, and height:

```
function centerToRect center,width,height
   get item 1 of center - width div 2 & "," & ¬
   item 2 of center - height div 2 & "," & ¬
   item 1 of center + width div 2 & "," & ¬
   item 2 of center + height div 2
   if odd(width) then add 1 to item 3 of it
   if odd(height) then add 1 to item 4 of it
   return it
end centerToRect
```

Return with message handlers: You use **return** within a message handler typically to report that something failed or that something else isn't OK. The string following the **return** keyword goes into the **result** function.

The following two-handler example assumes that the current card has a field named "balance" containing a customer's current balance, and a field "cash on hand" containing the amount of cash an automatic teller machine currently has available:

```
on atm
   ask "How much money would you like?"
   withdraw it -- Value of "it" passed to the "withdraw" handler
   get the result -- Result function set by Return in "withdraw"
   if it is not empty
   then answer "I'm sorry but" && it
   else answer "Here's your money."
end atm

on withdraw amount -- "amount" gets value of "it", passed from "atm"
   if amount > field "balance"
   then return "your balance is only" && field "balance"
   if amount > field "cash on hand"
   then return "this branch can't cover that withdrawal"
   subtract amount from field "balance"
   subtract amount from field "cash on hand"
end withdraw
```

The following handlers assume that each card in a stack describes a book in a library. It passes messages to the library patron through the **result** function using **return:**

```
 on mouseUp
   ask "What book would you like?"
   if it is empty then exit mouseUp
   checkOut it
   get the result -- set in the checkOut handler
   if it is not empty
   then answer "I'm sorry but " & it
   else answer "Please return the book in two weeks."
end mouseUp

on checkOut bookName
   find bookName in field "title"
   if the result is not empty
   -- "return" sets result function
   then return "we don't have that book"
   if field "reserved"  is true
```

```
  then return "that book is on reserve"
  if field "Copies On Hand" <= 0
  then return "that book is checked out"
  subtract 1 from field "Copies On Hand"
end checkOut
```

Also See:

FUNCTION keyword, page 128
ON keyword, page 142

SEND

Forms

```
send message {parameterList} {to [object | window expr]}

send "testHandler" to card button 5
send variableHoldingMessage to this card
send "initializeColumn 5" to card "Spreadsheet"
send "expandField" && quote & "National Debt" & quote to next card
send field "Do This"
send it -- same as "send it to me"
```

Action

The **send** keyword sends a message and any accompanying parameters directly to the named object or window without going through HyperCard's normal message passing path. If the destination object or window doesn't catch the message or if it passes the message, the message continues on the message passing path from that point.

If you don't name a destination, the message goes to the object containing the currently running script (that is, "me").

The following handler lets you add visual effects to card changes done through the arrow keys: it traps arrow key presses and then redirects control to prev and next buttons that already use visual effects. (This handler would also be useful when you wanted to make the prev and next buttons go somewhere besides the immediately previous and next cards.)

```
on arrowKey whichKey
   if the commandKey is down then pass arrowKey -- preserve go first / go last
   if whichKey is "right" then send "mouseUp" to bkgnd button "Next"
   else if whichKey is "left" then send "mouseUp" to bkgnd button "Prev"
   else pass arrowKey -- up and down arrows
end arrowKey
```

The background button "Next", for example, might have the script:

```
on mouseUp
   visual effect wipe left
   go to next card
```

```
end mouseUp
```

or

```
on mouseUp
  go to first card of next bkgnd
end mouseUp
```

Comments

object is HyperCard, any stack, me, the target, or any card or button or field or background in the current stack. *Message* is any valid HyperCard message (either built-in or user-defined). *Expr* is any expression that evaluates to the name of a window created by an external (that is, an xwindoid).

Essentially, **send** changes the start of the message passing path for a particular message.

The following handler sends a `mouseUp` message to every button on the current card (a useful way to find syntax errors in button scripts, or to entertain yourself late at night):

```
on tryAllButtons
  repeat with thisCdBtn = 1 to the number of card buttons
    push card -- in case button does a "go"
    send "mouseUp" to button thisCdBtn
    pop card
  end repeat
  repeat with thisBgBtn = 1 to the number of bkgnd buttons
    push card
    send "mouseUp" to bkgnd button thisBgBtn
    pop card
  end repeat
end tryAllButtons
```

About send x-ref to window *expr*: New for 2.0, this syntax applies only to external windows such as the **palette navigator** window (page 286) or windows displayed by the **picture** command (page 288).

Send and the message passing path: Send delivers its message directly to an object without using the message passing path, so no handler can intercept the sent message. But if no handler catches the message once the message reaches its target, the message continues normally from that point through the rest of the message passing path.

When you use **send**, you don't change cards. So HyperCard doesn't send open or close messages to cards, backgrounds, or stacks. For example, if you're on the first card of a stack, and you send a message to a button on the fifth card of that stack, the card holding the destination button doesn't get an `openCard` message:

```
send "mouseUp" to button "init" of fifth card
```

Send from the Message box: **Send** is a great boon to debugging, especially when you want to test things like hidden buttons (`send "mouseUp" to button "HiddenWayDown"`) or a particular handler in a script of many handlers (`send "handler7" to field 12`).

Send and defined functions

You can't use **send** to activate a function handler. But you can use **send** to activate a message handler which in turn activates a function handler. The following **send** statement ultimately activates a function handler in card button 1 that adds up a list of numbers (in this case, stored in background field 1):

```
send "callSum field 1" to button 1 -- sends message with params
on callSum list -- gets param "list" from the send statement
    put sum(list) -- this line calls the defined function "Sum"
end callSum

function sum list -- here's the indirectly called function
    put 0 into adder
    repeat with i = 1 to number of items in list
        add item i of list to adder
    end repeat
    return adder -- value of adder passed back to function caller
end sum
```

Send and Do are nearly identical: The keywords **do** and **send** do nearly the same thing. The only difference is that you can direct the message that **Send** delivers to a particular object, whereas **do** always delivers its message to the object containing the currently running script. (In effect, "do" means "send to me.")

Because anything on the line is automatically sent to "me" anyway, the only time you'd want to use `send <whatever> to me` or `do <whatever>` is to force a level of evaluation:

```
Fred -- sends message "Fred"
send Fred -- sends message that Fred contains
```

Also See:

ME, page 84
Message Passing, page 12
MESSAGES, page 13

Chapter 8

Commands

This chapter lists all HyperCard commands alphabetically with detailed definitions and examples.

Commands are statements that tell HyperCard to do something (unlike functions which are questions that HyperCard answers). Additionally, commands are messages that ordinarily travel the message passing path; if they make it all the way to HyperCard without being intercepted by a handler, HyperCard responds to command messages as if it had built-in handlers for them. You can send all commands from the Message box.

For a summary listing of all HyperTalk vocabulary words with brief definitions, see Appendix E. For a listing of commands and other vocabulary words grouped by type (arithmetic, painting, and so on), see Appendix F.

For commands and functionality added to commands at the very last moment of HyperCard 2.0's production schedule, see Commands in Appendix I, "Late Breaking News."

ADD

Forms

```
add numExpr to container

add 5 to it
add 1 to last word of field 1
add subtotal to total
add insult to field "Injury"
add field "State Taxes" to addItAll
```

Action

The **add** command adds the value of *numExpr* to the value of *container*, leaving the result in *container*. The old value of *container* is destroyed (but the value of *numExpr* is unaffected).

In the following handler, variable subHolder holds values in each of its lines for previously calculated subtotals. The handler adds those values together into the variable sum:

```
on AddEmUp
  global subHolder
  put 0 into sum
  repeat with subTotalLine = 1 to number of lines in subHolder
    add line subTotalLine of subHolder to sum -- Here's the action
    put sum into field Total
  end repeat
end AddEmUp
```

Comments

Add always puts its result into a container. If you try to add one number to another directly, as in add 7 to 12, you get a "Can't understand arguments" error, as shown in Figure 8-1.

You get this same dialog if you try to add containers that don't contain numbers. If the destination container doesn't contain a number, you get the dialog shown in Figure 8-2:

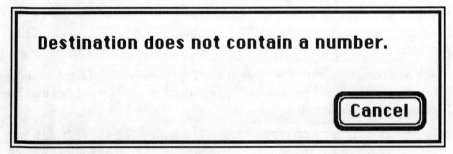

Can't understand arguments to command add

Cancel

Figure 8-1 "Can't understand" error dialog

Destination does not contain a number.

Cancel

Figure 8-2 "Bad contents" error dialog

If the container is a variable, it must already be initialized to some value (or be a global variable) or you'll get a "Can't understand arguments" error.

When the sum appears in a field or in the Message box, the format for the display depends upon the setting of the **numberFormat** property. (HyperTalk converts all numbers to strings before they're displayed.)

Points for techies: If both values to be added are integers, and if both have absolute values less than 1,073,741,823 (the highest value a 30 bit number can represent) HyperCard uses integer math to do the addition; otherwise, it uses SANE extended math.

The code for **add** and for the **"+"** operator is the same.

Also See:

NUMBERFORMAT property, page 585

ANSWER

Forms

```
answer expr {with reply1 {or reply2 {or reply3 } } }

answer "I'm sorry — that's not an option."
answer field 1 with field 2 or line 7 of field 3
answer "OK—what'll it be?" with "Door #1" or "Door #2" or "Door #3"
```

Action

The **answer** command displays a dialog box with a one-line question/statement string and up to three replies. The replies appear as button names: you click the button whose name is the reply you want to return. The reply goes into the local variable It.

This handler produces the dialog box that follows (see Figure 8-3):

```
on doMenu what
    if what is not "Quit HyperCard" then pass doMenu -- only works for "quit"
    answer "Print marked cards before quitting?" with "No" or "Yes"
    if It is "yes" then PrintMarkedCards -- a handler you've defined elsewhere
    pass doMenu -- Go ahead and quit
end doMenu
```

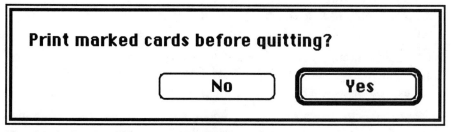

Figure 8-3 Answer dialog box with alternate answers

Comments

The dialog box stays on the screen until you click a reply, or until you press Return, Enter, or Command-Period. The reply farthest to the right (outlined with a bold border) is the default reply that's used if you press Return or

Enter. Command-Period cancels the command, puts the dialog box away, and aborts the rest of the script.

The only element your handler must supply for **answer** is the question/statement string. If you don't supply a reply, HyperCard provides an OK button as the only option (see Figure 8-4):

```
answer "I'm sorry, that's not an option."
```

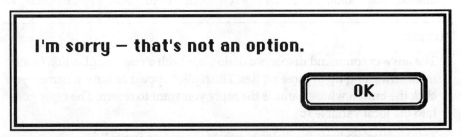

Figure 8-4   Answer dialog box with default answer

Answer temporarily converts the cursor to an arrow.

About the display: Text for both the question and the replies is in 12-point Chicago. The question/statement string has room to show about 38 characters in versions through 1.2.# and about 240 characters in 2.0, and each reply has room to show about 12 characters, depending on the character width. If you want to ask a more extensive question or if you want to offer more alternative answers, you'll need to construct your own questionnaire, perhaps using a field for the questions and a series of buttons for answers.

In versions through 1.2.#, if the question/statement *expr* refers to an expression with more than one line in it, HyperTalk shows as much of the *first* line of the expression as will fit, starting with the first character in that line.

If *reply* refers to an expression with more than one line in it, HyperTalk shows as much of the *last* line of the expression as will fit, starting with the center character in that line. (But the entire contents of the expression goes into the variable it.) The fact that it uses the last line instead of the first is a bug in all 1.2.# versions .

Get your priorities straight

This three-handler example helps you select the top priority from a range of choices. To extend the list, just modify the initProblems handler:

```
on changeTheWorld
  global theProblems
  if theProblems is empty then initProblems
  put item 1 of line 1 of theProblems into worstProblem
  put 1 into worstLine
  repeat with problemLine = 2 to the number of lines in theProblems
    put item 1 of line problemLine of theProblems into newProblem
    repeat
      answer "Which is worse?" with worstProblem or newProblem or "Give Up"
      if it is "Give Up" then
        play "harpsichord" tempo 180 "c c ch eq d ch eq f gh d d."
        answer "You really can make a difference." ¬
        with "I Quit" or "Press On"
        play stop
        if it is "Press On" then next repeat
        exit changeTheWorld
      end if
      if it is newProblem then
        put it into worstProblem
        put problemLine into worstLine
      end if
      exit repeat
    end repeat
  end repeat
  answer "Call " & item 2 of line worstLine of theProblems & ¬
  " at " & item 3 of line worstLine of theProblems
end changeTheWorld

on initProblems
  global theProblems
  put empty into theProblems
  addProblem("War,Beyond War,408-555-1212")
```

```
  addProblem("Injustice,Amnesty International,212-555-1212")
  addProblem("Famine,The Hunger Project,415-555-1212")
  addProblem("Disease,The Names Project,415-555-1212")
  addProblem("Alcoholism,Alcoholics Anonymous,212-555-1212")
end initProblems

on addProblem problem
  global theProblem
  put problem & return after theProblems
end addProblem
```

Sources: The question/statement string or replies can come from any expression, including functions like Date or Time.

Use quotation marks: If the question/statement string or reply isn't a container and if it includes any spaces, enclose it within quotation marks. (Actually, it's a good idea to enclose literals in quotation marks all the time; it's safer in that they can't be confused with variables, and it makes your code run faster.)

Replies not scriptable: You can't reply to an answer dialog box from a handler; you have to reply manually by clicking a button or by pressing Return, Enter, or Command-Period.

Pasting: You can't paste into an answer dialog box in versions through 1.2.#, but you have full editing functions starting in version 2.0.

Also See:

ASK command, page 174
IT variable, page 97

ANSWER FILE

Forms

```
answer file expr { of type factor { or factor { or factor }}}

answer file "Please choose a file" of type text
answer file myPicturePrompt of type TIFF or PICT or PNTG
```

Action

The **answer file** command, new for Hypercard 2.0, brings up the Macintosh's Standard GetFile dialog so that you can select the name of a file.

This handler produces the display in Figure 8-5:

```
editFile MacAuthor, MACA -- typical way you might call the handler
on editFile textEditor, fileType
   answer file "What file do you want to edit?" ¬
   of type fileType or text -- always accept text files into editor
   if It is empty then exit to HyperCard -- Cancel or Cmd-period
   open it with textEditor -- start textEditor with doc loaded
end editFile
```

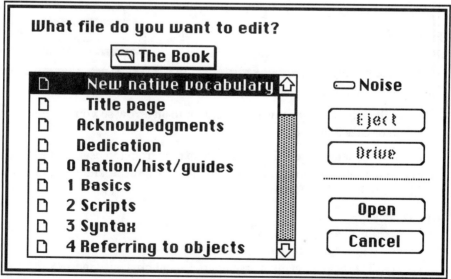

Figure 8-5 Answer File dialog

Comments

Expr is any expression that yields a prompting string. *Factor* is any factor that produces a file type.

The dialog stays on the screen until you click Open or Cancel, double-click a file name, or until you press Return, Enter, or Command-period.

When you click "Open" or double-click a file name, the full pathname of the selected file goes into the local variable It and the dialog goes away.

When you click "Cancel" or press Command-period, the **result** function is set to "Cancel" and the variable It is set to empty. Command-period cancels the command, but the rest of the script keeps running. (To cancel the rest of the script with a dialog showing, press Command-shift-period; to enter the Debugger, press command-option-period.)

The only element your handler must supply for **answer file** is the prompt string. If you forget to supply the prompt string, you'll get the **answer** command's dialog, with the word "file" as a prompt, as shown in Figure 8-6.

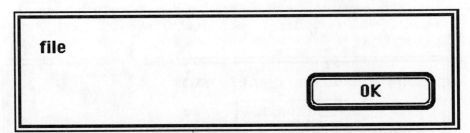

Figure 8-6 Probably not what you had in mind

Answer file temporarily converts the cursor to an arrow so you can make a selection or click a button.

The following handler gets the name of a text file from the user, imports the text from that file, strips any superfluous carriage returns, and finally puts the text into a field named "Imported Text":

```
on mouseUp
    -- prompt user for fileName
    answer file "Import text from:" of type text
    if it is empty then exit mouseUp -- check for Cancel
    set cursor to watch
```

```
-- import text
put it into fileName
open file fileName
put empty into fileText
repeat until it is empty
  read from file fileName for 16000
  put it after fileText
end repeat
close file fileName

-- strip returns
put empty into newText
repeat with lineNum = 1 to the number of lines in fileText
  get line lineNum of fileText
  if it is empty then get return & return
  put it after newText
end repeat

-- put into field
put newText into card field "Imported Text"
end mouseUp
```

About Type: All Macintosh files have a four-character type (case significant) that indicates the kind of file it is. For example, applications are type APPL, text files are type TEXT, and HyperCard stack files are type STAK. Usually you need a program like FEDIT or ResEdit to learn a file's type.

HyperTalk, in addition to recognizing all standard file types, also recognizes synonyms for several of the most common Macintosh file types, as shown in the following table:

Type	Synonym
APPL	application
PICT	picture
PNTG	paint, painting
STAK	stack
TEXT	text

Answer file doesn't open anything: This command doesn't open any file on its own; it just presents a convenient way to choose a file name. What you do with that name once **answer file** gets it is up to you.

About the display: Text for the prompt string and the file names appear in 12-point Chicago at the top of the dialog. The prompt string can be of any practical length; the dialog grows to accommodate it up to a size that still fits on a standard 9" Macintosh display.

Use quotation marks: If the prompt string isn't a container and if it includes any spaces, enclose it within quotation marks.

Also See:

ASK FILE command, page 178
IT variable, page 97
OPEN APPLICATION command, page 277
READ command, page 318

ARROWKEY

Forms

```
arrowkey [up|down|left|right]

arrowkey left
if it is "yes" then arrowkey right
```

Action

The **arrowKey** command is invoked by the action of the arrow keys. Its action depends upon the setting of the **textArrows** property.

When the **textArrows** property is false, **arrowKeys** goes to another card:

left	previous card in current stack (wrapping at the start)
right	next card in current stack (wrapping at the end)
down	card viewed immediately before current one
up	card viewed immediately after current one (only meaningful after a "down" action)

When the **textArrows** property is true and there's a selection (or just an insertion point), **arrowKeys** moves the insertion point:

left	left 1 character
right	right 1 character
down	down 1 line (or to end of text if already on last line)
up	up 1 line (or to start of text if already on first line)

The following handler sets up the arrow keys for editing in a field, and moves the insertion point around:

```
on moveInsertion
  put the textArrows into oldValue -- save textArrows state
  set the textArrows to true -- edit in a field
  select before text of field 1 -- insertion point to start of text
  repeat 3
    arrowkey down
    wait 10
```

```
     arrowkey right
     wait 10
   end repeat
   set the textArrows to oldValue -- restore textArrows state
end moveInsertion
```

Comments

The parameter for **arrowkey** must be one of the four words left, right, up, or down.

Arrowkey is also a message sent to the current card. With the following handler installed in a card script and **textArrows** set to true, pressing one of the arrow keys selects text in a group of three card fields as if they comprised a spreadsheet (as in Figure 8-7):

```
on arrowKey direction
   get the selectedLine -- line x of card field y
   if it is empty then pass arrowKey
   if direction is "right" then
     add 1 to last word of it
   else if direction is "left" then
     subtract 1 from last word of it
   else if direction is "down" then
     add 1 to word 2 of it
   else if direction is "up" then
     subtract 1 from word 2 of it
   end if
   put number of lines in card field 1 into lineCount
   if word 2 of it < 1 then put lineCount into word 2 of it
   if word 2 of it > lineCount then put 1 into word 2 of it
   if last word of it < 1 then put 3 into last word of it
   if last word of it > 3 then put 1 into last word of it
   select it
end arrowKey
```

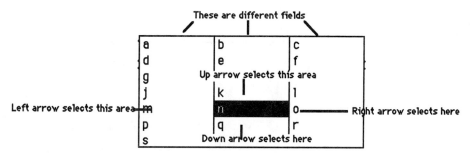

Figure 8-7 Arrowkey emulation of spreadsheet

ArrowKey with textArrows false: **ArrowKey down** can bring you through up to the last 100 cards viewed. **ArrowKey up** has no effect until you've backed up through cards by using the **ArrowKey down** command, pressing esc or the tilde (~) key, and/or choosing the **Back** command from the Go menu.

Reviewing one of the last 100 cards doesn't add that card again to the list of cards seen.

Also See:

BACK, *HyperCard User's Guide*
TEXTARROWS property, page 624

ASK

Forms

```
ask {password} stringExpr {with preset answer}

ask "Please type your name"
ask "Who discovered water?" with "Somebody who wasn't a fish."
ask questionString with card field 2
ask password "What's the password?"
```

Action

The **ask** command puts up a dialog box with a question at the top, an optional preset answer selected in a typeable text window, and two buttons — one labeled "Cancel" and one labeled "OK". (See Figure 8-8, below.) When a user clicks OK (or presses Return or Enter), the contents of the text window goes into the local variable It; when a user presses Cancel (or Command-Period, which aborts the handler), HyperTalk puts empty into It.

The variation **ask password** does the same thing, except that HyperTalk encrypts the answer (insensitive to case) into a number before the answer goes into local variable It. (See "About Passwords," below.)

The following handler asks for the name of the person at the keyboard, using the contents of global variable UserName (from the User Preference card) as *preset answer*:

```
on getTheName
  global userName
  ask "Please type your name:" with userName
  if it is not empty then put it into userName
end getTheName
```

Comments

The only element you're required to supply for **ask** is the question (as in `ask "Please type your name."`). If you don't propose a reply, HyperCard leaves the text window empty.

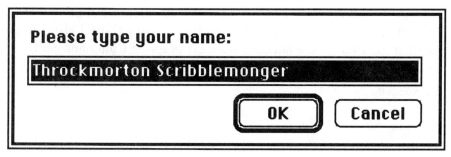

Figure 8-8   Ask dialog box

The dialog box stays on the screen until the user clicks a reply, or until the user presses Return, Enter, or Command-Period. The OK button (outlined with a bold border) becomes the default reply if the user presses Return or Enter.

The question or the default answer can come from any expression, including functions like **Date** or **Time.**

Ask temporarily converts the cursor to an arrow.

Reply not scriptable: You can't reply to an ask (or any) dialog box from a handler.

Use quotation marks: If the question or reply isn't an expression, and if it's more than one word or contains characters that might be misinterpreted, enclose it within quotation marks. (Actually, it's a good idea to enclose literals in quotation marks all the time; it's safer in that they can't be confused with variables, and it makes your code run faster.)

Format details: The question can be up to about 38 characters long in versions through 1.2.#, all on a single line. (Actually, it can be as long as you want, but only about the first 38 characters will fit in the display space.) In versions starting with 2.0, the question can be up to about 240 characters. The text window for the reply can hold up to 255 characters, but only the first 38 or so will be visible. (You can drag-left and drag-right in the text window to see hidden answer characters, but most users don't know about this feature.) The entire single-line answer will go into the local variable "it" unless the Cancel button is clicked.

Cancel vs. Command-Shift-Period: Cancel puts away the dialog box and puts empty into the variable it, but doesn't exit the current routine.

Command-Shift-Period, however, performs the equivalent of an Exit to HyperCard. In the following silly handler, clicking Cancel just causes another iteration of the handler, whereas pressing Command-Shift-Period exits the handler:

```
on mouseUp
  repeat
    ask "Name:"
    if it is "Fred" then
      answer "thanks"
      exit mouseUp
    end if
  end repeat
end mouseUp
```

Pasting: You can't paste into an Answer dialog box in versions through 1.2.#, but you have full editing functions starting in version 2.0.

About passwords: Passwords that you set with **Ask** are in addition to and separate from the password you set with the Protect Stack command on the File menu. While Protect Stack's password applies to the entire stack, **Ask's** password lets a handler grant or deny access to any object(s) within a stack. Using handlers, you can set a separate password for every object within a stack.

To set up a password, you first have to create a handler to receive the original password and to perform encryption. The following handler accepts a word to be used as a password and stores the encrypted result in a card field (presumably hidden) called Key:

```
on createPassWord
  ask Password "What's the password gonna be?"
  put it into card field "Key" -- presumably a hidden field!
end createPassWord
```

The next handler asks for a password and checks it against the encrypted password previously stored in card field Key:

```
on checkPassWord
  ask password "Password: "
  if it is not card field "Key" then
    answer "Sorry. Please make yourself comfy... " with "Rats!"
```

```
      go to card "alertSecurity"
    else
      answer "Welcome, Friend!" with "Thank you."
      go to card "startSecretInfo"
    end if
  end checkPassWord
```

Passwords don't afford much protection. Every HyperCard BBS has a "depro-tect" stack, and most experienced HyperCardiacs can get around passwords if they have a mind to. (We leave it as an exercise to the reader...) Passwords will however slow down rank amateurs, preschool children, and politicians.

Also See:

ANSWER command, page 163
IT variable, page 97

ASK FILE

Forms

```
ask file promptExpr { with defaultExpr }

ask file "Please choose a file" with "To Do List"
ask file promptString
```

Action

The **ask file** command, new in version 2.0, brings up the Macintosh's Standard PutFile dialog so that you can type a name (typically for a file being saved) and choose a file path.

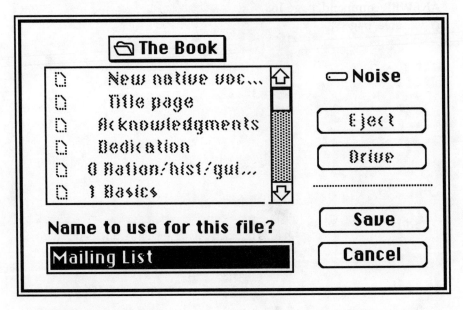

Figure 8-9   Ask File dialog

This handler produces the display in Figure 8-9:

```
on storeFile
  ask file "Name to use for this file?" with "Mailing List"
  if It is empty then exit to HyperCard -- Cancel or Cmd-period
  open file it -- "It" holds name that user typed
  repeat with cardNum = 1 to number of cards
    write field "Names & Addreses" of card cardNum to file it
  end repeat
  close file it
end storeFile
```

Comments

PromtExpr is any expression that yields a prompting string. *DefaultExpr* specifies a default name that goes into the editable field at the bottom of the dialog and is selected.

When you click "Save", the full pathname of the selected file goes into the local variable It, and the dialog goes away.

If you press Command-Period or click Cancel, empty goes into It, **the result** function is set to "Cancel", and the dialog goes away but the rest of the script keeps running. (To cancel the rest of the script with a dialog showing, press Command-Shift-Period; to enter the Debugger, press Command-Option-Period.)

The only element that your handler must supply for **ask file** is the prompt string. If you forget to add the prompt string, you'll get the **ask** command's dialog, with the word "file" as a prompt, as shown in Figure 8-10.

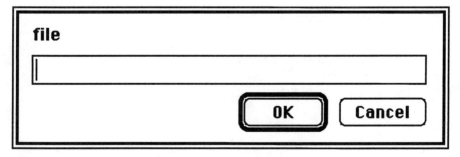

Figure 8-10   Accidental Ask dialog

Ask file temporarily converts the cursor to an arrow so that you can set a file path or click a button.

The following example creates a menu item in the File menu called "Save As..." (an extremely useful menu item, missing from the standard HyperCard File menu, that saves a copy of the current stack under a new name and then goes to the first card of that copy):

```
put "Save As..." after menuItem "Save a copy..." ¬
of menu "File" with menuMessage "userSaveAs"
```

When a user chooses the "Save As" command, the "Ask File" command is called into play:

```
on userSaveAs
  ask file "Save Stack As:"
  if it is not empty then
    save this stack as it
    go to it
  end if
end userSaveAs
```

Ask file doesn't save anything: This command doesn't save any file on its own; it just presents a convenient way to choose a file name. What you do with that name once **ask file** returns it is up to you.

About the display: Text for the prompt string appears in 12-point Chicago. The prompt string can be of any practical length; the dialog grows to accommodate it up to a size that still fits on a standard 9" Macintosh display.

Use quotation marks: If the prompt string isn't a container and if it includes any spaces, enclose it within quotation marks.

Also See:

ANSWER FILE command, page 167
IT variable, page 97
WRITE command, page 372

BEEP

Forms

```
beep {integer}
beep
beep 2
beep card field "beepcount"
```

Action

The **beep** command sends a tone to the Macintosh's speaker, or to the sound output port if something is plugged into it. If you give an integer value (or source of an integer value) as a parameter to **beep,** the speaker produces that many tones.

The following handler makes the speaker beep twice to alert the user that a dialog needs attention:

```
on panic
  beep 2
  answer "Commies! What should we do?" with "Run away" or "Bomb 'em"
  if It is "Run away" then evacuateSystem
  else launchCounterAttack
end panic
```

Comments

The beep sound is the same as the alert sound as set in the control panel. To use another tone or to change duration, you'll need to use an XCMD.

If the speaker volume is set to 0, the menu bar blinks once for each beep.

To stop in-progress beeping, press Command-Period.

Watch the beep count: Beeping can be a terrible annoyance. For the sake of your users, in most situations keep integer's value low (like, for example, 1). For a refreshing alternative, consider using `play harpsichord` or `play boing`; both of these sounds are built into every version of HyperCard:

```
play "harpsichord" tempo 180 "e4 d c d dh a3h aq c4 f f ew"
play "harpsichord" tempo 150 "ae g gh be4 c5# d5# e f# g f# e eh"
play "harpsichord" tempo 180 "fe f f fq fe f gq fe fq f f fe b4bq b4be c5q."
play "harpsichord" tempo 200 "g bb bb bb abh gq bbh.."
play "harpsichord" tempo 180 "c c ch eq d ch eq f gh d d."
play "harpsichord" dq dq b3e d4q. ee f#e ge aq ge eq.
```

Beep cancels playing: A beep cancels the playing of queued sounds.

Points for techies: Beep calls Sysbeep(1) *integer* times.

Also See:

PLAY command, page 292
XCMDs, page 694

CHOOSE

Forms

```
choose toolname tool
choose tool integerExpr

choose lasso tool
choose tool 5
choose userChosen tool
```

Action

The **choose** command selects a tool as if a user had clicked it from the Tools menu. *toolname* or *integerExpr* can come from any source, and must be (or resolve to) one of the following:

Table 8-1: Parameters for Choose command

integer	name	integer	name
1	browse	10	spray {can}
2	button	11	rect{angle}
3	field	12	round rect{angle}
4	select	13	bucket
5	lasso	14	oval
6	pencil	15	curve
7	brush	16	text
8	eraser	17	reg{ular} poly{gon}
9	line	18	poly{gon}

The following handler chooses the Pencil tool to sign a name using a prewritten handler called Signature (not included here — you'll have to write your own):

```
on signTheCheck
   put the tool into oldTool -- get the tool in use
   choose Pencil tool
   Signature -- a routine that hand-writes a name (for example)
   choose oldTool -- restore original tool
end signTheCheck
```

Comments

To choose one of the paint tools, the userlevel must be set to at least 3. To choose the field or button tool, the userlevel must be set to at least 4. When the userlevel is set too low to choose the tool that **choose** summons, an error dialog appears (see Figure 8-11).

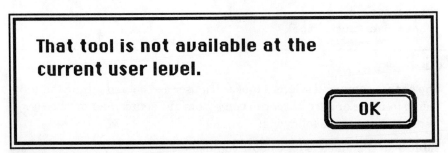

That tool is not available at the current user level.

OK

Figure 8-11   Tools error dialog

A tool's number corresponds to that tool's position on the Tools menu, moving left to right and top to bottom, as shown in Figure 8-12.

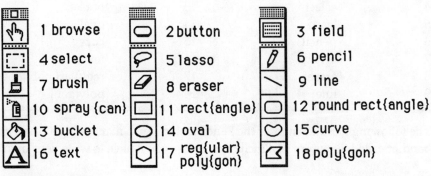

1 browse	2 button	3 field
4 select	5 lasso	6 pencil
7 brush	8 eraser	9 line
10 spray {can}	11 rect{angle}	12 round rect{angle}
13 bucket	14 oval	15 curve
16 text	17 reg{ular} poly{gon}	18 poly{gon}

Figure 8-12   Tools

The following handler chooses tools both randomly and purposefully:

```
on scribble
    repeat until the mouseClick -- Clicking the mouse stops the action
        get "rectangle tool, round rectangle tool, oval tool, brush tool"
```

```
    choose any item of it -- Chooses a random tool from the list
    set pattern to random(40)
    set filled to random(2) = 2 -- if random is 1, false; if 2, true
    drag from random(512),random(342) to random(512),random(342)
  end repeat
  choose select tool
  doMenu "Select All"
  doMenu "Clear Picture"
  choose browse tool
end scribble
```

The following handler (by Robin Shank) hides the message box whenever a paint tool is chosen so that power keys will work even when there's no paint selection. (Power keys don't work on nonselected items if the message box is visible because the typing goes into the message box):

```
on choose tool,toolNumber
  if toolNumber > 3 then hide msg
  pass choose
end choose
```

Effects of choosing: Choosing a new tool puts empty into the various **found** functions and removes the Selection. In version 1.2.#, if the new tool is the Browse tool, Background mode is turned off (if it was on).

Poly not available: You can choose the poly tool (tool 18), but you can't do anything with it within a script. You can, however, draw polygons from a script using the line tool, and then fill the polygons using the bucket tool.

Choose message sent/not sent: The **choose** command sends the message `choose,` as does manually clicking on a tool in the tool menu. (But in versions prior to 1.2.2, clicking on a tool when the tool windoid is torn off doesn't send the `choose` message.)

Some manual shortcuts: Pressing Command-Tab chooses the Browse tool. Starting with version 1.2, pressing Command-Tab twice in rapid succession (within 1/2 second) chooses the Button tool; pressing Command-Tab three times chooses the Field tool.

CLICK

Forms

```
click at location {with key1 {,key2 {, key3 } } }

click at the mouseloc
click at 250, 300 with optionkey, cmdkey
```

Action

The **click** command programmatically clicks the mouse at *location*, optionally "holding down" the shift, option, and/or command keys.

The following handler clicks every button on the current card:

```
on testButtons
  repeat with toTest = 1 to number of card buttons
    put "Testing card button " & toTest
    click at the loc of button toTest
  end repeat
  put "Finished!"
end testButtons
```

Comments

location is a point on the card, expressed as two integers separated by a comma: the integers represent respectively the horizontal and vertical offsets of the point (in pixels) from the upper-left corner of the card window.

key can be shiftkey, optionkey, and/or commandkey (or cmdkey).

Messages sent: When the **click** command executes, HyperCard sends the messages mouseDown, mouseStillDown (10 times), mouseUp, and mouseLeave. But HyperCard does *not* send the messages mouseEnter or mouseWithin, even if *location* is over a button or a field.

Click not an exact substitute for manual clicking: You can't use the click command to simulate manual shortcuts. Thus you can't use

```
click at 200, 200 with optionkey, commandkey
```

to bring up the handler of the button at 200, 200. (HyperCard needs to see the physical keys go down before it allows such shortcuts.)

Click can add lines to fields: When you click below the last line in a field, you add empty lines to that field in the form of Return characters (as many as it takes to fill the space to the vertical position of where you clicked). To avoid adding lines and to place the insertion point at the end of existing text, use the form

```
click at location with shiftkey -- shiftKey avoids extra lines
```

Using Click to simulate buttons in any type of field: HyperText support in the form of functions such as **the clickline, clickChunk,** and **clickText** came into HyperCard in version 2.0. But in versions through 1.2.#, you can simulate that support by using the **click** command to identify and isolate a single word or a complete line of text in a locked field of any type (including scrolling). Once you have text identified, you can do anything you want with it – and that includes anything you can do with a button.

The following handlers work for all versions starting with 1.2. This first handler belongs in the script of a locked field (or, if you're going to be using it a lot, in the script of an object farther along the message passing path). When somebody clicks on a word in the field, thus sending a mouseUp message, the handler double-clicks the word to select it (first unlocking the field so that the double-click works), and then puts the word into the variable it. Then the handler shows you the word in the Message box (just to prove that the word is in fact captured). This handler works just as well in scrolling fields as in nonscrolling fields:

```
on mouseUp
   set lockText of me to false -- to allow selection
   click at the clickLoc -- double click to select one word
   click at the clickLoc
   get the selection -- picks up the word you clicked on
   set lockText of me to true
   put "You picked " & quote & it & quote -- You'd do something more sensible
end mouseUp
```

This next handler works much like the last one, except that it picks up an entire line. It too belongs in the script of a locked field:

```
on mouseUp
   set lockText of me to false
      click at the clickLoc -- single click to identify a line
```

```
    get value of the selectedLine
    set lockText of me to true
    put "You picked " & quote & it & quote -- or whatever you need
end mouseUp
```

For 2.# Users

New functions available starting with version 2.0 let you create simulated buttons with a lot less code. The following handlers accomplish the
same end as the previous ones, but more efficiently:

```
on mouseUp
    get the clickText -- What word or group was clicked?
    put "You picked " & quote & it & quote -- You'd do something else
end mouseUp

on mouseUp
    get value of the clickLine -- text of clicked line
    put "You picked " & quote & it & quote -- or whatever you need
end mouseUp
```

Click with graphics: You can duplicate most of the things that **click** can do
by using other commands (most notably, send "mouseUp" to *object*).
The following handler demonstrates something that only **click** can do: the
handler draws overlapping shapes, and then uses the bucket tool and **click** to
fill the intersection:

```
on picture
    reset paint -- restores all paint properties to default values
    set lineSize to 4 -- nice, broad borders
    choose oval tool
    drag from 100,120 to 200,200 with shiftKey -- circle
    choose rectangle tool
    drag from 150,150 to 250,250
    choose bucket tool
    set pattern to 13
    click at 175,165 -- click at intersection to fill it with current pattern
```

```
  choose browse tool
end picture
```

Points for techies: **Click** is implemented internally as dragging from one point to the same point.

Also See:

CLICKH function, page 389
CLICKLINE function, page 391
CLICKLOC function, page 393
CLICKTEXT function, page 395
CLICKV function, page 397
MOUSELOC function, page 435

CLOSE FILE

Forms

```
close file filename

close file "Mailing list"
close file fileNameHolder
close file "File Number " & thisFileNumber
close file "BigDisk:BigFolder:BigFile"
```

Action

The **close file** command closes the named file(s) previously opened with the **Open File** command.

The following handler closes three previously opened files named "File 1", "File 2", and "File 3":

```
on closeThoseFiles
  repeat with thisFile = 1 to 3
  close file "File " & thisFile -- File 1, File 2, File 3
  end repeat
end closeThoseFiles
```

Comments

If *filename* is not in the same folder with HyperCard, you must provide a path-name to *filename* each time you reference it. So it makes sense to put the path-name into a variable for easy reference.

The following example assumes the existence of a file of student records and two auxiliary handlers:

```
on distributeScholarships
  put "University:Main Campus:Student Records" into students-- pathname in var
  open file students
  repeat
    read from file students until return -- one record/student
    if it is empty then exit repeat -- no more records
    put item 1 of it into studentName
    put item 2 of it into gradePointAverage
```

```
      put item 3 of it into nameAndAddress
      put item 4 of it into activities
      if gradePointAverage < 2.0 then
        if activities contains "varsity football"
        then sendScholarshipOffer nameAndAddress
        else alertDraftBoard nameAndAddress
      end if
    end repeat
    close file students
end distributeScholarships
```

Don't close unopened files: Trying to close an unopened file generates an error dialog, as shown in Figure 8-13.

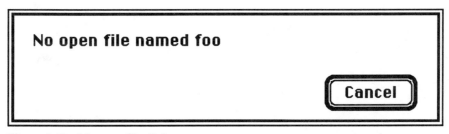

Figure 8-13   No open file dialog

Automatic file closing: HyperTalk automatically closes all open files under the following circumstances:

• You press Command-Period.
• HyperCard puts up a complaint dialog.
• An **exit to HyperCard** statement executes.
• You quit HyperCard.

Even so, you should explicitly close a file when you've finished with it because (1) no other program can access a file that's already open (as you might want to do under MultiFinder), (2) only three files can be open under HyperTalk at the same time, and (3) leaving open files lying about is Bad Form and makes written code difficult to follow.

"Close file" only for "open file": Use **close file** only with **open file**. The **Open printing** command must be paired with **close printing,** and the

open application command takes no closing command. (You close the application when you quit it.)

Also See:

EXIT TO HYPERCARD keyword, page 126
OPEN FILE command, page 280

CLOSE PRINTING

Forms

```
close printing

close printing
```

Action

The **close printing** command sends the last partial page to the printer.

The following handler prints 35 cards:

```
on printCards
   open printing -- starts the print job
   print 35 cards -- actually only prints 32 if dialog says 8/page
   close printing -- sends last three cards to printer and ends job
   answer "Printing completed!"
end printCards
```

Comments

This command effectively flushes the print buffer to the printer and ensures that any cards that would make up a partial page in a print job are immediately printed. (**Open printing** used alone prints only full pages.)

For example, assuming that the Printing Dialog is set to print 8 cards to the page, a job set to print 35 cards would immediately print only 32 cards without **close printing.** The remaining partial page wouldn't be printed until you quit HyperCard.

The following handler demonstrates how to search for and selectively print cards immediately, even if the selected cards make up a partial page:

```
on printBestSellers
  open printing
  repeat for the number of cards -- every card in the stack
    if field "total sales" > 500000
    then print this card
    go to next card
  end repeat
```

```
   close printing
end printBestSellers
```

Also See:

OPEN PRINTING command, page 283
PRINT CARD command, page 302

CONTROLKEY

Forms

```
controlkey integerExpr

controlkey 7 -- sends message: "Key G pressed"
if choice = 5 then controlKey 96
controlKey varName
```

Action

The **controlkey** command passes a numeric parameter that identifies a key-press.

The keypress identified is the key you pressed in combination with the control key. Numeric representation for all identifiable keys appears in the chart on page 197.

The following handler shows how to trap all possible control key combination keypresses, and one possible response:

```
on controlkey whichkey -- grabs the keypress combo
   if whichkey = 5 then put "Yup. Uh-huh. That's it." -- control-E pressed
end controlkey
```

Comments

Meaningful values for *integerExpr* are in the range 1 to 127 when such a value represents a key on the Macintosh keyboard.

Not all numbers have corresponding keys; for example, numbers in the range 97 through 126 don't correspond to any key. No representation exists for combinations of keypresses (for example, option-G), and certain num-bers represent several keys (for example, 28 for both backslash [\] and the left arrow, and 16 for all the function keys).

Controlkey is also a message sent to the current card. If you don't trap the message and do something with it, HyperCard ignores this command entirely.

Simulating function keys: You can write handlers for **controlkey** combina-tions just as you can for function keys. To do it, write handlers that trap specific control keys. The following form intercepts the **controlkey** message, determines which key was pressed, and then does something appropriate:

```
on controlkey whichkey
   if whichkey=5 then edit script of this card
   if whichkey=6 then edit script of this bkgnd
   -- and so on
   if whichkey=15 then doMenu "quit hypercard"
end controlkey
```

If you're writing longer, more complex instructions for control keys, you might want to write separate handlers for each key. The following form calls different handlers depending on the keys pressed (or simulated with the **controlkey** command); each handler is named myControlKey*var* where *var* is a valid **controlKey** number:

```
on controlkey whichKey
   do "myControlKey" & whichKey
end controlkey
...
on myControlKey7
  put "You pressed the G key (passing parameter 7)"
end myControlKey7
```

Not all Macs have a control key: Only Macintoshes with Apple Desktop Bus keyboards have control keys. Unless you're writing scripts exclusively for computers that have such keyboards (thus ruling out all Macintosh Plus models), use control keys as shortcuts for tasks that you provide other ways of doing — for example, make Control-*whatEver* a substitute for clicking a button or making a menu choice.

ControlKey parameter values: The following tables show the keys that match **controlkey's** parameter values (Tables 8-2 and 8-3). The second table isolates keys that produce no printable characters. Gaps in the chart represent numbers with no corresponding keys. All keys appear on the Apple extended keyboard; some keys don't exist on other Macintosh keyboards.

Table 8-2: Controlkey parameter values

Key pressed	Value	Key pressed	Value
A, home	1	], right arrow	29
B	2	up arrow	30
C, enter	3	- (dash), down arrow	31
D, end	4	' (single quote)	39
E, help	5		
F	6	*	42
G	7	+	43
H, delete	8	,	44
I, tab	9	– (keypad minus)	45
J	10	. (period)	46
K, page up	11	/	47
L, page down	12	0	48
M, return	13	1	49
N	14	2	50
O	15	3	51
P, function keys	16	4	52
Q	17	5	53
R	18	6	54
S	19	7	55
T	20	8	56
U	21	9	57
V	22		
W	23	;	59
X	24		
Y	25	=	61
Z	26		
[, esc, clear	27	~	96
\, left arrow	28	del (forward delete)	127

Table 8-3: Controlkey parameter values for nonprinting keys

Key pressed	Value	Key pressed	Value
clear	27	home	1
del (forward delete)	127	left arrow	28
delete	8	page down	12
down arrow	31	page up	11
end	4	return	13
enter	3	right arrow	29
esc	27	tab	9
function keys (all)	16	up arrow	30
help	5		

Also See:

CONTROLKEY command, page 195
FUNCTION keyword, page 128

CONVERT

Forms

```
convert expr to format {and format}

convert theDate to long date
convert line 1 of field "Time" to seconds -- since 01/01/04
convert 2667139260 to short date and time -- yields: 7/7/88 4:01 PM
convert last item of version of this stack to date and time
convert the seconds to dateItems -- get date, time in dateItems format
```

Action

The **convert** command converts a given date and/or time *(expr)* to a specific format or formats (see chart), usually to do calculations or to construct special displays.

The following handler takes a birth date and converts it to the seconds format for ease of calculation:

```
on bouncer
  ask "When were you born?" with the short date
  convert it to seconds
  if the seconds - it < 18 * 365 * 24 * 60 * 60 -- yrs * dys/yr * hrs/dy *...
  then answer "Sorry, you're under 18."
  else answer "Come on in."
end bouncer
```

Comments

If *expr* is a container the result of the conversion goes into *expr* ; if *expr* is not a container, the result goes into the local variable It.

The following function returns the long date of the day after today, i.e., tomorrow.

```
function tomorrow
  convert the seconds + 60*60*24 to long date -- 60*60*24 = seconds in day
  return it
end tomorrow
```

Table 8-4 shows the valid format specifications and their meanings in the United States. (The formats might be localized in other countries.)

Table 8-4: Formats for convert

Format	Meaning
dateItems	comma-separated list of items representing (in order) year, month, day number in month, hour, minute, second, text day of week (e.g., Monday): 1988,7,7,16,1,11,5 is 4:01:11 PM Thursday, July 7, 1988
seconds	seconds since midnight, January 1, 1904 (Don't ask): 2667139260
short time	time in colon-separated form without seconds: 4:01 PM (or 16:01)
long time	time in colon-separated form with seconds: 4:01:11 PM (or 16:01:11)
short date	month number, day number, last two digits of year: 7/7/88
abbr{ev{iated}} date	abbreviated date information: Thu, Jul 7, 1988
long date	fully expanded date information: Thursday, July 7, 1988

(25 bonus points if you can guess when this command's explanation was originally written.)

Abbreviated days are: Sun, Mon, Tue, Wed, Thu, Fri, Sat

Abbreviated months are: Jan, Feb, Mar, Apr, May, Jun, Jul, Aug, Sep, Oct, Nov, Dec

You can choose between a 12- or 24-hour clock in the Control Panel.

Local formats observed: The format for date and time are localizable, so they might not be the same as they appear in the chart. Seconds, however, are international, and will be the same in every format.

Avoid ambiguity: If *expr* is a literal that contains ambiguous characters, enclose the literal within quotation marks; otherwise HyperTalk tries to carry out meaningless calculations on what it thinks to be an expression to be evaluated:

convert 05/12/44 to seconds -- divide 5 by 12; divide result by 44; convert
convert "05/12/44" to seconds -- you get what you want

The following handler calculates a future date by adding days to a given date:

```
on addDays
  repeat
    ask "What's the starting date?" with the date -- default is today
    if it is empty then exit addDays -- abort if Cancel clicked
    convert it to dateItems
    if the result is empty then exit repeat
    answer "That's not a date."
  end repeat
  put it into whichDate
  ask "Add how many days?" with 13
  if it is empty then exit addDays
  add it to item 3 of whichDate
  convert whichDate to long date
  answer "That would be " & whichDate
end addDays
```

Convert and the result: If you supply an invalid date to **convert,** it puts the string "invalid date" into the **result** without complaining. But this string is likely to change in future versions of HyperCard, so it's not wise to use it to check for success. If the **result** is empty, however, you can be sure that **convert** has been successful.

Also See:

DATE function, page 403
RESULT function, page 454
TIME function, page 482

CREATE MENU

Forms

```
create menu expr

create menu "Utilities"
create menu word 2 of field 3
```

Action

The **create menu** command, new in HyperCard 2.0, adds a menu to the menu bar.

The following handler, which belongs in the script of an Address and Phone Number stack, creates a menu of names: choose a name, and the phone number appears in the Message box.

```
on callIt
  create menu "Quick Calling"
  repeat with i = 2 to number of cards -- 1st card is title card
    put line 1 of field "Name and Address" of card i ¬
    after menu "Quick Calling" with menuMessage ¬
    "put line 1 of field Telephone of card " & i
  end repeat
end callIt
```

Comments

The name of a menu is truncated to 29 characters.

To add items to the new menu, use the **put into menu** command.

To delete a menu, use the **delete menu** command.

To find the names of all menus on the menu bar, use the **menus** function:

```
on makeMyMenu
  if "Quick Calling" is in the menus then exit makeMyMenu
  callIt -- creates "Quick Calling" menu using handler listed above
end makeMyMenu
```

If the menu you're trying to create already exists, you get an error dialog.

Also See:

DELETE MENU command, page 215
DISABLE command, page 223
ENABLE command, page 238
ENABLED property, page 530
MENUS function, page 426
NUMBER function, page 438
PUT INTO MENU command, page 312
RESET MENUBAR command, page 322

CREATE STACK

Forms

```
create stack expr {with bgExpr} {in {a} new window}

create stack "myStack" in a new window
create stack variableName with background 3
create stack "Expenses" with background "Spreadsheet"
create stack Fred with this background -- copy current background
```

Action

The **create stack** command, new for 2.0, creates a new stack without presenting a dialog, optionally using any background of the current stack. If you use the form "in a new window" then **create stack** will display the newly created stack in a newly created window rather than displaying it in the current window.

The following handler creates a new stack called "Dog Breeds" using the third background of the current stack as a template:

```
on newDogs
  create stack "Dog Breeds" with background 3
end newDogs
```

Comments

Expr is any expression that yields a valid stack name. *BgExpr* is any background in the current stack.

This command presents no dialog. It just creates the new stack on disk, takes you to it, and sends a newStack message to it.

The following handler creates a new stack made up of all the marked cards in the current stack:

```
on extractMarkedCards
  if the number of marked cards is zero then
    answer "No cards are marked."
    exit extractMarkedCards
  end if
```

```
ask file "Save marked cards in stack:"
if it is empty then exit extractMarkedCards
put it into newStack
lock screen
go to first marked card
create stack newStack
go back
repeat with cardNum = 1 to the number of marked cards
  set cursor to busy
  go to marked card cardNum
  push card
  doMenu "Copy Card"
  go to last card of stack newStack
  doMenu "Paste Card"
  pop card
end repeat
go to stack newStack
doMenu "Delete Card" -- "create stack" makes blank card
end extractMarkedCards
```

Card size in created stack: Card size for the created stack is the standard 512 by 342 pixels. But if you use the `with bgExpr` option, the card size of the new stack is the same as the card size of the current stack.

To set the card size programmatically,use the **rect** property:

```
set rect of card to 0,0,200,200 -- left, top, right, bottom
```

Also See:

DOMENU command, page 229
RECT property, page 593

DEBUG

Forms

```
debug [ hintBits | pureQuickDraw logical | checkPoint ]

debug hintBits
debug pureQuickDraw true
debug checkPoint
```

Action

The form `debug hintBits` modifies the **Compact Stack** menu command such that the user can modify the effectiveness and efficiency of the **find** command by changing the way that HyperCard stores compressed information about the textual content of cards. This form is useful only to developers of stacks for CD-ROM or other media that hold very large read-only stacks.

The form `debug pureQuickDraw true` makes HyperCard use QuickDraw instead of its own drawing routines when it moves graphical information from an internal buffer onto the screen, in order to overcome problems sometimes associated with monitors not marketed by Apple Computer Inc. This form is useful only to monitor developers or to technicians diagnosing monitor compatibility problems.

The following handler turns on hintBits before compacting the stack:

```
on mouseUp
   debug hintBits
   doMenu "compact stack"
end mouseUp
```

The form `debug checkPoint` sets a permanent checkpoint in a script such that, each time the handler containing this command is run, the Debugger is invoked as soon as `debug checkPoint` executes.

Comments

Debug hintBits is initially off; it reverts to off whenever you change stacks. PureQuickDraw is initially false, but maintains whatever setting you give it.

Hint bits and fast searches: HyperCard creates a hash value for all the text on a given card each time you edit a field. The hash value is made up of 32-bit

longwords. Certain bits are set to give hints about the contents of the text —
for example, words that end with H, or that are five characters long. These
make up the hint bits after which the command is named. (Precisely how the
hash works is secret, at least for the moment.)

When you issue a Find command, HyperCard first does a hash on the text
you want to find, creating a set of hint bits for it. After the hash is created,
HyperCard begins its search — but for matching hint bits, rather than
matching text. If the hint bits on a particular card don't match the hint bits
of the search text, there's no possibility that the text you're looking for will
be on that card; so HyperCard rejects that card and goes on to the next one.
If the hint bits do match, then it's possible that this card has text that matches the search text; so HyperCard looks at all the text on that card looking for
a match.

Hint bits are kept in RAM, so a hint bit search is quick; cards, on the other
hand, mainly live on disk, and retrieving cards from disk is relatively slow.
(Typically, hint bits for hundreds of cards can be taken from disk in a single
read.) It's this pre-search for hint bits that accounts for HyperCard's speed in
searching through stacks.

About debug hintBits: debug hintBits changes the operation of the
Compact Stack and **Find** commands until you leave the current stack.

After you've issued a **debug hintBits** command, the menu item **Compact
stack** produces the dialog shown in Figure 8-14 before compacting begins.

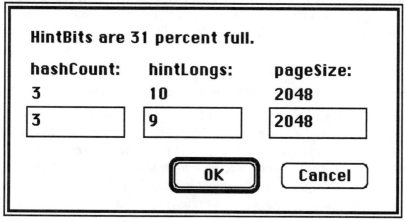

Figure 8-14 Hint bits dialog

HashCount, hintLongs, and pageSize are internal variables. The numbers immediately below these variable names in Figure 8-16 indicate the values that HyperCard used the last time it created hash values. The numbers in the editable text boxes are the values HyperCard will use in the new stack that **compact stack** creates. (**Compact stack** creates a new stack and deletes the old one. To the user, it looks like the stack stays the same.)

The joys of redundancy

In prerelease versions, HyperCard made compactions within the original stack. This proved dangerous because a bug or power failure during compaction would destroy the stack. Now that HyperCard creates a new compacted stack before destroying the original, you can't lose data even during a power loss — HyperCard just reverts to the original stack.

HashCount governs how many hint bits are set for text on each card. Increasing hashCount increases the sensitivity of the search: the higher this number, the more cards are rejected from consideration for actual searching. (But too high a number saturates the hint bits and the rejection rate declines again; you need to experiment to find the balance point.)

HintLongs governs the number of longwords allocated per card for holding hint bits. In especially large stacks, the longwords can quickly become saturated increasing the need for long words. The cost here is RAM and disk space: the greater the number of hintLongs, the greater the amount of disk space and memory needed.

PageSize is the number of bytes allocated per page of hint bits. The less available memory you have, the smaller you need to make pageSize.

In Figure 8-16, the phrase "HintBits are 31 percent full" means that 31percent of the bits that can be used to mark hint bits are turned on. This is close to an ideal percentage. A much lower number would mean that the number of longwords as set in the hintLong box is too high; this wastes both RAM and disk space. A much higher number would indicate that HyperTalk isn't being that effective in rejecting cards, which produces lots of false matches.

Find and hint bits: Each time a **find** command operates, debug hintBits reports the number of hint matches that occurred in the course of the find operation, whether or not the find operation was successful. This lets you know how well the hint bits are rejecting (see Figure 8-15).

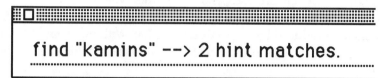

find "kamins" --> 2 hint matches.

Figure 8-15 Matches

At most, one of those matches reflects a card that really has what you're looking for; all the rest are false matches. HyperCard only looks up to the next real match. So a lower number of matches means that HyperCard is rejecting a higher number of cards — which is what you're after.

The following handler issues the debug hintBits command each time a **find** command executes so that all finds in this stack will show hint matches information:

```
on find
  debug hintBits  -- turn on hintDebug
  pass find       -- so find will report number of hint matches
end find
```

Debug hintBits is for CD-ROM developers

This command was designed as an aid to CD-ROM developers so they could create hashes in their huge read-only stacks to achieve the most efficient searches.

HyperCard does all this stuff automatically, making debug hintbits largely redundant for people who aren't making really large, read-only stacks with huge amounts of text in them.

Because hand-tuned values get lost on subsequent compacts, this command is essentially useless for stacks that can be recompacted.

About debug pureQuickDraw *logical*:   Added for version 1.2.2, this command determines what routines HyperCard uses to move graphics onto the screen from its internal graphics buffer. With `pureQuickDraw false` (the default condition when the Monitors area in the Control Panel is set to two colors/grays), HyperCard uses its own routines which are fast and which allow visual effects to work, but which cause compatibility problems for a few monitors not produced by Apple Computer Inc. With `pureQuickDraw false`, HyperCard uses the QuickDraw copyBits call which all monitors can handle.

The only time you'd use this command is when your monitor is displaying bizarre symptoms (for example, instead of seeing a proper card, you see eight little images of the card smeared across the display).

About debug checkPoint: New for 2.0, this command emerged when the HyperCard development team at Apple needed a way to set a checkpoint in a script that would remain even after HyperCard quit. (Checkpoints marked with a ✔ character disappear when HyperCard quits.) They needed this permanent checkpoint mostly as a way to show off the Debugger to Apple executives. Later, they discovered that it made sense to leave it in the language as a way for scripters to mark incomplete handlers.

The following sophisticated application of this command implements a conditional checkpoint. The handler **rangeCheck** tests an input parameter to see if it's within a low and high bound. if it's out of bounds, then rangeCheck enters the Debugger so you can figure out what went wrong. Otherwise rangeCheck simply returns and the calling handler continues normally:

```
on mouseUp
   rangeCheck 41,0,100 -- your would likely use variables
   rangeCheck 7,1,10
   rangeCheck -1,0,5 -- this one will enter the debugger
   -- because -1 is not between 0 and 5 inclusive
end mouseUp

on rangeCheck num,low,high
   if num < low or num > high
   then debug checkPoint -- conditional checkpoint
end rangeCheck
```

Debug checkPoint and the Message box: Typing `debug checkPoint` into the Message box has no effect unless an `on idle` handler resides somewhere between the card script and the Home stack script (inclusive) on the message passing path. In such a case, the debugger turns on with the first line of the `on idle` handler boxed. This `on idle` behavior is a side effect rather than a planned feature of this command (which wasn't designed to be used from the Message box); so it's liable to go away in future versions.

Also See:

FIND command, page 246

DELETE

Forms

```
delete chunkOfContainer

delete item 2 of PizzaOrder
delete word 3 to 5 of field 7 of card "lists"
delete last char of the Selection
delete the foundchunk
```

Action

The **delete** command removes specific character(s), word(s), item(s) or line(s) from a specific container.

The following handler removes a line of text from a field:

```
on killName
  Ask "Name to remove:"
  if it is not in field "phone book" then
    answer "Sorry -- " & it & "'s not listed."
    exit killName
  end if
  find It in field "phone book"
  delete the foundLine -- Here's where the deletion happens
end killName
```

(You can add this handler to the auto-dialer script described under **Dial,** page 218, to increase that script's functionality.)

Comments

If you don't name the card that the container is on, HyperTalk assumes you want to make the deletion from the current card. If you *do* specify a card, it must be in the current stack.

Delete is intelligent about commas and spaces:

• Deleting a word takes the space(s) after it.

• Deleting the last word deletes the space before it.

- Deleting an item takes the item's comma.

- Deleting the last item takes the preceding comma.

- Deleting a line takes the Return character at the end of the line.

Delete works on text (including the text in locked fields), but not on whole containers. To delete an entire field, for example, use a form like:

```
on killField
  ask "What field goes away?"
  select field It
  doMenu "Clear field"
end killField
```

Deleting all text in a field: To delete all the text in a field, use a form like:

```
on killText
  ask "What field do you want to clear?"
  put empty into field it
end killText
```

"delete line" different from "put empty into line":   A form like

```
delete line 5 of field 1
```

totally removes line 5 from the field; old line 6 becomes new line 5. The form

```
put empty into line 5 of field 1
```

leaves the Return character marking the end of line 5; old line 6 remains as line 6. The form

```
put empty into field 1
```

clears the field of all text, including Return characters.

"delete line 0" has strange results

The following forms delete the first <u>character</u> of *container*:

```
delete line 0 of container
delete line 0 to anyNumber of container
```

This is a bug and is likely to change in future versions.

Also note that a line in HyperTalk is defined as the text between Return characters (or between the start of a container and the first Return character, or between the last Return character and the end of the container). A line that goes beyond the right edge of a field might wrap; so several screen lines can (and often do) make up a single HyperTalk line.

Also See:

CHUNKS, page 102
EMPTY constant, page 91
PUT command, page 309
SELECT command, page 331

DELETE MENU

Forms

```
delete {menuItem expr [ of | from ] } menu menuName
delete {ordinal menuItem} [ of | from ] ordinal menu

delete menu "Companies"
delete menu 7
delete last menu
delete menuItem theMenuItem of menu myMenu
delete menuItem 3 from menu "file"
```

Action

The **delete menu** command, new for 2.0, removes menu items or menus from the menu bar.

The following handler prevents low level users from creating or deleting cards or from using any item on the File menu:

```
on mouseUp
  set the userLevel to 2
  delete menu "File"
  delete menuItem "Delete Card" of menu "Edit"
  delete menuItem "New Card" of menu "Edit"
  delete last menuItem of menu "Edit" -- get rid of the grey line
  -- can't refer to menuItem "-" because that would get the first one
  -- and we want the last
end mouseUp
```

Comments

You can delete standard menus and menu items (that is, all menus and menu items that come with HyperCard) or user-defined menus and menu items. But deleted standard menu items still respond to HyperTalk code:

```
delete menu Apple -- Removes Apple menu
doMenu Calculator -- Calculator still appears!
```

(In the above example, the Apple icon appears and the entire Apple menu is accessible while a desk accessory is the front window; but when you put the desk accessory away, the Apple icon disappears.)

You can't delete a specific menu item from HyperCard's Apple, Font, Tools, Style, or Patterns menus (but you can delete any HyperCard menu and create your own).

The following example creates a menu called "Parts" containing the names of all the buttons and fields on the current card. Choosing a menu item edits the script of the specified button or field. Buttons or fields that have no script are shown in italics on the menu (Figure 8-16):

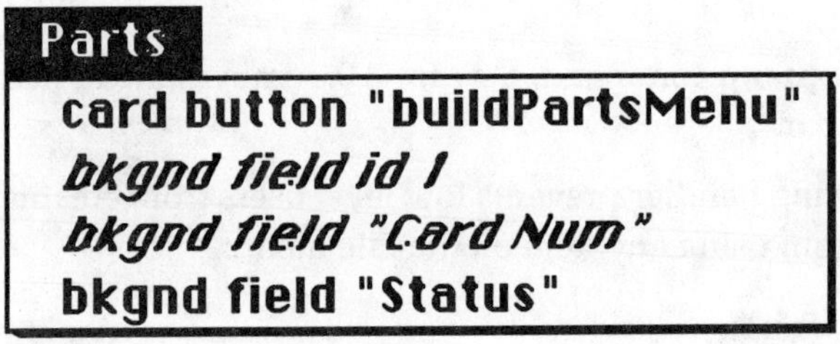

Figure 8-16 Parts menu with "empty objects" italicized

```
on buildPartsMenu
   if "Parts" is in the menus then delete menu "Parts"
   create menu "Parts"

   -- card buttons
   repeat with btnNum = 1 to the number of buttons
     put name of button btnNum after menu "Parts" with ¬
     menuMessage "edit script of button " & btnNum
   end repeat

     -- card fields
   repeat with cdFldNum = 1 to the number of cd fields
     put name of cd field cdFldNum after menu "Parts" with ¬
     menuMessage "edit script of cd field " & cdFldNum
   end repeat

   -- bkgnd buttons
   repeat with bgBtnNum = 1 to the number of bg buttons
```

```
      put name of bg button bgBtnNum after menu "Parts" with ¬
      menuMessage "edit script of bg button " & btnNum
   end repeat

   -- bkgnd fields
   repeat with fldNum = 1 to the number of fields
      put name of field fldNum after menu "Parts" with menuMessage ¬
      "edit script of field " & fldNum
   end repeat

   -- italicize items with no script
   repeat with itemNum = 1 to the number of menuItems in menu "Parts"
      if script of (name of menuItem itemNum of menu "Parts") is empty
      then set textStyle of menuItem itemNum of menu "Parts" to italic
   end repeat
end buildPartsMenu
```

Also See:

PUT INTO MENU command, page 312

DIAL

Forms

```
dial phoneNumber {with [{modem} modemCommands|modem] }

dial "415-767-1212"
dial Tim_Pozar -- The guy who told us the Truth about modems
dial Email with "ATZM1E1S0=0" -- modem commands in quotation marks
dial Martha with modem "ATSO=OS7=30DT"
dial field "Phone number"
dial it
```

Action

The **dial** command produces telephone tones through the Macintosh speaker. When you use any of the modem options, you dial through the modem serial port.

The following handler dials a long distance number using a credit card. The handler assumes that the field named "dialNumber" contains the number to dial, and that the field named "Credit Card" contains the credit card number:

```
on longDistanceCall
  dial "0" & field "dialNumber"
  wait 90 ticks -- until phone company computer asks for credit card
  dial field "Credit Card"
end longDistanceCall
```

Comments

When you dial without using the modem option, HyperTalk sets the speaker volume to maximum for dialing; when the dialing's finished, HyperTalk restores the old volume.

Dial command not meant for telecom programming: The **Dial** command was originally conceived to make dialing the telephone for voice communication easier. The form `dial with modem` dials through the modem port; but HyperTalk expects you to pick up the telephone as soon as dialing starts — otherwise it hangs up one second after dialing. For more complex calling, or to send tones to a modem that isn't Hayes-compatible, use the form dial *phoneNumber* with *modemCommands*

If you're using a Hayes-compatible modem (which most modems are these days, including all of the ones from Apple Computer Inc.), for best results use the form

    dial *phoneNumber* with modem "ATSO=OS7=30DT"

In any event, the entire dialing line must be less than 255 characters.

Modem dialing unreliable

The Dial command is unreliable for complex modem dialing. For serious dialing through a modem, you'll need the *Serial ToolKit* package from APDA. The kit comes complete with a sample BBS stack. See the end of Chapter 13 for APDA's address.

Points for techies: The form dial *phoneNumber* with modem calls through the modem at 1200 baud, and sends the string "ATSO=OS7=1DT". This string sets up the modem to

- use TouchTone rather than pulse (DT at the end)
- ignore incoming calls (S0=0)
- wait one second for a connection after dialing (S7=1)

The problem is that one second usually isn't enough time for a carrier to come up. (Default standard for most modems — including Hayes — is 30 or 45 seconds). In most situations, you'll need to change S7 to 30:

dial *phoneNumber* with modem "ATSO=OS7=30DT"

Phone number's contents: The phone number can contain any or all of the following:

- Digits 0 through 9

- Special characters * and #

- Uppercase A, B, C, and D (the extra set that appears on telephone company and ham radio keypads)

- Commas, each one representing a one-second pause

• Semicolons, each one representing a 10-second pause

• Hyphens (-), parentheses, and spaces (all of which are ignored when quoted)

The following example uses the modem to get an outside line, waits three seconds, and then makes a call:

```
dial "9,,, (415) 555-1212" with modem "ATSO=OS7=30DT"
```

Dial is smart enough to strip out junk. Thus you can say

```
dial line 1 of field 3
```

although line 1 of field 3 contains "555-1212 Office Number" or "Office Number 555-1212" or even "555 in New Jersey 1212." In all these cases, HyperTalk dials "555-1212."

Avoid subtraction: Enclose literal telephone numbers and modem commands within quotation marks to prevent HyperTalk from interpreting hyphens as minus signs. This step is not necessary if you're referencing telephone numbers typed directly into fields, but is necessary when you assign a literal telephone number to a variable:

```
put 617-555-1212 into BostonInfo   yields -1150
put "617-555-1212" into BostonInfo   yields 617-555-1212
```

An auto-dialing system

The following handlers make up a simple auto-dialing system. Put them into a card, background, or stack script.

The first handler responds to the message `call` *name:* it looks up *name* in the phone book, finds that *name's* number, and dials it (or puts up some appropriate message). When *name* is more than one word long, enclose it within quotation marks (as in `call "The bookie"`).

The second handler responds to the message `phonebook`. It builds a phone book in a background field named "phone book" by soliciting information from the user. It stores each name and number set on a separate line of the field.

Much of the code checks for user error (bad input, name not in list).

```
on call who
  repeat
    if who is in card field "Phone Book" then exit repeat
    comment "No entry for " & who & ". Add one?","No","Yes"
    phoneBook who
  end repeat
  dial item 2 of getLine(who,card field "Phone Book") -- with modem
end call

on phoneBook who
  if who is not empty then get who & ", (111) 111-1111"
  else get "San Francisco Info, (415) 555-1212"
  repeat
    ask "Add to phone book:" with it
    if it is empty then exit phoneBook
    if "," is in it then exit repeat
    comment "Form is name, number","Give Up","Try Again"
  end repeat
  put it into newNumber
  if item 1 of newNumber is in card field "Phone Book" then
    comment "That name exists. Update entry?","No","Yes"
    put deleteLine(item 1 of newNumber,card field "Phone Book") ¬
    into card field "Phone Book"
  end if
  if item 2 of newNumber is in card field "Phone Book"
  then comment "That number exists. Continue anyway?","No","Yes"
  put newNumber & return after card field "Phone Book"
end phoneBook

on comment what, quitChoice, continueChoice
  if quitChoice is empty then put "Quit" into quitChoice
  if continueChoice is empty then put "Continue" into continueChoice
  answer what with quitChoice or continueChoice
```

```
   if it is quitChoice then exit to HyperCard -- aborts handler
end comment

function getLine pattern,string
  put offset(pattern,string) into startChar
  put length(string) into endChar
  get char startChar to endChar of string
  return line 1 of it
end getLine

function deleteLine pattern,string
  put offset(pattern,string) into startChar
  put length(string) into endChar
  put char 1 to startChar - 1 of string into beforeMatch
  put char startChar to endChar of string into afterMatch
  delete line 1 of afterMatch
  return beforeMatch & afterMatch
end deleteLine
```

Also See:

MODEM commands, in your modem's reference manual

DISABLE

Forms

```
disable {menuItem expr of} menu menuName
disable {ordinal menuItem of} ordinal menu

disable menu "Companies"
disable menu 7
disable last menu
disable menuItem theMenuItem of menu myMenu
disable menuItem 3 of menu "file"
```

Action

The **disable** command, new for 2.0, disables a menu or menu item, preventing a user from working with it.

The following handler stops the user from using the Quit command:

```
on noQuit
    disable menuItem "Quit HyperCard" of menu "File"
end noQuit
```

Comments

Menu is the name or number of a specific menu. *MenuItem* is the name or number of a specific menu item on a specific menu.

A disabled menu item is greyed out and can't be chosen. When a menu title appears greyed out on the menu bar, no item within that menu can be chosen. But all greyed menu items still respond to **doMenu** commands.

This command sets the **enabled** property of the specified menu or menu item to false. It has exactly the same effect as set enabled of {menuItem expr of} menu menuName to false.

You can't disable any item on the Apple, Tools, Font, Style, or Patterns menu (but you can disable any whole menu).

The following example (which for greatest effectiveness belongs in the stack script) creates a menu that, when the insertion point is in a field, lets you set some or all the letters in that field to upper- or lowercase (Figure 8-17):

Figure 8-17   Capitalize menu

```
on openField
  if "Capitalize" is not in the menus then
    -- create the menu if it does not exist already
    create menu "Capitalize"
    Put "Words" after menu "Capitalize" ¬
    with menuMessage "capitalize words"
    Put "Sentences" after menu "Capitalize" ¬
    with menuMessage "capitalize sentences"
    Put "Everything" after menu "Capitalize" ¬
    with menuMessage "capitalize everything"
    Put "Nothing" after menu "Capitalize" ¬
    with menuMessage "capitalize nothing"
  end if
  enable menu "Capitalize" -- and enable it
end openField

on closeField
  disableCapsMenu
end closeField

on exitField -- new message in 2.0
  disableCapsMenu
end exitField

on disableCapsMenu
  disable menu "Capitalize"
end disableCapsMenu

on capitalize what
  -- get the selection if there is one, else the whole field
  put the selection into sourceText
```

```
  if sourceText is empty
  then put the value of the selectedField into sourceText

  put true into sentenceStart
  put true into wordStart
  put empty into destText
  repeat with charNum = 1 to length of sourceText
    set cursor to busy
    get char charNum of sourceText
    if it is space then put true into wordStart
    else if it is "." then put true into sentenceStart
    else if what is "Words" then
      if wordStart then
        get toUpper(it)
        put false into wordStart
      else get toLower(it)
    else if what is "Sentences" then
      if sentenceStart then
        get toUpper(it)
        put false into sentenceStart
      else get toLower(it)
    else if what is "Everything" then get toUpper(it)
    else if what is "Nothing" then get toLower(it)
    put it after destText
  end repeat

  -- replace the selection if there is one, else the whole field
  get the selectedChunk
  if the selection is empty
  then put destText into the selectedField
  else put destText into the selection
  select it -- preserve the selection
end capitalize

function toUpper whichChar
  put charToNum(whichChar) into thisNum
  put charToNum("a") into firstLower
  put charToNum("A") into firstUpper
  put thisNum -- firstLower into charIndex
```

```
    if charIndex >= 0 and charIndex < 26
    then put firstUpper + charIndex into thisNum
    return numToChar(thisNum)
end toUpper

function toLower whichChar
  put charToNum(whichChar) into thisNum
  put charToNum("a") into firstLower
  put charToNum("A") into firstUpper
  put thisNum - firstUpper into charIndex
  if charIndex >= 0 and charIndex < 26
  then put firstLower + charIndex into thisNum
  return numToChar(thisNum)
end toLower
```

Also See:

ENABLE command, page 238
ENABLED property, page 530

DIVIDE

Forms

```
divide container by numExpr

divide thePot by numberOfPlayers

divide field "Total State Allocation" by totalCounties
```

Action

The **divide** command divides *container* by *numExpr*, leaving the result in *container*. The old value of *container* is trashed (but the value of *numExpr* is unaffected).

The following handler computes the share of the national debt for each of the United States:

```
on debt
  ask "What's the national debt (in trillions)?"
  divide it by 50
  answer "That's $" & it & " trillion per state. (So little!)"
end debt
```

Comments

container must contain a numeric value before a divide can happen or you'll get an error dialog like this one (Figure 8-18):

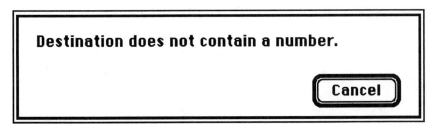

Destination does not contain a number.

Cancel

Figure 8-18 Wrong type

HyperTalk treats the contents of *container* as a floating- point value.

HyperTalk divides with up to 19 decimal places of precision (if the computation demands it); but the number of characters displayed in a field or in the Message box depends upon the setting of the **numberFormat** property.

INF & NAN: A result of INF in *container* most likely indicates that *numExpr* held 0. A result of NAN means "Not a number"; you'll get this if you do something like divide 0 by 0.

Points for techies: **Divide** and the "/" operator use the same internal code. Both use SANE to do floating-point division.

Also See:

NUMBERFORMAT property, page 585

DOMENU

Forms

```
doMenu menuItem
doMenu menuItem {,menuName} {without dialog} -- version 2.0 and later

doMenu "Open stack..."
doMenu "Calculator", "Utilities" -- calculator in the Utilities menu
doMenu itemChoice
domenu "delete stack..." without dialog
```

Action

The **doMenu** command executes a command *(menuItem)* from a HyperCard menu as if you had chosen the command using the mouse. In version 2.0 and later, you can specify (1) the name of the menu that the command is in (using the *menuName* option), and/or (2) that the command is to be performed without presenting the dialog that usually goes with that command (using the `without dialog` option).

The following handler executes various Apple menu commands depending on the control key combination pressed:

```
on controlKey whatEver
  if whatEver = 1 then doMenu "Alarm clock" -- 1 is letter A
  if whatEver = 3 then doMenu "Calculator" -- 3  is letter C
  if whatEver = 16 then doMenu "Puzzle" -- 16 is letter P
  pass controlkey
end controlKey
```

Comments

For **doMenu** to work, the summoned menu item must be available at the current user level and in the stack's current locked or unlocked condition.

Text for *MenuItem* must match the menu item character-for-character (but case is insignificant). The following form generates an error dialog (see Figure 8-19) because it lacks the three dots on the end, as they appear in the menu:

Figure 8-19   Menu item error dialog

```
doMenu "Open Stack"
```

The following form brings up the "Open Stack..." dialog. It has three dots on the end (*not* the ellipses generated by option-semicolon):

```
doMenu "Open Stack..."
```

About *menuName*: Version 2.0's *menuName* option lets you solve the problem that arises when an item in one of the menus you create using the **create menu** and **put into menu** commands (pages 202 and 312) has the same name as an item in a native HyperCard menu.

Assume for example that you've created a special calculator listed as an item in your Utilities menu. The form `domenu "Calculator"` gets you the first instance of "Calculator" in any menu, going from right to left and top to bottom. So a call for the calculator would always get the "Calculator" in the Utilities menu.

Version 2.0 lets you use the form domenu "Calculator", "Apple" to specify the calculator in the desk accessory menu.

Pass doMenu: When you trap for a specific menu command, be sure to use the form `pass doMenu` to let other commands execute:

```
on doMenu whatEver
  if whatEver is not "Quit HyperCard" then pass doMenu
  answer "You sure you want to quit HyperCard?" with "Yes" or "Cancel"
  if it is "yes" then pass doMenu
end doMenu
```

Menu items change: The text of menu items changes from time to time. For example, the Cut menu item can read "Cut," "Cut Picture," "Cut Text", "Cut Button," and so on, depending on what's selected. Further, users are liable to remove standard desk accessories, so calling specific ones with **doMenu** might not work.

To avoid worrying about the exact text of the cut, copy, and paste menus, use the following substitutes:

```
type "x" with commandKey -- cuts whatever is selected
type "c" with commandKey -- copies whatever is selected
type "v" with commandKey -- pastes whatever is on the clipboard
```

UserLevel affects available doMenu items: Lower **userLevel** settings mean fewer available menu commands. When the **userLevel** is below what you need it to be to access a particular command, you can temporarily set it to use the command and then reset it when you've finished:

```
put userLevel into oldLevel -- save the old userLevel
set userLevel to 4 -- set the userLevel where you need it
createMyButton -- do a procedure of some kind
set userLevel to oldLevel -- restore the old userLevel
```

See the **userLevel** property (page 639) for a chart of the menus and menu commands available at the various user levels.

Edit menu bug alert!

Sometimes HyperCard doesn't properly update the edit menu. This makes explicit cut, copy, and paste commands fail. You can patch this bug in a global way by putting the following handler into your home script:

```
on doMenu what
  global overrideEditMenu
  if overrideEditMenu is true then pass doMenu
  put true into overrideEditMenu
  if what contains "paste" then type "v" with commandKey
  else if what contains "card" then pass doMenu
  else if what contains "copy" then type "c" with commandKey
  else if what contains "cut" then type "x" with commandKey
  else pass doMenu
  put false into overrideEditMenu
end doMenu
```

Points for techies: **Domenu** looks for a summoned item first in the standard English HyperCard menus, then in localized menus, and finally in the Apple menu.

Also See:

CONTROLKEY command, page 195
DOMENU command, page 229

DRAG

Forms

```
drag from location1 to location2 {with key1{, key2{, key3 }}}

drag from 10,10 to 120, 350
drag from the loc of button 5 to the clickloc with cmdkey
```

Action

The **drag** command programmatically drags the mouse from *location1* to *location2*, optionally "holding down" the shiftkey, optionkey, and/or command-key as the dragging happens.

The following handler draws a small rounded rectangle at the upper-left corner of the card window:

```
on dragit
   set pattern to 13 -- get a pattern to fill a shape
   set filled to true -- fill it as you draw
   choose round rect tool -- choose the shape
   drag from 10,10 to 75,75 -- draw the shape by dragging
end dragit
```

Comments

location is a point on the display, expressed as two integers separated by a comma: the integers represent respectively the horizontal and vertical coordinates of the point in pixels, using the upper-left corner of the card window (under the title bar) as a frame of reference. *Location1* is the starting point for the drag. (You don't have to click there; the **drag** command includes the click.)

key can be `shiftkey`, `optionkey`, and/or `commandkey` (or `cmdkey`).

No-drag tools: You can't drag with the bucket, polygon, or lasso tools. You can drag with the curve tool, but you'll just get a straight line.

Selecting text: To select text with the **drag** command, use the form

```
drag from location1 to location2 with shiftkey
```

The field over which you're dragging must be unlocked for text to be selected.

(Most people find the **select** command, page 331, more convenient for selecting text.)

Dragging and selecting: When the field or button tool is active, you don't have to use the **select** command before dragging a field or button (assuming it's not covered by another object):

```
on moveThisField
  choose Field tool
  drag from the loc of field 3 to 150, 200 -- selects field 3 for you
  choose Browse tool
end moveThisField
```

Actually, it's more economical to use **set loc** to move a field or button:

```
on moveThisField
  set loc of field 3 to 150, 200
end moveThisField
```

Creating buttons and fields: You can create buttons and fields using **drag** with the Command Key (a handy way to "install" a button from a script):

```
 on newButton
  choose Button tool
  drag from 100,100 to 180, 120 with commandKey
  -- newly created button is last button, so next 3 lines work
  set the name of last button to "Dragged"
  set the showName of last button to true
  set the style of last button to roundRect
  choose Browse tool
end newButton
```

Also See:

DRAGSPEED property, page 526
SELECT command, page 331

EDIT

Forms

```
edit {the} script of object

edit script of bkgnd btn "Fred"
edit the script of field foo of card 3 -- foo is a variable
edit script of background 3
edit script of card "whacko"
edit script of cd 2 of bg 2
edit script of me -- handler edits its own script (bizarre, eh?)
```

Action

The **edit** command opens the script of the specified object for editing.

The following handler opens the script of the current card for editing when you press the Tab key:

```
on tabKey
   edit script of this card
end tabKey
```

Comments

Edit is more commonly used from the Message box than from within a handler.

When **edit** is called from within a handler, handler execution is suppressed while the editor is open; control returns to the executing handler when the script editor is closed, and the handler continues to run. Any changes you make to a running handler take effect after the handler finishes running.

The following handler checks the script of the current card, background, and stack to find out who would catch a particular message. The handler assumes that the name of the message in question is passed to it as its parameter. (For example, whoGets openCard opens the scripts that have handlers for the openCard message.

```
on whoGets msgName
  put "this card,this bkgnd,this stack" into objects
  repeat with i = 1 to 3
  if script of item i of objects contains msgName
  then edit script of item i of objects
  end repeat
end whoGets
```

To search every script in the current stack for a particular message, use
`searchScript` (one of the handlers in the script of the Home stack), discussed in Chapter 1.

Opening a script manually: Table 8-5 shows more ways to open an object's
script.

Table 8-5: Some ways to open a script

Script	How to open it
Any script	Click the script button in the object's Info dialog box.
Button	Press command-option and click over button (Browse, button tool selected)
Field	Press command-shift-option and click over field (Browse tool selected)
Stack	Press command-option-S
Background	Press command-option-B
Card	Press command-option-C

Edit's limits: The **edit** command lets you open the script editor for any
script in the current stack. When you close the editor after editing the script of
a noncurrrent background or noncurrent card, you go back to the card you
were on when you summoned the editor.

You can also open the script editor for the stack script of any stack:

```
edit script of stack "home"
```

No system messages sent: No system messages are sent while an **edit** command is carried out. So when you edit the script of a remote stack, the usual
system messages (`closeCard`, `closeBackground`, `closeStack`,
`openStack`, `openBackground`, `openCard`) are all suppressed (even in
versions through 1.2.#, where the first card of the remote stack becomes the
current card when you close the editor):

```
edit script of stack "Not This Stack" -- sends no messages
```

(The fact that you don't come back to the card you were on when you edit the script of a remote stack is a bug in versions through 1.2.#, and is fixed in later versions.)

Bitter complaints: The **edit** command complains with an error dialog when any of the following conditions are true:

• The **userLevel** is less than 5 (scripting).

• You try to edit the script of HyperCard (which doesn't have a script).

• The object whose script you want to edit doesn't exist.

• There's not enough memory available for editing.

Also See:

DEBUG command, page 206
SCRIPT EDITOR, page 34
SCRIPT property, page 599

ENABLE

Forms

```
enable {menuItem expr of} menu menuName
enable {ordinal menuItem of} ordinal menu

enable menu "Companies"
enable menu 7
enable last menu
enable menuItem theMenuItem of menu myMenu
enable menuItem 3 of menu "file"
enable third menu
```

Action

The **enable** command, new for 2.0, enables a menu or menu item, allowing a user to work with it

Comments

Menu is the name or number of a specific menu. *MenuItem* is the name or number of a specific menu item on a specific menu.

An enabled menu title or menu item is solid black and can be chosen. (When the user clicks an enabled menu item, some message is sent.) When a menu title appears greyed out on the menu bar, no item within that menu can be chosen.

This command sets the **enabled** property of the specified menu or menu item to true. It has exactly the same effect as `set enabled of {menuItem expr of} menu menuName to true`.

The following handlers, which belong in the card script (or higher), make sure that the Font and Style menus are enabled only when a field is open for editing or when the field tool is active:

```
on openField
  enableFieldMenus
end openField
```

```
on closeField
  disableFieldMenus
end closeField

on exitField
  disableFieldMenus
end exitField

on choose tool,toolNum
  send the params to HyperCard -- let the close/exitField happen
  if toolNum is 3 -- field tool
  then enableFieldMenus
  else disableFieldMenus
end choose

on disableFieldMenus
  disable menu "Font"
  disable menu "Style"
end disableFieldMenus

on enableFieldMenus
  enable menu "Font"
  enable menu "Style"
end enableFieldMenus
```

Also See:

DISABLE command, page 223
ENABLED property, page 530

ENTERINFIELD

Forms

```
enterInField

enterInField
```

Action

EnterInField has the same effect as pressing the Enter key when the insertion point or other selection is within a field. If **EnterInField** is untrapped and allowed to reach HyperCard, it closes the field.

This following script, which belongs in the script of a field, ensures that the field will only accept the values "Male" and "Female" as the field's entire contents:

```
on enterInField
  if first char of me is "M" then put "Male" into me
  else if first char of me is "F" then put "Female" into me
  else
    beep
    select text of me
  end if
end enterInField
```

(This script works because, in a field, the special word "me" refers to the object as a container. See Chapter 4 for details.)

Comments

EnterInField goes as the message `enterInField` to the field holding the insertion point or the selection.

The following field script ensures that the field will only accept valid dates, or the words "yesterday," "today," or "tomorrow" (which it then converts to valid dates). Note that nothing else except the date (or the words "yesterday," "today" , or "tomorrow") can be in the field:

```
on enterInField
  get me
```

```
    if it is "yesterday" then get the seconds - 60*60*24
    else if it is "today" then get the seconds
    else if it is "tomorrow" then get the seconds + 60*60*24
    convert it to date
    if the result is empty -- valid date
    then put it into me
    else -- invalid date
      beep
      select text of me
    end if
end enterInField
```

Also See:

ENTERKEY

Forms

```
enterKey

enterKey
```

Action

If the insertion point is not in any field, **enterKey** sends the message in the Message box to the current card (or, if the contents of the Message box is an expression, evaluates the expression and leaves the results in the Message box). If a field contains the insertion point or other selection, **enterKey** deselects any selected text and removes the insertion point from the field, and the message `enterInField` is sent to the field.

The following handler assumes that the current card has a field named "My Message Box" that you want to act like the message box:

```
on enterKey
   if field "My Message Box" is not empty
   then send field "My Message Box" to this card
   else pass enterKey
end enterKey
```

Comments

If the Message box appeared as a result of choosing the Find menu command, the **enterKey** command hides the Message box.

EnterKey is seldom used on its own as a command; it's useful more as a message.

This command and the **returnKey** command do exactly the same thing (that is, they call the same internal code).

Also See:

CLOSEFIELD message, page 661
ENTERINFIELD command, page 240

EXPORT PAINT

Forms

```
export paint to file expr

export paint to file "New Paint Document"
export paint to file pictureName
```

Action

The **export paint** command, new for 2.0, stores a copy of the current card or background picture to disk under the name you provide.

The following handler loops through the current stack exporting the picture on every card to a generated file name called "Paint from *name*":

```
on dumpPaint
  -- don't trigger open/closeCard handlers
  set lockMessages to true
  repeat with cardNum = 1 to the number of cards
    go to card cardNum
    put "Paint from " & name of this card into fileName
    export paint to file fileName
  end repeat
end dumpPaint
```

Comments

Expr is any expression that yields a valid file name.

This command works just like domenu "export paint...", except that (1) no dialog is presented, and (2) you don't have to choose a paint tool to make it work (and so it works in less memory).

If background mode is in effect (that is, if **background** is checked on the Edit menu), the background picture is exported. Otherwise, the card picture is exported.

The following example uses **mark cards** to select a group of cards that meet a user defined condition. It then loops through all the marked cards exporting pictures to a generated file name:

```
on mouseUp
   dumpPaintWhere "hasPicture()"
   -- function has to be quoted or else we'd be
   -- passing the value of the function, not the function itself

   -- Could also do things like: dumpPaintWhere "dog is in field 1"
   -- in order to export all your doggie pictures to MacPaint files
end mouseUp

on dumpPaintWhere expr
   unmark all cards
   mark cards where value of expr is true
   -- evaluates expr for every card
   set lockMessages to true -- don't trigger open/closeCard handlers
   push card
   repeat with cardNum = 1 to the number of marked cards
      go to marked card cardNum
      put "Paint from " & name of this card into fileName
      export paint to file fileName
   end repeat
   pop card
end dumpPaintWhere

function hasPicture
   -- return true if the current card has a picture, else false
   -- this function is from "Cooking With HyperTalk 2.0",
   -- by Dan Winkler and Scott Knaster
   put the tool into saveTool
   put the lockScreen into saveLockScreen
   lock screen
   choose select tool
   doMenu "Select All"
   doMenu "Select"
   -- if there's a picture, HyperCard chooses the lasso tool
   -- otherwise the tool remains the select tool
   -- This trick discovered by Robin Shank
   get the tool is "lasso tool"
   choose saveTool
```

```
   set lockScreen to saveLockScreen
   return it
end hasPicture
```

File info: When **export paint** executes, HyperCard creates a MacPaint file (type PNTG) named *expr*. If *expr* already exists in the destination folder, the old file is overwritten without warning. If you don't specify a pathname, HyperCard puts the file in the current folder.

Also See:

DOMENU command, page 229
EXPORT PAINT, *HyperCard User's Guide*
IMPORT PAINT command, page 267

FIND

Forms

```
find {normal|chars|word{s}|string|whole} expr {in field}
find "space case"
find chars "account" in field "Professions"
find words "bell book candle"
find string "gular dist" -- as in "angular distribution"
find whole "pushes me through another door"
find foo -- tried first as variable; if uninited, it's a literal
```

Action

The **find** command searches for a string throughout all the fields of the current card and background, or through a specific background or (starting in 2.0) card field. If no match is found on the current card, searching continues on each card through the stack either until a match is found or until all cards in the stack have been searched.

The following handler looks for a string that the user supplies:

```
on findIt
   ask "What do you want to look for?"
   if it is empty then exit findIt -- in case user presses Cancel
   find it
   if the result is not empty then answer "Sorry — can't find " & It
end findIt
```

Comments

The way that **Find** operates depends on the form of **Find** that you use.

• Find normal (or just find) makes HyperTalk look for *expr* at the start of words. (A word is any group of characters separated from other groups of characters by a space.) So if *expr* were "bark", HyperTalk would find "barking" but not "embarked". If *expr* is more than one word, HyperTalk looks for a match for each of the words someplace on the card. If it finds all the words it goes to that card; but the words don't need to be contiguous, or even in the same field — each one just has to appear someplace on that card at the start of a word. For example, if this paragraph were in the field of a card, find "start bark some" would find a match.

- Find chars looks for *expr* anywhere inside words. So if *expr* were "bark," HyperTalk would match "barking," "embarked" , or "birchbark." If *expr* is more than one word, HyperTalk looks for a match for each of the groups of characters on a card. If it finds all the groups it signals a match; but the groups don't need to be contiguous, or even in the same field — each one just has to appear someplace on the current card.

- Find word{s} looks for *expr* as a perfect match against other complete words (as opposed to parts of words). If *expr* were "book" HyperTalk would not find a match in "books," "bookends," or "redbook" — it would accept only "book." When *expr* is more than one word, HyperCard looks for instances of all the words on the same card; but the words can be in different fields and in any order, as long as they're on the same card.

- Find string searches for a complete word or phrase, including any imbedded spaces, in the exact order listed. The string can be anywhere within a word or group of words, but all the letters must be contiguous. For example, find string "ring can be any" would match "The string can be anywhere."

- Find whole searches for a complete word or phrase, including any imbedded spaces, in the exact order listed, and *as whole words*. All the letters must be contiguous. For example, find Whole "ring can be any" would not find a match in "The string can be anywhere"; only "ring can be any" would do.

In all cases, diacritical marks and capitalization are ignored.

Hidden fields searched: Searching goes on, and matches are possible, in fields whose **visible** property is currently false or whose **location** property holds coordinates outside card boundaries. When a match appears in a hidden field, searching stops as it does when a match occurs on a visible card; but the hidden field remains hidden, and no enclosing box is drawn around the found text. (If a tree falls in the forest...)

A form like the following makes such a field visible, then hides it again when the mouse button is pressed (but the enclosing box still doesn't show):

```
on findString
  global whatEver
  find chars whatEver
  if the visible of the foundfield is false then
    set the visible of the foundfield to true -- show the field...
    wait until the mouse is down -- ...until mouse button pressed...
    set the visible of the foundfield to false -- ...then hide field.
  end if
end findString
```

The **dontSearch** property (page 521), new in version 2.0, prevents searching in a given field, card, or background. The following handler , useful for stacks running in HyperCard versions earlier than 2.0, overrides **find** and prevents it from finding in any hidden field, or one that has the phrase

```
-- Don't Search
```

anywhere in its script:

```
on find
  lock screen
  put the id of this card into startCard
  send the params to HyperCard
  if the result is not empty then exit find
  put the id of this card into firstCard
  put the foundChunk into firstField
  repeat while "-- Don't Search" is in the script of the foundField ¬
  or visible of the foundField is false -- Skip hidden fields
    set cursor to busy
    send the params to HyperCard
    if the id of this card is firstCard ¬
    and the foundChunk is firstField then
      go to startCard
      send "find empty" to HyperCard -- deselect find rectangle
      exit find
    end if
  end repeat
end find
```

Failed finds: When Find finds nothing, it sets the result to "not found." If Find was executed from the Message box, HyperCard also beeps. If the user level is set lower than 4 (authoring), HyperCard puts up a dialog box (see Figure 8-20):

Find and the result: The system function **result** holds the string "not found" when the result of a search is unsuccessful, and is empty when a search is successful. (The string "not found" might change in future versions.)

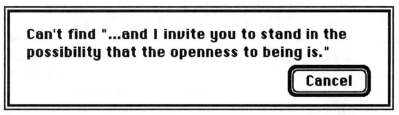

Figure 8-20   Dialog box for Find failures

How searching progresses: Unless you specify a particular field to which **Find** must confine a search, HyperTalk looks through all background and card fields on a card for a match. If it finds no match on the current card, it goes to the next card and looks there. If it finds a match, HyperTalk stops at that card and (if the field is visible) draws a rectangle around the matching string (Figure 8-21).

If an **unlock screen with visual** command is operating, you won't see the rectangle.

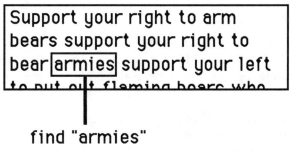

Figure 8-21   Find's rectangle

If *expr* is a single word with the form **find word,** or if the form is **find string** or **find whole,** HyperTalk shows each match on a card; otherwise, HyperTalk shows only matches for the first word in *expr*.

1.2.# Find anomaly

Specific background field searched by number, not name: When you specify a background field to search, HyperTalk identifies that field by locational number (as in field 5) and not by name or ID. (If you ask for a search by name or ID, HyperTalk converts the request to the field number.) So if searching progresses to the next card, which might in fact have a different background, HyperTalk looks in the same-*numbered* background field, and not necessarily in the field with the same *name* or ID. If that field number doesn't exist on a background, HyperCard reverts to searching all fields.

For example, if on the calling card you specify a field named "hayStack" (which is, in fact, field 5) and searching progresses to the next card (which might be a different background), field 5 of that background is searched — whether on not any field on that background is named "hayStack":

```
find "needle" in fld "hayStack" -- searches by number of fld "hayStack"
```

Special ordinals don't work: In versions through 2.0, the special ordinals `middle, last,` or `any` work unpredictably in searching. So don't use forms like this:

```
find thisString in last field -- this won't work.
```

Continued searching after a successful find: If the **find** command is executed from the Message box and the search is successful, you can press Return or Enter to continue searching for more matches on the same and subsequent cards.

Speeding up searches: If you're using HyperCard version 1.2.# on a stack modified by an earlier version of the product, executing the Compact Stack command two or three times considerably speeds up searching because of the way that the hint bits work. (The exact mechanism is proprietary.)

Find is far faster when you give it words of three characters or more to locate. (The hint bits, described on page 206, aren't used for words of fewer than three characters.) So:

```
find "fre smi"
```

is much faster than

```
find "fr sm"
```

The more words with three or more characters you supply, the faster **find** will be. So:

```
find "fred smith san francisco"
```

is faster than the previous two examples.

Find chars and **find string** don't use hint bits and are always slower than the other **find** forms. Hint bits only work on word-start searches, but **find chars** and **find string** look for matches that are not necessarily aligned to word starts.

Some special Find handlers

Find and replace: The following handler locates every occurrence of the first parameter and replaces it with the second parameter. This find-and-replace action occurs in every field of every card of the entire stack . (For example,

```
Replace "Republican", "Democrat"
```

finds every instance of "Republican" in every field of the current stack, and replaces it with "Democrat." (The authors are not sure that this makes any existential difference.)

```
on replace old,new
  repeat
    find string old -- "string" matches exact string, not word starts
    if the result is not empty then exit replace -- done
    do "put new into " & the foundChunk
  end repeat
end replace
```

Find selected text: The following handler finds the current selection:

```
on findSelection
  get the selection
  lock screen
  go to next card -- so we won't just find the same one
  find it
  put "find " & quote & it & quote -- set up so return will find next
end findSelection
```

(Power users can type Command-F and then use text pickup —
Command-Drag — to fill in the search string.)

Search other stacks: The following handler traps the **find** command
and searches in a second stack if the first search fails to find any matches.
If you're using a version of HyperCard earlier than 1.2.2, substitute the
code after the comment symbols for the second and fifth lines:

```
on find how,what
  send the params to HyperCard -- send "find " & what to HyperCard
  if the result is empty then exit find
  lock screen
  go to stack "My other address book" -- insert stack name here
  send the params to HyperCard -- send "find " & what to HyperCard
  if the result is not empty then go back
end find
```

FLASH

Forms

```
flash {integerExpr}

flash
flash 5
```

Action

The **flash** command inverts the screen image twice per call, effectively flashing the screen image.

The following handler flashes the screen five times as the **answer** dialog appears:

```
on wrongAnswer
  flash 5
  answer "Sorry -- that's not the right answer."
end wrongAnswer
```

Comments

IntegerExpr has a meaningful range of 0 through 32766.

If you issue **flash** with no parameter, the screen flashes once in HyperCard 1.2.#, and 3 times in 2.0.

Beware of runaway flashes: You can't stop flashes once they start without resetting the system. So keep *integerExpr* to some low value (such as 5).

Technically **Flash** isn't a built-in command; it's an XCMD shipped with every version of HyperCard. When you call for an XCMD, HyperCard turns over control to that XCMD; so things that usually get you out of trouble (such as pressing Command-period) have no effect.

Points for Techies: The source for the **flash** XCMD appears in Chapter 14, "Glue Routine Reference," as an example for the `StrToNum` callback.

Also See:

OVERVIEW OF EXTERNALS, Chapter 13
GLUE ROUTINE REFERENCE, Chapter 14

FUNCTIONKEY

Forms

```
functionkey integerExpr

functionkey 5
```

Action

The **functionkey** command is never used on its own as a command. It exists in the language as a handy way to pass a numeric parameter with the message functionKey. The effect (of the message, not the command) is the same as pressing one of the 15 function keys on the Apple extended keyboard, and running any handlers associated with that function key:

```
functionkey 7 -- simulates key F7 being pressed
functionkey whichKey -- activates functionkey whose number is whichKey
```

The following button script makes the button move itself to the next card:

```
on mouseUp
  select me
  functionKey 2 -- cut me
  go to next card
  functionKey 4 -- paste me
end mouseUp
```

The above script is contrived; in actual practice, **functionKey** is useful only as a message. Honest.

Comments

Useful values for *integerExpr* range from 1 through 15. HyperCard predefines function keys 1 through 4 to be undo, cut, copy, and paste (respectively). You can program all the function keys; this includes reprogramming the first four keys.

Writing scripts for function keys: The following form intercepts the functionKey message, determines which key was pressed, and then does something appropriate:

```
on functionkey whichkey
   if whichkey=5 then edit script of this card
   if whichkey=6 then edit script of this bkgnd
   ...
   if whichkey=15 then doMenu "quit hypercard"
end functionkey
```

If you're writing longer, more complex instructions for some or all of the function keys, you might want to write separate handlers for each key. In the following example, the first handler determines which function key was pressed, and then calls for another handler to do the intended job; the second handler is a sample of what a particular function key might do:

```
on functionkey whichKey
   do "myFunctionKey" & whichKey
end functionkey

-- other handlers go here.
on myFunctionKey6
   ask "What name do you want for the new button?"
   if it is empty then exit to HyperCard -- if user clicks cancel
   doMenu "New button"
   set name of last button to it
   choose browse tool
end myFunctionKey6
```

Creating extra function keys: You can create simulated function keys by trapping control key combinations; see the **controlKey** command for more information.

Not all Macs have function keys: Only Macintoshes that have the Apple extended keyboard have function keys. Unless you're writing scripts exclusively for computers that have such keyboards (thus ruling out the Macintosh Plus), you should use function keys only for tasks a user can also do in other ways.

Also See:

CONTROLKEY command, page 195
FUNCTIONKEY message, page 254
TABKEY command, page 358

GET

Forms

```
get value

get field 3
get lotsOfDough
get number of chars in message box
get hilite of card button 16
```

Action

The **get** command puts the value of any source or expression into the variable It.

The following button script uses **get** to get a phone number:

```
on mouseUp
  lock screen
  get field "Phone Number"
  go to stack "Phone"
  dial it
  go back
end mouseUp
```

(In the above handler, **Get** retrieves the phone number *before* leaving the current stack; the remote stack — where the number would otherwise be unavailable — is where the dialing is actually done. This is how dialing works when you click the telephone icon in the Address stack shipped with HyperCard.)

Comments

The phrase get `expr` is the same as `put expr into it`.

Get with properties: When you use Get to retrieve the value of a global property, you can use the form

```
get property
```

as opposed to

```
get the property
```

An historical note

Get is a vestige of a time when HyperTalk had only one variable, It. It was originally a global variable. Later, when local and global variables came along, It was demoted to local variable status but was still the first place where the retrieved value of properties went: you'd first have to **get** the value of some property, and then move the value of It to some more convenient container. (**Get** was the only way to find out the value of a property, parallel to **set**.) Eventually, Dan allowed property values to be retrieved directly into any expression. **Get** is no longer indispensable, and remains in the language for purposes of compatibility and convenience.

Also See:

IT variable, page 97
PUT command, page 309

GO

Forms

```
go {to} card {of background} {of stack}
go {to} destination {in {a} new window}{without dialog} -- new in 2.0
go {to} marked card -- 2.0
go {to} background {of stack}
go {to} stack
go {to} [help|home|back|next|prev{ious}]

go any card -- random card in current stack go back
go bkgnd foo -- first cd of bkgnd named by variable foo
             -- (or stays at current card if already in bg foo)
go card 6 of background 3 of stack "buried folder:great art"
go next -- next card in current stack
go prev -- card before this one in current stack
go to third marked card -- 2.0
go to stack Home in new window -- 2.0: keeps old stack on screen
go to stack Whatever without dialog -- 2.0: in case stack isn't there
go to "button ideas" -- note that the form is "go to", not "goto"
go to card 23 -- no stack named, so card 23 of this stack
go to field "Destination" -- holds stack name
```

Action

The **go** command lets you change cards. It is the primary command for navigation.

The following handler sends HyperCard to the next card in the current stack. It is one of the most common handlers in all HyperCardom:

```
on mouseUp
  go to next card
end mouseUp
```

The following handler endlessly shows random cards in the current stack until the mouse button is pressed:

```
on goAny
  repeat until the mouse is down
```

```
      go to any card
   end repeat
end goAny
```

Comments

The syntax for describing where you want to go is extremely flexible, and is tied to the naming of objects. The designation can be an ID number, positional number, or name, or a container holding the ID number, positional number, or name. For more details, see Chapter 4, "Referring to Objects."

The following handler goes to a preset card each time the stack is opened, as if the stack were a book with a bookmark on a particular page. The handler depends on the existence of a card field named "bookmark" on card 1 of the stack. The bookmark is set automatically when you leave the stack:

```
on openStack
  get card field "bookmark" of card 1
  go to card it
end openStack

on closeStack
  put the id of this card into card field "bookmark" of card 1
end closeStack
```

Go failures: When you use **go** from a handler, HyperTalk gives no audible or visible warning if it can't find the card given as **go**'s destination; but the **result** function is set.

When you try to go to a nonexistent card from the Message box, you get an error dialog (see Figure 8-22).

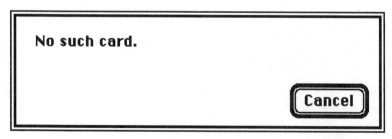

Figure 8-22   Trying to go to a nonexistent card from the Message box

In versions starting with 2.0, you can prevent this dialog from appearing by using the form `go to stack Whatever without dialog`. If **the result** is empty, you know that the **go** command succeeded.

The following handler looks up the number of wins of a given baseball team in a given year, illustrating how **go** can put a value besides empty into the **result** function. (This handler assumes the existence of a stack dedicated to the purpose):

```
on wins teamName,year
  lock screen
  go to card "wins " & year -- cards are named by year
  if the result is not empty then -- couldn't find the card
    answer "Sorry, no stats for that year."
    exit lookUp
  end if
  get field teamName -- assumes this field exists
  answer teamName & " won " & it & " games."
  go back
end wins
```

If HyperCard can't find a stack, it puts up a dialog box asking for directions, as in Figure 8-23.

If HyperCard thinks that the stack doesn't exist, the **result** gets "No such stack"; this happens if the user somehow specifies a file that isn't a stack, or a stack already in use by another user on a multiuser system , or a stack on a volume that suddenly goes off-line (because, for example, an airplane crashed into the disk drive between the command delivery and the command execution).

If the user clicks Cancel, the **result** gets "Cancel."

Because strings delivered by the **result** are likely to change in future versions of HyperCard, you're safer to check for **go** success rather than failure: when **go** is successful, the **result** is empty.

Go and lockMessages: When **lockMessages** is true, the **go** command causes no open or close messages for card, background, or stack.

Go and visual effects: You can show a variety of visual effects as you go from card to card. See the **visual** command, page 367, and the **unlock screen with** *visual* command, page 363, for details.

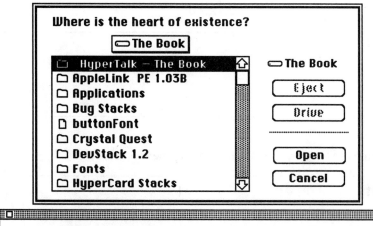

Figure 8-23 Spiritual stacks

Also See:

MARKED property, page 567
Naming objects, page 75
RESULT function, page 454

HELP

Forms

```
help

help
```

Action

The **help** command brings you to the first card of the Help stack.

Comments

Help goes to any stack called "Help," not necessarily the one shipped with HyperCard.

The following handler traps the Help message, no matter how it is sent (menu, Message box, keyboard, handler):

```
on help
  answer "What kind of help do you need?" ¬
  with "HyperCard" or "This stack" or "Cancel"
  if it is "Hypercard" then go to Help -- Help stack
    else if it is "This stack" then getHelp -- your help stuff
end help
```

The following handler lets you go to a specific topic in the help stack:

```
on help
  ask "What topic are you interested in?"
  if it is empty then exit help
  push card
  lock screen
  go to stack "help" -- only thing the built-in Help command would do
  find it
  if the result is empty then
    put "find " & quote & it & quote -- set up for subsequent finds
    exit help -- success
  end if
  answer "Sorry, no help on that topic."
```

```
  pop card
end help
```

Where's Help?   If your Help stack is in a different folder than the HyperCard application, HyperCard might have trouble finding it. (HyperCard puts up the standard file dialog box, asking you to locate Help.) Once you tell HyperCard where Help is, and assuming you don't move Help to another folder (or move the folder that Help is in to nest within some other folder), HyperCard will remember Help's location.

Points for techies: In 1.2.#, the name of the stack that Help goes to is determined by string #46 in the STR# resource named `TalkErrors`.

HIDE

Form

```
hide menubar
hide window
hide {the} [message|msg] {window|box}
hide [localButton|localField]
hide [background|card] pict{ure}
hide pict{ure} of [localCard|localBackground]

hide msg -- hides the message box
hide tool window
hide scroll window -- 2.0 and higher versions
hide pict of background 4 -- hides background picture
hide field "Confidential info"
hide button secretBtn -- hides btn whose identity is in secretBtn
```

Action

The **hide** command hides the designated element. To show the element again, use the **show** command.

The following handler hides a field with a visual effect. It assumes that you can press a button to show this field again:

```
on mouseUp
  lock screen
  hide field "extra info"
  unlock screen with visual effect dissolve
end mouseUp
```

To show this field, you'd have a button with the following script:

```
on mouseUp
  lock screen
  show field "extra info"
  unlock screen with visual effect dissolve
end mouseUp
```

Comments

A prefix of *local* in one of the form lines restricts the designation to an item in the current stack:

```
hide pict of card 3 of background 2
```

The **hide** command hides elements without affecting their locations.

Hide sets the **visible** property to false. It sets the **showPict** property of affected cards or backgrounds to false.

The following handler, placed in the script of the card, background, or stack, hides the menu bar when the stack opens on a Macintosh (where the card window fills the whole screen):

```
on openStack
  if the rect of card window is the screenRect -- full screen
  then hide menuBar
end openStack
```

Unless you use an external, there's no way to tell if the menu bar is hidden already.

Points for techies: An XFCN can tell if the menu bar is hidden: check to see if the low memory global `MBarHeight` is set to 0 by using the `MBarHeight` routine.

About hidden objects: You can write to and read from hidden fields, but hidden fields are not in the Tabbing order.

You can move hidden objects using forms like

```
set the loc of field "Hidden assets" to 220, 10
```

You can't select hidden objects, and you can't select the text of hidden fields. You can, however, examine and change the properties of hidden objects to the extent that you can examine and change the properties of visible ones. (Some properties, like the **ID** property, can't be changed whether they're visible or not.)

Hidden objects don't respond to manual mouse manipulations, even if you knew where to click; if you want to send a mouse message to a hidden object, you must use the **send** keyword.

Hidden objects stay hidden when you move them or when you close and reopen a card, background, and/or stack unless you explicitly show them.

About hidden pictures: You can use scripts to use paint tools on hidden pictures.

Hidden pictures stay hidden when you close and reopen a card, background, and/or stack unless you explicitly show them.

If you try to use a paint tool manually (as opposed to programmatically) on a hidden picture, a dialog appears asking if you want to show the hidden picture: you must answer OK to modify the picture (see Figure 8-24).

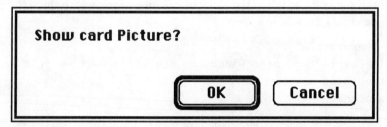

Figure 8-24 This pops up when you try to paint manually on a hidden card picture

About Find: The **find** command locates strings in a hidden field (unless the **dontSearch** property of such a field is set to true), but doesn't make hidden fields visible and doesn't draw a find rectangle around located strings.

Also See:

FIND command, page 246
SEND key, page 155
SHOW command, page 339
SHOW picture command, page 344
SHOWPICT property, page 613
TABBING ORDER, page 359
VISIBLE property, page 648

IMPORT PAINT

Forms

```
import paint from file expr

import paint from file "My Hard Disk:My Pics:My Favorites"
import paint from file thePictureName
```

Action

The **import paint** command, new for 2.0, retrieves a copy of a paint or PICT format document, and pastes it onto the current card or background.

The following example selects a random choice from a list of PICT and/or MacPaint file names, and imports that file's image to the current background:

```
on randomArt
  put any item of "Picture of Wally,Forest Scene,Apple Logo" ¬
  into fileName -- or whatever pictures you have
  set lockScreen to true
  set editBkgnd to true
  import paint from file fileName
  set editBkgnd to false
  set lockScreen to false
end randomArt
```

Comments

Expr is any expression that yields a valid file name.

This command works just like doMenu "Import Paint...", except that (1) no dialog is presented; (2) you don't have to choose a paint tool to make it work (so it works in less memory); and (3) you can import PICT as well as PNTG (MacPaint) pictures. (PICT files are converted to bitmaps on the way into HyperCard.)

Importing starts from the top left of the file. If the card size is smaller than the imported picture, the picture is clipped to the card's bottom right coordinates. If the card size is bigger than the imported picture, the imported picture covers only as much of the current picture as it needs to.

If background mode is in effect (that is, if **background** is checked on the Edit menu), the picture is pasted onto the background. Otherwise, the picture is pasted onto the card.

The following example demonstrates how to use a database of images. The script has a list of MacPaint documents with names like "small black dog 7," "medium black horse 6," "big white fish 3"; it prompts the user for a size, a color, and an animal (any of which may be "anything"), and imports all the paint documents whose name contains the category names:

```
on animalBase
   put "small black dog 7,medium black horse 6,big white fish 3" ¬
   into files

   ask "What size animals do you want?" with Anything
   put it into size
   ask "What color animals do you want?" with Anything
   put it into color
   ask "What kind of animals do you want?" with Anything
   put it into kind

   repeat with fileNum = 1 to the number of items in files
      get item fileNum of files
      if size is not "Anything" and size is not word 1 of it
      then next repeat
      if color is not "Anything" and color is not word 2 of it
      then next repeat
      if kind is not "Anything" and kind is not word 3 of it
      then next repeat
      doMenu "New Card"
      import paint from file it
   end repeat
end animalBase
```

Higher resolution displays: To show pictures in their own windows (including higher resolution PICT images in the PICT format), use the **picture** command.

Also See:

DOMENU command, page 229
EXPORT PAINT command, page 243
IMPORT PAINT, *HyperCard User's Guide*
PICTURE command, page 288

LOCK SCREEN

Forms

```
lock screen

lock screen
```

Action

The **lock screen** command keeps the current image on the display until HyperTalk executes a corresponding **unlock screen** (or **set lockscreen to false**) command, or until idle time.

The following handler locks the screen and then initializes three fields; then it unlocks the screen, and all three fields are updated on the screen at the same time:

```
on mouseUp
  lock screen
  put empty into field "Name"
  put empty into field "Phone Number"
  put "NeXT" into field "Favorite Computer"
  unlock screen
end mouseUp
```

Comments

Lock screen prevents the display from changing as you switch cards, make elements visible and/or invisible, programmatically use paint tools, or any other activities that usually make a visible difference.

After you've made changes to the display, use **unlock screen with** *visual* (page 363) to show your changes in the most aesthetically pleasing way.

Lock screen is useful both for aesthetics and for speed. When the screen is locked no time is spent drawing the screen. The following handler presumably goes to lots of cards, all of which would have to be drawn on the screen if the screen weren't locked:

```
on accountsReceivable
  lock screen
```

```
    put 0 into total
    repeat with i = 1 to the number of cards -- assumed to be some high number
        set cursor to busy -- so user knows system isn't locked up
        go to card i
        add field "balance" to total
    end repeat
    put "The total is " & total
end accountsReceivable
```

Lock screen has no effect on the Message box.

Lock screen's counter: HyperTalk keeps track of the number of times you've used the **lock screen** command (or its equivalent, **set lockscreen to true**). Each **lock screen** must be balanced with an **unlock screen** command (or with **set lockscreen to false**) or the display remains locked. This scheme lets all the drawing happen in the following scripts with the display locked:

```
on drawOne
    lock screen
    -- code to draw some stuff goes here
    drawTwo
    -- code to draw yet more stuff goes here
    unlock screen with visual dissolve -- display now really unlocked
end drawOne
```

```
on drawTwo
    lock screen -- second lock
    -- code to draw even more stuff goes here
    unlock screen -- display still has 1 lock!!
end drawTwo
```

You can omit `unlock screen` when you're sure the handler will never be called by something that has already locked the screen (and that will therefore try to unlock it when the call returns). Such cases include button `mouseUp` handlers. The screen will automatically unlock at idle time.

Be kind to your users: When you lock a screen to prevent changes from being visible and if those changes take more than a second or so to happen, be sure to set the **cursor** property to "watch" or to "busy" so that your users know that something is happening. (You can change the cursor, even when the screen is locked.) It's easy to assume the system is hung up when it seems that everything has just gone away — which is the visible impression when you've used **Lock Screen.**

Screen-locked visited cards not in Recent, but still recorded: When **lock screen** is in effect, screen images are not added to Recent. But even though you don't see cards when Lock Screen is in effect, all cards that HyperCard goes to (up to 100 or so) are in the "back" buffer. You can see such cards by choosing Back from the Go menu.

Also See:

LOCKSCREEN property, page 562
UNLOCK SCREEN command, page 363
VISUAL command, page 367

MARK

Forms

```
mark [cardExpr | cards where expr | all cards]

mark this card
mark card 7
mark card 7 of bg 3
mark cards where field "City" is "Amsterdam"
mark cards where fld "zip" is "94101" and hilite of btn "call" is true
mark cards where fld "phone" contains "415" or fld "address" is empty
mark all cards
```

Action

The **mark** command, new in HyperCard 2.0, marks the card or cards you specify for some later action (usually printing, display, or further filtering).

The following handler prints all the recipes in a recipe stack that contain garlic and are low in sodium:

```
on calCuisine
  unmark all cards -- clear results of previous mark commands
  mark cards where "garlic" is in field "Ingredients" ¬
  and hilite of bkgnd button "Low Sodium" is true
  print marked cards
end calCuisine
```

Comments

CardExpr refers to a card in the current stack.

Mark sets the **marked** property of the specified card(s) to true. It has no effect on cards already marked.

The following example finds all the people in your address book who live in the 408 area code, but who *don't* work at a computer company; the example then writes the information from the culled cards to a file. (The example assumes "Computer" is somewhere in the "name and address" field of people who work in the computer industry.)

```
on noNerds
  unmark all cards
  mark cards where "408" is in field "Phone Number" and ¬
  "Computer" is not in field "Name and Address"
  put "408 Friends" into fileName
  open file fileName
  repeat with cardNum = 1 to the number of marked cards
    write field "Name and Address" of marked card cardNum ¬
    to file fileName
  end repeat
  close file fileName
end noNerds
```

Mark tolerates missing fields: The **mark** command won't complain when it can't find missing fields. So you can use a form like

```
mark cards where field 3 is empty
```

even though it might pass through some backgrounds that don't have three background fields.

Commands using marked cards: HyperCard commands that can use marked cards directly include **go, print,** and **show.**

Also See:

MARKED property, page 567
NUMBER function, page 438
PRINT CARD command, page 302
SHOW command, page 339
UNMARK command, page 365

MULTIPLY

Forms

```
multiply container by numExpr

multiply planetCount by 43
multiply field "Individual assessment" by sagensOfTaxpayers
multiply radiusSquared by pi -- pi is a HyperTalk constant: 3.14159...
```

Action

The **multiply** command multiplies *container* by *numExpr,* leaving the result in *container.* The old value of *container* is trashed (but the value of *numExpr* is unaffected).

The following handler updates a specific aspect of your stock portfolio records. It assumes you have a field "shares" containing the number of shares you own of a stock that has just split 2 for 1. (Market surveys show that many people bought this book specifically for this example.)

```
on stockSplit
  multiply field "shares" by 2 -- incredible.
end stockSplit
```

Comments

container must contain a numeric value if **multiply** is to work.

HyperTalk multiplies with up to 19 decimal places of precision (if the computation demands it); but the number of characters displayed in a field or in the Message box depends upon the setting of the **numberFormat** property.

The following handlers let you check up on your bank by computing what the daily balance should be in an account whose balance compounds daily, given a starting balance and a daily interest rate. It assumes three card fields: Initial Balance, Annual Interest Rate, and Statement:

```
on dontTrustEm
  put card field "Initial Balance" into dailyBalance
  put 1.00 + (card field "Annual Interest Rate" / 100 / 365) into growthFactor
  put empty into card field "Statement"
```

```
  repeat with i = 1 to 31
    set numberFormat to "#"
    get "Day " & i & " balance is "
    set numberFormat to "0.00"
    get it & dailyBalance & return
    put it after card field "Statement"
    multiply dailyBalance by growthFactor
  end repeat
end dontTrustEm
```

(When we used the **compound** function for this example, we found that **compound** awarded about 0.3 percent more money than did the **multiply** command. Figures for $50,000 @ 6.23 percent after 30 days were $50,256.56 using **multiply,** versus $50,265.24 using **compound. Compound** is probably more accurate.

Points for techies: Multiply and the "*" operator work exactly the same way internally.

HyperTalk uses integer math if the absolute value of both of the values is less than 32767 (that is, the maximum value a 15 bit number can express); otherwise, it uses SANE to do extended precision multiplication.

Also See:

NUMBERFORMAT property, page 585

OPEN APPLICATION

Forms

```
open {document with} application

open SuperWriter
open "Martha's Pony" with "GreatPaint"
open foo with bar
open card field 7 with line 3 of background field 12
```

Action

The **open application** command opens a specific application, optionally with a specific document.

The following handler opens the MacWrite word processing application with the compatible document "Congressional Letter":

```
on getThatLetter
  open "CongressionalLetter" with "MacWrite"
end getThatLetter
```

Comments

Application must be a valid Macintosh application. *Document* must be compatible with (although not necessarily created by) *application*. The names of both *application* and *document* must be exactly as they appear in the Finder, complete with any special characters (such as ® or ©).

Open application is the equivalent of double-clicking a document or application in the Finder.

The name of the application appears at the top of the screen as HyperCard launches it, just as it does when you launch an application from the Finder (except that in this case it's HyperCard that draws the name).

The following handler lets you fill a card with named buttons (none of which can have any scripts); when a button is clicked, this card script handler opens the application that has the same name as the button:

```
on mouseUp
  if "button" is not in the target then pass mouseUp
```

```
    open the short name of the target
end mouseUp
```

Search paths: The **open application** command looks at the global variables Documents and Applications that are initialized by the Home stack to know where to look for the files it needs. These search paths are updated automatically each time HyperCard asks you where to find a document or application.

There have been reports that HyperCard sometimes can't find the named application, named document, or both. These problems go away, however, when you give full pathnames for everything.

Open application failures: If **Open Document** can't find the application or document you request, it puts "No such document" or "No such application" (as appropriate) into the **result** function. But because this string is likely to change in future versions of HyperCard, it's wiser to check for "empty" in the **result** function, indicating success. (Also see the note following the "Mac II Anomaly Alert," below.)

If the file you request isn't an application (that is, isn't type APPL), you get an error dialog (Figure 8-25).

Figure 8-25   Error dialog when you ask for a file that isn't application

Open application under MultiFinder: If MultiFinder is running, when you open another application HyperCard continues to be open (although inactive) and all global variables are maintained.

When you use the form open *document* with *application,* if the application is already open the document you ask for won't appear; you'll have to load it manually. (And yes, this *is* a bug.)

When you close the application you opened, you return to the card you were on in HyperCard. If the **cantModifyStack** and **userModify** properties are both set to true, changes made to the current card before you summoned the external application are not yet discarded.

Mac II anomaly alert!

When Multifinder is active in a Mac II, all the statements in the handler holding the **open** *application* statement are carried out *before* the application is opened, no matter where the **open** *application* statement appears in the handler.

In 1.2.#, if there's not enough room to run the application you asked for under MultiFinder, the application simply doesn't run. You get no alert, and nothing goes into the **result** function (as you'd have a perfect right to expect).

Open application under Finder: If MultiFinder is off, when you open another application HyperCard sends the suspend message. When you quit the external application, you return to the card you were on in HyperCard and HyperCard sends the resume message; but volatile properties and functions (like **lockMessages** and **userModify**) return to their default values and all variables are reset. Any commands remaining in the handler between **open application** and the end of the handler and any pending handlers are not executed.

Points for techies: This command calls the Macintosh operating system routine Launch, as does **print document.**

Also See:

NUMBERFORMAT property, page 585

OPEN FILE

Forms

```
open file filename

open file "Big Disk:Correspondence:Addresses"
open file myAddressFile
open file line 12 of field "Address Field"
```

Action

The **open file** command opens *filename* for use with the **read** and **write** commands. (If HyperTalk can't find a file named *filename*, it creates one.)

The following handler writes all the background fields of the current card into the same file:

```
on dumpCard
  put "my disk:myFile" into fileName -- your full pathname goes here
  open file fileName
  repeat with i = 1 to the number of fields
    write field i & return to file fileName -- return char separates fields
  end repeat
  close file fileName
end dumpCard
```

Comments

The file commands **open, close, read,** and **write** were designed for importing and exporting text. So information exchanged with these commands is treated as ASCII text.

To close a file that **open file** opened, use the **close file** command (page 190).

The following handler writes the contents of every background field of every card in the current stack to a file. It automatically separates fields with tabs:

```
on dumpStack
  put "My Disk:Dump File" into fileName -- Use your own full pathname
  open file fileName
  repeat with cardNum = 1 to the number of cards
```

```
    go to card cardNum
    repeat with fieldNum = 1 to the number of fields
      write field fieldNum & tab to file fileName
    end repeat
  end repeat
  close file fileName
end dumpStack
```

The following handler restores the contents of a stack that was dumped with the preceding handler. It assumes that the card you're currently on has the correct number of background fields, and so can act as a model for the handler (which creates a new card for each set of fields in the file):

```
on restoreStack
  put "My Disk:Dump File" into fileName
  open file fileName
  repeat
    doMenu "New Card"
    repeat with i = 1 to the number of fields
      read from file fileName until tab
      if it is empty then -- done
        close file fileName
        doMenu "Delete Card" -- get rid of extra card
        exit restoreStack
      end if
      delete last char of it -- strip tab
      put it into field i
    end repeat
  end repeat
end restoreStack
```

Three–file maximum: You can have up to three files open at the same time. If you try to open more than that, you get an error dialog, as in Figure 8-26.

But an error condition always closes all open files, so the three files already open automatically close. As soon as you put away the error dialog, you can open the fourth (now the first) file. Isn't that convenient?

Full pathname needed: You must provide a full pathname to *filename* each time you reference it; otherwise, HyperTalk assumes that *filename* is at the same level of the hierarchical file system as the HyperCard application.

Figure 8-26   Too many files open

Points for techies: The file that HyperTalk creates (when it can't find the one you name) is a MacWrite document: it has Creator MACA and Type TEXT. But you can open it with virtually any text editor or word processor.

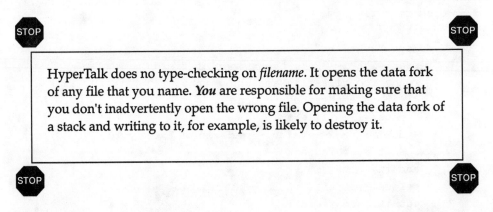

HyperTalk does no type-checking on *filename*. It opens the data fork of any file that you name. *You* are responsible for making sure that you don't inadvertently open the wrong file. Opening the data fork of a stack and writing to it, for example, is likely to destroy it.

Also See:

CLOSE FILE command, page 190
READ command, page 318
WRITE command, page 372

OPEN PRINTING

Forms

```
open printing {with dialog}
open report printing {with [template expr | dialog] } -- new in 2.0

open printing
open printing with dialog
open report printing with template "Boston" -- 2.0
```

Action

The **open printing** command starts the process of printing cards. The form **open report printing with dialog** (new in 2.0) brings up the Print Report dialog. If you don't use the with dialog option, HyperCard uses the last template you used; if you haven't used one this session, HyperCard uses the first one on the list; and if no list exists, HyperCard uses the default values.

The form **open report printing with template** *expr* starts the printing process using a report template you've previously created and saved using the Print Report dialogs.

The following handler prints five cards — the current card and the four that follow it:

```
on printFive
  open printing
  print five cards
  close printing
end printFive
```

Comments

You can't respond programmatically to the dialog box produced by **open {report} printing with dialog.**

The form **open printing with dialog** brings up the Print Stack dialog box so you can manually change print settings (otherwise HyperTalk assumes you want to use the current settings on the Print Stack dialog box).

Open printing buffers card images when you issue the **print card** command. When the buffer has enough card images to make up a full page (as determined by the current settings on the Print Stack dialog box), it prints the page. When you pair an **open printing** command with a **close printing** command, the print buffer flushes to the printer so that any cards that would make up a partial page in a print job are printed immediately. (Without **close printing,** a partial page isn't printed until you quit HyperCard.)

The following profitable handler prints all cards of the current stack whose background field "Sex" matches the user's preference:

```
on computerDating
  ask "What sex do you prefer?" with "Male" or "Female"
  put it into searchSex
  open printing
  repeat for the number of cards
    if field "Sex" is searchSex then print this card
    go to next card
  end repeat
  close printing
  answer "Have a great time! That'll be $195.00, please."
end computerDating
```

Open printing with dialog and the result: When the user clicks the Cancel button on the Printing dialog box, the string "Cancel" goes into the **result** function.

Report printing in 2.0 is powerful and complex: Report printing has been totally revamped for 2.0. Where the old report printing was pretty wimpy and limited, the new report printing is flexible, powerful, and complex. Special menus appear on the menu bar to assist you and to give you options, and there are a several dialogs to deal with — all of which is beyond the scope of this book. See the HyperCard 2.0 reference manual for the details, or experiment on your own.

One print job at a time: Complete **open printing** with **close printing** before you use the **print document** command. While the architecture of the language says that you shouldn't have to do this, there are reports that mysterious things happen when you try to mix print jobs. (Mean people would call this a bug.)

Also See:

CLOSE PRINTING command, page 193
PRINT command, page 299
PRINT CARD command, page 302
PRINT STACK command, *HyperCard User's Guide*

PALETTE NAVIGATOR

Forms

```
palette navigator

palette navigator
```

Action

The **palette navigator** command, new for HyperCard 2.0, brings up the navigation palette.

The following startling handler shows the palette navigator at startUp time:

```
on startUp
  palette navigator
end startUp
```

Comments

The navigation palette holds graphics representing the navigation commands from the Go menu. Its use eliminates the need for the Next, Previous, and Go Back arrows from most stacks (Figure 8-27).

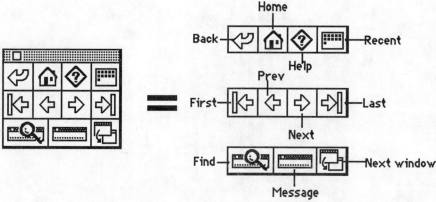

Figure 8-27 Navigation palette

The following example (which belongs in the stack script) appends "Navigator" to the Go menu. It adds the functionality of pressing Command-G to hide and show the palette:

```
on startUp
  put "Navigator" after menu "Go" with menuMessage toggleNavigator
  set commandChar of menuItem "Navigator" of menu "Go" to "G"
  pass startUp
end startUp

on toggleNavigator
  if there is a window "Navigator"
  then close window "Navigator"
  else palette navigator
end toggleNavigator
```

Clicking an image on the navigation palette sends the menu command corresponding to that image as a message. (If you like, you can catch the message and determine what happens.)

Points for techies: Palette is actually an XCMD that can display many palettes; the Navigator palette is just an example.

PICTURE

Forms

```
picture name {,source {,windowStyle {,"rect" {,"scroll" {,dither}}}}}

picture Dog -- file "Dog"
picture Dog, clipboard -- clipboard picture; gives it name "Dog"
picture Dog, clipboard, dialog -- in dialog-style window
picture Dog, clipboard, dialog, "50,50,100,100" -- frame size
picture Dog, clipboard, dialog, dogRect, "20,20" -- starts at 20,20
```

Action

The **picture** command (actually an XCMD new for HyperCard 2.0) displays a black and white or color PICT or MacPaint image up to 32-bits deep in its own window.

The following example displays a picture to give the user something to look at while a stack sort is going on:

```
on pictureSort
   picture "MyDisk:Pictures:Sorting...",file,rect,rect of card window
   sort by sortKey()
   close window "MyDisk:Pictures:Sorting..."
end pictureSort
```

Comments

At the time of this writing, the **picture** command is not yet complete so the final version may differ slightly from the description given here.

Name is the name of a MacPaint file, a PICT file or resource, or the name you want to use for the picture on the clipboard. If you don't give a name (that is, if you just say Picture with no parameters), the Macintosh's standard file dialog appears letting you choose either a PICT or PNTG (MacPaint) file.

Source can be `file`, `resource`, or `clipboard`. The default is `file`. If you use clipboard and the `clipboard` has no picture in it, you get nothing (but **the result** is set).

WindowStyle can be `dialog`, `plain`, `rect`, `roundRect`, `shadow`, `windoid`, or `zoom`. The default is zoom. (See Figure 8-28.)

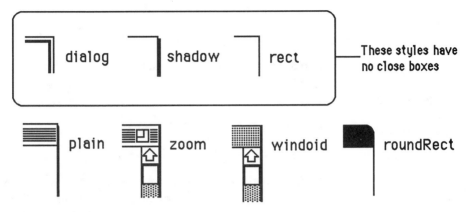

Figure 8-28   Window styles

The dialog, rect, and shadow styles have no close-boxes (but see the handler under "Unique Picture function," below).

Use the `rect` or `shadow` styles to create pop-up picture windoids. (Windoids appear on top of the card layer.)

Rect is the starting rectangle of the picture's window in global coordinates. This parameter must appear within quotation marks. If you set the rect to "0,0,0,0" or to coordinates that put it outside the desktop (either of which can happen when you use computed values), HyperCard uses the default rectangle – which is whatever HyperCard decides is appropriate to your monitor and system.

Scroll is the point of the picture, expressed in pixel coordinates local to the picture and enclosed within quotation marks, that appears at the top left corner of the window. The default is "0,0".

Dither is either true or false. The default is false. Dithering is a process whereby existing colors are mixed to create the illusion of a third color ordinarily unavailable on a particular screen — for example, when you display a 16-bit color image on an 8-bit monitor. You'll have to experiment to see what effect dithering has in a particular environment.

Picture window properties: You can set (and get) certain properties of the picture's window:

```
set loc of window name to left, top
set rect of window name to left, top, right, bottom
set scroll of window name to left, top
set zoom of window name to [in | out]
set magnification of window name to integer
```

For `magnification`, *integer* is a number between 0 and 5; the integer is treated as a power of two. Thus if *integer* is 3, the image is 8 times its normal size.

Closing a window: To close a window, use the command

```
close window windowName
```

Unique picture function: When you click the mouse on a **picture** window, the XCMD that created the window (and *not* HyperCard) sends the function `pictureClick()` through the HyperCard message passing path with three parameters: the name of the window you clicked on, the horizontal position of the click (local to the window), and the vertical position of the click (local to the window).

The following handler, placed in the home stack script, closes any window opened by **picture** when you click on that window:

```
function pictureClick
  return close
end pictureClick
```

By the way, the name of the last window you clicked is kept in the global variable `pictureGlobal`.

Pictures not editable: **Picture** is actually an XCMD shipped with HyperCard 2.0, and not technically a HyperTalk command. The picture is displayed in an xwindoid, and is not editable with the usual HyperCard tools.

Empty windows: You get an empty window when you try to display a picture deeper than eight pixels in a system that doesn't have 32-bit Quickdraw installed.

Memory: To get the most out of **picture**, run HyperCard in a memory partition of at least two megabytes.

Fun fact to know and tell: The source code for this XCMD shows a *windowStyle* called windoidZoom. As of this writing, it produces a windoid with a zoom box in the upper right corner — but no grow box in the lower right corner. Maybe it's fixed now...

Points for techies: You can use numbers representing window definition functions and variation codes for the *windowStyle* parameter.

Also See:

OVERVIEW OF EXTERNALS, Chapter 13

PLAY

Forms

```
play voice { {tempo integerExpr} notes}
play stop

play "harpsichord"
play myVoice myNotes
play "boing" c4e c dq c f eh
```

Action

The **play** command sends one or a series of digitized sounds to the Macintosh speaker (or to the sound port if anything is plugged into it). The form **play stop** aborts the sound.

The following handler plays the opening notes from a once-popular television series:

```
on bookHimDanno
  play "harpsichord" tempo 200 "ge g bb d5 cq. g4h. ge g f bb g"
end bookHimDanno
```

Comments

Voice is the name of a digitized sound (or an expression that resolves to a name) stored as a resource in one of the stacks on the current message passing path, or in the system file. You can think of the voice as the characteristic sound of an electronic instrument — like the sound you think of when you read the name "piano" or "tuba" or "1957 Chevy." HyperCard comes with two voices — "harpsichord" and "boing."

Tempo *integerExpr* is the speed at which the sound plays. The default tempo is 120. The higher the value of *integerExpr*, the faster the sound plays. (But a value of 0 acts as if the value were 120.)

The note string for a single **play** command is limited to 255 characters.

What you cannot do: You can't change the volume through any HyperTalk command (although you can set the volume using the SetSoundVolume external from Chapter 13). You can play only a single voice; you can't play chords. You can't run for president of the United States if you're a naturalized citizen.

How a note is constructed: *Notes* is a list of notes. The default note for *voice* is considered to be Middle C. Otherwise you must supply a name (d, e, f, etc.) for each note. Notation is standard: The notes are (case insignificant)

a   b   c   d   e   f   g

with the number 0 or letter r indicating a rest.

You can also supply an accidental, octave number, and duration for each note: any note that doesn't have an octave number is assumed to be in the same octave as the previous note, and a note with no specific duration is assumed to have the same duration as the previous one. Each note in the list is separated from its neighbors by a space.

The symbols for accidentals are also standard: sharp is #, flat is b; no symbol means the note is natural. (For example, d-sharp, b-flat and c-natural appear as d#, bb, and c.)

Octaves are numbered, with middle C's octave noted as 4 (for example, c4 or d5). The default octave is 4.

Duration can be from a whole note to a sixty-fourth note, represented by a letter (case insignificant):

w = whole	e = eigth	x= sixty-fourth
h = half	s = sixteenth	
q = quarter	t = thirty-second	

The default duration is a quarter-note.

Add a period (.) after a duration symbol to indicate a doted note; the note will play 1 1/2 times its normal duration (for example, ah. or ft.). To indicate a triplet (2/3 normal duration), type a 3 in place of the period.

The longest possible note duration, in real time, is 16.3835 seconds.

Order insignificant, but...: You can state the qualities of a note in any order, but when a note starts with "e" or "b", HyperTalk considers "b" or "e" to be the note name; otherwise "e" means "eighth note" and "b" means "flat." To avoid ambiguity in your writing, use the order *name accidental octave duration* (for example c3h or d#3q.).

Sound buffering: Sounds take time to load from disk. You can preload sounds at openStack time by using the following form:

```
on openStack
  play "mySound" r -- r means rest, so sound loads without playing
end openStack
```

Play failures: If the sound volume is set to 0 in the Control Panel, or if **Play** can't find the voice you give it, nothing happens — the result is *not* set, and the menuBar does *not* flash.

Stopping what's playing: HyperCard buffers the sounds you call for, starts playing the sounds, and goes on to execute the rest of the handler while the sound continues to play. Sometimes the buffered sound can be so long that it continues to play long after you want it to. **Play stop** stops the sound immediately.

A beep (or any system-caused beep, as in an error notification) clears any queued sounds.

Matching sounds and actions: HyperTalk buffers sounds and starts to play them immediately. As soon as it starts playing a sound, HyperTalk goes on to the next statement in a handler. So in the following example, HyperTalk goes to the next card as soon as the first Harpsichord starts, with four more Harpsichords buffered:

```
on mouseUp
  repeat 5
    play "harpsichord"
  end repeat
  go next
end mouseUp
```

To make HyperTalk wait until the harpsichord recital is finished before going to the next card, use the **sound** function (discussed in detail on page 472):

```
on mouseUp
  repeat 5
    play "harpsichord"
  end repeat
  wait until the sound is "done" -- this controls the action
  go next
end mouseUp
```

A notation alternative: You can use a number to represent a note's name, accidental, and octave. If the first character of *notes* is a number, HyperTalk assumes you're using numbers throughout and ignores any nonnumeric characters.

Middle C is 60; each note a half-step up or down the scale adds or subtracts 1 from the number. The note number is converted to the proper note and octave, as shown in the following example using 60 as an example:

octave = (noteNumber DIV 12) - 1 -- (60 DIV 12) - 1 = 5 -1 = 4 (middle octave)
note = noteNumber MOD 12 -- 60 MOD 12 = 0 (base note in the octave, C)
See the chart on page 296 for 6 octaves worth of notes.

When you use numbers instead of full notation, enclose the notes list within quotation marks.

The following handler plays the middle C octave:

```
on Rubenstein
  repeat with i = 60 to 71
    play "harpsichord" i
  end repeat
end Rubenstein
```

Chopin time: If you have an extended keyboard, you can assign notes to different function keys and pretend to be a big-time rock star. The following handler assigns F below middle C to the F1 function key, middle C to F8, and G above middle C to F15. Put it into a card script and rock on:

```
on functionkey whatEver
  play "boing" whatever + 52 -- Middle C is note value 60, F8
end functionkey
```

Six Octaves of Notes by Number

C 3 below Middle C		C 1 below Middle C		C 1 above Middle C	
24	C	48	C	72	C
25	C#	49	C#	73	C#
26	D	50	D	74	D
27	D#	51	D#	75	D#
28	E	52	E	76	E
C 3 below Middle C		**C 1 below Middle C**		**C 1 above Middle C**	
29	E#	53	E#	77	E#
30	F	54	F	78	F
31	G	55	G	79	G
32	G	56	G#	80	G#
33	A	57	A	81	A
34	A#	58	A#	82	A#
35	B	59	B	83	B
C 2 below Middle C		**Middle C**		**C 2 above Middle C**	
36	C	60	C	84	C
37	C#	61	C#	85	C#
38	D	62	D	86	D
39	D#	63	D#	87	D#
40	E	64	E	88	E
41	E#	65	E#	89	E#
42	F	66	F	90	F
43	G	67	G	91	G
44	G#	68	G#	92	G#
45	A	69	A	93	A
46	A#	70	A#	94	A#
47	B	71	B	95	B

Also See:

SOUND function, page 472

POP

Forms

```
pop card { [before|into|after] container}

pop card -- go to card whose ID is at top of pushed cards list
pop card after fld "Print List" -- remove ID from top of pushed cards
   -- list and place it at end of text
   -- in field "Print List"
pop card into storedCard -- creates variable storedCard if necessary
```

Action

The **pop card** command retrieves the long ID of the card most recently stored with the **push** command, removing the ID from the stored push list. If you don't specify a container to hold the card's ID, you go immediately to that card.

The following handler looks up a name in an address stack and reports the corresponding street address. It uses **push card** and **pop card** to return to the current card after visiting the address stack:

```
on lookUp cardCarrier
  lock screen
  push card
  go to stack "ACLU Members"
  find cardCarrier
  get the result   -- could be "not found"
  if it is empty then get field "Street Address" -- successful find
  else get "not available" -- unsuccessful find
  pop card
  put "That address is " & it
  unlock screen
end lookUp
```

Comments

When you pop a card into a container, its long ID gets stored in that container — in front of any information already in that container (before), after any information already there (after), or replacing what's there (into).

When you quit HyperCard, the list of pushed cards is emptied. It is maintained, however, when you leave HyperCard under MultiFinder by clicking on another application or by issuing an **open application** command.

If you issue a **pop card** command when the pushed cards list is empty, you get the long ID of the Home card.

The following pair of handlers ensures that a return button works correctly. The first handler belongs in the stack script; it pushes the recent card when the stack is opened. The second handler belongs in a return button; it returns you to where you were before you entered this stack:

```
on openStack
  push recent card -- push the long id of where we came from
end openStack
```

```
on mouseUp
  pop card -- go back whence we were before we entered this stack
end mouseUp
```

Important style note: For the above handlers to work properly, you must have employed good style in designing your scripts: no script pushes things that don't get properly popped, and you don't allow use of the go back key (~) to get out of a stack that has pushed something.

Pop card, messages, and push card commands: When you go to a card as a result of popping its ID, messages such as openCard, openBackground, and openStack occur as they normally do; but if handlers evoked by these messages contain **push card** commands, the **push card** lines are ignored.

Also See:

PUSH command, page 307

PRINT

Forms

```
print [field | expr]

print field 5 -- prints field 5 of this card with formatting intact
print (field 5) -- prints field 5 of this card without formatting
print field 5 of card 6
print totals
print line 3 to 5 of myFavoriteVariable
print the selection
print the stacksInUse
```

Action

The **print** command, new for version 2.0, prints the contents of any field or container, or the value of any expression.

The following example prints all the non-empty fields in a stack:

```
on dumpFieldsToPrinter
  open printing
  repeat with cardNum = 1 to the number of cards
    go to card cardNum
    repeat with fieldNum = 1 to the number of fields
      if field fieldNum is not empty
      then print field fieldNum
    end repeat
    repeat with fieldNum = 1 to the number of card fields
      if card field fieldNum is not empty
      then print card field fieldNum
    end repeat
  end repeat
  close printing
end dumpFieldsToPrinter
```

Comments

Expr is any valid HyperCard expression.

Expressions are evaluated before they're printed:

```
print fld 3 - 12 -- prints (numeric contents of fld 3) minus 12
print 12 + 38 -- prints 50
print "John" && "Scribblemonger" -- prints John Scribblemonger
```

When you print a field using the form `print field`, you print the entire contents of the field including any text scrolled out of sight. The fonts, sizes, and/or styles assigned to text are maintained. Word wraps in the field are printed as if they were carriage returns, so the essential shape of the text is also retained (Figure 8-29).

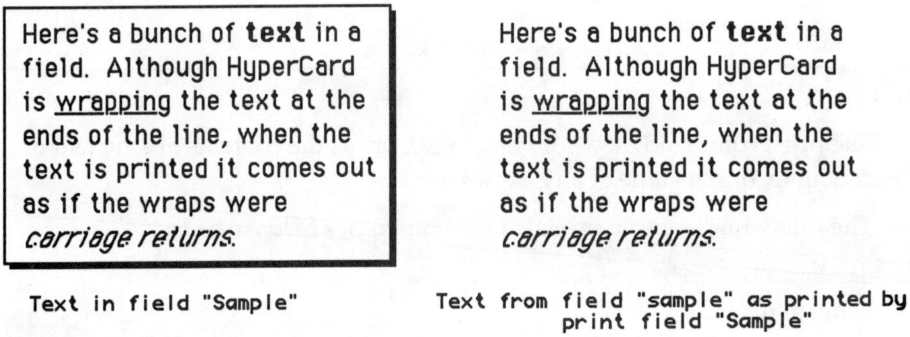

> Here's a bunch of **text** in a field. Although HyperCard is <u>wrapping</u> the text at the ends of the line, when the text is printed it comes out as if the wraps were *carriage returns.*

Here's a bunch of **text** in a field. Although HyperCard is <u>wrapping</u> the text at the ends of the line, when the text is printed it comes out as if the wraps were *carriage returns.*

```
     Text in field "Sample"              Text from field "sample" as printed by
                                                  print field "Sample"
```

Figure 8-29   Text, in field and printed

When you print a field using the form `print (expr)` — that is, with the field description enclosed within parentheses — the straight text of the field is printed, without any formatting or styles retained. Text printing is controlled by the printing properties discussed in Appendix I, "Late Breaking News."

The following example prints a text file by reading it into a variable and then printing the variable:

```
on dumpFileToPrinter
  ask file "Print which file?"
  if it is empty then exit mouseUp
  put it into fileName
  put empty into textVar
  open file fileName
  repeat
    read from file fileName for 16000
```

```
      if it is empty then exit repeat
      put it after textVar
   end repeat
   close file fileName
   print textVar
end dumpFileToPrinter
```

For information specifically geared to the printing of cards, see the **print card** command.

Fields and the dontWrap property: When a field's **dontWrap** is set to true, printing the field with the form `print field fieldExpr` prints only the visible portion of the field, with the field's fonts and text styles maintained. To print all the text in the field (but without any styles or other formatting), use the form `print (field fieldExpr)`.

Also See:

PRINT CARD

Forms

```
print [number |all] card{s}
print card from leftTop to rightBottom -- new in 2.0
print {[ordinal|next|prev]} marked card -- new in 2.0
print card

print card -- print current card
print all cards -- print all cards in current stack
print 12 cards -- print this card, plus next 11
print card ID 12 of stack "Evil Perpetrators of 1937"
print line 2 of field "print list" -- print the card identified
print marked cards -- prints cards whose marked property is true (2.0)
print 5 cards from 10,10 to 250, 310 -- prints designated area (2.0)
```

Action

The **print card** command prints the designated card or cards.

The following handler prints the cards whose ID numbers are stored in global
variable PrintList:

```
on printCards
  global printList
  open printing
    repeat with i = 1 to number of lines in PrintList
     print line i of PrintList
    end repeat
  close printing
end printCards
```

Comments

The form print card prints the current card. The form print marked
cards prints cards whose **marked** property is true. The form print card
from point to point (with the points stated in local coordinates) prints
the specified area of the card or cards. The form print number cards
prints *number* consecutive cards, starting at the current card.

If **open printing** is in effect, nothing gets printed until a page is full, a **close printing** command executes, or you quit HyperCard. If **open printing** is not in effect, HyperTalk flushes the buffer to the printer after each **print card** command.

The number of cards making up a full page is determined by a setting on the Print Stack dialog box.

The following handler demonstrates how to print cards selectively. It looks in background field *fieldName* of each card; if it finds *matchValue* in that field, the card is printed. (For example, if you send `printMatches` `"Publisher"`, `"Bantam"`, this handler would search field "Publisher" in every card in the stack for instances of the name "Bantam"; cards with matches would be printed:

```
on printMatches fieldName,matchValue
  unmark all cards
  marked cards by finding matchValue in field fieldName
  print marked cards
end printMatches
```

Print card and messages: When you print cards, you go to each card as it's printed (returning to the card that called for the printing when the printing's finished), but no system messages of any kind are generated.

To stop card changes from being visible, set the **lockScreen** property to true (but be sure to set the **cursor** property to "watch" or to "busy" so that your users know that something is happening).

Also See:

CLOSE PRINTING command, page 193
MARKED property, page 567
OPEN PRINTING command, page 283
POP command, page 297
PRINT STACK command, *HyperCard User's Guide*
PUSH command, page 307

PRINT DOCUMENT

Forms

```
print document with application

print "Collected Poems" with "WordMaster 9.5"
print Foo with Bar -- Foo holds doc name; Bar holds app name
print "Doc Number " & thisDocNumber with "MacWord"
```

Action

The **print document** command prints *document* using *application*. It simulates the Print command in the Finder when you have a single document and a printing application selected.

The following handler, which assumes that the current card has background fields named "Document Name" and "Application Name," prints the document whose name is in field "Document Name" using the application whose name appears in field "Application Name":

```
on mouseUp
  print field "Document Name" with field "Application Name"
end mouseUp
```

Comments

Application must be a valid Macintosh Application that supports printing. *Document* must be compatible with (although not necessarily created by) *application*. The names of both *application* and *document* must be exactly as they appear in the finder, complete with any special characters (such as ® or ©).

Print document provides the only way you can programmatically print the contents of individual fields from individual cards and/or backgrounds in all versions through 1.2.#. (Starting with version 2.0, you can use the **Print** command described on page 299.) The following handler writes a field into a file, and then prints the file with a word processor. The field name is passed to the handler:

```
printField "Classical CD's" -- prints contents of field "Classical CD's"

on printField fieldName
  put "My disk:temp printing" into fileName -- pathname goes here
  open file fileName
  write field fieldName to file fileName -- can repeat this for many fields
  close file fileName
  print fileName with "My Favorite Word Processor"
end printField
```

Print document under MultiFinder: If MultiFinder is active, HyperCard continues to run while printing is going on, although it becomes inactive. When printing is completed, HyperCard resumes active operation.

If *application* is already open when you call for it, HyperCard goes to *application* but doesn't load *document*. You must quit *application* manually, after which you return to HyperCard.

When you return to HyperCard, variable values are intact; if the stack is locked but the **userModify** property is set to true, changes made to the current card before you summoned the external application are not yet discarded. If **print application** was executed from within a handler that has unexecuted commands, the remaining commands are executed.

Mac II bug alert!

When Multifinder is active in a Mac II, all the statements in the handler holding the **print** *document* statement are carried out *before* the application is opened, no matter where the **print** *document* statement appears in the handler.

Print document under Finder: If Multifinder is inactive, HyperCard sends the message `suspend`, runs the application you've named, and prints the document. When printing is completed, you return to HyperCard (which sends the `resume` message); but HyperTalk global variables are reset to empty. Any commands remaining in the handler between **Print application** and the end of the handler, plus any commands remaining unexecuted in a calling handler, are ignored.

Keep print jobs separate: It's not advisable to use this command if an **Open Printing** command is still pending. While the architecture of the language says that you shouldn't have to do this, there are reports that mysterious things happen when you try to mix print jobs.

Print document and the result: If you give the name of a document or application that doesn't exist, HyperTalk puts the string "no such document" or "no such application" into the **result**. No error dialog appears.

This string is likely to change in future versions of HyperCard, so it's not wise to use it to check for success. If the **result** is empty, however, you can be sure that **print document** has been successful.

Points for techies: This command uses the same code as **open application**. See that command for further information.

Also See:

OPEN APPLICATION command, page 277
PRINT CARD command, page 302

PUSH

Forms

```
push card

push card
push back -- card we were on before this one (historically)
push recent card -- same as "push back"
push card 3 of background 5 of stack "Remote Locations"
push line 4 of field "Print List" -- pushes card named in line 4
```

Action

The **push card** command stores the long ID of a card on the top of a last-in first-out list (maintained by HyperCard) for later retrieval with **pop card**.

The following handler retrieves the top priority item from a to do list. It uses push/pop card to return to its starting card after visiting the "To Do" stack (not shown here):

```
on whatToDo
  lock screen
  push card
  go to stack "To Do"
  get line 1 of field "Hot Items"
  pop card
  put "You'd better work on " & it
  unlock screen
end whatToDo
```

Comments

If you don't indicate what card to push, HyperTalk pushes the current card.

If you use the form push recent card and there are no cards in recent, HyperTalk pushes the ID of the Home card.

The following openstack handler pushes the recent card so that its go back buttons (which say pop card) will work. Additionally, if the version isn't recent enough to run the current stack properly, the handler immediately pops the card it just pushed, thus returning whence it came:

```
on openStack
  push recent card
  if the version < 2.0 then
    answer "Please upgrade to version 2.0"
    pop card
  end if
end openStack
```

Point for techies: The push list is actually a circular stack. When the list is full and you push another card, the ID of the just-pushed card replaces the ID of the first-pushed card; if you push another card, it replaces the ID in position 2, and so on.

Also See:

POP command, page 297
PRINT CARD, page 302

PUT

Forms

```
put source  { [before|into|after] container}

put userName before card field 1
put sqrt(-1) after nonNumber
put long ID of this card into line 4 of field "Print List"
put line 4 of field "Print List" into the Selection
put field "data" of card 1 into card field "bozo" of card 4
put empty into char 3 to 12 of it
put it
```

Action

The **put** command puts a copy of *source* into *container.* If you don't name a specific container, HyperTalk puts *source* into the Message box (and shows the Message box if it's hidden).

The following handler puts some convenient default values into several fields on the current card (assumed to be a form of some kind):

```
on defaults
  put "USA" into field "Birth Place"
  put "N/A" into field "Selective Service Number"
  put "None" into field "Contagious Diseases"
end defaults
```

Comments

The preposition before inserts text from *source* immediately before any other text in the container; into replaces any old text in the container with the text from *source;* and after puts the text from *source* immediately after any other text in the container.

When *container* is a variable that doesn't yet exist in the current handler, HyperCard creates it as a local variable. Use **put** to create local variables used as *container* components of the **add, subtract, multiply,** or **divide** commands.

When *container* is a field, **put** doesn't send openField or closeField messages.

The following very tricky handler comprises a miniature mailmerge function. It assumes three background fields named "customer," "lastPurchase," and "city." Each card in the mailMerge stack takes care of a single customer, and so holds a different customer name, a different most recently purchased item, and perhaps a different city (see Figure 8-30). The script that calls the function might have these two lines in it:

```
get card field 1 of card "template" -- holds the template letter
put mailMerge(it) into field "letter"
```

```
function mailMerge formLetter
  repeat until offset("$",formLetter) is 0 -- until no more $'s
    put offset("$",formLetter) into startChar -- start of substitution
    delete char startChar of formLetter -- delete first $
    put offset("$",formLetter) into endChar
    delete char endChar of formLetter -- delete second $
    subtract 1 from endChar -- end of substitution
    put char startChar to endChar of formLetter into fieldName -- get fieldName
    put field fieldName into char startChar to endChar of formLetter
  end repeat
  return formLetter
end mailMerge
```

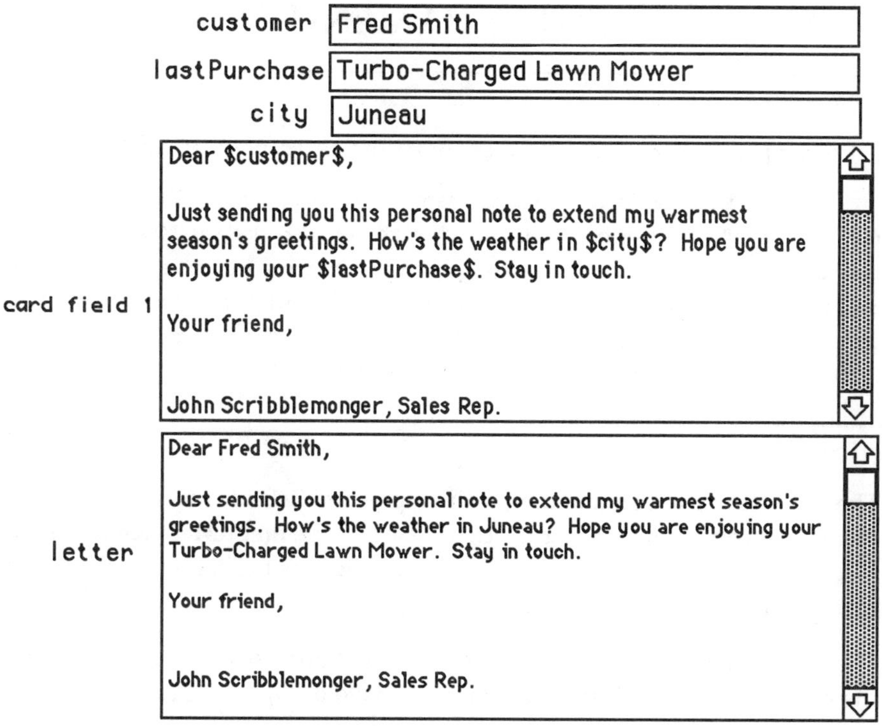

customer	Fred Smith
lastPurchase	Turbo-Charged Lawn Mower
city	Juneau

card field 1

Dear $customer$,

Just sending you this personal note to extend my warmest season's greetings. How's the weather in $city$? Hope you are enjoying your $lastPurchase$. Stay in touch.

Your friend,

John Scribblemonger, Sales Rep.

letter

Dear Fred Smith,

Just sending you this personal note to extend my warmest season's greetings. How's the weather in Juneau? Hope you are enjoying your Turbo-Charged Lawn Mower. Stay in touch.

Your friend,

John Scribblemonger, Sales Rep.

Figure 8-30   Mailmerge function at work

Put creates globals from Msg: When you use **put** from the message box and *container* is a variable that doesn't yet exist, HyperCard creates it as a global variable.

Also See:

GET command, page 256
READ command, page 318
SET command, page 336
WRITE command, page 372

PUT INTO MENU

Forms

put *expr preposition* {*menuItemExpr* of} menu {with menuMessage{s} *expr*}

```
put myItem into menu 3 -- third menu from left, Apple menu is first
put "Goodbye" after menu "Additions" with menuMsg doMenu "Open stack..."
put word 2 of the short name of bg btn 4 before menuItem 3 of menu 8
put word 2 of fld 3 before menu "Print Options" with menuMessage printIt
put "Fred,John,Martha" into menu "Addresses" with menuMessages ¬
   "go card Fred,go card John,go card Martha"
```

Action

The **put into menu** command, new in HyperCard 2.0, adds menu items to menus. The optional with *menuMsg* clause sets the **menuMessage** property to a message of your choice, usually one that defines the actions of the chosen menu item.

The following handler, which belongs in your Addresses stack script, creates the menu "Emergency" and adds three items to it (Figure 8-31):

```
on openStack
   -- install Emergency menu
   create menu "Emergency"
   put "Police" into menu "Emergency" ¬
   with menuMessage "find Police"
   put "Fire" after menu "Emergency" ¬
   with menuMessage "find Fire"
   put "Pizza" after menu "Emergency" ¬
   with menuMessage "find Pizza"
end openStack
```

Figure 8-31   New Addresses menu

Comments

Preposition is before, into, or after. Use before to insert a menu item or list of items before any menu item or at the start of the menu. Use after to place a menu item or list of items after any menu item or at the end of the menu. Use into to replace the current contents (if any) of the menu. You can also use into to replace the contents of an individual menu item:

```
put "Stop" into menuItem "Go" of menu "Engine Room"
```

MenuItemExpr is ordinal menuItem or menuItem *expr*.

Menu is a named or numbered menu. (The Apple menu at the far left is menu 1.)

Expr can be a single item or a quoted list. The item or list can be any container or expression. The list can be comma-separated or return-separated.

The length and width of a menu extends and expands as appropriate to fit the number and width of items and item names. If there are more items than will fit in a menu's screen space, the menu scrolls to accommodate the extra items. There's no practical limit to the number of items you can have in any menu.

The name of a menu item can be of any practical length (that is, well over 50 characters).

To change the name of an existing menu item, use the **name of** *menuItem* property.

You can't add an item to HyperCard's Font, Tools, or Patterns menus (but you can delete any HyperCard menu and create your own).

To draw a thin line across a menu, add a menu item named "-" (the minus sign):

```
put "-" after menu "Utilities"
```

About the "With" option: A menu item can have only one message assigned to it. The message is sent to the current card and continues through the message-passing path, where it can be caught like any other message.

The message most recently assigned to a menu item applies. For more information, see the **menuMessage** property.

You can add a list of menu items to a menu as well as a list of menu messages. When you do so, elements in corresponding positions in the two lists match; that is, the third menu item goes with the third message. Here's the example from the **action** section (above) rewritten to take advantage of this feature:

```
on openStack
  -- install Emergency menu
  create menu "Emergency"
  put "Police,Fire,Pizza" into menu "Emergency" ¬
  with menuMessages "find Police,find Fire,find Pizza"
end openStack
```

The following example creates a menu that lets you move the current card to any position in the current stack. It includes all necessary support handlers (Figure 8-32):

```
on makeCardMenu
  create menu "Card"
  put "Move To First,Move to Last,Move..." into menu "Card" ¬
  with menuMessage "moveToFirst,moveToLast,moveCardTo"
end makeCardMenu

on moveToFirst
  moveCardTo 1
end moveToFirst

on moveToLast
  moveCardTo the number of cards
end moveToLast

on moveCardTo newNumber
  if newNumber is empty then
    ask "New number of this card:"
```

```
    put it into newNumber
  end if
  put max(newNumber,1) into newNumber
  put min(newNumber,the number of cards) into newNumber
  if newNumber is the number of this card -- already done
  then exit moveCardTo
  set lockMessages to true -- prevent any background changes
  lock screen
  doMenu "Cut Card"
  if newNumber is 1 then -- have to handle first card specially
    go to card 1
    doMenu "Paste Card" -- this makes it card 2
    go to card 1
    doMenu "Cut Card"
    doMenu "Paste Card"
    go to card 1
  else
    go to card newNumber - 1
    doMenu "Paste Card"
  end if
end moveCardTo
```

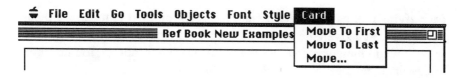

Figure 8-32 Moves card to any place in stack

Changing menu items: Menus and menu items stay intact until you quit
HyperCard, or issue a **reset menuBar** command. (**Reset menuBar** removes all
menus and menu items created by the **create menu** command, and restores
any deleted menus or menu items removed by the **delete menu** command.)
To remove an individual menu use the **delete menu** command.

To change the wording or spelling of a menu item, use the **name of** *menuItem* property. To change the style of a menu item, use the **textStyle of** *menuItem* property. To precede a menu item with a checkmark or other special character, use the **checkMark** or **markChar** property. To associate a command character with a menu item, use the **commandChar** property. To enable and disable a menu item, use the **enabled of** *menuItem* property or the **enable** and **disable** commands. To create a new menu, use the **create menu** command.

Cleaning up after yourself: In most cases, and especially when you use an `on openStack` handler to create new menus, it's a good idea to use **reset menuBar** (or **delete menu**) at closeStack time. This prevents redundant menu items from being added the next time the stack is opened in the same HyperCard session.

New menu items with old HyperCard names: When a user-created menu item has the same name as a standard HyperCard menu item and the new menu item has no **menuMessage** assigned to it, choosing the new item causes the same behavior as choosing the standard menu item. For example, if you create a new menu item called "Home" without a message, choosing that item sends you to the Home stack. (But HyperCard doesn't check, uncheck, enable, disable, or automatically assign the "standard" command key to the new item.)

Identifying menus and menu items: To get the number of menus or the number of items in a given menu, use the **number** function. To find the name of a specific menu item or menu, use the **name of** *menu* property. To find the names of all menus, use **the menus** function.

Also See:

MENUMESSAGE property, page 568
MENUS function, page 426
NAME OF *MENUITEM* property, page 576
NUMBER function, page 438
RESET MENUBAR command, page 322
TEXTSTYLE property, page 632

READ

Forms

```
read from file filename [until character|for numberOfCharacters]

read from file "Big Disk:Correspondence:Addresses" for 16384
read from file myFile until "Jim" -- stops at letter J
read from file myFile until Jim -- stops at 1st char of Jim's value
read from file (line 12 of field "Address Field") until Return
read from file whatEver until line 3 of characterLimit
```

Action

The **read** command retrieves text from the data fork of file *filename,* previously opened by the **open file** command, into the variable It. Reading starts at the beginning of the file; each successive **read** command picks up where the last one ended, replacing the contents of variable It. The pointer is reset to the start of the file each time the file is opened.

The following handler reads all the data from a file into the global variable infoHolder. (The variable is a global one so that you can do something with the information once it's captured.)

```
on getTheInfo fileName
  global infoHolder
  open file fileName
  repeat -- Until all text is retrieved
    read from file fileName for 16384 -- Get maximum characters
    if it is empty then exit repeat -- Stop if file is all read
    put it after infoHolder -- Add these chars to the buffer
  end repeat
  close file fileName
end  getTheInfo
```

Comments

The form until *character* reads from file *filename* through *character,* where *character* is any ASCII character (except null), including the values of the constants `formfeed`, `linefeed`, `quote`, `return`, `space`, and `tab`, or the first character that results from the evaluation of any expression. The case of a letter *is* significant (that is, the letter "A" is different from the letter "a").

If you specify more than one character for *character* (for example, `until "Fred"`), reading stops at the first character (in the example, `F`); if you use an expression like pi (where the expression evaluates to 3.1415...), reading stops at the first character of the value (that is, 3).

Null characters (ASCII 0) in the file are converted to spaces. (You can't specify nulls in the `read until` string — or anywhere else in HyperTalk for that matter.)

The form `for numberOfCharacters` reads for the number of characters (or bytes) specified.

The following handler is a simple spelling checker. (It assumes that the current stack is a dictionary.) The handler reads each word from a file that you specify, and uses the **find** command to see if that word is in the dictionary. It records all unique unknown words in a global variable:

```
on checkSpelling fileName
  global spellingErrors
  put empty into spellingErrors
  open file fileName
  repeat
    read from file fileName until return -- get one line
    if it is empty then exit repeat
    repeat with wordNum = 1 to the number of words in it
      find word wordNum of it
      if the result is not empty then -- not found: misspelled or not there
        put word wordNum of it into error
        if error is not in spellingErrors -- don't report duplicates
        then put error & return after spellingErrors
      end if
    end repeat
  end repeat
  close file fileName
end checkSpelling
```

Reading limits: The maximum number of bytes per **read** command is 16,384 (including spaces, tabs, and Return characters). Bytes beyond 16,384 are ignored, and the pointer remains just past 16,384 for the next read.

Other limits: Each time a **read** executes, retrieved characters go into the variable It, replacing any old value of It. So after each **read** you need to move the contents of It to another container, lest the old contents be lost.

Fields can hold up to 32,000 characters. If you're moving code from large files into fields, use a form such as the one in the following code segment:

```
on importFile fileName, fieldName -- names for source, destination passed in
  open file fileName
  repeat
    doMenu "New Card"
    repeat two times
      read from file fileName for 15000 -- maximum minus 1K (safety factor)
      put it after field fieldName
    end repeat
    if it is empty then exit repeat
  end repeat
  close file fileName
end importFile
```

Reading Tab characters: HyperTalk reads Tab characters the same as it does other characters. But if you move text with tab characters into a field, each tab is converted into a double space.

Full pathname needed: You must provide a full pathname to *filename* each time you reference it; otherwise, HyperTalk assumes that *filename* is in the same folder with the HyperCard application. If HyperTalk can't find a file named *filename*, it creates a MacWrite-compatible text file (Creator MACA, Type TEXT).

The following handler checks to see if a file has any data in it. If the file is empty, you've probably just created it:

```
on checkFile myFile
  open file myFile
  read from file myFile for 1000 -- An arbitrary number
  close file myFile
```

```
  if it is empty then put myFile & " is empty."
  else put myFile & " has live data!"
end checkFile
```

Points for techies: Every file in the Macintosh has two "forks," a data fork and a resource fork. The resource fork contains data of various types (like sounds, icons, windows, menus, code, controls, inits, fonts, cdev, strings); this data is maintained by the resource manager. The data fork keeps an untyped sequence of bytes that any program can read or write. You can put your own resources into the resource fork of a stack, but HyperCard uses the data fork of the stack for its own mysterious reasons. The moral is that, while the file commands can be useful for manipulating text in nonstack files, you're taking the life of a stack in your hands if you mess around with a stack's data fork.

Also See:

CLOSE FILE command, page 190
OPEN FILE command, page 280
WRITE command, page 372

RESET MENUBAR

Forms

```
reset menuBar

reset menuBar
if beenHereAlready then reset menuBar
```

Action

The **reset menuBar** command, new in HyperCard 2.0, restores HyperCard's standard menu bar throwing away any changes made with the **create menu, put into menu,** or **delete** commands.

The following handler resets the menu bar at closeStack time:

```
on closeStack
  reset menuBar
  pass closeStack -- may be other closeStack handlers in path
end closeStack
```

Comments

The standard HyperCard menu bar that appears after **reset menuBar** executes is appropriate to the current user level.

Also See:

CREATE MENU command, page 202
DELETE command, page 212
PUT INTO MENU command, page 312
USERLEVEL property, page 639

RESET PAINT

Forms

```
reset paint

reset paint
```

Action

The **reset paint** command restores all paint properties to their default values.

Changes you make to paint properties aren't automatically reset until you quit and restart HyperCard. The following handler resets the painting properties when you leave a stack. (Use it in a stack that gives unusual settings to the paint properties so that the properties are restored to normal before leaving.)

```
on closeStack
  reset paint -- remove any unusual paint settings
  pass closeStack
end closeStack
```

Comments

Table 8-6 shows default values for painting properties.

Table 8-6: Default values for painting properties

Property	Default value
brush	8
centered	false
filled	false
grid	false
lineize	1
multiple	false
multispace	1
pattern	12 (black)
polysides	4
textalign	left
textfont	application font (probably Geneva)
textheight	4 * textSize DIV 3 (probably 16)
textsize	system font size (probably 12)
textstyle	plain

The following handler uses **reset paint** to set all the painting properties to
their defaults before drawing a picture:

```
on mouseUp
  reset paint
  choose brush tool
  drag from 210,150 to 250,105
  drag from 250,105 to 250,300
  drag from 200,300 to 300,300
  choose browse tool
end mouseUp
```

RETURNINFIELD

Forms

```
returnInField

returnInField
```

Action

ReturnInField adds a carriage return to an open field. If no field is open for editing (that is, if the insertion point isn't in any field), nothing happens.

This command isn't good for much; it's only useful as a message. For example, the following field script prevents users from typing return characters into the field:

```
on returnInField
end returnInField
```

Comments

If the selection is in the bottom visible line of an unlocked nonscrolling field with its **autoTab** property set to true, **returnInField** sends the message `tabKey` and autoTab events are triggered. If the selection is anyplace else in a nonscrolling field, or anywhere in a scrolling field, **returnInField** adds a Return character to the field, updating scrolling as necessary.

When the user presses the return key, the message `returnInField` is sent to an open field.

An automated menu

The following handlers turn a nonscrolling locked field into a menu. Pressing the return key selects successive lines of a field. (As a bonus having nothing to do with **returnInField**, the up and down arrow keys also select successive lines.) If pressing return puts you past the bottom of the list, you go back to the top of the list automatically. Pressing the enter key gets the selected line into the variable it. These handlers can go

---

in the script of the card or background where you want them to work.
Note the comments if you're using version 2.0. (To start things off, you
click on any line in the field):

```
on mouseUp
  if "field" is not in the target then pass mouseUp
  if "menu" is not in the target then pass mouseUp
  set lockText of the target to false -- don't need in 2.0
  click at the clickLoc -- don't need in 2.0
  select the selectedLine -- "select the clickLine" in 2.0.
  set lockText of the target to true -- don't need in 2.0
end mouseUp

on returnInField
  moveSelectedLine 1
end returnInField

on arrowKey direction
  if the selectedField is empty then pass arrowKey
  if "menu" is not in name of the selectedField then pass arrowKey
  if direction is "down"
  then send "moveSelectedLine 1" to the selectedField
  else if direction is "up"
  then send "moveSelectedLine -1" to the selectedField
  else pass arrowKey
end arrowKey

on moveSelectedLine amount
  get the selectedLine
  add amount to word 2 of it
  if word 2 of it>the number of lines in value of the selectedField
  then put 1 into word 2 of it
  if word 2 of it < 1
  then put the number of lines in value of the selectedField into word 2 of it
  select it
end moveSelectedLine
```

```
on enterInField
  get the selection
  put "You chose " & it -- or whatever you want to do with the menu choice
  select empty -- deselect
end enterInField
```

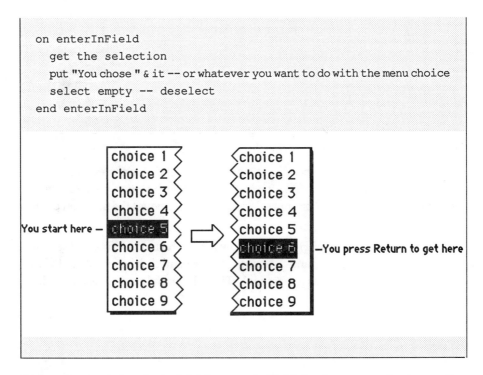

If the selection is in a locked field, **returnInField** deselects any selection and does nothing .

Also See:

RETURNINFIELD command, page 325
RETURNKEY command, page 328

RETURNKEY

Forms

```
returnKey

returnKey
```

Action

Returnkey, if the insertion point is not in any field, sends the contents of the Message box to the current card. If a field contains the insertion point or other selection, **returnkey** deselects any selected text and removes the insertion point from the field.

In pre-release versions of HyperCard, pressing return did a **find** of the contents of the message box, and pressing enter executed the contents of the message box (that is, sent it as a message). The following handler recreates that behavior:

```
on returnKey
  find the message box
end returnKey
```

Comments

If the Message box appeared as a result of choosing the Find menu command, the **returnkey** command hides the Message box.

This command and the **enterKey** command do exactly the same thing.

ReturnKey is more useful as a message than it is as a command. The following handler routes messages from the message box through a library stack of handlers:

```
on returnKey
  send the message box to stack "My Command Library"
end returnKey
```

Also See:

RETURNINFIELD command, page 325
RETURNKEY message, page 328
TABKEY command, page 358

SAVE AS

Forms

```
save [ {this} stack | stack expr ]  as {stack} expr

save stack as "My Backup"
save this stack as someVariableName
save stack variableName as stack "My Backup"
```

Action

The **save as** command, new for 2.0, saves a copy of a stack under the name you provide.

The following handler saves a copy of the stack "Original" in a pre-existing folder called "Backups" on the current disk:

```
on mouseUp
   save stack "Original" as ":BackUps:Copy of Original"
end mouseUp
```

Comments

Expr is any expression that yields a valid stack name.

If you don't provide the name of a stack before the required word **as**, HyperCard saves the current stack:

```
save stack as "exact copy" -- copies current stack
```

This command works just like domenu "Save a copy...", except that no dialog is presented.

The following example adds the "Save as..." command to the File menu:

```
on mouseUp
   put "Save As..." after menuItem "Save A Copy" ..." of menu "File" ¬
   with menuMsg "userSaveAs"
end mouseUp

on userSaveAs
   ask file "Save Stack As:"
   if it is not empty then
```

```
    save this stack as it
      go to it
   end if
end userSaveAs
```

Also See:

DOMENU command, page 229

SELECT

Forms

```
select {before|after} {text of|chunk of} [field|message]
select [button|field]

select after word 3 of field 5 -- Places insertion point after word 3
select text of field thisField -- Selects all text in field
select field thisField -- Chooses field tool, selects field
-- whose identifier is held in variable thisField
select button "Move me" -- chooses button tool, selects button
select word 2 to 5 of the msg -- Try this from the Message box
select empty -- deselects whatever's selected; removes insertion point
select the clickLine -- works in 2.0 and later versions
```

Action

The **select** command selects the specified text or object. It does *not* select graphics.

The following handler selects the text of a field named "Name and Address" when a card is opened, useful in situations where you expect the user to enter or change the value of this field:

```
on openCard
  select text of field "Name and Address"
end openCard
```

Comments

Button or *field* must be on the current card for this command to do anything. (You won't get an error if *button* or *field* is on another card, but nothing happens.)

Select will select text in a locked field; you can manipulate such selected text with commands like doMenu "Copy Text" or put the Selection or get the selectedText, and you can programmatically change the text of the selection while the field is locked.

Selecting objects: **Select** works only on objects whose **visible** property is set to true. Selecting an object automatically chooses the appropriate tool.

Dragging and selecting: When the field or button tool is active, you don't have to use the **select** command before dragging a field or button (useful for animation):

```
on moveTheButton thisButton
  choose button tool
  set dragSpeed to 72
  drag from the loc of btn thisButton to 150, 200 -- selects button for you
  choose Browse tool
end moveTheButton
```

Selecting text: **Select** works on text in a field whose **visible** property is set to true. When you select text that's scrolled out of sight in a scrolling field, the text scrolls into view; but because of a bug (aurggh!) in versions through 1.2.1, the scrolling changes neither the thumb's position nor the value of the **scroll** property.

Select adds extra lines to a field if you select a line that doesn't exist. (For example, the code `select line 7 of field 2` adds four empty lines if field 2 contains only three lines of text.) This command will not, however, pad to fill chars, words, items, or ranges: so if you say `select char 7 of word 2 of field 2` when word 2 has 7 or fewer characters, **Select** places the insertion point just after word 2.

And by the way: the correct form is `select text of field "Foo"`. In all versions through 2.0, it is never correct to say `select the text of field foo`, even though any right-thinking person would assume it would be correct to do so. ("Anomaly, thy name is HyperTalk.")

Yet another HyperTalk anomaly (YAHA)

In versions 1.2.# and 2.0, when the line of text you select comprises a button or field identifier (for example, the text reads `card field 12` or `button "Fred"`), HyperCard assumes that the identifier is an expression to be evaluated — and so that object is selected, rather than the specified line of text in the field.

For example, line 3 of card field 3 is this:

```
button 3
```

Assume that this statement executes (either from a handler or from the Message box):

```
select line 3 of card field 3
```

The result is that the button tool is chosen and card button 3 is selected, as in Figure 8-33.

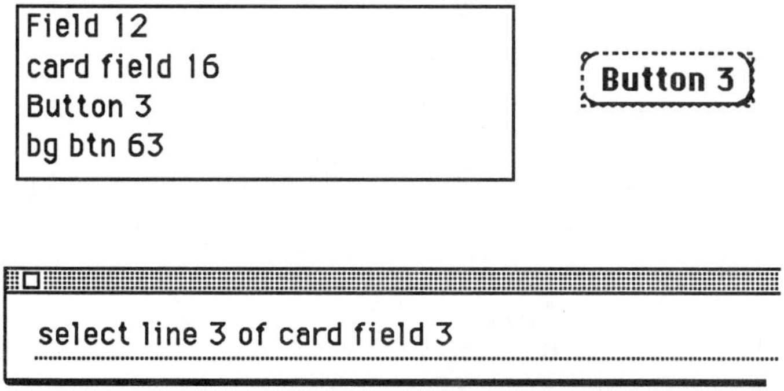

```
Field 12
card field 16
Button 3
bg btn 63
```

[Button 3]

```
select line 3 of card field 3
```

Figure 8-33   Selecting a button through a line reference

To ensure that the text line in card field 3 is selected, and *not* the object that it names, enclose the parameters to the **select** command within quotation marks (see Figure 8-34):

```
select "line 3 of card field 3"
```

```
Field 12
card field 16
Button 3
bg btn 63
```

(Button 3)

```
select "line 3 of card field 3"
```

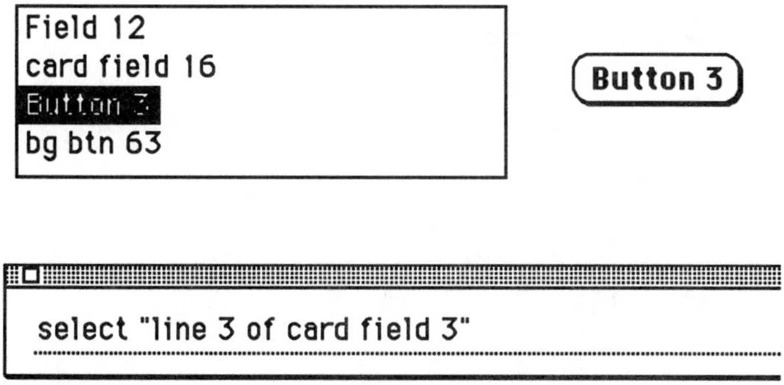

Figure 8-34   Selecting a line through a line reference

This anomaly doesn't occur if anything else appears on the line in addition to the object identifier:

```
button 3 is my favorite button
```

"Selecting" graphics: You can't use the **select** command to select graphics. Use **drag** instead:

```
choose rectangle tool -- or lasso tool for a tight selection
drag from 10,10 to 250, 300 -- or whatever points contain the image
```

Select empty: The form `select empty` deselects the selected object or text and removes the insertion point. (The insertion point is, by definition, the smallest selection possible.)

Select and Find handlers

The following handler simulates the effect of doMenu "Find":

```
on myFind
  put "find " & quote & quote
  select before last char of the message box
end myFind
```

The following slightly more complicated version also specifies the kind of find (char,word,normal,string,whole). You call it with a form such as `myFind "string"`:

```
on myFind how
  put "find " & how & " " & quote & quote
  select before last char of the message box
end myFind
```

The following pair of handlers find text the way a word processor does — it selects the found text so you can type over it:

```
on tabKey
  if the shiftKey is not down then pass tabKey -- works with shift-Tab
  ask "Find what?"
  findAndSelect it
end tabKey

on findAndSelect searchStr
  find searchStr
  select the foundChunk
end findAndSelect
```

Reversing numbers: Reversing numbers in a **select** command sets the insertion point to the left of the first number. Thus `select char 4 to 3` sets the insertion point to the left of the fourth character (the same effect as `select before char 3`), and `select char 8 to 2` sets the insertion point to the left of the eighth character (the same effect as `select before char 8`).

UserLevel must be high: To select an object, the userLevel property must be set to 4 or 5.

Also See:

CHOOSE command, page 183
DRAG command, page 233
SCROLL property, page 603
SELECTEDCHUNK function, page 461
SELECTEDFIELD function, page 463
SELECTEDLINE function, page 465
SELECTEDTEXT function, page 467

SET

Forms

```
set {the} logicalProperty of object to logical
set {the} integerProperty of object to integer
set {the} stringProperty of object to string

set the userLevel to 5
set hilite of button 2 to true
set dragSpeed to userSpeed
set the script of background button "Executive Decisions" to empty
```

Action

The **set** command changes the value of a property.

The following button script makes the button follow the mouse. To make it work, press the mouse with the pointer over the button, and drag:

```
on mouseStillDown
   set the loc of me to the mouseLoc
end mouseStillDown
```

Comments

LogicalProperty is a property whose value is true or false. *IntegerProperty* is a property whose value is an integer. *StringProperty* is a property whose value is a string. *Object* is any HyperCard object, including me, the target, or HyperCard itself.

When HyperCard is the object, as in the case of all global properties (including Paint properties), you can omit the object reference and use the form

```
set {the} property to [logical|integer|string]
```

using a logical, integer, or string value, as appropriate.

The following script, placed in a card or background or stack script, changes the defaults for a newly created button:

```
on newButton
   set the name of the target to empty
   set the showName of the target to false
```

```
    set the style of the target to transparent
    set the width of the target to 60
    set the height of the target to 60
end newButton
```

For details on all HyperCard properties, see Chapter 10, Properties.

Using set to create a sliding gauge: The following pair of button scripts operate a sliding gauge. The scripts go (respectively) into a left-facing button and a right-facing button. The gauge itself is constructed from two other buttons: a hilited (black) button named "Gauge background" behind an opaque (white) button named "gauge." The scripts work by adjusting the left side of the white button to expose more or less of the underlying black button (see Figure 8-35).

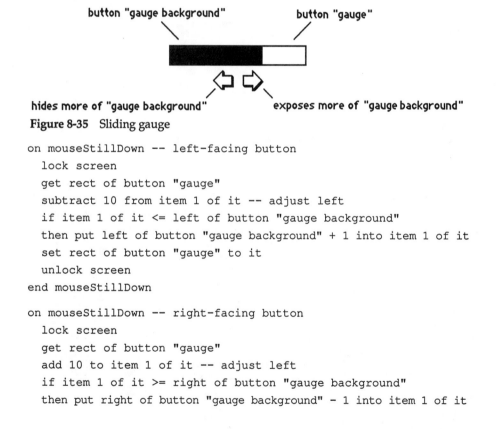

Figure 8-35 Sliding gauge

```
on mouseStillDown -- left-facing button
  lock screen
  get rect of button "gauge"
  subtract 10 from item 1 of it -- adjust left
  if item 1 of it <= left of button "gauge background"
  then put left of button "gauge background" + 1 into item 1 of it
  set rect of button "gauge" to it
  unlock screen
end mouseStillDown

on mouseStillDown -- right-facing button
  lock screen
  get rect of button "gauge"
  add 10 to item 1 of it -- adjust left
  if item 1 of it >= right of button "gauge background"
  then put right of button "gauge background" - 1 into item 1 of it
```

```
    set rect of button "gauge" to it
    unlock screen
end mouseStillDown
```

Properties in Info boxes: Many of the properties of an object appear as items in an object's Info dialog box.

Also See:

PROPERTIES, Chapter 10

SHOW

Forms

```
show window {at location}
show [button|field] {at location}
show menubar
show {the} [message|msg] {window|box} {at location}

show tool window at 20, 200
show msg at hor,vert
show background button "Awake!"
show field "Declassified Info" at 150,30
show scroll window
```

Action

The **show** command shows the named element, optionally at a specific location. The visible property of the element is set to true.

The following button conditionally shows a hidden field, as appropriate:

```
on mouseUp
  if field "Sex" is "Male" and field "Age" >= 18
  then show field "Draft Registration Instructions" -- Yuch!
  else show field "Skateboard Power Tips" -- Yea!
end mouseUp
```

Comments

If you don't give a location, the element appears at the location most recently set for it (that is, it uses the current value of its location property). To hide an element, use the **hide** command.

If the element is a button or field, it must be in the current stack.

location is a point on the display, expressed as two integers separated by a comma. The integers represent (respectively) horizontal and vertical coordinates (in pixels). Table 8-7 describes the location of point 0,0 (offset source) for a type of element, and where the point described by **show** is located on an element. (All locations start immediately below the title bar.) Table 8-8 shows the default positions for non-card windows.

Table 8-7: Offset sources for Loc

Element	Offset source	Point location
object	top-left corner of card window	center of object
noncard windows	top-left corner of card window	top-left corner, active area
card window	top-left corner of screen	top-left corner of card

Table 8-8: Default positions for noncard windows

Window	Position
Tool	200, 70
Pattern	300, 70
Message	22, 300

The following handlers keep the tool window in the same location relative to the card window. It assumes that the user's preferred location for the tool window is stored in the global theToolLoc:

```
on openStack
  global theToolLoc
  put loc of tool window into theToolLoc
end openStack

on idle
  global theToolLoc
  show tool window at theToolLoc
end idle
```

(You might have a little trouble as you install these guys; the idle handler complains because it has no initial value for theToolLoc. Just put away the error dialog and send the message openStack via the message box, and everything will be fine forever after. Trust us.)

Visible boundaries: Locations 0,0 through 511,341 are within a standard card's area and are therefore visible on all Macintosh displays. Points outside those boundaries may or may not be visible, depending upon the size of the display you're using.

When Show doesn't show anything: You can issue a command such as `show field 1`, and you still might not be able to see the element you asked for. The element might be covered by a picture or a window or an object, or its current location might be outside the visible boundaries of the current display. When that happens, move the pointer to some convenient bare spot on the card and enter `show field 1 at the mouseLoc` through the Message box.

If an object doesn't exist at all, HyperCard puts up an error dialog, as in Figure 8-36.

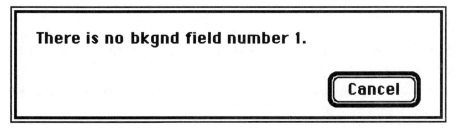

Figure 8-36 Error dialog for missing elements

Also See:

HIDE command, page 264
SEND keyword, page 155
SHOW PICTURE command, page 344
VISIBLE property, page 648

SHOW CARDS

Forms

```
show {all | marked | integer} cards

show all cards -- display all cards in the stack once
show cards -- cycle through all cards until mouseclick
show 5 cards -- show the next five cards in rapid succession
show theseMany cards
show marked cards -- show cards with marked property true (2.0)
```

Action

The **show cards** command shows a series of cards from the current stack in rapid succession, beginning with the card after the current one.

The following handler repeatedly plays a five card flipbook animation until the mouse is clicked:

```
on flipBook
  repeat until the mouseClick
    go to card "flip book start"
    show five cards
  end repeat
end flipBook
```

Comments

The form show *integer* cards shows the given number of cards proceeding from the current one and then stops. (You end up *integer* cards from where you started.)

Clicking the mouse stops all forms of **show cards**.

HyperCard doesn't send any system messages when **show card** operates, and visual effects aren't displayed as cards pass by. To show a series of cards with visual effects, use the following form:

```
on showCards numberOfCards
  repeat numberOfCards -- substitute any number
    visual dissolve to black
```

```
      visual dissolve to card
      go next
   end repeat
end showCards
```

The following handler makes HyperCard cache as many of the cards in the current stack as it has memory for. This "prewarming" makes cards more quickly accessible for animation sequences:

```
on preWarm
   lock screen
   show all cards
end preWarm
```

HyperCard automatically prewarms the next card (the card after the current one) at idle time because it knows you are very likely to go to it.

Points for techies: The form `show cards` isn't really an infinite loop, although it might as well be. Actually, it shows *bigNumber* cards, where *bigNumber* is the maximum value of a 32 bit number — 4,294,967,295 — enough (according to calculations performed by one of the authors) to keep a Macintosh II busy for at least 10 years.

Only the card where you started and the card you end up on are added to Recent.

Also See:

OPENCARD message, page 663
RECENT menu command, *HyperCard User's Guide*
VISUAL command, page 367

SHOW PICTURE

Forms

```
show [background|card] pict{ure}
show pict{ure} of [localCard|localBackground]

show card picture
show picture of card "Jennings" of background "Photos"
```

Action

Show picture shows the designated picture, previously hidden either with the **Hide picture** command or with the command form

```
set showpict of [card|background] to false
```

The following handler makes the card picture dissolve onto the screen:

```
on showIt
  lock screen
  show card picture
  unlock screen with visual effect dissolve
end showIt
```

Comments

Local designates a picture in the current stack.

To show the picture of the current background or card, use the form

```
show [background|card] pict{ure}
```

To show the picture on another card or background in the current stack, use the form

```
show pict{ure} of [localCard|localBackground]
```

Show Picture sets the **showPict** property of affected pictures to true.

Show doesn't Go: Although you can show the picture of a noncurrent card or background, you don't automatically go to that card or background when you make its picture visible:

```
on showRemote
  lock screen
```

```
   show picture of card 12 -- shows picture of some other card
   go card 12 -- goes to that card
   unlock screen with visual effect dissolve
end showRemote
```

Also See:

HIDE command, page 264
SHOW command, page 339
SHOW PICTURE property, page 344
UNLOCK SCREEN command, page 363

SORT

Forms

```
sort {ascending|descending} {type} by expr

sort by line 3 of field 4
sort descending numeric by line 3 of field partNumber
sort numeric by random(number of cards) -- scramble cards
sort by mySortKey() -- sort by user-defined function
sort dateTime by field "Hire date"
```

Action

sort sorts the cards in the current unlocked stack according to the criteria you specify.

The following handler sorts a stack of names (including non-English ones) from Z to A by the last word (presumably somebody's last name) of a field called "Name":

```
on sortNames
  sort descending international by last word of field "Name"
end sortNames
```

Comments

Type can be text, numeric, international, or dateTime. (See "About Types," below.) *Expr* can be any expression.

The default values for **sort** are ascending and text.

About types: Here are the types available for sorting:

• Text sorts according to the ASCII value of *expr* (the default).

• Numeric sorts in numeric order.

• International sorts in the order shown on the International Sort Chart in Inside Macintosh (volume 1), and is primarily useful for sorting text in languages containing ligatures and characters with diacritical marks.

- `DateTime` sorts by the date and/or time given, as long as the date and/or time are in an acceptable format. If the time doesn't appear, HyperCard assumes the time is Midnight (start of day). If the date doesn't appear, HyperCard uses today's date.

Cards that are unsortable by the given criteria use empty as a sort key, and so appear at the start of the stack (or the end of the stack, if the order is *descending*) in the order they appeared before the most recent sort. Thus you can sort several times on the same or different field.

HyperCard's sort is stable (cards with the same key stay in the same order); so you can sort by both primary and secondary criteria. The following example produces a stack sorted alphabetically by county, with cities sorted alphabetically within counties:

```
on mouseUp
  sort by field "city"
  sort by field "county"
end mouseUp
```

Supplying your own sort key: The following handler is an example of a user-defined sort key function. It sorts all the cards in a stack (presumably created by the records-keeping division of a district court) into four categories:

```
sort by mySortKey()

function mySortKey
  -- arrange cards in order of eligibility for prison furlough program
  get field "rap sheet"
  if it contains "MS-DOS Use" then return "Z" -- throw away the key
  if it contains "Cat Juggling" then return "M"
  -- keep away from small pets
  if it contains "Skateboarding" then return "A" -- skateboarding not a crime
  return "D" -- all other crimes go in this category
end mySortKey
```

The cards are sorted into four groups — Z, M, A, and D — but unsorted beyond that. To sort by alphabetic order by name within groups, use a form like this:

```
if it contains "MS-DOS Use" then return "Z" & field "name"
```

Compact after sorting: HyperCard keeps an internal list of the order of cards in a stack, telling where each card is. The **sort** command changes the list, but doesn't change the physical ordering of the cards: physically, card 2 might follow card 8, and card 1 might follow card 300. When you compact a stack, the physical cards get moved to match the logical list; and when that happens, going from card to card takes less time.

Sorting within containers

Sort works *only* on stacks. The following multihandler function will sort a multiple line expression into ascending order. For example,

```
put quickSort(field "data") into field "data"
```

will sort the lines of field "data" into ascending order.

This routine will sort 100 lines of 15 characters each in about 30 seconds on a Mac II using 1.2.#:

```
function quickSort data
   -- quick sort lines into ascending order
   -- uses bubble sort for small cases because it's faster
   -- and uses less recursion
   set cursor to watch
   put number of lines in data into lineCount
   if lineCount <= 10 then return bubbleSort(data)
   return merge(quickSort(line 1 to lineCount div 2 of data),¬
   quickSort(line lineCount div 2 + 1 to lineCount of data))
end quickSort

function merge list1,list2
   -- merge two sorted lists into one sorted list
   -- called by quickSort
   put empty into resultList
   put 1 into ptr1
   put 1 into ptr2
   put number of lines in list1 into lineCount1
   put number of lines in list2 into lineCount2
   repeat until ptr1 > lineCount1 and ptr2 > lineCount2
     if ptr1 > lineCount1 then -- use list2
```

```
      put line ptr2 of list2 & return after resultList
      add 1 to ptr2
    else if ptr2 > lineCount2 then -- use list1
      put line ptr1 of list1 & return after resultList
      add 1 to ptr1
    else if line ptr1 of list1 < line ptr2 of list2 then
      put line ptr1 of list1 & return after resultList
      add 1 to ptr1
    else
      put line ptr2 of list2 & return after resultList
      add 1 to ptr2
    end if
  end repeat
  return resultList
end merge

function bubbleSort data
  -- bubble sort lines into ascending order
  -- called by quickSort to handle small cases for best efficiency
  repeat with i = 1 to the number of lines in data
    repeat with j = i to the number of lines in data
      if line i of data > line j of data then
        get line j of data
        put line i of data into line j of data
        put it into line i of data
      end if
    end repeat
  end repeat
  return data
end bubbleSort
```

For an external that sorts lines far faster than this code, see the
`sortLines` XFCN in Chapter 13.

Points for techies: The actual sort time in the **sort** command happens during the brief cursor spin. The rest of the time is spent gathering keys and writing out the card list structure.

Also See:

ASCII CHART, Appendix A
DATE function, page 403
RANDOM function, page 452
TIME function, page 482

START USING

Forms

```
start using stackExpr

start using stack newStack
start using stack "The Latest Stuff"
start using this stack
```

Action

The **start using** command, new in HyperCard 2.0, adds as many as ten stacks to the message passing path.

The following example adds a stack to the message passing path at startup time:

```
on startUp
   start using stack "My Favorite Handlers"
end startUp
```

Comments

StackExpr is the name of any stack, optionally including a Hierarchical File System (HFS) path. If the stack name contains any spaces, the name must appear within quotation marks.

Start using extends the message passing path, giving you access to the scripts and resources of the added stack. The stack named as the parameter to this command is appended to the end of the read-only **stacksInUse** property list, and is inserted into the message passing path just before the Home stack.

A stack name appears in **stacksInUse** only once. If you issue the command `start using stackName` when `stackName` is already in **stacksInUse**, HyperCard moves `stackName` to the first item in **stacksInUse**. (The first item in **stacksInUse** is the first stack in the message passing path extension.)

You can add up to ten stacks to the message passing path. If you try to add an eleventh, you won't get an error message (except when you add the eleventh stack through the Message box), but **the result** is set.

If HyperCard can't find the stack that you want to start using, it puts up a dialog asking you to locate the stack.

When you quit HyperCard, the message passing path is reset to its unextended version.

The following simple example shows the proper way to clean up after yourself: it adds a stack to the path on openstack, and removes it from the path on closeStack:

```
on openStack
  start using stack "Shared Handlers"
end openStack

on closeStack
  stop using stack "Shared Handlers"
end closeStack
```

About compacting: You can't compact a stack currently in the extended path. To compact the stack, use `stop using stackNeedingCompacting`; after compaction, call `start using` again to put the stack back on the path.

How extending the path works: When you add a stack to the message passing path, HyperCard keeps information about that stack's handlers in memory. Each time a message goes through the path (assuming the message isn't caught before it reaches the extension), HyperCard looks in its RAM cache to see if that message has any handlers to catch it in the path extension.

Extending the message passing path has little impact on the time it takes for a given message to traverse the path. So you'll seldom notice a degradation in performance, even in slower machines.

Duplicate name errors: One stack might have a handler with the same name as, but with different functionality than, a handler in another stack. If both stacks are in the message passing path extension, be sure that the stack with the proper version is earlier in the path to avoid calling the wrong handler.

To avoid duplicate name errors: (1) use unique handler names whenever possible; and (2) add a stack to the path only when you need it (thus moving the stack to the start of the extension) and remove the stack from the path as soon as you've finished using it.

Also See:

PASSING ALONG THE MESSAGE (Chapter 0), page 18
STACKSINUSE property, page 615
STOP USING command, page 354

STOP USING

Forms

```
stop using stackExpr

stop using stack newStack
stop using stack "The Latest Stuff"
stop using this stack
```

Action

The **stop using** command, new in HyperCard 2.0, removes from the message passing path a stack previously added to it by the **start using** command.

The following example resets the stacksInUse to a known list stored in a global:

```
on resetStacksInUse
  -- make sure that some stack didn't leave
  -- unwanted stacks on the stacksInUse list
  -- by restoring it to the contents of a global variable
  global stacksAlwaysInUse
  setStacksInUse stacksAlwaysInUse
end resetStacksInUse

on setStacksInUse newList
  -- the stacksInUse is a read-only property
  -- this handler makes it read/write
  repeat with stackNum = 1 to the number of items in newList
    start using stack item stackNum of newList
  end repeat
  repeat with stackNum = 1 to ¬
  the number of items in the stacksInUse
    get item stackNum of the stacksInUse
    if it is not in newList
    then stop using stack it
  end repeat
end setStacksInUse
```

Comments

StackExpr is the name of any stack, optionally including a Hierarchical File System (HFS) path. If the stack name contains any spaces, the name must appear within quotation marks.

You can't use **stop using** to prevent messages from going to a stack in the usual static or dynamic paths.

Stop using doesn't harm a stack in any way; it just removes the stack from the extension to the message passing path. When you remove a stack from the path, you lose access to its scripts and resources. To regain access, use the **start using** command.

When you quit HyperCard, all stacks added to the message passing path by **start using** are automatically removed from the path. To clear all stacks from the message passing path extension while HyperCard is running, use this:

```
on clearStacks
  repeat for the number of items in the stacksInUse
    stop using stack (first item of the stacksInUse) -- always 1st!
  end repeat
end clearStacks
```

Also See:

PASSING ALONG THE MESSAGE (Chapter 0), page 18
STACKSINUSE property, page 615
START USING command, page 351

SUBTRACT

Forms

```
subtract numExpr from container

subtract 5 from it
subtract 3 from word 2 of line 5 of field 6
subtract refund from total
subtract value from field "Bargains"
subtract field "Federal taxes" from fairIncome
```

Action

The **subtract** command subtracts *numExpr* from *container*, leaving the result in *container*. The old value of *container* is destroyed (but the value of *numExpr* is unaffected).

The following handler displays a countdown counter in a field:

```
on countDown
  put 10 into field "Counter"
  repeat until field "Counter" is zero
    wait one second
    subtract 1 from field "Counter"
  end repeat
  play "boing"
end countDown
```

Comments

container must contain a numeric value before a subtraction can happen.

When the result of the subtraction appears in a field or in the Message box, the format for the display depends upon the setting of the **numberFormat** property. (HyperTalk converts all numbers to strings before they're displayed.)

The following handler tells you how many days you have left to meet a deadline:

```
on mouseUp
  ask "When's the deadline?"
  convert it to seconds
  subtract the seconds from it
  answer "You have about " & round(it/60/60/24) & " days left."
end mouseUp
```

Points for techies: If both values are integers, and if both have absolute values less than 1,073,741,823 (the highest value a 30-bit number can represent) HyperCard uses integer math to do the subtraction; otherwise, it uses SANE extended math.

Subtract and the "-" operator do the same thing arithmetically, and share exactly the same code internally.

Also See:

NUMBERFORMAT property, page 585

TABKEY

Forms

```
tabKey

tabKey
```

Action

The **tabKey** command has the same effect as pressing the Tab key.

TabKey is most useful as a message, not as a command. But the following handler shows a rare use of it as a command and simulates the effect of pressing the tab key when a new card is created. (It selects the text of the first field — the same effect as `select text of field 1`):

```
on newCard
  tabKey
end newCard
```

Comments

TabKey closes the current field (sending the message `closeField` if any text in the field has changed, or in 2.0 `exitField` if no text has changed) and selects all the text in the next visible unlocked field in the tabbing order, opening that field for editing (and sending the message `openField`). If that field is empty, **tabKey** puts the insertion point at the start of the first line. If no field holds the selection, then **tabKey** selects text in the lowest-numbered, visible, unlocked, background field. When the Background is open, **tabKey** does nothing.

The following handler catches tabKey and selects the text of the Message box. Thus this handler provides a handy way to go quickly from editing a field to entering text in the message box:

```
on tabKey
  select text of the message box
end tabKey
```

Backwards tabbing: If the shift key is down when **tabKey** executes, then **tabKey** closes the current field and selects all the text in the *previous* visible unlocked field in the tabbing order; but the form `tabKey with shiftKey` generates an error dialog. To tab backwards, use the statement

```
type Tab with shiftkey
```

Tabbing order: All tabbing happens on the same card. When you tab, you go to the next higher-numbered unlocked field of the type you left (background or card) whose visible property is set to true. If there's no higher-numbered available field of that type, you go to the lowest-numbered field of the other type.

To change the tabbing order, use the menu items **Bring closer** and **Send farther.** These commands change the positional number of a selected field, bringing it closer to or farther away from the front in its domain (that is, relative to other background or card fields).

Note that the card plane is closer to the front than is the background plane; so the closest background field will always be farther away from the front than the farthest card field.

Also See:

AUTOTAB property, page 494
MOVING BETWEEN FIELDS, *HyperCard User's Guide*
RETURNINFIELD command, page 325

TYPE

Forms

```
type expr {with key1 {,key2 {,key3 } } }

type "B" with commandKey -- toggle background mode
type field "Original" -- copies text from field "Original"
type Foo -- types contents of variable Foo at the insertion point
```

Action

The **type** command types at the insertion point, as if you were pressing keys by hand.

The following handler types a friendly greeting in large letters:

```
on mouseUp
  choose text tool
  set textSize to 24
  click at 100,200
  type "Welcome to HyperTalk!"
  choose browse tool
end mouseUp
```

Comments

Key can be `shiftkey`, `optionkey`, **and/or** `commandkey` (or `cmdkey`). *Expr* <u>is</u> case-sensitive.

When the Browse tool is chosen, **Type** sends text characters to an unlocked field or to the Message box at the insertion point. When the Text tool is chosen **type** sends text characters to the card or background picture at the insertion point.

If you have neither the browse tool nor the text tool chosen, or if there's no insertion point, HyperTalk tries to type into the Message box.

If the message box is not visible and **blindTyping** is set to false, the Macintosh beeps once for each character in *expr* and the typing goes nowhere. Any remaining commands in the handler continue to execute.

Type is useful for entering paint text from a script, and for programmatically performing cut, copy, and paste operations (as in `type x with commandKey`) without knowing the kind of element being operated upon.

Bring closer, send farther: To move a field or button closer to or farther away from the front in its domain, use **type** with "+" or "-". The following example moves a card field 5 layers closer to the front, assuming that there are five layers (that is, any combination of buttons and/or fields) between it and the front. (If there are fewer than five layers, the field moves to the front.)

```
on mouseUp
  select cd field 1
  repeat 5
    type "+" with cmdkey
  end repeat
  select browse tool
end mouseUp
```

Choosing Browse tool: The statement `type Tab with commandKey` chooses the Browse tool (that is, has the same effect as `choose browse tool`).

253-character limit: The **type** command types up to the first 253 characters of *expr.* Characters beyond the 253rd are ignored.

Type not a precise manual simulation: You can't use the **Type** command to simulate everything you'd do by hand. Thus you can't use

```
type "." with commandkey
```

to abort a running handler, nor can you convert from lower to uppercase letters by using the form

```
type lots_of_lower_case_characters with shiftKey
```

You can, however, simulate any menu command that has a keyboard equivalent (for exampe, `type "M" with commandKey` to toggle the Message box).

Being creative with Type: While Put sends its information all at once, Type sends text one character at a time. You can use this trait to create animated text displays (sort of):

```
on flashy
   set the textalign of field 1 to center -- Type around a central point
   set the textstyle of field 1 to bold -- Anything distinctive will do
   set the lockText of field 1 to false -- Type needs unlocked field
   repeat until the shiftkey is down -- Do until user presses shift
      select before text of field 1 -- Place insertion point properly
      type "Am I being artistic yet?" -- Here's the action
      wait 30 -- Keep it on screen
      delete line 1 of field 1 -- clear the field
   end repeat
end flashy
```

Also See:

UNLOCK SCREEN

Forms

```
unlock screen {with visual}

unlock screen
unlock screen with dissolve slowly to white
unlock screen with visual effect zoom open
```

Action

The **unlock screen** command sets the **lockScreen** property to false and updates the display with all visual changes that occurred since the last time the **lockScreen** property was set to true. (But see "Lock Screen's Counter" later in this description.)

The following button handler makes the field "comments" alternately visible and invisible with a dissolve visual effect:

```
on mouseUp
  lock screen
  set visible of field "Comments" to not visible of field "Comments"
  unlock screen with dissolve
end mouseUp
```

Comments

visual can be any one visual effect as described later on. The full syntax is:

```
unlock screen {with {visual {effect}} effectname {speed} {to image}}
```

Making all your changes to the screen at once is less jarring on the user than making your changes one at a time.

Creating visual effects using this method doesn't send the `visual` message.

Using `unlock screen` on a screen that isn't locked is harmless.

Visual effects without changing cards: Using the `with visual` option, you can show visual effects without changing cards:

```
on fade
  lock screen
```

```
   hide field 1
   hide card button 1
   show card picture
   unlock screen with visual iris open very slowly
end fade
```

Speed considerations: The command pair **lock screen** and **unlock screen** save time when you need to gather information from a number of different cards; HyperCard can run a lot faster if it doesn't have to update the screen all the time.

Lock screen's counter: HyperTalk keeps track of the number of times you've used the **lock screen** command (or its equivalent, set lockScreen to true). Each **lock screen** must be balanced with an **unlock screen** command (or with set lockScreen to false) or the display remains locked. This scheme lets all the drawing in the following scripts happen with the display locked:

```
on drawOne
   lock screen
   -- draw some stuff
   drawTwo
   -- draw yet more stuff
   unlock screen with visual dissolve -- display now really unlocked
end drawOne

on drawTwo
   lock screen -- second lock
   -- draw even more stuff
   unlock screen -- display still has 1 lock!!
end drawTwo
```

At idle time HyperCard sets the lockscreen property to false and resets the counter.

Also See:

LOCK SCREEN command, page 270
LOCKSCREEN property, page 562
VISUAL command, page 367

UNMARK

Forms

```
unmark [cardExpr | cards where expr | all cards]

unmark this card
unmark card 7
unmark cards where field "City" is "Milpitas"
unmark cards where field "name" is "Winkler" or fld "address" is empty
unmark all cards
```

Action

The **unmark** command, new for HyperCard 2.0, sets the **marked** property of one or more cards to false.

The following example, designed for a real estate stack, prints all the cards whose price per sqare foot is below a given limit:

```
on mouseUp
  rentalSpace 1.20 -- $1.20 per square foot
end mouseUp

on rentalSpace maxPrice
  unmark all cards
  mark cards where ¬
  (field "Price Per Month" / field "Square Feet") < maxPrice
  print marked cards
end rentalSpace
```

Comments

cardExpr refers to a card in the current stack.

A card's **marked** property isn't reset to false when you quit HyperCard. So if you want it reset, you must do it yourself with **unmark.**

Unmark has no effect on a card whose **marked** property is already set to false.

The following example shows how to cull out duplicates in a data base. It's designed to work in a stack of cards representing songs on compact disks.

Each card in the stack includes fields for the song title, the artist, and a list of topics — the example finds all artists who have performed a song about a given topic:

```
on findArtists
  ask "What topic are you interested in?"
  if it is empty then exit mouseUp
  unmark all cards
  mark cards by finding it in field "Topic"
  put empty into artists
  push card
  repeat until the number of marked cards is zero
    go to next marked card
    put field "Artist" & return after artists
    -- unmark all other cards of this same artist
    unmark cards where field "Artist" contains field "Artist"
  end repeat
  pop card
  put artists into field "Artists"
end findArtists
```

Also See:

MARK command, page 273
MARKED property, page 567

VISUAL

Forms

```
visual [effect] effectname {speed} {to image}

visual dissolve
visual effect wipe up
visual iris open very fast
visual effect barn door close very slowly to inverse
```

Action

The **visual** command displays up to 10 visual effects when you change cards with a **Go** command or when a **Find** command is successful.

Here's the canonical `go next card` button script:

```
on mouseUp
   visual effect wipe left
   go to next card
end mouseUp
```

Comments

effectname is the effect itself:

barn door close	barn door open	checkerboard	dissolve
iris close	iris open	plain (or cut)	scroll down
scroll left	scroll right	scroll up	stretch to bottom
stretch to center	shrink to top	shrink to bottom	shrink to center
stretch to top	venetian blinds	wipe down	wipe left
wipe right	wipe up	zoom close	zoom in
zoom open	zoom out		

speed is the speed at which the effect occurs (the faster the machine — for example, the Macintosh II compared with a Macintosh Plus — the more obvious the speed difference):

```
{very} fast           slow{ly}              very slow{ly}
```

In 1.2.# `fast` and `very fast` have the same effect, but `slow` and `very slow` have different effects.

image covers the entire card area at the end of the effect, but before the card reappears (but see the comments on the card image) :

black	card	gray (or grey)	inverse	white

The card image is special in that it's meant to be used in the second line of a two-line visual effect. In the following handler, the old card first goes white and then the new card fades in:

```
on fadeWhite
  visual dissolve to white slowly
  visual dissolve to card slowly
  go next
end fadeWhite
```

You can stack up to 10 visual effects, all of which are executed on the next **go** command. Effects beyond the tenth are ignored, and the list is cleared at idle time:

```
on lotsOfEffects
  visual zoom open
  visual zoom close
  visual barn door open
  visual barn door close
  visual dissolve to white
  visual dissolve to card
  go next
end lotsOfEffects
```

Visual effects on Mac II

To see visual effects on a Macintosh II when you're using any HyperCard version earlier than 2.0, set the number of colors (or gray scales) to 2 in the Monitors section of the Control Panel. If you have more than one monitor, the entire card must be on the main monitor to see visual effects. These restrictions don't apply if you're using version 2.0 or higher.

Nonscripted card changes: Visual effects don't work when you change cards with menu commands or with the arrow keys unless you write a handler trapping the appropriate message:

```
on arrowkey thisKey
  if thisKey <> "right" then pass arrowKey
  visual scroll right
  go next
end arrowkey
```

Find: When a Find is successful, the visual effect works but the rectangle that usually encloses the found text is invisible.

Visual with Unlock Screen: You can use a modified form of Visual with the **unlock screen** command to show visual changes to the current card.

Also See:

FIND command, page 246
LOCK SCREEN command, page 270
LOCKSCREEN property, page 562
UNLOCK SCREEN command, page 363

WAIT

Forms

```
wait {for} integerExpr {tick{s}} -- 1 tick = 1/60th second
wait {for} integerExpr sec{ond}{s}
wait [until | while] condition

wait for 30 -- waits for 30 ticks (1/2 second)
wait stall seconds -- stall is a variable whose value is an integer
wait until the mouse is down -- pause until mouse button is pressed
wait while the mouse is down -- pause as long as mouse btn is pressed
wait while the mouseClick -- clears the click buffer
```

Action

The **wait** command makes HyperCard pause before executing the rest of the running handler for *integerExpr* units, or until or while *condition* is true.

The following handler shows a sequence of cards for a specified number of repetitions, pausing slightly after each card (useful for some kinds of coarse animation):

```
on slowShow howManyCards
  repeat howManyCards times
    go to next card
    wait 10 ticks
  end repeat
end slowShow
```

Comments

integerExpr evaluates to an integer.

You can cancel an operating **wait** by pressing Command-Period.

The following handler prevents HyperCard from leaving a card until all sounds have finished playing:

```
on closeCard
  wait until the sound is "done"
end closeCard
```

The following handler plays a song that has been divided into several different sound resources. (You often have to split a song up like this because the whole thing won't fit in memory.) This handler keeps two sounds in the queue at all times and enqueues another sound as soon as the second one starts playing:

```
smoothSound "cut1,cut2,cut3,cut4" -- sample way to call handler

on smoothSound playList
  play item 1 of playList
  repeat with soundNum = 2 to the number of items in playList
    play item soundNum of playList
    wait until the sound is item soundNum of playList
  end repeat
end smoothSound
```

Also See:

SOUND function, page 472

WRITE

Forms

```
write source to file filename

write field nextField to file "Big Disk:Correspondence:Addresses"
write thisInfo to file myAddressFile
write "No more data available" to file (line 12 of field "Address")
```

Action

The **write** command copies text from *source* to file *filename*, previously opened with the **open file** command. (See "Points for techies.")

The following handler writes the contents of a field to a file:

```
on sendOutData
  open file "Mailing List"
  write field "Names & Addresses" to file "Mailing List"
  close file "Mailing List"
end sendOutData
```

Comments

The data pointer is reset to the start of the file each time the file is opened, and the **write** operation writes from the current position of the data pointer. Each successive **write** command continues from where the last one ended.

The following handler writes the text of every field on every card in the current stack to a file whose name you pass to it. Fields are separated by tabs, and cards are separated by carriage returns:

```
on writeToFile fileName
  open file fileName
  repeat with j = 1 to number of cards
    go card j
    repeat with i = 1 to number of fields
      write field i & tab to file fileName
    end repeat
    repeat with i = 1 to number of cd fields
```

```
      write cd field i & tab to file fileName
    end repeat
    write Return to file fileName
  end repeat
  close file fileName
end writeToFile
```

Appending text: You can't directly append new text to the end of an existing file. You have to read all the text in the file in order to move the data pointer to the bottom of the file, and then add new text:

```
on addToBottom string,fileName
  open file fileName
  repeat -- skip over existing text
    read from file fileName for 16384
    if it is empty then exit repeat
  end repeat
  write string to file fileName -- append new text
  close file fileName
end addToBottom
```

ASCII text: The file commands **open, close, read,** and **write** were designed to be used for importing and exporting text. So information exchanged with these commands is treated as ASCII text.

Automatic file closing: HyperTalk automatically closes all open files when you press Command-Period, when an error occurs, when an **exit to HyperCard** statement executes, or when you quit HyperCard. Even so, you should explicitly close a file when you've finished with it because (1) no other program can access a file that's already open (as you might want to do under MultiFinder), (2) only three files can be open under HyperTalk at the same time, and (3) leaving open files lying about is bad form and makes code difficult to read and to follow.

Write cannot write nulls to a file: When you use either of the following forms, HyperTalk assumes that you're writing the empty string — and so it won't write anything at all:

```
write empty to file "Current" -- the file name is arbitrary
write numToChar(0) to file "Current"
```

Only an external can write a null to a file for you.

Full pathname needed: You must provide a full pathname to *filename* each time you reference it; otherwise, HyperTalk assumes that *filename* is in the same folder as the HyperCard application. If HyperTalk can't find a file named *filename*, it creates one (Creator MACA, Type TEXT — as if MacWrite had made it).

> HyperTalk does no type-checking on *filename*. It opens and writes to the data fork of any file that you name. *You* are responsible for making sure that you don't inadvertently open and write to the wrong file. Opening the data fork of a stack and writing to it, for example, is liable to destroy the stack.

Points for techies: Every file in the Macintosh has two "forks," a data fork and a resource fork. The resource fork contains data of various types (like sounds, icons, windows, menus, code, controls, inits, fonts, cdevs, strings); this data is maintained by the resource manager. The data fork keeps an untyped sequence of bytes that any program can read or write. You can put your own resources into the resource fork of a stack, but HyperCard reserves the data fork of the stack for its own reasons. While the file commands can be useful for manipulating text in nonstack files, you're taking the life of a stack in your hands if you mess around with a stack's data fork.

Also See :

CLOSE FILE command, page 190
OPEN FILE command, page 280
READ command, page 318

Chapter 9

Functions

A function returns a value, usually based on one or more arguments passed to it. Certain system functions such as **the date** and **the time** require no argument; these functions return a value reflecting the current state of the system. In either case, the value of a function is changeable, and is calculated at the time that it's called.

Functions have up to three forms: (1) the *functionName*, (2) *functionName()*, and (3) {the} *functionName* of *factor*. (Legal forms for each function are listed with that function.) When you use a form that ends with parentheses (), the function is sent as a message through the message passing path and can be intercepted (and perhaps redefined) by a handler. When you use one of the other forms, the function is not sent as a message but rather goes directly to HyperCard; because the function call doesn't go through the message passing path, it can't be trapped.

This chapter lists all of HyperCard's built-in functions in alphabetical order. Each function description includes complete syntax and examples that show how to use it, plus any appropriate technical notes and comments about anomalies.

For information on defining your own functions, see the **function** keyword (page 128). To read about the message passing path, see Chapter 1. For a listing of functions and other vocabulary words grouped by type (arithmetic, painting, and so on), see Appendix F. For a summary of all HyperTalk vocabulary words with brief definitions, see Appendix E.

Some functions were added to the language so late that their descriptions couldn't be included in the main body of this book. See "Functions" in Appendix I, "Late Breaking News."

ABS()

Forms

```
the abs of numFactor
abs(numExpr)

abs(-3) -- yields 3
abs(sin(x))
abs(h1-h2)
abs of it
```

Action

The **abs** function returns the absolute value of its argument.

The following example reports the difference in temperature between two locations:

```
on weather
  ask "What's the temperature in San Francisco?"
  put it into sanFranTemp
  ask "What's the temperature in Boston?"
  put it into bostonTemp
  put abs(sanFranTemp-bostonTemp) into tempChange
  answer "That's a difference of" && tempChange && "degrees."
end weather
```

Comments

The absolute value of a number is the numerical value without regard to sign.

The following handler computes the horizontal and vertical difference between two points (very useful for computing offsets):

```
on measure
  put "Click at first point..."
  wait until the mouseClick
  put the clickLoc into click1
  put "Click at second point..."
  wait until the mouseClick
  put the clickLoc into click2
```

```
    put abs(item 1 of click1 - item 1 of click2) into deltaH
    put abs(item 2 of click1 - item 2 of click2) into deltaV
    put "That's" && deltaH && "pixels horizontally and" ¬
    && deltaV && "pixels vertically."
end measure
```

Points for techies: Abs uses integer math if the expression is already in that form from previous calculations, as in `abs (1 - 3 + 2)` or `abs(number of this card - number of card "Fred")`. Otherwise, it uses floating-point math.

ANNUITY()

Forms

```
annuity(interest, periods)

annuity(0.091,12)
```

Action

The **annuity** function returns the present value of an ordinary annuity with payments of one unit, given the interest rate per period and the number of periods.

Comments

Interest is a floating-point value; so you must convert percentages (for example, 8.5 percent) to their floating-point equivalents (.085).

The formula for **annuity** is $(1-(1+interest)-periods)/interest$

The following example calculates amortized monthly payments for any loan amount:

```
on mortgagePayments
  ask "What's the loan amount?" with "150000"
  put it into loan
  ask "What's the interest rate?" with "9.5"
  put it/100 into interest -- convert to floating point value
  ask "How many years?" with "30"
  put it into years
  put loan / annuity(interest/12, years*12) into payment
  set numberFormat to "0.00"
  answer "Your monthly payment is $" & payment with "Yikes!"
end mortgagePayments
```

Also See:

NUMBERFORMAT property, page 585

ATAN()

Forms

```
{the} atan of numFactor

atan(numExpr)
atan(-1)*-4 -- yields 3.141593 (that is, π)
atan(sqrt(3))*3 -- ditto
atan(tan(1)) -- yields 1
```

Action

The **atan** function returns the arctangent (inverse tangent) of its argument.
The result (which is the angle whose tangent equals the given value) is
expressed in radians in the range $\pm\pi/2$.

Comments

One radian is $180/\pi$ degrees. To end up with the result in degrees, use the
formula

```
atan(numExpr)*(180)/pi
```

HyperTalk doesn't have arcsine or arccosine functions: but using the algo-
rithms presented in the Apple Numerics Manual, you can write them like this:

```
function asin x
  put abs of x into y
  if y <= 2^-33 then return x
  if y <= 0.5 then put 1-y*y into y
  else
    put 1-y into y
    put 2*y-y*y into y
  end if
  return atan of (x / sqrt of y)
end asin

function acos x
  return 2 * atan of sqrt of ((1-x)/(1+x))
end acos
```

Also See:

COS function, page 400

AVERAGE()

Forms

```
average(numList)

average(100,85,97,90) -- yields 93
average(num1,num2,num3) -- yields average of values of variables
average(line 2 of field "Grades") -- average of items in line 2
```

Action

The **average** function returns the average of its arguments.

The following example computes the average score:

```
on testResults
  put "88,94,87,79,89,98,97,86" into scores
  put "Average score =" && average(scores)
end testResults
```

Comments

NumList is a comma-separated list of expressions, each of which resolves to a numeric value.

The following handlers draws a bar chart. The line across the chart marks the average point, with the average numeric value noted (Figure 9-1):

```
on mouseUp
  -- make some data
  put empty into data
  repeat with i = 1 to 5+random(30)
    put random(100) into item i of data
  end repeat

  -- make a bar chart of the data
  if the shiftKey is down
  then barChart quickSort(data)
  else barChart data
end mouseUp
```

```
on barChart data
  put 10 into top
  put 10 into left
  put 300 into bottom
  put 500 into right

  -- clear screen, set up tools etc.
  reset paint
  choose select tool
  doMenu "Select All"
  doMenu "Clear Picture"
  doMenu "Select All"
  doMenu "Opaque"
  choose rect tool
  set pattern to 14
  set filled to true

  -- draw chart
  put left into h
  put max(data) into maxValue
  put the number of items in data into dataCount
  put round((right-left)/dataCount) into horizStep
  put round(horizStep * 3/4) into width
  repeat with i = 1 to dataCount
    put round((bottom-top) * item i of data / maxValue) into height
    drag from h,bottom-height to h+width,bottom
    add horizStep to h
  end repeat

  -- draw average line
  choose line tool
  set lineSize to 3
  put round((bottom-top) * average(data) / maxValue) into height
  drag from left,bottom-height to h+width-horizStep,bottom-height
  choose text tool
  click at left+50,bottom-height+5
  type "  Average = " & average(data) & "  "
  choose browse tool
end barChart
```

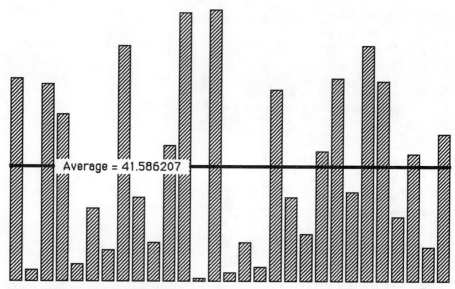

Average = 41.586207

Figure 9-1   Using average with a bar chart

Also See:

MAX function, page 424
MIN function, page 429

CHARTONUM()

Forms

```
{the} charToNum of factor
charToNum(stringExpr)

charToNum("A") -- yields 65
charToNum(fred) -- yields ASCII of value of variable fred
chrToNum of "g" -- yields 103
charToNum(5) -- yields 53
charToNum("abc") -- yields 97, ASCII value of "a"
```

Action

The **charToNum** function returns an ASCII value, given a quoted literal, a digit, or a string expression.

The following function returns true if its argument is an uppercase letter, else false:

```
get isUpperCase(char 1 of fld 1) -- tests 1st character of bg field 1

function isUpperCase letter
  get charToNum(letter)
  return it >= charToNum("A") and it <= charToNum("Z")
end isUpperCase
```

Comments

CharToNum is the inverse of the **numToChar** function (page 440).

If the argument is a quoted literal with more than one character or is a container whose value is longer than one character, **charToNum** operates on the first character and ignores the rest.

The following function takes a string and makes it either all uppercase or lowercase:

```
get changeCase(field 1,toLower) -- get fld 1 as a lower case string
get changeCase(field 1,toUpper) -- get fld 1 as an upper case string
```

```
function changeCase string,direction
  if direction is "toLower" then
    put charToNum("A") into lowBound
    put charToNum("Z") into highBound
    put charToNum("a") - charToNum("A") into index
  else
    put charToNum("a") into lowBound
    put charToNum("z") into highBound
    put charToNum("A") - charToNum("a") into index
  end if
  repeat with i = 1 to the number of chars in string
    get charToNum(char i of string)
    if it >= lowBound and it <= highBound then
      add index to it
      put numToChar(it) into char i of string
    end if
  end repeat
  return string
end changeCase
```

Also See:

ASCII CHART, Appendix A
NUMTOCHAR function, page 440

CLICKCHUNK()

Forms

```
the clickChunk
clickChunk()

put the clickChunk into it
```

Action

The **clickChunk** function, new for HyperCard 2.0, returns the positions of the starting and ending characters of the word or group most recently clicked in a locked field.

Comments

A group of characters is any single word or any contiguous run of text assigned the text style "group" (described under the **textStyle** property).

ClickChunk reports using the form

```
char start to finish of [card|bkgnd] field integer
```

where *start* is the first character selected, *finish* is the last character, and *integer* is the number of a card or background field in the current stack.

To learn the actual text of the chunk clicked, use the **clickText** function or the **value** function:

```
put the clickText
put the value of the clickLine -- returns text of whole line
```

For this function to work the field either must be locked, or you must command-click over the field.

The following example uses **clickChunk** to locate cross-references and annotations. In the fields affected by this script, text that goes to a cross-reference when clicked appears in boldface, and text that displays an annotation in a pop-up field appears in italic. The script uses the **textStyle** of the **clickChunk** to determine what to do:

```
on mouseUp
  -- this mouseUp handler goes in the stack script
  if "field" is not in the target
  then pass mouseUp -- only works on fields
  get the textStyle of the clickChunk
  if it is italic -- annotation
  then show card field the clickText
  else if it is bold -- cross reference
  then find the clickText
  else answer "Sorry, no more info on " & the clickText
end mouseUp
```

Also See:

CLICK command, page 186
CLICKTEXT function, page 395
TEXTSTYLE property, page 632
VALUE function, page 487

CLICKH()

Forms

```
the clickH
clickH()

put the clickH into it
```

Action

The **clickH** function returns the distance (in pixels) of the most recent mouse click from the left edge of the card window.

The following button script will tell you on which side of the button you clicked (useful for dividing a button into distinct areas as shown in Figure 9-2):

```
on mouseUp
  if the clickH < item 1 of loc of me -- loc is center point
  then put "You clicked on the left side."
  else put "You clicked on the right side."
end mouseUp
```

<- Left Side   Right Side ->

Figure 9-2   Button with distinct areas

(For another example of breaking a button up into multiple areas, see Figure 10-8.)

Comments

The number that **clickH()** returns is the first item of the **clickLoc** function.

When you use the `clickH()` form, put nothing between the parentheses or you'll get an error message.

The following handler measures the horizontal distance between two points. It reports its result in the message box; press the Enter key to measure something else:

```
on measure
  put "Click at the left edge..."
  wait until the mouseClick
  put the clickH into left
  put "Click at the right edge..."
  wait until the mouseClick
  put the clickH into right
  put "measure -- That distance is " & right - left & " pixels."
end measure
```

ClickH is not necessarily mouseH: The horizontal location of the last mouse click is not necessarily the same as the current horizontal position of the mouse, because the mouse might have moved since the click. To find the current horizontal position of the mouse, use the **mouseH** function.

Also See:

CLICK command, page 186
CLICKLOC function, page 393
CLICKV function, page 397
LOC property, page 556
MOUSEH function, page 433
MOUSELOC function, page 435

CLICKLINE()

Forms

```
the clickLine
clickLine()

put the clickLine into it
```

Action

The **clickLine** function, new in HyperCard 2.0, identifies the line most recently clicked in a locked field.

Comments

clickLine reports using the form

```
line integer of [card|bkgnd] field integer
```

with the field always in the current stack.

The following example, which belongs in a field script, removes an item (when you click on it) from a "to do" list and puts it into a "done" list. The handler belongs in the script of the "to do" field:

```
on mouseUp
  get the value of the clickLine
  if it is empty then exit mouseUp
  delete the clickLine
  put it & return after card field "Done"
end mouseUp
```

To learn the actual text of the line clicked, use the **value** function:

```
put the value of the clickLine -- returns text of line clicked
```

Line defined: To HyperTalk, a line is that which ends with a Return character. So "line 3" means "the line of text between the second and third Return characters in the field". Because text can wrap in a field unless its dontWrap property is set to true, many *screen* lines of text can make up a single line ending in a Return character.

Also See:

CLICK command, page 186
VALUE function, page 487

CLICKLOC()

Forms

```
the clickLoc
clickLoc()

put the clickLoc into it
```

Action

The **clickLoc** function returns the location of the most recent mouse click.

The following handler repeatedly tells you where you clicked until you click with the shift key down:

```
on mouseUp
  repeat forever
    wait until the mouseClick
    put the shiftKey is down into done
    put "You clicked at " & the clickLoc
    if done then exit mouseUp
  end repeat
end mouseUp
```

Comments

This function returns two numbers separated by a comma, representing the distance in pixels from, respectively, the left and top edges of the card window.

The two items that **clickLoc** returns correspond to the **clickH** and **clickV** functions, respectively.

When you use the `clickLoc()` form, put nothing between the parentheses or you'll get an error message.

The following example draws a circle whose diameter you define by clicking at two points on the screen:

```
on mouseUp
  -- get points
  set cursor to plus
```

```
wait until the mouseClick
put the clickLoc into point1
wait until the mouseClick
put the clickLoc into point2

-- compute center and radius
put (item 1 of point1 + item 1 of point2) div 2 into midH
put (item 2 of point1 + item 2 of point2) div 2 into midV
put abs(item 1 of point1 - midH) into deltaH
put abs(item 2 of point1 - midV) into deltaV
put round(sqrt(deltaH^2+deltaV^2)) into radius

-- draw a circle
choose oval tool
set lineSize to 2
set centered to true
drag from midH,midV to midH+radius,midV+radius
choose browse tool
end mouseUp
```

ClickLoc is not necessarily mouseLoc: The location of the last mouse click is not necessarily the same as the current position of the mouse because the mouse might have moved since the click. To find the current mouse location, use the **mouseLoc** function.

Also See:

CLICK command, page 186
CLICKH function, page 389
CLICKV function, page 397
MOUSELOC function, page 435

CLICKTEXT()

Forms

```
the clickText
clickText()

put the clickText into it
```

Action

The **clickText** function, new in HyperCard 2.0, returns the word or group of characters most recently clicked in a locked field.

Comments

A group of characters is any single word, or a contiguous run of text assigned the text style "group" (described under the **textStyle** property).

When you click on white space, **clickText** returns empty.

The following handler looks up a clicked word or group in a glossary:

```
on mouseUp
  -- this mouseUp handler goes in the stack script
  if field is not in the target
  then pass mouseUp -- only works on fields
  get the clickText
  lock screen
  go to stack "Glossary"
  find it
  if the result is not empty then
    go back
    answer "Sorry, no further information on " & it
  end if
end mouseUp
```

Also See:

CLICK command, page 186
CLICKCHUNK function, page 387
TEXTSTYLE property, page 632

CLICKV()

Forms

```
the clickV
clickV()

put the clickV into it
```

Action

The **clickV** function returns the distance of the last mouse click from the top edge of the card window (just below the window's title).

Comments

The **clickV**, which is measured in pixels, is the second item of the **clickloc.**

When you use the `clickV()` form, put nothing between the parentheses or you'll get an error message.

ClickV is not necessarily mouseV: The vertical location of the last mouse click is not necessarily the same as the current vertical position of the mouse because the mouse might have moved since the click. To find the current vertical position of the mouse, use the **mouseV** function.

The following handler shows the difference between clickV and mouseV as you move the mouse around. (Press the shift key when you've had enough):

```
on mouseUp
  repeat until the shiftKey is down
    get the mouseClick
    put "ClickV = " & the clickV & ", MouseV = " & the mouseV
  end repeat
end mouseUp
```

Also See:

CLICK command, page 186
CLICKH function, page 389
MOUSELOC function, page 435
MOUSEV function, page 437

COMMANDKEY()

Forms

```
the commandKey
the cmdKey
commandKey()
cmdKey()

put the commandKey into it
```

Action

The **commandKey** (or **cmdKey**) function returns the state of the command key (up or down).

Comments

When you use the `commandKey()` form, put nothing between the parentheses or you'll get an error message.

The following handler adds a level of safety to HyperCard's **delete** functions: If you don't have the command key pressed, it asks you to confirm deletions:

```
on doMenu what
  if the commandKey is down then pass doMenu
  if "Clear" is not in what and "Delete" is not in what
  then pass doMenu
  answer "OK to delete?" with "OK" or "Cancel"
  if it is "OK" then pass doMenu
end doMenu
```

COMPOUND()

Forms

```
compound(interest, periods)

put compound(percentRate/100,1) * principal into newValue
put compound(0.05,4) * 10000 -- yields 12155.0625
```

Action

The **compound** function returns the principal plus accrued interest on an investment of 1 unit, given the interest rate and number of periods.

Comments

Interest is a floating-point value; so you must convert percentages (for example, 8.5 percent) to their floating-point equivalents (.085).

The formula for **compound** is (1+*interest*) * *periods*.

The following example returns the value of an investment over any period of years at any interest rate:

```
on futureValue
   ask "What's the investment amount?" with "1000"
   put it into investment
   ask "What's the interest rate?" with "7.5"
   put it/100 into interest
   ask "How many years?" with "3"
   put it into years
   put compound(interest, years) * investment into value
   set numberFormat to "0.00"
   answer "The compounded value is $" & value with "Thank you!"
end futureValue
```

COS()

Forms

```
{the} cos of numFactor
cos(numExpr)

cos(pi) -- yields -1
cos(theta)
```

Action

The **cos** function returns the cosine of its argument.

HyperTalk has no secant function but you can write one as follows:

```
function sec x
   return 1 / cos of x
end sec
```

Comments

The argument must be in radians. One radian is $180/\pi$ degrees (about 57.3 degrees).

Cosine is defined as the ratio of the length of the adjacent side of an acute angle in a right triangle to the length of the hypothenuse.

The following excessive two-handler example draws a pie chart (see Figure 9-3):

```
on mouseUp
  put empty into data
  repeat with i = 1 to 4+random(8) -- number of wedges
    put random(100) into item i of data -- value for each wedge
  end repeat
  pieChart data
end mouseUp

on pieChart data
   -- compute total of values, and top,left,bottom,right of chart
   put 250 into pieCenterH
   put 160 into pieCenterV
```

```
put 150 into pieRadius
put the number of items in data into dataCount
put zero into total
repeat with i = 1 to dataCount
  add item i of data to total
end repeat
put pieCenterV - pieRadius into pieTop
put pieCenterV + pieRadius into pieBottom
put pieCenterH - pieRadius into pieLeft
put pieCenterH + pieRadius into pieRight

-- clear screen, draw bounding circle, draw first line
reset paint
choose select tool
doMenu "Select All"
doMenu "Clear Picture"
choose oval tool
set lineSize to 2
drag from pieLeft,pieTop to pieRight,pieBottom
choose line tool
drag from pieCenterH,pieCenterV to pieCenterH,pieCenterV-pieRadius

-- draw a wedge for each value and fill it in
put zero into angle
repeat with i = 1 to dataCount
  put pi * item i of data / total into halfChange
  add halfChange to angle
  put pieCenterH + round((pieRadius-3) * sin(angle)) into halfH
  put pieCenterV - round((pieRadius-3) * cos(angle)) into halfV
  add halfChange to angle
  put pieCenterH + round(pieRadius * sin(angle)) into h
  put pieCenterV - round(pieRadius * cos(angle)) into v
  choose line tool
  drag from pieCenterH,pieCenterV to h,v
  if halfChange > .01 then -- don't try to fill very small wedges
    set pattern to item (i mod 12)+1 ¬
    of "2,13,11,3,14,6,21,17,31,18,4,32"
    choose bucket tool
    click at halfH, halfV
```

```
      end if
   end repeat
   choose browse tool
end pieChart
```

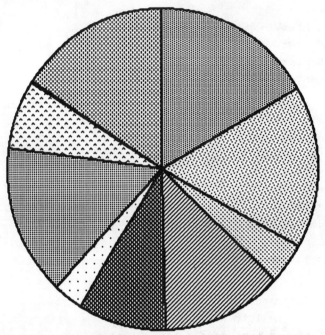

Figure 9-3   Pie chart (yours will look different because of random function)

Also See:

ATAN function, page 380

DATE()

Forms

```
the {long|short|abbr{ev{iated}}} date
date()

put the long date into it
```

Action

The **date** function returns the current date.

The following background handler records the date that the text in any field on a card has been changed. (It assumes the existance of a background field named "Last Modified"):

```
on closeField
  put the date into field "Last Modified"
end closeField
```

Comments

The form `date()` gets a response in the form `mm/dd/yy`.

When you use any variation of the form `the {long|short|abbr{ev{iated}}} date,` the response you get depends upon the modifier (but because of a bug in versions through 1.2.#, all adjectives are ignored when you use parentheses). Table 9-1 shows the possibilities:

Table 9-1:   Date formats

Modifier	Response
short date	7/7/88
abbr{ev{iated}} date	Thu, Jul 7, 1988
long date	Thursday, July 7, 1988
date	7/7/88

The **date** is a localizable function; so how it actually appears will differ from country to country. **Seconds,** however, is universal. If your stacks are being used internationally, store the date in seconds and convert it back:

```
on closeField
  get the seconds
  put it into field "Last Modified Seconds" -- presumably hidden
  convert it to date
  put it into field "Last Modified Date" -- so the user can see it
end closeField
```

```
on openCard
  get field "Last Modified Seconds" -- hidden field
  convert it to date
  put it into field "Last Modified Date" -- so the user can see it
end openCard
```

Keep parentheses empty: When you use the `date()` form, put nothing between the parentheses or you'll get an error message.

Also See:

CONVERT command, page 199
TIME function, page 482

DISKSPACE()

Forms

```
the diskSpace
diskSpace()

put the diskSpace into it
```

Action

The **diskSpace** function returns the space in bytes remaining on the volume holding the current stack.

The following closeStack handler compacts a stack if its free size is greater than 1/10 the total free disk space:

```
on closeStack
  if the freeSize of this stack > 1/10 * the diskSpace
  then doMenu "Compact Stack"
end closeStack
```

Comments

When you use the `diskSpace()` form, put nothing between the parentheses or you'll get an error message.

Also See:

DEBUG command, page 206
FREESIZE property, page 536
HEAPSPACE function, page 417
SIZE property, page 614
STACKSPACE property, page 475
VERSION property, page 645

EXP()

Forms

```
{the} exp of numFactor
exp(numExpr)

exp(1) -- yields the constant e (2.718282)
```

Action

The **exp** function returns the natural exponential of its argument.

Comments

The exponential is the constant e raised to the power of the argument, where e is 2.718281828 (or so).

The following example computes exponential population growth:

```
on mouseUp
  ask "What's the starting population?" with 200000000
  put it into startPop
  ask "What's the growth rate per period?" with 0.023
  put it into growthRate
  ask "How many periods?" with 20
  put it into timePeriods
  put startPop*exp(growthRate*timePeriods) into endPop
  answer "Ending population will be " & trunc(endPop)
end mouseUp
```

Also See:

EXP1 function, page 407
LN function, page 421
LN1 function, page 422

EXP1()

Forms

```
{the} exp1 of numFactor
exp1(numExpr)

put exp1(10^-5) -- yields 0.00001
```

Action

The **exp1** function returns the natural exponential of its argument -1, such that $exp1(x) = exp(x) - 1$

Comments

The exponential is the constant *e* raised to the power of the argument, where *e* is 2.718281828.

This function has been designed such that accuracy near zero won't be lost.

The following handler computes a compound interest rate given a simple interest rate. It uses a formula (supplied by Paul Finlayson of Apple Computer) that gives very precise results even when the rate is very small or the frequency of compounding is very large, or both:

```
on mouseUp
  ask "What's the simple interest rate?" with 7
  put it/100 into simpleRate
  ask "Compounded how many times a year?" with 4
  put it into periods
  put exp1(periods*ln1(simpleRate/periods)) into compoundRate
  answer "That's a compound rate of " & compoundRate*100
end mouseUp
```

Also See:

EXP function, page 406
LN function, page 421
LN1 function, page 422

EXP2()

Forms

```
{the} exp2 of numFactor
exp2(numExpr)

put exp2(32) -- yields 4294967296, the number of possibilities in 32 bits
put exp2(16) -- yields 65536, what computers used in the old days
```

Action

The **exp2** function returns the value 2 raised to the power of its argument. It's the same as $2^{\wedge}numExpr$.

The following handler produces a terribly useful chart showing the highest values possible for numbers from 1 to 16 bits long:

```
on bitValues
   set textFont of field 1 to Monaco
   put "              " into spaces -- 14 spaces
   put "Bit count" & "     " & "Highest value" into field 1-- 5 spaces
   repeat with bits = 1 to 16
      put return & "    " & bits & spaces & exp2(bits) - 1 after field 1—4 spaces
   end repeat
end bitValues
```

Comments

This function is in the language only because the Standard Apple Numeric environment (SANE) offers it.

Also See:

EXP function, page 406
LN function, page 421
LN1 function, page 422

FOUNDCHUNK()

Forms

```
the foundChunk
foundChunk()

put empty into the foundChunk -- delete what was found
```

Action

The **foundChunk** function returns the starting and ending positions of the chunk of text located by the most recent Find command.

Comments

FoundChunk always uses the form

```
char start to finish of [card|bkgnd] field integer
```

where *start* is the first character found, *finish* is the last character, and *integer* is the number of the card or background field in the current stack.

The following functions report all occurrences of a given string throughout the current stack:

```
on mouseUp
   ask "Find all occurrences of what?"
   put findAll(it) into card field 1
end mouseUp

function findAll whatToFind
   push card
   lock screen
   find whole whatToFind
   put the foundChunk into startChunk
   put empty into matches
   repeat until the foundChunk is empty
      set cursor to busy
      put the foundChunk & " of card " & number of this card & return ¬
      after matches
      find whole whatToFind
```

```
    if the foundChunk is startChunk then exit repeat
  end repeat
  pop card
  unlock screen
  return matches
end findAll
```

Keep parentheses empty: When you use the `foundChunk()` form, put nothing between the parentheses or you'll get an error message.

When foundChunk returns empty: **foundChunk** returns empty when the **Find** command finds nothing, or when any one of the following events happens between the most recent **Find** and when you ask for the **foundChunk:**

• HyperCard moves from one card to another.

• The tool changes.

• A character is typed, either at the keyboard or with the **Type** command.

• A mouseDown event happens, either by a physical mouse click or by a **Click** command.

Also See:

FIND command, page 246
FOUNDFIELD function, page 411
FOUNDLINE function, page 413
FOUNDTEXT function, page 415
RESULT function, page 454

FOUNDFIELD()

Forms

```
the foundField
foundField()

put value of the foundField into thePoop
-- puts entire contents of field that was found in
```

Action

The **foundField** function identifies the field where the most recent **Find** command located text.

Comments

FoundField always uses the form

```
[card|bkgnd] field integer
```

where *integer* is the number of the field holding the found text.

In versions through 1.2.#, there's no built-in way to stop HyperCard from searching in certain fields. (The **dontSearch** property was added for version 2.0.) The following handler implements this missing "dontSearch" feature; it overrides find and prevents it from finding in any field that has the phrase

```
-- Don't Search
```

anywhere in its script. As a bonus, it also has a line that prevents searching in hidden fields.

```
on find
  lock screen
  put the id of this card into startCard
  send the params to HyperCard
  if the result is not empty then exit find
  put the id of this card into firstCard
  put the foundChunk into firstField
  repeat while "-- Don't Search" is in the script of the foundField ¬
    or visible of the foundField is false -- Skip hidden fields
    set cursor to busy
```

```
      send the params to HyperCard
      if the id of this card is firstCard ¬
      and the foundChunk is firstField then
         go to startCard
         send "find empty" to HyperCard -- deselect find rectangle
         exit find
      end if
   end repeat
end find
```

Keep parentheses empty: When you use the `foundField()` form, put nothing between the parentheses or you'll get an error message.

When foundField returns empty: FoundField returns empty when the **Find** command finds nothing, or when any one of the following events happens between the most recent **Find** and when you ask for the **foundField:**

• HyperCard moves from one card to another.

• The tool changes.

• A character is typed, either at the keyboard or with the **Type** command.

• A mouseDown event happens, either by a physical mouse click or by a **Click** command.

Also See:

FIND command, page 246
FOUNDCHUNK function, page 409
FOUNDLINE function, page 413
FOUNDTEXT function, page 415
RESULT function, page 454

FOUNDLINE()

Forms

```
the foundLine
foundLine()

get the foundLine
put foundLine() into whichLine
```

Action

The **foundLine** function identifies the line in which text was located by the most recent **Find** command.

Comments

FoundLine always uses the form

```
line integer of [ [card|bkgnd] field integer ]
```

The **foundLine** is a location, not the text at that location. In the following example, line 3 of field 7 holds "The way the world ends." The search is for "world":

```
on searchIt
   find "world"
   put the foundline into fld 1 -- gives "line 3 of bkgnd field 7"
   wait 2 seconds
   put value of the foundline into fld 2 -- gives "The way the world ends"
end searchIt
```

When foundLine returns empty: foundLine returns empty when the **Find** command finds nothing or when any one of the following events happens between the most recent **Find** and when you ask for the **foundLine:**

• HyperCard moves from one card to another.

• The tool changes.

• A character is typed, either at the keyboard or with the **Type** command.

• A mouseDown event happens, either by a physical mouse click or by a **Click** command.

Keep parentheses empty: When you use the `foundLine()` form, put nothing between the parentheses or you'll get an error message.

Line defined: To HyperTalk, a line is that which ends with a Return character. So "line 3" means "the line of text between the second and third Return characters in the field." Because text wraps in a field, many *screen* lines of text can make up a single line ending in a Return character.

Also See:

FIND command, page 246
FOUNDCHUNK function, page 409
FOUNDLINE function, page 413
RESULT function, page 454

FOUNDTEXT()

Forms

```
the foundText
foundText()

put the foundText into actualMatch
if the foundText is not the value of the foundChunk then beep 3
```

Action

The **foundText** function returns the text located by the most recent **Find** command.

Comments

The information returned by **foundText** depends upon the form of the **Find** command used to locate the found text. But it always returns what **find** encloses in its found box. (See page 246 for information on **Find**.)

The following handler tries to find exactly what you asked for. If it can't, the handler tries to find what you asked for as a word start. If the second try succeeds, it informs you of the difference between what it found and what you asked for:

```
on mouseUp
  ask "What do you want to find?"
  put it into whatToFind
  find whole whatToFind -- see if we can match exactly
  if the result is not empty then -- try wordstart now
    put "Couldn't find " & whatToFind into report
    find whatToFind
    if the result is empty
    then put ", only " & the foundText after report
    answer report
  end if
end mouseUp
```

Keep parentheses empty: When you use the foundText() form, put nothing between the parentheses or you'll get an error message.

When foundText returns empty: foundText returns empty when the **Find** command finds nothing or when any one of the following events happens between the most recent **Find** and when you ask for the **foundText:**

• HyperCard moves from one card to another.

• The tool changes.

• A character is typed, either at the keyboard or with the **Type** command.

• A mouseDown event happens, either by a physical mouse click or by a **Click** command.

Also See:

FIND command, page 246
FOUNDCHUNK function, page 409
FOUNDFIELD function, page 411
FOUNDLINE function, page 413
RESULT function, page 454

HEAPSPACE()

Forms

```
the heapSpace
heapSpace()

if the heapSpace < 20000 then answer "Not enough RAM for that sound."
put "There's " & heapSpace() div 1024 & "K available"
```

Action

The **heapSpace** function returns the maximum contiguous amount of space in the application heap (in bytes) that would be available if all purgeable handles were purged and all relocateable handles were relocated.

Comments

HeapSpace is one of several commands, functions, and properties built into the language as aids to the development of HyperCard itself, and therefore of primary use only to the HyperCard programming team at Apple Computer Inc. So you don't have to feel guilty about ignoring it.

The following handler repeatedly checks an XCMD to see if it's allocating memory without releasing that memory later. (Any number greater than 0 means it's leaking memory):

```
on testXCMD xcmd,count
  if count is empty then put 100 into count
  put the heapSpace into startSpace
  repeat count times
    do xcmd
  end repeat
  put (startSpace -- the heapSpace) div 1024 & "K change in heap space."
end testXCMD
```

Keep parentheses empty: When you use the form heapspace(), put nothing within the parentheses; otherwise you'll get an error message.

Also See:

DEBUG command, page 206
STACKSPACE function, page 475
VERSION property, page 645

LENGTH()

Forms

```
{the} length of stringExpr
length(stringExpr)

sort by the length of field 1
if length(it) is not number of chars in it
then answer "Something's wrong."
```

Action

The **length** function returns the number of characters in the value of its argument.

Comments

If **length's** argument is not in quotation marks, HyperTalk assumes that the argument is a container, a chunk expression, property, or function call.

The following handler warns you when a field is nearing its character limit (a total of 29,996 characters):

```
on closeField
  if the length of me > 28000
  then put "This field is getting full."
end closeField
```

When you read text from a file, tabs are converted to double spaces as the text goes into a field. In the following example, the second handler expands tabs to spaces such that the text looks right in a field. It's assumed that the text you're de-tabbing comes from the file read in the first handler:

```
on mouseUp
  open file "tab file"
  read from file "tab file" for 2000
  close file "tab file"
  put deTab(it,8) into card field 1
end mouseUp

function detab text,tabSize
```

```
    put 1 into column
    put empty into cleanText
    repeat with i = 1 to the number of chars in text
      set cursor to busy
      get char i of text
      if it is tab then
        get " "
        repeat
          add 1 to column
          if column mod tabSize is zero then exit repeat
          put " " after it
        end repeat
      else if it is return then put 1 into column
      else add 1 to column
      put it after cleanText
    end repeat
    return cleanText
end detab
```

LN()

Forms

```
{the} ln of numFactor
ln(numExpr)

put ln(exp(1))  -- puts 1
```

Action

The **ln** function returns the natural logarithm of the value of the argument.

Comments

This function, like all HyperCard math functions, uses SANE extended precision arithmetic.

The following handler tells you how many digits it takes to represent a given number in a given base:

```
on mouseUp
  ask "What's your number?" with 65535
  put it into number
  ask "What base?" with 2
  put it into base
  put 1+trunc(ln(number)/ln(base)) into digitCount
  answer "That requires " & digitCount & " digits."
end mouseUp
```

Also See:

EXP function, page 406
LN1 function, page 422

LN1()

Forms

```
{the} ln1 of numFactor
ln1(numExpr)

get ln1 of 0.00001
```

Action

The **ln1** function returns the natural logarithm of the sum of 1 plus the value of the argument.

Comments

The formula for this function is

```
ln1(numExpr)= ln(numExpr + 1)
```

For values close to 0, this function is more accurate than **ln**.

The following handler computes a compound interest rate given a simple interest rate. It uses a formula (supplied by Paul Finlayson of Apple Computer) that gives very precise results even when the rate is very small or the frequency of compounding is very large, or both:

```
on mouseUp
  ask "What's the simple interest rate?" with 7
  put it/100 into simpleRate
  ask "Compounded how many times a year?" with 4
  put it into periods
  put exp1(periods*ln1(simpleRate/periods)) into compoundRate
  answer "That's a compound rate of " & compoundRate*100
end mouseUp
```

Also See:

EXP function, page 406
LN function, page 421

LOG2()

Forms

```
{the} log2 of numFactor
log2(numExpr)

put log2(2^32) -- yields 32
```

Action

The **log2** function returns the base 2 logarithm of its argument.

Comments

The following handler returns the log of a value to any base:

```
put logx(16,4) -- returns 2

function logx value, base -- thanks to Giovanni Paoletti
  return log2(value)/log2(base)
end logx
```

MAX()

Forms

```
max(numList)

max(3,4,5)
max(it) -- it contains an item list
```

Action

The **max** function returns the highest numeric value in a comma-separated list.

Comments

When *numList* has more than one line, max ignores every line beyond the first.

Every item in the list must evaluate to a number. If any item in *numList* evaluates to nonnumeric data, **max** gives an error message.

NumList can contain a mixture of integer and floating-point numbers:

```
    put max(13, 126.7, thisVar/thatVar)
```

But it can't contain a mixture of single and list values. For example, if the variable thisList contains "2,5,6,7" you can't say:

```
    put max(23, thisList, thisVar/thatVar) -- this ain't right
```

The following example computes a greatest common divisor using Euclid's algorithm:

```
on mouseUp
  ask "First number?"
  put it into num1
  ask "Second number?"
  put it into num2
  answer "Greatest common divisor is " & gcd(num1,num2)
end mouseUp

function gcd num1,num2
  -- compute greatest common divisor using Euclid's algorithm
```

```
   put max(num1,num2) into highValue
   put min(num1,num2) into lowValue
   repeat
      put highValue mod lowValue into remainder
      put lowValue into highValue
      put remainder into lowValue
      if remainder = 0 then exit repeat
   end repeat
   return highValue
end gcd
```

Also See:

AVERAGE function, page 382
MIN function, page 429

MENUS()

Forms

```
the menus
menus()

put the menus into field 1
answer the menus
```

Action

The **menus** function, new for HyperCard 2.0, returns a return-separated list of the menu names currently on the menu bar.

Comments

Each time you create or delete a menu, or when you issue the **reset menuBar**, the list returned by **the menus** is liable to change (because what appears on the menu bar is liable to change).

Line 1 of the list that **the menus** returns is the leftmost menu name; the last line in the list is the rightmost menu name. The first five menu names in **the menus** are usually Apple, File, Edit, Go, and Tools (unless one or more of these menus has been deleted).

The following handler checks **the menus** to see if a menu already exists before trying to create it:

```
on makeUtilities
  if "Utilities" is in the menus then exit to HyperCard
  create menu "Utilities"
  -- Code to create rest of menu goes here
end makeUtilities
```

The following more sophisticated example extends the clipboard: it creates a menu that lets you paste the last five text selections that have been cut or copied:

```
on doMenu whichItem,whichMenu
  global cut1,cut2,cut3,cut4,cut5

  if whichMenu is "Paste" then -- do the paste
```

```
    if the selectedChunk is empty
    then answer "Nowhere to paste"
    else
      get value("cut" & word 2 of whichItem)
      put it into the selection
    end if
    exit doMenu
  end if

  if whichItem is not "Cut Text" ¬
  and whichItem is not "Copy Text"
  then pass doMenu

  -- make room for the latest cut
  repeat with i = 4 down to 1
    do "put cut" & i & " into cut" & i+1
  end repeat
  put the selection into cut1

  -- make sure the paste menu is there
  if "Paste" is not in the menus then
    create menu "Paste"
    put "Paste 1,Paste 2,Paste 3,Paste 4,Paste 5" into menu "Paste"
  end if

  -- update the menu names
  repeat with i = 1 to 5
    get value("cut" & i)
    if the number of words in it > 1
    then get word 1 of it & "..."
    if it is not empty
    then get " (" & it & ")"
    set name of menuItem i of menu "Paste" to ¬
    "Paste " & i & it
  end repeat

  -- do the cut
  pass doMenu
end doMenu
```

To learn the name of an individual menu or menu item, use the **name of menu** property.

Only HyperCard Menus Returned: Menus returns the names of menus created by HyperCard (including the ones you create with the **create menu** command). It doesn't return menus created by desk accessories or ancillary programs.

Also See:

CREATE MENU command, page 202
DELETE MENU command, page 215
NAME OF *MENU* property, page 576
PUT INTO MENU command, page 312
RESET MENUBAR command, page 322

MIN()

Forms

```
min(numList)

put min(score1,score2) into losingScore
put min(5,3,9) -- yields 3
```

Action

The **min** function returns the lowest numeric value in a comma-separated list.

Comments

When *numList* has more than one line, **min** ignores every line beyond the first.

Every item in the list must evaluate to a number. If any item in *numList* evaluates to nonnumeric data, **min** gives an error message.

NumList can contain a mixture of integer and floating-point value:

```
put min(13, 126.7, thisVar/thatVar)
```

But it can't contain a mixture of single and list values. For example, if the variable thisList contains "2,5,6,7" you can't say:

```
put min(23, thisList, thisVar/thatVar)
```

Min operates only on the first line of an expression. Here's a function that finds the minimum line among all the lines of an expression:

```
function minLine list
  put line 1 of list into result
  repeat with i = 2 to the number of lines in list
    put min(line i of list,result) into result
  end repeat
  return result
end minLine
```

Also See:

AVERAGE function, page 382
MAX function, page 424

MOUSE()

Forms

```
the mouse
mouse()

repeat until the mouse is down
if the mouse is up then exit repeat
```

Action

The **mouse** function returns the state of the mouse button (up or down).

Comments

When you use the `mouse()` form, put nothing between the parentheses or you'll get an error message.

The following handler continually draws lines radiating from the button holding the handler to the current pointer location. It stops drawing when you release the mouse button:

```
on mouseDown
   choose line tool
   reset paint
   repeat until the mouse is up
      drag from the loc of me to the mouseLoc
   end repeat
   choose browse tool
end mouseDown
```

MOUSECLICK()

Forms

```
the mouseClick
mouseClick()

wait until the mouseClick -- wait for the user to click
```

Action

The **mouseClick** function returns either true or false, reflecting whether the mouse has been clicked since the last idle message.

Comments

MouseClick works well with the wait command:

```
wait until the mouseClick
```

This is the same as

```
wait until the mouse is down
wait until the mouse is up
```

MouseClick is especially useful for killing extra clicks in unwanted double clicks:

```
wait while the mouseClick -- clears the click buffer
```

MouseClick returns true if there's a mouse click in the event queue and, as part of its intrinsic action, it removes the click. So you can use it to kill inadvertent clicks. The following handler uses this technique to get rid of any mouseclicks that might acumulate as a card is flashing by. (Such stray clicks would ordinarily accumulate during a running handler; when the handler stopped running, the clicks would take effect on the current card.)

```
on mouseUp
  go to next card
  wait 20 ticks -- user might click during these 20 ticks
  go to next card
  wait while the mouseClick -- discard any mouseClicks
end mouseUp
```

Keep parentheses empty: When you use the form `mouseClick()`, put nothing within the parentheses; otherwise you'll get an error message.

Also See:

WAIT command, page 370

MOUSEH()

Forms

```
the mouseH
mouseH()

get the mouseH
if the mouseH > right of me then go to next card
```

Action

The **mouseH** function returns the distance (in pixels) from the pointer to the left edge of the card window.

Comments

MouseH, which is measured in pixels, is the first item of the **mouseloc** function.

The following handler returns the location of the mouse in global coordinates (that is coordinates relative to the corners of the display device). Use this handler to position the card window on large screens:

```
show card window at globalMouseLoc() -- A possible call

function globalMouseLoc
  return the mouseH + left of card window & "," & ¬
  the mouseV + top of card window
end globalMouseLoc
```

Keep parentheses empty: When you use the `mouseH()` form, put nothing between the parentheses or you'll get an error message.

Points for techies: The window is pinned to multiples of 16 pixels horizontally so that it will always be at an even address in memory. Additionally, the card window is a whole number of longwords wide. These facts allow HyperCard to copy its internal buffer onto the screen using a very tight loop that moves whole longwords at a time.

Also See:

CLICK command, page 186
CLICKLOC function, page 393
CLICKV function, page 397
MOUSELOC function, page 435
MOUSEV function, page 437

MOUSELOC()

Forms

```
the mouseLoc
mouseLoc()

put the mouseLoc into thisLoc
if the mouseLoc is within rect of me then beep
```

Action

The **mouseLoc** function returns the current location of the pointer.

Comments

This function returns two numbers separated by a comma, representing the distance in pixels between the left and top edges of the card window and the pointer's current location.

The top of the card window is just below the title bar.

The following example reports what field or button the pointer is over, even if the field or button is hidden:

```
on mouseUp
  repeat until the mouseClick
    get the mouseLoc
    -- find what button or field the mouse is over
    put empty into list
    repeat with i = 1 to the number of buttons
      if it is within rect of button i
      then put name of button i & ", " after list
    end repeat
    repeat with i = 1 to the number of bkgnd buttons
      if it is within rect of bkgnd button i
      then put name of bkgnd button i & ", " after list
    end repeat
    repeat with i = 1 to the number of fields
      if it is within rect of field i
      then put name of field i & ", " after list
```

```
    end repeat
    repeat with i = 1 to the number of card fields
       if it is within rect of card field i
       then put name of card field i & ", " after list
    end repeat
    if list is empty then put "No button or field here"
    else put char 1 to length(list)-2 of list
  end repeat
end mouseUp
```

MouseLoc is mouseH and mouseV: The two items that **mouseLoc** returns correspond to the **mouseH** and **mouseV** functions, respectively.

Keep parentheses empty: When you use the `mouseLoc()` form, put nothing between the parentheses or you'll get an error message.

Also See:

CLICK command, page 186
CLICKLOC function, page 393
CLICKV function, page 397
MOUSEH function, page 433
MOUSEV function, page 437

MOUSEV()

Forms

```
the mouseV
mouseV()

if the mouseV < top of me then beep 3 -- mouse is above me
```

Action

The **mouseV** function returns the location of the pointer relative to the top edge of the card window (just below the window's title).

Comments

MouseV, which is measured in pixels, is the second item of the **mouseloc.**

The following handler continually reports the vertical position of the pointer until you click the mouse:

```
on mouseUp
  repeat until the mouseClick
    put "The pointer's at vertical position" && the mouseV
  end repeat
end mouseUp
```

Keep parentheses empty: When you use the mouseV() form, put nothing between the parentheses or you'll get an error message.

Also See:

CLICK command, page 186
CLICKH function, page 389
MOUSEH function, page 433
MOUSELOC function, page 435

NUMBER()

Forms

```
{the} number of [card|background] [buttons|fields]
number ([card|background] [buttons|fields])
{the} number of backgrounds
number(backgrounds)
{the} number of cards [in background]
number(cards [in background])
{the} number of chunks in stringExpr
number(chunks in stringExpr)
{the} number of [menus | menuItems | marked cards] -- new in 2.0
number ( [ menus | menuItems | marked cards ] ) -- new in 2.0

put the number of words in it into wordCount
repeat with i = 1 to the number of lines in string
if x > the number of items in it then next repeat
put number(menus) into menuCount -- 2.0
put number of menuItems in menu 3 -- includes lines across menus
```

Action

The **number** function tells you how many of a given element are in its domain.

Comments

Everything refers to the current stack. Chunks must be one of the following:

chars	characters	words	items	lines

The following example retrieves the same information displayed in a card's info box:

```
on mouseUp
  put cardInfo() into card field 1
end mouseUp

function cardInfo
  put "Card Name: " & short name of this card & return into report
```

```
   put "Card Number: " & number of this card & ¬
   " out of " & the number of cards & return after report
   put "Card ID: " & short id of this card & return after report
   put "Contains " & number of card fields & " card fields." & ¬
   return after report
   put "Contains " & number of card buttons & " card buttons." & ¬
   return after report
   put "Can't Delete Card: " & cantDelete of this card & return after report
   return report
end cardInfo
```

About words: Words are separated by ASCII 32 space characers, by the start of a line plus an ASCII 32 space character, or by an ASCII 32 space character and the end of a line. Within a container, all characters enclosed within a set of quotation marks (including imbedded spaces) are counted as a single word.

Line defined: To HyperTalk, a line is that which ends with a Return character. So "line 3" means "the line of text between the second and third Return characters in the field." Because text wraps in a field, many *screen* lines of text can make up a single line ending in a Return character.

Positional analysis: To find out the positional number of an object in its domain (for example, the position the current card holds relative to other cards in the current stack), use the number *property* (page 583).

Also See:

NUMBER property, page 583

NUMTOCHAR()

Forms

```
{the} numToChar of integerFactor
numToChar(integerExpr)

numToChar(65) -- yields A
numToChar(thisChar) -- character based on value of variable thisChar
numToChar of 103 -- yields g
numToChar(3 + 7)
```

Action

The **numToChar** function returns an ASCII character, given a numeric value.

Comments

Meaningful values for **numToChar** are in the range 0 through 255 (although many numbers might not have corresponding characters).

NumToChar is the inverse of the **charToNum** function (page 385).

The following handler displays all the characters of a given font in a given font size. It assumes the existence of a field called "Font Test":

```
fontTest "Geneva", 12 -- for example

on fontTest fontName,fontSize
  put empty into card field "Font Test"
  set textFont of card field "Font Test" to fontName
  if fontSize is not empty
  then set textSize of card field "Font Test" to fontSize
  repeat with charNum = 1 to 255
    set cursor to busy
    if charNum is 13 -- special case for Carriage Return
    then put "<return>" into thisChar
    else put numToChar(charNum) into thisChar
    put charNum & ": " & thisChar & return after card field "Font Test"
  end repeat
  set scroll of card field "Font Test" to zero
end fontTest
```

Characters yielded depends on font: The character produced by **numToChar** depends upon the value of the **textFont** property currently set for the destination. For example, the statement

```
put numToChar(92) into field myField
```

yields "\" when `myField` has a **textFont** property of New York, but yields "∴" when `myField` is set to Symbol.

⌘ and available: ⌘ and , the symbols on the Command key, are respectively `charToNum(17)` and `charToNum(20)` in the Chicago font.

ASCII chart: For a complete list of all meaningful numbers and their equivalent characters in the Geneva font (the default font for fields), see the ASCII chart on page 837.

Also See:

ASCII CHART, Appendix A
CHARTONUM function, page 385
TEXTFONT property, page 625

OFFSET()

Forms

```
offset (patternString, sourceString)

offset ("pen", "appendix") -- returns 3
offset (customer, field 7)
```

Action

The **offset** function returns an integer representing the offset from the start of *sourceString* to the first character of *patternString*.

Comments

PatternString is the string to locate. *SourceString* is the place to look for *patternString*. Case is insignificant.

If *patternString* isn't within *sourceString*, **offSet** returns 0.

The following handler deletes any string from field 1 by computing the offset of the start of the string from the beginning of the field, and then removing characters from that point through the length of the string to be deleted:

```
on deleteChars
   ask "Delete what string?"
   put offset (it, field 1) into start
   if start is zero then exit deleteChars
   put start + length(it) into finish
   delete char start to finish of field 1
end deleteChars
```

The next handler returns the entire line of any string that starts with the given search pattern. (The **find** functions do this only for fields):

```
function getLine pattern, string
   put offset (pattern, string) into firstChar
   put offset (return, char firstChar to length of string of string) - 1 ¬
   into lineLength
   return char firstChar to firstChar+lineLength of string
end getLine
```

The following handler returns the line after the line that contains the given pattern. This handler is useful for cycling through a sequence of lines where you have a given line (or part of it) and you want the next line (or the first if you've reached the end):

```
function getNextLine pattern,string
  put offset(pattern,string) into firstChar
  put offset(return,char firstChar to length of string of string) - 1 ¬
  into lineLength
  put firstChar+lineLength+1 into firstChar
  put offset(return,char firstChar to length of string of string) - 1 ¬
  into lineLength
  if lineLength <= 0
  then return line 1 of string
  else return char firstChar to firstChar+lineLength-1 of string
end getNextLine
```

First occurrence returned: The offset function returns the first occurrence of a string that might appear multiple times:

```
offset("ana", "banana") -- returns 2
```

Offset is for English: Offset ignores diacritical marks. Further, when your text contains diphthongs (like œ), you'll get surprising results if the English base letter comes before the diphthong in the source:

```
offset ("œ", "Who's seen Bœrnie?")
-- yields 3 (for the base letter "o")
```

OPTIONKEY()

Forms

```
the optionKey
optionKey()

if the optionKey is down then exit mouseUp
put the optionKey is down into optionDown -- check now for later use
set hilite of me to the optionKey is down
```

Action

The **optionKey** function returns the state of the option key (up or down).

Comments

When you use the `optionKey()` form, put nothing between the parentheses or you'll get an error message.

OptionKey is great for making a button perform two functions. The following function lets you drag a button with the browse tool if the optionKey is down:

```
on mouseDown
   if the optionKey is up then pass mouseDown
   repeat until the mouse is up
     set loc of me to the mouseLoc
   end repeat
   exit to HyperCard -- suppress mouseUp
end mouseDown

on mouseUp
   -- here's where the functionality of the button goes
   play "boing"
end mouseUp
```

PARAM()

Forms

```
{the} param of integerFactor
param(integerExpr)

put param(3) into chucko
-- assigns 3rd value in param list to variable chucko
```

Action

The **param** function returns the value of a parameter that you specify, chosen from those passed to the current handler. Param's argument is an integer indicating which value in the list to retrieve (1 gets the first parameter, 2 gets the second one, and so on.)

Comments

Param(0) returns the name of the message that invoked the handler. (This message is also the name of the currently executing handler.)

This function returns empty (the value, not the word) if the parameter you call for is a higher number than the number of parameters passed. It always returns empty when you try to use it from the Message box.

The following function definition uses **param** to add as many as 50 numeric values:

```
put sum(cityTax,stateTax,federalTax,autoDeposit) into deductions

function sum
  put 0 into total
  repeat with i = 1 to the paramCount
    add param(i) to total
  end repeat
  return total
end sum
```

Prior knowledge required: Before you can understand this function completely, you need to be familiar with how HyperTalk passes parameters. See the section on parameters and parameter passing on page 99.

How long can a parameter list be?

The maximum number of parameter values depends upon the amount of space available at any given time to HyperTalk's internal stack. But at any time, you can have at least 50 parameter values.

Also See:

HANDLERS (section on PARAMETERS), page 99
PARAMCOUNT function, page 447
PARAMS function, page 449
RETURN keyword, page 151

PARAMCOUNT()

Forms

```
the paramCount
paramCount()

put the paramCount into it
```

Action

The **paramCount** function returns the number of values from the parameter list actually passed to the current handler.

Comments

ParamCount doesn't include the name of the message that carried the parameter list.

Because the parameter list is a comma-separated list of expressions, you can think of **paramCount** as passing the count of items from the list of parameters actually passed.

ParamCount is especially useful when you don't know in advance how many parameters a handler is going to receive. The following handler clears all the fields that you tell it to:

```
clearField "Date","Total","Name" -- Add as many names as you need

on clearFields
  repeat with i = 1 to the paramCount
    put empty into field param of i
  end repeat
end clearFields
```

Parameters evaluated before passing: The expressions in the parameter list are evaluated before they're passed. The number that **paramCount** returns is the count of values after evaluation. For example, the passing line might have the expression 3 * 4 + 5; when the expression is passed, it's passed as the single value 17 and not as a list of five elements in a string.

Watch your parentheses: When you use the form `paramCount()`, put nothing within the parentheses; otherwise you'll get an error message.

Prior knowledge required: Before you can understand this function completely, you need to be familiar with how HyperTalk passes parameters. See the section on parameters and parameter passing in Chapter 5.

Also See:

Parameter Passing, page 99
PARAM function, page 445
PARAMS function, page 449
RETURN keyword, page 151

PARAMS()

Forms

```
the params
params()

put the params into it
```

Action

The **params** function returns the entire list of parameters passed to the current handler.

Comments

The first word of the value that **params** returns is the name of the message carrying the parameter list. Following the message name are the parameter values, presented as a comma-separated list of quoted literals:

```
theList "3.141593","4.571429","fred","7","12"
```

All the elements in the parameter list are evaluated before they're passed to the named handler. Here's the original command that passed the list shown above:

```
theList  pi + 0, 32 / 7, fred, number, 3 + 4 + 5
```

(Number is a variable that holds the value 7.)

In versions below 2.0 when your home stack script gets too full, you can move handlers from it into an auxilliary stack and still have them accessible from anywhere in HyperCard by placing "stubs" for each of them in the Home stack. This gets around the 32K maximum characters per script:

```
on myMessage
   send the params to stack "Auxilliary Handlers" -- redirect message
end myMessage
```

(In version 2.0, use the **Start Using** command, page 351, to do the same thing.)

Params not fully implemented: Although this function works fine for all user-defined messages, **params** isn't fully implemented for several command and function messages in versions 1.2.#.

Here's a list of commands and functions for which **params** is not fully implemented in 1.2.#:

add	ask	convert	delete	dial	divide
edit	go	hide	multiply	open	play
pop	print	push	put	select	set
show	sort	subtract	visual	wait	
annuity	compound	max	min	number	offset

For example, Figure 9-4 shows what you get from 1.2.# when the message add 3 to field 1 is trapped by the following handler:

```
on add
  put the params
end add
```

Figure 9-4   What Params might show

Here's a test you can implement before you use a command to see if **params** will yield the result you want:

```
on <commandName>
  send the params to HyperCard
end <commandName>
```

If HyperCard complains with a "Can't understand arguments to command" dialog, **Params** isn't implemented for *commandName*.

Don't write scripts based on your discoveries about how **params** works with commands and functions on the above list: the way that they work is *guaranteed* to change in future versions.

Keep the parentheses empty: When you use the form params(), put nothing within the parentheses; otherwise you'll get an error message.

Prior knowledge required: Before you can understand this function completely, you need to be familiar with how HyperTalk passes parameters. See the section on parameters and parameter passing in Chapter 5.

Also See:

HANDLERS (section on PARAMETERS), page 99
PARAM function, page 445
PARAMCOUNT function, page 447
RETURN keyword, page 151

RANDOM()

Forms

```
{the} random of Factor
random(numExpr)

put random(52) into yourCard -- pick a card, any card
```

Action

The **random** function returns a random number in the range 1 through 32768, or 1 through the value of the argument, whichever is lower.

Comments

The argument for **random** can be any positive whole number up to 10 digits long, but the highest number that **random** returns is 32,768 (the highest value that a 15-bit number can express).

The following handler draws a random bar chart (Figure 9-5). (For your added amusement, run this one with the pattern window torn off.)

```
on mouseUp
  put empty into data
  repeat with i = 1 to 5+random(30)
    put random(100) into item i of data
  end repeat
  barChart data
end mouseUp

on barChart data
  put 10 into top
  put 10 into left
  put 300 into bottom
  put 500 into right
  reset paint
  choose select tool
  doMenu "Select All"
  doMenu "Clear Picture"
  doMenu "Select All"
```

```
  doMenu "Opaque"
  choose rect tool
  set filled to true
  put left into h
  put max(data) into maxValue
  put the number of items in data into dataCount
  put round((right-left)/dataCount) into horizStep
  put round(horizStep * 3/4) into width
  repeat with i = 1 to dataCount
    put round((bottom-top) * item i of data / maxValue) into height
    set pattern to random(40)
    drag from h,bottom-height to h+width,bottom
    add horizStep to h
  end repeat
  choose browse tool
end barChart
```

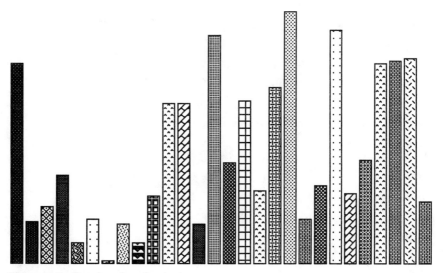

Figure 9-5 Random bar chart

RESULT()

Forms

```
the result
result()

put the result into field 1
```

Action

The **result** function either indicates the success of one of several commands, or it holds the value just sent by the **return** keyword in a message handler.

Comments

In 1.2.#, the commands that the **result** function works for are **convert, find, go, open application, open printing with dialog,** and **print document.** (See "How Commands Might Fail.")

When the **result** is empty, the last command either was successful or has no error message to put into the **result.**

Result is most useful when you use it to measure the success of the **find** or **go** commands. This first example is for find:

```
on findIt searchString,searchField
  find whole searchString in field searchField
  if the result is not empty
  then put "Sorry -- can't find" && searchString
end findIt
```

You can use a similar form for **go:**

```
on goToCard cardID
  go to card id cardID
  if the result is not empty
  then put "Sorry -- card id" && cardID && "not here."
end goToCard
```

Result quickly reset: This function is reset before every command. Most of the time, commands fail because of syntax or runtime errors. Such errors are immediately reported in dialog boxes, aborting the running handler; by the time you close the error dialog box, the handler isn't running any longer and you can't find out what the **result** held. (Thus you can't use **result** to construct "on error" handlers.)

How commands might fail: Table 9-2 shows the reasons a command might fail, plus the resulting string that **the result** returns in versions through 1.2.5 for the failures.

Table 9-2:   Result strings and their causes

Command	String	Cause
convert	invalid date	bad date format
find	not found	can't find string
go to	no such card	card doesn't exist
	cancel	cancel clicked on dialog asking for stack location
	no such stack	stack chosen from dialog not really a stack (seldom appears)
open application	no such application	application doesn't exist
open printing with dialog	cancel	cancel clicked on printing dialog
print document	no such document	document doesn't exist
print document with application	no such application	application doesn't exist

But the strings that failing commands give to the **result** function are likely to change in future HyperTalk versions; so it's not a good idea to write scripts based on today's strings. You can always be sure, however, that when a command is successful it puts empty into the **result.**

Keep parentheses empty: When you use the form result (), put nothing within the parentheses; otherwise you'll get an error message.

Also See:

RETURN keyword, page 151

ROUND()

Forms

```
{the} round of numFactor
round(numExpr)

put round of 3.5 -- puts 4
put round of 4.5 -- also puts 4!
put round of 4.6 -- puts 5
```

Action

The **round** function returns its argument rounded off to the nearest integer (but see comments, below).

Comments

Rounding occurs by the criteria in Table 9-3.

Table 9-3 Rounding criteria

Value	Direction	Example
0.5	down	.5 becomes 0
0.51	up	.51 becomes 1
any even value + .5	down	36.5 becomes 36
any even value + .51	up	36.51 becomes 37
any odd value + .5	up	37.5 becomes 38
any value +.4	down	99.4 becomes 99
any value + .6	up	99.6 becomes 100

To round off decimal digits, use the **numberFormat** property (page 585).

To truncate decimal digits, use the **trunc** function (page 486).

To round .5 up all the time use this defined function:

```
function round X
  if X < 0
  then return trunc (X - .5) -- for values less than 0
```

```
   else return trunc (X + .5) -- for values greater than 0
end round
```

Points for techies: This function calls the SANE `Num2LongInt` routine, with rounding set to `ToNearest`.

The highest value you can use for round's argument is 2147483647, the highest signed integer -1 representable in 31 bits — that is, exp2(31)-1. Higher numbers get back -2147483648, no matter what you put in.

Points for trekkies: Mr. Spock is half-human.

Also See:

NUMBERFORMAT property, page 585
TRUNC function, page 486

SCREENRECT()

Forms

```
the screenRect
screenRect()

put the screenRect into it
```

Action

The **screenRect** function returns a comma-separated list of four items representing respectively, the left, top, right, and bottom coordinates (in pixels) of the current display device. The first two coordinates are both always zero; the third coordinate tells you the width of the screen; and the fourth coordinate tells you the screen height.

Comments

Use this function to determine where you'll place windows that you open as you use HyperCard. If you know you have room, you can place windows around the card rather than over it:

```
on checkScreenSize
  if item 4 of the screenRect ≥ 480 then
    show msg at 10, 364
    show tool window at -69, 58
    show card window at 64, 69
  end if
end checkScreenSize
```

In versions earlier than 2.0, if the **screenRect** of the current display device is the same as the **rect** of the card window, you've got yourself a standard-sized Macintosh screen.

Keep parentheses empty: When you use the form `screenRect()`, put nothing within the parentheses; otherwise you'll get an error message.

SECONDS()

Forms

```
the seconds
seconds()

put the seconds into it
```

Action

The **seconds** (or **secs**) function returns the number of seconds since 12:00:00 AM January 1, 1904 (based on the current time as set on the Macintosh's clock).

Comments

Most people use this function to measure elapsed time between events.

The following handler measures the time it takes to sort a stack:

```
on elapsedTime
  put the seconds into oldTime
  sort by last word of field "Name"
  put the seconds - oldTime
end elapsedTime
```

Why January 1, 1904?

The original Macintosh development team (circa 1983) determined that January 1, 1904, would be the Day that Time Began. That date was chosen for several reasons:

- A long word seemed like an adequate amount of memory to allocate to date-keeping; its 32 bits can produce an unsigned number high enough to represent just over 130 years worth of seconds.

- The team wanted to include the birthdays of most Macintosh users; so a date somewhere around the turn of the century looked like a great target.

- Projecting from the beginning of this century forward for 130 years brought the date to 2030, which meant that clocks in Macs would work for 46 years before Time would run out (and reset to 1/1/04); nobody wanted to speculate on the life of the Mac (or of the current operating system) beyond that point.

- For calculation purposes, it was arithmetically convenient to have time start on a leap year (which 1900 wasn't, being a century year — 19 — not divisible by 4).

The philosophical implications of these facts are dizzying. The authors are therefore taking a short nap.

For finer granularity, use the **ticks** function (page 480).

Keep parentheses empty: When you use the form `seconds()`, put nothing within the parentheses; otherwise you'll get an error message.

Also See:

CONVERT command, page 199
TICKS function, page 480
TIME function, page 482

SELECTEDCHUNK()

Forms

```
the selectedChunk
selectedChunk ()

put the selectedChunk into it
```

Action

The **selectedChunk** function returns the positions of the starting and ending characters of the selected text.

Comments

SelectedChunk reports using the form

```
char start to finish of [[[card|bkgnd] field integer|message box]
```

where *start* is the first character selected, finish is the last character, and *integer* is the number of a card or background field in the current stack.

If no text is selected but there is an insertion point, then **selectedChunk** reports the position of the insertion point as in the following example :

```
char afterInsPt to beforeInsPt of [[card|bkgnd] field integer|message box]
```

```
char 14 to 13 of card field 1
```

In the example, the insertion point is between the 13th and 14th characters in card field 1. The reversed numbers show that no character is selected.

If there's no selection (not even an insertion point), the **selectedChunk** returns empty.

Text deselected: Text is deselected when any of the following happen:

• A **find, enterInField, enterKey, returnInField, returnKey, tabKey,** or sort command executes.

• The **hilite** or **cantModify** property changes.

• The **lockScreen** property is set to true.

• A new tool is chosen.

• HyperCard moves from one card to another.

• the Enter key or the Return key is pressed (the latter of which removes the selected item or text).

• Anything else that forces HyperCard to redraw the card.

If any of these events happen before you use **selectedChunk,** then **selectedChunk** returns empty.

In the following example, the name of a button is set to the number of characters in a particular field each time you press return while typing in that field; the selection is *not* lost:

```
on returnInField
  get the selectedChunk
  set name of button 1 to length of me
  select it
  pass returnInField
end returnInField
```

Keep parentheses empty: When you use the `selectedChunk()` form, put nothing between the parentheses or you'll get an error message.

Also See:

SELECT command, page 331
SELECTEDFIELD function, page 463
SELECTEDLINE function, page 465
SELECTEDTEXT function, page 467

SELECTEDFIELD()

FORMS

```
the selectedField
selectedField()

put the selectedField into it
```

ACTION

The **selectedField** function identifies the field holding the selection (or the insertion point, which is the smallest possible selection). When the selection is in the Message box, **selectedField** returns message box.

COMMENTS

SelectedField reports using the form

```
[card|bkgnd] field integer | message box
```

The field is in the current stack.

The following card handler selects everything in that field when you press shift-enter:

```
on enterInField
  if the shiftKey is down
  then select text of the selectedField
  else pass enterInField
end enterInField
```

Text deselected: Text is deselected when any of the following happen:

• A **find, enterInField, enterKey, returnInField, returnKey, tabKey,** or **sort** command executes.

• The **hilite** or **cantModify** property changes.

• The **lockScreen** property is set to true.

• A new tool is chosen.

• HyperCard moves from one card to another.

• The Enter key or the Return key is pressed (the latter of which removes the selected item or text).

• anything else that forces HyperCard to redraw the card

If any of these events happen before you use **selectedField,** then **selectedField** returns empty.

Keep parentheses empty: When you use the `selectedField()` form, put nothing between the parentheses or you'll get an error message.

Also See:

SELECT command, page 331
SELECTEDCHUNK function, page 461
SELECTEDLINE function, page 465
SELECTEDTEXT function, page 467

SELECTEDLINE()

Forms

```
the selectedLine
selectedLine()

put the selectedLine into it
```

Action

The **selectedLine** function identifies the line holding the selection (or the insertion point, which is the smallest possible selection).

Comments

SelectedLine reports using the form

```
line integer of [[card|bkgnd] field integer | message box]
```

with the field always in the current stack.

The following field handler selects the current line when you press shift-enter:

```
on enterInField
  if the shiftKey is up then pass enterInField
  get the selectedLine
  if the selectedText is the value of it then -- select next
    add 1 to word 2 of it
    if word 2 of it > number of lines in the value of the selectedField
    then put 1 into word 2 of it
  end if
  select it
end enterInField
```

Line defined: To HyperTalk, a line is that which ends with a Return character. So "line 3" means "the line of text between the second and third Return characters in the field." Because text wraps in a field, many *screen* lines of text can make up a single line ending in a Return character.

Text deselected: Text is deselected when any of the following happen:

- A **find**, **enterInField**, **enterKey**, **returnInField**, **returnKey**, **tabKey**, or **sort** command executes.

- The **hilite** or **cantModify** property changes.

- The **lockScreen** property is set to true.

- A new tool is chosen.

- HyperCard moves from one card to another.

- The Enter key or the Return key is pressed (the latter of which removes the selected item or text).

- Anything else that forces HyperCard to redraw the card.

If any of these events happen before you use **selectedLine,** then **selectedLine** returns empty.

Keep parentheses empty: When you use the `selectedLine()` form, put nothing between the parentheses or you'll get an error message.

Also See:

SELECT command, page 331
SELECTEDCHUNK function, page 461
SELECTEDFIELD function, page 463
SELECTEDTEXT function, page 467

SELECTEDTEXT()

Forms

```
the selectedText
selectedText()

put the selectedText into it
```

Action

The **selectedText** function returns the selected text.

Comments

The statement `put the selectedText` has the same result as but executes faster than the statement `put the selection` or `put the value of the selectedChunk`.

In the following example, the first handler saves the currently selected text when you type shift-enter. It writes into a global variable, so you can collect chunks of text together no matter where you are in HyperCard. Later, you'd use the second handler to put the collected notes into a field:

```
on enterInField
  global notes
  if the shiftKey is not down then pass enterInField
  put the selectedText & return after notes
end enterInField

on mouseUp -- Use this later to retrieve the notes
  global notes
  put notes into card field 1
end mouseUp
```

If the **selectedText** is empty, either there is no selection or the selection is only the insertion point.

Text deselected: Text is deselected when any of the following happen:

• A **find, enterInField, enterKey, returnInField, returnKey, tabKey,** or **sort** command executes

- The **hilite** or **cantModify** property changes

- The **lockScreen** property is set to true

- A new tool is chosen.

- HyperCard moves from one card to another.

- The Enter key or the Return key is pressed (the latter of which removes the selected item or text).

- Anything else that forces HyperCard to redraw the card.

If any of these events happen before you use **selectedText**, then **selectedText** returns empty. So, for example, if you assign a selection-manipulating handler to a button whose **autoHilite** property is set to true, the handler returns empty.

Keep parentheses empty: When you use the selectedText() form, put nothing between the parentheses or you'll get an error message.

Also See:

SELECT command, page 331
SELECTEDCHUNK function, page 461
SELECTEDFIELD function, page 463
SELECTEDLINE function, page 465
THE SELECTION, page 101

SHIFTKEY()

Forms

```
the shiftKey
shiftKey()

put the shiftKey into it
```

Action

The **shiftKey** function returns the state of the shift key (up or down).

Comments

When you use the `shiftKey()` form, put nothing between the parentheses or you'll get an error message.

The following handler makes a field display the number of words in it on shift-enter but retains the normal functionality of enterKey if the shiftKey is not down:

```
on enterInField
  if the shiftKey is up then pass enterInField
  get the selectedChunk
  put the number of words in target & " words."
  select it
end enterInField
```

SIN()

Forms

```
{the} sin of numFactor
sin(numExpr)

put the sin of pi into it
```

Action

The **sin** function uses SANE extended precision arithmetic to return the sin of the angle given as its argument.

Comments

The argument must be in radians, where 1 radian = $180/\pi$ degrees.

The **sin** function is especially useful for creating amusing graphics (see Figure 9-6):

```
on spiro
  reset paint
  choose regular polygon tool
  put 100 into startH
  put 300 into endH
  put 100 into startV
  put 180 into maxHeight
  put startH into h
  repeat 30
    add 5 to h
    put sin((h-startH)/(endH-startH)*pi)*maxHeight into height
    drag from 200,150 to h,round(startV+height)
  end repeat
  choose browse tool
end spiro
```

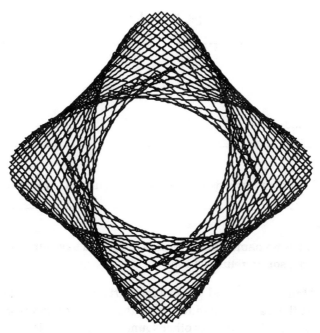

Figure 9-6   Sin is useful for graphic design

SOUND()

Forms

```
the sound
sound()

put the sound into it
```

Action

The **sound** function returns the name of the currently playing sound.

Comments

If the sound has no name, **sound** returns the sound's resource ID. If there's no sound playing, **sound** returns `"done"`.

HyperCard buffers the sound you call for, starts playing the sound, and goes on to execute the rest of the handler while the sound continues to play. (During this process, HyperCard buffers other sounds as they are played.)

Sound is especially useful for synchronizing a series of **play** commands with other actions in a handler by letting your handler know when a sound is complete:

```
on checkTiming
  repeat
    if the sound is not "done" then next repeat
    exit checkTiming
  end repeat
end checkTiming
```

A simpler version of the same handler is:

```
on checkTiming
  wait until the sound is "done"
end checkTiming
```

Keep parentheses empty: When you use the form sound(), put nothing within the parentheses; otherwise you'll get an error message.

Also See:

PLAY command, page 292

SQRT()

Forms

```
{the} sqrt of numFactor
sqrt(numExpr)

put sqrt of -1 -- yields NAN(001)
put sqrt of 2 -- yields 1.414214
```

Action

The **sqrt** function uses SANE extended precision arithmetic to return the square root of its positive argument.

Comments

If the argument is a negative number, **sqrt** returns NAN(001), meaning "not a number."

The following handler calculates the distance between you and the horizon, given your height. The handler assumes you're standing at sea level (formula by Paul Finlayson of Apple Computer):

```
on mouseUp
  ask "How tall are you in feet?" with 5.5
  put it into h
  put sqrt(h*(7926.41*5280+h))/5280 into horizon
  set numberFormat to "0.####"
  answer "The horizon is " & horizon & " miles away for you."
end mouseUp
```

The following handler calculates the length of the hypotenuse of a right triangle given the other two sides, using the Pythagorean theorem. (We knew you'd want this one.)

```
on mouseUp
  -- compute hypotenuse of a right triangle given two sides
  -- using the Pythagorean theorem c^2 = sqrt(a^2+b^2)
  ask "Side 1?"
  put it into a
  ask "Side 2?"  put it into b
  answer "Hypotenuse is " & sqrt(a^2+b^2)
end mouseUp
```

STACKSPACE()

Forms

```
the stackSpace
stackSpace()

put the stackSpace into it
```

Action

The **stackSpace** function returns the amount of space left on the system memory stack (as opposed to the HyperCard stack).

Comments

HyperTalk uses this memory stack to do internal housekeeping. The **stackSpace()** function is a debugging tool for the HyperCard system programmers at Apple Computer Inc. It is listed here for the sake of completeness.

The following example displays how stack space decreases as a handler recurses (or calls another handler). HyperTalk versions through 2.0 abort all pending handlers when the stack space has dropped below 8,000 bytes and give the message "Too much recursion"; this example checks the stackspace to make sure there's more than 8,000 bytes left before it recurses:

```
on mouseUp
  test
end mouseUp

on test
  put the stackSpace
  wait 10 ticks
  if the stackSpace > 8000 then test -- recursive call
  else put "Can't recurse anymore!"
end test
```

Keep parentheses empty: When you use the form stackSpace(), put nothing within the parentheses; otherwise you'll get an error message.

Also See:

HEAPSPACE function, page 417
VERSION property, page 645

TAN()

Forms

```
{the} tan of numFactor
tan(numExpr)

put tan(pi) -- yields 0
put tan of alpha into alphaTan
```

Action

The **tan** function uses SANE extended precision arithmetic to return the tangent of its argument.

Comments

The argument is the angle whose tangent equals the given value. The result is expressed in radians in the range $\pm\pi/2$.

One radian is $180/\pi$ degrees. To end up with the result in degrees, use the formula

```
(tan(numExpr)*180)/pi
```

This handler calculates how tall a structure is, given (1) the angle at which you look to see the top, and (2) your distance away from it. (This example does require you to have a sextant, but that's better than crawling up the outside of the building with a measuring tape.)

```
on mouseUp
  ask "Distance to the building in feet?"
  put it into distance
  ask "Angle to the top in degrees?"
  put it/180*pi into angle
  put distance*tan(angle) into height
  answer "That building is " & height & " feet tall."
end mouseUp
```

Also See:

ATAN function, page 380
COS function, page 400

TARGET()

FORMS

```
the target
target()

put the target into it
```

Action

The **target** function returns the name of the object that first received the current message. (But see the note on fields, below.)

Comments

When you click on an object, that object is `the target`. Whether or not it contains a mouseUp handler has no bearing on its being the target.

Fields get special handling: When `the target` is a field, the form `target` returns the contents of the field, and the form `the target` returns the name of the field receiving the message.

The following example adds another level of Undo to HyperCard: it lets you restore the former contents of a field even after you've closed the field:

```
on openField
   global saveField, saveFieldContents
   put the target into saveField
   put target into saveFieldContents
end openField

on restoreField
   global saveField, saveFieldContents
   do "put saveFieldContents into " & saveField
end restoreField
```

The following field handler displays the difference between "the target" (a function) and "target" (an object). (You'll have to lock the field or hold down the command key to be able to click the field):

```
on mouseUp
  put "the target = " & the target & ", target = " & target
end mouseUp
```

Target() bug alert

Because of a bug in HyperTalk, when the target is a field (and only when the target is a field) the form `target()` gets an error message in all versions through 1.2.#.

Keep parentheses empty: When you use the form `target()`, put nothing within the parentheses; otherwise you'll get an error message.

Also See:

Message Passing, page 13
THE TARGET, page 86

TICKS()

Forms

```
the ticks
ticks()

put the ticks into it
```

Action

The **ticks** function returns the number of ticks that have elapsed since the computer was last turned on or reset.

Comments

A tick is 1/60th of a second.

The following handlers show how to use the ticks to benchmark your code. As examples, these two handlers measure the time it takes to do a stack change and the time it takes to do a card change. On a Macintosh II using 1.2.#, these handlers show that stack changing takes about seven times as long as card changing:

```
on mouseUp
  -- measure how long card changes take
  lock screen -- don't want to measure screen drawing time
  put the ticks into startTime
  repeat with i = 1 to 10
    go next
    go back
  end repeat
  put (the ticks - startTime)/60/20 & " seconds per card change."
end mouseUp

on mouseUp
  -- measure how long stack changes take
  lock screen -- don't want to measure screen drawing time
  put the ticks into startTime
  repeat with i = 1 to 10
    go home
```

```
    go back
  end repeat
  put (the ticks - startTime)/60/20 & " seconds per stack change."
end mouseUp
```

This handler reports the time between mouse clicks:

```
on timeClicks
  global timeBetweenClicks
  wait until the mouseClick -- Start clock
  put the ticks into currentTicks
  wait until the mouseClick -- Stop clock
  put ticks() -- currentTicks into timeBetweenClicks
end timeClicks
```

Keep parentheses empty: When you use the form `ticks()`, put nothing within the parentheses; otherwise you'll get an error message.

Also See:

SECONDS function, page 459
TIME function, page 482

TIME()

Forms

```
the {long|short|abbr{ev{iated}}} time
time()

get the long time
```

Action

The **time** function returns the current time.

Comments

When you use any variation of the form `time()`, you get a response in the form `hh:mm`. (If you've set the clock in the Control Panel to report 12-hour time, the time is followed by AM or PM.)

```
14:42
 2:42 PM
```

The form `the short time` reports the hour and minute. The form `the long time` reports the hour, minute, and second:

`the short time`   4:01 PM (or 16:01, if you use the 24-hour setting)

`the long time`   4:01:11 PM (or 16:01:11)

Any other form gets the same response as the short time.

The following handler shows how to display the time in two time zones, given the difference in hours between them:

```
on mouseUp
  put the time into card field "Time Here"
  convert the seconds + card field "Time Difference"*60*60 to time
  put it into card field "Time There"
end mouseUp
```

The **time** is a localizable function; so how it actually appears will differ from country to country. **Seconds,** however, is portable and constant from country to country.

Keep parentheses empty: When you use the `time()` form, put nothing between the parentheses or you'll get an error message.

Also See:

CONVERT command, page 199
DATE function, page 403
SECONDS function, page 459

TOOL()

Forms

```
the tool
tool()

put the tool into it
```

Action

The **tool** function returns the name of the currently selected tool.

Comments

Tool returns one of the following:

browse tool	spray tool
button tool	rectangle tool
field tool	round rect tool
select tool	bucket tool
lasso tool	oval tool
pencil tool	curve tool
brush too	text tool
eraser tool	regular polygon tool
line tool	polygon tool

Figure 9-7 shows what tool name goes with what tool.

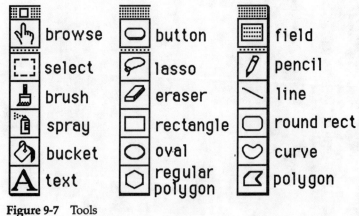

Figure 9-7   Tools

The following example shows how to save the current tool before you change it so you can later restore it:

```
on mouseUp
  choose oval tool
  repeat with i = 1 to 10
    drag from 30*i,30*i to 30*i+20,30*i+20
    fill 30*i+10,30*i+10,i -- this handler uses a different tool
  end repeat
  choose browse tool
end mouseUp

on fill h,v,fillPattern
  -- fill with a pattern at h,v
  put the tool into saveTool
  choose bucket tool
  set pattern to fillPattern
  click at h,v
  choose saveTool -- so the handler that called us will work
end fill
```

Keep parentheses empty: When you use the `tool()` form, put nothing between the parentheses or you'll get an error message.

Also See:

CHOOSE command, page 183

TRUNC()

Forms

```
{the} trunc of numFactor
trunc(numExpr)

put trunc(84847.48375) -- yields 84847
put trunc of 1 -- yields 1
```

Action

The **trunc** function returns the whole number part of its argument.

Comments

Trunc doesn't do any rounding; it merely throws away any fractional part of its argument.

You can use **trunc** to tell if you're dealing with whole numbers or not. (How many families really have 2.3 kids?) The following handler returns "true" if the number you pass it is a whole number, or "false" if the number has a fractional part:

```
function isInteger x
  return x = trunc(x)
end isInteger
```

Points for techies: This function calls the SANE Num2LongInt routine with rounding set to TowardZero.

The highest value you can use for **trunc**'s argument is 2147483647, the highest signed integer -1 representable in 31 bits — that is, exp2(31)-1. Higher numbers get back -2147483648, no matter what you put in.

Also See:

DIV operator, page 144
MOD operator, page 114
ROUND function, page 456

VALUE()

Forms

```
{the} value of factor
value(expr)

get value(it)
put value of field "Formula" into field "Value"
```

Action

The **value** function evaluates its argument and returns the result.

Comments

The argument can be any kind of expression.

The following handler returns the numeric value of a string passed to the variable It:

```
on doCalculation
  ask "Type an expression for me to evaluate:" with "4 * 3 + 2 - 1"
  answer "The value is " & value (it) & "."
end doCalculation
```

The following handler returns the contents of a whole line of text located by the Find command (even though only a single word was found):

```
on putFoundInfo
  find "nauseated" in field ElectionYear
  put the value of the foundLine
end putFoundInfo
```

The following handler looks for a card that meets any condition or conditions you specify. The example asks for a card whose first field has nothing in it, and whose second field contains at least 11 characters:

```
findCard "field 1 is empty and length(field 2) > 10"

on findCard where
  repeat with i = 1 to the number of cards
    go to card i
```

```
    if value of where is true then exit findCard
  end repeat
  put "Can't find card where " & where
end findCard
```

Chapter 10

Properties

A property reflects the current state of some attribute of an object or window. Properties return a logical, numeric, or string value, depending on the specific attribute. Many properties can be set using the **set** command (page 336).

Every HyperTalk property is listed in this chapter, with the complete syntax and appropriate examples for each one.

For a listing of properties and other vocabulary words grouped by type (arithmetic, painting, and so on), see Appendix F. For a summary of all HyperTalk vocabulary words with brief definitions, see Appendix E.

Some functions were added to the language so late that their descriptions couldn't be included in the main body of this book. See "Functions" in Appendix I, "Late Breaking News."

AUTOHILITE

Forms

```
set {the} autoHilite of button to logical

set autoHilite of button 12 to true
```

Action

The **autoHilite** property reflects whether a button's highlight changes each time you click at that button's location.

The following handler makes a new check box with the name you supply and sets its **autoHilite** property to true:

```
newCheckBox "Werner" -- Here's how to call the handler

on newCheckBox boxName
  doMenu "New Button"
  set style of last button to checkBox
  set name of last button to boxName
  set autoHilite of last button to true
  choose browse tool
end newCheckBox
```

Comments

Button must be in the current stack.

You click at a button's location manually by clicking it with the mouse or programmatically by using the form

```
click at the location of button
```

When **autoHilite** is true, a button is hilited while the mouse is pressed over that button; if the button is any type except radio button or check box, when the mouse is released the button appears not hilited.

The following handler creates, vertically aligns, and names a bank of radio buttons. The first two parameters are the top and left coordinates for the button bank; the rest of the parameters (as many as you choose) are button names:

```
newRadioGroup 40,200,"Dan","Bill","Scot" -- Here's how to call it

on newRadioGroup topCoord, leftCoord
  repeat with i = three to the paramcount
    if i is not three -- not the first button
    then add height of last button to topCoord
    doMenu "New Button"
    set style of last button to radioButton
    set autoHilite of last button to true
    set name of last button to param(i)
    set left of last button to leftCoord
    set top of last button to topCoord
  end repeat
  choose browse tool
end newRadioGroup
```

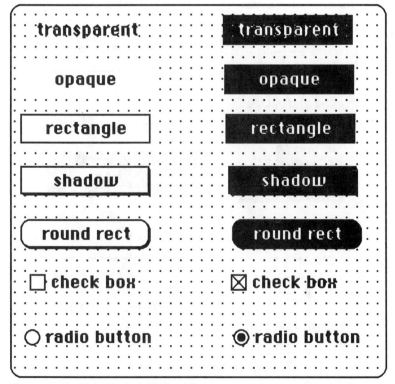

Figure 10-1   Unhilited and hilited buttons

See the **hilite** property (page 543) for a handler to make this bank of radio buttons behave like standard Macintosh radio buttons — only one button in a bank hilited at a time.

Default values: The default value of **autoHilite** for a new button is false; the default value of this property for a button created by option-dragging another button (the source) is the same as the value of **autoHilite** in the source.

What "hilited" means: Different styles of buttons are hilited in different ways: a hilited check box has an X in it; a hilited radio button has a dot in its center; all other hilited buttons appear in inverse video (that is, light text on a dark background). (See Figure 10-1.)

When a transparent icon button hilites, the text and icon portion appear in inverse video; the rest appears as it does when the button is unhilited (Figure 10-2).

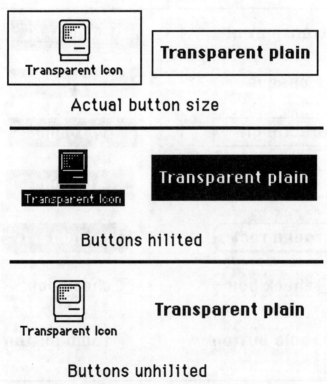

Figure 10-2   Iconic hiliting

AutoHilite and the Selection: Clicking a button whose autoHilite property is true deselects whatever is selected. In fact, anytime a button's hilite is changed you lose the selection. The following handler lets you change the hilite of a button and keep the selection:

```
on mouseUp
  get the selectedChunk
  set hilite of me to true
  wait 10 ticks -- delay so user can see the hiliting
  set hilite of me to false
  select it
end mouseUp
```

Setting autoHilite manually: You can set the autoHilite property of a button manually by clicking the appropriate option in that button's Info dialog box.

Also See:

HILITE property, page 543
SHAREDHILITE property, page 607

AUTOTAB

Forms

```
set {the} autoTab of field to logical

set autoTab of field "Tabby" to true
```

Action

The **autoTab** property determines what happens when you press Return with the insertion point in the last line of a nonscrolling field.

The following handler will set the autoTab property of all nonscrolling fields of the current background to true:

```
on mouseUp
  repeat with i = 1 to the number of fields
    if style of field i is not "scrolling"
    then set autoTab of field i to true
  end repeat
end mouseUp
```

Comments

Field must be in the current stack.

If **autoTab** is true and the insertion point is on the last line, pressing Return selects the text of the next field in the Tabbing order. If it is false, the insertion point remains in the current field (although it moves below the field's visible bottom and is therefore partially or completely hidden).

This property is extremely useful when you want a user to fill out an on-screen form.

autoTab has no effect on scrolling fields.

Default value: The default value of **autoTab** for a new field is false. The following handler makes new fields default to having the autoTab property set to true:

```
on newField
  set autoTab of the target to true
end newField
```

The default value of this property for a field created by option-dragging another field (the source) is the same as the value of **autoTab** in the source.

Beware the automatic selection: Because all the text in a field that is **autoTab's** destination becomes selected, pressing any character key (and any of several other keys) deletes that text. The following handler placed in the script of the destination field eliminates the danger; it deselects the text and places the insertion point immediately after the field's last character:

```
on openField
   select after text of me
   -- change "after" to "before" to put insertion point at text's start
end openField
```

Setting autoTab manually: You can set the **autoTab** property of a field manually by clicking the appropriate option in that field's Info dialog box.

Also See:

SELECT command, page 331
TABBING order, page 395

BLINDTYPING

Forms

```
set {the} blindTyping to logical

set blindTyping to true
```

Action

The **blindTyping** property reflects whether you can type into the Message box while it's hidden.

The following handler sets blindTyping to a user-specific value on openStack:

```
on openStack
  global userName
  if userName is "Dan Winkler" or userName is "Scot Kamins"
  then set blindTyping to false
  else set blindTyping to true
end openStack
```

Comments

To change the value of **blindTyping,** the userLevel property must first be set to 5. This property is normally set at startup and then not changed.

When **blindTyping** is false or **userLevel** is not 5, trying to type to the Message box while it's invisible makes the Macintosh beep. If that happens, press Command-M to bring up the Message box and enter the following (<CR> = press Return):

```
set userlevel to 5 <CR>
set blindTyping to true <CR>
```

Default value: The default value of this property depends upon the options set on the User Preferences Card of the Home stack.

Also See:

USERLEVEL property, page 639

BOTTOM

Forms

```
set {the} bottom of [button|field|card|window] to integerExpr

set bottom of msg to 450
```

Action

The **bottom** property describes the distance of the bottom edge of an object or window from some source. The source depends on the element:

Element	Source
object	top of card window
noncard windows	top of card window
card window or card	top of screen

The top of the card window is immediately below the card's title bar. (The title bar on a standard-sized card is invisible in the Macintosh Plus and Macintosh SE built-in displays.)

The following handler vertically aligns all the buttons on the current card by setting their bottoms to be the same. This is useful if you have several buttons scattered across a card and you want them all to rest on the same horizontal plane:

```
on vertAlign
  repeat with i = 2 to the number of buttons
    set bottom of button i to bottom of button 1
  end repeat
end vertAlign
```

Comments

IntegerExpr evaluates to a positive or a negative integer. *Button* or *field* must be in the current stack. The top of a card window is located just below the title bar.

Normally, repeatedly choosing the new button command from the objects menu piles the new buttons on top of each other. The following handler puts new buttons at a random place on the card:

```
on newButton
  set the loc of last button to random(480), random(320)
end newButton
```

Visible boundaries: Locations 0,0 through 511, 341 are within a standard card's area and are therefore visible on all Macintosh displays. Points outside those boundaries might or might not be visible, depending upon the size of the display you're using. Moving an element outside the visible boundaries of the display doesn't change its **visible** setting, and is harmless.

Bottom and Rectangle: The value of **bottom** is the same as item 4 of the rectangle property of the same element. (But note that changing the bottom of an element will move the element, while putting a new number into item 4 of that element will change its size.)

Changing bottom's value: Anything that moves an element changes its **bottom** value. Such methods include (but are not limited to) dragging the element either programmatically or manually, setting its **location** property, changing its **rectangle** property, or using the **show** command with a different value following **at**.

Also See:

BOTTOMRIGHT property, page 499
LOCATION property, page 556
RECTANGLE property, page 593
SHOW command, page 339
TOP property, page 635
TOPLEFT property, page 637

BOTTOMRIGHT

Forms

```
set {the} bot{tom}Right of [button|field|card|window] to location

set botright of field "Listings" to right, bottom
```

Action

The **bottomRight** property describes an element's right-bottom corner, expressed as two integers separated by a comma. (See chart in"Comments" below.)

The following handler aligns all the buttons on the current card in a diagonal line:

```
on diagAlign
  repeat with i = 2 to the number of buttons
    set topLeft of button i to botRight of button (i - 1)
  end repeat
end diagAlign
```

Comments

Button or *field* must be in the current stack. *Location* is a point on the display, expressed as two integers separated by a comma. The integers represent respectively horizontal and vertical distances (in pixels) from the left and top edges of a source. The source depends on the element:

Element	Source
object	top-left corner of card window
noncard windows	top-left corner of card window
card window or card	top-left corner of screen

The top of the card window is immediately below the card's title bar (invisible for standard-sized or larger cards in the Macintosh Plus and Macintosh SE built-in displays).

The following button handler makes the button drag itself to the mouseLoc as the mouse moves:

```
on mouseDown
  repeat until the mouse is up -- stops when you release the mouse
    set botRight of me to the mouseLoc
  end repeat
end mouseDown
```

Backward name: The name of this property does *not* reflect the correct order of coordinates. Although the name is **botRight,** you must give the coordinates in the order right, bottom.

Visible boundaries: Locations 0,0 through 511,341 are within a standard card's area and are therefore visible on all Macintosh displays. Points outside those boundaries might or might not be visible, depending upon the size of the display you're using. Moving an element outside the visible boundaries of the display doesn't change its **visible** setting, and is harmless.

BottomRight and sources of values: The **bottomRight** is expressed as two integers separated by a comma. So you can refer to **bottomRight's** values as items:

```
put item 1 of the bottomRight of field 6 into Horizontal
```

which is the same as:

```
put right of field 6 into horizontal
```

To assign **bottomRight's** two-item value to a variable, put the assignment in quotation marks:

```
put "110, 130" into botRt
```

BottomRight and Rectangle: The value of **bottomRight** is the same as items 3 and 4 of the rectangle property of the same element.

Changing bottomRight's value: Anything that moves an element changes its **bottomRight** value. Such methods include (but are not limited to) dragging the element either programmatically or manually, setting its **location** property, changing its **rectangle** property, or using the **show** command with a different value following **at.**

Also See:

BOTTOM property, page 497
LOCATION property, page 556
RECTANGLE property, page 593
SHOW command, page 339
TOP property, page 635
TOPLEFT property, page 637

BRUSH

Forms

```
set {the} brush to integerExpr

set the brush to 8
```

Action

The **brush** property reflects the current shape of the brush tool. (See Figure 10-3.)

The following handler draws a stacatto line:

```
on stacattoLine
  choose brush tool
  set the brush to 32
  put 200 into v1
  put 20 into h1
  put v1 into v2
  put h1 into h2
  repeat until h2 > 400
    add random(21)-11 to v2
    add random(10) to h2
    drag from h1,v1 to h2,v2
    put h2 into h1
    put v2 into v1
  end repeat
  choose browse tool
end stacattoLine
```

Comments

IntegerExpr is a positive integer in the range 1 through 32. The default value for **brush** is 8.

Changing the value of the brush property changes the current brush shape. The shape determines the trail that the brush leaves as you drag it across a card. The brush shapes are the same as the ones in the Brush Shape dialog box; that dialog appears when you choose Brush Shape from the Options window (or when you double-click on the brush tool on the Tool window). Figure 10-3 shows that box, with numbers for the **brush** property added:

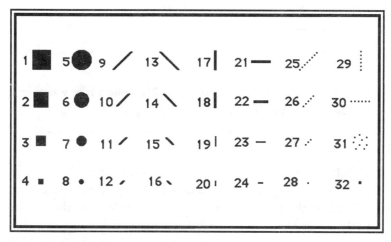

Figure 10-3   Brush property values

The following handler lets you paint with randomly changing brushes (which makes it easy to produce clever forgeries of Ralph Steadman works):

```
on mouseDown
  choose brush tool
  repeat until the mouse is up
    set brush to random(32)
    click at the mouseLoc
  end repeat
  choose browse tool
end mouseDown
```

Out of range values: Setting a value of 0 for Brush selects brush shape 1. Setting a value in the range 32 through 32767 selects brush shape 32. Values above 32767 select brush shape 1, but this is liable to change in future versions.

CANTABORT

Forms

```
set {the} cantAbort of stack to logical

set the cantAbort of stack "No Exit" to true
```

Action

The **cantAbort** property, new in HyperCard 2.0, determines whether pressing Command-period aborts the action of a running script.

Comments

When **cantAbort** is true, pressing Command-period has no effect on a running script. (Ordinarily, pressing Command-period has the same effect as a handler executing the command `exit to HyperCard` — the running script immediately aborts.)

Changing the setting of this property makes a corresponding change to the Can't Abort option in a stack's "Protect Stack" dialog.

The following example uses **cantAbort** to bracket critical sections of code where interruption could create an inconsistent state:

```
on dontStop
   -- this handler moves the current card to the end of the stack
   -- it uses cantAbort to make sure that the script is not
   -- aborted after cutting the card but before pasting it
   set cantAbort of this stack to true
   doMenu "Cut Card"
   go to last card
   doMenu "Paste Card"
   set cantAbort of this stack to false
end dontStop
```

CantAbort is dangerous: Once you've set **cantAbort** to true, the only way to stop a runaway script is to reboot the machine:

```
on timeToReboot
   set cantAbort of this stack to true
```

```
   repeat
     ask "Shall I stop now?" with "Never!"
     -- if it is not "Never!" — Oops! Forgot to uncomment!!!
     -- then exit to HyperCard
   end repeat
end timeToReboot
```

This can be particularly unnerving if you're running HyperCard under MultiFinder with unsaved work in a simultaneously running application. (This is the Voice of Bitter Experience talking.)

Also See:

PROTECT STACK Command, *HyperCard User's Guide*
RESET SWITCH, *Macintosh Owner's Guide*

CANTDELETE

Forms

```
set {the} cantDelete of [stack|bkgnd|card] to logical

set the cantDelete of this stack to true
set cantDelete of card "Set Up" to true
```

Action

The **cantDelete** property reflects whether a particular object can (false) or cannot (true) be deleted.

The following handler, which belongs in the stack or background script, causes the cantDelete property of the current card to be set to true as soon as text is entered into any of its fields:

```
on closeField
  set cantDelete of this card to true
end closeField
```

Comments

Bkgnd or *card* describe objects in the current stack, while *stack* can be any stack. *logical* must evaluate either to true or to false; its default value is false.

CantDelete checks (when true) or unchecks (when false) the related option in the Info dialog box of a particular background or card, or in the Protect Stack dialog box of a particular stack. If the related option is changed manually, the property's value is also changed.

The following handler sets the cantDelete property of all cards that have card scripts to true:

```
on mouseUp
  repeat with i = 1 to the number of cards
    if script of card i is not empty
    then set cantDelete of card i to true
  end repeat
end mouseUp
```

This next handler, which belongs in the background or stack script, prevents users who aren't scripters from deleting the current card:

```
on openCard
  set cantDelete of this card to the userLevel < 5
end openCard
```

Handler aborted on error: If the **cantDelete** of an object is set to true and a command within a running handler tries to delete the object, a "Can't delete object" message appears and the remainder of the handler is aborted. To avoid this problem, use a form like the following before you try to delete the object:

```
set cantDelete of theDoomedObject to false
```

CantDelete doesn't work in the Finder: No matter what the setting of **cantDelete**, the user can still throw the stack away from the Finder (unless the stack's Locked option is checked in the Finder's Get Info window).

Also See:

CANTMODIFY property, page 508

CANTMODIFY

Forms

```
set {the} cantModify of this stack to logical

set the cantModify of this stack to true
```

Action

The **cantModify** property reflects whether a particular stack can be changed. If **cantModify** is true, the object can't be permanently modified (but see the **userModify** property, page 642).

The following handler sets the cantModify property of the current stack to true:

```
on ship_It
  set cantModify of this stack to true
end ship_It
```

Comments

logical must evaluate either to true or to false.

When **cantModify** is true, HyperTalk puts a check in both the "Can't modify stack" and "Can't delete stack" options in the Protect Stack dialog box of the named stack, and puts the cutest little padlock next to the rightmost menu on the menubar. If **cantModify** is later set to false, the "Can't modify stack" option is unchecked and the padlock disappears; but if a user manually checked "Can't delete stack" before **cantModify** changed, "can't delete stack" remains checked.

When "Can't modify stack" is changed manually, the value of **cantModify** changes to match.

CantModify is useful when you want to change some data, graphic, or setting temporarily, but then have everything revert to its former state. The following handler moves a button around, playing sounds as the button moves, and then puts the button back where it was originally:

```
on mouseUp
  set cantModify of this stack to true -- all changes temporary
  repeat 5 times
    play boing 48+random(35)
    set loc of me to random(512),random(342)
    wait until the sound is "done"
  end repeat
  set cantModify of this stack to false -- revert to initial state
end mouseUp
```

Write-protected stacks: Although **cantModify** might be set to false, you can't change a stack that's locked in other ways, such as when the lock box in the stack's Get Info dialog in the Finder is checked, or when the media that holds the stack is read–only media (locked disk, CD ROM, restricted privileges on a file server, etc.), or when you're runnng a 1.2.# unconverted stack with 2.# HyperCard.

Handler aborted on error: If **cantModify** is set to true and a command within a running handler tries to change a stack, a "Can't modify this stack" message appears and the remainder of the handler is aborted. To avoid this problem, use a command like this before you make any changes:

```
set cantmodify of stack toBeChanged to false
```

CantModify of card or background doesn't work in 1.2.#

In version 1.2.#, you can set and retrieve the **cantModify** property of any card or background; but setting **cantModify** of that card or background doesn't affect whether that card or background can be changed. Isn't that special?

CantModify and the Selection: If you change **cantModify**'s setting and if the new setting is different from the old one, any selected object or text is deselected.

Points for techies: When the setting for **cantModify** changes, it purges all objects from HyperCard's virtual memory.

Restoring lost changes can be tricky

Changes made to a read-only stack are lost as soon as you leave the card. When you return to the stack, restoring any lost changes (like hiding or showing buttons) isn't always as simple as it sounds.

You might think that you can cover the situation by using an openCard handler to do the job. But sometimes HyperCard will leave the card (thus losing your changes) and come back without sending any open or close messages:

```
on mouseUp -- in stack "This Stack"
  go to stack "Other Stack"
  put "hello" into field 1
end mouseUp

on openCard -- in stack "Other Stack"
  hide button 1
end openCard
```

The **put** statement after the **go** forces HyperCard to go back to "This Stack" to see what the **put** command is about; this loses the changes in "Other Stack." Because no messages are sent, the **hide** statement in the openCard handler for stack "Other Stack" doesn't get executed when HyperTalk comes back from "This Stack."

To avoid this problem, make the **go** that change stacks be the last statement executed. If you must have a statement after a **go**, send the post-**go** statement to HyperCard in order to avoid going back to the old stack for the handler:

```
on mouseUp
  go to stack "Other Stack"
  send "put " & quote & "hello" & quote & "into field 1" to HyperCard
end mouseUp
```

Also See:

USERMODIFY property, page 642

CANTPEEK

Forms

```
set {the} cantPeek of stack to logical

set the cantPeek of stack "Somewhat Protected" to true

set cantPeek of this stack to false
```

Action

The **cantPeek** property, new in HyperCard 2.0, determines whether you can see buttons and fields by pressing Command-option and Command-shift-option, and whether you can open the scripts of buttons and fields by using Command-option-click and Command-shift-option-click.

Comments

When **cantPeek** is true, you can't "peek" at the script of a button or a field — a feature especially useful in the construction of games.

You can edit the script of any button or field by using the command `edit script of objectName`, regardless of **cantPeek**'s setting.

The following example turns **cantPeek** on when you enter a specific card, and turns it off when you leave the card:

```
on openCard
  set cantPeek of this stack to true
end openCard

on closeCard
  set cantPeek of this stack to false
end closeCard
```

Changing the setting of this property makes a corresponding change to the Can't Peek option in a stack's "Protect Stack" dialog.

Also See:

Keyboard commands, *Macintosh User's Guide*
PROTECT STACK command, *HyperCard User's Guide*

CENTERED

Forms

```
set {the} centered to logical

set centered to true
```

Action

The **centered** property reflects whether certain tools subsequently draw from the center (true) or from the edge (false) of a starting point.

The following button handler draws an oval around the button that holds the handler in its script:

```
on mouseUp
   choose oval tool
   set centered to true
   set lineSize to 3
   drag from loc of me to right of me + 10, bottom of me + 10
   choose browse tool
end mouseUp
```

Comments

Tools affected by this property are:

Line   Rectangle   Round Rectangle   Oval   Curve   Poly   Reg Poly

When **centered** is true, a checkmark in appears next to the Draw Centered item in the Options menu. Choosing Draw Centered toggles the value of **centered.**

The default value for **centered** is false.

The following handler draws a bullseye:

```
on bullsEye
   choose oval tool
   set centered to true
   set lineSize to 2
   put "100,100" into center
```

```
   put center into point
   repeat 10 times
      add 5 to item 1 of point
      add 5 to item 2 of point
      drag from center to point
   end repeat
end bullsEye
```

Also See:

Draw Centered, *HyperCard User's Guide*

CHECKMARK

Forms

```
set {the} checkMark of menuItem to logical

set checkMark of menuItem 3 of menu "Additions" to true
```

Action

The **checkmark** property, new in HyperCard 2.0, determines whether a check-mark (✔) appears to the left of a menu item.

Comments

MenuItem identifies a specific menu item of a specific menu in the current stack.

Typically you'd use the **checkMark** property to indicate that some option was currently operating, as HyperCard does with the **Power Keys** menu choice on the options menu.

CheckMark is a special case of the **markChar** property. To use any character besides ✔, use the **markChar** property.

The following handler executes one of two routines (not included), depending on whether the chosen menu item was checked or unchecked:

```
on doMenu what
  if what is "Add Name" then
    if checkMark of menuItem "Add Name" of menu "Additions" is true
    then doFirstOption
    else doSecondOption
  else pass doMenu
end doMenu
```

The following example creates a userLevel menu on a specific card with a checkmark next to the current user level. (To change the user level, choose the appropriate menu item):

```
on openCard
  create menu "UserLevel"
```

```
    put "1,2,3,4,5," into menu "UserLevel"
    get the userLevel
    set checkMark of menuItem it of menu "UserLevel" to true
end openCard

on closeCard
  -- remove UserLevel menu
  delete menu "UserLevel"
end closeCard

on doMenu whichItem, whichMenu
  if whichMenu is not "UserLevel" then pass doMenu
  get the userLevel
  set checkMark of menuItem it of menu "UserLevel" to false
  set the userLevel to whichItem
  set checkMark of menuItem whichItem of menu "UserLevel" to true
end doMenu
```

CheckMark reverts to false when you issue the **reset menuBar** command.

You can't set the **checkMark** property for any item on the Apple, Tools, Font, Style, or Patterns menu.

Also See:

MARKCHAR property, page 566
RESET MENUBAR command, page 322

COMMANDCHAR

Forms

```
set {the} [ commandChar|cmdChar ] of menuItem to character

set cmdChar of first menuitem of last menu to "D"
```

Action

The **CommandChar** (or **cmdChar**) property, new in HyperCard 2.0, determines what command character (if any) you can press from the keyboard to execute a specific menu command.

Comments

MenuItem refers to a specific menu item of a specific menu.

The command character appears to the right of the menu item, after the symbol ⌘.

A command character is any character you press in conjunction with the Command key (the one with the symbols and/or ⌘ on it). When the character is a letter, case is insignificant; but the case you specify is the one that appears in the menu.

The following handler creates a menu and adds command characters:

```
on mouseUp
  create menu "Directions"
  put "Left,Right,Up,Down,Forward,Back" into menu "Directions"
  put "L,R,U,D,F,B" into cmdCharList
  repeat with i = 1 to number of items in cmdCharList
    set commandChar of menuItem i of menu "Directions" ¬
    to item i of cmdCharList
  end repeat
end mouseUp
```

You can't set the **CommandChar** property for any item on the Apple, Tools, Font, Style, or Patterns menu.

To eliminate a command key character already on the menu, set it to empty (*""*).

Command key order: HyperCard checks for command key assignments by looking at menus going from right to left, and top to bottom. So programmatically assigned command characters in new menus take precedence over command characters assigned by HyperCard.

For example, If you assign **C** to a menu item in a menu that appears to the right of the Edit menu, ⌘ **C** works for the new item (but you can no longer use ⌘ **C** to copy a selection).

When you assign a command key that duplicates (and therefore disables) a HyperCard command key, be sure to eliminate the one that doesn't work:

```
set cmdchar of menuItem 3 of menu "Edit" to empty
```

(We used `menuItem 3` here rather than Cut because the exact text of this item changes. Also note that it's item #3; the blank line between "Undo" and "Cut" in the menu is also a menu item.)

In order to maintain HyperCard's functionality most closely, use only unassigned letters and characters wherever possible. Letters not used by HyperCard are **D, G, J, X, Y**. Additionally, HyperCard uses the letters **A** and **S** only when a paint tool is chosen.

HyperCard uses only the following special characters: ~ . ? + - (freeing you to use any others without fear).

When command keys revert: All programmatically assigned command characters are canceled when you use the **reset menuBar** command or when you quit HyperCard.

Also See:

RESET MENUBAR command, page 322

CURSOR

Forms

```
set {the} cursor to expr

set cursor to 4
set cursor to watch
set cursor to none
```

Action

The **cursor** property reflects the graphic currently representing the pointer.

Comments

Expr is the name or (if available) number of the graphic assigned to the pointer. Figure 10-4 shows the available pointers.

Name	Number	Graphic
Ibeam	1	⌶
cross	2	+
plus	3	⊹
watch	4	⌚
hand		 ☝
arrow		➤
busy		◓
none		

Figure 10-4 Cursors

You can progammatically change the shape of the pointer, even if the screen is locked.

At idle time the shape for the pointer reverts to whatever HyperCard's normal updating procedures says it should be.

Courtesy to users: Users panic easily. Whenever your code is doing something that's going to take more than a couple of seconds, set the cursor to either `watch` or to `busy` so that the user knows that something is happening.

Spinning busy: The `busy` graphic turns 1/8th of a rotation each time you call it. The following handler spins the busy graphic one full rotation:

```
on spinThatPuppy
  repeat 8 times
    set the cursor to busy -- turn 1/8th rotation
    wait 5 ticks -- slow things down
  end repeat
end spinThatPuppy
```

The following handler illustrates how to spin the busy graphic during time-consuming operations. This handler assumes that every card has a background field named "balance":

```
on mouseUp
  put 0 into maxBalance
  repeat with i = 1 to the number of cards
    set cursor to busy
    get field "Balance" of card i
    if it > maxBalance then put it into maxBalance
  end repeat
  put "Maximum balance is " & maxBalance
end mouseUp
```

What "User Interface Guidelines"?

Alert readers know that the Macintosh has no cursors, just different pointers. One of the authors of this book begged and pleaded with the language designer (obviously to no avail) to name this property "pointer." We apologize for any inconvenience.

Quiet failures: HyperTalk doesn't notify you if it can't supply the cursor
you ask for, nor does it set the **result** function. Further, there's no way to find
out what the current cursor is (that is, you can't say `get the cursor` or
`put the cursor into field whatEver`). Sorry.

DONTSEARCH

Forms

```
set {the} dontSearch of [ field | card | bkgnd ] to logical

set the dontSearch of field "Skip Me" to true
set the dontSearch of third marked card to logicalValue
set the dontSearch of background 3 to false
```

Action

The **dontSearch** property, new in HyperCard 2.0, determines whether the **find** command searches a specific field, or any field on a given card or background.

Comments

Card, bkgnd, and *field* are restricted to the current stack.

Find doesn't look in an object whose **dontSearch** property is set to true. The default setting of this property is false.

When a card's **dontSearch** is set to true, none of the card or background fields on that card is searched. When a background's **dontSearch** is set to true, none of the cards in that background is searched.

The following handler, which belongs in the background script, stops a field from being searched if it has the string "secret" typed into it:

```
on closeField
  set dontSearch of me to "secret" is in me
end closeField
```

Changing the setting of this property makes a corresponding change to the Don't Search option in the object's "Info..." dialog. (But setting a card's or background's **dontSearch** to true does *not* make a corresponding change to the settings of Don't Search options on contained fields or cards.)

Impact on search speed negligible: The setting of a given object's **dontSearch** property has little noticeable effect on **find**'s speed. **Find** doesn't know if a card's **dontSearch** property is set to true until **find** gets to that card.

Further, a card doesn't know what background it's in until you get to that card. (You can think of a background as a property of a card.) And if a card or background's **dontSearch** is false, **find** doesn't know if an individual field can be searched until it reaches that field.

Shared text not searched: Setting **sharedText** of a field to true changes the setting of the **Don't Search** option in the target field's Info box (but, interesting enough, doesn't change the **dontSearch** property of that field). The **find** command doesn't look for text in fields whose **sharedText** property is set to true. When (and only when) **sharedText** for a given field is set to false, **find** can look in the *unshared* text of that field.

Also See:

FIND command, page 246
SHAREDTEXT property, page 608

DONTWRAP

Forms

```
set {the} dontWrap of field to logical

set the dontWrap of field "Skip Me" to true

set the dontWrap of cd fld 3 of bg 2 to false
```

Action

The **dontWrap** property, new in HyperCard 2.0, determines whether the text of a given field wraps at the boundary of that field's viewing window.

Comments

Field is any field in the current stack.

When a field's **dontWrap** property is set to true, text doesn't wrap at the visible right edge of that field; rather, text trails off out of sight past the field's right edge. A carriage return, however, marks the end of a line and moves the insertion point (and any subsequent text) back to the left edge of the field. (See Figure 10-5.)

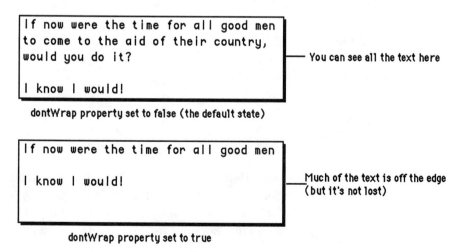

Figure 10-5   Same field with dontWrap set false (top) and true

The default setting of this property is false.

When a card's **dontWrap** is set to true and text trails off the edge, that text isn't lost; it's merely hidden from view. If you set the **dontWrap** of such a field to false, or if you increase the field's width, the hidden text comes into view.

Changing the setting of this property makes a corresponding change to the "Don't wrap" option in the "Field Info..." dialog.

The following utility script is useful in index fields where each line contains a series of ordered items. For example, the first item in the line might be a name — the only item that you need to see to locate a particular line for editing. (Subsequent items in the line might be data that's used by various scripts, but that you don't need to see.) The script changes the **dontWrap** of the field when you open and/or close it:

```
on openField
   -- set up for editing
   get the selectedChunk -- save the selectedChunk
   select empty -- trigger the closeField
   set dontWrap of me to false
   select it -- restore the selectedChunk
end openField

on closeField
   -- set up for use
   set dontWrap of me to true
end closefield

on exitField
   -- set up for use
   set dontWrap of me to true
end exitField
```

The script deals with some hairy HyperTalk issues. Setting properties of buttons or fields loses the selection *after* the property is set. So if an `openField` handler sets a property, HyperCard loses the selection, which then triggers a `closeField` message, which in this example undoes the set that the `openField` did.

Printing impact: When a field's **dontWrap** is set to true, printing the field with the form `print` *`fieldExpr`* prints only the visible portion of the field, with the field's fonts and text styles maintained. To print all the text in the field without any styles or other formatting (in Courier 10, with a lineHeight of 13), use the form `print (`*`fieldExpr`*`)`.

Also See:

PRINT command, page 299

DRAGSPEED

Forms

```
set {the} dragspeed to integerExpr

set dragSpeed to 100
set dragSpeed to 0
```

Action

The **dragSpeed** property reflects the rate, in pixels per second (more or less), that the pointer moves in response to the **drag** command.

The following handler illustrates slow dragging with a painting tool:

```
on slowTriangle
  choose brush tool
  set dragSpeed to 60
  drag from 100,100 to 200,200
  drag from 200,200 to 100,300
  drag from 100,300 to 100,100
  choose browse tool
end slowTriangle
```

Comments

DragSpeed affects all the painting tools except the bucket and text tools.

At idle time **dragSpeed** is set to 0, the fastest possible speed. If you set **dragSpeed** to less than 0, it's set to 0.

At a speed of 72, the pointer covers about an inch per second.

If you set **dragSpeed** to any speed other than the maximum and then execute a **drag** command with the browse tool selected, the browse tool doesn't move; rather, the Macintosh acts as though it were in a wait state until the "drag" is completed. ("No, that's actually a feature.")

The following handler illustrates dragging a selected card picture at a slow drag speed. It assumes the existence of a small graphic, such as the triangle drawn by the preceding example. This is a popular way to do simple animation:

```
on slowDrag
  choose select tool
  doMenu "Select" -- lassos the whole card picture
  set dragSpeed to 100
  drag from 150,150 to 500,150
  choose browse tool
end slowDrag
```

Also See:

DRAG command, page 233

EDITBKGND

Forms

```
set {the} editBkgnd to logical

set editBkgnd to true
set editBkgnd to false
```

Action

The **editBkgnd** property reflects where editing takes place: if **editBkgnd** is set to true, editing takes place on the background; if it is false, editing takes place on the card.

The following handler creates a new background field:

```
on newBgFld
  set editBkgnd to true
  doMenu "New Field"
  set style of last field to rectangle
  set editBkgnd to false
  choose browse tool
end newBgFld
```

Comments

If the userLevel is set below 3, you can set **editBkgnd** to true but you won't be able to do any editing.

In 1.2.#, choosing the Browse tool or changing cards sets **editBkgnd** to false.

Moving objects to the background: The following two handlers move objects from the card level to the background level.

This handler moves a named button from the card to the background:

```
on btnToBkgnd buttonName
  select button buttonName
  type "x" with commandKey
  set editBkgnd to true
  type "v" with commandKey
  set editBkgnd to false
```

```
    choose browse tool
end btnToBkgnd
```

This handler moves a card field and any of its text to the background:

```
on fldToBkgnd fieldName
  get card field fieldName -- save text
  select card field fieldName
  type "x" with commandKey
  set editBkgnd to true
  type "v" with commandKey
  set editBkgnd to false
  choose browse tool
  put it into field fieldName -- restore text
end fldToBkgnd
```

If you have version 1.2.2 or later, the following shorter handler does the same thing:

```
on fldToBkgnd fieldName
  select card field fieldName
  type "x" with commandKey
  set editBkgnd to true
  type "v" with commandKey, shiftKey -- Shift-Paste pastes text, too
  set editBkgnd to false
  choose browse tool
end fldToBkgnd
```

ENABLED

Forms

```
set {the} enabled of [menu | menuItem] to logical

set enabled of menuItem 3 of menu "additions" to true
set enabled of menu "Edit" to false
```

Action

The **enabled** property, new in HyperCard 2.0, determines whether you can choose a particular menu item, or any item on a given menu.

Comments

Menu is the name or number of a specific menu. *MenuItem* is the name or number of a specific menu item on a specific menu.

You can't choose a menu item whose **enabled** property is set to false, or any item on a menu whose **enabled** property is set to false. Such items appear greyed out. (See Figure 10-6.)

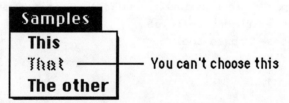

```
set the enabled of menuItem 2 of menu "Samples" to false
```

Figure 10-6 You can't choose a greyed-out menu item

The following example disables the menu items "First" or "Last" on the Go menu when you're on the first or last card:

```
on openCard
  -- put this handler in the stack script
  set the enabled of menuItem "First" of menu "Go" to ¬
  number of this card is not 1
  set the enabled of menuItem "Last" of menu "Go" to ¬
```

```
    number of this card is not the number of cards
end openCard
```

The default value for **enabled** is true.

You can't set the **enabled** property for any item on the Apple, Tools, Font, Style, or Patterns menu (but you can set the **enabled** of all menus).

The following handler disables an item on a menu if the user level is 3 or below:

```
on openStack
  if userLevel <= 3
  then set enabled of menuItem "Debug" of menu "Utilities" to false
end openStack
```

Overruling HyperCard Enables & Disables: You can disable a standard menu item enabled by HyperCard by setting its **enabled** property to false (except for items on the Apple, Tools, Font, Style, or Patterns menu), but you *can't* enable a standard menu item disabled by HyperCard by setting its **enabled** property to true. (In any event, the **result** function is unaffected.):

```
-- works fine all the time
set enabled of menuItem "New Stack..." of menu "File" to false

-- sometimes gets error, other times just doesn't work
set enabled of menuItem "Text style..." of menu "Edit" to true
```

To restore all standard HyperCard menu settings, use the **reset menuBar** command.

Also See:

DISABLE command, page 223
ENABLE command, page 238
RESET MENUBAR command, page 322

FILLED

Forms

```
set {the} filled to logical

set filled to true
```

Action

The **filled** property reflects whether shape-drawing painting tools draw hollow shapes (false) or shapes filled with the current pattern (true).

The following handler draws five filled blocks:

```
on fiveBlocks
  set filled to true
  choose rectangle tool
  put "20,50" into topLeft
  put "50,230" into botRight
  repeat 5 times
    set pattern to random(40)
    drag from topLeft to botRight
    add 40 to item 1 of topLeft
    add 40 to item 1 of botRight
  end repeat
  choose browse tool
end fiveBlocks
```

Comments

Tools affected by the **filled** property are:

rectangle   round rectangle   oval   curve   polygon   regular   polygon

The following two handlers use (respectively) filled regular polygons and filled circles to create designs:

```
on regPolys
  set filled to true
  set centered to true
  choose regular polygon tool
```

```
    repeat until the mouse is down
      set polySides to any item of "3,4,5,6,8"
      set pattern to random(40)
      drag from 200,200 to 200+random(100),200+random(100)
    end repeat
    choose browse tool
end regPolys

on circles
  set filled to true
  choose oval tool
  set centered to true
  put "200,200" into center
  repeat until the mouse is down
    put center into point
    put 15 into count
    put 10 into size
    add count * size to item 1 of point
    add count * size to item 2 of point
    repeat count times
      subtract size from item 1 of point
      subtract size from item 2 of point
      set pattern to random(40)
      drag from center to point
    end repeat
  end repeat
  choose browse tool
end circles
```

Filled with the Curve tool: When **filled** is set to true and you're currently drawing with the Curve tool, HyperCard draws a straight line connecting the starting and ending points of the shape and fills it with the current pattern.

Other ways to set Filled: double-clicking any of the affected tools on the Tools window chooses that tool and toggles the **filled** property. You can also change the state of **filled** by choosing the Draw Filled item on the Options menu.

Default value: The default value for **filled** is false.

Also See:

Draw Filled, *HyperCard User's Guide*

FIXEDLINEHEIGHT

Forms

```
set {the} fixedLineHeight of field to logical

set the fixedLineHeight of field 1 to true
```

Action

The **fixedLineHeight** property, new in HyperCard 2.0, reflects whether HyperCard automatically adjusts the spacing above and below lines of text of different sizes (that is, adjusts the leading) in a given field.

Comments

Field is any card or background field. *Logical* is any expression that evaluates to true or false.

The default value for **fixedLineHeight** is false, meaning that the line spacing in the field adjusts to the text typed into it.

set fixedLineHeight of field 1 to TRUE   set fixedLineHeight of field 1 to FALSE

Figure 10-7   fixedLineHeight property, TRUE (left) and FALSE for the same field

Changing the setting of this property makes a corresponding change to the Fixed Line Height option in the field's "Field Info..." dialog.

ShowLines and fixedLineHeight related: If the **showLines** property is true, the **fixedLineHeight** property is automatically set to true.

Also See:

SHOWLINES property, page 610
TEXTHEIGHT property, page 628

FREESIZE

Forms

```
put {the} freeSize of stack {into container}

put the freeSize of this stack into slop
```

Action

The **Freesize** property tells how many wasted bytes are locked within a stack. (Its only practical use is to decide whether or not to use the **compact stack** menu command.)

The following handler compacts the current stack at close time if it has more than 20,000 bytes free in it:

```
on closeStack
  if the freeSize of this stack > 20000
  then doMenu "Compact Stack"
end closeStack
```

Comments

Locked bytes accumulate within a stack each time you add or delete an item in that stack. Locked bytes waste space and slow down a stack's performance. (Think of them as stack cholesterol.)

You can't set **freeSize** with the **set** command; but you can set **freeSize** to 0 for the current stack (assuming the **userLevel** property is set above 2) by using the command

```
domenu "Compact Stack"
```

Sophisticated slop checking: Use the percentage of the size of the stack or a percentage of the size of the free space on the disk to determine when to compact a stack:

```
if the freeSize of this stack > .10 * the size of this stack
then doMenu "Compact Stack"
```

or

```
if the freeSize of this stack > .10 * the diskSpace
then doMenu "Compact Stack"
```

Also See:

COMPACT stack, *HyperCard User's Guide*
SIZE property, page 614
USERLEVEL property, page 639

GRID

Forms

```
set {the} grid to logical

set grid to true

set grid to false
```

Action

The **grid** property when true constrains the movements of selected bitmaps and many painting tools to increments of 8 pixels (about 1/9th of an inch).

Comments

The default value for **grid** is false.

You can also toggle **grid**'s value by choosing the **grid** item on the Options menu.

Grid is almost never used from a script because scripts can drag to exact coordinates. It's in the language essentially because Winkler and Atkinson decided to make every paint command available to scripts in some way, even if they couldn't think of a use for a particular command at the time.

(And no, you don't win a toaster if you come up with a good use for **grid**.)

Also See:

DRAG command, page 233

HEIGHT

Forms

```
set {the} height of [field|button|card] to integerExpr

set height of last button to 100
```

Action

The **height** property reflects the distance in pixels between the top and bottom of an element.

The following handler sets the height of all buttons on the card to be the same as the height of the first button:

```
on alignHeight
  repeat with i = 2 to the number of buttons
    set height of button i to height of button 1
  end repeat
end alignHeight
```

Comments

Button or **field** must be in the current stack.

When you set the height of an element, that object grows or shrinks vertically around its center such that its center point (described by the **location** property) doesn't change. If the height is an odd number, the odd pixel is added to the bottom half.

The heights of some windows (tool, pattern, msg) are all fixed, so you can't set them (but you can examine them).

Heights don't include the title bar or other perimeters.

The actual height of the Message box is 13 pixels more than is reported by

```
height of the Message box.
```

The following three handlers by Robin Shank make a field adjust its size based on how much text is in it. As written, all three handlers belong in the script of the field to be adjusted:

```
on closeField
  adjustHeight
end closeField

on returnInField
  put return after the selection
  get the selectedChunk
  adjustHeight
  select it
end returnInField

on adjustHeight
  lock screen
  put topLeft of me into saveTopLeft
  if number of lines in me > 1 then
    set height of me to number of lines in me * textHeight of me + 6
    set topLeft of me to saveTopLeft
  end if
  unlock screen
end adjustHeight
```

Hiding an object with Height: When you assign a value of 0 or a negative value to the height of an object, that object disappears. When it's in that state, you can send messages to the object but it won't respond to manual mouse actions. If the hidden object is a field, you can programmatically type into it and manipulate a selection within it, but you can't see what's going on. A field thus hidden remains in the Tabbing order, but is apt to confuse users (because when you tab to a hidden field, you can't see the selection); it's better to hide the object by setting its **visible** to false, thus taking it out of the tabbing order.

An object hidden by giving its **height** property a negative value responds differently than does an object whose **visible** property is set to false; see the **visible** property (page 648) for details.

Other ways to change Height: You can also change an object's height programmatically by changing its **rectangle** property. (**Height** is the same as item 4 minus item 2 of **rectangle**.)

Using Height to set up button zones: The following handler automatically divides a button into a number of vertical zones, and computes which of the

540

zones was clicked on. The button must be precisely aligned over the zones it is intended to control, such that the very top of the button lies at the top of the topmost zone and the very bottom of the button lies at the bottom of the bottommost zone. (The width is not critical.) In the case of this example, shown in Figure 10-8, there are 26 zones — one for each letter of the English alphabet. Use it as the edge of an alphabetically indexed stack:

```
on mouseUp -- based on an idea by Gary Bond
    put (the clickV - top of me)/height of me into ratio
    put numToChar(charToNum("A")+trunc(ratio*26)) -- where you clicked
end mouseUp
```

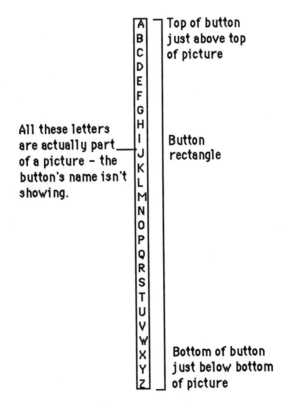

Figure 10-8   One button acts like 26 buttons (or as many as you want)

Also See:

HILITE

Forms

```
set {the} hilite of button to logical

set hilite of me to true

set hilite of button 1 to false
```

Action

The **hilite** property determines whether a button appears normal (false) or hilited (true).

Comments

The value for **hilite** of a new button is false. *Button* must be in the current stack.

When the **sharedHilite** property of a button is true, the hilite property of a background button has the same value across all cards of that background. So if you hilite a background button on card 1, that same button is also hilited on (for example) card 5 of that background.

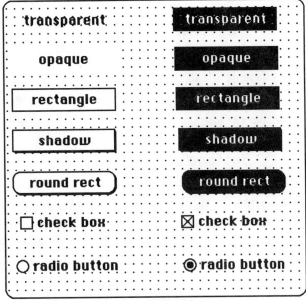

Figure 10-9   Unhilited and hilited buttons

What "hilited" means: Different styles of buttons are hilited in different ways: a hilited check box has an X in it; a hilited radio button has a dot in its center; all other hilited buttons appear in inverse video (that is, light text on a dark background).

When a transparent iconic button hilites, the text and icon portion appear in inverse video; the rest appears as it does when the button is unhilited (Figure 10-10):

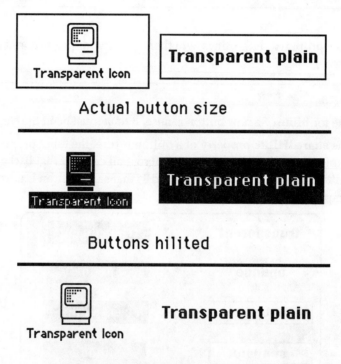

Figure 10-10   Iconic hiliting

Text deselected: When the **hilite** property of a button changes, any selected text is deselected and the insertion point is removed. The following button handler shows how a button can be hilited and the selection restored:

```
on mouseUp
  get the selectedChunk
  set hilite of me to true
```

```
    wait 10 ticks -- delay so user can see the hiliting
    set hilite of me to false
    select it
end mouseUp
```

Other spellings: Alternate spellings for **hilite** are `highlite, hilight,` and `highlight`.

One radio button hilited at a time: Apple's human interface standards suggest that only one button in a bank of radio buttons be hilited at any given time. The following handler placed in script of the card, background, stack or home stack makes sure that the object that was clicked on is a radio button, and then loops through all radio buttons on the current card unhiliting every one except the one just clicked on. (The handler assumes that there's only one bank of radio buttons on the card):

```
on mouseUp
  if "button" is not in the target then pass mouseUp
  if style of the target is not "radioButton" then pass mouseUp
  repeat with i = 1 to the number of buttons
    if style of button i is not "radioButton" then next repeat
    set hilite of button i to i = number of the target
  end repeat
end mouseUp
```

Also See:

AUTOHILITE property, page 490
SHAREDHILITE property, page 607

ICON

Forms

```
set {the} icon of button to expr

set icon of button 7 to -15859 -- icon numbers often negative

set icon of button Fred to "ideas"
```

Action

The **icon** property reflects what icon (if any) HyperCard uses as the graphic for a particular button.

Comments

Button must be in the current stack. *Expr* is the ID number or name (if any) of an ICON resource that resides in the current stack, Home stack, HyperCard, or the System file.

When you **get** or **put** the icon of a button, you end up with the icon's ID number, even if it has a name:

```
put icon of button "My Icon" -- yields 20965, although icon's name is "Memo"
```

See page 796 for the iconName external, which yields an icon's name.

Macintosh icons are all 32 pixels square.

A button has no icon when icon is set to 0 (zero).

Iconic animation: Usually you set the icon at button creation time by clicking the proper box in the button's info dialog. Under most circumstances, you'd only change the icon when you're doing animation.

The following script performs a simple animation by cycling through a series of icons (illustrated in Figure 10-11):

```
on mouseUp
  repeat until the mouse is down
    repeat with i = 1 to 4
      set icon of me to item i of "Up Arrow,Next Arrow,Down Arrow,Prev Arrow"
      wait 10 ticks
```

```
      end repeat
    end repeat
  end mouseUp
```

Up Arrow   Next Arrow   Down Arrow   Prev Arrow

Figure 10-11   Icons for button animation

Limit on button styles: An icon is invisible when the button's style is radio button or check box.

For best results, always use "transparent" as the style of a button that uses an icon.

Getting icons: You can see what icons are available in the current stack by clicking the "icon" button on the Info box of any button; when you click on any icon from the dialog box that appears, that icon's resource ID and name (if any) appears at the top of the dialog box. (An icon is available to a stack if the icon is part of that stack or is part of the Home stack.) You can move icons from one stack to another, or from any resource file to any other resource file, by using Apple Computer's resCopy stack. This stack is available free from user's groups and from electronic information utilities like Compuserve®.

Fantastic icon editor: Version 2.0 has an insanely great icon editor. You can move any icon in the system to the current stack, edit an existing icon, or create your own icons from scratch without leaving HyperCard. To get to the icon editor, click "Icon..." on any button's Info dialog; then click "Edit..." on the dialog that appears. See the 2.0 HyperCard reference manual for the details of this really great new feature.

When you paste a button with an icon to a stack, the button takes its icon with it and the icon thereafter is part of that stack if it isn't already available to the stack.

Also See:

STYLE property, page 617

ID

Forms

```
put {the} id of [background|field|button] {into container}
put {the}{adjective}id of card {into container}

put the id of this bkgnd
put the long id of next card into it
```

Action

The **ID** property reflects the unique identification number of a particular object.

The following handler illustrates how a card, background, or stack can tell if a message was sent directly to it or whether the message got to it through the message passing path:

```
on mouseUp
  if id of the target is id of me -- message did not go through path
  then put "message was sent to me"
  else put "message got to me through message passing path"
end mouseUp
```

Comments

You can't set the ID of an object.

Adjective can be long, short, abbr, abbrev, or abbreviated:

Long: card id 5684 of stack "The Book:A HyperTalk - The Book:test"

Abbr{ev{iated}}: card id 5684

Short: 5684

Using Abbr{ev{iated}} or using no adjective has the same result.

HyperCard creates unique IDs for all objects except stacks and HyperCard itself.

How IDs are reported: The IDs of noncard objects look like the short ID of a card — that is, the property "ID of this bkgnd" or "ID of button myButton" or "ID of field myField" is reported as an unlabeled number.

While several objects of the same type might have the same name, they'll never have the same ID in places where such a similarity might cause confusion. For example, no two buttons on the same card will have the same ID, although all buttons can have the same name.

When you delete an object in a stack, that object's ID is unlikely to recur for the life of that stack.

About adjective with noncards: You won't get an error message if you use the *adjective* option to get the ID of objects other than cards, but the result is the same as not using *adjective*. Because either of these facts is liable to change in future versions, it's best to restrict using *adjective* only for cards.

Also See:

NAME property, pages 576, 579
NUMBER property, page 583

LANGUAGE

Forms

```
set {the} language to expr

set language to "French"
```

Action

The **language** property reflects the language in which you read and write scripts.

The following handler catches edit script messages and warns if the language is not English:

```
on edit
  if the language is "English" then pass edit
  answer "The language is " & the language & ". Set to English?" with ¬
  the language or "English"
  if it is "English" then set the language to it
  pass edit
end edit
```

Comments

The default language is English.

To use a language other than English, a translator resource for that language must be available in the current stack, in the Home stack, or in HyperCard. When you try to use a language for which there is no translator resource, you get the message "Don't have a translator for that language."

Points for techies: Scripts are always stored on the disk in English. The translator translates scripts just before the script editor displays them, and then translates them back to English just before the scripts are stored on the disk again.

Translators can perform any transformation on a script, including turning it into Pascal or BASIC or C and back again. For an example of how a translator can be used to allow block comments within a handler, see Chapter 15, "Translators."

Also See:

TRANSLATORS, Chapter 15

LEFT

Forms

```
set {the} left of [button|field|card|window] to integerExpr

set left of msg to 25
set left of pattern window to left of tool window
```

Action

The **left** property tells the distance between the left edge of an element and some reference location:

Element	Reference location
object	left edge of card window
noncard windows	left edge of card window
card window or card	left edge of screen

(That is, all object locations are relative to the card window location; the card and card window locations are relative to the screen.)

Comments

Expr evaluates to a positive or a negative integer.

The following handler repeatedly increments and decrements the left of the message box, making it shake on the screen until you click the mouse:

```
on friscoDisco
  get left of message box
  repeat until the mouse is down
    set left of message box to it + 1
    set left of message box to it - 1
  end repeat
end friscoDisco
```

Visible boundaries: Locations 0 through 511 are within a standard card's width and are therefore visible on all Macintosh displays when the card window is at 0,0. Points outside those boundaries might or might not be visible, depending upon the size of the display you're using. Moving an element outside the visible boundaries of the display doesn't change its **visible** setting, and is harmless (but the only way to get it back within visible boundaries is through a script).

Left of card windows: Left of card window is constrained to multiples of 16 for efficiency of graphics updating. If you try to set this property to something that is not a multiple of 16, the value the property actually gets will be the multiple of 16 closest to the number you requested.

Left of Rectangle: The value of **left** is the same as item 1 of the rectangle property of the same element.

Changing left's value: Anything that moves an element changes its **left** value. Such methods include (but are not limited to) dragging the element either programmatically or manually, setting its **location** property, changing its rectangle property, or using the **show** command with a different value following **at.**

Also See:

BOTTOM property, page 497
BOTTOMRIGHT property, page 499
RECTANGLE property, page 593
RIGHT property, page 597
TOP property, page 635
TOPLEFT property, page 637

LINESIZE

Forms

```
set {the} lineSize to integerExpr

set lineSize to 2
```

Action

The **lineSize** property reflects the thickness of borders and lines drawn with painting tools.

The following handler draws several concentric circles with a diminishing lineSize. (It's supposed to look like ripples caused by a rock dropped into a pond, but hey...):

```
on ripples
  choose oval tool
  set centered to true
  put 200 into h
  put 175 into v
  put h & "," & v into center
  repeat with i = 1 to 10
    set lineSize to 10 - i
    add 10+the lineSize to h
    add 10+the lineSize to v
    drag from center to h,v
  end repeat
end ripples
```

Comments

The thickness of a line is measured in pixels.

Meaningful values for *integerExpr* are 1, 2, 3, 4, 6, and 8. Other positive integers set lineSize to the next lower valid number (so 5 gets 4, and 32767 gets 8).

Changing lineSize affects only subsequent creations: When you change the value of **lineSize,** you affect only future creations; existing graphics keep the borders and line thicknesses in effect at the time of their creation.

Default lineSize: The default setting for **lineSize** is 1.

Setting lineSize manually: You can set **lineSize** manually by clicking the appropriate line on the dialog box that appears when you double-click the line tool on the tool window or when you choose the Line Size command from the Options menu.

LOCATION

Forms

```
set {the} loc{ation} of [button|field|card|window] to location

set loc of button 1 to 100, 200
```

Action

The **location** (or **loc**) property reflects the location of a particular button, field, card, or window.

Comments

Button or *field* must be in the current stack.

Location is a point on the display, expressed as two integers separated by a comma, at the center of any resizable item or at the upper-left corner of the content region of nonresizable items. The integers represent respectively the horizontal and vertical distances (in pixels) from the left and top edges of a source:

Element	Source
object	top-left corner of card window
noncard windows	top-left corner of card window
card window or card	top-left corner of screen

Setting the location of an object is likely to move the object; it doesn't, however, affect the object's width or height.

The following handler places the card window, the tool window, the pattern window, and the message box at convenient locations for use on a Mac II 13" screen:

```
on startUp
   set loc of card window to 96,57
   show message box at 19,362
   show tool window at -77, 13
   show pattern window at -77,183
end startUp
```

Loc and sources of values: The **location** is expressed as two integers separated by a comma. So you can refer to **loc's** values as items:

```
put item 1 of the loc of button 6 into Horizontal
```

To assign a value to a variable that you'll later use to set a location, be sure to put the assignment in quotation marks:

```
put "110, 130" into buttonLoc
```

Visible boundaries: Locations 0,0 through 511,341 are within a card's area and are therefore visible on all Macintosh displays. Points outside those boundaries might or might not be visible, depending upon the size of the display you're using. Moving an element outside the visible boundaries of the display doesn't change its **visible** setting, and is harmless.

Other properties affected: When you change the location of an object, you might also be changing a number of other properties including **rectangle, top, left, right, bottom, topLeft,** and **bottomRight.**

Also See:

BOTTOM property, page 497
BOTTOMRIGHT property, page 499
LEFT property, page 552
RECTANGLE property, page 593
RIGHT property, page 597
TOP property, page 635
TOPLEFT property, page 637

LOCKMESSAGES

Forms

```
set {the} lockMessages to logical

set lockMessages to true
```

Action

The **lockMessages** property reflects whether HyperCard automatically sends open and close system messages to stacks, backgrounds, or cards. When **lockMessages** is true, no open or close messages are sent to these objects, and handlers that normally run when they receive these messages don't execute.

Comments

Because it takes time for messages to go through the message passing path, setting **lockMessages** to true increases the speed at which handlers execute. Speed is also increased when **lockMessages** is true because handlers ordinarily executed by open or close messages don't operate.

The following handler sets lockMessages to true to speed up the process of traversing all cards in the stack:

```
on countVotes
  set lockScreen to true
  set lockMessages to true
  go to stack "Polling Places" -- each card holds results from one poll
  put empty into totals
  repeat for the number of cards
    repeat with i = 1 to the number of fields
      add field i to item i of totals -- each field is one candidate
    end repeat
    go to next card
  end repeat
  put "Winner got " & max(i) & " votes."
end countVotes
```

Certain handlers won't automatically execute: Because **lockMessages** prevents certain open and close system messages from being sent, handlers that depend upon such messages won't execute as long as **lockMessages** is in effect. Such messages include:

```
openCard    openBackground    openStack

closeCard   closeBackground   closeStack
```

But **lockMessages** doesn't stop any messages that your handler sends:

```
on mouseUp
   set lockMessages to true
   go card 5 -- no closeCard or openCard system message automatically sent
   openCard -- openCard message sent along message path, so an
   -- openCard handler further along the path will execute!
   go card 6 -- no closeCard or openCard system message automatically sent
end mouseUp
```

LockMessages is reset to false (the default state) at idle time.

Creating a Lock Messages command: The **lockScreen** property has the covenient commands **lock screen** and **unlock screen** to set it to true and false, respectively. The following handlers (which should be placed in the script of the Home stack) provide the same convenience for **lockMessages:**

```
on lock what
   if what is "messages" -- Is this a lockMessages command?
   then set lockMessages to true -- Yes, so set lockMessages
   else pass lock -- No, must be some other lock (screen, ness, etc.)
end lock

on unlock what
   if what is "messages" -- Is this a lockMessages command?
   then set lockMessages to false -- Yes, so clear lockMessages
   else pass unlock -- No, must be some other unlock
end lock
```

Also See:

MESSAGES, Chapter 1
SPEED, Chapter 12

LOCKRECENT

Forms

```
set {the} lockRecent to logical

set lockRecent to true
```

Action

The **lockRecent** property reflects whether the images of newly encountered cards are added to the Recent display.

Comments

Setting **lockRecent** to true stops images from being added to Recent, and slightly increases the speed of handlers that include card-changing commands.

HyperCard acts as if **LockRecent** is set to true when the **lockScreen** property is set to true (no matter what the actual setting of **lockRecent**). So the **lockRecent** property is, in actual practice, rarely explicitly set.

Reset at idle time: **lockRecent** is reset to false (the default state) at idle time.

About Recent: Recent, brought up when you choose the Recent command from the Go menu (or when you press Command-R), lets you go immediately to a card by clicking on that card's image. Recent holds images of up to the last 42 different cards encountered.

Recent's actions are totally separate from the **push card** and **pop card** commands (which can store and retrieve the addresses of up to 20 cards), from the actions of the **go back** and **go forth** HyperTalk commands, and from the up and down arrow keys (which, with the **textArrows** property set to false, can review the last 100 cards encountered).

Also See:

ARROWKEY command, page 171
LOCKSCREEN property, page 562
POP card command, page 297

PUSH card command, *HyperCard User's Guide*
RECENT command, *HyperCard User's Guide*
SPEED, Chapter 12
TEXTARROWS property, page 624

LOCKSCREEN

Forms

```
set {the} lockScreen to logical

set lockScreen to true
set lockScreen to false
set lockScreen to x < 10
set lockScreen to it
```

Action

The **lockscreen** property reflects whether changes to the visual interface take place on the display.

Comments

Setting **lockScreen** to true has exactly the same effect as the **lock screen** command: until **lockScreen** is set to false, (1) the current image stays on the display no matter what visual changes are taking place behind the scenes, and (2) no additional card images are added to Recent.

Setting **lockScreen** to true can significantly increase the speed of handlers that include card-changing commands.

LockRecent is automatically set to true when **lockScreen** is set to true.

The following handler illustrates how to create a new card with several default values filled in. It locks the screen while filling in the values so that they all appear at once rather than one at a time:

```
on mouseUp
  set lockScreen to true
  doMenu "New Card"
  repeat with i = 1 to the number of fields
    put short name of field i into field i -- or whatever
  end repeat
  unlock screen with dissolve
end mouseUp
```

All visited cards recorded: Even though you don't see cards when **lockScreen** is set to true, all cards that HyperCard goes to (up to 100 or so) are in the "back" buffer. You can see such cards by choosing Back from the Go menu.

Lockscreen's counter: HyperTalk keeps track of the number of times you've used `set lockscreen to true` (or its equivalent, lock screen). Each `set lockScreen to true` must be balanced with a `set lockscreen to false` or the display remains locked.

Default value: The default value for **lockScreen** is false.

Be kind to your users: When you lock a screen to prevent changes from being visible, be sure to set the **cursor** property to "watch" or to "busy" so that your users know that something is happening. It's easy to assume the system is hung up when it seems that everything has just gone away — which is the visible impression when you've set **LockScreen** to true.

Also See:

RECENT command, *HyperCard User's Guide*
SPEED, Chapter 12

LOCKTEXT

Forms

```
set {the} lockText of field to logical

set lockText of me to false

set lockText of field 1 to true
```

Action

The **lockText** property determines whether the user can edit text in a field.

The following handler (which belongs in the card, background, or stack script) toggles the **lockText** property of a field when you click on it. (To click on a field that's unlocked, hold down the command key.)

```
on mouseUp
  if "field" is not in the target then pass mouseUp
  set lockText of the target to not lockText of the target
end mouseUp
```

Comments

Field must be in the current stack.

When **lockText** is false (the default state) and the browse tool is the active tool, the following is true:

- The pointer takes on the I-beam shape when it's over the field.

- Clicking in the field sends the message `openField` to the field and sets the insertion point.

- Dragging in the field produces a selection.

- The field holding the insertion point responds to presses of the return and enter keys and sends `returnInField` and `enterInField` messages.

- The field is in the Tabbing order.

- The Lock Text option in the field's Info dialog box is unchecked.

When **lockText** is true and the browse tool is the active tool, the following is true:

- The pointer shape stays the same when it's moved over the field.

- No manual editing can take place in the field (although you can edit programmatically).

- The field receives the mouse messages `mouseDown` `mouseStillDown` `mouseUp` when you click on it.

- The field is removed from the Tabbing order.

- The Lock Text option in the field's Info dialog box has an X in it.

The setting for **lockText** remains unchanged until you explicitly change it.

Send always gets through: You can send any message to a field using the keyword **send** no matter what the setting for **lockText.**

More about editing in fields: When the **cantModify** property for the current stack is true and the **userModify** property is false, you can't make even temporary changes to a field.

When **cantModify** is true, **userModify** is true, and **lockText** for a particular field is false, the user can edit text in the field; but the editing is discarded as soon as HyperCard goes to another card.

Also See:

CANTMODIFY property, page 508
SEND keyword, page 155
USERMODIFY property, page 642

MARKCHAR

Forms

```
set {the} markChar of menuItem to character

set markChar of menuItem 3 of menu 6 to "•" -- option-8
```

Action

The **markChar** property, new in HyperCard 2.0, determines what character (if any) appears to the left of a specific menu item.

Comments

MenuItem refers to a specific menu item of a specific menu.

Character is any character you can type from the keyboard or assign programmatically.

You can't set the **markChar** property for any item on the Apple, Tools, Font, Style, or Patterns menu.

Typically you'd use the **markChar** property to set off menu items particularly useful for some specific function, to group related menu items visually, or to note that some option was currently operating (as HyperCard does with the **Power Keys** menu choice on the options menu).

When MarkChar characters revert: All programmatically assigned **markChar** characters are canceled when you quit HyperCard.

Also See:

CHECKMARK property, page 514
COMMANDCHAR property, page 516
RESET MENUBAR command, page 322

MARKED

Forms

```
set {the} marked of card to logical

set marked of last card to true
```

Action

The **marked** property, new in HyperCard 2.0, determines whether a card is marked for possible action (usually printing, display, or further filtering) sometime in the future.

Comments

Card is any card in the current stack.

Changing the setting of this property makes a corresponding change to the Marked option in the card's "Card Info..." dialog.

Use "set marked of *card*" for single cards: If you want to mark more than one card, it's far more efficient to use the **mark** command instead of **set marked**. The following two handlers accomplish the same end:

```
on inefficient
  repeat with i = 1 to number of cards
    if (char 1 of field 1 of card i) is "J"
    then set marked of card i to true
  end repeat
end inefficient

on farBetter
  mark cards where char 1 of field 1 is "J"
end farBetter
```

Commands using "Marked": HyperCard commands that directly use this property include **go, print card,** and **show.**

Also See:

MARK command, page 273
UNMARK command, page 365

MENUMESSAGE

Forms

```
set {the} [menuMessage|menuMsg] of menuItem to message

set menuMsg of menuItem "Full Power" of menu "Actions" to meltDown
set menuMsg of last menuItem of second menu to answer "No quitting!"
```

Action

The **menuMessage** (or **menuMsg**) property, new in HyperCard 2.0, determines what message, if any, is sent when you choose a particular menu item.

Comments

MenuItem names a specific menu item of a specific menu.

A menu item can have only one message assigned to it. (Of course, a message can call a user-defined handler that issues a host of messages of its own.) The most recent message assigned to a menu item applies.

You can't set the **menuMessage** property for any item on the Apple, Tools, Font, Style, or Patterns menu.

The following example, which belongs in the script of the Home stack, creates a "customized Recent" menu. (Be sure to call the handler name "History" from your startUp handler to make the script take effect.) Once the menu is created, you choose "Add" (or, to make it easy, Command-A) to add the current card to the bottom of the menu; later, you can click on the entry to go back to that card. It's like having your own Recent list where you choose the entries:

```
on History
  put "Add,Delete,-" into menu "History" with menuMessages ¬
  "addToHistory,deleteFromHistory," -- last item empty
  set commandChar of menuItem "Add" of menu "History" to "A"
  set commandChar of menuItem "Delete" of menu "History" to "D"
end History

-- the following two handlers should go in the home stack or
-- a "start using" stack so they'll always be found
```

568

```
on addToHistory
   put the long name of this card into goDest
   put the short name of this card into itemName
   put itemName after menu "History" with menuMsg "go to " & goDest
end addToHistory

on deleteFromHistory
   get the short name of this card

   -- make sure it's in the menu
   repeat with i = 1 to the number of menuItems in menu "History"
      if (name of menuItem i of menu "History") is it then
         delete menuItem i of menu "History"
         exit deleteFromHistory
      end if
   end repeat
   answer "This card is not on the History menu."
end deleteFromHistory
```

A message is only one word long. If you set the **menuMsg** to an item's name and that name is several words long, HyperCard sees the first word as the message and the second and subsequent words as parameters. (And if what HyperCard thinks are parameters aren't separated from each other by commas, you'll get an error message.)

Overruling HyperCard Messages: You can use **menuMessage** to redefine the actions of standard HyperCard menu items, but this is liable to confuse regular HyperCard users. For the sake of your users, it's often better to disable a particular menu item by setting its **enabled** property to false (as described on page 530), and by using **put** to create a new menu item.

DoMenu takes precedence: A **doMenu** handler takes precedence over **menuMessage**, and **menuMessage** takes precedence over a built-in command.

When you choose an item from a menu, doMenu *itemName, menuName* goes through the message passing path. Only after the **doMenu** call has traversed the complete path uncaught (or passed) does HyperCard check to see if the **menuMessage** property for that item has been set.

Also See:

DOMENU command, page 229
ENABLED property, page 530

MESSAGEWATCHER

Forms

```
set {the} messageWatcher to expr

set messageWatcher to myCustomWatcher
```

Action

The **messageWatcher** property, new in HyperCard 2.0, reflects the name of the current message watcher XCMD, HyperCard's facility for displaying messages for debugging.

Comments

The default message watcher (the one that comes with HyperCard) is named `MessageWatcher`.

If you set the **messageWatcher** property to a message watcher that doesn't exist, HyperCard uses the default message watcher.

This property is seldom used. Custom message watchers are XCMDs written by Pascal, C, and assembly language programmers who also provide installer scripts to set this property if necessary; most scriptwriters find that the default message watcher serves adequately.

For details about the resident message watcher, see Chapter 2.

Also See:

DEBUG command, page 206
EXTERNALS OVERVIEW, Chapter 13
SCRIPTEDITOR property, page 602
SCRIPTS, Chapter 2
VARIABLEWATCHER property, page 644

MULTIPLE

Forms

```
set {the} multiple to logical

set multiple to true
set multiple to false
set multiple to hilite of button "multiple"
```

Action

The **multiple** property reflects whether certain painting tools produce multiple (true) or single images (false).

The following handler uses multiple to draw concentric rectangles

```
on mouseUp
  choose rectangle tool
  set centered to true
  set multiple to true
  set dragSpeed to 200
  set multiSpace to 5
  drag from 250,200 to 450,300
  choose browse tool
end mouseUp
```

Comments

Tools which draw multiple images when **multiple** is set to true are

```
line, rectangle rounded, rectangle, oval, regular polygon
```

Setting the **multiple** property to true puts a checkmark next to the Draw Multiple item on the Options menu. Choosing Draw Multiple toggles the value of **multiple.**

Multiple has no effect if dragSpeed is 0.

Multiple gets set to false each time you enter the paint tools or issue the command `reset paint.`

Also See:

Draw Multiple, *Hypercard User's Guide*
MULTISPACE property, page 574

MULTISPACE

Forms

```
set {the} multispace to integerExpr

set multiSpace to 10
set multiSpace to field 1
```

Action

The **multiSpace** property determines the space between images subsequently drawn in a single sweep when the multiple property is set to true.

Comments

Meaningful values for *integerExpr* range from 1 through 100 or so. Tools affected are

```
line, rectangle, rounded rectangle, oval, regular polygon
```

The default value for **multiSpace** is 1. The higher the value that you set, the more space appears between images. A value of 0 has the same effect as the value 1; values above 150 yield silly results.

The following handler shows a typical use for the **multiSpace** property, and produces the image shown in Figure 10-13:

```
on thingee
  reset paint
  choose oval tool
  set multiple to true
  set dragSpeed to 200
  set multiSpace to 15
  put "128,80" into topLeft
  put "320,272" into botRight
  put "320,80" into topRight
  put "128,272" into botLeft
  drag from topLeft to botRight with shiftKey
  drag from botRight to topLeft with shiftKey
```

```
   drag from botLeft to topRight with shiftKey
   drag from topRight to botLeft with shiftKey
end thingee
```

Figure 10-13   MultiSpace at work

Effects on dragging: Dragging a selected image with the option and command keys pressed produces a multiple image. The setting for **multiSpace** affects these images the same way that it affects the images drawn with the listed tools.

Also See:

MULTIPLE property, page 572

NAME OF [*MENU* | *MENUITEM*]

Forms

```
set {the} name of menuItem to expr
get {the} name of menu

set name of menuItem "Utilize alphabetics" of menu 4 to "Use letters"
set the name of menuItem "upper" of menu "Choices" to "lower"
set name of first menuItem of last menu to "Check Seismograph"
get name of menu 7
```

Action

The **name of menu** property, new in HyperCard 2.0, reflects the names of individual menus and menu items.

Comments

Menu identifies a specific menu, and *menuItem* identifies a specific menu item of a specific menu, currently available on the menu bar.

Menu or *menuItem* must be in the menu bar when you use this property or you'll get an error message.

Name of *menu* is read-only. **Name of** *menuItem* is read-write.

You use **name** to learn the name of an existing menu, or to identify or change the name of an existing menu item. (You can't use **name** to change the name of a menu.) To create a menu or menu item, use the **create** and **put into menu** commands.

To change the name of a menu, delete the old menu and create a new one with a different name.

The width of a menu expands or contracts as appropriate to fit the width of an item's name. The name of a menu item can be of any practical length (that is, well over 50 characters).

The following handler toggles the name of a menu item between "Residence" and "Office". The menu item is item 3 of a menu called "Locations":

```
on doMenu itemName
  if itemName is not "Residence" and itemName is not "Office"
  then pass doMenu
  if itemName is "Residence"
  then put "Office" into itemName
  else put "Residence" into itemName
  set name of menuItem 3 of menu "Locations" to itemName
end doMenu
```

Figure 10-14   The Incredible Stretching Menu

You can set the **textStyle, textFont,** and **textSize** properties of a menu item name. The name of a menu, however, always appears in 12 point chicago plain.

Setting the name of a menu item to "-" (the minus sign) draws a thin line across the menu in place of the name. Setting it to " " (a single space) or to "" (empty) leaves the menu item blank, as if you had typed a row of space characters across the width of the menu.

You can't retrieve or set the name of any item on the Tools or Patterns menu. You can't set the name of any item on the Apple menu.

A rose by any other name...: When you change the name of an item on the Font menu, that change is reflected in the Text Style dialog. But changing the name of an item doesn't change its functionality; all you're changing is its name.

Changed items with old HyperCard names: When you set the name of a menu item to the same name as a standard HyperCard menu item, choosing the new item causes the same behavior as choosing the standard menu item (unless the new item has a different message assigned to its **menuMessage** property). For example, if you change an existing menu item to "Home,"

choosing that item takes you to the Home stack. HyperCard does not, however, automatically check, uncheck, enable, disable, or assign the "standard"
command key to the new item.

Also See:

CREATE MENU command, page 202
DELETE MENU command, page 215
MENUMESSAGE property, page 568
TEXTSTYLE property, page 632

NAME OF *OBJECT*

Forms

```
set {the} name of object to expr

set name of last button to "Fred"

set name of me to it
```

Action

The **name** property reflects the name of an object.

The following handler gives the name "Button *n*" to each new button, where *n* is the button's number on the card. (Ordinarily, HyperCard assigns the name "New Button" to each new button.) This handler belongs in the card, background, or stack script:

```
on newButton
  set name of last button to "Button " & number of last button
end newButton
```

Comments

If an object has no name, HyperTalk uses the object's ID as the name.

You can change the name of any object by using the **set** command or by typing the name manually into that object's Info dialog box.

You can store type information about a button or field in the name property. The following handler (which belongs in the card, background, or stack script) looks at the name of a button to know what to do — if the name starts with the word "application," HyperTalk considers the rest of the name to be an application to sublaunch; if the name starts with any other word, then HyperTalk assumes that the name of the button is the name of a stack to go to:

```
on mouseUp
  if "button" is not in the target then pass mouseUp
  get short name of the target
  if word 1 of it is "Application" then
    delete word 1 of it
    open it
```

```
    else go to it
end mouseUp
```

Name forms: There are three forms of the **name** property— the short name, the name, or the long name. (You can always refer to an object using the name or the long name forms; whether you can use the short name form varies from object to object, as detailed later in this chapter):

The form `short name` is just the name of the object:

```
myButton
myField
myBackground
```

If the object doesn't have a name, the short name is the object's type and ID:

```
card button id 4
card id 3745
bkgnd id 5170
```

The form `name` is the object's type plus its `short name`:

```
card button "myButton"
bkgnd field "myField"
stack "myStack"
```

The form `long name` is the object's `name` plus its full path:

```
stack "myHardDisk:myFolder:myStack"
bkgnd "myBackground" of stack "myHardDisk:myFolder:myStack"
card "myCard" of stack "myHardDisk:myFolder:myStack"
```

Name bug alert #1: Name length

Keep the names of objects (other than stacks) to 29 or fewer characters. A bug in all HyperCard versions through 1.2.# lets HyperCard match only the first 29 characters of a name when you reference that object. If the real name has 30 or more characters in it, a reference to that object by name will fail all the time (but a reference to it by ID or number will succeed).

No matter what form you use for the object HyperCard, you always get HyperCard.

For details on naming specific objects, see Chapter 4, "Referring to Objects."

Name bug alert #2: Renaming stacks

When you rename a stack in an open directory under MultiFinder, the Finder won't know about the name change until you close that directory. HyperCard might not be able to find a stack whose name change is yet to be recognized .

About button names: You can set the name of a button to a source that contains carriage returns, but the returns won't show (Figure 10-15):

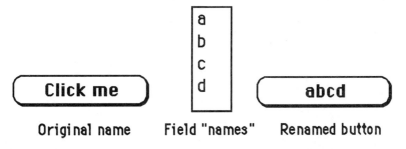

Original name   Field "names"   Renamed button

Figure 10-15 Set name of button "Click me" to field "names"

Banner button names: The following handler turns the name of a button into a banner that streams through the button:

```
on mouseUp -- based on an idea by XCMD wizard Gary Bond
  set showName of me to true
  set textAlign of me to left
  put "              Buy another copy...    " into banner
  repeat with i = 1 to length(banner)
    set name of me to char i to length(banner) of banner
    wait 5 ticks
  end repeat
end mouseUp
```

Also See:

ID property, page 548
REFERRING TO OBJECTS, Chapter 4
SHOWNAME property (for buttons), page 611

NUMBER

Forms

```
put {the} number of [button|field|card|background] {into container}

put the number of button id 3 into it
```

Action

The **number** property tells you the object's position in its domain:

- A card's number is the card's position in a stack.

- A button's number is its layer from back to front in its background or on its card (higher numbers closer to the front).

- A field's number is its layer from back to front in its background or on its card (higher numbers closer to the front).

- A background's number reflects its birth order in the family of backgrounds for that stack.

Comments

HyperCard gives numbers to objects sequentially within a type as the objects are created, starting with the number 1.

When you delete a card, field, or button whose number isn't the highest of its type, HyperCard renumbers all the objects of that type having a higher number than the one deleted.

You can change the number of a card by cutting that card and pasting it someplace else in a stack. You can change the number of a field or button by selecting that object and using the Send Farther and Bring Closer commands from the Objects menu.

You can't change the number of any object with the **set** command. You can't change the number of a background at all.

The following handlers show how to construct "go next" and "go prev" buttons that will not wrap around past the ends of the stack. The idea is to hide the "go next" button if you're on the last card, and to hide the "go prev" button if you're on the first card:

```
on mouseUp -- goes in "go next" button
  lock screen -- allow openCard to set visible of buttons before drawing
  go to next card
end mouseUp

on openCard -- goes in background script
  set visible of button "Next" to the number of this card is not ¬
  the number of cards
  set visible of button "Prev" to the number of this card is not 1
  pass openCard
end openCard
```

Number implemented as function

Although an object's number is logically a property (which is why it's listed here and not with the **number** function in Chapter 9), it's actually implemented as a function. So when you ask for

```
number of field id 6
```

you're really calling a function. This means you can use parentheses to call it:

```
number(field id 6)
```

Also See:

ID property, page 548
REFERRING TO OBJECTS, Chapter 4
NUMBER function, page 438

NUMBERFORMAT

Forms

```
set {the} numberFormat to quotedExpr

set numberFormat to "000.###"
```

Action

The **numberFormat** property determines how HyperTalk shows the results of numeric calculations in display areas (such as fields, the Message box, and — if you're given to wild fits of creativity — the names of buttons).

The following handler shows how to set numberFormat to handle dollars and cents:

```
on bucksPerSucker
  ask "What's the jackpot?"
  put it into jackpot
  ask "How many tickets were sold?"
  put it into suckers
  set numberFormat to "0.00"
  answer "That's $" & jackpot/suckers & " per ticket."
end bucksPerSucker
```

Comments

HyperTalk does all calculations internally using up to 19 digits of accuracy. **NumberFormat** reflects how many of those digits appear when it's time to show the results of a calculation.

QuotedExpr is a quoted string in the form "0...0.#...#" or "0...0.0...0".

The zeros to the left of the decimal indicate the *minimum* number of integer digits you want to appear. HyperTalk always puts at least as many digits to the left of the decimal as there are digits in the calculation's result — extra zeros in **numberFormat** beyond the number of digits in the result tells HyperCard to pad digits.

The pound signs to the right of the decimal indicate the *maximum* number of decimal digits to appear in the final display, but only if the digit has value.

Zeros to the right of the decimal in the format indicate the *exact* number of decimal digits to appear.

The following list shows examples based on the result 123.456789. The first example is the default for **numberFormat:**

NumberFormat	Result
"0.######"	123.456789
"000.###"	123.457
"0000.##"	0123.46
"0.########"	123.456789
"0000.00000000"	0123.45678900
"0"	123

NumberFormat reverts to its default value at idle time.

Calculation necessary: For **numberFormat** to work at all, the value to be displayed must have had some calculation performed upon it. For example, using the default format:

```
put pi into msg          yields   3.14159265358979323846
put pi + 0 into msg       yields   3.141593
```

Maximum length: The maximum number of characters that **numberFormat** can handle is 31. Any character beyond the 31st is ignored.

Rounding can be curious: Rounding is usually up, but when the only digit to be rounded is a 5, rounding is down. Thus in the format "0.#", the expression 5.55 + 0 yields 5.5, but 5.555 + 0 yields 5.6.

Rounding occurs by the criteria in Table 10-1:

Table 10-1: Rounding values

Value	Direction	Example
0.5	down	.5 becomes 0
0.51	up	.51 becomes 1
any even value + .5	down	36.5 becomes 36
any even value + .51	up	36.51 becomes 37
any odd value + .5	up	37.5 becomes 38
any value +.4	down	99.4 becomes 99
any value + .6	up	99.6 becomes 100

To round .5 up all the time, use this defined function:

```
function round X
  if X < 0
  then return trunc (X - .5) -- for values less than 0
  else return trunc (X + .5) -- for values greater than 0
end round
```

See the **round** function (page 456) for more information on rounding.

Also See:

ROUND function, page 456

PATTERN

Forms

```
set {the} pattern to integerExpr

set pattern to 1 -- white
```

Action

The **pattern** property reflects the current pattern used by the painting tools.

Comments

Meaningful values for *integerExpr* are in the range 1 through 40, and reflect one of the patterns on the Patterns menu. Numbering on the Patterns menu goes from top to bottom, left to right, such that the pattern at the top left is 1, bottom left is 10, top right is 31, and the pattern at the bottom right is 40 (see Figure 10-16):

1	11	21	31
2	12	22	32
3	13	23	33
4	14	24	34
5	15	25	35
6	16	26	36
7	17	27	37
8	18	28	38
9	19	29	39
10	20	30	40

Figure 10-16   Patterns menu with numeric equivalents

The numbering system represents patterns occupying specific positions on the Patterns menu rather than the patterns themselves because you can change individual patterns by using the Edit Pattern item on the Options menu, by using pattern pickup, and so on. See the *HyperCard User's Guide* for more information about editing patterns.

The default pattern setting is 12 (black). You can change this setting by using the **set** command or by clicking on the appropriate pattern on the Patterns menu.

The following handler draws 40 circles, each filled with a different pattern (shown in Figure 10-17):

```
on balloons
  choose oval tool
  set filled to true
  set centered to true
  put 60 into h
  put 60 into v
  repeat with i = 1 to 40
    set pattern to i
    drag from h,v to h+40,v+40 with shiftKey
    add 50 to h
    if h > 450 then
      put 60 into h
      add 50 to v
    end if
  end repeat
end balloons
```

Figure 10-17 Patterns

Other values for Pattern: The value 0 and values between 41 and 65536 are ignored. Values 65537 and 65576 repeat patterns 1 through 40, but this is an anomaly and might change in future versions.

POLYSIDES

Forms

```
set {the} polysides to integerExpr

set polysides to 5
```

Action

The **polySides** property reflects the number of sides on an image produced with the Regular Polygon tool.

Comments

IntegerExpr has a meaningful range of 3 through 50, plus 0 for a circle shape, with 4 being the default (but see "getting a circle," below). The higher the number of sides, the more that the drawn shape looks like a circle. Values greater than 50 set **polySides** to 50; values 1 and 2 are ignored.

The following handler draws lots of polygons with different numbers of sides filled with different patterns:

```
on mouseUp
  choose regular polygon tool
  set dragSpeed to 300
  repeat until the mouse is down
    set polySides to any item of "3,4,5,6,8"
    set filled to true
    set pattern to random(40)
    drag from 250,170 to 500,300
  end repeat
  choose browse tool
end mouseUp
```

Getting a circle: To get the circle shape, you can set **polysides** to 0. But sometimes HyperTalk balks, and converts 0 to 3. Another, more reliable way to get a circle shape is to choose the oval tool, set centered to true, and drag with shiftkey.

POWERKEYS

Forms

```
set {the} powerKeys to logical

set powerKeys to true

set powerKeys to false
```

Action

The **powerKeys** property reflects whether the user can perform common painting actions from the keyboard that ordinarily must be done through menu choices.

Comments

Power key actions include most of those listed under the Paint and Options menu, plus selecting the white or black patterns from the Patterns menu.

You can also set the **powerKeys** property by choosing the Power Keys option on the Options menu or by checking the Power Keys box on the User Preference card in the Home stack.

PowerKeys works only when a paint tool is active. For a paint tool to be active, the **userLevel** property must be set to 3 or higher.

Changing the **powerKeys** value programmatically also puts a check next to the Power Keys item on the Options menu, and changes the setting on the User Preference card of the Home stack.

This property seldom programmatically set: This property exists in the language so that it can be set by the Preferences card in the Home stack. Ordinarily there's no need to mess with it from a script.

Also See:

Power Keys, *HyperCard User's Guide*

RECTANGLE

Forms

```
set {the} rect{angle} of card window to leftH, topV, rightH, bottomV --2.0
set {the} rect{angle} of [field|button|card] to leftH, topV, rightH, bottomV
put {the} rect{angle} of [field|button|window] {into container}

set rect of button 1 to 100,100,200,200
```

Action

The **rectangle** property (or **rect**) reflects the size and location of any HyperCard field, button, card, or window.

Comments

Button or *field* must be in the current stack.

`LeftH, topV, rightH,` and `bottomV` are four comma-separated integers representing the upper-left corner (`leftH, topV`) and lower-right corner (`rightH, bottomV`) of the specified element, expressed as the distance in pixels from a particular source:

Element	Source
object	top-left corner of card window
noncard windows	top-left corner of card window
card window or card	top-left corner of screen

The top of the card window is immediately below the card's title bar. (The title bar for standard-sized cards is invisible in the Macintosh Plus and Macintosh SE built-in displays.)

Whenever you move an element, you change its **rectangle** property.

The following handlers use the **rectangle** property to show when the pointer is over any button or field. (Use it to locate hidden buttons or fields.) Click to get a report; shift-click to stop the action:

```
on mouseUp
  repeat until the shiftKey is down
    wait until the mouseClick
```

```
    put hitTest(the clickLoc)
  end repeat
end mouseUp

function hitTest point
  repeat with i = 1 to the number of buttons
    if point is within rect of button i
    then return name of button i
  end repeat
  repeat with i = 1 to the number of card fields
    if point is within rect of card field i
    then return name of card field i
  end repeat
  repeat with i = 1 to the number of fields
    if point is within rect of field i
    then return name of field i
  end repeat
  repeat with i = 1 to the number of bkgnd buttons
    if point is within rect of bkgnd button i
    then return name of bkgnd button i
  end repeat
  return "No button or field"
end hitTest
```

Imbedded properties: The four items in the **rectangle** property are the same as the **left, top, right,** and **bottom** properties, respectively. The **width** property is item 3 (**right**) minus item 1 (**left**); the **height** property is item 4 (**bottom**) minus item 2 (**top**). Figure 10-18 shows these properties for a button, field, or noncard window.

Impact of changing Rectangle: When you change one or more items of **rectangle** you change the value of one or more of its related properties (**top, bottom, left, right, topLeft, botRight, location**). Additionally, when you change one of the items in the **rectangle** property of a field or button, you change the size of that object. Figure 10-19 shows a field whose current rect is 115, 59, 342, 187. These are local coordinates, relative to the card.

Figure 10-20 shows this rectangle with its *leftH* coordinate (formerly 115) changed to 40 — thus making the field wider:

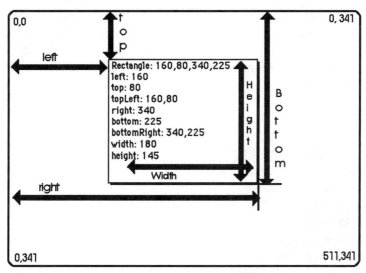

Figure 10-18   **Rectangle** and its derived properties on a standard sized card

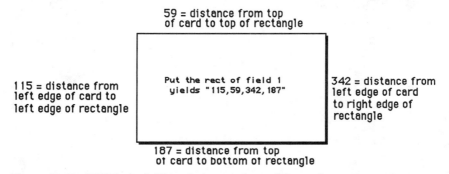

59 = distance from top
of card to top of rectangle

115 = distance from
left edge of card to
left edge of rectangle

Put the rect of field 1
yields "115,59,342,187"

342 = distance from
left edge of card
to right edge of
rectangle

187 = distance from top
of card to bottom of rectangle

Figure 10-19   RECT of a field is relative to edges of the card

```
set rect of field 1 to 40,59,342,187
widens the field by moving its left side closer
to the left edge of the card, but leaving its
other coordinates intact.
```

Figure 10-20   Changing an item of a field's RECT changes the object's size

Changing an object's size or location: To make explicit changes to the size of an object without changing its basic location, change its **height** (page 539) and/or **width** (page 651) properties. To change the location of an object without impacting its size, change one of these properties: **location, top, bottom, left, right, topLeft, botRight.**

Also See:

BOTTOM property, page 497
BOTTOMRIGHT property, page 499
HEIGHT property, page 539
LEFT property, page 552
LOCATION property, page 556
RIGHT property, page 597
TOP property, page 635
TOPLEFT property, page 637
WIDTH property, page 651

RIGHT

Forms

```
set {the} right of [button|field|card|window] to integerExpr

set right of the message box to 491
set right of field 1 to left of field 2
```

Action

The **right** property describes the distance in pixels of the right edge of the element from a source:

Element	Source
object	right edge of card window
noncard windows	right edge of card window
card window or card	right edge of screen

Comments

IntegerExpr evaluates to a positive or a negative integer. *Button* or *field* must be in the current stack.

The following handler moves a button off the screen and then back on by adjusting its **right** property. (The **lock screen** and **unlock screen** commands get rid of distracting screen flicker):

```
on mouseUp -- With yet another thanks to Gary "XCMD" Bond
  repeat 50
    lock screen -- deflickering device
    set right of me to right of me + 5 -- 5 controls increment of move
    unlock screen
  end repeat
  repeat 50
    lock screen
    set right of me to right of me -- 5
    unlock screen
  end repeat
end mouseUp
```

Visible boundaries: Locations 0 through 511 are within a standard card's width and are therefore visible on all Macintosh displays. Points outside those boundaries might or might not be visible, depending upon the size of the display you're using and where the card window is on that display. Moving an element outside the visible boundaries of the display doesn't change its **visible** setting, and is harmless; but the only way to get the element back into view is programmatically.

Right of card windows: `Right of card window` is constrained to multiples of 16 for efficient graphics updating. If you try to set this property to something that is not a multiple of 16, the value the property actually gets will be the multiple of 16 closest to the number you requested.

Right and Rectangle: The value of **right** is the same as item 3 of the rectangle property of the same element.

Changing Right's value: Anything that moves an element changes its **right** value. Such methods include (but are not limited to) dragging the element (either programmatically or manually), setting its **location** or its **rectangle** property, or using the **show** command with a different value following **at**.

Also See:

LOCATION property, page 556
RECTANGLE property, page 593
SHOW command, page 339

SCRIPT

Forms

```
set {the} script of object to expr

set script of button 1 to script of button 2
```

Action

The **script** property reflects the contents of a particular object's script.

Comments

object is any button or field on the current card, any background or card in the current stack, or any stack.

You can retrieve part or all of a script:

```
put line 3 to 5 of the script of this card into field 3
put the script of button "Click me" into scriptVar
```

But when you set the script of an object, you set the entire script:

```
set the script of this card to wholeNewScript
set script of button 7 to script of card field 5
set script of stack "Home" to myScript & script of stack "Home"
```

The following button script installs the button that contains it on the Home card, and then deletes the installation code (the entire first handler, plus the "∗∗∗" line):

```
on mouseUp
  choose button tool
  select me
  doMenu "Copy Button"
  go home
  type "v" with commandKey
  get script of me
  delete char 1 to offset("***"&return,it) of it
  delete line 1 of it
  set script of last button to it
  put "Drag the button where you want and type cmd-tab."
```

```
end mouseUp
*** real script begins here ***
on mouseUp
  play "boing"
end mouseUp
```

When you set the script of an object that has a handler running (as would happen, for example, with the statement `set script of me to field newScript`), the replacement takes place when all handlers running from that object have completed their actions.

For complete information on writing scripts, see Chapter 2.

Low memory bug alert

Under certain low memory conditions with HyperCard versions 1.2.1 and earlier, transferring a script from one object to another partially fails: the symptom is that the top part of the script in the destination object is truncated. It happens in certain (mostly unpredictable) conditions when you're low on RAM and you issue a command such as this one:

```
set script of button destination to script of button source
```

HyperTalk gives no warning when this happens, but the script of the destination object won't work. The solution is move to version 1.2.2 or higher.

Script limit: The script of an object can have up to 30,000 characters. If you reach this limit (HyperTalk complains if you do), move some of your handlers to another object (perhaps a hidden button called MyHandlerLibrary) and send messages to it as required:

```
send myRemoteHandler to background button myHandlerLibrary
```

In versions 2.0 and higher, you can use the **start using** command (page 351) to add stacks to the message passing path. So you can also put ancillary handlers in the scripts of such stacks.

Closely guarded commenting secrets: Ordinarily, you have to add comment marks (--) at the start of any comment. But you don't have to use comment marks with comments that you write outside of handlers.

Avoid starting comment lines outside of handlers with the words "on" or "function." If you must start a line with one of these words, precede it with an option-space character.

HyperTalk eliminates leading ASCII-32 spaces from all lines when it stores a script. (ASCII-32 spaces are the ones you make when you press the spacebar.) When it redisplays a script, HyperTalk provides its own indentation. But HyperTalk sees option-spaces (ASCII-202) as valid characters, and leaves them alone.

Also See:

SCRIPTS, Chapter 2
START USING command, page 351

SCRIPTEDITOR

Forms

```
set {the} scriptEditor to expr

set scriptEditor to myScriptEditor
```

Action

The **scriptEditor** property, new in HyperCard 2.0, determines the current script editor.

Comments

The default script editor (the one that comes with HyperCard) is cleverly named `ScriptEditor`. **ScriptEditor** is reset to the default each time you quit HyperCard.

This property is seldom used. Custom script editors are XCMDs (Chapter 13) written by Pascal, C, and assembly language programmers and are therefore not discussed in polite company.

For complete details about the resident script editor, see Chapter 2.

When you ask to see or edit the script of some object, a script appears in a script editor. If you set the script editor to one that doesn't exist, HyperCard uses the built-in editor instead.

Also See:

DEBUG command, page 206
EXTERNALS OVERVIEW, Chapter 13
MESSAGEWATCHER property, page 571
SCRIPTS, Chapter 2
VARIABLEWATCHER property, page 644

SCROLL

Forms

```
set {the} scroll of scrollingField to integerExpr

set the scroll of field "Comments" to zero
```

Action

The **scroll** property reflects the number of pixels that have scrolled off the top of a scrolling field.

Comments

Field is a field in the current stack.

A scroll of 0 means that the top line of the field is visible.

The following handler scrolls data smoothly:

```
scrollField "Field 1" -- field's name in quotation marks

on scrollField whichField -- Thanks again, Gary Bond!
  set scroll of whichField to 0
  put height of whichField div textHeight of whichField ¬
  into linesPerField -- gets number of visible screen lines
  put textHeight of whichField * ¬
  (number of lines in value of whichField + 1 - linesPerField) ¬
  into totalPixels -- tells how many pixels we're dealing with
  repeat with i = 1 to totalPixels
    set scroll of whichField to i -- what's at the top of the field
    wait 2 ticks -- slow things down a bit
  end repeat
end scrollField
```

How many lines have scrolled?   The following two-handler example computes the number of lines that have scrolled off the top of a particular field (in this case, a background field named "Comments"):

```
on mouseUp
  send linesOffTop to field "Comments"
```

```
   put the result
end mouseUp

on linesOffTop
   return trunc(scroll of the target/textHeight of the target)
end linesOffTop
```

Moving the scroll thumb: You can move the thumb in a scrolling field by setting the scroll property to any value higher than 0:

```
set the scroll of field 12 to 30 -- scrolls 30 pixels out of sight
```

Version 1.2.1 thumb bug

In HyperCard versions through 1.2.1, you cannot move the thumb by selecting text that's scrolled out of sight in a scrolling field. Selecting such text scrolls the text into view, but changes neither the thumb's position nor the value of the **scroll** property. This bug is fixed for versions 1.2.2 and higher.

Error on nonscrolling fields: Trying to use the scroll property with a non-scrolling field gets the error dialog box "Not a scrolling field."

Also See:

SELECT command, page 331
TEXTHEIGHT property, page 628

SCROLL OF CARD WINDOW

Forms

```
set {the} scroll of card window to point

set scroll of card window to 10,20
```

Action

The **scroll of card window** property, new in HyperCard 2.0, describes the horizontal and vertical scroll of the card within the card window.

Comments

The **scroll** is a point reported in the form *horizontal, vertical.* Card window is the card window of the current stack.

Scroll reflects the top left corner of the card window within the scroll window (visible when you choose the Scroll command from the Go menu). The card window defines how much of the card you can see; the origin of the card window (that is, the **scroll**) reflects where your view of the card begins relative to the top left corner of the card (Figure 10-21):

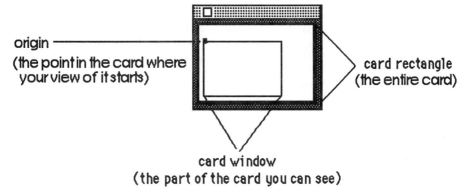

origin —
(the point in the card where your view of it starts)

card rectangle
(the entire card)

card window
(the part of the card you can see)

Figure 10-21 Scroll palette, showing **origin** of a standard-size card at about 32, 70

When the origin coincides with the card's top left corner (always the case when the card window is the same size as the card), **scroll** is 0,0.

You shrink the view window by dragging a corner within the scroll palette, or by pressing Command-Shift-E and dragging from the bottom right corner of the card window (Figure 10-22).

Figure 10-22   Size box revealed when you press Command-Shift-E

Once the card window is shrunk (and therefore smaller than the card itself), you can scroll the card within the card window by dragging or by setting **scroll** to anything other than 0,0.

Also See:

RECTANGLE property, page 593

SHAREDHILITE

Forms

```
set {the} sharedHilite of bgBtn to logical

set the sharedHilite of bg btn "Choice" to false
```

Action

The **sharedHilite** property, new in HyperCard 2.0, determines whether a background button hilited on one card of a given background is hilited on every card of that background or whether the hiliting is card-specific.

Comments

BgBtn is any button in the current background.

The default for **sharedHilite** is true — a background button hilited on one card is hilited on all cards.

Changing the setting of this property makes a corresponding change to the Shared Hilite option in the button's "Button Info..." dialog.

This feature is especially useful when the background button's style is checkbox.

But what's it for? This property lets a background button act like a card button — setting the hilite of a background button on a card affects the hilite of that button only on that one card, so you don't have to create a new button on every card.

In a typical case, a collection of buttons in a given background comprises a form of some kind. Each card sharing that background represents information about a different person. Assume that the third checkbox of such a background is labeled "Click this box if you have children": childless Fred Ferfee would leave the box unchecked, while Mary Scribblemonger (mother of 16) would check it. The **sharedHilite** property of such a background button would be set to false.

Also See:

AUTOHILITE property, page 490
HILITE property, page 543

SHAREDTEXT

Forms

```
set {the} sharedText of bgFld to logical

set the sharedText of field "Show this text everywhere" to true
```

Action

The **sharedText** property, new in HyperCard 2.0, reflects whether text typed into a background field appears on all cards in that background.

Comments

BgFld is any field in the current background.

To enter or edit shared text:

1. Set the **sharedText** property of the field to true (or check "Shared Text" on that field's Info box).

2. Set the **editBackground** property to true (or choose "Background" from the Edit menu).

3. Click in the field with the Browse tool and edit as usual.

Shared text is uneditable unless you're in the background. (The field acts as if its **lockText** property were set to true.)

Changing the setting of this property makes a corresponding change to the Shared Text option in the field's "Field Info..." dialog.

Shared and unshared text can co-exist: Each background field can have both shared (or common) and unshared text. Shared text is visible in a background field on every card in the background when that field's **sharedText** property is set to true, while unshared is visible only on the card on which it was typed, and only when that field's **sharedText** property is set to false.

When **sharedText** is set to false, shared text is invisible and uneditable (but still there); when **sharedText** is set to true, unshared text is invisible and uneditable (but again, still there).

The following handler, which goes in the script of a field, toggles between shared and unshared text when you command-click the field.

```
on mouseUp
  if the commandKey is down
  then set sharedText of me to not sharedText of me
end mouseUp
```

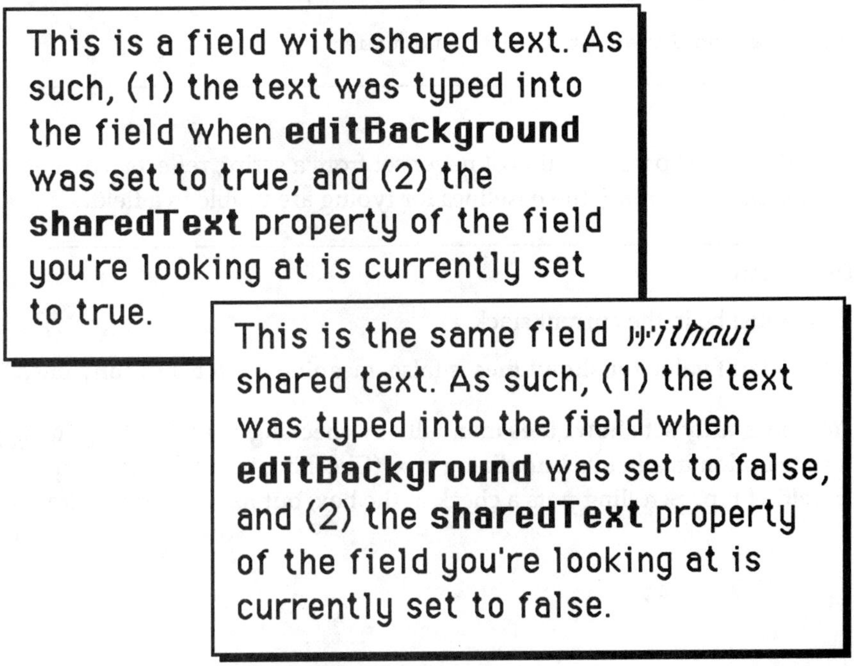

This is a field with shared text. As such, (1) the text was typed into the field when **editBackground** was set to true, and (2) the **sharedText** property of the field you're looking at is currently set to true.

This is the same field *without* shared text. As such, (1) the text was typed into the field when **editBackground** was set to false, and (2) the **sharedText** property of the field you're looking at is currently set to false.

Figure 10-23   Same field with sharedText property set to TRUE (top) and FALSE

Shared text not searched: Setting **sharedText** of a field to true changes the setting of the **Don't Search** option in the field's Info box (but doesn't change the **dontSearch** property of that field, although it behaves as if it had been changed). The **find** command doesn't look for text in fields whose **sharedText** property is set to true. When (and only when) **sharedText** for a given field is set to false, **find** can look in the *unshared* text of that field.

Also See:

DONTSEARCH property, page 521
FIND command, page 246

SHOWLINES

Forms

```
set {the} showLines of field to logical

set the showLines of field 1 to true
```

Action

The **showlines** property, almost never set from a script, reflects whether dotted lines that mark the baselines for typing are visible in a field.

Comments

Field must be in the current stack.

The default value for **showLines** is false, meaning "don't show any lines."

You ordinarily set **showLines** manually by checking or unchecking the appropriate option in a field's Info dialog box. (Checking the Show Lines option for a field of type Scrolling puts a check in the box, but has no further effect.)

SHOWNAME

Forms

```
set {the} showName of button to logical

set showName of button 1 to true
```

Action

The **showName** property reflects whether the button's name appears in the button.

Comments

Button must be in the current stack, and can be any style.

The default value for **showName** is false, meaning "don't show the name."

You can set **showName** manually by checking or unchecking the appropriate option in a button's Info dialog box.

The following handler gets the user's attention by toggling the **showName** property of a button:

```
on mouseUp -- Yet another astounding Gary Bond example (What a guy!)
  repeat until the mouseClick -- click to stop the flashing
    set showName of me to not showName of me
    wait 10 ticks
  end repeat
  set showName of me to true
end mouseUp
```

Where name appears: Where a button's name appears depends upon the style of the button:

- When a button has an icon associated with it, the button's name appears at the bottom of the button, below the icon.

- When the button is a radio button or check box, the name appears to the right of the button.

- In all other cases, the name appears in the center of the button.

Default name properties: The default values for properties of a nonicon button's name are:

Property	Default
textAlign	center
textFont	Chicago
textSize	12
textStyle	plain

You can change each of these properties with the **set** command.

An icon button is always displayed in Geneva 9, no matter what settings you use.

Also See:

TEXTALIGN property, page 622
TEXTFONT property, page 625
TEXTSIZE property, page 630
TEXTSTYLE property, page 632

SHOWPICT

Forms

```
set {the} showPict of [card|background] to logical

set the showPict of last card to true
```

Action

The **showPict** property reflects whether the picture on a particular card or background is visible.

The following handler detects hidden card pictures. You can put this handler in your home stack if you want to be alerted to hidden pictures in any stack (assuming the stack passes openCard):

```
on openCard
  if showPict of this card is true then pass openCard
  play "Boing"
  answer "Hidden card picture!"
end openCard
```

Comments

Card or *background* must be in the current stack.

The original value for **showPict** is true, meaning the picture is visible; if **showPict** is set to false, the affected picture remains hidden until its **showPict** is explicitly set to true again.

The value for **showPict** can be changed by the **set, hide picture, or show picture** commands.

Also See:

HIDE command, page 264
SHOW PICTURE command, page 344

SIZE

Forms

```
put {the} size of stack {into container}

put freeSize of this stack / size of this stack > 0.20 into compactMe
```

Action

The **size** property reflects the size in bytes of a particular stack.

Comments

You can't use the **set** command with this property.

The following handler checks to see if a stack can fit on an 800K disk (leaving a margin for overhead):

```
on closeStack
  if size of this stack > 793600
  then put "This stack no longer fits on a floppy disk."
end closeStack
```

The following handler catches doMenu "Compact Stack" and makes sure that you have enough disk space for the compaction to succeed. (You need enough disk space to copy a stack in order to compact it — HyperCard compacts into a copy, deletes the original, and finally renames the copy. This is safer than compacting in place in case something goes wrong during the compaction.)

```
on doMenu what
  if what is not "Compact Stack" then pass doMenu
  if the size of this stack < the diskSpace then pass doMenu
  answer "Sorry, not enough disk space to compact this stack"
end doMenu
```

Also See:

FREESIZE property, page 536

STACKSINUSE

Forms

```
get {the} stacksInUse

get the stacksInUse
```

Action

The **stacksInUse** property, new in HyperCard 2.0, reflects what stacks (if any) have been added to the message passing path by the **start using** command.

Comments

This property holds a return-separated list of up to ten stacks inserted in the message passing path before the Home stack. It's set to empty when you quit HyperCard.

stacksInUse produces full path names. The statement

```
put the stacksInUse into cd field 1
```

might produce the list in Figure 10-24.

```
Noise:H20:Stacks:Background art
Noise:H20:Stacks:addresses
```

Figure 10-24   Typical **stacksInUse** list

This list of stacks is an extension of, and not a replacement to, the standard message passing path as described in Chapter 1.

The following handler, designed as a quick debugging aide, puts the **stacksInUse** list into a field whenever the message watcher is visible:

```
on idle
  if  visible of the message watcher
  then put the stacksInUse into field "Extended Path"
  pass idle
end idle
```

Untrapped (or passed) messages travel from the current stack to the first stack in **stacksInUse,** then to the second stack in **stacksInUse,** and so on through to Home and the rest of the message passing path. The last item in **stacksInUse** is the last stack that messages go to before going to the Home stack.

A stack name appears in **stacksInUse** only once. If you issue the command `start using` *stackName* when *stackName* is already in **stacksInUse,** HyperCard moves *stackName* to the beginning of **stacksInUse.**

Changing stacksInUse: You can't directly **set** this property. Use the **start using** command to add a stack to the beginning of the stacksInUse, or the **stop using** command to remove a stack from it:

```
start using newStackName
```

The **stacksInUse** is cleared when you quit HyperCard. To clear all stacks from the message passing path extension (and so to clear the **stacksInUse** property) while HyperCard is still running, use this:

```
on clearStacks
  repeat for the number of lines in the stacksInUse
    stop using stack (first line of the stacksInUse) -- always 1st!
  end repeat
end clearStacks
```

Quick look at StacksinUse: For a quick look at a list of stacks currently in use, enter

```
answer the stacksInUse
```

through the Message box. Or enter

```
get the stacksInUse
```

with the Variable Watcher window on the display.

Also See:

PASSING ALONG THE MESSAGE, page 18
START USING command, page 351
STOP USING command, page 354

STYLE

Forms

```
set {the} style of [field | button] to expr

set the style of last button to radioButton
set style of card field 1 to scrolling
```

Action

The **style** property reflects the style of a particular field or button.

Comments

Field or *button* must be in the current stack.

For a field, *expr* must evaluate to one of the following:

```
transparent     opaque      rectangle      shadow      scrolling
```

For a button, *expr* must evaluate to one of the following:

```
transparent        opaque          rectangle        shadow
roundRect          checkBox        radioButton
```

You can also set this property by making choices from the object's Info dialog box.

The following handler, most effectively placed in a stack script and called from the Message box, cycles through each style available for a given button or field. Each time you call it, the named button or field gets the next style in the list. (Keep calling it until you get the style that works best):

```
cycleStyles "card field 1"  -- call repeatedly to try all styles

on cycleStyles whichPart
  if whichPart contains "field"
  then put "transparent,opaque,rectangle,shadow,scrolling" into styles
  else put ¬
  "transparent,opaque,rectangle,roundRect,checkBox,radioButton" ¬
  into styles
  get style of whichPart
```

```
repeat with i = 1 to the number of items in styles
   if item i of styles is it then exit repeat
end repeat
add 1 to i
if i > the number of items in styles then put 1 into i
set style of whichPart to item i of styles
end cycleStyles
```

Default styles: For fields, the default **Style** is transparent. For buttons, the default **style** depends upon the method used to make the button: if you use command-drag with the button tool chosen, the default style is transparent; If you create a new button using the New Button command from the Objects menu, the default style is roundrect.

The following handler changes the default style of newly created fields to rectangle rather than transparent. (It belongs in the stack or Home script):

```
on newField
   set style of the target to rectangle
end newField
```

The following three handlers, written by Gary Bond, make a field have a scroll bar only when it has enough text in it to need one. Put them in the script of the Home stack for maximum effectiveness:

```
on openField -- remember starting style so can restore later
   global oldStyle
   put style of me into oldStyle
end openField

on returnInField -- check if we now need a scroll bar
   put height of me div textHeight of me into visibleLines
   if word 2 of the selectedLine > visibleLines - 1 and ¬
   style of me is not "scrolling" then
      select empty -- to trigger closeField before we set the style
      set style of me to scrolling
      select after text of me
   end if
   pass returnInField
end returnInField
```

```
on closeField -- restore old style if scroll bar no longer needed
  global oldStyle
  put height of me div textHeight of me into visibleLines
  if word 2 of the selectedLine <= visibleLines - 1
  then set style of me to oldStyle
end closeField
```

SUSPENDED

Forms

```
get {the} suspended

get the suspended
```

Action

The **suspended** property, new in HyperCard 2.0, reflects whether HyperCard is running in the background under MultiFinder.

Comments

Suspended returns true when HyperCard is running in the background (while some other application is running in the foreground), and false when HyperCard is running in the foreground.

You can use **suspended** to control HyperCard's interface. For example, you might not want to use visual effects or play sounds while HyperCard is runnning in the background. Such effects distract the user; and one assumes that, if the user wanted to be distracted, he'd be running HyperCard in the foreground.

The following utility handlers suppress sounds, visual effects, and wait states in a stack when it's running in the background:

```
on play
  if not the suspended then pass play
end play

on visual
  if not the suspended then pass visual
end visual

on wait
  if not the suspended then pass wait
end wait

on beep
  if not the suspended then pass beep
end beep
```

You can't use **set** to change **suspended**.

About background running: In version 2.0, handlers continue to run in the background under MultiFinder after you switch out of HyperCard to work with another application. HyperCard gives time to MultiFinder while the "busy" pointer is spinning under HyperCard's direct control (during sorts, stack compaction, and printing, as opposed to under the control of your scripting), after executing every line of HyperTalk code, and during the **Show Cards** and **Wait** commands.

If, while running in the background, HyperCard needs you to respond to a dialog (for an **ask** dialog, for example), it puts the symbol ◊ next to HyperCard in the Apple menu, an icon flashes on the menu bar, and the speaker beeps once. When you switch back to HyperCard, the dialog appears.

TEXTALIGN

Forms

```
set {the} textAlign of [button|field] to [left|center|right]
set {the} textAlign to [left|center|right] -- for paint text
put {the} textAlign {of [button|field]} {into container}

set textAlign of field 1 to left
```

Action

The **textAlign** property reflects the alignment of text around an insertion point as the text is created.

Comments

Button or *field* must be in the current stack.

The default alignment for radio buttons, check boxes, text in fields, and paint text is `left`. The default alignment of text in all other styles of button names is `center`.

Radio buttons and check boxes: The text alignment of radio buttons and check boxes is always left, no matter what value you set for their **textAlign** property.

Retrieving a setting: You can both set and retrieve the alignment of text in buttons and fields. HyperTalk can't tell you the alignment for a particular group of paint text characters once they're fixed as bit maps, but the form

```
put {the} textAlign {into container}
```

reports the current setting for paint text **textAlign.** (Paint text gets set as bitmapped images when you change tools or when you click the mouse any-place on the screen except in the menubar.)

Also See:

SHOWNAME property, page 611
TEXTFONT property, page 625
TEXTHEIGHT property, page 628
TEXTSIZE property, page 630
TEXTSTYLE property, page 632

TEXTARROWS

Forms

```
set {the} textArrows to logical

set the textArrows to true
```

Action

The **textArrows** property reflects whether the arrow keys move the insertion point in a field.

Comments

The default value for **textArrows** is false (as set by the Home stack script, and by the User Preferences card).

When **textArrows** is false, pressing the arrow keys takes you through the stack: left-arrow to the previous card, right-arrow to the next card, up-arrow forward through recently seen cards, down-arrow backward through recently seen cards.

When **textArrows** is true, pressing the arrow keys moves the insertion point in the appropriate direction through text.

The following handler makes **textArrows** active only when there's a text selection:

```
on arrowKey
  set textArrows to the selectedChunk is not empty
  pass arrowKey
end arrowKey
```

Best of both worlds: When **textArrows** is true, pressing the optionkey at the same time as an arrow key makes the arrow key perform as though **textArrows** were false.

Also See:

ARROWKEY command, page 171

TEXTFONT

Forms

```
set {the} textFont of [button|field|textExpr] to expr
set {the} textFont to expr -- for paint text
put {the} textFont {of [button|field|textExpr]} {into container}

set the textFont of field 1 to Geneva
```

Action

The **textFont** property determines the font used for text.

Comments

Button or *field* must be in the current stack. *TextExpr* is any expression that describes a chunk of text (versions 2.0 and later). *Expr* can be any font installed in the current stack, Home stack, HyperCard, or the System file.

The default font for button names is Chicago; default font for text in fields and paint text is Geneva.

You can change the **textFont** at any time for button names and text in fields; but you can change the **textFont** for paint text only at the time of the text's creation.

You can't get to the text properties dialog box for a button from a script; you can only get as far as button info. But you *can* get to the paint text properties from a script. The following handler lets you adjust the text style of a button using the text style dialog box. It operates on the numbered (or named) button specified; if no button is specified, it operates on the one most recently created:

```
on buttonStyle buttonNum
  if buttonNum is empty -- operate on last button
  then put the number of buttons into buttonNum

  -- set the paint text properties to the properties of this button
  set the textFont to textFont of button buttonNum
  set the textStyle to textStyle of button buttonNum
```

```
    set the textAlign to textAlign of button buttonNum
    set the textSize to textSize of button buttonNum
    set the textHeight to textHeight of button buttonNum

    -- display paint text properties
    choose text tool
    doMenu "Text Style..."

    -- set the properties of this button to the paint text properties
    set textFont of button buttonNum to the textFont
    set textStyle of button buttonNum to the textStyle
    set textAlign of button buttonNum to the textAlign
    set textSize of button buttonNum to the textSize
    set textHeight of button buttonNum to the textHeight
    choose browse tool
end buttonStyle
```

Retrieving a setting: You can both set and retrieve the font for text in buttons and fields at any time. You can't retrieve the font of a particular group of paint text characters once they're created, but the form

```
    put {the} textFont {into container}
```

reports the current setting for **textFont** used with paint text.

Changing textFonts: When you change the **textFont** for an entire field in 2.0, each run of text that has the old default font for that field changes. But text whose font is different retains that difference:

```
set textFont of field 3 to "Geneva" -- all text is Geneva
set textFont of word 3 to 5 of field 3 to "Chicago"
set textFont of field 3 to "Monaco" -- all except words 3 to 5 now Monaco
```

Moving text with Put loses formatting: When you copy or move text from one field to another through the clipboard, all formatting (including **textFont** settings) is maintained. When you move text using **put** (as in put field 1 into field 2), the text takes on the default formats of the field into which it's pasted. (At the time of this writing the team is considering changing the **put** command so that it will retain styles. Check the product to see if they did it.)

Substitute fonts: If you set the **textFont** to one that doesn't exist, HyperCard substitutes the System font (Chicago).

Points for techies: You can set **textFont** by using a FOND family ID resource number:

```
set the textFont of word 3 of field 1 to 4 -- Monaco
```

When you ask for the font you just set (put the textFont of word 3 of field 1), HyperTalk returns the font name (Monaco) if the font is in the system.

If you set **textFont** using the ID of a font that isn't in the system, HyperTalk uses Geneva, but returns the font number you gave:

```
set the textFont of field 1 to 12 -- Los Angeles (But it ain't here)
put the textFont of field 1 -- 12
```

Use a program like ResEdit or ResCopy to find out the FOND family ID resource number of a font. Some of the most common ones are shown in Table 10-2.

Table 10-2: FOND numbers and fonts

FOND	Font
0	Chicago (system)
1	Geneva
2	New York
3	Geneva (application)
4	Monaco
5	Venice
6	London
7	Athens

Also See:

SHOWNAME property, page 611
TEXTALIGN property, page 622
TEXTHEIGHT property, page 628
TEXTSIZE property, page 630
TEXTSTYLE property, page 632

TEXTHEIGHT

Forms

```
set {the} textHeight of field to integerExpr
set {the} textHeight to integerExpr -- for paint text
put {the} textHeight {of field} {into container}

set the textHeight of field 1 to 10
```

Action

The **textHeight** property reflects the vertical space (in pixels) allowed for each line of text. (A pixel is about 1/72" high.)

Comments

field must be in the current stack.

The smaller you make the **textHeight,** the less distance between lines of text.

The default for **textHeight** is the result of the formula `(textSize * 4) DIV 3`.

The smallest value you can set for **textHeight** is the **textSize** of the current font. Smaller settings are automatically reset.

You can change the **textHeight** at any time for text in fields; but you can change the **textHeight** for paint text only at the time of the text's creation.

Retrieving a setting: You can both set and retrieve the **textHeight** for text in fields. You can't retrieve the **textHeight** for a particular group of paint text characters once they're created, but the form

```
put {the} textHeight {into container}
```

reports the current setting for **textHeight** used with paint text.

TextHeight and buttons: You can both set and retrieve **textHeight** for buttons. But **textHeight** only makes sense when you use it as a measure of distance between lines of text. Because a button can show only one line of text in its name, **textHeight** for a button isn't useful.

Also See:

TEXTSIZE

Forms

```
set {the} textSize of [field|textExpr] to integerExpr
set {the} textSize to integerExpr -- for paint text
put {the} textSize {of [button|field]} {into container}

set the textSize of field 1 to 12
```

Action

The **textSize** property reflects the height of a character in pixels. (A pixel is about 1/72" high.)

Comments

Field must be in the current stack. *TextExpr* is any expression that describes a chunk of text (versions 2.0 and higher).

TextSize measures from the top of the tallest ascender on any character to the bottom of the longest descender on any character.

You can set **textSize** to any setting; but HyperCard disables font scaling so you won't see jagged fonts. If it doesn't have the size you ask for HyperCard uses the closest existing smaller font size surrounded by extra white space. To see available sizes, look in the TextStyle dialog box (Command-T). To enable font scaling, use the setFontScaling external listed on page 784.

You can change the **textSize** at any time for text in fields; but you can change the textSize for paint text only at the time of the text's creation.

Set textSize before textHeight: When you set **textSize, textHeight** is set to (4 * textSize) DIV 3. So the order of setting these two properties should be:

```
set the textSize of field 1 to wantedSize
set the textHeight of field 1 to wantedHeight
```

Retrieving a setting: You can both set and retrieve the **textSize** for text in fields and in button names. You can't retrieve the **textSize** for a particular group of paint text characters once they're created, but the form

```
    put {the} textSize {into container}
```

reports the current setting for **textSize** used with paint text.

Moving field text with Put command loses formatting: When you copy or move text from one field to another through the clipboard, all formatting (including **textSize** settings) is maintained. When you move text using **put** (as in `put text of field 1 into field 2`), the text takes on the default formats of the field into which it's pasted. (At the time of this writing the team is considering changing the **put** command so that it will retain styles. Check the product to see if they did it.)

Also See:

FIXEDLINEHEIGHT property, page 535
SHOWNAME property, page 611
TEXTALIGN property, page 622
TEXTFONT property, page 625
TEXTHEIGHT property, page 628
TEXTSTYLE property, page 632

TEXTSTYLE

Forms

```
set {the} textStyle of [button|field|textExpr|menuItem] to expr {, expr}
set {the} textStyle to expr {, expr} -- for paint text
put {the} textStyle {of [button|field|textExpr|menuItem]} {into container}

set textStyle of last field to bold,italic,outline
```

Action

The **textStyle** property reflects the style used for text.

Comments

Button or *field* must be in the current stack. *TextExpr* is any expression that describes a chunk of text (versions 2.0 and higher). *MenuItem* is a specific menu item in a specific menu currently visible on the menu bar.

Expr can be any combination of the following:

```
plain  bold  italic  underline  outline  shadow  condense  extend
```

Additionally, *textExpr* in versions 2.0 and higher can also be set to style group. (See "About Group," below.)

The default **textStyle** is plain.

To set multiple styles for the same text in the same command, separate style names with a comma, as shown in Figure 10-25.

```
set the textStyle of btn 1 to bold, italic, underline
```

Figure 10-25 Button with aesthetically questionable multiple styles

When plain is used in combination with other styles, the other styles override it:

```
set the textStyle of field 1 to bold, italic, plain, underline
```

```
-- plain is ignored here
```

But the command

```
set textStyle to plain
```

cancels all styles except plain.

Changing textStyles: When you change the **textStyle** for an entire field, each run of text that has the old default style for that field changes. But text whose style is different retains that difference:

```
set textStyle of field 3 to italic -- all text is italic
set textStyle of word 3 to 5 of field 3 to underline
set textStyle of field 3 to bold -- words 3 to 5 still underlined
```

Moving field text using Put loses formatting: When you copy or move text from one field to another through the clipboard, all formatting (including **textStyle** settings) is maintained. When you move text using **put** (as in `put field 1 into field 2`), the text takes on the default formats of the field into which it's pasted. (At the time of this writing the team is considering changing the **put** command so that it will retain styles. Check the product to see if they did it.)

Retrieving a setting: You can both set and retrieve the **textStyle** for text in buttons and fields and menu items at any time. You can't change or retrieve the **textStyle** of a particular group of paint text characters once they're created, but the form

```
put {the} textStyle {into container}
```

reports the current setting for **textStyle** used with paint text.

About Group: New for HyperCard 2.0, the **group** textStyle lets you band together any contiguous run of text characters (as in `word 3 to 5` or `char 12 to 56` or `line 5`). Once a run of text in a field has been grouped, and a user clicks anywhere within that group, you can use the 2.0 functions **clickText**, **clickChunk**, and **clickLine** to determine what happens next.

Group appearance unchanged: Setting a bunch of characters to the **group** textstyle doesn't change the appearance of that text; it just changes the way the text might behave when somebody clicks on it.

Also See:

TOP

Forms

```
set {the} top of [button|field|card|window] to integerExpr

set top of msg to 100
```

Action

The **top** property describes the distance between a source and the top edge of an element:

Element	Source
object	top of card window
noncard windows	top of card window
card window or card	top of screen

The top of the card window is immediately below the card's title bar (invisible in the Macintosh Plus and Macintosh SE built-in displays).

Comments

IntegerExpr evaluates to a positive or a negative integer. *Button* or *field* must be in the current stack.

Visible boundaries: Locations 0,0 through 511, 341 are within a standard card's area and are therefore visible on all Macintosh displays. Points outside those boundaries might or might not be visible, depending upon the size of the display you're using and the location of the card window on the display. Moving an element outside the visible boundaries of the display doesn't change its **visible** setting, and is harmless (but the only way you can bring it back into a visible area is programmatically).

Top and Rectangle: The value of **top** is the same as item 2 of the **rectangle** property of the same element.

Changing Top's value: Anything that moves an element changes its **top** value. Such methods include (but are not limited to) dragging the element (either programmatically or manually), setting its **location** property or its

rectangle property, or using the **show** command with a different value following **at.**

Also See:

BOTTOM property, page 497
BOTTOMRIGHT property, page 499
LOCATION property, page 556
RECTANGLE property, page 593
TOPLEFT property, page 637

TOPLEFT

Forms

```
set {the} topLeft of [button|field|card|window] to left, top

set topLeft of field "Listings" to left, top
```

Action

The **topLeft** property describes an element's top-left corner, expressed as two integers separated by a comma.

Comments

Button or *field* must be in the current stack. *Left* and *top* represent respectively horizontal and vertical distances (in pixels) from the left and top edges of a source. The source depends on the element:

Element	Source
object	top-left corner of card window
noncard windows	top-left corner of card window
card window or card	top-left corner of screen

The top of the card window is immediately below the card's title bar (often invisible in the Macintosh Plus and Macintosh SE built-in displays).

Backward name: The name of this property does *not* reflect the correct order of coordinates. Although the name is **topLeft,** you must give the coordinates in the order left, top.

Visible boundaries: Locations 0,0 through 511,341 are within a standard card's area and are therefore visible on all Macintosh displays. Points outside those boundaries might or might not be visible, depending upon the size of the display you're using. Moving an element outside the visible boundaries of the display doesn't change its **visible** setting, and is harmless.

TopLeft and sources of values: The **topLeft** is expressed as two integers separated by a comma. So you can refer to **topLeft's** values as items:

```
put item 1 of the topLeft of field 6 into Horizontal
```

which has the same effect as, but executes more slowly than

```
put left of field 6 into Horizontal
```

To assign **topLeft's** two-item value to a variable, put the value in quotation marks:

```
put "110, 130" into upperLeft
```

TopLeft and Rectangle: The value of **topLeft** is the same as item 1 to 2 of the rectangle property of the same element.

Changing topLeft's value: Anything that moves an element changes its **topLeft** value. Such methods include (but are not limited to) dragging the element (either programmatically or manually), setting its **location** or **rectangle** property, or using the **show** command with a different value following **at.**

Also See:

BOTTOM property, page 497
BOTTOMRIGHT property, page 499
LOCATION property, page 556
RECTANGLE property, page 593
TOP property, page 635

USERLEVEL

Forms

```
set {the} userLevel to integerExpr

set the userLevel to 5
set userLevel to field "User Level"
set the userLevel to saveUserLevel
```

Action

The **userLevel** property reflects the User Level setting on the User Preferences card, defining the power a user has while interacting with HyperCard.

Comments

IntegerExpr has meaning in the range 1 through 5. In version 2.0 setting *integerExpr* to 0 or below gets 1, and 6 through 32767 gets 5. Meanings for the settings are shown in Table 10-3.

Table 10-3:   User levels and their powers

Setting	Name	Powers
1	browsing	Use of browse tool, Go menu, short File and Edit menus.
2	typing	Level 1 plus text editing in existing fields.
3	painting	Level 2 plus full File and Edit menus, tools menu, painting menus, use of painting tools.
4	authoring	Level 3 plus object menu, button and field tools.
5	scripting	All HyperCard and HyperTalk powers, including ability to write and edit scripts. HyperGodHood.

Generally, you change the user level to make sure that the tools you need are available. After you set **userLevel,** check to make sure you got what you want. (The stack could limit it, as noted in "Local versus Global User Levels," below.)

The following handler sets the user level as appropriate to the task of a given handler. Part of this example's action is to make sure that the stack allows access to the level you need; if not, it warns you so you can make appropriate changes:

```
doHandler "makeButtons",4 -- You need level 4 to make buttons
doHandler "drawStuff",3 -- paint tools require level 3
doHandler "showScripts" -- default is 5

on doHandler handler,level -- get handler name, level to set
   if level is empty then put 5 into level -- the default
   put the userLevel into saveUserLevel -- preserves userlevel
   set the userLevel to level
   if the userLevel is not level then
      put "This stack limits user level"
      exit doHandler
   end if
   do handler -- forces execution of parameter "handler"
   set userLevel to saveUserLevel -- restores old userlevel
end doHandler
```

Restore userLevel if you change it: The **userlevel** is set below 5 to provide minimal stack protection or to ensure simplicity. If your stack changes the value of **userLevel,** be sure to restore the original **userLevel** value when your stack closes:

```
on openStack
   global oldUserLevel
   put the userLevel into oldUserLevel
   -- add other openStack statements here
end openStack

on closeStack
   global oldUserLevel
   set the userLevel to oldUserLevel
```

```
  -- add other closeStack statements here
end closeStack
```

Local versus global user levels: You can limit the user level for a particular stack in the Protect Stack dialog box. The **userLevel** property reflects the setting on the User Preference card, and not that of the Protect Stack dialog box; if the settings of the User Preference card and the Protect Stack dialog box are in conflict, the lower setting takes precedence.

USERMODIFY

Forms

```
set {the} userModify to logical

set userModify to true
set userModify to false
```

Action

The **userModify** property reflects whether a user can make temporary changes to a stack (insofar as the **userLevel** setting allows such changes) even though the stack is locked.

Comments

The default value for **userModify** is false. HyperCard resets **userModify** to false as soon as the user leaves the current stack.

When a stack is locked and **userModify** is true, the user can make any changes to the current card that the effective User Level setting allows, except that no scripts can be changed in any way. (The effective User Level setting is the lower of the **userLevel** property and the User Level setting in the Protect Stack dialog box.) But as soon as you leave the current card, all user changes to that card are discarded.

Ordinarily when a stack is locked (**cantModify** is set to true, the LOCK box in the stack's Get Info dialog in the Finder is checked, the media holding the stack is READ ONLY, etc.), a user can do nothing but browse.

When a stack is not locked, HyperCard ignores the **userModify** property.

The following field script lets the user enter text into that field even if the stack is locked. The script is intended to work under the following circumstances: (1) the stack is locked; (2) you want to restrict temporary modifications to specific fields; (3) the word "editable" appears somewhere in the script (including a comment) of each field in which you want to allow editing; and (4) you as the programmer take responsibility for saving/using changes to the field, because the changes all go away as soon as you leave the current card:

```
on openField
  set userModify to script of the target contains "editable"
end openField
```

Also See:

CANTMODIFY property, page 508
USERLEVEL property, page 639

VARIABLEWATCHER

Forms

```
set {the} variableWatcher to expr

set variableWatcher to myCustomWatcher
```

Action

The **variableWatcher** property, new in HyperCard 2.0, reflects the name of the current variable watcher XCMD, HyperCard's facility for tracking variables.

Comments

The default variable watcher (the one that comes with HyperCard) is named `VariableWatcher`.

If you set the **variableWatcher** property to a watcher that doesn't exist, HyperCard uses the default variable watcher.

This property is seldom used. Custom variable watchers are XCMDs written by Pascal, C, and assembly language programmers; most scriptwriters find that the default variable watcher serves adequately.

For details about the resident variable watcher, see Chapter 2.

Also See:

DEBUG command, page 206
EXTERNALS OVERVIEW, Chapter 13
MESSAGEWATCHER property, page 571
SCRIPTEDITOR property, page 602
SCRIPTS, Chapter 2

VERSION

Forms

```
put the version {into container}
put the long version {into container}
put {the} version of stack {into container}

if the version < 2.0 then go home
put the long version into field "Version"
if char 5 of the long version ≠ 8 then put "this is not final software"
get the version of this stack
```

Action

The **version** property supplies information about the version of the running HyperCard application, or about the version(s) of HyperCard used to modify the current stack.

Comments

The form the version reports the family name of the running HyperCard application (for example, 1.2). The form the long version returns an 8-digit hexidecimal number representing the major revision number, minor revision number, bug-fix number, and software state (development, alpha, beta, or release version) of the running HyperCard application. (See Figure 10-26.)

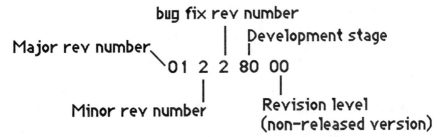

Figure 10-26 HyperCard long version number

So 01 2 3 60 01 is version 1.2.3b1, and 01 2 2 80 00 is version 1.2.2

The following function converts a version number into human readable form:

```
put versToStr(the long version)
function versToStr version
   if version is zero then return "1.0" -- could be anything before 1.2.1
   put char 1 to 2 of version + 0 into majorRev -- strip leading zero
   put char 3 of version into minorRev
   put char 4 of version into bugFixRev
   put char 5 to 6 of version into stageNum
   put char 7 to 8 of version + 0 into nonRelNum -- strip leading zero
   get majorRev & "." & minorRev
   if bugFixRev is not zero then put "." & bugFixRev after it
   if stageNum is not 80 then
      if stageNum is 20 then put "d" & nonRelNum after it
      if stageNum is 40 then put "a" & nonRelNum after it
      if stageNum is 60 then put "b" & nonRelNum after it
   end if
   return it
end versToStr
```

The form `version of this stack` returns a list of five comma-separated 8-digit numbers. The first four numbers, which are in the same format as the number explained in Figure 10-17, respectively report the version of HyperCard used to create the stack; the version of HyperCard that last compacted the stack; the oldest version of HyperCard used to modify the stack since its last compaction; and the version of HyperCard that last modified the stack. In most cases, at least three of these numbers will be the same. (See Figure 10-27.)

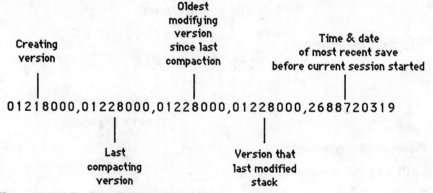

Figure 10-27   Version of this stack number

(An item 00000000 indicates a version before 1.2.1.) The last number is probably the most useful: it's the time (in seconds format) of the the last save made to the stack before the current session started. To convert this number to a meaningful time and date, use this:

```
convert last item of version of this stack to date and time
put it
```

The following function converts a stack version into human readable form. It uses the versToStr function, defined earlier:

```
put stackVersToStr(version of this stack) into card field 1

function stackVersToStr version
  get "Created By: " & versToStr(item 1 of version) & return
  put "Compacted By: " & versToStr(item 2 of version) & return after it
  put "Oldest: " & versToStr(item 3 of version) & return after it
  put "Latest: " & versToStr(item 4 of version) & return after it
  put "Modified: " & last item of version & return after it
  convert last word of it to long date
  return it
end stackVersToStr
```

Does your stack match HyperCard?   HyperCard's vocabulary has grown from release to release. While it seems easy to update HyperCard to the current version, for a variety of reasons not everybody does so. Many scripts written with version 1.2, for example, won't work in earlier HyperCard versions, particularly if those scripts use the current version's latest features. And all stacks written in a version earlier than 2.0 must be converted before their contents can be modified under 2.0 and later versions.

To make sure that the stack you've created works with the version of HyperCard your user is running, compare your version of HyperCard to your user's:

```
on openStack
  if the version < 2.0 then pass openStack -- 2.0 or higher
  answer "Sorry — you need to upgrade." with "Rats!"
  go home
end openStack
```

Version not settable: You can't set the version value; you can only retrieve it.

VISIBLE

Forms

```
set {the} visible of [button|field|window] to logical

set the visible of button 1 to it
```

Action

The **visible** property reflects whether a button, field, or window is visible when it's within normally visible boundaries.

Comments

The **hide** command sets the **visible** property of a window, button, or field to false. The **show** command sets the **visible** property of a window, button, or field to true.

About Find: The **find** command locates strings in hidden fields (assuming the field's **dontSearch** property is set to false), but doesn't make hidden fields visible.

About hidden objects: You can write to and read from hidden fields, but tabbing does not step through hidden fields. You can move hidden objects using forms like

```
set the loc of field "Hidden assets" to 220, 10
```

Hidden objects stay hidden when you move them, or when you close and reopen a card, background, and/or stack unless you explicitly show them.

You can't select hidden objects, nor can you select the text of hidden fields. You can, however, examine and change the properties of hidden objects insofar as you can examine and change the properties of visible ones.

Hidden objects don't respond to mouse manipulations; if you want to send a Mouse message to a hidden object, you must use the **send** keyword.

Hiding without changing Visible: Because an element's **visible** property is true doesn't mean you can see that element. Other things that will make an object invisible besides setting **visible** to false include (but are not limited to) the following:

- Set **height** or **width** of buttons, fields, and windows to a negative number.
- Set **location, rect, left, top,** or any similar property to a number off the screen (for example, 9000).
- Draw opaque card pictures over background fields or background buttons.

Also See:

DONTSEARCH property, page 521
HIDE command, page 264
SHOW command, page 339
SHOWPICT property, page 613

WIDEMARGINS

Forms

```
set {the} wideMargins of field to logical

set the wideMargins of field 1 to true
```

Action

The **wideMargins** property, seldom used in a script, reflects whether HyperCard leaves extra space for a field's top and left margins.

Comments

field must be in the current stack.

HyperCard ordinarily leaves a border five pixels wide around the top and left edges of a field using 12-point Geneva text. Setting **wideMargins** to true increases the size of the margins to nine pixels.

The purpose for **wideMargins** is purely aesthetic. Its setting has no impact on performance. Its only effect is that you have a few less pixels in a field for display space than you otherwise would have.

WIDTH

Forms

```
set {the} width of [field|button|card] to integerExpr
put {the} width of [field|button|window] {into container}

set width of button 1 to 100
```

Action

The **width** property reflects the distance in pixels between the left and right sides of an element.

Comments

Button or *field* must be in the current stack.

When you set the width of an element, that element grows or shrinks horizontally around its center such that its center point (described by the location property) remains fixed. If the width is an odd number, the odd pixel is added to the right side.

The widths of some windows — tool, pattern, msg, and (in version 1.2.#) card — are all permanent, so you can't set them. (But in versions starting with 2.0, you can set the width of the card or card window.)

Hiding an object with Width: When you assign a value of 0 or a negative number to the width of an object, that object disappears and it won't respond to mouse actions. You can, however, send messages to it. If it's a field you can type into it and manipulate a selection within it. A field thus hidden remains in the Tabbing order. (An object's **visible** property is unaffected by its **width** property.)

Other ways to change Width: You can also change an object's width programmatically by changing its **rectangle** property. (**Width** is the same as item 3 minus item 1 of the **rectangle** property.)

Also See:

HEIGHT property, page 539
LOCATION property, page 556
RECTANGLE property, page 593
TABKEY command, page 358
VISIBLE property, page 648

Chapter 11

System Messages

This chapter describes every message that HyperCard sends. It tells what event triggers a particular message and the meaning of any parameters to the message.

When a single event elicits more than one message, the event's description includes the order in which the messages are sent.

Before this chapter can make any real sense, you need to understand how the message passing path works, covered in Chapter 1.

In addition, some messages were added to the language so late that their descriptions couldn't be included in the main body of this book. See "Messages" in Appendix I, "Late Breaking News."

HyperCard sends a message when some event of significance has happened while the Browse tool is active. These **system messages** (so called because they're sent by the HyperCard system itself rather than by your handlers) fall into certain broad categories based on the events that make them happen. These categories are associated with the mouse, the keyboard, and HyperCard objects.

But first: are you experienced?

To understand this chapter, you need a working knowledge of what a message is and how message passing works. These subjects are covered in Chapter 1. Here's a synopsis of the static and dynamic message passing paths that a message might follow if it were sent to a button:

1. that button

2. the card that button is on

3. the background of that card

4. the stack of that background

5. the current card (if different from the card in step 2 — the card that was the destination of a **go** command, for example)

6. the current background (if different from the background in step 3)

7. the stack of the current background (if different from the stack in step 4)

8. stacks added to the message passing path by the **start using** command (page 351)

9. the Home stack

10. HyperCard itself

Additionally, you should be clear on the definitions of the different kinds of messages. Here's a quick reminder:

- **System messages** are sent by HyperCard when some event occurs in the HyperCard environment (for example, mouseUp when the mouse button is released or newCard when a new card is created) or when nothing is happening (idle). These messages are effects rather than causes

---

and are more like news flashes about something that's already happened or in the process of happening, as opposed to announcements of upcoming events. Of course, these messages can cause further behaviors; for example, one of your handlers might catch a `mouseUp` message and send a series of command messages.

- **Command messages** are messages that HyperCard itself can respond to (`put, read, go`). These messages tend to be causes rather than effects in that they make HyperCard do something.

- **User-defined messages** are messages you create (for example: `myMessage, sendToDisk, foo`). Usually such messages set off handlers that ultimately send command messages to Hypercard.

THE MOUSE

The object that first gets a mouse message depends on where the pointer is (as with the message `mouseEnter`), or where the pointer is when the mouse is clicked (as with the message `mouseUp`). The target of a mouse message can be a button, a field, or the current card.

If the pointer is over a button, mouse messages get sent to that button. If the pointer is over a field, some mouse messages are sent to the field depending on the field's condition (see Table 11-1). Mouse messages that aren't sent to a button or a field are sent to the current card.

Table 11-1: Mouse messages and their meanings

Message	What happened
mouseEnter	Pointer just moved over a button or a field.
mouseWithin	Pointer is over a button or a field.
mouseDown	Mouse button has just been pressed. (This message isn't sent to an unlocked field unless the command key is being held down.)
mouseStillDown	Mouse button is being held down. (This message isn't sent to an unlocked field.)

Message	What happened
mouseUp	Mouse button has just been released. (This message isn't sent to an unlocked field unless the command key is being held down.)
mouseLeave	Pointer has just been moved out of a button or field.

Table 11-2 shows the mouse messages that a field can capture, depending on the field's condition:

Table 11-2: Field conditions for capturing mouse messages

Message	Field locked	Field unlocked	Command key pressed, field unlocked
mouseEnter	X	X	X
mouseWithin	X	X	X
mouseDown	X*		X*
mouseStillDown	X		
mouseUp	X		X
mouseLeave	X	X	X

* When the command key is pressed at the same time that you press the mouse button with the pointer over either a locked or an unlocked field, that field gets a mouseDown message *immediately followed by a mouseUp message* whether or not you release the mouse button. Strange to say, holding down the mouse button in these situations produces no mouseStillDown message. (Also see "Fields," later in this chapter.) This is neither a bug nor a feature; it's just the way things are.

MouseWithin and mouseLeave are the only messages sent for pointer action within the scrollbar area of scrolling fields.

About mouseDown: When a mouseDown handler in a card, background, or stack script forces a change to another card in the same stack, the mouseUp message goes to the current card and *not* to the card where the action initiated. For example, if card A has the handler

```
on mouseDown
  go to card "B"
end mouseDown
```

and the script of card B has the handler

```
on mouseUp
  put "This is a different card"
end mouseUp
```

when the mouse button is released the `mouseUp` message goes to card B (executing the mouseUp handler in card B's script).

When you mouseDown in a button that goes to another card, the mouseUp goes to the button on the original card if the pointer is still within that button's rectangle on the current card. If you move the pointer out of that button's region, no `mouseUp` message is sent.

When a mouseDown handler forces a change to a card in a different stack, `mouseUp` won't be sent when the mouse button is released.

About mouseWithin: When the pointer travels over a button or a field, it generates a `mousewithin` message even when the button or field is hidden by the message box or by a windoid (that is, a menu that's been torn off the menu bar).

About the Click command: When the **click** command executes, HyperCard sends the messages `mouseDown`, `mouseStillDown` (10 times), `mouseUp`, and `mouseLeave`. But HyperCard does *not* send `mouseEnter` or `mouseWithin`.

THE KEYBOARD

Keyboard messages are usually sent to the current card (but note the possible exceptions for enterKey, tabKey, and returnKey shown in Table 11-3).

Table 11-3: Keyboard messages and their meanings

Message	What happened
arrowKey *var*	One of the arrow keys has just been pressed, or the **arrowKey** command was sent. *var* is up, down, left, or right. Sent only if the **textArrows** property is false. See the **arrowKey** command (page 171) for more information.
controlKey *var*	The control key and some other key have just been pressed, or the **controlKey** command was sent. *var* is an integer in the range 1 through 127. See the **controlKey** command (page 195) for more information.
enterKey	The enter key has been pressed with no selection — not even the insertion point — in a field. (When a selection exists in some field, pressing the enter key sends the enterInField message to that field.) See the **enterKey** command (page 242) for more information.
functionKey *var*	One of the function keys on the Apple Extended Keyboard has been pressed, or the **functionKey** command was sent. *var* is an integer in the range 1 through 15. See the **functionKey** command (page 254) for more information.
returnKey	The return key has been pressed with no selection — not even the insertion point — in a field. (When a selection exists in some field, pressing the return key sends the returnInField message to that field.) See the **returnKey** command (page 328) for more information.
tabKey	The tab key was just pressed, autoTab action was initiated, or the tabKey command was sent. (The tabkey message is sent to the currently open field if there is one; if there is no open field, then tabKey goes to the current card.) See the **tabkey** command (page 358) for more information.

BUTTONS

Button messages are sent to the button in question (see Table 11-4).

Table 11-4: Button messages and their meanings

Message	What happened
newButton	Button has just been created.
deleteButton	HyperCard has started the deletion process and the button is about to disappear.

About newButton: A newly created button can't catch its own `newButton` message because new buttons don't have scripts. (The exception is a new button copied from an existing button that already has a script.) But you can place a newButton handler other places in the message passing path (card script, background script, etc.) so that as soon as a button is created that handler will operate. For example, the following handler placed in the background script brings up the Info box of a new button as soon as it's created (so you can set its properties):

```
on newButton
  doMenu "Button info..."
end newButton
```

Also see "The Mouse," earlier in this chapter.

Preventing button deletions

You can catch the `deleteButton` message (which is sent to the doomed button) and, by sleight of hand, prevent the button's demise. To do it, you need a handler like this:

```
on deleteButton -- Trap deleteButton message
  select empty -- Deselect the doomed button
end deleteButton
```

The order of events that HyperCard ordinarily goes through to carry out a button deletion are

1. Receive command message to delete a button.

2. Send message deleteButton.

3. Look for selected button.

4. Delete it.

The sample handler prevents step 3 in this process from succeeding because no button is selected. If the command to delete the button came from a handler, HyperCard beeps as a notification of an error condition, carries out the remaining commands of the handler that tried to delete the button, and returns control to the caller.

To prevent the destruction of a particular button, put the handler in that button's script. To prevent the deletion of all buttons, put the script later in the message passing path (for example, in the background or stack script).

FIELDS

All the messages in Table 11-5 go to the field in question, unless otherwise noted.

Table 11-5: Field messages and their meanings

Message	What happened
newField	Field has just been created.
deleteField	HyperCard has started the deletion process and the field is about to disappear.
enterInField	The enter key was pressed while a selection existed in a field. (When a selection — including the insertion point — doesn't exist in any field, pressing the enter key sends the enterKey message to the card.)
returnInField	The return key was pressed while a selection existed in a field. (When a selection — including the insertion point — doesn't exist in any field, pressing the return key sends the returnKey message to the card.)
openField	You or a command (e.g., **click**) clicked in an unlocked field, or the insertion point moved to that field from the previous field in the tabbing order because somebody pressed the tab key, a **tabKey** command was executed, a **select text** or **select** *<chunk>* command executed, or an autoTab happened.
closeField	The selection (including the insertion point) has been removed from an open field, *and some text has been changed in that field.* Actions that remove the selection include (but are not limited to) opening another field, pressing the enter key, tabbing, clicking outside the field, toggling the Message box, switching into the background mode, and changing cards.
exitField	New in HyperCard 2.0: acts like closeField (above) in that the insertion point has been removed from an opened field, but *no text has been changed in that field.*

For more messages that go to the target field, see "The Mouse," earlier in this chapter.

When the **put** or **pop** commands write text into a field, they send no `openField` message.

About returnInField: A returnInField handler prevents the Return character from being entered in the field (unless it passes the `returnInField` message).

Preventing field deletions

You can catch the `deleteField` message (which is sent to the doomed field) and prevent the field's demise. To do it, you need a handler like this:

```
on deleteField -- Trap deleteField message
   select empty -- Deselect the doomed field
end deleteField
```

The order of events that HyperCard ordinarily goes through to carry out a field deletion are:

1. Receive command message to delete a field

2. Send message `deleteField`

3. Look for selected field

4. Delete it

The sample handler prevents step 3 in this process from succeeding because no field is selected. If the command to delete the field came from a handler, HyperCard beeps as a notification of an error condition, carries out the remaining commands of the handler that tried to delete the field, and returns control to the user.

To prevent the destruction of a particular field, put the handler in that field's script. To prevent the deletion of all fields, put the script later in the message passing path (for example, in the background or stack script).

CARDS

All the messages in Table 11-6 are sent to the current card:

Table 11-6: Card messages and their meanings

Message	What happened
newCard	Card has just been created (including one that comes into being when you create a new background). In 1.2.#, this message is always preceded by the message openCard.
deleteCard	HyperCard has started the deletion process and the card is about to disappear.
openCard	Card becomes current because of a **go** command, the card itself was just created, a background has just been created (thus creating a new card), or the system has just started. If MultiFinder is off, you get this message (among others) when execution of HyperCard has been resumed after an **open application** operation. You *don't* get this message while scanning cards with the **show cards** command or when printing cards with the **print cards** command.
closeCard	You just left the card because of a **go** command, **Quit HyperCard** menu choice, or because a stack was deleted. If MultiFinder is off, you get this message (among others) when execution of HyperCard has been suspended for an **open** *application* operation. You *don't* get this message while scanning cards with the **show cards** command or when printing cards with the **print cards** command.

BACKGROUNDS

All the messages in Table 11-7 are first sent to the current card (and *not* to the current background). In most cases background messages are accompanied by other messages; these other messages are noted where appropriate.

System messages are never automatically sent to backgrounds (although you can send messages to backgrounds using **send**).

Table 11-7: Background messages and their meanings

Message	What happened
newBackground	Background was just created.
deleteBackground	Background was just deleted and is about to disappear.
openBackground	The card that just opened has a different background from the card that just closed (including the card that's created when a new background is created).
closeBackground	You just moved to a card whose background is different from the last card you were on.

STACKS

All these messages are first sent to the current card (and *not* to the current stack). In most cases stack messages are accompanied by other messages; these other messages are noted where appropriate.

System messages are never automatically sent to stacks (although you can send messages to stacks using **send**).

Table 11-8: Stack messages and their meanings

Message	Action
newStack	A stack was just created.
deleteStack	A stack is in the process of being deleted and is about to disappear. After sending this message, HyperCard deletes the stack and goes to the first card of the Home stack.
openStack	A stack opened because HyperCard just started, because a new stack was just created, or because a **go** command changed stacks.
closeStack	A stack closed because a **go** command changed stacks, because a stack was deleted, or because you quit HyperCard. This message is usually preceded by the messages closeCard closeBackground and followed by the messages openStack openBackground openStack.

HYPERCARD SYSTEM

All the messages in Table 11-9 first go to the current card (not to HyperCard). In some cases these messages are accompanied by other messages, and are noted where appropriate.

Table 11-9: HyperCard general messages and their meanings

Message	What happened
hide menuBar	Somebody pressed command-spacebar when the menubar was showing, or the **hide menuBar** command executed.
show menuBar	Somebody pressed command-spacebar when the menubar was hidden, or the **show menuBar** command executed.
idle	No other message is being sent, no handler is running, and the browse tool is the current tool. (See Table 11-10.)
startUp	The HyperCard application has just been started.
suspend	HyperCard is in the process of executing an **open** *application* command, and is about to suspend operation so that *application* can run. This message is only sent when MultiFinder is turned off.
suspendStack	New in HyperCard 2.0: another stack opened in a new window, or somebody clicked in the window of another stack already on the screen.
resume	HyperCard has just resumed operation after an application launched by the **open** *application* command has quit. This message is only sent when MultiFinder is turned off.
resumeStack	New in HyperCard 2.0: a previously suspended stack has become active. (See suspendStack, above.)
quit	Somebody just issued a **Quit HyperCard** command and HyperCard is about to quit.

Idle time resets: When the `idle` message is sent, any pending visual effects are cleared and the properties in Table 11-10 are reset to the listed values:

Table 11-10:   Properties reset at Idle time

Property	Value
numberFormat	0.######
dragSpeed	0
lockRecent	false
lockMessages	false
lockScreen	false

SENDING ORDER

Many events make HyperCard send multiple messages. Table 11-11 lists multiple message events, and shows the order in which the messages are sent.

Table 11-11: Message order in events that send multiple messages

Event	Version	Message order
Start HyperCard	1.2.#	openStack openBackground openCard startup
	2.#	startup openStack openBackground openCard
Suspend for launch*	All	closeCard closeBackground closeStack suspend
Resume from launch*	1.2.#	openStack openBackground openCard resume
	2.#	resume openStack openBackground openCard
Quit HyperCard	All	closeCard closeBackground closeStack quit
Stack change	All	closeCard closeBackground closeStack openStack openBackground openCard
Background change	All	closeCard closeBackground openBackground openCard
Card change	All	closeCard openCard
New stack	1.2.#	closeCard closeBackground closeStack openStack openBackground openCard newStack

Event	Version	Message order
	2.#	closeCard closeBackground closeStack newStack newBackground newCard openStack openBackground openCard
New stack in new window	2.#	suspendStack newStack newBackground newCard openStack openBackground openCard
New background	1.2.#	closeCard closeBackground openBackground openCard newBackground newCard
	2.#	closeCard closeBackground newBackground newCard openBackground openCard
New card	1.2.#	openCard newCard
	2.#	closeCard newCard openCard
Delete stack	1.2.#	deleteStack closeCard closeBackground closeStack
	2.#	closeCard closeBackground closeStack deleteStack
Delete background	1.2.#	deleteBackground deleteCard
	2.#	closeCard closeBackground deleteCard deleteBackground
Delete card	1.2.#	deleteCard closeCard
	2.#	closeCard {closeBackground} deleteCard {deleteBackground openBackground} openCard
Paste card	1.2.#	openCard
	2.#	{newBackground} newCard {openBackground} openCard

Event	Version	Message order
Cut card	1.2.#	(No messages sent)
	2.#	closeCard {closeBackground} deleteCard {deleteBackground openBackground} openCard

* These messages are sent only when MultiFinder is *NOT* running.

ADDITIONAL MESSAGE-SENDING ANOMALIES

Choosing a tool by clicking on the tools menu sends the message `choose tool <integer>` to the current card; but in versions through 1.2.1 clicking on the tools windoid sends no message. This bug is fixed in version 1.2.2. (For information on the **choose** command, see page 183.)

Opening and closing scripts doesn't send any messages, even if the script you're opening is the script of a remote card or stack. (See page 235 for more information on the **edit** command.)

Chapter 12

Speed and Style Issues

Too often in computer languages, your code can have speed or it can have good style. HyperTalk lets you have both.

The chapter is divided into three sections. The first section, "Writing the Fastest Code Possible," concentrates on how to get the most speed from a script, even when the code is compiled (as it is in version 2.#). The second section, "Style Issues," shows how you can write your scripts so that they're orderly and easy to read without sacrificing speed. The final section, "Organizing a Script," is a special style issue, and deals with the placement of handlers in the message passing path and the order of handlers within a script.

WRITING THE FASTEST CODE POSSIBLE

HyperTalk 2.0 is a compiled language, so it's pretty fast. (Earlier versions were *interpreted*, and were slower.) But many of the other operations that HyperCard does are by their nature slow. This is especially true for disk-accessing operations, and HyperCard is disk-intensive. But there are ways to get the most speed possible out of it — in some cases making scripts run up to an order of magnitude faster. This section tells you what operations are slow and should be used sparingly, and how you can modify your scripts to make them faster.

Time savings are relative

This section quotes different time savings for different techniques. The actual performance you get will vary from machine to machine and from situation to situation. But what you can count on is that all these techniques work. If you follow all the recommendations in this chapter, your code *will* run as fast as possible.

Here's a quick summary of principles to follow to make your stacks run (or seem to run) as fast as possible. They're listed in order of importance. (The comments about script design — in-line statements rather than handler calls, using externals wherever speed is essential, and so on — apply more to interpreted versions of HyperTalk than to compiled versions.) You'll find details and examples for all of these principles later in the chapter:

- Change stacks as seldom as possible.

- Use variables instead of fields for all operations.

- Migrate to Externals for highly repetitive tasks (such as sorting).

- Refer to a remote card rather than going there.

- Take unnecessary code out of loops.

- Set lockScreen to true to avoid needless redrawing.

- Set lockMessages to true to save time during card-to-card data collection.

- Combine multiple messages.

- Use quoted instead of unquoted literals.

- Use in-line statements rather than handler calls.

- Do complex calculations once.

- Refer to variables as infrequently as possible.

- Do visible work first.

Change Stacks as Seldom as Possible

Changing stacks requires HyperCard to read from some external storage device (for example, a disk or CD-ROM). And this takes more time than any other Macintosh operation (not counting getting through to the Technical Support department).

So it makes more sense to keep all related data in the same stack to minimize stack changes. This includes data that you regularly sort, search, or move between. If you have substantially different interfaces (for example, one interface to take phone orders, another interface to do inventory, etc.) and you need to cross boundaries frequently, use multiple backgrounds in the same stack rather than separate stacks.

When you need to read or write data from another stack, make the trip to that stack only once. Get or put everything you need at the same time. (But see later comments about data collection.)

The following script shows how to do everything in one trip. It scans a stack of phone company customer records and creates a new stack with the names, addresses and phone numbers of those that have the highest phone bills:

```
on windBags
  lock screen
  repeat with i = 1 to the number of cards
    go to card i
    if field "Phone Bill" > 100 then -- found a big spender
      put field "Name" into name
      put field "Address" into address
      put field "Phone Number" into phoneNum
      -- got everything we need
      -- now go put it in the other stack
      push card
      go to last card of stack "WindBags"
      doMenu "New Card"
      put name & return & address into field "Name and Address"
```

```
      put phoneNum into field "Phone"
      pop card -- return to other stack
   end if
  end repeat
end windBags
```

There are always exceptions: There are a few valid reasons to use more than one stack for closely related data. The prime one is stack size — you might want to make sure that each stack fits on a single floppy to make transport or backup easier. Another is command operations — a few commands (like **sort** and **find**) work on the entire stack, and sometimes you don't want the entire stack affected.

Warning to giant stack makers

A bug in versions through 1.2.2 corrupts stacks larger than 8 megabytes. This bug has been fixed for versions 1.2.5 and higher.

Use Variables, not Fields, for All Operations

As much as possible, do all operations — sorting, data collecting, calculations — in variables rather than in fields. Operations happen much faster in variables than they do in fields.

Fields are for the display of data and for long-term storage; HyperCard keeps field information stored on disk and draws that information onto the screen. Variables, on the other hand, live in RAM and are for the storage and manipulation of transient data — data that you don't see on the screen and that disappears when you quit HyperCard. And (as you probably know) information stored in RAM is available quickest.

Sometimes you can't use this method: you might not have enough RAM to hold all the information in variables. But this method is the best one to use where circumstances allow.

Sorting a list shows most dramatically the difference in using variables instead of fields for operations. This first example compares sorting data in a field to sorting data in a variable. Assume you're sorting a few items (maybe 20) in field "data," each item on its own line. The following code uses a bubble sort to sort the data in a field:

```
on sort
  repeat with i = 1 to the number of lines in field "data"
```

```
      repeat with j = i to the number of lines in field "data"
        set cursor to busy -- shows computer isn't brain-dead
        if line i of field "data" > line j of field "data" then
          get line j of field "data"
          put line i of field "data" into line j of field "data"
          put it into line i of field "data"
        end if
      end repeat
    end repeat
end sort
```

The code above sorts 20 items in about 21 seconds on a Mac II using 1.2.#. But the following code, which does all its sorting in a variable, is much faster:

```
on sort
  put field "data" into data -- Sorting in a variable is faster
  repeat with i = 1 to the number of lines in data
    repeat with j = i to the number of lines in data
      set cursor to busy -- shows computer isn't brain-dead
      if line i of data > line j of data then
        get line j of data
        put line i of data into line j of data
        put it into line i of data
      end if
    end repeat
  end repeat
  put data into field "data" -- Put sorted list back into field
end sort
```

This code, doing its work in a variable, sorts the same 20 items about three times as fast as sorting in a field.

About the sort code

The bubble sort is a lot slower than most other sorts when you get above 20 items or so. (The time it takes to do a sort rises exponentially.) For sorting larger numbers of items, use the QuickSort function listed on page 348 or the sortLines XCMD on page 706.

Collecting data on different cards into a variable is at least 50 percent faster than collecting it into a field. For example, assume that you want to collect the names from the Name and Address field of your Address stack. This first example, collecting the names from 100 cards into a field, takes about 6 1/2 seconds on a Mac II using 1.2.#:

```
on mouseUp
  lock screen
  push card
  set cursor to watch
  repeat with i = 2 to number of cards
    go card i
    put line 1 of field "Name and Address" & return after ¬
    card field "Collector" of card 1
  end repeat
  pop card
  unlock screen
end mouseUp
```

This next example, collecting the data into a variable and, after the collecting is done, putting all the data at once into a field, takes about four seconds on a Mac II using 1.2.#:

```
on mouseUp
  set cursor to watch
  put empty into allNames
  repeat with i = 2 to number of cards
    put line 1 of (field "Name and Address" of card i) & return ¬
    after allNames
  end repeat
  put allNames into card field "Collector"
end mouseUp
```

You get even better results using variables when you're doing calculations (for example, adding the contents of a series of fields from different cards): Everything that goes into a field is converted to a string, no matter what its original format was; the numeric content of variables, on the other hand, is nearly always stored in binary format, which makes calculations more efficient and more precise.

Migrate to Externals for Repetitive Tasks

(This one might be number one on the list, depending on the number of iterations in the task.) No matter how efficient your code is, sorting 500 items is still going to take a long time. For repetitive time-intensive tasks, use externals. They have the same calling interface as other commands (that is, you use them the same as any HyperTalk command), so they're no harder to use.

If you don't know Pascal, C, or Assembly, you can still find externals for your stacks. The information utilities (CompuServe, MacNet, and so on) all have HyperCard libraries packed with public domain and shareware externals.

For more information on Externals, see Chapter 13.

Referring to a Remote Card is Often Faster than Going There

For collecting data from fewer than 10 fields, referring to a remote card in the current stack is faster than going to it. For collecting data from 10 fields or more, it's faster to go to that card and then to collect the data.

The following three examples illustrate collecting data in a field, collecting data in a variable, and collecting data in a variable by referring to a remote field. For retrieving data from up to 10 fields, each successive handler is faster:

```
on mouseUp
  -- collect one data item in a field
  -- time on a Mac+ using 1.2.# = 159 seconds for 338 cards
  put empty into card field "Collector"
  get the ticks
  lock screen
  push card
  set cursor to watch
  repeat with i = 2 to the number of cards
    go card i
    put line 1 of field "Name and Address" & return after ¬
    card field "Collector" of card 1
  end repeat
  pop card
  unlock screen
  put (the ticks - it)/ 60 & " seconds."
end mouseUp

on mouseUp
```

```
  -- collect one data item in a variable
  -- time on a Mac+ using 1.2.# = 90 seconds for 338 cards
  put empty into card field "Collector"
  get the ticks
  lock screen
  push card
  set cursor to watch
  put empty into allNames
  repeat with i = 2 to the number of cards
    go card i
    put line 1 of field "Name and Address" & return after allNames
  end repeat
  pop card
  put allNames into card field "Collector"
  unlock screen
  put (the ticks - it)/ 60 & " seconds."
end mouseUp

on mouseUp
  -- collect one data item in a variable by referring to remote field
  -- average time on a Mac+ = 34 seconds for 338 cards
  put empty into card field "Collector"
  get the ticks
  set cursor to watch
  repeat with i = 2 to the number of cards
    put line 1 of (field "Name and Address" of card i) & return ¬
    after allNames
  end repeat
  put allNames into card field "Collector"
  put (the ticks - it)/ 60 & " seconds."
end mouseUp
```

Take Unnecessary Code Out of Loops

While differences in speed will be more apparent in versions before 2.0, this is still important for running the fastest code: shorter handlers take less time to run than do longer ones. This is magnified in loops: you can think of a loop that's six lines long and that runs six iterations as being roughly the equivalent of 25 lines of code (roughly, because loops have two extra lines — the opening and closing

— that wouldn't be there if you "unwrapped" the code, plus a certain amount of overhead). So every extra line in that 6-iteration loop counts as six lines.

The **lockScreen** line in the following code should precede the loop. In its present position, it wastes many multiples of the amount of time it actually needs:

```
on collectNames
  -- this is where "set lockScreen to true" should be
  repeat with i = 1 to 300
    set lockScreen to true --No! Get out of the loop! Bad line!!! Bad!!!
    put line 1 of field 1 & return after dataCollector
  end repeat
end collectNames
```

An exception to the rule

It's faster to move an object or window than it is to check if it's already where you intend to move it to. For example, even if the Message box is already at 10, 364 it takes longer to say

```
if the loc of msg ≠ "10,364" then set the loc of msg to 10,364
```

than it does to say

```
set the loc of msg to 10,364
```

And if you're checking in a loop, the time difference can add up. This is especially true in versions earlier than 2.0.

Use Quoted Literals Instead of Unquoted Literals

When HyperTalk comes across an ambiguous word — that is, one that might be a literal, function call, variable, or whatever — it must check all the possibilities to discover what the word really is. The first possibility that HyperTalk considers is that the word is a quoted literal; the last thing it considers is that the word is an unquoted literal. In several tests on the Mac II, quoted literals ran 20 percent faster than unquoted literals. So enclosing literals in quotation marks can result in considerable time savings — up to 20 percent in some cases of highly repetitive loops running in versions earlier than 2.0.

Set lockScreen to True to Avoid Redrawing

Redrawing the screen takes time. It makes no sense to let the screen change when all you're doing is collecting data (unless you want to wow the user and you think that's worth the time that redrawing takes). This is especially true when you decide to collect data by going from card to card or from stack to stack.

The bubble sort in the example earlier in this chapter runs about 20 percent faster when the screen is locked. The data collection examples take far longer to traverse the hundreds of cards when the card changes are visible.

Lock Messages During Data Collection

The **lockMessages** property allows you to prevent HyperCard from sending the six open and close messages associated with cards, backgrounds, and stacks. When a stack has handlers keyed to open and close messages, **lockMessages** can save lots of time and confusion; when a stack has no such handlers but you're using 1.2.#, **lockMessages** still saves time — the time that it takes for such messages to traverse the message-passing path (made longer by a third if you're collecting data from a remote stack when the dynamic path comes into play).

Combine Multiple Messages

In 1.2.# message-sending is relatively expensive because each message traverses the entire message passing path. So here are a bunch of techniques that, when taken together, can save lots of time:

Use operators: Operators are interpreted directly and don't incur the cost of message sending. They're quite fast compared to everything else. So "is in," "is not in," and "contains" are faster than `offset()` because they're not sent as messages.

Use "the" for functions: Similarly, calling a built-in function with "the" or "of" is faster than calling with "()" because "()" functions traverse the message path. So using `date()` is slower than `the date`

Assign values directly: Getting a value and putting it somewhere is slower than putting it directly, because two statements take longer to execute than does one. So

```
add 1 to x
divide x by 4
```

is slower than

```
put (x+1)/4 into x
```

A highly technical point: Sometimes the journey is the reward

Because an entire handler is converted to executable code before it starts running, normal in-line message sending doesn't require additional analysis. But when you use the **send** keyword, the message being sent must be converted before the **send** keyword can execute and so is slower:

```
foo
```

is faster than

```
send "foo"
```

Handler Calls Take More Time than In-line Statements

It always takes time to get from here to there and back again. When you call remote code, you're adding travel time. And every time you pass a parameter, you not only do some traveling, but you have to load up your backpack before you leave and unpack it again when you arrive. (Don't you love these California outdoorsy metaphors?)

To save time, put all your code in-line. The problem, however, is that this can make your code hard to follow. Consider this easy-to-read module:

```
on checkSchedule
    ... -- bunch of other code
    getTheDayAndTime
    getNewAppointment day, time
    checkForConflicts
    addToSchedule
    askForOtherAppointments
end checkSChedule
```

The utility handlers take slightly more time to execute than they would if they were all in-line, but they're very easy to read. The speed increase you get by having harder to read code might not be worth it. The best solution is probably to save straight in-line work for repetitive, time-intensive stuff that you haven't relegated to Externals.

Another good compromise is to call handlers only when you have to — that is, test for the necessity of going to a handler in the main module, rather than in the utility handler. For an example of this, see "Use Structures Judiciously" in the Style section.

Do Complex Calculations Once

This includes retrieving parameter values once rather than many times (assuming you know that the values haven't changed). Once you've figured something out, stick the results in a variable, and then refer to the variable. And again, the time saved is magnified within loops.

This first handler is pretty slow because it continually recomputes the value of the user-defined function `sortLines(values)` (function not shown):

```
on findADuplicate values
  repeat with i = 2 to the number of lines in sortLines(values)
    if line i of sortLines(values) is line i - 1 of sortLines(values) then
      put line i of sortLines(values) & " is a duplicate."
      exit findDuplicates
    end if
  end repeat
  put "No duplicates."
end findADuplicate
```

This handler, however, is much faster; it computes the value of `sortLine(values)` only once:

```
on findADuplicate values
  get sortLines(values)
  repeat with i = 2 to the number of lines in it
    if line i of it is line i - 1 of it then
      put line i of it & " is a duplicate."
      exit findDuplicates
    end if
  end repeat
  put "No duplicates."
end findADuplicate
```

Refer to Variables as Infrequently as Possible

Although variables are the fastest way to access data, the statement `add x to` y is slightly faster than `put x + y into y` because the former has fewer variable references (two) than does the latter (three).

Do Visible Work First

Give the user something to look at or play some music just before you do some heavy-duty, time-consuming work. This technique is strictly sleight-of-hand Houdini stuff: it doesn't make your code any faster, but it occupies the user's attention so he doesn't notice the time so much. Thus the actual runtime is the same, but the perceived runtime is much better.

Here's a code fragment (rest of the code not shown) from a script that shuffles a deck of cards before dealing:

```
on shuffle
  global theDeck
  put empty into field "Your Hand" -- user thinks we're done now
  repeat with i = 1 to 100 -- but we keep working to shuffle the deck
    put random(52) into cardA
    put random(52) into cardB
    get line cardA of theDeck
    put line cardB of theDeck into line cardA of theDeck
    put it into line cardB of theDeck
  end repeat
end shuffle
```

SOME MYTHS ABOUT SPEED

There are lots of strange concepts going around about how to make HyperTalk code run faster. These are our top five all-time favorites.

Myth #1: Fewer comments means more speed. Comments, blank lines, and both leading and unquoted imbedded spaces are all stripped out before runtime, when all handler text is converted to executable form. So the number and length of comments makes absolutely no difference in a handler's speed.

Myth #2: Card changes are slow, so always pre-warm a stack. Initial card changes are sort of slow; but after a card appears, HyperCard caches it in RAM. (It also automatically caches the next card in the stack, figuring you'll want to go there soon.) And if you lock the screen (as we recommend) when you're going through a stack to collect data programmatically, the amount of time it takes to go from card to card even the first time through isn't that great. You can use the following code to pre-warm a stack for bursts of speed (effective if you're doing animation), but in most cases it isn't necessary:

```
on openStack
  go card "Show Me First" -- Give user something to look at
  lock screen
  set lockMessages to true
  show all cards
  ...-- other openStack stuff goes here
  pass openStack
end openStack
```

Myth #3: Short variable names make handlers run faster. Pah! The variable name `This_Is_My_Fave_Variable_Name` has the same impact on speed as does the name `T7` — practically none.

Myth #4: Placement of a handler impacts speed. Wrong again! Placement of a handler in a script or in the hierarchy has no noticable impact on how quickly that handler reacts to a message or on how quickly the statements in that handler execute.

When Prewarming Helps in 2.0

HyperCard compiles a handler the first time it's called. The compiled code is kept in memory (as memory allows) until you quit HyperCard. So a handler runs somewhat faster the second (and subsequent) time that you call it. You can prewarm handlers this way:

```
on myHandler what
  if what is "prewarm" then exit myHandler
  -- rest of code for this handler goes here
end myHandler
```

To prewarm the handler without actually running it, call it using the form `myHander prewarm`. The next time you call it, the handler will already have been compiled and so will execute immediately.

The best time to prewarm is when you have something on the screen for the user to read, such as just after you've displayed the opening card; that way, the user is occupied and doesn't notice the time it takes to do the compilation.

Myth #5: It's faster to use Get than it is to use Put. In actual practice, they take about the same time. Because Get references a single variable automatically (that is, the local variable "it"), it seems slightly faster. But when you start moving values around, Put is faster; it takes two statements to say

```
get 5 * 3
put it into foo
```

but it takes just one statement to say

```
put 5 * 3 into foo
```

STYLE ISSUES

Robustness in programming means that code works right in all possible cases now, and can stand changes to its environment in the future. This section makes style suggestions that produce robust, elegant, and efficient scripts that are easy to debug and maintain through all versions of HyperCard.

Quote All Literals

HyperTalk lets you use unquoted literals. But if you use variable names that are the same as unquoted literals, you can get in trouble.

For example, assume you have a field called "Names" as well as a variable called names:

```
put "John Scribblemonger" into names
put names into field Names
```

HyperCard tries to evaluate a word as a variable before it tries to evaluate it as an unquoted literal. So, because the variable "names" has a value (defined in the first line of code), HyperTalk assumes that the unquoted word Names (at the end of the second line of code) is also variable, and treats it as such. Unless you have a field called "John ScribbleMonger," this code generates an error dialog.

Compare Result Function Contents to Empty

Some commands, such as **Find** or **Go,** set the **result** function to a string. When such a command is successful, it always sets the **result** function to empty. When the command fails, it generally sets the **result** function to a useful error message (like "No such card.").

But the string that each command sets the **result** to is liable to change from version to version of HyperCard, so you can't rely on it. It makes sense, then, to look at the contents of **result** only in terms of its being empty or *not* empty, and not in terms of its actual contents.

For example if you're checking to see whether a **go** command worked, the phrase:

```
if the result is not empty -- This will always be reliable
then answer "Sorry - " & the result
```

will always work; but the phrase

```
if the result is "no such card" -- Message might change in later versions!
then answer "Sorry - " & the result
```

might work only with the current version of HyperCard.

You have been warned.

Use Structures Judiciously

Test for success (or failure) as early in a structure as you can. This makes constructing the rest of the code cleaner and easier to deal with, because you'll have the "no-go" cases taken care of first and you won't have to think about them any more:

```
on mouseUp
  if "field" is not in the target
  then exit mouseUp -- get out here
  put me after field 2
  beep
  answer the target && "appended."
end mouseUp
```

Keep a Handler's Interface and Implementation Separate

The interface to a handler should be as simple as possible, with the handler itself doing the work. As you find better ways of doing things, all you have to change is the implementation rather than every place that you call it.

The call to a sort routine, for example, might pass the source to be sorted and the order of the sort:

```
sortExpr(field 6, descending)
```

This way the sort handler can accept input from any source, and decide what type of sort is most appropriate.

Similarly, if you have a stack that does a lot of telephone dialing, all the interface should do is get the number to be dialed, and then pass it to the implementing handler. The dialing handler ought to supply all the other information (outside dialing codes, necessary pauses, credit card number if necessary and so on). For an example of this, see the Address stack that came with HyperCard.

Keep Handlers General and Reusable

This suggestion follows naturally from the last one. Handlers need to be flexible so that they can handle as many situations as possible within their domain. So a sort routine, for example, shouldn't refer to specific containers, and shouldn't expect the names of containers to be passed to them: rather, it should expect to get, and to pass back, values in a simple parameter:

```
function sortExpr data, direction
   -- sort code goes here
  return data -- returns the data all sorted to the caller
end sortExpr
```

The point here is that a handler that operates on any expression can take parameters from and return results to anywhere.

Standardize Naming Conventions

This makes your code easy to read (and therefore easy to debug and to modify). It doesn't matter what forms you ultimately decide on, just as long as you're consistent. Here are a few suggestions (none of which have any intrinsic value, beyond the fact that together they consitute a consistent system):

- Start all variables and handler names with lowercase letters, but capitalize imbedded words:

```
myVarName       mouseLocation      lastName      newData
```

- Start global variables with the word "the" to indicate that they're unique throughout HyperCard:

687

```
theUserName    thePayrollList    theBook
```

- Always use descriptive names for variables and handlers. It costs you nothing more to use 25 characters for a name than it does to use two:

```
sortContainer      goodPoliticians      makeNewButton
```

- Avoid using negative forms in names. These are bound to be confusing. For example, when you're dealing with situations that need to know whether the Mac running your stack is a fast one or not, use forms like `if fastMac then callA` or `if slowMac then callB`, rather than `if not slowMac then...` or (by far the worst case) `if not nonFastMac then....`

Use Globals Sparingly

The great thing about globals is that they stay alive throughout all of HyperCard until you quit. And that's also the problem with globals. Because they're always around, they're easy both to clobber and to forget to clobber. This is especially true if you have some favorite global names: you're liable to use the same ones in several stacks, perhaps forgetting to reset them to zero or to empty when you close the stack.

Where appropriate, write code that passes parameters from handler to handler rather than code that depends upon the value of global variables.

ORGANIZING A SCRIPT

Organization deals with deciding what handlers to keep in a script and determining the order in which you list those handlers. You organize a stack to make editing and reading code easier. To this end, most people find that a top-down organization works best. The brief suggestions in this section assume a top-down approach.

Handlers that Belong in a Particular Script

The handlers in a script should be called from that script's object, or from objects earlier on the message passing path. The only handlers in a card script, for example, should be those that respond to card messages (`on openCard`, `on closeCard`, `on newCard`), to messages that might be passed to it or inherit to it from earlier in the message passing path (on `mouseEnter`, on `mouseDown`, on `mouseStillDown`), and to **utility** messages (messages that activate custom handlers) whose handlers you've created specifically to serve a main handler.

For suggestions about where in the message passing path to place a particular handler, see Chapter 1.

Order of Handlers Within a Script

The top handler in a script should be the handler first called from outside the object. In most cases, that handler is the one that first initiated the action (for example, on `mouseUp` for a button or on `openCard` for a card) followed by the utility handlers used by the activating handler.

List utility handlers in the order that you use them in the calling handler. In the case of nested utility handlers, follow the order of the nesting. So if the order of calls looks like this:

```
call mainHandler
call subHandler1
call subHandler2
call subUnderHandler1
call subUnderHandler2
call subUnderHandler3
call subHandler3
```

then list the handlers in the script in the same order:

```
mainHandler
subHandler1
subHandler2
subUnderHandler1
subUnderHandler2
subUnderHandler3
subHandler3
```

An alternate organization is to have handlers after the top one in alphabetical order. This makes handlers easier to find in very long scripts.

Performance effects of organization

Organization is actually a matter of personal convenience: HyperTalk doesn't care in what order handlers occur (except that, as noted in Chapter 2, if two handlers with the same name appear in the same script, the handler earlier in a script is the one that responds to a message); and the **send** keyword lets you execute any handler in the current stack or in any stack script.

The only measurable effect on performance is that summoning a handler in another stack using **send** does a `go to stack` before the named handler is executed, and changing stacks takes a lot of time.

Part Three Advanced Material

Chapter 13

Overview of Externals

This chapter covers the theoretical basis of
XCMDs and XFCNs, resources that contain executable machine language. These
external commands and functions (or
more simply, externals) give you a way to
extend the language, adding features that
HyperTalk doesn't provide directly.

For detailed information on the glue
routines — the practical side of externals
— turn to Chapter 14, "Glue Routine
Reference."

HyperCard external commands and functions (or more simply, **externals**) are
resources that contain executable machine language. Because they're resources,
externals can reside in the resource fork of any stack, of the HyperCard application itself, or of the System file.

You use externals to do things either that HyperTalk doesn't let you do (such
as gaining access to some aspect of the hardware or operating system that you
can't get to directly from HyperTalk) or that HyperTalk doesn't do very well
(such as sorting large amounts of information in a container).

Attention new scripters

Much of the material in this chapter is pretty heady stuff. To make complete sense of it, you need a basic knowledge of programming the Macintosh in Pascal, C, or Assembler. But scripters without such arcane knowledge can still benefit from the general discussions in this chapter about how externals work.

XCMDs VERSUS XFCNs

HyperTalk has two types of externals, external commands and external functions.

External commands have resource type "XCMD". To invoke an XCMD in HyperTalk, you use it as you would a command. For example, assume you've written an XCMD named SetSoundVolume that sets the volume of the speaker to some number that you pass:

```
on speakerVolume
  repeat -- loop until you get a valid volume
    ask "What volume (between 1 and 10) ?" with 5
    if it ≥1 and it ≤10 then exit repeat -- check range
    beep 2 -- get user's attention if range illegal
  end repeat
  SetSoundVolume it -- call XCMD setSoundVolume with value of it
end speakerVolume
```

(The complete Pascal code for this XCMD is on page 703.)

External functions have resource type "XFCN". To invoke an XFCN in HyperTalk, you use it as if it were a function. For example, the XFCN menuBarShowing() returns true if the menubar is visible or false if the menubar is hidden:

```
on openStack
  global theMenuBarCondition
  put menuBarShowing() into theMenuBarCondition -- so you can restore it later
  hide menuBar
end openStack
```

(The complete Pascal code for this XFCN is on page 699.)

Both types of externals are identical except for their resource types and calling mechanisms.

EXTERNAL PROCESSING

When HyperTalk comes upon a call to an external, it does the following three things in the order listed:

1. HyperTalk creates a parameter block (the contents of which is described in the next section).

2. It puts the address of that block on the processor stack.

3. It turns control over to the external's code.

The only thing that the external is required to do is to remove the parameter block's address from the stack. (Pascal does this automatically.) So the simplest possible external (written in Pascal) is

```
PROCEDURE EntryPoint (paramPtr: XCmdPtr);
BEGIN
END;
```

As far as HyperCard is concerned, this code comprises a complete external: although it doesn't do anything, it runs and returns and doesn't crash. You can fill in your own statements and make it do something useful without knowing anything else about externals (but you do need to know how to program the Macintosh).

Freedom and responsibility department

HyperCard relinquishes control of the computer to the called external. You can tell that HyperCard loses control once an external starts because command-period has no effect on running externals.

If your external doesn't follow the rules of Macintosh programming, it can destroy the current stack. As James Redfern (HyperCard tester and one of the original members of the HyperCard development team) once said, "We've got to stop these people before they kill again!"

It's vital that you know the basics of Macintosh programming and that you test every external in a variety of situations before you unleash it on the world.

THE PARAMETER BLOCK

All the features of externals are accessed through the single parameter pointer that HyperTalk passes to it. Here's what the parameter block looks like:

```
XCmdPtr = ^XCmdBlock;
XCmdBlock =
    RECORD
        { receiving parameters }
        paramCount:  INTEGER;
        params:      ARRAY[1..16] OF Handle;

        { returning a result }
        returnValue: Handle;

        { passing the message }
        passFlag:    BOOLEAN;

        { calling back to HyperCard }
        entryPoint:  ProcPtr;
        request:     INTEGER;
        result:      INTEGER;
        inArgs:      ARRAY[1..8] OF LongInt;
```

```
    outArgs:        ARRAY[1..4] OF LongInt;
  END;
```

(The structure for this parameter block is available in C and assembler from Apple Computer. It comes with MPW and is available from APDA on the Magic Hooks disk. See the end of this chapter for APDA's address.)

The parameter pointer provides four categories of functionality:

• receiving parameters

• returning a result

• passing the message

• calling back to HyperCard.

Each of these elements works independently. You can entirely ignore any or all of these categories and HyperTalk will do the Right Thing; and what you don't care to use won't hurt you.

Receiving Parameters

The first two fields of the parameter block let externals receive up to 16 parameters from scripted handlers or from other externals:

```
paramCount:    INTEGER;
params:        ARRAY[1..16] OF Handle;
```

Don't write to read-only fields

These first two fields are read-only. They are initialized and disposed of for you by HyperTalk. If you write to them, you'll probably crash the computer and lose data.

The `paramCount` field (an integer in the range 0 to 16) indicates how many parameters were passed to the external. The `params` field is an array of handles containing one handle for each parameter. These are always handles to zero-terminated strings, even for parameters that are the result of arithmetic or logical operations. For example, the call:

```
myXCMD "hello",3+4,5<10
```

would make the first three handles in params contain the following three zero-terminated strings:

```
"hello","7","true"
```

(HyperTalk evaluates all expressions before sending them.) Whenever fewer than 16 parameters exist for params, HyperTalk puts NIL into all unused handles.

The following XCMD demonstrates passing parameters. It sets the title of the card window to the string passed to it.

```
(*
   SetWindowTitle -- XCMD to set title of card window.

   Sample HyperTalk line:

      SetWindowTitle "Pay Attention!"

   To compile and link this file using MPW:

      Pascal SetWindowTitle.p
      Link -rt XCMD=15 -m ENTRYPOINT -sg SetWindowTitle ∂
      -o "XCMD's" SetWindowTitle.p.o "{Libraries}HyperXLib.o"

*)
{$R-}   { no range checking }
{$D-}   { no Macsbug symbols }

UNIT DummyUnit;

INTERFACE

USES Types,Windows,HyperXCmd;

PROCEDURE EntryPoint(paramPtr: XCmdPtr);

IMPLEMENTATION

PROCEDURE SetWindowTitle(paramPtr: XCmdPtr); FORWARD;

PROCEDURE EntryPoint(paramPtr: XCmdPtr);
BEGIN
   SetWindowTitle(paramPtr);
END;

PROCEDURE SetWindowTitle(paramPtr:XCmdPtr);
VAR title: Str255;
```

```
   port:       GrafPtr;
BEGIN
  IF paramPtr^.paramCount <> 1 THEN title := ''
  ELSE ZeroToPas(paramPtr,paramPtr^.params[1]^,title);
  GetPort(port);
  SetWTitle(WindowPtr(port),title);
END;

END.
```

Returning a Result

The parameter block's third field (a write-only field) lets an external return a result:

```
returnValue: Handle;
```

ReturnValue is analogous to the **return** keyword for scripted handlers (page 151). When an XCMD returns, the value of returnValue is available through the HyperTalk function the result; when an XFCN returns, returnValue is returned as the value of the function.

When HyperTalk first calls your external, returnValue contains NIL. If returnValue is still NIL when your external returns, HyperTalk treats it as a result of empty. (If you want to return a result other than empty in such a situation, set returnValue to a handle containing the zero-terminated string you want to return.)

HyperTalk deallocates this handle for you after using its value.

The following XFCN demonstrates returning a value. It returns true if the menu bar is showing and false if it is not. (It determines this by checking the current menu bar height; If the height is 0, then the menu bar must be hidden.)

```
(*

MenuBarShowing -- XFCN to check if the menu bar is showing.

Sample HyperTalk line:

  if MenuBarShowing() then hide menuBar

To compile and link this file using MPW:

  Pascal MenuBarShowing.p
  Link -rt XFCN=19 -m ENTRYPOINT -sg MenuBarShowing ∂
  -o "XCMD's" MenuBarShowing.p.o "{Libraries}HyperXLib.o"
```

```
*)

{$R-}   { no range checking }
{$D-}   { no Macsbug symbols }

UNIT DummyUnit;

INTERFACE

USES Types,Script,HyperXCmd;

PROCEDURE EntryPoint(paramPtr: XCmdPtr);

IMPLEMENTATION

PROCEDURE MenuBarShowing(paramPtr: XCmdPtr); FORWARD;

PROCEDURE EntryPoint(paramPtr: XCmdPtr);
BEGIN
  MenuBarShowing(paramPtr);
END;

PROCEDURE MenuBarShowing(paramPtr:XCmdPtr);
VAR str: Str255;
BEGIN
  BoolToStr(paramPtr,GetMBarHeight <> 0,str);
  paramPtr^.returnValue := PasToZero(paramPtr,str);
END;

END.
```

Passing Messages

The parameter block's fourth field (a write-only field) lets an external pass the message that invoked it:

```
passFlag:    BOOLEAN;
```

passFlag is analogous to HyperTalk's **pass** keyword .

When HyperTalk first calls your external, passFlag contains false, or in binary 0000000000000000 (that's 16 zeros). If passFlag is still false when your external returns, HyperTalk assumes that your external has caught and handled the message that invoked it. But If you've changed passFlag to anything other than false, HyperTalk assumes that your external has *not* handled the message;

so the message continues along the normal message passing path looking for a receiver.

The following XFCN demonstrates passing the current message from an external. It overrides the **shiftKey** function and returns down if the caps lock key is down; otherwise it passes the message and lets shiftKey return its normal value.

```
(*

  shiftKey -- XFCN to override and enhance the shiftKey function.

  Sample HyperTalk line:

    get shiftKey() -- returns true if shift key or caps lock down

  To compile and link this file using MPW:

    Pascal shiftKey.p
    Link -rt XFCN=17 -m ENTRYPOINT -sg shiftKey -o ∂
    "XCMD's" shiftKey.p.o "{Libraries}HyperXLib.o"

*)

{$R-}  { no range checking }

{$D-}  { no Macsbug symbols }

UNIT DummyUnit;

INTERFACE

USES Types,Events,HyperXCmd;

PROCEDURE EntryPoint(paramPtr: XCmdPtr);

IMPLEMENTATION

PROCEDURE MyShiftKey(paramPtr: XCmdPtr); FORWARD;

PROCEDURE EntryPoint(paramPtr: XCmdPtr);
BEGIN
  MyShiftKey(paramPtr);
END;

PROCEDURE MyShiftKey(paramPtr:XCmdPtr);
VAR theKeys: KeyMap;
  PROCEDURE Return(value: Str255);
  BEGIN
    paramPtr^.returnValue := PasToZero(paramPtr,value);
```

```
      EXIT(MyShiftKey);
   END;

BEGIN
   IF paramPtr^.paramCount <> 0 THEN Return('Form is: shiftKey()');
   GetKeys(theKeys);
   IF theKeys[57] THEN Return('down');
   paramPtr^.passFlag := true; { pass to the built-in function }
END;

END.
```

Calling Back to HyperCard

The last five fields of the parameter block let externals call a variety of useful routines that are built into HyperCard. In essence, your external asks HyperCard for information (the result of a function, the value of a property, and so on) which the external then uses to do its work:

```
entryPoint:   ProcPtr;
request:      INTEGER;
result:       INTEGER;
inArgs:       ARRAY[1..8] OF LongInt;
outArgs:      ARRAY[1..4] OF LongInt;
```

Actually, your external doesn't write to these fields. Instead, you call a **glue routine** (so called because it "glues" together the external, no matter what its language — Pascal, C, whatever — to one of HyperCard's internal routines) which does the work for you. The glue routine writes appropriate information into the parameter block.

For example, the routine `EvalExpr` lets an external evaluate any HyperTalk expression. This lets an external get any value that a scripted handler can get. Assume you have an external that needs to determine the font of field "Fred" :

```
myHandle := EvalExpr('textFont of field "Fred"');
```

Chapter 14, "Glue Routine Reference," describes and shows how to use all the routines implemented through version 1.2.#.

The following XCMD is an example of calling back to HyperCard. It sets the speaker volume to the parameter it was passed. The parameter is passed as a string and it uses a call back to HyperCard to turn the string into an integer.

```
(*
   SetSoundVolume -- XCMD to the sound volume.
   Sample HyperTalk line:
     SetSoundVolume 3 -- set sound volume to level 3
   To compile and link this file using MPW:
     Pascal SetSoundVolume.p
     Link -rt XCMD=11 -m ENTRYPOINT -sg SetSoundVolume ∂
     -o "XCMD's" SetSoundVolume.p.o "{Libraries}Interface.o" ∂
     "{Libraries}HyperXLib.o"
*)
{$R-}   { no range checking }
{$D-}   { no Macsbug symbols }
UNIT DummyUnit;

INTERFACE

USES Types,OSUtils,Sound,HyperXCmd;

PROCEDURE EntryPoint(paramPtr: XCmdPtr);

IMPLEMENTATION

PROCEDURE SetSoundVolume(paramPtr: XCmdPtr); FORWARD;

PROCEDURE EntryPoint(paramPtr: XCmdPtr);
BEGIN
  SetSoundVolume(paramPtr);
END;

PROCEDURE SetSoundVolume(paramPtr: XCmdPtr);
VAR newVol: LongInt;
    volStr: Str255;
    p: SysPPtr;
    err: INTEGER;

  PROCEDURE Abort;
  BEGIN
    paramPtr^.returnValue :=
      PasToZero(paramPtr,'Form is: SetSoundVolume <0..7>');
    EXIT(SetSoundVolume);
  END;
```

```
BEGIN
  IF paramPtr^.paramCount <> 1 THEN Abort;
  ZeroToPas(paramPtr,paramPtr^.params[1]^,volStr);
  newVol := StrToNum(paramPtr,volStr);
  IF (newVol < 0) OR (newVol > 7) THEN Abort; { out of range }
  SetSoundVol(newVol); { set it in memory }
  p := GetSysPPtr; { and in parameter RAM }
  WITH p^ DO volClik := BOR(BAND(volClik,$F8FF),BSL(newVol,8));
  err := WriteParam;
END;

END.
```

You need glue routines for callbacks

The pre-compiled glue routines that you use for callbacks must be included in a library file accompanying the externals that use them. (You compile the external; then the linker finds the glue routines that it needs, puts them together with your external, and finally combines them into a final resource of type XCMD or XFCN.)

A collection of HyperTalk glue routines (written here in Pascal) appears at the end of Chapter 14. If you don't want to type these routines into a library file, or if you want them in C, you can get them on disk from the Apple Programmer's and Developer's Association (APDA) whose address appears at the end of this chapter.

(They also come with Apple's MPW, Think's C and Pascal, and most other packages.)

Checking for success: After calling a routine, it's up to the external to check the result field to see if the call was successful. The glue routines don't check the result field for you. Three result codes currently exist, indicating whether the call succeeded, failed, or isn't implemented in this version of HyperCard. The result codes are

```
xresSucc     = 0;
xresFail     = 1;
xresNotImp   = 2;
```

To check if a call is successful, the external would use a statement such as this:

```
IF paramPtr^.result = xresSucc THEN ...
```

The result code for a successful call is `xresSucc` and the handle you get back contains the value of the expression.

Some callbacks set the result field to `xresFail` and return NIL if the call fails. These callbacks are EvalExpr, SendCardMessage, SendHCMessage, and StrToBool.

Externals and error trapping

Ordinarily when a HyperTalk handler does something that results in an error condition (such as trying to evaluate an invalid expression), the handler aborts with an error dialog. But when a callback fails, *the external continues to run.* This ability to do something that causes an error, to detect the error, and to continue executing is unique to externals and presents great opportunities for you to write error trapping procedures as you need them.

`xresNotImp` means that the routine you've requested isn't implemented in the running version of HyperCard.

Beware new routines: New routines might be added at any time. For example, HyperCard version 1.2.1 saw the addition of two new routines, `GetMaskAndData` and `ChangedMaskAndData` (described in detail in Chapter 14). If your recently written external were run in an earlier version of HyperCard, your external would fail and you'd get the result code `xresNotImp`. An external can easily check what version of HyperCard it's running under:

```
myHandle := EvalExpr('the version');
```

SPEED INCREASES — AN EXTERNAL'S FINEST HOUR (OR MINUTE)

One of the prime uses for externals is to increase HyperTalk's execution speed. This is especially true if you're using any version of HyperTalk earlier than 2.0. The following external (with short assembly language appendage to handle upper/lower case issues) sorts lines much faster than the most efficient HyperTalk sorting algorithm:

```
(*
   sortLines --
      XFCN to text sort lines of an expression into
      ascending or descending order.
   Sample HyperTalk line:

   get sortLines(field 1)
   put sortLines(x,descending) into field 2 — second param can be "descending"

      To compile and link this file using MPW:

      directory "Reno:XCMD's:"
      asm :Src:lowerCase.a -o :Obj:lowerCase.a.o
      Pascal :Src:sortLines.p -o :Obj:sortLines.p.o
      Link -rt XFCN=17 -m ENTRYPOINT -sg sortLines -o ∂
      "XCMD's" :Obj:sortLines.p.o :Obj:lowerCase.a.o "{Libraries}HyperXLib.o" ∂
      "{Libraries}Interface.o"

      By Dan Winkler, March 1989.

*)
{$R-}   { no range checking }
{$D-}   { no Macsbug symbols }

UNIT DummyUnit;
INTERFACE

USES Types,Memory,Packages,HyperXCmd;

PROCEDURE EntryPoint(paramPtr: XCmdPtr);

IMPLEMENTATION

PROCEDURE SortLines(paramPtr: XCmdPtr); FORWARD;
FUNCTION  LowerCase(byte: SignedByte): SignedByte; EXTERNAL;

PROCEDURE EntryPoint(paramPtr: XCmdPtr);
{ The entryPoint must be the first procedure and so cannot       }
{ have local procedures, so we have it call a later procedure    }
{ which can have local procedures. The reason that the first     }
{ procedure cannot have local procedures is that the compiler    }
{ places local procedures before the procedure that contains them. }
BEGIN
```

```
    SortLines(paramPtr);
END;

PROCEDURE SortLines(paramPtr:XCmdPtr);
TYPE  PtrPtr = ^Ptr; { pointer to a pointer to a line }
VAR   lineCount: LongInt;
      keys,sortedList: Handle;
      descendingFlag: BOOLEAN;

  PROCEDURE Abort(errorMsg: Str255);
  { return to caller with an error message as the return value }
  BEGIN
    paramPtr^.returnValue := PasToZero(paramPtr,errorMsg);
    EXIT(SortLines);
  END;

  PROCEDURE CheckInput;
  CONST formErr = 'Form is: sortLines(<expr> {, descending })';
  VAR str: Str255;
  BEGIN
    IF (paramPtr^.paramCount < 1) OR (paramPtr^.paramCount > 2)
    THEN Abort(formErr);
    descendingFlag := FALSE;
    IF (paramPtr^.paramCount = 2) THEN
      BEGIN
        ZeroToPas(paramPtr,paramPtr^.params[2]^,str);
        IF NOT StringEqual(paramPtr,str,'descending')
        THEN Abort(formErr);descendingFlag := TRUE;
      END;

  END;

  FUNCTION CountLines(strPtr: Ptr): LongInt;
  { count how many lines there are in the input string }
  { this will determine how many pointers we need to allocate }
  VAR count: LongInt;
  BEGIN
    count := 0;
    WHILE strPtr^ <> 0 DO
      BEGIN
```

```
        count := count + 1;
        ScanToReturn(paramPtr,strPtr);
        IF strPtr^ <> 0
        THEN strPtr := Pointer(ORD(strPtr)+1);
      END;
    CountLines := count;
END;

PROCEDURE AllocateMemory;
{ All memory that this external will ever need is allocated here }
{ before it does anything else.  This makes it very easy for it  }
{ to abort if it couldn't get enough memory.                     }
CONST notEnoughMemoryMsg = 'Error: Not enough memory to sort.';
BEGIN
    keys := NewHandle(lineCount*4); { need one four-byte pointer per line }
    IF keys = NIL THEN Abort(notEnoughMemoryMsg);
    sortedList := NewHandle(StringLength(paramPtr,paramPtr^.params[1]^)+2);
      { Length of output string is length of input string plus 1 byte null }
      { terminator plus 1 byte carriage return in case last line of input  }
      { string is not return terminated                                    }
    IF sortedList = NIL THEN
      BEGIN
        DisposHandle(keys);
        Abort(notEnoughMemoryMsg);
      END;
    paramPtr^.returnValue := sortedList;
      { set up return value here, before it contains anything useful }
END;

PROCEDURE BuildKeys;
{ Build a list of pointers to the lines to be sorted. }
{ Then we'll sort the pointers instead of the lines.  }
VAR i: LongInt;
    scanPtr: Ptr;
    keyPtr: PtrPtr;
BEGIN
  scanPtr := paramPtr^.params[1]^;
  keyPtr := PtrPtr(keys^);
  FOR i := 1 TO lineCount DO
```

```
      BEGIN
        keyPtr^ := scanPtr;
        keyPtr := Pointer(ORD(keyPtr)+4);
        ScanToReturn(paramPtr,scanPtr);
        scanPtr := Pointer(ORD(scanPtr)+1);
      END;
  END;

  FUNCTION CompareLine(ptr1,ptr2: Ptr): INTEGER;
  LABEL 9;
  { Does a case insensitive string compare of two lines. }
  { Returns +1 if first > second, -1 if first < second,  }
  { and 0 if first = second.                             }
  VAR byte1,byte2,result: INTEGER;
  BEGIN
    WHILE TRUE DO
      BEGIN
        byte1 := LowerCase(ptr1^);
        byte2 := LowerCase(ptr2^);
        IF byte1 > byte2 THEN
          BEGIN
            result := +1;
            GOTO 9;
          END;
        IF byte1 < byte2 THEN
          BEGIN
            result := -1;
            GOTO 9;
          END;
        IF byte1 = 13 THEN { end of line }
          BEGIN
            result := 0;
            GOTO 9;
          END;
        ptr1 := Pointer(ORD(ptr1) + 1);
        ptr2 := Pointer(ORD(ptr2) + 1);
      END;
```

```
9:
  IF descendingFlag THEN CompareLine := - result
  ELSE CompareLine := result;
END;

PROCEDURE InsertionSort(startLine,endLine: PtrPtr);
VAR swapPtr,scanPtr: PtrPtr; swapValue: Ptr;
BEGIN
  swapPtr := Pointer(ORD(startLine)+4);
  WHILE ORD(swapPtr) <= ORD(endLine) DO
    BEGIN
      swapValue := swapPtr^;
      scanPtr := swapPtr;
      WHILE (ORD(scanPtr) > ORD(startLine))
      & (CompareLine(PtrPtr(ORD(scanPtr)-4)^,swapValue) = 1) DO
        BEGIN
          scanPtr^ := PtrPtr(ORD(scanPtr)-4)^;
          scanPtr := PtrPtr(ORD(scanPtr)-4);
        END;
      scanPtr^ := swapValue;
      swapPtr := Pointer(ORD(swapPtr)+4);
    END;
END;

FUNCTION Partition(lowLine,highLine: PtrPtr): PtrPtr;
{ median of three partitioning method }
VAR savePtr,pivot: Ptr; midLine,i,j: PtrPtr;
BEGIN
  { sort the low middle and high lines to determine their median }
  midLine := PtrPtr(ORD(lowLine)
             + BAND(BSR((ORD(highLine)
             - ORD(lowLine)),1),$FFFFFFFC));
  IF CompareLine(lowLine^,midLine^) = 1 THEN
    BEGIN
      savePtr := lowLine^;
      lowLine^ := midLine^;
      midLine^ := savePtr;
    END;
  IF CompareLine(lowLine^,highLine^) = 1 THEN
```

```
    BEGIN
      savePtr := lowLine^;
      lowLine^ := highLine^;
      highLine^ := savePtr;
    END;
  IF CompareLine(midLine^,highLine^) = 1 THEN
    BEGIN
      savePtr := midLine^;
      midLine^ := highLine^;
      highLine^ := savePtr;
    END;
  { now partition around the median of the low, middle, and high lines }
  highLine := Pointer(ORD(highLine)-4);
  savePtr := midLine^;
  midLine^ := highLine^;
  highLine^ := savePtr;
  lowLine := Pointer(ORD(lowLine)+4);
  pivot := highLine^;
  i := Pointer(ORD(lowLine)-4);
  j := highLine;
  REPEAT
    REPEAT
      i := Pointer(ORD(i)+4);
    UNTIL CompareLine(i^,pivot) <> -1;
    REPEAT
      j := Pointer(ORD(j)-4);
    UNTIL CompareLine(j^,pivot) <> 1;
    savePtr := i^;
    i^ := j^;
    j^ := savePtr;
  UNTIL ORD(j) <= ORD(i);
  j^ := i^;
  i^ := highLine^;
  highLine^ := savePtr;
  Partition := i;
END;
PROCEDURE QuickSort(startLine,endLine: PtrPtr);
```

```
{ Call InsertionSort if we are sorting fewer than 20 lines    }
{ else partition and recursively sort each half of the partition. }
VAR midLine: PtrPtr;
BEGIN
  IF ORD(endLine) - ORD(startLine) < 80 { 80 bytes of key = 20 lines }
  THEN InsertionSort(startLine,endLine)
  ELSE
    BEGIN
      midLine := Partition(startLine,endLine);
      QuickSort(startLine,Pointer(ORD(midLine)-4));
      QuickSort(Pointer(ORD(midLine)+4),endLine);
    END;
END;

PROCEDURE ConcatResult;
{ Now that the pointers have been sorted, we just need to }
{ concatenate together the lines they point to to make a  }
{ sorted output string.                                   }
VAR inPtr: PtrPtr;
    outPtr: Ptr;
    i: LongInt;

  PROCEDURE CopyOneLine(srcPtr: Ptr; VAR dstPtr: Ptr);
  { copy the input line pointed to by srcPtr to the }
  { output line pointed to by dstPtr }
  BEGIN
    WHILE srcPtr^ <> 0 DO
      BEGIN
        dstPtr^ := srcPtr^;
        dstPtr := Pointer(ORD(dstPtr)+1);
        IF srcPtr^ = 13 THEN EXIT(CopyOneLine);
        srcPtr := Pointer(ORD(srcPtr)+1);
      END;
    dstPtr^ := 13;
    dstPtr := Pointer(ORD(dstPtr)+1);
  END;
BEGIN
  inPtr := PtrPtr(keys^);
```

```
    outPtr := sortedList^;
    FOR i := 1 to lineCount DO
      BEGIN
        CopyOneLine(inPtr^,outPtr);
        inPtr := Pointer(ORD(inPtr)+4);
      END;
    outPtr^ := 0;
  END;
BEGIN

  CheckInput;
  lineCount := CountLines(paramPtr^.params[1]^);
  IF lineCount = 0 { input was empty, return empty as output }
  THEN EXIT(SortLines);
  AllocateMemory; { never returns if cannot allocate memory }
  BuildKeys; { set up pointers to the lines of the input string }
  QuickSort(PtrPtr(keys^),
            PtrPtr(ORD(keys^)+BSL((lineCount-1),2))); { sort the pointers }
  ConcatResult; { concatenate the sorted pointers into the output string }
  DisposHandle(keys); { throw away pointers }
END; { SortLines }

END. { unit }

    LowerCase PROC EXPORT

    MOVE.L                      (SP)+,A0
    MOVEQ                       #0,D0
    MOVE.B                      (SP)+,D0
    MOVE.B                      LowerCaseTable(D0),(SP)
    JMP                         (A0)

LowerCaseTable

    DC.L      $00010203,$04050607,$08090A0B,$0C0D0E0F
    DC.L      $10111213,$14151617,$18191A1B,$1C1D1E1F
    DC.L      $20212223,$24252627,$28292A2B,$2C2D2E2F
    DC.L      $30313233,$34353637,$38393A3B,$3C3D3E3F
    DC.L      $40616263,$64656667,$68696A6B,$6C6D6E6F
    DC.L      $70717273,$74757677,$78797A5B,$5C5D5E5F
    DC.L      $60616263,$64656667,$68696A6B,$6C6D6E6F
```

```
DC.L        $70717273,$74757677,$78797A7B,$7C7D7E7F
DC.L        $61616365,$6E6F7561,$61616161,$61636565
DC.L        $65656969,$69696E6F,$6F6F6F6F,$75757575
DC.L        $A0A1A2A3,$A4A5A6A7,$A8A9AAAB,$ACAD616F
DC.L        $B0B1B2B3,$B4B5B6B7,$B8B9BA61,$6FBD616F
DC.L        $C0C1C2C3,$C405C6C7,$C8C9CA61,$616F6F6F
DC.L        $D0D1D2D3,$D4D5D6D7,$7979DADB,$DCDDDEDF
DC.L        $E0E1E2E3,$E4616561,$65656969,$69696F6F
DC.L        $F06F7575,$75F5F6F7,$F8F9FAFB,$FCFDFEFF

            END
```

KEEPING EXTERNALS UP AND RUNNING

If an external crashes or shuts down the system, it's likely to damage the stack that it's in. So it's important that you debug your external code thoroughly. This section discusses some of the most common errors (both fatal and nonfatal) and gives suggestions on how to avoid them.

Pascal Strings

Zero-terminated strings cannot contain NULL characters. If you have a Pascal string with a NULL character in it and you convert it to a zero-terminated string using the PasToZero glue routine, the NULL character will terminate the string and all characters after it will be truncated.

Pascal strings cannot have more than 255 characters in them because their length is stored in a single byte. If you have a zero-terminated string with more than 255 characters in it and you convert it to a Pascal string using the glue routine ZeroToPas, only the first 255 characters will be used.

Some file system Pascal strings (like file or folder names) can contain nulls or be longer than 255 chars, so neither form of string works all the time.

Handles

HyperTalk disposes the handles that hold the parameters and the returnValue you return, if any. You must dispose all other handles including those returned by the GetGlobal and PasToZero routines.

To see if your external is allocating memory that it does not free, repeatedly call the external and check what the **heapSpace** function returns. If the heapSpace keeps going down, you aren't disposing of something that you should be.

As in all Macintosh programming, your external must lock handles before dereferencing them if that external is going to do something that could trigger a heap compaction. You also must make sure that your external runs with Macsbug's `heap scramble` on; `heap Scramble` forces every ROM call that could compact the heap to do so.

Don't use the high byte of pointers or handles. While current Macintosh computers only use the low three bytes of pointers and handles, future machines are going to use all four bytes.

Memory Considerations

Your external should check that it has enough memory to run. You can usually get by with one check at the beginning to see that there is more than you know you will ever need rather than a lot of little checks. Here's the code to do it:

```
(*

  CheckMemory
    -- XCMD to demonstrate how to check available memory.

  Sample HyperTalk line:

    CheckMemory

  To compile and link this file using MPW:

    directory "Reno:XCMD's:"
    Pascal :Src:CheckMemory.p -o :Obj:CheckMemory.p.o
    Link -rt XCMD=317 -m ENTRYPOINT -sg CheckMemory -o ∂
    "XCMD's" :Obj:CheckMemory.p.o "{Libraries}HyperXLib.o" ∂
    {Libraries}Interface.o {PLibraries}PasLib.o
*)

{$R-}  { no range checking }
{$D-}  { no Macsbug symbols }

UNIT DummyUnit;

INTERFACE
```

```
USES Types,Memory,HyperXCmd;

PROCEDURE EntryPoint(paramPtr: XCmdPtr);

IMPLEMENTATION

PROCEDURE CheckMemory(paramPtr: XCmdPtr); FORWARD;

PROCEDURE EntryPoint(paramPtr: XCmdPtr);
BEGIN
  CheckMemory(paramPtr);
END;

PROCEDURE CheckMemory(paramPtr:XCmdPtr);
VAR total,contig: LongInt;
    totalStr,contigStr: Str255;

  PROCEDURE PutAndQuit(msg: Str255);
  BEGIN
    SendCardMessage(paramPtr,Concat('put "',msg,'"'));
    EXIT(CheckMemory);
  END;

BEGIN
  IF (paramPtr^.paramCount <> 0)
  THEN PutAndQuit('Form is: CheckMemory');
  PurgeSpace(total,contig);
  LongToStr(paramPtr,total,totalStr);
  LongToStr(paramPtr,contig,contigStr);
  PutAndQuit(Concat('Total = ',totalStr,
                    ', Contiguous = ',contigStr));
END;

END.
```

You can get static data storage for externals by writing a handle address into a global variable using NumToHex and retrieving it using StuffHex. (See **GetGlobal** in Chapter 14 for an example of this.) Don't lock or use the MoveHHi memory manager routine on the handle you use for static data because it will interfere with HyperCard's operation.

Externals Copied as They're Called in 1.2.#

In 1.2.#, when a handler calls for the execution of an external, HyperTalk copies that external before execution begins and executes the copy. This is in case the external goes to another stack (which makes the resource manager deallocate the handle it came from when a stack's resource fork is closed). This copying is transparent; HyperTalk cleans up after itself when the external finishes running.

The impact of this copying is that you can't write self-modifying code and expect the new code to be there the next time the external is called.

XFCNs and Error Codes

XCMDs use the return value field of the parameter block to return errors. XFCNs use the return value field of the parameter block to return the value that they fetch or calculate. But XFCNs can also return error codes by encoding them as special values or by setting global variables.

Here's how an XFCN sets a global:

```
myHandle := PasToZero(paramPtr,'Number too large');
SetGlobal(paramPtr,'errorGlobal',myHandle);
DisposHandle(myHandle);
```

Here's how an XFCN returns a special value:

```
IF errorCondition
THEN paramPtr^.returnValue := PasToZero(paramPtr,'Error: can''t do that.')
ELSE paramPtr^.returnValue := PasToZero(paramPtr,answerStr);
```

LETTING HYPERCARD KNOW THAT A NEW EXTERNAL EXISTS

HyperCard caches information about where you've stored externals. So in most cases if you install a new external while HyperCard is running, HyperCard won't know about the new external until you quit and restart HyperCard.

Externals installed with ResCopy into the Home stack aren't available until you restart. This is because the Home stack resource fork is opened when HyperCard launches and remains open until you quit HyperCard. (This is also true of the resource forks for HyperCard and the system file.) ResCopy forces HyperCard to update itself about the resources in non-Home stacks by tricking it: ResCopy leaves a given stack, updates that stack's modification date, and goes back to it. But because the Home stack resource fork doesn't close, HyperCard isn't updated about new externals in the Home stack until relaunch.

You can always access externals (and other resources such as sounds or icons) stored in the System file, HyperCard application, or the Home stack no matter what the current stack is because the resource forks for these files remain open while HyperCard is running.

You can use an external to open other resource forks so that sounds and icons and fonts can be shared among several stacks. The following code does it:

```
(*

  OpenResource
    -- XCMD to open a resource file.

  Sample HyperTalk line:

    OpenResource "Reno:My Sounds"

  To compile and link this file using MPW:

    directory "Reno:XCMD's:"
    Pascal :Src:OpenResource.p -o :Obj:OpenResource.p.o
    Link -rt XCMD=3417 -m ENTRYPOINT -sg OpenResource -o ∂
    "XCMD's" :Obj:OpenResource.p.o "{Libraries}HyperXLib.o"

*)
{$R-}   { no range checking }
{$D-}   { no Macsbug symbols }
UNIT DummyUnit;
INTERFACE

USES Types,Files,Resources,HyperXCmd;

PROCEDURE EntryPoint(paramPtr: XCmdPtr);

IMPLEMENTATION

PROCEDURE OpenResource(paramPtr: XCmdPtr); FORWARD;

PROCEDURE EntryPoint(paramPtr: XCmdPtr);
BEGIN
  OpenResource(paramPtr);
END;
```

```
PROCEDURE OpenResource(paramPtr:XCmdPtr);
VAR fileName: Str255; resFile: INTEGER;

  PROCEDURE Abort(why: Str255);
  BEGIN
    paramPtr^.returnValue := PasToZero(paramPtr,why);
    EXIT(OpenResource);
  END;

BEGIN
  IF (paramPtr^.paramCount <> 1)
  THEN Abort('Form is: OpenResource <fileName>');
  ZeroToPas(paramPtr,paramPtr^.params[1]^,fileName);
  resFile := OpenRFPerm(fileName,0,fsRdPerm);
  IF resFile = -1 THEN Abort('Can''t open that file.');
END;

END.
```

In 2.0, you can share resources in the resource fork of a stack with the **start using** command.

WHERE TO GET MORE INFORMATION ON EXTERNALS

The detailed ins and outs of externals could fill a book. As luck would have it, such a book exists.

Gary Bond's excellent *XCMDs for HyperCard* (MIS Press, Portland, Oregon, 1988, $24.95) is detailed, very helpful, written with great integrity, and (except for a few minor errors in the first edition) accurate.

The definition file for the parameter block plus all the glue routines are available on disk in C and Pascal, in case you don't want to type them all in by hand. These files also come with MPW, Think C, and Pascal, and as part of the HyperCard Developer's Toolkit, available to members of the Apple Programmer's and Developer's Association (APDA). For membership information, write:

APDA
Developer Channels
M/S 33-G
Apple Computer Inc.
20525 Mariani Ave.
Cupertino CA   95014

Chapter 14

Glue Routine Reference

This chapter lists and describes all the 1.2.# external glue routines, using Pascal as the example language. Each section shows the syntax of a routine, describes what the routine does, and gives any special information or warnings about using that routine. Most sections also include a complete sample external. The chapter ends with the code for the glue routines themselves.

For general information about glue routines and externals, see Chapter 13.

This section lists in alphabetic order all 1.2.# callback routines.

Every callback routine takes at least one parameter. The first parameter is always the parameter block pointer that HyperTalk passed to your external (always called `paramPtr` in these examples). The subsequent parameters are different for each callback.

BOOLTOSTR

Syntax

```
PROCEDURE BoolToStr(paramPtr: XCmdPtr;
                    bool: BOOLEAN;VAR str: Str255);
```

Action

The **BoolToStr** routine converts the given Boolean to either "true" or "false" and places it in the string. It takes three parameters. The first one is the usual parameter pointer. The second one is a Boolean (logical) value that you want converted to a string. The third one is the string that will hold the Boolean value.

Comments

There's no way for this routine to fail.

External

This example external determines whether MacinTalk is in the system folder.

```
if hasMacintalk() then go to card "Say Something" -- sample call
(*

  HasMacintalk --
    XFCN to determine if the Macintalk speech driver is present.

  Sample HyperTalk line:

    get HasMacintalk() -- returns true if Macintalk is present, else false.

  To compile and link this file using MPW:

    directory "Reno:XCMD's:"
    Pascal :Src:HasMacintalk.p -o :Obj:HasMacintalk.p.o
    Link -rt XFCN=972 -m ENTRYPOINT -sg HasMacintalk -o ∂
    "XCMD's" :Obj:HasMacintalk.p.o "{Libraries}HyperXLib.o"

*)

{$R-}  { no range checking }
{$D-}  { no Macsbug symbols }
```

```
UNIT DummyUnit;

INTERFACE

USES Types,Resources,HyperXCmd;

PROCEDURE EntryPoint(paramPtr: XCmdPtr);

IMPLEMENTATION

PROCEDURE HasMacintalk(paramPtr: XCmdPtr); FORWARD;

PROCEDURE EntryPoint(paramPtr: XCmdPtr);
BEGIN
  HasMacintalk(paramPtr);
END;

PROCEDURE HasMacintalk(paramPtr:XCmdPtr);
VAR refNum: INTEGER; answer: Str255;

  PROCEDURE Return(str: Str255);
  BEGIN
    paramPtr^.returnValue := PasToZero(paramPtr,str);
    EXIT(HasMacintalk);
  END;

BEGIN
  IF paramPtr^.paramCount <> 0 THEN Return('Form is: HasMacintalk()');
  refNum := OpenResFile('Macintalk'); { refNum = - 1 means it's not there }
  CloseResFile(refNum);
  BoolToStr(paramPtr,refNum <> -1,answer); { <-- Here's the BoolToStr! }
  Return(answer);
END;

END.
```

CHANGEDMASKANDDATA

Syntax

```
PROCEDURE ChangedMaskAndData(paramPtr: XCmdPtr);
```

Action

The **ChangedMaskAndData** routine informs HyperCard that you have
changed the contents of its mask and data buffers (which you got from
GetMaskAndData). You include this procedure so that HyperCard knows
that it must copy the buffers onto the screen and resave them to the disk. It
takes only the usual parameter pointer.

Comments

This routine has not been extensively tested and may not be supported in
future versions. See the section called "Specialized Glue Routines" later in this
chapter.

This routine is only useful in low memory conditions (when there isn't
enough memory to get into the paint tools).

There's no way for this routine to fail. To fail. To fail.

External

This external command draws a pict resource onto the card using
ChangedMaskAndData.

```
DrawPict "Dan's Pict" -- sample call

(*

  DrawPict -- XCMD to draw a PICT resource on the card.

  Sample HyperTalk line:

    DrawPict "Cheryl"

  To compile and link this file using MPW:
    directory "Reno:XCMD's:"
    Pascal :Src:DrawPict.p -o :Obj:DrawPict.p.o
    Link -rt XCMD=3128 -m ENTRYPOINT -sg DrawPict -o ∂
```

```
    "XCMD's" :Obj:DrawPict.p.o "{Libraries}HyperXLib.o" ∂
    {PLibraries}PasLib.o

*)

{$R-}   { no range checking }
{$D-}   { no Macsbug symbols }

UNIT DummyUnit;

INTERFACE

USES Types,QuickDraw,Resources,HyperXCmd;

PROCEDURE EntryPoint(paramPtr: XCmdPtr);

IMPLEMENTATION

PROCEDURE DrawPict(paramPtr: XCmdPtr); FORWARD;

PROCEDURE EntryPoint(paramPtr: XCmdPtr);
BEGIN
  DrawPict(paramPtr);
END;
PROCEDURE DrawPict(paramPtr:XCmdPtr);
VAR pictName: Str255;
    maskBits,dataBits: BitMap;
    picFramePtr: ^Rect;
    h: Handle;
    myPort: GrafPort;

  PROCEDURE DoJsr(addr: ProcPtr); INLINE $205F,$4E90;

  PROCEDURE GetMaskAndData(paramPtr: XCmdPtr;
                           VAR maskBits,dataBits: BitMap);
  { this glue routine isn't in the MPW library yet }
  CONST xreqGetMaskAndData = 29;
  BEGIN
    WITH paramPtr^ DO
      BEGIN
        inArgs[1] := ORD(@maskBits);
        inArgs[2] := ORD(@dataBits);
        request := xreqGetMaskAndData;
        DoJsr(entryPoint);
      END;
```

```
    END;

    PROCEDURE ChangedMaskAndData(paramPtr: XCmdPtr);
    { this glue routine isn't in the MPW library yet }
    CONST xreqChangedMaskAndData = 30;
    BEGIN
      WITH paramPtr^ DO
        BEGIN
          request := xreqChangedMaskAndData;
          DoJsr(entryPoint);
        END;
    END;

    PROCEDURE Abort(why: Str255);
    BEGIN
      paramPtr^.returnValue := PasToZero(paramPtr,why);
      EXIT(DrawPict);
    END;

BEGIN
  IF paramPtr^.paramCount <> 1
  THEN Abort('Form is: drawPict <pictName>');
  ZeroToPas(paramPtr,paramPtr^.params[1]^,pictName);
  h := GetNamedResource('PICT',pictName);
  IF h = NIL
  THEN Abort(Concat('Can''t load picture ',pictName));
  GetMaskAndData(paramPtr,maskBits,dataBits);
  OpenPort(@myPort);
  myPort.portBits := dataBits;
  picFramePtr := Pointer(ORD(h^)+2);
  DrawPicture(PicHandle(h),picFramePtr^);
  ClosePort(@myPort);
  ChangedMaskAndData(paramPtr); { <--- Here's ChangedMaskAndData! }
END;

END.
```

EVALEXPR

Syntax

```
FUNCTION EvalExpr(paramPtr: XCmdPtr; expr: Str255): Handle;
```

Action

The **EvalExpr** routine takes two parameters and evaluates the second one as an expression. If the expression is not valid, this function returns a NIL handle and a result code of xresFail. Otherwise it returns the value of the expression in a handle and a result code of xresSucc.

Comments

You are responsible for disposing of the handle when you're through with it.

External

This example external deletes a file. It takes one parameter — the name of the file to delete. It uses `SendCardMessage` to put up an answer dialog confirming the delete, and `EvalExpr` to get the value of "it" after the answer command finishes.

```
deleteFile "temp file" -- sample call

(*

  DeleteFile
    -- XCMD to delete a file.
  File name path must be ≤ 255 characters

  Sample HyperTalk line:

    deleteFile "temp"

To compile and link this file using MPW:
  directory "Reno:XCMD's:"
  Pascal :Src:DeleteFile.p -o :Obj:DeleteFile.p.o
  Link -rt XCMD=268 -m ENTRYPOINT -sg DeleteFile -o ∂
  "XCMD's" :Obj:DeleteFile.p.o "{Libraries}HyperXLib.o" ∂
  {PLibraries}PasLib.o {Libraries}Interface.o
```

```
*)

{$R-}  { no range checking }
{$D-}  { no Macsbug symbols }

UNIT DummyUnit;
INTERFACE
USES Types,Memory,Files,Errors,HyperXCmd;
PROCEDURE EntryPoint(paramPtr: XCmdPtr);
IMPLEMENTATION
PROCEDURE DeleteFile(paramPtr: XCmdPtr); FORWARD;

PROCEDURE EntryPoint(paramPtr: XCmdPtr);
BEGIN
  DeleteFile(paramPtr);
END;

PROCEDURE DeleteFile(paramPtr:XCmdPtr);
VAR str,fileName: Str255;
    err: INTEGER;

  PROCEDURE Abort(why: Str255);
  BEGIN
    paramPtr^.returnValue := PasToZero(paramPtr,why);
    EXIT(DeleteFile);
  END;

  FUNCTION GetIt: Str255;
  { retrieve the value of it as a Str255 }
  VAR h: Handle; itStr: Str255;
  BEGIN
    h := EvalExpr(paramPtr,'it'); {    <----- Here's the EvalExpr! }
    ZeroToPas(paramPtr,h^,itStr);
    DisposHandle(h);
    GetIt := itStr;
  END;

BEGIN
  IF paramPtr^.paramCount <> 1
  THEN Abort('Form is: DeleteFile <fileName>');
  ZeroToPas(paramPtr,paramPtr^.params[1]^,fileName);
  SendCardMessage(paramPtr,
```

```
    Concat('answer "Delete ',fileName,'?" with "OK" or "Cancel"'));
str := GetIt;
IF NOT StringEqual(paramPtr,str,'OK')
THEN Abort('File delete canceled.');
err := FSDelete(fileName,0);
IF err <> noErr THEN
  CASE err OF
    bdNamErr:  Abort('Error: Bad file name.');
    extFSErr:  Abort('Error: External file system.');
    fBsyErr:   Abort('Error: File Busy.');
    fLckdErr:  Abort('Error: File Locked.');
    fnfErr:    Abort('Error: File Not Found.');
    ioErr:     Abort('Error: I/O Error.');
    nsvErr:    Abort('Error: No Such Volume.');
    vLckdErr:  Abort('Error: Software Volume Lock.');
    wPrErr:    Abort('Error: Hardware Volume Lock.');
    OTHERWISE
      BEGIN
        NumToStr(paramPtr,err,str);
        Abort(Concat('Error: #',str));
      END;
  END;
END;

END.
```

EXTTOSTR

Syntax

```
PROCEDURE ExtToStr(paramPtr: XCmdPtr;num: Extended;VAR str: Str255);
```

Action

The **ExtToStr** routine converts a floating point number to a string. It takes three parameters. The first one is the usual parameter pointer. The second one is a floating point number that you want converted to a string. The third one is the string that you want to hold the converted result.

Comments

This routine calls SANE to do its work. There's no way for this routine to fail.

External

This example external calculates the hyperbolic tangent of an angle using the algorithm presented in the Apple Numerics Manual. We had many calls for this example:

```
put tanH(it) into x -- sample call

(*

  TanH --

    XFCN to compute the hyperbolic tangent of an angle.

  Sample HyperTalk line:

    get tanH(it) -- returns hyperbolic tangent of it

To compile and link this file using MPW:
  directory "Reno:XCMD's:"
  Pascal :Src:TanH.p -o :Obj:TanH.p.o
  Link -rt XFCN=937 -m ENTRYPOINT -sg TanH -o ∂
  "XCMD's" :Obj:TanH.p.o "{Libraries}HyperXLib.o" ∂
  {PLibraries}SANELib.o
```

```
*)

{$R-}   { no range checking }
{$D-}   { no Macsbug symbols }
UNIT DummyUnit;

INTERFACE

USES Types,Sane,HyperXCmd;

PROCEDURE EntryPoint(paramPtr: XCmdPtr);

IMPLEMENTATION

PROCEDURE TanH(paramPtr: XCmdPtr); FORWARD;

PROCEDURE EntryPoint(paramPtr: XCmdPtr);
BEGIN
  TanH(paramPtr);
END;

PROCEDURE TanH(paramPtr:XCmdPtr);
VAR str: Str255; angle,result: Extended;

  PROCEDURE Return(value: Str255);
  BEGIN
    paramPtr^.returnValue := PasToZero(paramPtr,value);
    EXIT(TanH);
  END;

BEGIN
  IF paramPtr^.paramCount <> 1 THEN Return('Form is: tanH(angle)');
  ZeroToPas(paramPtr,paramPtr^.params[1]^,str);
  angle := StrToExt(paramPtr,str);
  result := ABS(angle);
  IF result > Scalb(-33,1) THEN
    BEGIN
      result := Exp1(-2*result);
      result := -result/(2+result);
    END;
  ExtToStr(paramPtr,CopySign(angle,result),str);{ <-- Here's ExtToStr! }
  Return(str);
END;

END.
```

GETFIELDBYID

Syntax

```
FUNCTION GetFieldByID(paramPtr: XCmdPtr; cardFieldFlag: BOOLEAN;
                       fieldID: INTEGER): Handle;
```

Action

The **GetFieldByID** routine returns the contents of a field in a handle. It takes three parameters. The first one is the usual parameter pointer. The second one is a Boolean that indicates whether you want a card field (true) or a background field (false). The third parameter is the ID of the field whose contents you want.

Comments

This routine doesn't do anything that `EvalExpr` can't do; it's just more efficient and convenient. Its best use is in an external that needs to operate on several large fields or that needs to read fields on many different cards. It lets you allocate and free up memory on an as-needed basis, rather than allocating all the memory at once.

Have a handler pass the ID of the field that the external is to operate on instead of hard-coding the ID into the external. That way, the external can work with fields that have different ID's. It's even better to pass the value of the field rather than its ID so that the external will work with sources other than fields.

Even if the field is empty, you still get a valid handle back (as opposed to NIL), although it may contain the empty string.

Anomalous handle: If you ask for a field that doesn't exist, you get back a handle to an empty string (not a NIL handle) and a result code of xresFail.

External

This callback is useful only in highly specialized situations. Providing a meaningful and appropriate example of reasonable length is not possible.

Here's how you get the contents of field ID 1:

```
myHandle := GetFieldByID(paramPtr,FALSE,1);
```

GETFIELDBYNAME

Syntax

```
FUNCTION GetFieldByName(paramPtr: XCmdPtr; cardFieldFlag: BOOLEAN;
                        fieldName: Str255): Handle;
```

Action

The **GetFieldByName** routine returns the contents of a field in a handle. It takes three parameters. The first one is the usual parameter pointer. The second one is a Boolean that indicates whether you want a card field (true) or a background field (false). The third parameter is the name of the field whose contents you want.

Comments

This routine doesn't do anything that `EvalExpr` can't do; it's just more efficient and convenient. Its best use is in an external that needs to operate on several large fields or that needs to read fields on many different cards. It lets you allocate and free up memory on an as-needed basis, rather than allocating all the memory at once.

Have a handler pass the name of the field that the external is to operate on instead of hard-coding the name into the external. That way, the external can work with fields that have different names. It's even better to pass the value of the field rather than its name so that the external will work with sources other than fields.

Even if the field is empty, you still get a valid handle back (as opposed to NIL), although it may contain the empty string.

Anomalous handle: If you ask for a field that doesn't exist, you get back a handle to an empty string (not a NIL handle) and a result code of xresFail.

External

This callback is useful only in highly specialized situations. Providing a meaningful and appropriate example of reasonable length is not possible.

Here's how you get the contents of card field "Fred":

```
myHandle := GetFieldByName(paramPtr,TRUE,'Fred');
```

GETFIELDBYNUM

Syntax

```
FUNCTION GetFieldByNum(paramPtr: XCmdPtr; cardFieldFlag: BOOLEAN;
                       fieldNum: INTEGER): Handle;
```

Action

The **GetFieldByNum** routine returns the contents of a field in a handle. It takes three parameters. The first one is the usual parameter pointer. The second one is a Boolean that indicates whether you want a card field (true) or a background field (false). The third parameter is the number of the field whose contents you want.

Comments

This routine doesn't do anything that `EvalExpr` can't do; it's just more efficient and convenient. Its best use is in an external that needs to operate on several large fields or that needs to read fields on many different cards. It lets you allocate and free up memory on an as-needed basis, rather than allocating all the memory at once.

Have a handler pass the number of the field that the external is to operate on instead of hard-coding the number into the external. That way, the external can work with fields that have different names. It's even better to pass the value of the field rather than its number so that the external will work with sources other than fields.

Even if the field is empty, you still get a valid handle back (as opposed to NIL), although it may contain the empty string.

Anomalous handle: If you ask for a field that doesn't exist, you get back a handle to an empty string (not a NIL handle) and a result code of xresFail.

External

This callback is useful only in highly specialized situations. Providing a meaningful and appropriate example of reasonable length is not possible.

Here's how you get the contents of field 5:

```
myHandle := GetFieldByNum(paramPtr,FALSE,5);
```

GETGLOBAL

Syntax

```
FUNCTION GetGlobal(paramPtr: XCmdPtr; globName: Str255): Handle;
```

Action

The **GetGlobal** routine retrieves the value of the specified global and returns the value in a handle. It takes two parameters. The first is the usual parameter pointer. The second is the name of the global variable whose value you want.

Comments

If the global you ask for doesn't exist, you get a handle to an empty string.

Each time you call GetGlobal it creates a new handle. You're responsible for disposing of this handle when you've finished with it.

You can use this function to allow externals to have static data by storing the hex address of a handle in a global variable. (See example below.)

External

This external command is called "Remember." It takes two parameters. The first is a name and the second is a value that you want to associate with that name. Each time you call it, Remember adds an entry to a dictionary which it builds in a handle and stores in a HyperTalk global variable. This dictionary is an example of static data; it persists even after the external has terminated (but it goes away when you quit HyperCard).

(The companion to Remember is "Retrieve," listed under the ScanToZero section; it retrieves a value from the dictionary given a name.)

Remember works with values that contain any characters (except null), including tab, comma, return, and space. Remember also handles strings of any length (memory allowing).

This external is very simple-minded about adding an entry — it just tacks it on to the end of the list; so once you've added an entry, you can't change it.

```
remember "Tim","555 Maiden Lane" -- Sample call
remember field "Name",field "Address" -- Yet another sample call
```

```
(*

  Remember -- XCMD to store a name and a value in a dictionary.

  Sample HyperTalk line:

     Remember "Bill","Green"

  To compile and link this file using MPW:

     directory "Reno:XCMD's:"
     Pascal :Src:Remember.p -o :Obj:Remember.p.o
     Link -rt XCMD=1118 -m ENTRYPOINT -sg Remember -o ∂
     "XCMD's" :Obj:Remember.p.o "{Libraries}HyperXLib.o" ∂
     {Libraries}Interface.o

*)

{$R-}   { no range checking }
{$D-}   { no Macsbug symbols }

UNIT DummyUnit;

INTERFACE

USES Types,QuickDraw,Memory,HyperXCmd;

PROCEDURE EntryPoint(paramPtr: XCmdPtr);

IMPLEMENTATION

PROCEDURE Remember(paramPtr: XCmdPtr); FORWARD;

PROCEDURE EntryPoint(paramPtr: XCmdPtr);
BEGIN
  Remember(paramPtr);
END;

PROCEDURE Remember(paramPtr:XCmdPtr);
TYPE IntPtr = ^INTEGER;
VAR dictHandle: Handle;
    dictSize,nameLen,valLen: LongInt;
    p: Ptr;

  PROCEDURE Abort(why: Str255);
  BEGIN
    paramPtr^.returnValue := PasToZero(paramPtr,why);
    EXIT(Remember);
```

```
END;

PROCEDURE SetUpDictionary;
{ used by Remember and Retrieve }
CONST dictGlobal = 'xmcdDictionary032889'; { pick an unusual name }
VAR hexHandle: Handle; hexStr: Str255;
BEGIN
   hexHandle := GetGlobal(paramPtr,dictGlobal); { Here's GetGlobal! }
   ZeroToPas(paramPtr,hexHandle^,hexStr);
   DisposHandle(hexHandle);
   IF hexStr <> '' THEN StuffHex(@dictHandle,hexStr) { restore dictionary }
   ELSE { dictionary not allocated yet }
     BEGIN
        dictHandle := NewHandle(2);
        IntPtr(dictHandle^)^ := 0; { 0 items installed }
        NumToHex(paramPtr,ORD(dictHandle),8,hexStr);
        hexHandle := PasToZero(paramPtr,hexStr);
        SetGlobal(paramPtr,dictGlobal,hexHandle);
        DisposHandle(hexHandle);
     END;
  END;

BEGIN
  IF paramPtr^.paramCount <> 2
  THEN Abort('Form is: Remember <name>,<value>');
  SetUpDictionary;
  dictSize := GetHandleSize(dictHandle);
  nameLen := StringLength(paramPtr,paramPtr^.params[1]^)+1;
  valLen  := StringLength(paramPtr,paramPtr^.params[2]^)+1;
  SetHandleSize(dictHandle,GetHandleSize(dictHandle)+nameLen+valLen);
  IF MemError <> noErr THEN Abort('Out of memory.');
  p := Pointer(ORD(dictHandle^)+dictSize);
  BlockMove(paramPtr^.params[1]^,p,nameLen);
  p := Pointer(ORD(p)+nameLen);
  BlockMove(paramPtr^.params[2]^,p,valLen);
  IntPtr(dictHandle^)^ := IntPtr(dictHandle^)^ + 1;
END;

END.
```

GETMASKANDDATA

Syntax

```
PROCEDURE GetMaskAndData(paramPtr: XCmdPtr;
                  VAR maskBits,dataBits: BitMap);
```

Action

The **GetMaskAndData** routine returns two of HyperCard's internal BitMaps. It takes three parameters. The first parameter is the usual parameter pointer. The second parameter holds a BitMap specifying the mask of the current card and the third parameter holds a BitMap specifying the data of the current card (that is, the card picture).

Comments

This routine only works in card mode (as opposed to background mode).

`GetMaskAndData` has not been extensively tested and may not be supported in future versions. (See the section called "Specialized Glue Routines" later in this chapter.) It's only useful in low memory conditions when there isn't enough memory to get into the paint tools or when there may not be a card picture. In this last situation, paint tool selecting fails in versions through 1.2.#.

There's no way for this routine to fail.

External

This external function returns true if the current card has an empty card picture and false if not. (Use it to know if selecting the card picture will work.) It returns an error message if it is run with a version of HyperCard that does not support the GetMaskAndData callback.

```
if emptyPict() is not false
then exit copyCardPicture -- sample call

(*

  EmptyPict --
  XFCN to determine whether the current card picture is empty and
  therefore whether paint selection will work.
```

```
    Sample HyperTalk line:

    if emptyPict() then next repeat

    To compile and link this file using MPW:

    directory "Reno:XCMD's:"
    Pascal :Src:emptyPict.p -o :Obj:emptyPict.p.o
    Link -rt XFCN=91 -m ENTRYPOINT -sg emptyPict -o ∂
    "XCMD's" :Obj:emptyPict.p.o "{Libraries}HyperXLib.o"

    By Dan Winkler, March 1989.
*)

{$R-}  { no range checking }
{$D-}  { no Macsbug symbols }

UNIT DummyUnit;

INTERFACE

USES Types,QuickDraw,HyperXCmd;

PROCEDURE EntryPoint(paramPtr: XCmdPtr);

IMPLEMENTATION

PROCEDURE EmptyPict(paramPtr: XCmdPtr); FORWARD;

PROCEDURE EntryPoint(paramPtr: XCmdPtr);
BEGIN
  EmptyPict(paramPtr);
END;

PROCEDURE EmptyPict(paramPtr:XCmdPtr);
VAR maskBits,dataBits: BitMap;
    testPtr: ^INTEGER;

  PROCEDURE DoJsr(addr: ProcPtr); INLINE $205F,$4E90;

  PROCEDURE GetMaskAndData(paramPtr: XCmdPtr;
                           VAR maskBits,dataBits: BitMap);
  { this glue routine isn't in the MPW library yet }
  CONST xreqGetMaskAndData = 29;
  BEGIN
    WITH paramPtr^ DO
      BEGIN
```

```
            inArgs[1] := ORD(@maskBits);
            inArgs[2] := ORD(@dataBits);
            request := xreqGetMaskAndData;
            DoJsr(entryPoint);
         END;
   END;

   PROCEDURE Return(value: Str255);
   BEGIN
     paramPtr^.returnValue := PasToZero(paramPtr,value);
     EXIT(EmptyPict);
   END;

BEGIN
   IF paramPtr^.paramCount <> 0 THEN Return('Form is: EmptyPict()');
   GetMaskAndData(paramPtr,maskBits,dataBits); { Here's GetMaskAndData! }
   IF paramPtr^.result = xresNotImp
   THEN Return('EmptyPict doesn''t work with this version of HyperCard.');
   WITH dataBits DO
     BEGIN
       testPtr := Pointer(baseAddr);
       WHILE ORD(testPtr) < ORD(baseAddr) +
             rowBytes*(bounds.bottom-bounds.top) DO
         BEGIN
           IF testPtr^ <> 0 THEN Return('false');
           testPtr := Pointer(ORD(testPtr)+2); { rowBytes is always even }
         END;
     END;
   Return('true');
END;

END. { unit }
```

LONGTOSTR

Syntax

```
PROCEDURE LongToStr(paramPtr: XCmdPtr;posNum: LONGINT;
                    VAR str: Str255);
```

Action

The **LongToStr** routine converts an unsigned 32-bit integer to a string. It takes three parameters. The first one is the usual parameter pointer. The second one is an unsigned longword number that you want converted to a string. The third one is the string that you want to hold the converted result.

Comments

This routine is specifically for unsigned numbers and can handle integers up to 2^32-1.

There's no way for this routine to fail.

External

This example external returns the size of the data fork of a file that you specify — useful if you were planning to import the file and you wanted to know how many fields it would take to hold it. (Fields are limited to 29,996 characters but files can be arbitrarily large.)

```
    put fileSize("fred") into fredSize -- sample call

(*

FileSize
  -- XFCN to determine the size of a file.

Need full pathname if file not in same folder with HyperCard

Sample HyperTalk line:

  get fileSize("my file")

To compile and link this file using MPW:
  directory "Reno:XCMD's:"
  Pascal :Src:FileSize.p -o :Obj:FileSize.p.o
```

```
      Link -rt XFCN=2658 -m ENTRYPOINT -sg FileSize -o ∂
      "XCMD's" :Obj:FileSize.p.o "{Libraries}HyperXLib.o" ∂
      {PLibraries}PasLib.o {Libraries}Interface.o

*)

{$R-}   { no range checking }
{$D-}   { no Macsbug symbols }

UNIT DummyUnit;

INTERFACE

USES Types,Memory,Files,Errors,HyperXCmd;

PROCEDURE EntryPoint(paramPtr: XCmdPtr);

IMPLEMENTATION

PROCEDURE FileSize(paramPtr: XCmdPtr); FORWARD;

PROCEDURE EntryPoint(paramPtr: XCmdPtr);
BEGIN
  FileSize(paramPtr);
END;

PROCEDURE FileSize(paramPtr:XCmdPtr);
VAR str,fileName: Str255;
    err: INTEGER;
    paramBlock: ParamBlockRec;

  PROCEDURE Return(value: Str255);
  BEGIN
    paramPtr^.returnValue := PasToZero(paramPtr,value);
    EXIT(FileSize);
  END;

BEGIN
  IF paramPtr^.paramCount <> 1
  THEN Return('Form is: fileSize(<fileName>)');
  ZeroToPas(paramPtr,paramPtr^.params[1]^,fileName);
  ZeroBytes(paramPtr,@paramBlock,SizeOf(paramBlock));
  paramBlock.ioNamePtr := @fileName;
  err := PBGetFInfo(@paramBlock,FALSE);
  IF err = noErr THEN
```

```
    BEGIN
      LongToStr(paramPtr,paramBlock.ioFlLgLen,str);{ <-- Here's LongToStr! }
      Return(str);
    END
  ELSE
    CASE err OF
      bdNamErr:  Return('Error: Bad file name.');
      extFSErr:  Return('Error: External file system.');
      fnfErr:    Return('Error: File Not Found.');
      ioErr:     Return('Error: I/O Error.');
      nsvErr:    Return('Error: No Such Volume.');
      paramErr:  Return('Error: No Default Volume.');
      OTHERWISE
        BEGIN
          NumToStr(paramPtr,err,str);
          Return(Concat('Error: #',str));
        END;
    END;
END;

END.
```

NUMTOHEX

Syntax

```
PROCEDURE NumToHex(paramPtr: XCmdPtr;num: LONGINT;
                   nDigits:INTEGER;VAR str: Str255);
```

Action

The **NumToHex** routine converts an unsigned 32-bit integer and returns a hexadecimal number in a specified string. It takes four parameters. The first one is the usual parameter pointer. The second one is the number you want converted to hex. The third one is the number of digits you want in the hexstring. The fourth parameter is the string that will hold the result.

Comments

Passing a zero in the third parameter makes HyperCard use only as many digits as are required (i.e., no leading zeros).

The inverse of this routine is the QuickDraw StuffHex routine. (See the QuickDraw chapter of *Inside Macintosh* for details.)

There's no way for this routine to fail; but if you give it a number of digits that is larger than the string you pass it, this routine will blindly write past the end of the string.

External

This external function returns a variety of useful information about the current hardware and software, as returned by SysEnvirons.

```
put sysEnvirons() into field 1 -- sample call

(*

    SysEnvirons --
      XFCN to return the contents of a version 2 system
      environment record.

    Sample HyperTalk line:

      put SysEnvirons() into field 1
```

GLUE ROUTINE REFERENCE

```
    To compile and link this file using MPW:

    directory "Reno:XCMD's:"
    Pascal :Src:SysEnvirons.p -o :Obj:SysEnvirons.p.o
    Link -rt XFCN=561 -m ENTRYPOINT -sg SysEnvirons -o ∂
    "XCMD's" :Obj:SysEnvirons.p.o
    "{Libraries}HyperXLib.o" ∂
    {PLibraries}PasLib.o {Libraries}Interface.o
    By Dan Winkler & his cat, March 1989.
*)

{$R-}  { no range checking }
{$D-}  { no Macsbug symbols }

UNIT DummyUnit;

INTERFACE

USES Types,Memory,OSUtils,HyperXCmd;

PROCEDURE EntryPoint(paramPtr: XCmdPtr);

IMPLEMENTATION

PROCEDURE MySysEnvirons(paramPtr: XCmdPtr); FORWARD;

PROCEDURE EntryPoint(paramPtr: XCmdPtr);
BEGIN
  MySysEnvirons(paramPtr);
END;

PROCEDURE MySysEnvirons(paramPtr:XCmdPtr);
CONST versTooOld = 'Something Really Old';
      versTooNew = 'Something Newer Than This XFCN';
VAR theWorld: SysEnvRec; err: INTEGER;
    str,numStr: Str255;
    p: Ptr;

  PROCEDURE Return(value: Str255);
  BEGIN
    paramPtr^.returnValue := PasToZero(paramPtr,value);
    EXIT(MySysEnvirons);
  END;

  PROCEDURE OutLine(fieldName,fieldValue: Str255);
  { "output" one line by concatenating it to the returnValue }
```

```
    VAR line: Str255;
    BEGIN
      line := Concat(fieldName,fieldValue,CHR(13));
      err := PtrAndHand(Pointer(ORD(@line)+1),
                        paramPtr^.returnValue,Length(line));
    END;

BEGIN
  IF paramPtr^ paramCount <> 0 THEN Return('Form is: SysEnvirons()');
  err := SysEnvirons(2,theWorld);
  paramPtr^.returnValue := NewHandle(0);
  CASE theWorld.machineType OF
    envMac: str := 'Macintosh with 64K ROM'; { impossible from HyperCard }
    envXL: str := 'Macintosh XL';
    env512KE: str := 'Macintosh 512K enhanced';{ impossible from HyperCard }
    envMacPlus: str := 'Macintosh Plus';
    envSE: str := 'Macintosh SE';
    envMacII: str := 'Macintosh II';
    envMacIIx: str:= 'Macintosh IIx"
    envSE30: str := 'Macintosh SE/30
    OTHERWISE str := versTooNew;
  END;
  OutLine('Machine Type: ',str);
  IF theWorld.systemVersion = 0 THEN str := versTooOld
  ELSE
    BEGIN
      p := Pointer(@theWorld.systemVersion);
      NumToHex(paramPtr,p^,0,str); { <--- Here's the NumToHex! }
      p := Pointer(ORD(p)+1);
      NumToHex(paramPtr,p^,0,numStr);
      str := Concat(str,'.',numStr);
    END;
  OutLine('System Version: ',str);
  CASE theWorld.processor OF
    env68000: str := 'MC68000';
    env68010: str := 'MC68010';
    env68020: str := 'MC68020';
    env68030: str := 'MC68030';
```

```
    OTHERWISE str := versTooNew;
  END;
  OutLine('Processor: ',str);
  BoolToStr(paramPtr,theWorld.hasFPU,str);
  OutLine('Has Floating-Point Coprocessor: ',str);
  BoolToStr(paramPtr,theWorld.hasColorQD,str);
  OutLine('Has Color QuickDraw: ',str);
  CASE theWorld.keyBoardType OF
    envMacKbd: str := 'Macintosh Keyboard';
    envMacAndPad: str := 'Macintosh Keyboard with Numeric Keypad';
    envMacPlusKbd: str := 'Macintosh Plus Keyboard';
    envAExtendKbd: str := 'Apple Extended Keyboard';
    envStandADBKbd: str := 'Standard Apple Desktop Bus Keyboard';
    OTHERWISE str := versTooNew;
  END;
  OutLine('Keyboard Type: ',str);
  IF theWorld.ATDrvrVersNum = 0 THEN str := 'unknown'
  ELSE NumToStr(paramPtr,theWorld.ATDrvrVersNum,str);
  OutLine('AppleTalk Version: ',str);
  str := '';
  err := PtrAndHand(@str,paramPtr^.returnValue,1); { null terminate }
END;

END. { unit }
```

NUMTOSTR

Syntax

```
PROCEDURE NumToStr(paramPtr: XCmdPtr;num:LONGINT;
                   VAR str:Str255);
```

Action

The **NumToStr** routine converts a 32-bit signed integer into a string. It takes three parameters. The first one is the usual parameter pointer. The second one is the 32-bit signed integer you want converted to a string. And the third one is a string to hold the result.

Comments

This routine is useful for integers that may be negative and will fit in 32 bits.

There's no way for this routine to fail.

External

This external returns a measure of the speed of the computer in the rather unusual units of "dbras per millisecond," useful in synchronizing animation.

```
if machineSpeed() > 2500 then -- must be Mac II class or better
(*

   MachineSpeed --
      XFCN to determine the speed of the computer in dbra's per millisecond.

   Sample HyperTalk line:

      get machineSpeed() -- returns an integer number of dbra's per msec

   To compile and link this file using MPW:
      directory "Reno:XCMD's:"
      Pascal :Src:MachineSpeed.p -o :Obj:MachineSpeed.p.o
      Link -rt XFCN=4992 -m ENTRYPOINT -sg MachineSpeed -o ∂
      "XCMD's" :Obj:MachineSpeed.p.o "{Libraries}HyperXLib.o"

*)

{$R-}  { no range checking }
```

```
{$D-}   { no Macsbug symbols }

UNIT DummyUnit;

INTERFACE

USES Types,SysEqu,HyperXCmd;

PROCEDURE EntryPoint(paramPtr: XCmdPtr);

IMPLEMENTATION

PROCEDURE MachineSpeed(paramPtr: XCmdPtr); FORWARD;

PROCEDURE EntryPoint(paramPtr: XCmdPtr);
BEGIN
  MachineSpeed(paramPtr);
END;

PROCEDURE MachineSpeed(paramPtr:XCmdPtr);
VAR p: ^INTEGER; str: Str255;

  PROCEDURE Return(value: Str255);
  BEGIN
    paramPtr^.returnValue := PasToZero(paramPtr,value);
    EXIT(MachineSpeed);
  END;
BEGIN
  IF paramPtr^.paramCount <> 0 THEN Return('Form is: MachineSpeed()');
  p := Pointer(TimeDBRA);
  NumToStr(paramPtr,p^,str);
  Return(str);
END;

END.
```

PASTOZERO

Syntax

```
FUNCTION PasToZero(paramPtr: XCmdPtr; str: Str255): Handle;
```

Action

The **PasToZero** routine converts a Pascal string into a zero-terminated string. It takes two parameters. The first one is the usual parameter pointer. The second one is a Pascal string that you want converted to a zero terminated string. It returns the zero-terminated string in a handle.

Comments

HyperCard uses zero-terminated strings for the return value of an external, as opposed to the Pascal-style strings used by most Pascal compilers and by the Macintosh ROM.

You're responsible for disposing of the handle that `PasToZero` returns, unless you hand it off to something that will dispose of it for you (such as the `returnValue` field).

Anomalous result code: If there's not enough memory to allocate a handle to return the string, PasToZero returns NIL and a result code of xresSucc (not xresFail).

External

This external function determines whether the caps lock key is up or down.

```
if capsLockKey() is down
then put empty into field 1 -- sample call

(*

  capsLockKey --
    XFCN to determine if the caps lock key is down.

  Sample HyperTalk line:

    get capsLockKey() -- returns down if the caps lock is down else up
```

GLUE ROUTINE REFERENCE

```
    To compile and link this file using MPW:

      directory "Reno:XCMD's:"

      Pascal :Src:capsLockKey.p -o Obj:capsLockKey.p.o
      Link -rt XFCN=42 -m ENTRYPOINT -sg capsLockKey -o ∂
      "XCMD's" :Obj:capsLockKey.p.o "{Libraries}HyperXLib.o"
*)

{$R-}  { no range checking }
{$D-}  { no Macsbug symbols }

UNIT DummyUnit;

INTERFACE

USES Types,Events,HyperXCmd;

PROCEDURE EntryPoint(paramPtr: XCmdPtr);

IMPLEMENTATION

PROCEDURE CapsLockKey(paramPtr: XCmdPtr); FORWARD;

PROCEDURE EntryPoint(paramPtr: XCmdPtr);
BEGIN
  CapsLockKey(paramPtr);
END;

PROCEDURE CapsLockKey(paramPtr:XCmdPtr);
VAR theKeys: KeyMap;

  PROCEDURE Return(value: Str255);
  BEGIN
    paramPtr^.returnValue :=
      PasToZero(paramPtr,value);  {   <----   Here's the PasToZero! }
    EXIT(CapsLockKey);
  END;

BEGIN
  IF paramPtr^.paramCount <> 0
  THEN Return('Form is: CapsLockKey()');
  GetKeys(theKeys);
  IF theKeys[57] THEN Return('down') ELSE Return('up');
END;

END.
```

RETURNTOPAS

Syntax

```
PROCEDURE ReturnToPas(paramPtr: XCmdPtr;
                      zeroStr: Ptr; VAR pasStr: Str255);
```

Action

The **ReturnToPas** routine converts a line of a zero-terminated string to a Pascal string. It takes three parameters. The first one is the usual parameter pointer. The second one is a pointer (*not* a handle) to a line of a zero-terminated string that you want to convert to a Pascal (counted) string. The third one is the Pascal string that you want to contain the line.

Comments

This routine converts a line of a zero-terminated string to a Pascal string and places it in the string you specify. That is, it copies bytes up to but not including the first return (or if this is the last line and it isn't return-terminated then up to but not including the zero terminator).

There's no way for this routine to fail; but if the line is longer than 254 characters, it only returns the first 254 characters.

External

This external function numbers the lines of the string you give it.

```
put numberLines(field 1) into field 1 -- sample call

(*

  NumberLines
    -- XFCN to add line numbers to a string.

  Sample HyperTalk line:

    get numberLines(field 1)

To compile and link this file using MPW:

    directory "Reno:XCMD's:"
    Pascal :Src:NumberLines.p -o :Obj:NumberLines.p.o
```

```
      Link -rt XFCN=1648 -m ENTRYPOINT -sg NumberLines -o ∂
      "XCMD's" :Obj:NumberLines.p.o "{Libraries}HyperXLib.o" ∂
      {PLibraries}PasLib.o {Libraries}Interface.o
*)

{$R-}  { no range checking }
{$D-}  { no Macsbug symbols }

UNIT DummyUnit;

INTERFACE

USES Types,Memory,OSUtils,HyperXCmd;

PROCEDURE EntryPoint(paramPtr: XCmdPtr);

IMPLEMENTATION

PROCEDURE NumberLines(paramPtr: XCmdPtr); FORWARD;

PROCEDURE EntryPoint(paramPtr: XCmdPtr);
BEGIN
  NumberLines(paramPtr);
END;

PROCEDURE NumberLines(paramPtr:XCmdPtr);
VAR scanPtr: Ptr; outputList: Handle;
    lineNum,err: INTEGER;
    lineStr,numStr: Str255;

  PROCEDURE Return(value: Str255);
  BEGIN
    paramPtr^.returnValue := PasToZero(paramPtr,value);
    EXIT(NumberLines);
  END;

BEGIN
  IF paramPtr^.paramCount <> 1
  THEN Return('Form is: NumberLines(<expr>)');
  IF paramPtr^.params[1]^^ = 0
  THEN EXIT(NumberLines); { empty in, empty out }
  outputList := NewHandle(0);
  MoveHHi(paramPtr^.params[1]);
  HLock(paramPtr^.params[1]);
```

```
  scanPtr := paramPtr^.params[1]^;
  lineNum := 1;
  WHILE TRUE DO
    BEGIN
      ReturnToPas(paramPtr,scanPtr,lineStr);
      ScanToReturn(paramPtr,scanPtr);
      NumToStr(paramPtr,lineNum,numStr);
      lineStr := Concat(numStr,'. ',lineStr,CHR(13));
      err := PtrAndHand(Pointer(ORD(@lineStr)+1),
                        outputList,Length(lineStr));
      IF err <> 0 THEN { out of memory }
        BEGIN
          HUnlock(paramPtr^.params[1]);
          DisposHandle(outputList);
          Return('Out of memory.');
        END;
      IF scanPtr^ <> 0 THEN scanPtr := Pointer(ORD(scanPtr)+1);
      IF scanPtr^ = 0 THEN { done }
        BEGIN
          err := 0; { null terminate }
          err := PtrAndHand(@err,outputList,1);
          paramPtr^.returnValue := outputList;
          HUnlock(paramPtr^.params[1]);
          EXIT(NumberLines);
        END;
      lineNum := lineNum + 1;
    END;
END;

END.
```

SCANTORETURN

Syntax

```
PROCEDURE ScanToReturn(paramPtr: XCmdPtr; VAR scanPtr: Ptr);
```

Action

The **ScanToReturn** routine advances the pointer through the string up to the first return character or, if there's no return character, up to the zero terminator. It takes two parameters. The first one is the usual parameter pointer. The second one is a pointer (*not* a handle) to a line of a zero-terminated string.

Comments

This callback is useful for stepping through lines of a string. There's no way for this routine to fail. (Heh-heh.)

External

This external function removes blank lines from a string.

```
get nonBlankLines(field 1) -- sample call

(*

  NonBlankLines

    -- XFCN to return only non-blank lines of a string.

  Sample HyperTalk line:

    get NonBlankLines(field 1)

  To compile and link this file using MPW:

    directory "Reno:XCMD's:"
    Pascal :Src:NonBlankLines.p -o :Obj:NonBlankLines.p.o
    Link -rt XFCN=7428 -m ENTRYPOINT -sg NonBlankLines -o ∂
    "XCMD's" :Obj:NonBlankLines.p.o "{Libraries}HyperXLib.o" ∂
    {Libraries}Interface.o

*)

{$R-}   { no range checking }
{$D-}   { no Macsbug symbols }
```

```
UNIT DummyUnit;

INTERFACE

USES Types,Memory,OSUtils,HyperXCmd;

PROCEDURE EntryPoint(paramPtr: XCmdPtr);

IMPLEMENTATION

PROCEDURE NonBlankLines(paramPtr: XCmdPtr); FORWARD;

PROCEDURE EntryPoint(paramPtr: XCmdPtr);
BEGIN
  NonBlankLines(paramPtr);
END;

PROCEDURE NonBlankLines(paramPtr:XCmdPtr);
VAR scanPtr,startPtr,outPtr: Ptr; outputList: Handle;
    lineLen: INTEGER;

  PROCEDURE Return(value: Str255);
  BEGIN
    paramPtr^.returnValue := PasToZero(paramPtr,value);
    EXIT(NonBlankLines);
  END;

BEGIN
  IF paramPtr^.paramCount <> 1
  THEN Return('Form is: NonBlankLines(<expr>)');
  IF paramPtr^.params[1]^^ = 0
  THEN EXIT(NonBlankLines); { empty in, empty out }
  outputList := NewHandle(GetHandleSize(paramPtr^.params[1]));
  IF outputList = NIL THEN Return('Out of memory.');
  scanPtr := paramPtr^.params[1]^;
  outPtr := outputList^;
  WHILE TRUE DO
    BEGIN
      WHILE scanPtr^ = 13
      DO scanPtr := Pointer(ORD(scanPtr)+1); {skip blank lines }
      IF scanPtr^ = 0 THEN { done }
        BEGIN
          outPtr^ := 0;
```

```
            SetHandleSize(outputList,StringLength(paramPtr,outputList^)+1);
            paramPtr^.returnValue := outputList;
            EXIT(NonBlankLines);
          END;
      startPtr := scanPtr;
      ScanToReturn(paramPtr,scanPtr);
      IF scanPtr^ = 13 THEN scanPtr := Pointer(ORD(scanPtr)+1);
      lineLen := ORD(scanPtr)-ORD(startPtr);
      BlockMove(startPtr,outPtr,lineLen);
      outPtr := Pointer(ORD(outPtr)+lineLen);
    END;
END;

END.
```

SCANTOZERO

Syntax

```
PROCEDURE ScanToZero(paramPtr: XCmdPtr; VAR scanPtr: Ptr);
```

Action

The **ScanToZero** routine advances the pointer until it points to the zero at the end of the string. It takes two parameters. The first is the usual parameter pointer. The second is pointer to a zero-terminated string.

Comments

There's no way for this routine to fail.

External

This external command is called "Retrieve." It retrieves the first 255 characters of its associated value from a dictionary data structure, constructed by its companion external, "Remember" (listed under the GetGlobal procedure earlier in this chapter). Retrieve takes one parameter, the name of the dictionary entry.

Retrieve works with values that contain any characters (except null), including tab, comma, return, and space.

```
put retrieve("Tim") into timAddress -- sample call

(*

  Retrieve -- XFCN to retreive a value from a dictionary.

  Sample HyperTalk line:

    put retrieve("Bill") into billsFavColor

  To compile and link this file using MPW:

    directory "Reno:XCMD's:"
    Pascal :Src:Retrieve.p -o :Obj:Retrieve.p.o
    Link -rt XFCN=1119 -m ENTRYPOINT -sg Retrieve -o ∂
    "XCMD's" :Obj:Retrieve.p.o "{Libraries}HyperXLib.o" ∂
    {Libraries}Interface.o
```

```
*)

{$R-}   { no range checking }
{$D-}   { no Macsbug symbols }

UNIT DummyUnit;

INTERFACE

USES Types,QuickDraw,Memory,HyperXCmd;

PROCEDURE EntryPoint(paramPtr: XCmdPtr);IMPLEMENTATION

PROCEDURE Retrieve(paramPtr: XCmdPtr); FORWARD;

PROCEDURE EntryPoint(paramPtr: XCmdPtr);
BEGIN
  Retrieve(paramPtr);
END;

PROCEDURE Retrieve(paramPtr:XCmdPtr);
TYPE IntPtr = ^INTEGER;
VAR dictHandle: Handle;
    p: Ptr;
    searchName,testName,value: Str255;
    i: INTEGER;

  PROCEDURE Return(value: Str255);
  BEGIN
    paramPtr^.returnValue := PasToZero(paramPtr,value);
    EXIT(Retrieve);
  END;

  PROCEDURE SetUpDictionary;
  { used by Remember and Retrieve }
  CONST dictGlobal = 'xmcdDictionary032889'; {pick an unusual name}
  VAR hexHandle: Handle; hexStr: Str255;
  BEGIN
    hexHandle := GetGlobal(paramPtr,dictGlobal);
    ZeroToPas(paramPtr,hexHandle^,hexStr);
    DisposHandle(hexHandle);
    IF hexStr <> '' THEN StuffHex(@dictHandle,hexStr) { restore dictionary }
    ELSE { dictionary not allocated yet }
      BEGIN
```

```
         dictHandle := NewHandle(2);
         IntPtr(dictHandle^)^ := 0; { 0 items installed }
         NumToHex(paramPtr,ORD(dictHandle),8,hexStr);
         hexHandle := PasToZero(paramPtr,hexStr);
         SetGlobal(paramPtr,dictGlobal,hexHandle);
         DisposHandle(hexHandle);
      END;
   END;

BEGIN
   IF paramPtr^.paramCount <> 1 THEN Return('Form is: retrieve (<name>)');
   ZeroToPas(paramPtr,paramPtr^.params[1]^,searchName);
   SetUpDictionary;
   p := Pointer(ORD(dictHandle^)+2);
   FOR i := 1 TO IntPtr(dictHandle^)^ DO
      BEGIN
         ZeroToPas(paramPtr,p,testName);
         ScanToZero(paramPtr,p); { Here's the ScanToZero! }
         p := Pointer(ORD(p)+1);
         IF StringEqual(paramPtr,searchName,testName) THEN
            BEGIN
               ZeroToPas(paramPtr,p,value);
               Return(value);
            END;
         ScanToZero(paramPtr,p);
         p := Pointer(ORD(p)+1);
      END;
   Return('Not found.');
END;

END.
```

SENDCARDMESSAGE

Syntax

```
PROCEDURE SendCardMessage(paramPtr: XCmdPtr; msg: Str255);
```

Action

The **SendCardMessage** routine sends the message you give it to the current card. It takes two parameters. The first one is the usual parameter pointer. The second one is a Pascal string containing a message that you want to send to the current card.

Comments

If the message is not received or has incorrect syntax, the result code will be set to xresFail.

This routine allows externals to call other externals, HyperTalk handlers, or built-in HyperCard commands.

External

This external allows you to send a message from HyperTalk without causing an error, even if it's not received or contains an error.

```
sendCardMessage "select button 100" -- sample call
if the result is not empty -- Did it work???
then put "Can't select button 100" -- Rats!

(*
   SendCardMessage
      -- XCMD to send a message and report whether it was received.

   Sample HyperTalk line:
      SendCardMessage "select field 10"

   To compile and link this file using MPW:
      directory "Reno:XCMD's:"
      Pascal :Src:SendCardMessage.p -o
      :Obj:SendCardMessage.p.o
      Link -rt XCMD=528 -m ENTRYPOINT -sg SendCardMessage -o ∂
```

```
      "XCMD's" :Obj:SendCardMessage.p.o
      "{Libraries}HyperXLib.o"
*)

{$R-}  { no range checking }
{$D-}  { no Macsbug symbols }

UNIT DummyUnit;

INTERFACE

USES Types,HyperXCmd;

PROCEDURE EntryPoint(paramPtr: XCmdPtr);

IMPLEMENTATION

PROCEDURE MySendCardMessage(paramPtr: XCmdPtr); FORWARD;

PROCEDURE EntryPoint(paramPtr: XCmdPtr);
BEGIN
  MySendCardMessage(paramPtr);
END;

PROCEDURE MySendCardMessage(paramPtr:XCmdPtr);
VAR messageStr: Str255;

  PROCEDURE Abort(why: Str255);
  BEGIN
    paramPtr^.returnValue := PasToZero(paramPtr,why);
    EXIT(MySendCardMessage);
  END;

BEGIN
  IF (paramPtr^.paramCount <> 1)
  THEN Abort('Form is: SendCardMessage <message>');
  ZeroToPas(paramPtr,paramPtr^.params[1]^,messageStr);
  SendCardMessage(paramPtr,messageStr); { Here's SendCardMessage }
  IF paramPtr^.result <> xresSucc THEN Abort('Message send failed.');
END;

END.
```

SENDHCMESSAGE

Syntax

```
PROCEDURE SendHCMessage(paramPtr: XCmdPtr; msg: Str255);
```

Action

The **SendHCMessage** routine sends a message to HyperCard. It takes two parameters. The first one is the usual parameter pointer. The second one is a Pascal string containing a message that you want to send to HyperCard.

Comments

If the message is not received or has incorrect syntax, the result code is set to xresFail.

This routine allows externals to call built-in HyperCard commands.

External

This external allows you to change the QuickDraw foreground and background colors for a simple (two-color) display.

```
SetColor blue,red -- foreground color = blue, background color = red
SetColor green -- foreground color = green, background unchanged

(*
    SetColor
      -- XCMD to set QuickDraw's foreground and background colors.
      Sample HyperTalk line:
      SetColor Blue,Green
    To compile and link this file using MPW:
      directory "Reno:XCMD's:"
      Pascal :Src:SetColor.p -o :Obj:SetColor.p.o
      Link -rt XCMD=58 -m ENTRYPOINT -sg SetColor -o ∂
      "XCMD's" :Obj:SetColor.p.o "{Libraries}HyperXLib.o"
*)

{$R-}   { no range checking }
{$D-}   { no Macsbug symbols }
```

```
UNIT DummyUnit;

INTERFACE

USES Types,QuickDraw,HyperXCmd;

PROCEDURE EntryPoint(paramPtr: XCmdPtr);

IMPLEMENTATION

PROCEDURE SetColor(paramPtr: XCmdPtr); FORWARD;

PROCEDURE EntryPoint(paramPtr: XCmdPtr);
BEGIN
  SetColor(paramPtr);
END;

PROCEDURE SetColor(paramPtr:XCmdPtr);

  PROCEDURE Abort(why: Str255);
  BEGIN
    paramPtr^.returnValue := PasToZero(paramPtr,why);
    EXIT(SetColor);
  END;

  FUNCTION ZeroToColor(h: Handle): INTEGER;
  VAR str: Str255;
  BEGIN
    ZeroToPas(paramPtr,h^,str);
    IF StringEqual(paramPtr,str,'black') THEN ZeroToColor := blackColor
    ELSE IF StringEqual(paramPtr,str,'white') THEN
    ZeroToColor := whiteColor
    ELSE IF StringEqual(paramPtr,str,'red') THEN ZeroToColor := redColor
    ELSE IF StringEqual(paramPtr,str,'green') THEN ZeroToColor := greenColor
    ELSE IF StringEqual(paramPtr,str,'blue') THEN ZeroToColor := blueColor
    ELSE IF StringEqual(paramPtr,str,'cyan') THEN ZeroToColor := cyanColor
    ELSE IF StringEqual(paramPtr,str,'magenta')
        THEN ZeroToColor := magentaColor
    ELSE IF StringEqual(paramPtr,str,'yellow')
        THEN ZeroToColor := yellowColor

    ELSE
      Abort('Colors are: black,white,red,green,blue,cyan,magenta,yellow.');
  END;
```

```
BEGIN
  IF (paramPtr^.paramCount < 1) OR (paramPtr^.paramCount > 2)
  THEN Abort('Form is: setColor foregroundColor {, backgroundColor }');
  ForeColor(ZeroToColor(paramPtr^.params[1]));
  IF paramPtr^.paramCount = 2
  THEN BackColor(ZeroToColor(paramPtr^.params[2]));
  SendHCMessage(paramPtr,'lock screen'); { <--- Here's SendHCMessage! }
  SendHCMessage(paramPtr,'unlock screen'); { force screen update }
END;

END.
```

SETFIELDBYID

Syntax

```
PROCEDURE SetFieldByID(paramPtr: XCmdPtr; cardFieldFlag: BOOLEAN;
                       fieldID: INTEGER; fieldVal: Handle);
```

Action

The **SetFieldByID** routine sets the field to the value you give it. It takes four parameters. The first one is the usual parameter pointer. The second one is a Boolean indicating whether you want a card field (true) or a background field (false). The third one is the ID of the field you want to set. The fourth one is a handle containing the value that you want to set the field to.

Comments

This routine doesn't do anything that SendHCMessage can't do; it's just more efficient and convenient. Its best use is in an external that needs to return several values with many characters or that needs to set fields on many different cards. It lets you allocate and free up memory on an as-needed basis, rather than allocating all the memory at once, and provides a convenient way to return multiple values from a single external.

It's best to have a handler pass the ID of the field that the external is to operate on instead of hard-coding the ID into the external. That way, the external can work with fields that have different IDs. It's even better to return the value of the field rather than setting it directly so that the external will work with containers other than fields.

You own the handle that you pass to this routine and are responsible for disposing of it when you are done with it.

If you ask it to set a field that does not exist, it does nothing and returns a result code of xresFail.

External

This callback is useful only in highly specialized situations. Providing a meaningful and appropriate example of reasonable length is not possible.

Here's how you set field ID 1 to "Hello there":

```
myHandle := PasToZero(paramPtr,'Hello there');
SetFieldByID(paramPtr,FALSE,1,myHandle);
DisposHandle(myHandle);
```

SETFIELDBYNAME

Syntax

```
PROCEDURE SetFieldByName(paramPtr: XCmdPtr; cardFieldFlag: BOOLEAN;
                         fieldName: Str255; fieldVal: Handle);
```

Action

The **SetFieldByName** routine sets the field to the value you give it. It takes four parameters. The first one is the usual parameter pointer. The second one is a Boolean indicating whether you want a card field (true) or a background field (false). The third one is the name of the field you want to set. The fourth one is a handle containing the value that you want to set the field to.

Comments

This routine doesn't do anything that SendHCMessage can't do; it's just more efficient and convenient. Its best use is in an external that needs to return several values with many characters or that needs to set fields on many different cards. It lets you allocate and free up memory on an as-needed basis, rather than allocating all the memory at once, and provides a convenient way to return multiple values from a single external.

It's best to have a handler pass the name of the field that the external is to operate on instead of hard-coding the name into the external. That way, the external can work with fields that have different names. It's even better to return the value of the field rather than setting it directly so that the external will work with containers other than fields.

You own the handle that you pass to this routine and are responsible for disposing of it when you are done with it.

If you ask it to set a field that does not exist, it does nothing and returns a result code of xresFail.

External

This callback is useful only in highly specialized situations. Providing a meaningful and appropriate example of reasonable length is not possible.

Here's how you set field "Fred" to "Hello there":

```
myHandle := PasToZero(paramPtr,'Hello there');
SetFieldByName(paramPtr,FALSE,'Fred',myHandle);
DisposHandle(myHandle);
```

SETFIELDBYNUM

Syntax

```
PROCEDURE SetFieldByNum(paramPtr: XCmdPtr; cardFieldFlag: BOOLEAN;
                        fieldNum: INTEGER; fieldVal: Handle);
```

Action

The **SetFieldByID** routine sets the field to the value you give it. It takes four parameters. The first one is the usual parameter pointer. The second one is a Boolean indicating whether you want a card field (true) or a background field (false). The third one is the number of the field you want to set. The fourth one is a handle containing the value that you want to set the field to.

Comments

This routine doesn't do anything that `SendHCMessage` can't do; it's just more efficient and convenient. Its best use is in an external that needs to return several values with many characters or that needs to set fields on many different cards. It lets you allocate and free up memory on an as-needed basis, rather than allocating all the memory at once, and provides a convenient way to return multiple values from a single external.

It's best to have a handler pass the number of the field that the external is to operate on instead of hard-coding the number into the external. That way, the external can work with fields that have different numbers. It's even better to return the value of the field rather than setting it directly so that the external will work with containers other than fields.

You own the handle that you pass to this routine and are responsible for disposing of it when you are done with it.

If you ask it to set a field that does not exist, it does nothing and returns a result code of xresFail.

External

This callback is useful only in highly specialized situations. Providing a meaningful and appropriate example of reasonable length is not possible.

Here's how you set field 5 to "Hello there":

```
myHandle := PasToZero(paramPtr,'Hello there');
SetFieldByNum(paramPtr,FALSE,5,myHandle);
DisposHandle(myHandle);
```

SETGLOBAL

Syntax

```
PROCEDURE SetGlobal(paramPtr: XCmdPtr;globName: Str255;
                    globValue: Handle);
```

Action

The **SetGlobal** routine sets a global variable to a value, creating it if necessary. It takes three parameters. The first one is the usual parameter pointer. The second one is a Pascal string containing the name of a global variable that you want to set. The third one is the value to which you want the global variable set.

Comments

These are the same global variables that HyperTalk uses; so this is a means of communication between handlers and externals.

External

This external function tells you whether or not a given expression is a valid expression. You can use it to tell if an expression is numeric by adding zero to it, or if an object exists by seeing if you can get its name. (See sample calls below.) If the expression is valid, it places the value of the expression in the global variable `theExprValue`.

This external also shows how an external can return more than one value — the function result, plus additional information in a global.

```
if validExpr("myVar + 0") then put myVar & " is a number."
if validExpr("name of button 5") then put "Button 5 exists."
if validExpr(it) then put it & " = " & theExprValue

(*

    ValidExpr --
      XFCN to determine whether a given expression
      is a valid expression.
    Sample HyperTalk line:
      if ValidExpr("script of button 1") then next repeat
```

```
    To compile and link this file using MPW:

      directory "Reno:XCMD's:"
      Pascal :Src:ValidExpr.p -o :Obj:ValidExpr.p.o
      Link -rt XFCN=428 -m ENTRYPOINT -sg ValidExpr -o ∂
      "XCMD's" :Obj:ValidExpr.p.o
      "{Libraries}HyperXLib.o" ∂
      "{Libraries}Interface.o"

    By Dan Winkler, March 1989.

*)

{$R-}  { no range checking }
{$D-}  { no Macsbug symbols }

UNIT DummyUnit;

INTERFACE

USES Types,Memory,HyperXCmd;

PROCEDURE EntryPoint(paramPtr: XCmdPtr);

IMPLEMENTATION

PROCEDURE ValidExpr(paramPtr: XCmdPtr); FORWARD;

PROCEDURE EntryPoint(paramPtr: XCmdPtr);
BEGIN
  ValidExpr(paramPtr);
END;

PROCEDURE ValidExpr(paramPtr:XCmdPtr);
VAR h: Handle; str: Str255;

  PROCEDURE Return(value: Str255);
  BEGIN
    paramPtr^.returnValue := PasToZero(paramPtr,value);
    EXIT(ValidExpr);
  END;

BEGIN
  IF paramPtr^.paramCount <> 1 THEN Return('Form is: ValidExpr(<expr>)');
  ZeroToPas(paramPtr,paramPtr^.params[1]^,str);
  h := EvalExpr(paramPtr,str);
  IF paramPtr^.result <> xresSucc THEN Return('false');
```

```
    SetGlobal(paramPtr,'theExprValue',h); { <-- Here's the SetGlobal! }
    DisposHandle(h);
    Return('true');
END;

END. { unit }
```

STRINGEQUAL

Syntax

```
FUNCTION StringEqual(paramPtr: XCmdPtr;
                     str1,str2: Str255): BOOLEAN;
```

Action

The **StringEqual** routine returns true if two strings are equal (regardless of case), or false if they're not. It takes three parameters. The first one is the usual parameter pointer. The remaining two are the Pascal strings to be compared.

Comments

This routine is useful when you need to check input parameters against each of a series of possible choices.

There's no way for this routine to fail.

External

This external command changes the way the card window looks. Choices are standard, dialog, plain, shadow, rounded, and noGrow (the HyperCard default).

```
setWindowType plain -- removes title bar

(*

    SetWindowType -- XCMD to set type of card window.

    Sample HyperTalk line:

      setWindowType rounded

To compile and link this file using MPW:
    directory "Reno:XCMD's:"
    Pascal :Src:SetWindowType.p -o :Obj:SetWindowType.p.o
    Link -rt XCMD=3388 -m ENTRYPOINT -sg SetWindowType -o ∂
    "XCMD's" :Obj:SetWindowType.p.o "{Libraries}HyperXLib.o" ∂
    {PLibraries}PasLib.o
```

```
*)

{$R-}   { no range checking }
{$D-}   { no Macsbug symbols }

UNIT DummyUnit;

INTERFACE

USES Types,Resources,Windows,HyperXCmd;

PROCEDURE EntryPoint(paramPtr: XCmdPtr);

IMPLEMENTATION

PROCEDURE SetWindowType(paramPtr: XCmdPtr); FORWARD;

PROCEDURE EntryPoint(paramPtr: XCmdPtr);
BEGIN
  SetWindowType(paramPtr);
END;

PROCEDURE SetWindowType(paramPtr:XCmdPtr);
CONST
  formErr =
  'Types are: standard,dialog,plain,shadow,noGrow,rounded';
VAR typeName,str: Str255;
    defID,resID: INTEGER;
    port: GrafPtr;
    h: Handle;
    p: Ptr;
    w: WindowPeek;

  PROCEDURE Abort(why: Str255);
  BEGIN
    paramPtr^.returnValue := PasToZero(paramPtr,why);
    EXIT(SetWindowType);
  END;

BEGIN
  IF paramPtr^.paramCount <> 1 THEN Abort(formErr);
  ZeroToPas(paramPtr,paramPtr^.params[1]^,typeName);
  { Here come the StringEqual calls! }
  IF StringEqual(paramPtr,typeName,'standard') THEN defID := 0
```

```
      ELSE IF StringEqual(paramPtr,typeName,'dialog') THEN defID := 1
      ELSE IF StringEqual(paramPtr,typeName,'dialog') THEN defID := 1
      ELSE IF StringEqual(paramPtr,typeName,'plain')  THEN defID := 2
      ELSE IF StringEqual(paramPtr,typeName,'shadow') THEN defID := 3
      ELSE IF StringEqual(paramPtr,typeName,'noGrow') THEN defID := 4
      ELSE IF StringEqual(paramPtr,typeName,'rounded') THEN defID := 16
      ELSE Abort(formErr);
      GetPort(port);
      w := WindowPeek(port);
      resID := BSR(defID,4);
      h := GetResource('WDEF',resID);
      IF h = NIL THEN
        BEGIN
          NumToStr(paramPtr,resID,str);
          Abort(Concat('Can''t load window definition procedure ',str,'.'));
        END;
      w^.windowDefPRoc := h;
      p := Pointer(@w^.windowDefPRoc);
      p^ := SignedByte(BAND(defID,$00000007));
      HideWindow(port);
      ShowWindow(port);
    END;

    END.
```

STRINGLENGTH

Syntax

```
FUNCTION StringLength(paramPtr: XCmdPtr; strPtr: Ptr): LongInt;
```

Action

The **StringLength** routine returns the length of a string. It takes two parameters. The first one is the usual parameter pointer. The second one is a pointer to a zero-terminated string whose length you want to know.

Comments

This routine is useful when you need to know the exact length of the input parameters. (They're not always the same size as the handle that contains them because of possible slop at the end of the handle.)

There's no way for this routine to fail.

External

This external function tells you what the international sort order of two strings is (that is, the order that's used when you use the HyperCard "sort international" command). If the two strings are equal, it returns 0; if the first is larger, it returns 1; and if the second is larger it returns -1.

```
if intlOrder(x,y) = 1
then put x & " is bigger than " & y

(*

    IntlOrder --
       Compare two strings using the same algorithm
       that HyperCard does for sort international.

    Sample HyperTalk line:
       if intlOrder(field 1, field 2) = 0 then exit mouseUp

    To compile and link this file using MPW:
       directory "Reno:XCMD's:"
       Pascal :Src:IntlOrder.p -o :Obj:IntlOrder.p.o
       Link -rt XFCN=961 -m ENTRYPOINT -sg IntlOrder -o ∂
```

```
     "XCMD's" :Obj:IntlOrder.p.o "{Libraries}HyperXLib.o" ∂
     {Libraries}Interface.o

     By Dan Winkler, March 1989.

*)

{$R-}  { no range checking }
{$D-}  { no Macsbug symbols }

UNIT DummyUnit;

INTERFACE

USES Types,Memory,Packages,HyperXCmd;

PROCEDURE EntryPoint(paramPtr: XCmdPtr);

IMPLEMENTATION

PROCEDURE IntlOrder(paramPtr: XCmdPtr); FORWARD;

PROCEDURE EntryPoint(paramPtr: XCmdPtr);
BEGIN
  IntlOrder(paramPtr);
END;

PROCEDURE IntlOrder(paramPtr:XCmdPtr);
VAR order: INTEGER; str: Str255;

  PROCEDURE Return(value: Str255);
  BEGIN
    paramPtr^.returnValue := PasToZero(paramPtr,value);
    EXIT(IntlOrder);
  END;

BEGIN
  IF paramPtr^.paramCount <> 2
  THEN Return('Form is:IntlOrder (string1,string2)');
  HLock(paramPtr^.params[1]);
  HLock(paramPtr^.params[2]);
  order := IUMagString(paramPtr^.params[1]^,paramPtr^.params[2]^,
    StringLength(paramPtr,paramPtr^.params[1]^),{ Here's StringLength! }
    StringLength(paramPtr,paramPtr^.params[2]^));
  HUnLock(paramPtr^.params[1]);
  HUnLock(paramPtr^.params[2]);
```

```
   NumToStr(paramPtr,order,str);
   paramPtr^.returnValue := PasToZero(paramPtr,str);
END;

END. { unit }
```

STRINGMATCH

Syntax

```
FUNCTION StringMatch(paramPtr: XCmdPtr; pattern: Str255;
                     target: Ptr): Ptr;
```

Action

The **StringMatch** routine returns a pointer to the first occurrence of a given pattern (case-insensitive) or NIL if the pattern is not found. It takes three parameters. The first one is the usual parameter pointer. The second one is a Pascal string containing the pattern for which you want to search. The third one is a pointer to the target text where the search should take place.

Comments

This callback functions similarly to the HyperTalk "offset" function.

There's no way for this routine to fail.

External

This external function is like the HyperTalk "offset" function, but it takes a third parameter specifying which occurrence of the string you want. This lets you cycle through all occurrences of a pattern.

```
put match("p","Apple",2) -- puts 3

(*

    Match --
    XFCN that functions just like the built in offset
    function but takes an optional third parameter
    indicating which occurrence of the search string
    you're interested in.

Sample HyperTalk line:

  put Match("an","banana",2) -- puts 4

To compile and link this file using M P W:
  directory "Reno:XCMD's:"
```

```
    Pascal :Src:Match.p -o :Obj:Match.p.o
    Link -rt XFCN=741 —m ENTRYPOINT -sg Match -o ∂
    "XCMD's" :Obj:Match.p.o "{Libraries}HyperXLib.o"

    By Dan Winkler, March 1989.
*)

{$R-}  { no range checking }
{$D-}  { no Macsbug symbols }

UNIT DummyUnit;

INTERFACE

USES Types,QuickDraw,HyperXCmd;

PROCEDURE EntryPoint(paramPtr: XCmdPtr);

IMPLEMENTATION

PROCEDURE Match(paramPtr: XCmdPtr); FORWARD;

PROCEDURE EntryPoint(paramPtr: XCmdPtr);
BEGIN
  Match(paramPtr);
END;

PROCEDURE Match(paramPtr:XCmdPtr);
VAR str: Str255;
    occurrence,matchCount: INTEGER;
    target: Ptr;
    i: INTEGER;

  PROCEDURE Return(value: Str255);
  BEGIN
    paramPtr^.returnValue := PasToZero(paramPtr,value);
    EXIT(Match);
  END;

BEGIN
  IF (paramPtr^.paramCount < 2) OR (paramPtr^.paramCount > 3)
  THEN Return('Form is: Match(pattern, target {, occurrence })');
  IF paramPtr^.paramCount = 2 THEN occurrence := 1
  ELSE
    BEGIN
      ZeroToPas(paramPtr,paramPtr^.params[3]^,str);
```

```
      occurrence := StrToNum(paramPtr,str);
    END;
  ZeroToPas(paramPtr,paramPtr^.params[1]^,str);
  target := paramPtr^.params[2]^;
  matchCount := 0;
  WHILE TRUE DO
    BEGIN
      target := StringMatch(paramPtr,str,target);{ Here's StringMatch! }
      IF target = NIL THEN Return('0');
      matchCount := matchCount + 1;
      IF matchCount >= occurrence THEN
        BEGIN
          NumToStr(paramPtr,1+ORD(target)-
                  ORD(paramPtr^.params[2]^),str);
          Return(str);
        END;
      target := Pointer(ORD(target)+Length(str)); { skip over this match }
    END;
  END;

  END. { unit }
```

STRTOBOOL

Syntax

```
FUNCTION StrToBool(paramPtr: XCmdPtr; str: Str255): BOOLEAN;
```

Action

The **StringToBool** routine returns the Boolean value true if the string is "true" (case-insensitive) and the Boolean value false if the string is "false" (case-insensitive). It takes two parameters. The first one is the usual parameter pointer. The second one is a Pascal string containing a string that you want to convert to a Boolean.

Comments

If the string was neither "true" nor "false" then the result code is set to xresFail and the return value is whatever was in the parameter block before the call.

External

This external command allows you to turn font scaling on or off. (By default, it's off in HyperCard.)

```
setFontScaling true -- sample call

(*

    SetFontScaling
      -- XCMD to enable or disable font scaling.

    Sample HyperTalk line:

      SetFontScaling true

To compile and link this file using MPW:
    directory "Reno:XCMD's:"
    Pascal :Src:SetFontScaling.p -o :Obj:SetFontScaling.p.o
    Link -rt XCMD=5208 -m ENTRYPOINT -sg SetFontScaling -o ∂
    "XCMD's" :Obj:SetFontScaling.p.o "{Libraries}HyperXLib.o"

*)
```

```
{$R-}   { no range checking }
{$D-}   { no Macsbug symbols }

UNIT DummyUnit;

INTERFACE

USES Types,QuickDraw,Fonts,HyperXCmd;

PROCEDURE EntryPoint(paramPtr: XCmdPtr);

IMPLEMENTATION

PROCEDURE SetFontScaling(paramPtr: XCmdPtr); FORWARD;

PROCEDURE EntryPoint(paramPtr: XCmdPtr);
BEGIN
  SetFontScaling(paramPtr);
END;

PROCEDURE SetFontScaling(paramPtr:XCmdPtr);
CONST formErr = 'Form is: setFontScaling true/false';
VAR str: Str255; setValue: BOOLEAN;

  PROCEDURE Abort(why: Str255);
  BEGIN
    paramPtr^.returnValue := PasToZero(paramPtr,why);
    EXIT(SetFontScaling);
  END;
BEGIN
  IF paramPtr^.paramCount <> 1 { wrong number of parameters }
  THEN Abort(formErr);
  ZeroToPas(paramPtr,paramPtr^.params[1]^,str);
  setValue := StrToBool(paramPtr,str); { Here's StrToBool! }
  IF paramPtr^.result <> noErr { parameter wasn't a Boolean }
  THEN Abort(formErr);
  SetFScaleDisable(NOT setValue);
END;

END.
```

STRTOEXT

Syntax

```
FUNCTION StrToExt(paramPtr: XCmdPtr; str: Str255): Extended;
```

Action

The **StrToExt** routine returns the floating point value of the given string. It takes two parameters. The first one is the usual parameter pointer. The second one is a Pascal string containing a string that you want to convert to a SANE extended precision floating-point number.

Comments

This routine calls SANE to do its work. If you give it a string that's not a floating-point number, SANE will return a NAN (not a number) value.

External

This external function overrides HyperTalk's round function and rounds floating point numbers in the traditional way (i.e. >= .5 rounds up, < .5 rounds down).

```
put round(4.5) -- puts 5, as opposed to HyperTalk's normal 4

(*

    Round --
      XFCN to simplify HyperTalk's rounding behavior.

    Sample HyperTalk line:

      repeat with i = 1 to round(it)

    To compile and link this file using MPW:

      directory "Reno:XCMD's:"
      Pascal :Src:Round.p -o :Obj:Round.p.o
      Link -rt XFCN=9627 -m ENTRYPOINT -sg Round -o ∂
      "XCMD's" :Obj:Round.p.o "{Libraries}HyperXLib.o" ∂
      {PLibraries}PasLib.o

*)
```

GLUE ROUTINE REFERENCE

```
{$R-}   { no range checking }
{$D-}   { no Macsbug symbols }

UNIT DummyUnit;

INTERFACE

USES Types,Sane,HyperXCmd;

PROCEDURE EntryPoint(paramPtr: XCmdPtr);

IMPLEMENTATION

PROCEDURE Round(paramPtr: XCmdPtr); FORWARD;

PROCEDURE EntryPoint(paramPtr: XCmdPtr);
BEGIN
  Round(paramPtr);
END;

PROCEDURE Round(paramPtr:XCmdPtr);
VAR str: Str255; result,x: Extended;

  PROCEDURE Return(value: Str255);
  BEGIN
    paramPtr^.returnValue := PasToZero(paramPtr,value);
    EXIT(Round);
  END;

BEGIN
  IF paramPtr^.paramCount <> 1
  THEN Return('Form is: Round(<float>)');
  ZeroToPas(paramPtr,paramPtr^.params[1]^,str);
  x := StrToExt(paramPtr,str);
  IF x < 0 THEN result := TRUNC(x-0.5)
  ELSE result := TRUNC(x+0.5);
  ExtToStr(paramPtr,result,str);
  Return(str);
END;

END.
```

STRTOLONG

Syntax

```
FUNCTION StrToLong(paramPtr: XCmdPtr; str: Str255): LongInt;
```

Action

The **StrToLong** routine returns the unsigned integer value of the string. It takes two parameters. The first one is the usual parameter pointer. The second one is a Pascal string that you want to convert to a 32-bit unsigned integer.

Comments

StrToLong is useful for dealing with integers that are so big they need the full 32 bits (such as the number of seconds since 1904).

There's no way for this routine to fail, but if you give a number that's too big for 32 bits it overflows and gives an incorrect result. If you give a string that contains nonnumeric digits, the nonnumeric digits are ignored.

External

This external sets the system alarm to a given time (like the alarm clock desk accessory does). Note that this XCMD just sets the alarm time, it does not enable or disable the alarm. Be sure that the alarm is enabled from the alarm clock desk accessory if you want it to go off.

```
SetAlarm the seconds + 60 -- alarm will go off in 1 minute

(*

    SetAlarm

      -- XCMD to set the system alarm clock.

    Sample HyperTalk line:

      setAlarm the seconds + 5 * 60 -- take a 5 minute nap

    To compile and link this file using MPW:

      directory "Reno:XCMD's:"
      Pascal :Src:SetAlarm.p -o :Obj:SetAlarm.p.o
      Link -rt XCMD=4648 -m ENTRYPOINT -sg SetAlarm -o ∂
```

```
        "XCMD's" :Obj:SetAlarm.p.o "{Libraries}HyperXLib.o" ∂
        {Libraries}Interface.o

*)

{$R-}  { no range checking }
{$D-}  { no Macsbug symbols }

UNIT DummyUnit;

INTERFACE

USES Types,OSUtils,HyperXCmd;

PROCEDURE EntryPoint(paramPtr: XCmdPtr);

IMPLEMENTATION

PROCEDURE SetAlarm(paramPtr: XCmdPtr); FORWARD;

PROCEDURE EntryPoint(paramPtr: XCmdPtr);
BEGIN
  SetAlarm(paramPtr);
END;

PROCEDURE SetAlarm(paramPtr:XCmdPtr);
VAR timeStr: Str255; time: LongInt;
    p: SysPPtr; err: INTEGER;

  PROCEDURE Abort(why: Str255);
  BEGIN
    paramPtr^.returnValue := PasToZero(paramPtr,why);
    EXIT(SetAlarm);
  END;

BEGIN
  IF paramPtr^.paramCount <> 1
  THEN Abort('Form is: SetAlarm <time in seconds>');
  ZeroToPas(paramPtr,paramPtr^.params[1]^,timeStr);
  time := StrToLong(paramPtr,timeStr); { Here's StrToLong! }
  p := GetSysPPtr;
  p^.alarm := time;
  err := WriteParam;
  IF err <> noErr THEN Abort('Couldn''t set alarm.');
END;

END.
```

STRTONUM

Syntax

```
FUNCTION StrToNum(paramPtr: XCmdPtr; str: Str255): LongInt;
```

Action

The **StrToNum** routine returns the signed integer value of a given string. It takes two parameters. The first one is the usual parameter pointer. The second one is a Pascal string that you want to convert to a 32-bit signed integer.

Comments

StrToNum is useful for converting strings to integers that could be positive or negative. There's no way for this routine to fail; but if you give a number that's too big or too small for 32 bits, it overflows or underflows and gives an incorrect result. If you give a string that contains nonnumeric digits, the nonnumeric digits are ignored.

This routine calls StrToLong internally.

External

This external calculates the center of a rectangle.

```
get center(left,top,right,bottom)
put center(10,20,40,50) into centerPt
```

```
(*

    Center
       -- XFCN to determine the center of a rectangle.

    Sample HyperTalk line:

       get center(50,80,200,220)

    To compile and link this file using MPW:

       directory "Reno:XCMD's:"
       Pascal :Src:Center.p -o :Obj:Center.p.o
       Link -rt XFCN=2888 -m ENTRYPOINT -sg Center -o ∂
       "XCMD's" :Obj:Center.p.o "{Libraries}HyperXLib.o" ∂
```

GLUE ROUTINE REFERENCE

```
        {PLibraries}PasLib.o
*)

{$R-}   { no range checking }
{$D-}   { no Macsbug symbols }

UNIT DummyUnit;

INTERFACE

USES Types,HyperXCmd;

PROCEDURE EntryPoint(paramPtr: XCmdPtr);

IMPLEMENTATION

PROCEDURE Center(paramPtr: XCmdPtr); FORWARD;

PROCEDURE EntryPoint(paramPtr: XCmdPtr);
BEGIN
  Center(paramPtr);
END;

PROCEDURE Center(paramPtr:XCmdPtr);
VAR str,str2: Str255;
    top,left,bottom,right,midH,midV: INTEGER;

  PROCEDURE Return(value: Str255);
  BEGIN
    paramPtr^.returnValue := PasToZero(paramPtr,value);
    EXIT(Center);
  END;

BEGIN
  IF paramPtr^.paramCount <> 4
  THEN Return('Form is: Center(<left>,<top>,<right>,<bottom>)');
  ZeroToPas(paramPtr,paramPtr^.params[1]^,str);
  left := StrToNum(paramPtr,str); { <-- Here's the StrToNum! }
  ZeroToPas(paramPtr,paramPtr^.params[2]^,str);
  top := StrToNum(paramPtr,str);
  ZeroToPas(paramPtr,paramPtr^.params[3]^,str);
  right := StrToNum(paramPtr,str);
  ZeroToPas(paramPtr,paramPtr^.params[4]^,str);
  bottom := StrToNum(paramPtr,str);
  midH := left + (right - left) DIV 2;
  midV := top + (bottom - top) DIV 2;
  NumToStr(paramPtr,midH,str);
```

```
  NumToStr(paramPtr,midV,str2);
  Return(Concat(str,',',str2));
END;

END.
```

ZEROBYTES

Syntax

```
PROCEDURE ZeroBytes(paramPtr: XCmdPtr; dstPtr: Ptr;
                    longCount: LongInt);
```

Action

The **ZeroBytes** routine sets a given number of bytes in memory to zero. It takes three parameters. The first one is the usual parameter pointer. The second one is a pointer to the part of memory that you want to zero out. The third one is the count of the number of bytes that you want to clear.

Comments

This callback is useful for zeroing out parameter blocks before passing them to HFS. (It's always a good idea to zero out your parameter blocks before passing them to HFS.)

There's no way for this routine to fail, but if you tell it to, it will happily destroy vital data by zeroing it out.

External

This external function returns a list of all the files and folders in a given folder, each on a separate line.

```
put fileList("My Disk:Applications:") into field 1 -- sample call

(*

    FileList --
      XFCN that returns a multiple-line list of files
      and folders in a given folder.

    Sample HyperTalk line:

      get fileList("Reno:System Folder:")

    To compile and link this file using MPW:
      directory "Reno:XCMD's:"
      Pascal :Src:FileList.p -o :Obj:FileList.p.o
      Link -rt XFCN=42 -m ENTRYPOINT -sg FileList -o ∂
```

```
    "XCMD's" :Obj:FileList.p.o "{Libraries}HyperXLib.o" ∂
    {Libraries}Interface.o {PLibraries}PasLib.o

*)

{$R-}  { no range checking }
{$D-}  { no Macsbug symbols }

UNIT DummyUnit;

INTERFACE

USES MemTypes,QuickDraw,OSIntf,ToolIntf,HyperXCmd;

PROCEDURE EntryPoint(paramPtr: XCmdPtr);

IMPLEMENTATION

PROCEDURE FileList(paramPtr: XCmdPtr); FORWARD;

PROCEDURE EntryPoint(paramPtr: XCmdPtr);
BEGIN
  FileList(paramPtr);
END;

PROCEDURE FileList(paramPtr:XCmdPtr);
VAR pathName,fileName: Str255;
    fileIndex,result,err: INTEGER;
    paramBlock: CInfoPBRec;
    wdParams: WDPBRec;
    fileList: Handle;

  PROCEDURE Return(value: Str255);
  BEGIN
    paramPtr^.returnValue := PasToZero(paramPtr,value);
    EXIT(FileList);
  END;

BEGIN
  IF paramPtr^.paramCount <> 1
  THEN Return('Form is: FileList(<path>)');
  ZeroToPas(paramPtr,paramPtr^.params[1]^,pathName);
  ZeroBytes(paramPtr,@wdParams,SizeOf(wdParams)); { Here's ZeroBytes! }
  WITH wdParams DO { set up working directory }
    BEGIN
      ioNamePtr := @pathName;
```

```
      ioWDProcID := $4552494B;   { 'ERIK' so finder will delete later }
      ioWDDirID := 2;
   END;
  result := PBOpenWD(@wdParams,FALSE);
  IF result <> 0 THEN Return('Couldn''t access that path.');
  fileList := NewHandle(0);
  fileIndex := 1;
  REPEAT { step through each file in this directory }
    ZeroBytes(paramPtr,@paramBlock,SizeOf(paramBlock));
    WITH paramBlock DO
      BEGIN
        fileName := '';
        ioNamePtr := @fileName;
        ioVRefNum := wdParams.ioVRefNum;
        ioFDirIndex := fileIndex;
      END;
    result := PBGetCatInfo(@paramBlock,FALSE);
    IF result = 0 THEN
      BEGIN
        IF BitTst(@paramBlock.ioFlAttrib,3)
        THEN fileName := Concat(fileName,':'); { it's a folder }
        fileName[Length(fileName)+1] := CHR(13);
        err := PtrAndHand(Pointer(ORD(@fileName)+1),
                          fileList,Length(fileName)+1);
      END;
    fileIndex := fileIndex + 1;
  UNTIL result = fnfErr;
  fileName := '';
  err := PtrAndHand(Pointer(@fileName),fileList,1); { null terminate }
  paramPtr^.returnValue := fileList;
END;

END.
```

ZEROTOPAS

Syntax

```
PROCEDURE ZeroToPas(paramPtr: XCmdPtr;zeroStr: Ptr;
                    VAR passStr: Str255);
```

Action

The **ZeroToPas** routine converts a zero-terminated string to a Pascal string. It takes three parameters. The first one is the usual parameter pointer. The second one is a pointer (*not* a handle) to a zero-terminated string that you want to convert to a Pascal (counted) string. The third one is the Pascal string that you want to contain the converted string.

Comments

This callback is useful for converting your parameters to Pascal strings.

There's no way for this routine to fail, but if you give a string that's longer than 254 characters, only the first 254 are used.

External

This external function returns the name of an icon given its ID number (useful because HyperCard stores icons by ID even if you set them by name).

```
put iconName(icon of button 1) into thisName -- sample call

(*

    iconName --
    XFCN to convert an icon ID to an icon name.

    Sample HyperTalk line:

      get iconName(icon of button 1)

    To compile and link this file using MPW:

      directory "Reno:XCMD's:"
      Pascal :Src:iconName.p -o :Obj:iconName.p.o
      Link -rt XFCN=41 -m ENTRYPOINT -sg iconName -o ∂
      "XCMD's" :Obj:iconName.p.o
```

```
     "{Libraries}HyperXLib.o"

   By Dan Winkler, March 1989.

*)

{$R-}  { no range checking }
{$D-}  { no Macsbug symbols }

UNIT DummyUnit;

INTERFACE

USES Types,Resources,HyperXCmd;

PROCEDURE EntryPoint(paramPtr: XCmdPtr);

IMPLEMENTATION

PROCEDURE IconName(paramPtr: XCmdPtr); FORWARD;

PROCEDURE EntryPoint(paramPtr: XCmdPtr);
BEGIN
  IconName(paramPtr);
END;

PROCEDURE IconName(paramPtr:XCmdPtr);
VAR str,iconName: Str255;
    iconHandle: Handle;
    iconID: INTEGER;
    iconType: ResType;

  PROCEDURE Abort(errorMsg: Str255);
  { return to caller with an error message as the return value }
  BEGIN
    paramPtr^.returnValue := PasToZero(paramPtr,errorMsg);
    EXIT(IconName);
  END;

BEGIN
  IF paramPtr^.paramCount <> 1
  THEN Abort('Form is: iconName(<iconID>)');
  ZeroToPas(paramPtr,paramPtr^.params[1]^,str); { Here's ZeroToPas }
  iconID := StrToNum(paramPtr,str);
  SetResLoad(FALSE);
  iconHandle := GetResource('ICON',iconID);
  SetResLoad(TRUE);
```

```
  GetResInfo(iconHandle,iconID,iconType,iconName);
  IF iconName <> ''
  THEN paramPtr^.returnValue := PasToZero(paramPtr,iconName);
END;

END. { unit }
```

SPECIALIZED GLUE ROUTINES

The way you get graphics onto the card using the painting tools is to create a QuickDraw picture, put it on the clipboard using the `PutScrap` call, and paste it onto the card using doMenu "Paste Picture." This method requires that you enter the Paint tools.

But sometimes there isn't enough memory to let you get into the Paint tools. Such a condition can exist even in machines that have lots of memory when that memory is being allocated for other purposes. For example, the HyperScan XCMD allocates a large amount of memory to hold data from the scanner.

Two glue routines new in version 1.2.1, `GetMaskAndData` and `ChangedMaskAndData`, let you paste graphics onto a card without entering the paint tools. HyperScan uses these routines to get the image onto the card.

A doubtful future

These routines, useful only in low-memory conditions, have not been thoroughly tested and might not be supported in future versions. If you use these routines, it's up to you to make sure the callback was successful by checking the result field of the `paramPtr`. Having been warned, read on.

How to Use These Routines

If you don't have enough memory to enter the paint tools, do the following:

1. Make sure that the editBackground property of HyperCard is false.

2. Make sure that nothing is selected (no text, no button, no field, nothing).

3. Call `GetMaskAndData` to get two QuickDraw bitmaps that point into the actual offscreen buffers that HyperCard uses to hold the card picture and its opacity mask.

4. Check the result field of the `paramPtr` to see if the callback was successful.

5. Make any changes to these buffers that you like.

---

6. Call `ChangedMaskAndData` to inform HyperCard that it should incorporate your changes.

7. Check the result field of the `paramPtr` to see if the callback was successful.

These routines give you only the card picture, not the whole image of the card; they don't give you the background picture, the image of buttons, or the image of fields.

To get the whole image of the card, use the following procedure instead:

1. Use the HyperCard command

```
debug pureQuickDraw true
```

to make HyperCard draw with QuickDraw using CopyBits call. (See the **debug** command, page 206.)

2. Hide and show the card window to make HyperCard recopy the card onto the screen from its internal buffer using QuickDraw's CopyBits routine.

QuickDraw versus HyperCard drawing

HyperCard has specialized routines that can draw a card faster than QuickDraw. Additionally, QuickDraw doesn't do visual effects.

For more information on QuickDraw and how CopyBits and the bottleneck routines work, see the QuickDraw section of volume I of *Inside Macintosh*.

DETAILS FOR LANGUAGE DESIGNERS

You don't need to know about this to make externals work; it's here for general interest and to provide necessary information for people writing glue routines for new languages.

How a Glue Routine Works

This section describes how glue routines do their job.

The example used is the code that makes up the `GetGlobal` glue routine. It assumes that a global variable named "theMarkedCards" contains a long list of card ids, and that you want your external to do something to every card in that list. The external gets the value of the global variable by using the `GetGlobal` glue routine:

```
myHandle := GetGlobal('theMarkedCards');
```

This code produces a handle containing a zero-terminated string with the same value as the HyperTalk global. The external gets a copy of the global variable and so is free to do anything it wants to this handle.

The glue routine for GetGlobal is as follows:

```
FUNCTION GetGlobal(globName: Str255): Handle;
BEGIN
   WITH paramPtr^ DO
     BEGIN
       inArgs[1] := ORD(@globName);
       request := xreqGetGlobal;
       DoJsr(entryPoint);
       GetGlobal := Handle(outArgs[1]);
     END;
END;
```

Here's how this glue routine works:

First, it puts a pointer to the name of the desired global into inArgs[1]; inArgs is a write-only field. (Glue routines only write to this field, and HyperTalk only reads from it.)

Then it sets the request field of the parameter block to the constant `xreqGetGlobal` so that HyperTalk will know that the GetGlobal routine is being requested.

Next, the glue routine does a JSR (without passing any parameters) to the address contained in the entryPoint field of the parameter block, making HyperTalk execute the requested routine. This works because HyperTalk keeps track of the location of the last parameter block it passed to any external and looks there for its parameters when a call is made to the entry point.

Finally, the glue routine returns the handle that HyperTalk placed in outArgs[1]; outArgs is a read-only field. (Glue routines only read from it and HyperTalk only writes to it.)

CallBack Reference

Here are the callback request codes for all the callbacks implemented through 1.2.#. The glue routines use these codes to do their jobs; so this list must appear in the header file (along with the result codes and the definition of the parameter block).

Apple Computer will create more callback request codes in the future. The numbers that Apple will use will ascend from these and are likely to go quite high. If you implement externals for a product that uses this same architecture and you want to define your own callback numbers, be sure to use numbers over 20,000.

The following are all the callbacks defined in version 1.2:

```
xreqSendCardMessage        = 1;
xreqEvalExpr               = 2;
xreqStringLength           = 3;
xreqStringMatch            = 4;
xreqSendHCMessage          = 5;
xreqZeroBytes              = 6;
xreqPasToZero              = 7;
xreqZeroToPas              = 8;
xreqStrToLong              = 9;
xreqStrToNum               = 10;
xreqStrToBool              = 11;
xreqStrToExt               = 12;
xreqLongToStr              = 13;
xreqNumToStr               = 14;
xreqNumToHex               = 15;
xreqBoolToStr              = 16;
```

```
xreqExtToStr              = 17;
xreqGetGlobal             = 18;
xreqSetGlobal             = 19;
xreqGetFieldByName        = 20;
xreqGetFieldByNum         = 21;
xreqGetFieldByID          = 22;
xreqSetFieldByName        = 23;
xreqSetFieldByNum         = 24;
xreqSetFieldByID          = 25;
xreqStringEqual           = 26;
xreqReturnToPas           = 27;
xreqScanToReturn          = 28;
xreqGetMaskAndData        = 29;
xreqChangedMaskAndData    = 30;
xreqScanToZero            = 39;
```

Note the gap between 30 and 39, the result of a typo on Dan Winkler's part when he was creating the original list. (Callbacks 29 and 30 didn't exist at the time; number 39 was supposed to be 29, but Dan's finger hiccupped.)

STANDARD RAW GLUE ROUTINES

Here are the raw Pascal glue routines. To use them, type them into a library file and call them as appropriate (as described throughout the first part of this chapter).

Note to do-it-yourselfers

If you're constructing your own files rather than using the ones provided on disk with MPW or Think C or Pascal or the HyperCard Developer's Toolkit from APDA (page 720), you also need a header file named HyperXCmd.p. That file must contain the request codes (page 802), the result codes (page 699), and the definition of the parameter block (page 696).

```
PROCEDURE DoJsr(addr: ProcPtr); INLINE $205F,$4E90;
{ You need this at the top of the file}

FUNCTION StringMatch(paramPtr: XCmdPtr; pattern: Str255; target: Ptr): Ptr;
BEGIN
  WITH paramPtr^ DO
    BEGIN
      inArgs[1] := ORD(@pattern);
      inArgs[2] := ORD(target);
      request := xreqStringMatch;
      DoJsr(entryPoint);
      StringMatch := Ptr(outArgs[1]);
    END;
END;

FUNCTION PasToZero(paramPtr: XCmdPtr; str: Str255): Handle;
BEGIN
  WITH paramPtr^ DO
    BEGIN
      inArgs[1] := ORD(@str);
      request := xreqPasToZero;
      DoJsr(entryPoint);
      PasToZero := Handle(outArgs[1]);
    END;
END;

PROCEDURE ZeroToPas(paramPtr: XCmdPtr; zeroStr: Ptr;
                    VAR pasStr: Str255);
BEGIN
  WITH paramPtr^ DO
    BEGIN
      inArgs[1] := ORD(zeroStr);
      inArgs[2] := ORD(@pasStr);
      request := xreqZeroToPas;
      DoJsr(entryPoint);
    END;
END;

FUNCTION StrToLong(paramPtr: XCmdPtr; str: Str255): LongInt;
BEGIN
  WITH paramPtr^ DO
    BEGIN
      inArgs[1] := ORD(@str);
      request := xreqStrToLong;
      DoJsr(entryPoint);
```

```
      StrToLong := outArgs[1];
    END;
END;

FUNCTION StrToNum(paramPtr: XCmdPtr; str: Str255): LongInt;
BEGIN
  WITH paramPtr^ DO
    BEGIN
      inArgs[1] := ORD(@str);
      request := xreqStrToNum;
      DoJsr(entryPoint);
      StrToNum := outArgs[1];
    END;
END;

FUNCTION StrToBool(paramPtr: XCmdPtr; str: Str255): BOOLEAN;
BEGIN
  WITH paramPtr^ DO
    BEGIN
      inArgs[1] := ORD(@str);
      request := xreqStrToBool;
      DoJsr(entryPoint);
      StrToBool := BOOLEAN(outArgs[1]);
    END;
END;

FUNCTION StrToExt(paramPtr: XCmdPtr; str: Str255): Extended;
VAR x: Extended;
BEGIN
  WITH paramPtr^ DO
    BEGIN
      inArgs[1] := ORD(@str);
      inArgs[2] := ORD(@x);
      request := xreqStrToExt;
      DoJsr(entryPoint);
      StrToExt := x;
    END;
END;

PROCEDURE LongToStr(paramPtr: XCmdPtr;posNum: LONGINT;
                    VAR str: Str255);
BEGIN
  WITH paramPtr^ DO
    BEGIN
```

```
        inArgs[1] := posNum;
        inArgs[2] := ORD(@str);
        request := xreqLongToStr;
        DoJsr(entryPoint);
     END;
  END;

PROCEDURE NumToStr(paramPtr: XCmdPtr;num: LONGINT;
                   VAR str: Str255);
BEGIN
  WITH paramPtr^ DO
    BEGIN
       inArgs[1] := num;
       inArgs[2] := ORD(@str);
       request := xreqNumToStr;
       DoJsr(entryPoint);
    END;
END;

PROCEDURE NumToHex(paramPtr: XCmdPtr;num: LONGINT;nDigits: INTEGER;
                   VAR str: Str255);
BEGIN
  WITH paramPtr^ DO
    BEGIN
       inArgs[1] := num;
       inArgs[2] := nDigits;
       inArgs[3] := ORD(@str);
       request := xreqNumToHex;
       DoJsr(entryPoint);
    END;
END;

PROCEDURE ExtToStr(paramPtr: XCmdPtr;num: Extended;VAR str: Str255);
BEGIN
  WITH paramPtr^ DO
    BEGIN
       inArgs[1] := ORD(@num);
       inArgs[2] := ORD(@str);
       request := xreqExtToStr;
       DoJsr(entryPoint);
    END;
END;
```

```
PROCEDURE BoolToStr(paramPtr: XCmdPtr;bool: BOOLEAN;VAR str: Str255);
BEGIN            ⟩
  WITH paramPtr^ DO
    BEGIN
      inArgs[1] := LongInt(bool);
      inArgs[2] := ORD(@str);
      request := xreqBoolToStr;
      DoJsr(entryPoint);
    END;
END;

PROCEDURE SendCardMessage(paramPtr: XCmdPtr; msg: Str255);
BEGIN
  WITH paramPtr^ DO
    BEGIN
      inArgs[1] := ORD(@msg);
      request := xreqSendCardMessage;
      DoJsr(entryPoint);
    END;
END;

PROCEDURE SendHCMessage(paramPtr: XCmdPtr; msg: Str255);
BEGIN
  WITH paramPtr^ DO
    BEGIN
      inArgs[1] := ORD(@msg);
      request := xreqSendHCMessage;
      DoJsr(entryPoint);
    END;
END;

FUNCTION EvalExpr(paramPtr: XCmdPtr; expr: Str255): Handle;
BEGIN
  WITH paramPtr^ DO
    BEGIN
      inArgs[1] := ORD(@expr);
      request := xreqEvalExpr;
      DoJsr(entryPoint);
      EvalExpr := Handle(outArgs[1]);
    END;
END;

FUNCTION StringLength(paramPtr: XCmdPtr; strPtr: Ptr): LongInt;
BEGIN
```

```
      WITH paramPtr^ DO
        BEGIN
          inArgs[1] := ORD(strPtr);
          request := xreqStringLength;
          DoJsr(entryPoint);
          StringLength := outArgs[1];
        END;
  END;

  FUNCTION GetGlobal(paramPtr: XCmdPtr; globName: Str255): Handle;
  BEGIN
    WITH paramPtr^ DO
        BEGIN
          inArgs[1] := ORD(@globName);
          request := xreqGetGlobal;
          DoJsr(entryPoint);
          GetGlobal := Handle(outArgs[1]);
        END;
  END;

  PROCEDURE SetGlobal(paramPtr: XCmdPtr; globName: Str255; globValue: Handle);
  BEGIN
    WITH paramPtr^ DO
        BEGIN
          inArgs[1] := ORD(@globName);
          inArgs[2] := ORD(globValue);
          request := xreqSetGlobal;
          DoJsr(entryPoint);
        END;
  END;

  FUNCTION GetFieldByName(paramPtr: XCmdPtr; cardFieldFlag: BOOLEAN;
                          fieldName: Str255): Handle;
  BEGIN
    WITH paramPtr^ DO
        BEGIN
          inArgs[1] := ORD(cardFieldFlag);
          inArgs[2] := ORD(@fieldName);
          request := xreqGetFieldByName;
          DoJsr(entryPoint);
          GetFieldByName := Handle(outArgs[1]);
        END;
  END;
```

```
FUNCTION GetFieldByNum(paramPtr: XCmdPtr; cardFieldFlag: BOOLEAN;
                          fieldNum: INTEGER): Handle;
BEGIN
  WITH paramPtr^ DO
    BEGIN
      inArgs[1] := ORD(cardFieldFlag);
      inArgs[2] := fieldNum;
      request := xreqGetFieldByNum;
      DoJsr(entryPoint);
      GetFieldByNum := Handle(outArgs[1]);
    END;
END;
FUNCTION GetFieldByID(paramPtr: XCmdPtr; cardFieldFlag: BOOLEAN;
                          fieldID: INTEGER): Handle;
BEGIN
  WITH paramPtr^ DO
    BEGIN
      inArgs[1] := ORD(cardFieldFlag);
      inArgs[2] := fieldID;
      request := xreqGetFieldByID;
      DoJsr(entryPoint);
      GetFieldByID := Handle(outArgs[1]);
    END;
END;
PROCEDURE SetFieldByName(paramPtr: XCmdPtr; cardFieldFlag:
                          BOOLEAN; fieldName: Str255; fieldVal: Handle);
BEGIN
  WITH paramPtr^ DO
    BEGIN
      inArgs[1] := ORD(cardFieldFlag);
      inArgs[2] := ORD(@fieldName);
      inArgs[3] := ORD(fieldVal);
      request := xreqSetFieldByName;
      DoJsr(entryPoint);
    END;
END;
PROCEDURE SetFieldByNum(paramPtr: XCmdPtr; cardFieldFlag: BOOLEAN;
                          fieldNum: INTEGER; fieldVal: Handle);
BEGIN
  WITH paramPtr^ DO
    BEGIN
```

```
        inArgs[1] := ORD(cardFieldFlag);
        inArgs[2] := fieldNum;
        inArgs[3] := ORD(fieldVal);
        request := xreqSetFieldByNum;
        DoJsr(entryPoint);
      END;
  END;

PROCEDURE SetFieldByID(paramPtr: XCmdPtr; cardFieldFlag: BOOLEAN;
                        fieldID: INTEGER; fieldVal: Handle);
BEGIN
  WITH paramPtr^ DO
    BEGIN
      inArgs[1] := ORD(cardFieldFlag);
      inArgs[2] := fieldID;
      inArgs[3] := ORD(fieldVal);
      request := xreqSetFieldByID;
      DoJsr(entryPoint);
    END;
END;

FUNCTION StringEqual(paramPtr: XCmdPtr; str1,str2: Str255): BOOLEAN;
BEGIN
  WITH paramPtr^ DO
    BEGIN
      inArgs[1] := ORD(@str1);
      inArgs[2] := ORD(@str2);
      request := xreqStringEqual;
      DoJsr(entryPoint);
      StringEqual := BOOLEAN(outArgs[1]);
    END;
END;

PROCEDURE ReturnToPas(paramPtr: XCmdPtr; zeroStr: Ptr;
                      VAR passStr: Str255);
BEGIN
  WITH paramPtr^ DO
    BEGIN
      inArgs[1] := ORD(zeroStr);
      inArgs[2] := ORD(@passStr);
      request := xreqReturnToPas;
      DoJsr(entryPoint);
    END;
END;
```

```
PROCEDURE ScanToReturn(paramPtr: XCmdPtr; VAR scanPtr: Ptr);
BEGIN
  WITH paramPtr^ DO
    BEGIN
      inArgs[1] := ORD(@scanPtr);
      request := xreqScanToReturn;
      DoJsr(entryPoint);
    END;
END;

PROCEDURE ScanToZero(paramPtr: XCmdPtr; VAR scanPtr: Ptr);
BEGIN
  WITH paramPtr^ DO
    BEGIN
      inArgs[1] := ORD(@scanPtr);
      request := xreqScanToZero;
      DoJsr(entryPoint);
    END;
END;

PROCEDURE ZeroBytes(paramPtr: XCmdPtr; dstPtr: Ptr; longCount: LongInt);
BEGIN
  WITH paramPtr^ DO
    BEGIN
      inArgs[1] := ORD(dstPtr);
      inArgs[2] := longCount;
      request := xreqZeroBytes;
      DoJsr(entryPoint);
    END;
END;

PROCEDURE GetMaskAndData(paramPtr: XCmdPtr; VAR maskBits,dataBits: BitMap);
BEGIN
  WITH paramPtr^ DO
    BEGIN
      inArgs[1] := ORD(@maskBits);
      inArgs[2] := ORD(@dataBits);
      request := xreqGetMaskAndData;
      DoJsr(entryPoint);
    END;
END;

PROCEDURE ChangedMaskAndData(paramPtr: XCmdPtr);
BEGIN
  WITH paramPtr^ DO
```

```
    BEGIN
      request := xreqChangedMaskAndData;
      DoJsr(entryPoint);
    END;
  END;
```

Chapter 15

Translators

The translator interface, which looks very much like the external interface with added provisions for static data, lets you write translators that convert what the user sees in the script editor to whatever form you want.

Typically, the translator interface is used to translate HyperCard's English language scripts into other languages. But you can use the translator to do much more than substitute one set of words for another; this chapter shows you how.

The language in which scripts are displayed in the HyperCard script editor window is controlled by the property **language**. By default, **language** is set to English. You can change the value of the language property by using the **set** command:

```
set language to French
```

For this command to work (and not cause an error message), the named script translator must exist as a Macintosh resource of type 'WTRN' (case significant) in the HyperCard application, the current stack, or the Home stack. WTRN stands for "WildTalk Translator"; WildTalk was the code name for HyperTalk during development, and would have been the released name for the language if some company besides Apple didn't already own the name.

HOW A TRANSLATOR WORKS

A WTRN resource is a code segment with no header bytes, like an XCMD or XFCN. It's written in a Macintosh development language such as Pascal, C, or 68000 assembly language. You attach it to the HyperCard application or a stack file using a resource editor such as ResEdit.

All scripts are always stored on disk in English and executed in English. When the language property is set to a value other than English, HyperCard invokes the appropriate translator whenever it displays or saves a script. So the user sees and edits the script in the language specific to the current translator, but the translator translates the script back to English before putting it away. If the user edits the script again, the translator translates it again into the current language (that is, the one that the **language** property calls for) before displaying it in the script editor window.

So HyperCard can execute any script, regardless of the language in which it was created, and regardless of the language translators available at execution time.

Figure 15-1 shows the position of the script translator in the script editing process.

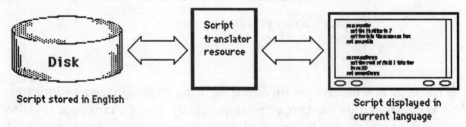

Script stored in English

Script displayed in current language

Figure 15-1   Position of script translator in script editing process.

When you use the **set** command to change the language property to a non-English value, HyperCard looks for a WTRN resource named the same as the requested value. Virtually any number of WTRN script translator resources can exist in a resource file, but only one language can be current at a time. (The default language, English, requires no translator resource.)

As long as their names are unique, there can be different translators for the same base language, although each constitutes a different "dialect" of HyperTalk and has its own language property value. For example, you could have a French1 WTRN that would do simple word substitution, plus a French2 WTRN that would also transpose adjectives to appear after, rather than before, modified words. A user who wanted to write scripts in a French dialect of HyperTalk could choose either French1 or French2.

When a Translator Is Invoked

HyperCard invokes a script translator at the following times:

- When the language property is set (using the **set** command) to a value other than English, HyperCard calls the appropriate script translator to initialize itself.

- When the language property is reset from non-English HyperTalk to English, HyperCard calls the departing script translator to deallocate static memory.

- When the current language isn't English and the script editor is opened, HyperCard calls the script translator to translate the script from English to the current language before displaying it.

- When the current language isn't English and a script is saved from the script editor, HyperCard calls the script translator to translate the displayed script back to English before writing it to the disk.

- When the current language isn't English and the user sends a message from the Message box, HyperCard calls the translator to translate the message into English before trying to execute it.

- When the current language isn't English and the user formats a script in the script editor window by pressing the Tab or Return key, HyperCard can call the script translator to indent the displayed script, rather than doing it itself. (At initialization time, the translator specifies whether or not it will do its own indenting.)

Interface Details

Script translators communicate with HyperCard through the translator data block, in the same way that external commands and functions communicate with HyperCard through the XCMD data block. The translator data block and its request and result codes have the following forms, expressed here in MPW Pascal:

```
UNIT HyperTrans;

INTERFACE

CONST

   { request codes }
   transInit    = 0;      { init the translator's static data }
   transQuit    = 1;      { deallocate static data before quit }
   transToEng   = 2;      { translate to English }
   transFromEng = 3;      { translate from English }
   transIndent  = 4;      { indent }

   { result codes }
   succTrans    = 0;      { success }
   failTrans    = 1;      { failure }
   cantTrans    = 2;      { not implemented }

   { flag masks }
   indentMask   = 1;      { BOR this onto flags to allow custom
   indenting }

TYPE
   TransPtr = ^TransBlock;
   TransBlock =
     RECORD
       request:   INTEGER;  { uses request codes defined above }
       result:    INTEGER;  { uses result codes defined above }
       srcHandle: Handle;   { zero terminated text to translate }
       dstHandle: Handle;   { zero terminated translation }
       selLoc:    INTEGER;  { location of insertion point }
       flags:     LongInt;  { bit 0 = indentFlag, others reserved }
       reserved:  LongInt;  { reserved for future use }
       userData:  ARRAY[1..16] OF LongInt; { for translator's static data }
     END;
END;
```

Data Fields

When HyperCard invokes a script translator, it passes only one parameter to the translator: a pointer to the translator data block. HyperCard then executes a JSR instruction to the translator, and the translator begins executing. Next, the translator examines the request field of the translator data block to see what HyperCard wants it to do. The fields of the translator data block are described in the following sections.

Request Codes

HyperCard puts one of the request codes (listed above among the constants) into this field to be examined by the translator. The request code transInit is made when the user executes a **set** command for the language specific to the translator. Typically, the translator initializes itself at this time, setting up tables of non-English words to substitute for English words, and so on. You can allocate these tables in the heap as static data that remains between invocations of the translator.

The ability to maintain static data, plus the fact that HyperCard calls WTRN resources automatically, differentiates WTRN resources from XCMD and XFCN resources. (But see **GetGlobal** in Chapter 14 for a description of how external commands can keep static data using global variables.) When you set the language again, HyperCard puts transQuit into the request field. (At this time, the translator should deallocate any static data.)

HyperCard puts the request transToEng into the request field when the user saves a script after editing in a non-English language or sends a non-English message from the Message box.

HyperCard puts the request transFromEng into the request field when the user invokes the script editor to view any script (and the language is not English).

If indentFlag is set in the flags field, HyperCard puts the request transIndent into the request field whenever the user presses the Tab or Return key and whenever he opens a script.

Result Codes

The translator places one of the result codes (listed above among the constants) into the result field when it returns control to HyperCard after executing a request. If, for example, the translator passes failTrans after HyperCard requests `transInit,` HyperCard displays the error message `Translator failed to initialize itself,` and the language reverts to English.

SrcHandle

When HyperCard calls the translator to translate a script, either to or from English, it places into this field a handle to the zero-terminated string where the untranslated script currently resides in memory. (So, for example, if the value of request is `transToEng,` the srcHandle field contains a handle to a non-English string.)

DstHandle

When the translator finishes translating a script, either to or from English, it writes the translated script to dstHandle (already allocated by HyperCard).

SelLoc

When an error occurs in English HyperTalk and you click the script button in the error dialog, HyperCard places the insertion point on the line that has the error when it opens the script editor. It uses the selLoc field to pass an integer that represents the location of the insertion point. It's the translator's responsibility to replace this value with one representing the appropriate point in the translated version of the script that HyperCard then displays.

The value of `selLoc` is an integer representing the number of characters from the beginning of the translated script to the cursor location. If `selLoc` is 1, then the cursor is after the first character.

Flags

If the translator sets bit 0 to 1 (by OR'ing the `indentMask` onto the flags field), HyperCard doesn't try to indent the translated script when it displays it: rather, the translator is called to indent the translated script by inserting space characters after each return character, and HyperCard displays the string exactly as received. If the flag isn't set to 1, HyperCard attempts to indent the translated script by finding non-English keywords that correlate to the English HyperTalk keywords at the beginning of each line.

The remainder of the flags field is reserved for future use.

Reserved

This field is reserved for future use.

UserData

This array comprises 16 long integer values that the translator can use to maintain data between invocations of itself.

For example, the French translator example included in a later section of this document uses three elements of this array. The first two long integers hold handles — the first to the string resource containing HyperTalk keywords and their French equivalents, the second to the hash table the translator builds in memory from the strings so that it can do fast translations. The third long integer is interpreted by the translator as two integers representing the number of entries in the hash table and its size.

The translator must dispose of its static data when HyperCard calls it with a transQuit request; otherwise the memory allocated by the translator is tied up until the user quits HyperCard.

Placement of WTRN Resources

HyperCard uses the standard resource hierarchy when it looks for a script translator. So your WTRN translator resource can be in the current stack, the Home stack, a "start using" stack, or the HyperCard application. (The WTRN could also be in the System file, but attaching it there would be pointless because no application other than HyperCard would ever use it.)

Place WTRNs highly

In versions of HyperCard through 2.0 (at least), placing the WTRN in a stack other than Home causes HyperCard to crash in the following situation:

1. Set the language to the non-English value of a WTRN in the current stack.

2. Go to another stack (so that the WTRN is no longer present).

3. Try to edit a script.

Blouie.

Thus the prudent programmer will attach his/her translator to the Home stack or to HyperCard itself.

The French Script Translator

The following listing illustrates a language translator created in MPW Pascal with a hash function written in 68000 assembly language. This translator also requires a 'STR#' resource, named French, containing strings of English HyperTalk and French HyperTalk vocabulary words in alternating sequence. The translator uses the string resource to build its hash table at initialization time, so the strings can be modified independent of the WTRN code.

```
{$R-}
{$D+}
{
      French -- a HyperCard language translator.

      To compile and link this file using Macintosh Programmer's Workshop,

          pascal French.p
          asm TransUtil.a
          link -o French -sn Main=French -sn STDIO=French ∂
              French.p.o TransUtil.a.o ∂
              -sn INTENV=French -rt WTRN=0 ∂
              reno:mpw:libraries:interface.o
      then paste the resulting WTRN into HyperCard or a HyperCard stack.
}

UNIT DummyUnit;

INTERFACE

USES MemTypes, QuickDraw, OsIntf, ToolIntf, HyperTrans;

IMPLEMENTATION

CONST return = 13;

TYPE WordPtr = ^INTEGER;

PROCEDURE FrenchTrans(arg: TransPtr);                    FORWARD;
FUNCTION TransHash(hashStart: WordPtr; modulo: INTEGER;
                   str: Str255): WordPtr; EXTERNAL;

PROCEDURE EntryPoint(arg: TransPtr);
{ entry point cannot have local procs, but forward routines can }
BEGIN
  FrenchTrans(arg);
END;
```

```
PROCEDURE FrenchTrans(arg: TransPtr);
TYPE
   Str255Ptr = ^Str255;

   { private interpretation of the block that HyperCard passes in }
   FrenchPtr = ^FrenchBlock;
   FrenchBlock =
      RECORD
         { fields used by HyperCard }
         request:  INTEGER;   { uses request codes defined above }
         result:   INTEGER;   { uses result codes defined above }
         srcHndl:  Handle;    { zero terminated text to translate }
         dstHndl:  Handle;    { zero terminated translation }
         selLoc:   INTEGER;   { location of insertion point }
         flags:    LongInt;   { bit 0 = indentFlag, others reserved }
         reserved: LongInt;   { reserved for future use }

         { fields for use by this translator only }
         strings:   Handle;
         hashTab:   Handle;
         hashCount: INTEGER;
         hashSize:  INTEGER;
      END;
CONST
   dstGrowSize = 2048;   { grow dest handle in chunks of this size }
   maxLineLen = 1024;
VAR
   blockPtr: FrenchPtr;
   selFixed: BOOLEAN;

   PROCEDURE Fail;
   BEGIN
      blockPtr^.result := failTrans;
      EXIT(FrenchTrans);
   END;

   PROCEDURE QuitTranslator;
   BEGIN
      WITH blockPtr^ DO
         BEGIN
            HPurge(strings);
            DisposHandle(hashTab);
         END;

   END;
```

```
PROCEDURE InitTranslator;
{ read in strings and build hash table }
VAR strNum,strCount,offset,i: INTEGER;
    strPtr,transPtr,basePtr: Ptr;
    hashEnd,hashStart,entryPtr: WordPtr;

  PROCEDURE AddHashEntry(strPtr: Ptr);
  VAR str: Str255;
      i,stepSize: INTEGER;
  BEGIN
    BlockMove(strPtr,@str,strPtr^+1);
    FOR i := 1 TO Length(str) DO IF str[i] = ' ' THEN Fail;
    UprString(str,FALSE);
    entryPtr := TransHash(hashStart,blockPtr^.hashCount,str);
    stepSize := BSL(strPtr^,1);  { cheap double hash }
    WHILE entryPtr^ <> 0 DO
      BEGIN
        entryPtr := Pointer(ORD(entryPtr)+stepSize);
        IF ORD(entryPtr) >= ORD(hashEnd)
        THEN entryPtr := Pointer(ORD(entryPtr)-blockPtr^.hashSize);
    END;
    entryPtr^ := offset;
END;


BEGIN
  WITH blockPtr^ DO
    BEGIN
        strings := GetNamedResource('STR#','French');
        IF strings = NIL THEN Fail;

        strCount := WordPtr(strings^)^;  { english and french strings are interleaved }

        IF strCount > 1000 THEN Fail; { can't handle that many strings }

        { pick a prime hash table size based on the number of strings }
        hashCount := 1361;
        IF strCount < 900 THEN hashCount := 1201;
        IF strCount < 800 THEN hashCount := 1069;
        IF strCount < 700 THEN hashCount := 937;
        IF strCount < 600 THEN hashCount := 809;
        IF strCount < 500 THEN hashCount := 673;
        IF strCount < 400 THEN hashCount := 541;
        IF strCount < 300 THEN hashCount := 401;
```

822

```
      IF strCount < 200 THEN hashCount := 269;
      IF strCount < 100 THEN hashCount := 137;
      hashSize := hashCount*2;        { two bytes per entry }
      hashTab := NewHandle(hashSize);
      IF hashTab = NIL THEN Fail;     { couldn't get enough RAM for hash table }

      hashStart := Pointer(hashTab^);
      entryPtr := hashStart;
      FOR i := 1 TO hashCount DO     { zero out the hash table }
        BEGIN
          entryPtr^ := 0;
          entryPtr := Pointer(ORD(entryPtr)+2);
        END;
      hashEnd := entryPtr;

      basePtr := strings^;  { offsets are from this base }
      strPtr := Ptr(ORD(strings^)+2); { skip count }
      transPtr := Pointer(ORD(strPtr)+strPtr^+1);
      FOR strNum := 1 TO strCount DIV 2 DO
        BEGIN
          offset := ORD(strPtr)-ORD(basePtr);
          AddHashEntry(strPtr);
          AddHashEntry(transPtr);
          strPtr := Pointer(ORD(transPtr)+transPtr^+1);
          transPtr := Pointer(ORD(strPtr)+strPtr^+1);
        END;
    END;
END;

PROCEDURE Translate;
VAR srcPtr,dstPtr: Ptr;
    srcOffset,dstOffset: INTEGER;
    size: LongInt;

  PROCEDURE CopyByte;
  BEGIN
    dstPtr^ := srcPtr^;
    dstPtr := Pointer(ORD(dstPtr)+1);
    srcPtr := Pointer(ORD(srcPtr)+1);
  END;
```

```
FUNCTION IdentChar(ch: INTEGER): BOOLEAN;
BEGIN
   ch := BAND($FF,ch);
   IdentChar := FALSE;
   IF (ch < ORD('A')) AND (ch <> ORD('''')) THEN EXIT(IdentChar);
   IF (ch >= ORD('[')) AND (ch <= ORD('^')) THEN EXIT(IdentChar);
   IF ch = ORD('≠') THEN EXIT(IdentChar);
   IF ch = $7F THEN EXIT(IdentChar);   { rubout char }
   IdentChar := TRUE;
END;

PROCEDURE CopyToIdent;
{ copy whitespace, literals, punctuation, numbers, and comments }
VAR ch: INTEGER;
BEGIN
   WHILE (srcPtr^ <> return) AND (srcPtr^ <> 0) DO
     BEGIN
       ch := srcPtr^;
       IF IdentChar(ch) THEN EXIT(CopyToIdent); { found start of ident }
       CopyByte;
       IF ch = ORD('"') THEN   { copy literal }
         BEGIN
           WHILE (srcPtr^ <> 0) AND (srcPtr^ <> return) AND (srcPtr^ <> ORD('"'))
           DO CopyByte;
             IF srcPtr^ = ORD('"') THEN CopyByte;
           END
         ELSE IF (ch = ORD('-')) AND (srcPtr^ = ORD('-')) THEN { copy comment }
           BEGIN
             CopyByte;   { copy second "-" }
             WHILE (srcPtr^ <> 0) AND (srcPtr^ <> return)
             DO CopyByte; { copy till end of line }
           END;
     END;
END;

PROCEDURE HashLookup(identPtr,transPtr: Ptr);
VAR entryPtr,hashStart,hashEnd: WordPtr;
    matchPtr,subsPtr,swapPtr,basePtr: Ptr;
    stepSize: INTEGER;
BEGIN
```

```
    basePtr := Pointer(blockPtr^.strings^);
    hashStart := Pointer(blockPtr^.hashTab^);
    hashEnd := Pointer(ORD(hashStart)+blockPtr^.hashSize);
    entryPtr := TransHash(hashStart,blockPtr^.hashCount,Str255Ptr(identPtr)^);
    stepSize := BSL(identPtr^,1);  { cheap double hash }
    WHILE entryPtr^ <> 0 DO
      BEGIN
        matchPtr := Pointer(ORD(basePtr)+entryPtr^);
        subsPtr := Pointer(ORD(matchPtr)+matchPtr^+1);
        IF blockPtr^.request = transToEng THEN
          BEGIN
            swapPtr := matchPtr;
            matchPtr := subsPtr;
            subsPtr := swapPtr;
          END;
        IF EqualString(Str255Ptr(identPtr) ^,
                    Str255Ptr(matchPtr) ^,FALSE,FALSE) THEN { found it }
          BEGIN
            BlockMove(subsPtr,transPtr,subsPtr^+1);
            EXIT(HashLookup);
          END;
        entryPtr := Pointer(ORD(entryPtr)+stepSize);
        IF ORD(entryPtr) >= ORD(hashEnd)
        THEN entryPtr := Pointer(ORD(entryPtr)-blockPtr^.hashSize);
      END;
END;

PROCEDURE TranslateIdent;
VAR len: INTEGER;
    ident,translation: Str255;
BEGIN
  len := 0;
  WHILE IdentChar(srcPtr^) DO
    BEGIN
      len := len + 1;
      ident[len] := CHR(srcPtr^);
      srcPtr := Pointer(ORD(srcPtr)+1);
    END;
```

```
    IF len = 0 THEN EXIT(TranslateIdent);
    ident[0] := CHR(len);
    BlockMove(@ident,@translation,len+1); { default is original ident }
    UprString(ident,FALSE);
    HashLookup(@ident,@translation);
    BlockMove(Pointer(ORD(@translation)+1),dstPtr,Length(translation));
    dstPtr := Pointer(ORD(dstPtr)+Length(translation));
  END;

PROCEDURE CheckSel;
VAR srcOffset,dstOffset: INTEGER;
BEGIN
  WITH blockPtr^ DO
    BEGIN
      srcOffset := ORD(srcPtr) - ORD(srcHndl^);
      IF srcOffset >= selLoc THEN
        BEGIN
          dstOffset := ORD(dstPtr) - ORD(dstHndl^);
          selLoc := selLoc + dstOffset - srcOffset;
          selFixed := TRUE;
        END;
    END;
END;

PROCEDURE TranslateLine;
BEGIN
  WHILE (srcPtr^ <> 0) AND (srcPtr^ <> return) DO
    BEGIN
      CopyToIdent;
      IF NOT selFixed THEN CheckSel;
      TranslateIdent;
    END;
  dstPtr^ := srcPtr^;  { copy the 0 or return }
  IF srcPtr^ <> 0 THEN
    BEGIN
      srcPtr := Pointer(ORD(srcPtr)+1);
      dstPtr := Pointer(ORD(dstPtr)+1);
    END;
END;
```

```
BEGIN
  WITH blockPtr^ DO
  BEGIN
    SetHandleSize(dstHndl,dstGrowSize);
    dstPtr := dstHndl^;
    srcPtr := srcHndl^;
    selFixed := FALSE;
    WHILE srcPtr^ <> 0 DO
      BEGIN
        TranslateLine;
        dstOffset := ORD(dstPtr) - ORD(dstHndl^);
        size := GetHandleSize(dstHndl);
        IF size - dstOffset < maxLineLen THEN
          BEGIN
            srcOffset := ORD(srcPtr) - ORD(srcHndl^);
            SetHandleSize(dstHndl,size+dstGrowSize);
            dstPtr := Pointer(ORD(dstHndl^)+dstOffset);
            srcPtr := Pointer(ORD(srcHndl^)+srcOffset);
          END;
      END;
    dstPtr^ := 0;
  END;
END;

BEGIN
  blockPtr := Pointer(arg);   { cast to type FrenchPtr }
  CASE blockPtr^.request OF
    transInit: InitTranslator;
    transQuit: QuitTranslator;
    transToEng,transFromEng: Translate;
    OTHERWISE
      blockPtr^.result := cantTrans; { can't satisfy that request }
  END;
END;

END.
```

The following listing is the hash function, written in 68000 assembly language, which is used by the foregoing translator to build its translate table.

```
;
;
;   TransUtil.a, assembly language for translators
;
;
              SEG  'Main'

              BLANKS ON
              STRING ASIS


TransHash FUNC  EXPORT
;------------------------------------------------------------
;
;   FUNCTION  TransHash(hashStart: WordPtr;
;                      modulo: INTEGER;
;                      str: Str255): WordPtr;
;
              MOVE.L    (SP)+,A0          ;POP RETURN ADDR
              MOVE.L    (SP)+,A1          ;GET STR
              MOVEQ     #0,D0             ;get ready for bytes
              MOVEQ     #0,D2             ;init hash
              MOVE.B    (A1)+,D2          ;to string length
              MOVE      D2,D1             ;copy string length
              LSL.W     #7,D2             ;start length in hi byte
              BRA.S     START             ;go to loop start
NEXTCHAR      ROL.W     #1,D2             ;rotate hash left
              MOVE.B    (A1)+,D0          ;get character
              EOR.B     D0,D2             ;xor into hash
START         DBRA      D1,NEXTCHAR       ;loop all chars in string
              DIVU      (SP)+,D2          ;DIVIDE BY MODULO
              CLR.W     D2                ;DISCARD QUOTIENT
              SWAP      D2                ;GET REMAINDER
              ADD       D2,D2             ;TIMES 2 FOR EACH ENTRY
              ADD.L     (SP)+,D2          ;ADD HASH START
              MOVE.L    D2,(SP)           ;UPDATE FCN RESULT
              JMP       (A0)              ;AND RETURN

              END
```

828

SECONDARY TRANSLATOR USES

As you saw in the first section of this chapter, the translator was designed to provide a mechanism by which HyperCard scripts can be displayed and created in dialects of HyperTalk other than English. Most commonly the translator takes text on its way to the script editor, "translates" it into some appropriate language from English, and then translates it back to English before the scripts is sent to the disk.

But the translator interface can transform scripts in other ways. To understand how, think of the translator as a filter that stands between the disk and the script editor: a script gets sent from the disk to the translator, it's somehow massaged, and finally it (presumably in some new form) gets sent to the script editor. But how the script is massaged is entirely up to the translator.

Block Comments "Translator"

The following fully functioning sample shows how to use the translator to do something besides translate from one language to another: it lets you use Pascal-style block comments in a script. You call it by setting the "language" to `blockComments`:

```
set language to blockComments
```

Figure 15-2   Summoning the blockComments "language"

Here's how you might write and see a script with the blockComments translator active. Pascal-style comment delimiters comment out the repeat loop:

```
on mouseUp
  get 1
  get 2
  {
  repeat 5
    beep 10
  end repeat
  }
  get 4
```

```
  if true then
    get 5
  end if
  play "boing"
end mouseUp
```

And here's how the same script would look with the language property set to
English, the version of the script that's actually stored to disk:

```
on mouseUp
  get 1
  get 2
--! {
--!    repeat 5
--!       beep 10
--!    end repeat
--!    }
  get 4
  if true then
    get 5
  end if
  play "boing"
end mouseUp
```

And here's the Pascal code to make it happen:

```
{$R-}
{$D+}
(*
     BlockComments --
        a HyperCard language translator to implement
        Pascal-style block comments.

    To compile and link this file using Macintosh Programmer's Workshop,

        directory "reno:reference book:translators:"
        pascal BlockComments.p
        link -o TestStack -sn Main=BlockComments ∂
            BlockComments.p.o -rt WTRN=5 {libraries}interface.o

    then paste the resulting WTRN into HyperCard or a HyperCard stack.
```

```
*)

UNIT DummyUnit;

INTERFACE

USES MemTypes, Memory, OSUtils, HyperTrans;

IMPLEMENTATION

PROCEDURE BlockComments(arg: TransPtr);

FORWARD;

PROCEDURE EntryPoint(arg: TransPtr);
{ entry point cannot have local procs, but forward routines can }
BEGIN
  BlockComments(arg);
END;

PROCEDURE BlockComments(arg: TransPtr);
CONST growSlop = 1024;
VAR srcPtr,dstPtr: Ptr;
    freeBytes: LongInt;
    commentStr: Str31;
    commentDone: BOOLEAN;

  PROCEDURE Fail;
  BEGIN
    arg^.result := failTrans;
    arg^.dstHndl^^ := 0; { return empty string }
    EXIT(BlockComments);
  END;

  PROCEDURE SetUp;
  BEGIN
    SetHandleSize(arg^.dstHndl,growSlop);
    IF MemError <> 0 THEN Fail;
    freeBytes := growSlop;
    srcPtr := arg^.srcHndl^;
    dstPtr := arg^.dstHndl^;
    commentStr := '--! ';
  END;

  PROCEDURE MakeRoom(count: INTEGER);
  VAR srcOffset,dstOffset: LongInt;
```

```
BEGIN
  IF count <= freeBytes THEN EXIT(MakeRoom);
  srcOffset := ORD(srcPtr) - ORD(arg^.srcHndl^);
  dstOffset := ORD(dstPtr) - ORD(arg^.dstHndl^);
  SetHandleSize(arg^.dstHndl,GetHandleSize(arg^.dstHndl)+count+growSlop);
  IF MemError <> 0 THEN Fail;
  freeBytes := freeBytes + count + growSlop;
  srcPtr := Pointer(ORD(arg^.srcHndl^)+srcOffset);
  dstPtr := Pointer(ORD(arg^.dstHndl^)+dstOffset);
END;

PROCEDURE Finish;
BEGIN
  MakeRoom(1);
  dstPtr^ := 0; { zero terminate }
END;

PROCEDURE OutBytes(fromPtr: Ptr; count: INTEGER);
BEGIN
  MakeRoom(count);
  BlockMove(fromPtr,dstPtr,count);
  dstPtr := Pointer(ORD(dstPtr)+count);
END;

PROCEDURE EchoBytes(count: INTEGER);
BEGIN
  MakeRoom(count);
  BlockMove(srcPtr,dstPtr,count);
  srcPtr := Pointer(ORD(srcPtr)+count);
  dstPtr := Pointer(ORD(dstPtr)+count);
END;

PROCEDURE EchoLine;
VAR endPtr: Ptr;
BEGIN
  endPtr := srcPtr;
  WHILE (endPtr^ <> 0) AND (endPtr^ <> 13) DO
    BEGIN
      IF endPtr^ = ORD('}') THEN commentDone := TRUE;
      endPtr := Pointer(ORD(endPtr)+1);
    END;
  IF endPtr^ = 13 THEN endPtr := Pointer(ORD(endPtr)+1);
  EchoBytes(ORD(endPtr)-ORD(srcPtr));
END;
```

```
PROCEDURE BlocksOut;
VAR commentPtr: Ptr;
BEGIN
  SetUp;
  REPEAT
    { find the start of the next comment }
    commentPtr := srcPtr;
    WHILE (commentPtr^ <> ORD('{')) AND (commentPtr^ <> 0)
    DO commentPtr := Pointer(ORD(commentPtr)+1);

    { copy up to the comment }
    EchoBytes(ORD(commentPtr)-ORD(srcPtr));

    IF srcPtr^ = ORD('{') THEN
      BEGIN
        { copy the comment, inserting commentStr }
        commentDone := FALSE;
        REPEAT
          OutBytes(Pointer(ORD(@commentStr)+1) , Length(commentStr));
          EchoLine;
        UNTIL commentDone OR (srcPtr^ = 0);
      END;
  UNTIL srcPtr^ = 0;
  Finish;
END;

PROCEDURE BlocksIn;
VAR commentPtr: Ptr;

  FUNCTION VerifyMatch: BOOLEAN;
  VAR i: INTEGER;
  BEGIN
    VerifyMatch := TRUE;
    FOR i := 1 TO Length(commentStr) DO
    IF ORD(commentStr[i]) <> Ptr(ORD(commentPtr)+i-1)^ THEN
      BEGIN
        VerifyMatch := FALSE;
        EXIT(VerifyMatch);
      END;
  END;
```

```
BEGIN
  SetUp;
  REPEAT
    { find next commentStr }
    commentPtr := srcPtr;
    WHILE (commentPtr^ <> 0) & NOT ((commentPtr^ = ORD('-')) & VerifyMatch)
    DO commentPtr := Pointer(ORD(commentPtr)+1);

    { copy up to commentStr }
    EchoBytes(ORD(commentPtr)-ORD(srcPtr));

    { jump over commentStr }
    IF srcPtr^ <> 0
    THEN srcPtr := Pointer(ORD(srcPtr)+Length(commentStr));

  UNTIL srcPtr^ = 0;
  Finish;
END;

BEGIN
  CASE arg^.request OF
    transInit,transQuit: { do nothing } ;
    transToEng: BlocksOut;
    transFromEng: BlocksIn;
    OTHERWISE
      arg^.result := cantTrans;  { can't satisfy that request }
  END;
END;

END.
```

Part Four Appendixes

Appendix A

ASCII Chart

The following chart shows the complete Monaco character set, with standard ASCII (American Standard Code for Information Interchange) control code listings for characters 0 through 31 and 127. Characters above 127 are *not* consistent throughout all fonts, and are included here for convenience. (But characters 218 through 255 are undefined in this font.)

To produce all the characters in a given font from HyperCard, use the following script (which we used to produce the chart for this appendix):

```
fontTest "Monaco",12 -- We used these parameters to get this chart

on fontTest fontName,fontSize
  put empty into card field "Font Test"
  set textFont of card field "Font Test" to fontName
  if fontSize is not empty
  then set textSize of card field "Font Test" to fontSize
  repeat with charNum = 1 to 255
    set cursor to busy
    put numToChar(charNum) into thisChar
    put charNum & ": " & thisChar & return after card field "Font Test"
  end repeat
  set scroll of card field "Font Test" to zero
end fontTest
```

0	NULL	34	"	68	D
1	SOH	35	#	69	E
2	STX	36	$	70	F
3	ETX	37	%	71	G
4	EOT	38	&	72	H
5	ENQ	39	'	73	I
6	ACK	40	(	74	J
7	BELL	41	)	75	K
8	BS	42	*	76	L
9	HT	43	+	77	M
10	LF	44	,	78	N
11	VT	45	-	79	O
12	FF	46	.	80	P
13	(RETURN)	47	/	81	Q
14	SO	48	0	82	R
15	SI	49	1	83	S
16	DLE	50	2	84	T
17	DC1	51	3	85	U
18	DC2	52	4	86	V
19	DC3	53	5	87	W
20	DC4	54	6	88	X
21	NAK	55	7	89	Y
22	SYN	56	8	90	Z
23	ETB	57	9	91	[
24	CAN	58	:	92	\
25	EM	59	;	93	]
26	SUB	60	<	94	^
27	ESC	61	=	95	_
28	FS	62	>	96	`
29	GS	63	?	97	a
30	RS	64	@	98	b
31	US	65	A	99	c
32	(SPACE)	66	B	100	d
33	!	67	C	101	e

102	f	136	à	170	™	
103	g	137	â	171	´	
104	h	138	ä	172	¨	
105	i	139	ã	173	≠	
106	j	140	å	174	Æ	
107	k	141	ç	175	Ø	
108	l	142	é	176	∞	
109	m	143	è	177	±	
110	n	144	ê	178	≤	
111	o	145	ë	179	≥	
112	p	146	í	180	¥	
113	q	147	ì	181	µ	
114	r	148	î	182	∂	
115	s	149	ï	183	Σ	
116	t	150	ñ	184	Π	
117	u	151	ó	185	π	
118	v	152	ò	186	∫	
119	w	153	ô	187	ª	
120	x	154	ö	188	º	
121	y	155	õ	189	Ω	
122	z	156	ú	190	æ	
123	{	157	ù	191	ø	
124	|	158	û	192	¿	
125	}	159	ü	193	¡	
126	~	160	†	194	¬	
127	DEL	161	°	195	√	
128	Ä	162	¢	196	f	
129	Å	163	£	197	≈	
130	Ç	164	§	198	Δ	
131	É	165	•	199	«	
132	Ñ	166	¶	200	»	
133	Ö	167	ß	201	…	
134	Ü	168	®	202	(OPTION-	
135	á	169	©		SPACE)	

203	À	208	–	213	′
204	Ã	209	—	214	÷
205	Õ	210	"	215	◊
206	Œ	211	"	216	ÿ
207	œ	212	`	217	Ÿ

1.2.# Error Messages

HyperTalk has nearly 90 error dialogs in version 1.2.#. This appendix lists the contents of each 1.2.# error dialog, tells what condition(s) produced each dialog, and makes suggestions for correcting the problem where such solutions are not obvious. In all cases, HyperTalk inserts the proper word where the contents of the error dialog includes a nonterminal (as in *<expr>*). This appendix does not apply to version 2.0 because at the time of this writing, 2.0's error messages were not finalized.

1.2.# DIALOG BOXES

HyperTalk error dialog boxes all look and act the same. When a run-time error occurs, a box appears. The dialog holds a message that describes the error. It also has one or two buttons — one labeled "Cancel" (Figure B-1) and, if the code that caused the problem was generated by a script that HyperTalk can locate and if the userLevel property is set to 5, a second button labeled "script" (Figure B-2).

Clicking the "Cancel" button or pressing Return or Enter puts the dialog away and returns control to the user. (The rest of the running handler is aborted.) Clicking the button marked "Script" opens the offending script; if HyperTalk can figure out the code that caused the error, it places the insertion point at the farthest point it was able to parse within the script.

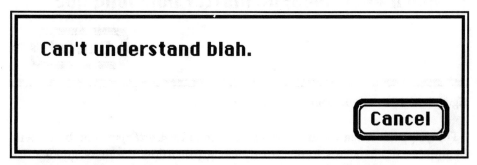

Figure B-1   Offending code probably sent from the Message box.

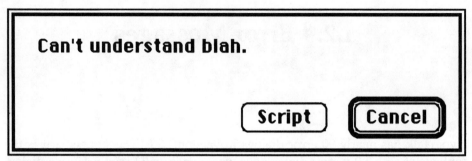

Figure B-2   Click "Script" to see what caused the problem.

"<fileName>" is not an application.

The "open" or "print" command has been used with a file that is not an application. <fileName> is replaced by the name of the file.

<sortExpr> was not a valid expression for any card.

The expression by which the sort command was supposed to sort didn't make sense for any card in the stack. You probably mistyped a field name or made some other simple error.

Sometimes you won't get the whole message in the box, and you'll get something mysterious, as in Figure B-3.

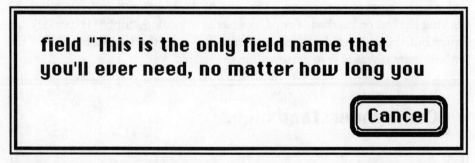

Figure B-3   Not enough room for the whole message

This happens when the number of characters in *<sortExpr>*, combined with the number of characters in the error message, overflow the message area that the dialog has available.

In Figure B-3, the name of the field is "This is the only field name that you'll ever need, no matter how long you script in HyperCard," and the code that generated the message (typed into the Message box) was

```
sort by field "This is the only field name that you'll ever need,
no matter how long you script in HyperCard"
```

<value> is not a point.

You tried to use the "is within" or "is not within" operator with a first argument that wasn't a point. *<value>* is replaced by what was found on the line where a point was expected. Common causes for this error are

- You've tried to use "is within" to find a string within another string (when in fact "is within" can only be used to find a point within a rectangle, and you should be using "is in" instead).

- You've used the wrong variable for <value>.

Sometimes the error message won't make any sense, as in Figure B-4.

Figure B-4 Not enough room for the whole message

This happens when the number of characters in *<value>*, combined with the number of characters in the error message, overflow the message area that the dialog has available.

The code that produced the dialog in Figure B-4 was

```
on mouseUp
  put "The quality of mercy is not strained, it droppeth as the
  gentle rain from heaven upon the place beneath." into myVar --
  all on one line, of course
  put myVar is within "10,10,100,100"
end mouseUp
```

<value> is not a rectangle.

You tried to use the "is within" or "is not within" operator with a second argument that wasn't a rectangle. *<value>* is replaced by what was found on the line where a rectangle was expected. Common causes for this error are

- You've tried to use "is within" to find a string within another string (when in fact "is within" can only be used to find a point within a rectangle, and you should be using "is in" instead).

- You've used the wrong variable for <value>.

Sometimes the error message won't make any sense, as in Figure B-5.

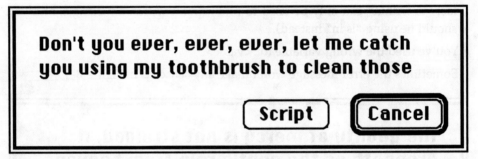

Figure B-5   Not enough room for the whole message

This happens when the number of characters in *<value>*, combined with the number of characters in the error message, overflow the message area that the dialog has available.

The code that produced the dialog in Figure B-5 was

```
on mouseUp
    put "Don't you ever, ever, ever, let me catch you using my
    toothbrush to clean those keys on that typewriter!" into myVar
    -- all on one line, of course
    put "10, 100" is within myVar
end mouseUp
```

\<value> is not the right type for \<operator>.

You tried to use an operator on a value with which that operator couldn't work. You'll get this dialog, for example, if you try to use a numeric operator when at least one of the elements isn't a number (as in `put "fred" + 12 into total`), or if you try to use a logical operator when at least one of the elements isn't a logical value (as in `put this and that into result` when either `this` or `that` doesn't hold a logical value).

Sometimes the error message won't make any sense, as in Figure B-6.

Figure B-6 Not enough room for the whole message

This happens when the number of characters in *\<value>*, combined with the number of characters in the error message, overflow the message area that the dialog has available.

The code that produced the dialog in figure B-6 was

```
on foo
   get "very very very very very very very very very very very very
   very very very very long string" + 9 -- all on one line
end foo
```

Already have a local variable named \<variableName>.

HyperCard has encountered a variable named \<variableName> in a global statement that has already been used as a local variable in the same handler.

The handler that produces this error might look like this:

```
on mouseUp
   put 0 into myVar -- here's the one to watch
   repeat with i = 1 to number of cards
```

```
      put field "Names" of card i & Return after namesCollector
      if length(namesCollector) < 30000
      then put field "Names" of card i & Return after namesCollector
      else
         global myVar -- this complains!
         add 1 to myVar
         do makeNew
      end if
   end repeat
   -- other code goes here
end mouseUp
```

You can prevent this error from ever occurring by declaring all globals at the top of a handler.

See global, page 132.

Can't DIV by zero.

You tried to use DIV with a divisor of zero. This error happens most often when you're using a variable for DIV's right-side operand, and through some calculation the variable ends up with a zero value.

To prevent this error, check for the value of that which will become DIV's right-side argument before you use it. For example:

```
on closeField
   put number of lines in me into lineCount
   put length of me into charCount
   if lineCount is zero then exit closeField -- so div won't blow up
   put charCount div lineCount into charsPerLine
   answer charsPerLine & " characters per line."
end closeField
```

Can't edit script of HyperCard.

You tried to edit the script of HyperCard:

```
edit script of HyperCard
```

HyperCard is the only object without a script.

Can't find "<findString>".

The find command could not find the requested string. This message appears only when find is used from the message box and the user level is set below authoring (that is, userLevel < 4). In other cases of failed find, no message appears but the **result** function is set.

Can't find icon named "<iconName>."

You tried to set the icon of a button to an icon that isn't in the resource fork of the current stack, Home stack, HyperCard, or the System file.

Can't find menu item "<item>."

You tried to use doMenu on a menu item that wasn't in the menu bar. (See **doMenu**, page 229.) The most common causes for this error are

• You misspelled the name of the menu item.

• You didn't type the menu item exactly as it appears in the menu (for example, Find with the three dots after it).

• You got caught by the bug in HyperCard where the edit menu fails to update properly. (See the box on page 32 for a workaround.)

• The menu item you called for doesn't appear at that user level, in that tool, or with that kind of selection.

Can't get that property.

You tried to get a property of an object or window which that kind of object or window doesn't have. (For example, you asked for the textHeight of the card window.)

Can't interpret that keyword in the message box.

You tried to execute a keyword other than send from the message box. Such keywords are do, end, exit, function, global, if, then, else, next, on, pass, repeat, and return.

Can't MOD by zero.

You tried to use MOD with a divisor of zero. This error happens most often when you're using a variable for MOD's right-side operand, and through some calculation the variable ends up with a zero value.

To prevent this error, check the value that will become MOD's right-side argument before you use it.

Can't open any more files.

The open file command has reached its limit for open files: three. To prevent this error, keep track of the number of files you're opening so that you don't try to have more than three files open at any one time. (See **open file,** page 280.)

Can't set properties of that object.

This indicates an internal error. You should never see this one.

Can't set that bkgnd property.

You tried to set a property of a background that is either read only or that backgrounds don't have. (For example, you tried to set the textFont of the background.)

The settable background properties in version 1.2.# are **cantDelete, name,** and **script.**

Can't set that button property.

HyperCard was unable to set the requested button property. The most common causes for this error are (1) the property you named isn't a settable button property (see list below); or (2) the disk is full, so HyperCard can't update its information on that button.

The settable button properties in version 1.2.# are **autoHilite, bottom, bottomRight, height, hilite, icon, left, location, name, rectangle, right, script, showName, style, textAlign, textFont, textHeight, textSize, textStyle, top, topLeft, visible,** and **width.**

Can't set that card property.

You tried to set a property of a card, and that property is read-only or isn't a property of a card.

The settable card properties in version 1.2.# are **cantDelete, name, script,** and **showPict.**

Can't set that field property.

HyperCard was unable to set the requested field property. The most common causes for this error are (1) the property you named isn't a settable field property (see list below); or (2) the disk is full, so HyperCard can't update its information on that field.

The settable field properties in version 1.2.# are **autoTab, bottom, bottomRight, height, left, location, lockText, name, rectangle, right, script, scroll, showLines, showPict, style, textAlign, textFont, textHeight, textSize, textStyle, top, topLeft, visible, wideMargins,** and **width.**

Can't set that HyperCard property.

You tried to set a property of HyperCard that is either read-only (such as **version** or **name**) or that HyperCard doesn't have.

The settable HyperCard nonpainting properties are **blindTyping, cursor, dragSpeed, editBkgnd, language, lockMessages, lockRecent, lockScreen, numberFormat, powerKeys, textArrows, userLevel,** and **userModify.**

The settable painting properties are **brush, centered, filled, grid, lineSize, multiple, multiSpace, pattern, polySides, textAlign, textFont, textHeight, textSize,** and **textStyle.**

Can't set that stack property.

You tried to set a property of a stack that is either read-only or that stacks don't have. You'll also get this message if you try to set a property of unpropertied things (for example, `set width of the Selection to 10` where the `Selection` doesn't evaluate to an object with a width property).

The settable stack properties are **cantDelete, cantModify, name,** and **script.**

Can't set that window property.

You tried to set a property of a window (tools window, patterns window, card window, Message box) that is either read-only or that windows don't have.

The settable window properties are **bottom, bottomRight, left, right, top,** and **topLeft.**

Can't take the value of that expression.

The value function was passed an argument that isn't a valid expression. You'll get this error when the code is something like value(x) where x is "3 + hello". (See **value,** page 487.)

Can't understand <message>.

A message that was neither a built-in command nor system message reached HyperCard. This usually happens when (1) you misspell either the name of the message or the name of the handler that's supposed to catch the message, or (2) you forget to write a handler for that message.

Can't understand arguments of <name>

HyperTalk couldn't understand the arguments to a function or handler, usually because you've used the wrong syntax (bad spelling, improper spacing, you forgot a comma, etc).

Can't understand arguments to command <commandName>

You've used the wrong syntax to enter arguments to a command. Lots of things are included here: spelling errors, failure to include a space where appropriate, using uninitialized variables, and so on. For example, you type add tax to total when either of these variables hasn't been initialized or tax doesn't contain a numeric value; or you try to set the value of a function.

Can't understand arguments to wait.

HyperCard encountered an error in the arguments to the **wait** command. You get this error, for example, if you type wait for the mouseClick instead of wait until the mouseClick.

Can't understand what's after "(".

HyperTalk was in the middle of parsing an expression that included parentheses but did not find a valid expression after the "(". This commonly happens when you forget the closing parenthesis.

Can't understand what's after "-".

HyperTalk was in the middle of parsing an expression that included unary negation ("-") but did not find a valid expression after the "-". This happens, for example, when "-" is followed by a variable name that hasn't been initialized (as in `add -total to newTotal`).

Can't understand what's after "<keyword>".

HyperCard found invalid arguments to or insufficient arguments for a keyword. For example:

```
on blah
  if x -- generates error "Can't understand what's after if"
end blah
```

Can't understand what's after "not."

HyperTalk was in the middle of parsing an expression that included "not" but didn't find a valid expression after the "not."

Can't understand what's after <operator>.

HyperCard succeeded in getting a left side and an operator but could not understand what's on the right side of the operator.

Can't use a reserved word as a variable name.

You tried to use a reserved word as a local, global, or parameter variable name. The following categories comprise the reserved words:

adjectives (long, short, abbrev)
chunk specifiers (char, word, item, line)
constants
keywords
literals (including quoted literals)
operators
ordinals (first...tenth, last, middle, any)
prepositions (before, after, into)
punctuation

Couldn't create file "<fileName>."

The open command couldn't create the named file. This often means that the disk is either full or locked.

Couldn't edit script of that object. Maybe it's been deleted.

You tried to edit the script of an object, but somehow that object is not available. Here's a way to evoke this message:

```
on mouseUp
  select me
  type "x" with commandKey
  edit script of me
end mouseUp
```

This error doesn't come up very often, and usually means you've selected the wrong object.

Couldn't load external command.

HyperCard got an error from the resource manager when trying to load an external command. This error usually means that you ran out of memory for some (usually not apparent) reason.

Couldn't set that field.

HyperCard was unable to put new text into a field. You see this error when the disk is full. (HyperCard stores information in fields to disk.)

Destination does not contain a number.

You tried to use add, subtract, multiply, or divide with a container that didn't contain a number.

Error writing to file "<fileName>."

The write command got an error code back from the file manager while writing to the specified file. This often means that the disk became full during the writing process, or was suddenly turned off.

Expected "(".

HyperCard expected a "(" after a function call but did not find it. However, since recognizing the "(" is the way that HyperCard knows it's dealing with a user function call, this error can never occur. (No kidding. This is really right there, in the code. Honest!)

Expected ")" but found "<whatWasFound>."

HyperTalk was in the middle of parsing an expression that had opened a set of parentheses using "(" but couldn't find a matching ")." *<whatWasFound>* is replaced by what was found; if nothing was found at all — that is, the end of the line was reached — the message is simply: Expected ")".

Expected ")".

HyperTalk was in the middle of parsing an expression that had opened a set of parentheses using "(" but either (1) HyperTalk reached the end of the line without finding a matching ")" or (2) it was in the middle of parsing the arguments to a function called with parentheses and found no closing ")".

Expected "of" but found "<whatWasFound>."

Chunk expressions must be followed by the word "of." Anything else evokes this message.

Expected comma between arguments.

There was no comma between arguments in a handler call, function call, or definition of a handler or function.

Expected end of line after <keyword>.

HyperCard found correct arguments for a keyword, but there were additional characters on the line after the arguments rather than the end of the line.

Expected expression but found "<whatWasFound>."

Any invalid chunk expression evokes this message.

Expected unsigned integer but found "<whatWasFound>."

Chunk expressions must use only expressions that evaluate to nonnegative integers. Any other value evokes this message.

Expression too complicated.

HyperCard has exceeded the number of elements it can hold on its internal expression stack: 128. If you get this message, break the expression up into two parts using a variable for the intermediate result.

External commands and functions cannot have more than 16 parameters.

An external was called with more than 16 parameters.

Failed to sort this stack.

HyperCard completed the sort of the keys but encountered an error when it tried to shuffle the cards into the correct order on the disk. This happens when you're out of memory or when there's a problem with the disk.

Fields can't hold more than 30,000 characters.

You tried to put more than 30,000 characters into a field.

Found "else" without "then."

HyperCard found an else statement without a preceding then statement (and possibly without an if statement).

Found "end if" without "if."

HyperCard found an end if statement outside of a multiple line **if...then** statement.

Found "end repeat" without "repeat."

HyperCard found an end repeat statement outside of a **repeat** statement.

Found "exit repeat" outside a repeat loop.

HyperCard found an **exit repeat** statement outside of a **repeat** statement.

Found "if" without "then."

HyperCard found an **if** statement with no **then** statement.

Found "next repeat" outside a repeat loop.

HyperCard found a **next repeat** statement outside of a **repeat** statement.

Found "then" without "if."

HyperCard found a **then** statement outside of an **if** statement.

Got error <errorNumber> while trying to open file "<fileName>."

The open command got an error code back from the file manager while trying to open the file. At this point, the **open** command has already verified that the file exists (or the open created a new file if the file didn't already exist).

Got file system error <errorNumber>.

The **read** command got an error code back from the file manager while reading from a file, or the **open** or **print** command got an error code back from the file manager while trying to open or print a file.

Need number after "-" but got "<whatWasFound>."

HyperTalk was in the middle of parsing an expression that included unary negation ("-") but didn't find a number after the "-".

Need true or false after "not" but got "<whatWasFound>."

HyperTalk was in the middle of parsing an expression that included "not" but didn't find a logical value after the "not."

Never heard of <part> <how> "<which>."

A reference has been made to a button or field that doesn't exist. Either the button or field was deleted or it never existed. You'll often get this error when your script refers to a button or field in the wrong domain. (For example, your script says card button and you mean background button.)

<part> is {card | bkgnd} [*button* | *field*]
<how> is the word "named," "number," or "id."
<which> is the name, number, or id of the button or field in question.

Never heard of that button or field.

You tried to retrieve a property of a button or field referred to as me or the
target, and that object doesn't exist anymore. The object most probably had
just been deleted:

```
on mouseUp
  select me  type "x" with commandKey
  put name of me
end mouseUp
```

No open file named "<name>."

You tried to use the read, write, or close command on a file that wasn't open.

No such button or field.

You tried to set a property of a button or field refered to as me or the target,
and that object doesn't exist. The object most probably had just been deleted:

```
on mouseUp
  select me
  type "x" with commandKey
  set name of me to "Fred"
end mouseUp
```

No such card.

HyperCard couldn't find the specified card. Usually you get this message when
you send a failed go command from the Message box. (**Go** failures from scripts
are silent, but they set the result function.)

No such stack.

HyperCard could not find the specified stack. HyperCard will always ask the
user if it can't find the stack it needs, so this message means that the user either
canceled or didn't choose a valid stack from the dialog box.

Not a scrolling field.

You tried to get or set the **scroll** property of a button or of a field that was not a scrolling field.

Not enough ends.

HyperCard reached the end of the handler while there was still an open **if** or **repeat** block. You need to add more "end if" or "end repeat" statements, or remove extraneous **if** or **repeat** statements.

Not enough memory to read from file.

The read command couldn't allocate enough memory to read the requested number of bytes. Because the buffer is clipped to 16384, you must have at least this amount of available memory regardless of how much or how little you asked it to read.

This error in effect means you have less than 16K of memory left. Lots of other things stop working when memory gets this low, so it's likely that you'll see some other error message before you get to this point (for example, "Out of memory").

Not enough memory to sort this stack.

HyperCard needs at least eight bytes per card to do a sort. This message means it couldn't get that much memory, even using MultiFinder temporary memory.

Only cards and backgrounds have pictures.

You tried to hide or show the picture of an object that wasn't a card or background.

Only fields, buttons, cards, and backgrounds have numbers.

The number function was passed a type of object that doesn't have a number (that is, either a stack or HyperCard).

Out of memory.

HyperCard didn't have enough memory to do the requested operation. There are dozens of different operations that can give this message if memory is low enough.

Script too silly to process.

HyperTalk looked at a script and determined that it couldn't in good conscience execute what it found, the style of the code being as poor as it was.

Sort by what?

The **sort** command wasn't told what expression to sort by. (See page 346 and Appendix I for information on the **sort** command.)

That property is read only.

You tried to set a read-only property (for example, `set size of this stack to 10000`).

There isn't any selection.

You tried to put something into the Selection at a time when there was no Selection.

Too many nested blocks.

HyperCard has reached its limit of nested blocks across all pending handlers: 128.

Too many pending messages.

HyperCard is has no room to cache a new object in order to send a message to it. This means that there are at least 64 pending handlers running, all from different objects. Because HyperCard gives the "Too much recursion" message before reaching 64 calls deep, this message never appears.

Too many repeats.

HyperCard has exceeded its limit of repeats across all pending handlers: 32.

Too much recursion.

There are too many handler calls pending (not necessarily recursive ones). You can have 54 calls to message handlers, and 18 calls to functions.

Translator failed to indent.

An installed language translator indicated at initialization that it wanted to do custom indenting. But when HyperTalk asked it to indent a script, the translator didn't return a successful result code.

The exact meaning of this message depends on the particular translator and the conditions under which the error occurred.

Translator failed to translate the message box into English.

The installed language translator, when asked to translate the message box into English, didn't return a successful result code.

The exact meaning of this message depends on the particular translator and the conditions under which the error occurred.

Translator failed to translate to English.

The installed language translator, when asked to translate the script into English so that the script editor could write it to the disk, didn't return a successful result code.

The exact meaning of this message depends on the particular translator and the conditions under which the error occurred.

Unexpected end of line.

HyperCard (1) reached the end of the line without getting valid arguments for a handler or function, or (2) couldn't find the end of the handler.

In the first instance, you might have forgotten to add a parameter variable after a comma:

```
on mouseUp
  test blah,blah, -- there's nothing after the comma!
end mouseUp
```

In the second instance, you plumb forgot to close the handler:

```
on mouseUp
-- no end of handler
```

User level is too low to edit scripts.

You tried to use the edit command when the userLevel **property** was set below 5.

Appendix C

Summary of Tables

These tables, taken from various places throughout the book, hold the information that scripters seem to refer to most often. Tables include:

Table C-1: Shortcuts to bring up script editor

Tool	Key press	Action
Browse tool	Command-Option	Displays outline of all visible buttons; click one to see its script.
	Shift-Command-Option	Displays outline of all visible buttons and fields; click one to see its script.
Field tool	Command-Option	Displays outline of all visible and invisible fields; click a visible field to see its script.

Table C-1: Shortcuts to bring up script editor (cont.)

Tool	Key press	Action
Button tool	Command-Option	Displays outline of all visible and invisible buttons; click a visible button to see its script.
Any tool	Command-Option-C	Displays script of current card.
	Command-Option-B	Displays script of current background.
	Command-Option-S	Displays script of current stack.

Table C-2: Shortcuts for editor and debugger operations

Operation	Keypress or Click
Enter line continuation char ¬ (all)	Option-Return
Reformat script (all)	Tab
Select entire line (2.#)	Triple-Click
Undo last edit (2.#)	Command-Z
Cut selected text (all)	Command-X
Copy selected text (all)	Command-C
Paste text (all)	Command-V
Select entire script (all)	Command-A
Print selected/entire script (all)	Command-P
Find text with dialog (all)	Command-F
Find selected text (all)	Command-H
Find again (all)	Command-G
Replace (2.#)	Command-R
Replace again (2.#)	Command-T
Comment selected line(s) (2.#)	Command-minus
Uncomment selected line(s) (2.#)	Command-equals
Set/Clear Checkpoint in editor (2.#)	Command-D or Option-Click on line
Set/Clear Checkpoint in Debugger (2.#)	Command-D
Break into Debugger (2.#)	Command-Option-period

Operation	Keypress or Click
Close editor, keep changes (all)	Enter
Close editor, kill changes (all)	Command-period
Close editor, get changes dialog (1.2.#)	Command-Option-*<any key>*
Close editor, get changes dialog (2.#)	Command-W
Break into Debugger (2.#)	Command-Option-period
Debugger Step (2.#)	Command-S
Debugger Step Into (2.#)	Command-I
Debugger Trace (2.#)	Command-T
Debugger Go (2.#)	Command-G
Debugger Set/Clear Checkpoint (2.#)	Command-D
Exit Debugger, Abort Handler (2.#)	Command-A

Table C-3: Syntactic symbols

Symbol	Meaning
< >	Enclose generic term meant to be substituted by a specific form (that is, enclose nonterminal)
|	Separates mutually exclusive alternatives indicating left-to-right precedence
{ }	Enclose optional elements
[ ]	Enclose group of terms, indicating left-to-right precedence
@	Indicates whether a phrase is expandable (1.2.# only)

Table C-4: Constants

Constant	Value/comment
up	The name *is* the value
	as in: if the shiftKey is up
down	
true	The logical value
false	The name is the value
empty	"" (ASCII 0)
space	" " (ASCII 32)
pi	3.14159265358979323846
zero	0
one	1
two	2
three	3
four	4
five	5
six	6
seven	7
eight	8
nine	9
ten	10
tab	ASCII 9
formfeed	ASCII 12
linefeed	ASCII 10
quote	ASCII 34
return	ASCII 13

Table C-5: Relational operators

Operator	Relationship
is, =	equal to
is not, <>, ≠	not equal to
>	greater than
<	less than
>=, ≥	greater than or equal to
<=, ≤	less than or equal to
contains	presence of
is in	presence of
is not in	absence of

Table C-6: Concatenation operator

Operator	Effect	Result
&	concatenates operands	single string
&&	concatenates operands, adding a space between them	single string

Table C-7: Arithmetic operators

Operator	Operation	Example	Yield
^	exponentiation	13 ^ 3	2197
*	multiplication	13 * 3	39
/	real division	13 / 3	4.333333
div	integer division	13 div 3	4
		-13 div 3	-4
mod	modulo division	13 mod 3	1
		-13 mod 3	-1
+	addition	13 + 3	16
-	subtraction	13 - 3	10

Table C-8: Truth table

Operator	1st operand	2nd operand	Yield
and	true	true	true
	true	false	false
	false	false	false
	false	true	false
or	true	true	true
	true	false	true
	false	false	false
	true	false	true

Table C-9: Operator precedence

Precedence	Operator
9	unary -, not
8	^
7	*, /, mod, div
6	+, -
5	&, &&
4	contains, >=, >, is in, is not in, is within, is not within, <=, <
3	=, <>
2	and
1	or

Table C-10: Default values for painting properties

Property	Default value
brush	8
centered	false
filled	false
grid	false
linesize	1
multiple	false
multispace	1
pattern	12 (black)
polysides	4
textalign	left
textfont	application font (probably Geneva)
textheight	4 * textSize DIV 3 (probably 16)
textsize	system font size (probably 12)
textstyle	plain

Table C-11: Properties reset at Idle time

Property	Value
numberFormat	0.######
dragSpeed	0
lockRecent	false
lockMessages	false
lockScreen	false

Table C-12:   Message order in events that send multiple messages

Event	Version	Message order
Start HyperCard	1.2.#	openStack openBackground openCard startup
	2.#	startup openStack openBackground openCard
Suspend for launch*	All	closeCard closeBackground closeStack suspend
Resume from launch*	1.2.#	openStack openBackground openCard resume
	2.#	resume openStack openBackground openCard
Quit HyperCard	All	closeCard closeBackground closeStack quit
Stack change	All	closeCard closeBackground closeStack openStack openBackground openCard
Background change	All	closeCard closeBackground openBackground openCard
Card change	All	closeCard openCard
New stack	1.2.#	closeCard closeBackground closeStack openStack openBackground openCard newStack
	2.#	closeCard closeBackground closeStack newStack newBackground newCard openStack openBackground openCard
New stack in new window	2.#	suspendStack newStack newBackground newCard openStack openBackground openCard
New background	1.2.#	closeCard closeBackground openBackground openCard newBackground newCard
	2.#	closeCard closeBackground newBackground newCard openBackground openCard
New card	1.2.#	openCard newCard
	2.#	closeCard newCard openCard

Event	Version	Message order
Delete stack	1.2.#	deleteStack closeCard closeBackground closeStack
	2.#	closeCard closeBackground closeStack deleteStack
Delete background	1.2.#	deleteBackground deleteCard
	2.#	closeCard closeBackground deleteCard deleteBackground
Delete card	1.2.#	deleteCard closeCard
	2.0	closeCard {closeBackground}deleteCard {deleteBackground openBackground} openCard
Paste card	1.2.#	openCard
	2.#	{newBackground} newCard {openBackground} openCard
Cut card	1.2.#	(no messages sent)
	2.#	closeCard {closeBackground} deleteCard {deleteBackground openBackground} openCard

* These messages are sent only when MultiFinder is *not* running.

Table C-13: Result strings and their causes

Command	String	Cause
convert	invalid date	bad date format
find	not found	can't find string
go to	no such card	card doesn't exist
	cancel	cancel clicked on dialog asking for stack location
	no such stack	stack chosen from dialog not really a stack (seldom appears)
open application	no such application	application doesn't exist
open printing with dialog	cancel	cancel clicked on printing dialog
print document	no such document	document doesn't exist
print document with application		no such application application doesn't exist

Table C-14: Rounding criteria

Value	Direction	Example
0.5	down	.5 becomes 0
0.51	up	.51 becomes 1
any even value + .5	down	36.5 becomes 36
any even value + .51	up	36.51 becomes 37
any odd value + .5	up	37.5 becomes 38
any value +.4	down	99.4 becomes 99
any value + .6	up	99.6 becomes 100

Appendix D

Boundaries and Limits

This appendix lists HyperTalk's various boundary conditions, size limitations, and the like. These numbers are valid for versions through 1.2.#, and might change in future upgrades.

Maximum number of stacks	limited only by file system
Maximum stack size	512 megabytes (but a bug in versions through 1.2.2 causes stacks above 8 megabytes to become corrupted)
Minimum stack size:	4,896 bytes
Maximum number of cards/ bkgnds/bitmaps per stack	16,777,216
Maximum stack name length	31 characters
Graphics	black and white bitmaps with opaque and transparent areas
Worst case card bitmap size	22K mask + 22K data
Worst case bkgnd bitmap size	22K
Maximum script length	30,000 characters
Maximum number of buttons & fields per card or bkgnd	32,767 (but bug in versions through 1.2.1 allows only 127 fields/card; fixed in 1.2.2)
Maximum characters per field	29,996 characters
Maximum card/bknd/button/ field name length	255 characters (but bug in versions through 1.2.# allows only 29)
Minimum card/bkgnd size	64 bytes
Minimum button/field overhead	30 bytes
Maximum number of variables	unlimited
Maximum variable value size	available memory

Maximum file i/o buffer size	16,384 bytes
Maximum number of nested repeats	32
Maximum variable name length	31 characterss
Maximum numberFormat length	31 characters
Maximum handler name length	254 characters
Standard card pixel size	512 horizontal, 342 vertical
	(exact size of original Macintosh screen)

Appendix E

Quick Dictionary

The Quick Dictionary provides a summary definition of every HyperTalk native vocabulary word, plus a reference to the page where you can find more detailed information (if more detailed information exists). For the definitions of HyperTalk conceptual terms, see the Glossary.

& is the concatenation operator; it joins two strings into one. (page 113)

&& is the modified concatenation operator; it joins two strings into one with a space in between them. (page 113)

* is the multiplication operator. (page 114)

+ is the addition operator. (page 114)

- is the subtraction operator. (page 114)

/ is the division operator. (page 114)

< is the relational operator for "less than." (page 112)

<= is the relational operator for "less than or equal to." (page 112)

<> is the relational operator for "not equal to." (page 112)

= is the relational operator for "equal to." (page 112)

> is the relational operator for "greater than." (page 112)

>= is the relational operator for "greater than or equal to." (page 112)

^ is the exponentiation operator. (page 114)

≠ is the relational operator for "not equal to" (with the same effect as <>). (page 112)

≤ is the relational operator for "less than or equal to" (with the same effect as <=). (page 112)

≥ is the relational operator for "greater than or equal to" (with the same effect as >=). (page 112)

¬ is the line-continuation character. (page 48)

Abbreviated (or **abbr** or **abbrev**) is an adjective that affects the way certain functions and properties (including date, time, name, and ID) report their values.

Abs function returns the value of its numeric argument without regard to sign. (page 377)

Add command adds the value of a numeric expression to the value of any container, leaving the result in the container. (page 161)

After is a preposition used to insert text at a specific point in a string or to position the insertion point in the message box or in a field. (page 309)

And operator combines two logical values to produce a logical result: if both operands are true, the result is true; otherwise the result is false. (page 114)

Annuity function returns the present value of an ordinary annuity with payments of one unit, given the interest rate per period and the number of periods. (page 379)

Answer command displays a dialog box with a one-line question and up to three reply buttons. (page 163)

Answer file command brings up the Macintosh's Standard GetFile dialog so that you can select the name of a file. Optionally, the script can specify a filter so only the names of files of a particular type (applications, stacks, textfiles, etc.) are displayed. (page 167)

Arrow is one of the values for the **cursor** property. (page 518)

ArrowKey as a command simulates the action of the arrow keys. It's also the system message that HyperCard sends when a user presses one of the arrow keys. (page 171)

Ascending is one of two orders (the other being **descending**) for sorting cards in a stack. (page 346)

Ask command puts up a dialog box with a one-line question at the top, an optional preset answer selected in a typeable text window, and two buttons — one labeled "Cancel" and one labeled "OK". (page 174)

Ask file command brings up the Macintosh's PutFile dialog (the one that lets you name a file) with an optional string prompt. You can also specify a default name to go in the editable PutFile field. (page 178)

Atan function returns the arctangent of its argument. (page 380)

AutoHilite property reflects whether a button's hilite changes each time you click at that button's location. (page 490)

AutoTab property reflects whether pressing Return when the insertion point is in the last line of a nonscrolling field selects the text of the next field in the Tabbing order. (page 494)

Average function returns the average of its arguments. (page 382)

Back, most usually used with the **go** and **push** commands, refers to the card that was most recently added to HyperCard's Recent list before the current one. Same as **recent card.** (page 258)

Background as a noun designates one of HyperTalk's objects. As an adjective it designates the owner of a button or field.

Barn door close is one of the visual effects used with the **visual** and **unlock screen with visual effect** commands. (page 367)

Barn door open is one of the visual effects used with the **visual** and **unlock screen with visual effect** commands. (page 367)

Beep command sends a tone to the Macintosh's speaker, or to the sound output port if something is plugged into it. (page 181)

Before is a preposition used to insert text at a specific point in a string or to position the insertion point in the message box or in a field. (page 309)

Bg is a synonym for **background** (*which see*).

Bkgnd is a synonym for **background** (*which see*).

Black is one of the optional images that covers an entire card when a visual effect finishes but before a card reappears. (page 368)

BlindTyping property reflects whether you can type into the Message box while it's hidden. (page 496)

Bold is one of the values for the style of text. (page 632)

Bottom property gives the location of the bottom of a button, field, or window. (page 497)

BottomRight or **BotRight** property gives the coordinates for the bottom-right corner of a button, field, or window. (page 499)

Box see **Message**

Browse is the name of one of the tools, chosen with the **choose** command or returned by the **Tool** function. (page 184)

Brush as a property reflects the current shape of the brush tool. (page 502)

Brush is the name of one of the tools, chosen with the choose command or returned by the **Tool** function. (page 184)

Btn is a synonym for **Button** (*which see*).

Bucket is the name of one of the tools, chosen with the **choose** command or returned by the Tool function. (page 184)

Busy is one of the values for the **cursor** property. (page 518)

Button designates one of HyperCard's objects. (page 84) It's also the name of one of the tools, chosen with the **choose** command (page 183) or returned by the **Tool** function. (page 184)

CantAbort property determines whether pressing Command-period aborts the action of a running script. (page 504)

CantDelete property reflects whether a particular background, card, or stack can be deleted. (page 506)

CantModify property tells whether a particular stack can be changed. (page 508)

CantPeek property determines whether you can see buttons and fields by pressing Command-option and Command-shift-option, and whether you can open the scripts of buttons and fields by using Command-option-click and Command-shift-option-click. (page 511)

Card (or **cd**) as a noun designates one of HyperTalk's objects. As an adjective it designates the owner of a button or field. (page 81)

Card is one of the optional images that covers an entire card when a visual effect is over but before a card reappears. (page 368)

Center is one of the values for the alignment of text in a field or a button. (page 622)

Centered property reflects whether certain tools subsequently draw from the center (true) or from the edge (false). (page 512)

Character (or **char**) is the smallest element of a chunk expression. (page 103)

Chars is a modifier used with the **Find** command allowing a match for the search string anywhere in the destination. (page 246)

CharToNum function returns the ASCII value of the first character of its argument's value. (page 385)

CheckBox is one of the values for the style of a button. (page 617)

Checkerboard is one of the visual effects used with the **visual** and **unlock screen with visual effect** commands. (pages 367, 363)

CheckMark property determines whether a checkmark (✔) appears to the left of a menu item. (page 514)

Choose command selects a tool as if you had clicked it on the Tools menu. (page 183)

Click command programmatically clicks the mouse at a specific location, optionally "holding down" the shift, option, and/or command key(s). (page 186)

ClickChunk function returns the positions of the starting and ending characters of the word or group most recently clicked in a locked field. (page 387)

ClickH function returns the distance between the left edge of the card window and the horizontal location of the most recent mouse click. (page 389)

ClickLine function identifies the line most recently clicked in a locked field. (page 391)

ClickLoc function returns the location of the most recent mouse click. (page 393)

ClickText function returns the word or group of characters most recently clicked in a locked field. (page 395)

ClickV function returns the distance between the top of the card window and the vertical location of the most recent mouse click. (page 397)

Close file command closes the file(s) previously opened with the **Open File** command. (page 190)

Close printing command flushes the printing buffer and brings the current print job (opened with the open printing command) to an orderly conclusion. (page 193)

CloseBackground is the system message that HyperCard sends when one of the arrow keys has just been pressed, or the **arrowKey** command was sent. (page 664)

CloseCard is the system message that HyperCard sends when you leave a card because of a **go** command, **Quit HyperCard** menu choice, or because a stack was deleted. (page 663)

CloseField is the system message that HyperCard sends when the selection (including the insertion point) has been removed from an open field, *and* some text has been changed in that field. (page 661)

CloseStack is the system message that HyperCard sends when a stack closes because a **go** command changed stacks, because a stack was deleted, or because you quit HyperCard. (page 665)

CmdChar is a synonym for the **commandChar** property (*which see*).

CommandChar property determines what command character (if any) you can press from the keyboard to execute a specific menu command. (page 516)

CommandKey function returns the state of the command key (up or down). (page 398)

Compound function returns the principal plus accrued interest on an investment of one unit, given the interest rate and number of periods. (page 399)

Condense is one of the values for the style of text. (page 632)

Contains is the relational operator testing whether the string operand to its left contains the string operand to its right. (page 112)

Controlkey as a command simulates pressing the control key in combination with some other key. (page 195) It's also the system message that HyperCard sends when the control key and some other key have just been pressed.

Convert command converts a date and/or time to one or more formats, usually to do calculations or to construct special displays. (page 199)

Cos function returns the cosine of its argument. (page 400)

Create menu command adds new menus to the menu bar. (page 202)

Create stack command creates a new stack without presenting a dialog, optionally using any background of the current stack. (page 204)

Cross is one of the values for the **cursor** property. (page 518)

Curve is the name of one of the tools, chosen with the **choose** command or returned by the **Tool** function. (page 184)

Cut is one of the visual effects used with the **visual** and **unlock screen with visual effect** commands. (pages 367, 363)

Date function returns the current date. (page 403)

DateItems is one of the formats used with the **convert** command. (page 200)

DateTime is a modifier used with the **sort** command to sort the cards in a stack by date and/or time. (page 347)

Debug command (1) modifies the **Compact Stack** menu command such that the user can modify the effectiveness and efficiency of the **find** command by changing the way that HyperCard stores compressed information about the textual content of cards; (2) makes HyperCard use QuickDraw instead of its own drawing routines when it moves graphical information from an internal buffer onto the screen in order to overcome problems sometimes associated with third party monitors; and (3) temporarily halts execution of the handler containing this command and enters the Debugger with this command boxed. (page 206)

Delete command removes one or more characters, words, items, or lines from a specific container. (page 212)

Delete menu command removes an entire menu, or a single menu item, from the menu bar. (page 215)

DeleteBackground is the system message that HyperCard sends when a background is about to be deleted. (page 664)

DeleteButton is the system message that HyperCard sends when a button is about to be deleted. (page 659)

DeleteCard is the system message that HyperCard sends when a card is about to be deleted. (page 663)

DeleteField is the system message that HyperCard sends when a field is about to be deleted. (page 661)

DeleteStack is the system message that HyperCard sends when a stack is about to be deleted. (page 665)

Descending is one of two orders (the other being **ascending**) for sorting cards in a stack. (page 346)

Dial command generates telephone tones through the Macintosh speaker or sends such tones to the modem serial port. (page 218)

Disable command disables a menu or a menu item, preventing a user from working with it. (page 223)

Diskspace function returns the space in bytes remaining on the current volume. (page 405)

Dissolve is one of the visual effects used with the **visual** and **unlock screen with visual effect** commands. (pages 367, 363)

Div operator divides the operand to its right into the operand to its left and returns an integer result. (page 114)

Divide command divides the contents of a container by the value of a numeric expression, leaving the result in the container. (page 227)

Do keyword executes any expression as one or more HyperCard statements. (page 120)

DoMenu command executes a command from a HyperCard menu as if you had chosen the command with the mouse. (page 229)

DontSearch property determines whether the **find** command searches in a given field, card, or background. (page 521)

DontWrap property determines whether the text in a given field wraps at that field's right edge, or if it trails off out of sight. (page 523)

Down is a constant, as in "if the shiftkey is down...". (page 92)

Drag command programmatically drags the mouse between locations, optionally "holding down" the shiftkey, optionkey, and/or commandkey(s) as the dragging happens. (page 233)

DragSpeed property reflects the rate, in pixels per second (approximately), that the pointer moves in response to the drag command. (page 526)

Edit command opens the script of an object for editing in a script editor window. (page 235)

EditBkgnd property reflects where editing takes place. (page 528)

Eight is the constant for the value 8. (page 92)

Eighth is a HyperTalk ordinal. (page 64)

Empty is the constant for the null string. (page 92)

Enable command enables a menu or a menu item, allowing a user to work with it. (page 238)

Enabled property determines whether you can choose a particular menu item, or any item in a given menu. (page 530)

End keyword starts the final line of every multiline structure. (page 122)

EnterInField as a command simulates pressing the Enter key when the insertion point or other selection is within a field. (page 240) It's also the system message that HyperCard sends when the Enter key has been pressed while a selection exists in a field. (page 661)

EnterKey as a command, when a field contains the insertion point or other selection and a change has been made to text in the field, closes the field and sends the closeField message to the field; when the insertion point is anywhere except in a field, it evaluates the contents of the Message box and, if it's an expression, shows the results, or if it's not an expression sends the contents to the current card. (Whew.) (page 242) It's also the system message that HyperCard sends when the enter key has been pressed with no selection in a field — not even the insertion point. (page 658)

Eraser is the name of one of the tools, chosen with the **choose** command or returned by the Tool function. (page 184)

Exit keyword immediately transfers flow of control out of the current handler or repeat structure. (page 123)

ExitField is the message that HyperCard sends when the insertion point is removed from an open field *and the text in that field has not changed.* Compare to **closeField** (*which see*). (page 661)

Exp function returns the natural exponential of its argument. (page 406)

Exp1 function returns the natural exponential of 1 less than its argument. (page 407)

Exp2 function returns the value 2 raised to the power of its argument. (page 408)

Export paint command stores a copy of the current card or background picture to disk under the name you provide. (page 243)

Extend is one of the values for the style of text. (page 632)

False is a constant, as in "set *property* to false." (page 92)

Fast is a speed at which a visual effect occurs. (page 367)

Field designates the only HyperTalk object that is also a container. (page 94) It's also the name of one of the tools, chosen with the **choose** command (page 183) or returned by the **Tool** function. (page 184)

Fifth is a HyperTalk ordinal. (page 64)

Filled property reflects whether shape-painting tools draw hollow shapes (false) or shapes filled with the current pattern (true). (page 532)

Find command searches fields for a match to a specific string. (page 246)

First is a HyperTalk ordinal. (page 64)

Five is the constant for the value 5. (page 92)

FixedLineHeight property reflects whether HyperCard automatically adjusts the spacing above and below lines of text of different sizes (that is, adjusts the leading) in a given field. (page 535)

Flash command (actually an external command) inverts the screen image several times, attracting the user's attention. (page 253)

Formfeed is the constant for the formfeed character (ASCII 12). (page 92)

Forth refers to the card that was added to HyperCard's Recent list after the current one. (page 258)

FoundChunk function returns the starting and ending positions of the chunk of text located by the most recent Find command. (page 409)

FoundField function returns the name of the field in which text was located by the most recent Find command. (page 411)

FoundLine function identifies the line in which text was located by the most recent Find command. (page 413)

FoundText function returns the text located by the most recent Find command. (page 415)

Four is the constant for the value 4. (page 92)

Fourth is a HyperCard ordinal. (page 64)

FreeSize property tells how many unused bytes are locked within a stack. (page 536)

Function keyword begins a handler that defines a function. (page 128)

FunctionKey as a command simulates pressing one of the 15 function keys on the Macintosh Extended keyboard. (page 254) It's also the system message that HyperCard sends when one of the function keys on the Apple Extended Keyboard has been pressed. (page 658)

Get command puts the value of any source or expression into the variable It. (page 256)

Global keyword creates one or more global variables, or imports values for existing ones. (page 132)

Go command brings you to a specific card or stack. (page 258)

Gray (or **grey**) is one of the optional images that covers an entire card at the end of a visual effect before a card reappears. (page 368)

Grid property, when true, constrains the movements of selected bitmaps and many painting tools to increments of 8 pixels (about 1/9th of an inch). (page 538)

Group is a value for the style of a chunk of text in a field, letting you treat any contiguous run of characters as a single unit. (page 633)

Hand is one of the values for the **cursor** property. (page 518)

HeapSpace function returns the maximum contiguous amount of space in bytes that would be available if all purgeable handles were purged and all relocatable handles were relocated. (page 417)

Height property gives the distance in pixels between the top and bottom of a button, field, or window. (page 539)

Help command brings you to the first card of the Help stack (assuming the message `help` isn't caught and redirected). (page 262)

Hide command hides a card, button, field, picture, window, or menuBar. (page 264)

Hide menuBar is the system message that HyperCard sends when somebody presses command-spacebar with the menubar showing. (page 666)

Hilite property reflects whether a button appears normal (false) or hilited (true) under a variety of conditions. (page 543)

Ibeam is one of the values for the **cursor** property. (page 518)

Icon reflects what icon (if any) HyperCard uses as the graphic for a particular button. (page 546)

ID property gives the unique identification number of a particular button, field, card, or background. (page 548)

Idle is the system message that HyperCard sends when no handler is running, when no action has been initiated through the Message box, and when the mouse isn't being manipulated. (page 666)

If...then...else keywords define conditional structure(s). (page 135)

Import paint command retrieves a copy of the paint document stored in the file whose name you provide, and pastes it onto the current card or background. (page 267)

In, see **is in**

International is a modifier used with the **sort** command to sort the cards in a stack by an international alphabet. (page 346)

Into is a preposition used to replace text in a container. (page 309)

Inverse is one of the optional images that covers an entire card at the end of a visual effect before a card reappears. (page 368)

Iris close is one of the visual effects used with the **visual** and **unlock screen with visual effect** commands. (page 367)

Iris open is one of the visual effects used with the **visual** and **unlock screen with visual effect** commands. (page 367)

Is in operator checks if the string on its left is a substring of the string on its right. (page 112)

Is not in operator checks if the string on its left is not a substring of the string on its right. (page 112)

Is not within operator checks if the point described on its left does not lie within the rectangle described on its right. (page 116)

Is within operator checks if the point described on its left lies within the rectangle described on its right. (page 116)

It is the local variable created by **get, answer, ask, read,** and (sometimes) **convert.** (page 97)

Italic is one of the values for the style of text. (page 632)

Item is the chunk of a source of value separated by commas. (page 104)

Language property reflects the language in which you read and write scripts. (page 550)

Lasso is the name of one of the tools, chosen with the **choose** command or returned by the **Tool** function. (page 484)

Last is a HyperTalk ordinal. (page 64)

Left property tells how far a window is from the left edge of the display that holds HyperCard's title bar, or how far the left edge of a button or field is from the left edge of the card. (page 552) It's also one of the values for the alignment of text in a field or a button. (page 622)

Length function returns the number of characters in the string value of its argument. (page 419)

Line is the chunk of a source of value terminated by a return character. (page 104) It's also the name of one of the tools, chosen with the **choose** command (page 183) or returned by the **Tool** function. (page 484)

Linefeed is the constant for the linefeed character (ASCII 10). (page 92)

LineSize property reflects the thickness of borders and lines drawn with painting tools. (page 554)

Ln function returns the natural logarithm of the value of its argument. (page 421)

Ln1 function returns the natural logarithm of the sum of 1 plus the value of its argument. (page 422)

Location (or **loc**) property reflects the location of a window relative to the upper-left corner of the display that holds HyperCard's title bar, or the location of the center of a button or field relative to the upper-left corner of the card. (page 556)

Lock screen command keeps the current image on the display until HyperTalk executes a corresponding **unlock screen** (or **set lockScreen to false**) command, or until idle time. (page 270)

LockMessages property reflects whether HyperCard automatically sends certain system messages to the HyperCard community of objects. (page 558)

LockRecent property reflects whether the images of newly encountered cards are added to the Recent display. (page 560)

LockScreen property reflects whether changes to the visual interface take place on the display. (page 562)

LockText property reflects whether the user can edit text in a field. (page 564)

log2 function returns the base 2 logarithm of its argument. (page 423)

Long is an adjective that affects the way certain functions and properties (including date, time, name, and ID) report their values.

Mark command marks the card or cards you specify for some later action (usually display, printing, or filtering). (page 273)

MarkChar property determines what character (if any) appears to the left of a specific menu item. (page 566)

Marked property determines whether a card is noted for some possible later action (usually printing, display, or filtering). (page 567)

Max function returns the highest numeric value in a comma-separated list. (page 424)

Me is the object containing the currently running handler. (page 84)

MenuMessage property determines what message, if any, is sent when you choose a particular menu item. (page 568)

MenuMsg is a synonym for the **menuMessage** property (*which see*).

Menus function returns a return-separated list of the menu names currently visible on the menu bar. (page 426)

Message (also called the **Message box** or **Msg**) is the single-line HyperTalk container most readily available for sending messages to the current card. (page 102)

MessageWatcher property reflects the name of the current message watcher XCMD, HyperCard's facility for tracking messages. (page 571)

Middle (or **mid**) is a HyperTalk ordinal refering to the middle element of a series. (page 64)

Min function returns the lowest numeric value in a comma-separated list (page 429)

Mod is the arithmetic operator that divides the operand on its right into the operand on its left, returning the remainder. (page 114)

Mouse function returns the state of the mouse button (up or down). (page 430)

MouseClick function returns true or false, depending on whether the mouse has been clicked. (page 431)

MouseDown is the system message that HyperCard sends when the mouse button has just been pressed. (pages 655, 656)

MouseEnter is the system message that HyperCard sends when the pointer has just moved over a button or field. (pages 655, 656)

MouseH function returns the distance between the left edge of the card window and the current location of the pointer. (page 433)

MouseLeave is the system message that HyperCard sends when the pointer has just moved out of a button or field. (page 656)

MouseLoc function returns the current location of the pointer. (page 435)

MouseStillDown is the system message that HyperCard sends when the mouse button is being held down. (pages 655, 656)

MouseUp is the system message that HyperCard sends when the mouse button has just been released. (page 656)

MouseV function returns the distance between the top edge of the card window and the current location of the pointer. (page 437)

MouseWithin is the system message that HyperCard sends when the pointer is over a button or field. (pages 655, 656)

Msg is a synonym for **Message** (*which see*).

Multiple property reflects whether certain painting tools produce multiple images (true) or single images (false). (page 572)

Multiply command multiplies the contents of a container by the value of a numeric expression, leaving the result in the container. (page 275)

MultiSpace property determines the space between images subsequently drawn in a single sweep with certain tools when the multiple property is set to true. (page 574)

Name property reflects the name of a specific object, menu, or menu item. (page 576)

NewBackground is the system message that HyperCard sends when a background has just been created. (page 664)

NewButton is the system message that HyperCard sends when a button has just been created. (page 659)

NewCard is the system message that HyperCard sends when a card has just been created. (page 663)

NewField is the system message that HyperCard sends when a field has just been created. (page 661)

NewStack is the system message that HyperCard sends when a stack has just been created. (page 665)

Next (or **next card**) refers to the next card in the current stack. (page 81)

Next background refers to the next background in the current stack. (page 80)

Next repeat keyword terminates the current execution of a repeat loop and sends control to the **repeat** statement at the top of the loop. (page 140)

Nine is the constant for the value 9. (page 92)

Ninth is a HyperTalk ordinal. (page 64)

None is one of the values for the **cursor** property. (page 518)

Normal is a modifier used with the **Find** command restricting the search to the start of words. (page 246)

Not is the logical negation operator; it negates the factor following it. Also see **is not in, is not within.** (page 115)

Number function returns how many of a given element are in its domain (as in `number of cards in this background`), or the number of a specific element (as in `number of this card`). (page 438)

NumberFormat property determines how HyperCard shows the results of numeric calculations in display areas. (page 585)

Numeric is a modifier used with the **sort** command to sort a stack in numeric order. (page 346)

NumToChar function returns an ASCII character, given a numeric value. (page 440)

Offset function returns an integer representing the number of characters from the start of a string to the first character of a pattern within that string. (page 442)

On keyword begins all message handlers. It immediately precedes the name of the message to which the handler responds. (page 142)

One is the constant for the value 1. (page 92)

Opaque is one of the values for the style of a button or field. (page 617)

Open application command opens an application, optionally with a particular document. (page 277)

Open file command opens the data fork of any file for use with the **read** and **write** commands. (page 280)

Open printing command starts the process of buffering cards for printing. (page 283)

OpenBackground is the system message that HyperCard sends when the card that just opened (including the card that's created when a new background is created) has a different background from the card that just closed. (page 664)

OpenCard is the system message that HyperCard sends when a card becomes current because of a **go** command, the card itself was just created, a background has just been created (thus creating a new card), or the system has just started. If MultiFinder is off, you get this message (among others) when execution of HyperCard has been resumed after an **open** *application* operation. (page 663)

OpenField is the system message that HyperCard sends when you or a command (e.g., **click**) clicks in an unlocked field, or the insertion point moves to that field from the previous field in the tabbing order because somebody pressed the tab key, a **tabKey** command was executed, a **select text** or **select** *<chunk>* command executed, or an autoTab happened. (page 661)

OpenStack is the system message that HyperCard sends when a stack opened because HyperCard just started, because a new stack was just created, or because a **go** command changed stacks. (page 665)

OptionKey function returns the state of the option key (up or down). (page 444)

Or combines two logical values to produce a logical result: if either operand is true, the result is true; otherwise the result is false. (page 115)

Outline is one of the values for the style of text. (page 632)

Oval is the name of one of the tools, chosen with the **choose** command or returned by the **Tool** function. (page 484)

Palette navigator command (actually an external command) brings up the navigation palette. (page 286)

Param function returns the value of a specific parameter, chosen from those passed to the current handler. (page 445)

ParamCount function returns the number of values in the parameter list passed to the current handler. (page 447)

Params function returns the entire list of parameters passed to the current handler. (page 449)

Pass keyword immediately transfers flow of control out of the current handler and passes the message that initiated the current handler along the inheritance path. (page 145)

Pattern property reflects the current pattern that painting tools use. (page 588)

Pencil is the name of one of the tools, chosen with the **choose** command or returned by the **Tool** function. (page 484)

Pi is the constant for the value 3.14159265358979323846. (page 92)

Picture command (actually an XCMD) displays a black and white or color PICT or MacPaint image up to 32-bits deep in its own window. (page 288)

Plain is one of the values for the style of text. (page 632) It's also one of the visual effects used with the **visual** (page 367) and **unlock screen with visual effect** commands. (page 363)

Play command sends one or a series of digitized sounds to the Macintosh speaker (or to the sound port if anything if plugged into it), or terminates playing sound(s). (page 292)

Plus is one of the values for the **cursor** property. (page 518)

Polygon is the name of one of the tools, chosen with the **choose** command or returned by the Tool function. (page 484)

PolySides property reflects the number of sides on an image that the Regular Polygon tool produces. (page 591)

Pop card command retrieves the long ID of the card most recently stored with the **push** command and, in the absence of a container to hold the ID, goes immediately to that card. (page 297)

PowerKeys property reflects whether the user can perform common painting actions from the keyboard that ordinarily must be done through menu choices. (page 592)

Prev (or prev card) refers to the previous card in the current stack. (page 81)

Prev background refers to the previous background in the current stack. (page 80)

Print command prints the contents of any field or container, or the value of any expression. (page 299)

Print card command buffers cards for printing if **open printing** is in effect, or immediately prints designated card(s) if **open printing** is not in effect. (page 302)

Print document command prints any document using the application that you specify. (page 304)

Push card command stores the long ID of a card on the top of a last-in first-out list maintained automatically by HyperTalk for later retrieval with the **pop card** command. (page 307)

Put command puts a copy of a source into any container. (page 309)

Put into menu command adds menu items (and, optionally, associated messages) to menus. (page 312)

Quit is the system message that HyperCard sends when it is about to quit. (page 666)

Quote is the constant for the double-quote character (ASCII 34). (page 92)

RadioButton is one of the values for the style of a button. (page 617)

Random function returns a random integer in the range 1 through the value of its argument (or 1 through 32768, whichever is lower). (page 452)

Read command retrieves bytes from the data fork of any file and places it into the variable It. (page 318)

Recent card, most usually used with the **go** and **push** commands, refers to the card that was most lately added to HyperCard's Recent list before the current one. Same as **Back**. (page 258)

Rectangle (or **rect**) property gives the coordinates of all four corners of a button, field, or window. (page 593) The form **rectangle** is also one of the values for the style of a button or field (page 617), as well as the name of one of the tools, chosen with the **choose** command (page 184) or returned by the **Tool** function. (page 484)

Regular polygon is the name of one of the tools, chosen with the **choose** command or returned by the Tool function. (page 484)

Repeat keyword begins a structure that repeats execution of the statements in a list until some condition is met or until an **exit, pass,** or **return** statement executes. How many times the statements are executed depends upon the form of **repeat** used. (page 147)

Reset menuBar — restores HyperCard's standard menu bar as appropriate to the current setting of the **userLevel** property. (page 322)

Reset paint command restores all paint properties to their default values. (page 323)

Result function either indicates the success of the most recently executed command, or holds the value just sent by the **return** keyword in a message handler. (page 454)

Resume is the system message that HyperCard sends when HyperCard has just resumed operation after an application launched by the **open** *application* command has quit. This message is only sent when MultiFinder is turned off. (page 666)

ResumeStack is the system message that HyperCard sends when a previously suspended stack has become active. (page 666)

Return keyword assigns a value to a defined function when **return** appears in a function handler, or assigns a value to the function **the result** when **return** appears in a message handler. (page 151) It's also the constant for the return character (ASCII 13).

ReturnInField is the message the current field gets when the Return key is pressed in a field that contains the insertion point or other selection. (page 661)

ReturnKey command, when a field contains the insertion point or other selection, adds a carriage return to the field at the insertion point and sends the returnInField message to the current field; when the insertion point is anywhere except in a field, it sends the contents of the Message box to the current card. (page 328) It's also the system message that HyperCard sends when the Return key has been pressed with no selection in a field— not even an insertion point. (page 658)

Right as a property tells how far a window or button or field is from the left edge of the card. (page 597) It's also one of the values for the alignment of text in a field or a button. (page 622)

Round function returns its argument rounded off to the nearest integer. (page 456)

Round Rectangle is the name of one of the tools, chosen with the choose command or returned by the Tool function. (page 484)

RoundRect is one of the values for the style of a button. (page 617)

Save as command saves a copy of a stack under the name you provide. (page 329)

ScreenRect function returns the bounding rectangle of the display that holds HyperCard's title bar. (page 458)

Script property reflects the contents of an object's script. (page 599)

ScriptEditor property determines the XCMD being used as the current script editor. (page 602)

Scroll down is one of the visual effects used with the **visual** and **unlock screen with visual effect** commands. (page 367)

Scroll left is one of the visual effects used with the **visual** and **unlock screen with visual effect** commands. (page 367)

Scroll property reflects the number of pixels that have scrolled off the top of a scrolling field or the horizontal and vertical scroll of the card within the card window. (page 603)

Scroll right is one of the visual effects used with the **visual** and **unlock screen with visual effect** commands. (page 367)

Scroll up is one of the visual effects used with the **visual** and **unlock screen with visual effect** commands. (page 367)

Scrolling is one of the values for the style of a field. (page 617)

Second is a HyperTalk ordinal. (page 64)

Seconds returns the number of seconds since midnight, January 1, 1904. (page 459)

Select as a command selects the specified text or object. (page 331) It's also the name of one of the tools, chosen with the **choose** command or returned by the **Tool** function. (page 484)

SelectedChunk function returns the positions of the starting and ending characters of the selected text. (page 461)

SelectedField function returns the name of the field that holds the selection. (page 463)

SelectedLine function identifies the line that holds the selection. (page 465)

SelectedText function returns the selected text. (page 467)

Selection is the HyperTalk container defined as the currently selected text or the insertion point. (page 101)

Send keyword sends a message and any accompanying parameters directly to the named object without traversing HyperCard's normal message passing path to get to that object. If you don't name an object, the message goes to the object containing the currently running script. (page 155)

Set command changes the state or value of a property of an object, window, menu, menu item, or chunk of text. (page 336)

Seven is the constant for the value 7. (page 92)

Seventh is a HyperTalk ordinal. (page 64)

Shadow is one of the values for the style of a button or field (page 617) and for the style of text. (page 632)

SharedHilite property determines whether a background button, highlighted on one card of a given background, is highlighted on every card of that background. (page 607)

SharedText property reflects whether text typed into a background field appears on all cards in that background. (page 608)

ShiftKey function returns the state of the shift key (up or down). (page 469)

Short is an adjective that affects the way certain functions and properties (including date, time, name, and ID) report their values.

Show cards command shows a series of cards from the current stack in rapid succession, beginning with the card after the current one. (page 342)

Show command shows a hidden button, field, picture, window, or menubar. (page 339)

Show menuBar is the system message that HyperCard sends when somebody presses command-spacebar with the menubar hidden, or the **show menuBar** command executes. (page 666)

Show picture command shows a hidden picture. (page 344)

ShowLines property reflects whether dotted lines marking baselines for typing are visible in a field. (page 610)

ShowName property reflects whether a button's name appears in the button. (page 611)

ShowPict property reflects whether the picture of a specific card or background is visible. (page 613)

Shrink to bottom is one of the visual effects used with the **visual** and the **unlock screen with visual effect** commands. (pages 367, 363)

Shrink to center is one of the visual effects used with the **visual** and the **unlock screen with visual effect** commands. (pages 367, 363)

Shrink to top is one of the visual effects used with the **visual** and the **unlock screen with visual effect** commands. (pages 367, 363)

Sin function returns the sin of the angle given as its argument. (page 470)

Six is the constant for the value 6. (page 92)

Sixth is a HyperTalk ordinal. (page 64)

Size property reflects the size of a specific stack in bytes. (page 614)

Slow (or **slowly**) is a speed at which a visual effect occurs. (page 367)

Sort command sorts the cards in the current unlocked stack. (page 346)

Sound function returns the name or resource ID of the playing sound, or, if no sound is playing, the literal "done." (page 472)

Space is the constant for the space character (ASCII 32), created when you press the spacebar. (page 92)

Spray can is the name of one of the tools, chosen with the **choose** command or returned by the **Tool** function. (page 484)

Sqrt function returns the square root of its positive argument. (page 474)

Stack designates one of HyperTalk's objects. (page 78)

StacksInUse property reflects what stacks (if any) have been added to the message passing path. (page 615)

StackSpace function reflects the amount of space left on the memory stack (as opposed to any HyperCard stack) inside the Macintosh. (page 475)

Start using command adds stacks to the message passing path just before the Home stack. (page 351)

StartUp is the system message that HyperCard sends when the HyperCard application opens. (page 666)

Stop using command removes a stack previously added to the message passing path by the **start using** command. (page 354)

Stretch from bottom is one of the visual effects used with the **visual** and the **unlock screen with visual effect** commands. (pages 363, 367)

Stretch from center is one of the visual effects used with the **visual** and the **unlock screen with visual effect** commands. (pages 363, 367)

Stretch from top is one of the visual effects used with the **visual** and the **unlock screen with visual effect** commands. (pages 363, 367)

String is a modifier used with the **Find** command restricting the search to a contiguous group of characters, including embedded spaces. (page 247)

Style property reflects the style of a specific button: transparent, opaque, rectangle, shadow, roundRect, checkBox, or radioButton. It also reflects the style of a specific field: transparent, opaque, rectangle, shadow, or scrolling. (page 617)

Subtract command subtracts the value of a numeric expression from any container, leaving the result in the container. (page 356)

Suspend is the system message that HyperCard sends when HyperCard is in the process of executing an **open** *application* command, and is about to suspend operation so that *application* can run. This message is sent only when MultiFinder is turned off. (page 666)

Suspended property returns true when HyperCard is running in the background (while some other application is running in the foreground), and false when HyperCard is running in the foreground. (page 620)

SuspendStack is the system message that HyperCard sends when another stack opens in a new window, or when somebody clicks in the window of another stack already on the screen. (page 666)

Tab is the constant for the tab character (ASCII 9). (page 92)

Tabkey as a command simulates pressing the Tab key. (page 358) It's also the system message that HyperCard sends when the tab key was just pressed, or an autoTab action was initiated. (page 658)

Tan function returns the tangent of its argument. (page 477)

Target function returns either the name of the object first receiving a message, or if that object is a field (depending on the syntax of target), the field's contents. (page 478)

Ten is the constant for the value 10. (page 92)

Tenth is a HyperTalk ordinal. (page 64)

Text is a modifier used with the **sort** command to sort the cards in a stack by ASCII ordering. (page 346) It's also the name of one of the tools, chosen with the **choose** command (page 184) or returned by the **Tool** function. (page 484)

TextAlign property reflects the alignment of text around a starting point as text is created. (page 622)

TextArrows property reflects whether the arrow keys move the insertion point in a field. (page 624)

TextFont property reflects the font used for text created with the browse or text tool. (page 625)

TextHeight property reflects the vertical space allowed for each line of text. (page 628)

TextSize property reflects a character's height in pixels. (page 630)

TextStyle property reflects the style used for text. (page 632)

The is an article that may optionally appear before any of the following: `target`, `selection`, `message` (or `msg`), the name of any property (as in `the size`), and references to any function that uses the `of` form (as in `the number of cards in this stack`). It's required before argumentless functions (for example `the time` or `the date`) when you don't follow the function name with parentheses. These comprise the only legal uses of **the** in all versions through 2.0.

Third is a HyperTalk ordinal. (page 64)

This is an adjective used to refer to the current card, background, or stack.

Three is the constant for the value 3. (page 92)

Ticks function returns the number of ticks (units of 1/60th of a second) since the system was last reset or turned on. (page 480)

Time function returns the current time. (page 482)

To is the preposition used to define the limits of a range in a chunk expression, as in "word 2 **to** 5" (page 103), as a preface to the image word in visual effects, as in "dissolve slowly **to** black" (page 368), before the destination object with **send,** as in "send myMessage **to** button 5" (page 155), and optionally after **go** for a more natural sounding syntax, as in "go **to** card 5." (page 258)

Tool returns the name of the currently chosen tool. (page 484)

Top property gives the location of the top of a button, field, or window. (page 635)

TopLeft property gives the coordinates for the top-left corner of a button, field, or window. (page 637)

Transparent is one of the values for the style of a button or field. (page 617)

True is a constant, as in "set *property* to true." (page 92)

Trunc function returns the integer part of its argument. (page 486)

Two is the constant for the value 2. (page 92)

Type command types into an unlocked field at the insertion point when the Browse tool is chosen, and onto the card or background picture at the insertion point when the Text tool is chosen. (page 360)

Underline is one of the values for the style of text. (page 632)

Unlock screen command sets the **lockScreen** property to false and updates the display with all visual changes that occurred since the last time the **lockScreen** property was set to true. (page 363)

Unmark command can set the **marked** property of one or more cards to false. (page 365)

Up is a constant, as in "the shiftKey is up." (page 92)

UserLevel property reflects the User Level setting on the User Preferences card, defining a user's power. (page 639)

UserModify property reflects whether a user can make temporary changes to a stack (insofar as the **userLevel** setting allows such changes) even though the stack is locked. (page 642)

Value function returns the fully resolved value of its argument. (page 487)

VariableWatcher property determines the current **variable watcher** XCMD, HyperCard's facility for tracking variables. (page 487)

Venetian blinds is one of the visual effects used with the **visual** and **unlock screen with visual effect** commands. (page 367)

Version property supplies information about the version of HyperCard or about the version(s) of HyperCard used to modify the current stack. (page 645)

Very fast is a speed at which a visual effect occurs. (page 367)

Very slow (or **very slowly**) is a speed at which a visual effect occurs. (page 367)

Visible property reflects whether a button, field, or window is visible when it's within normally visible boundaries. (page 648)

Visual command displays one or more visual effects when you change cards with a **Go** or **pop card** command, or when a successful **Find** command causes a card change. (page 367)

Wait command suspends HyperCard for a specific period or until some condition is met. (page 370)

Watch is one of the values for the **cursor** property. (page 518)

White is one of the optional images that covers an entire card at the end of a visual effect before a card reappears. (page 367)

Whole is a modifier used with the **Find** command restricting the search to a complete word or phrase, including embedded spaces. (page 247)

WideMargins property reflects whether a field has extra border space along its top and left sides. (page 650)

Width property reflects the distance in pixels between the left and right sides of a button, field, or window. (page 651)

Wipe down is one of the visual effects used with the **visual** and **unlock screen with visual effect** commands. (page 363)

Wipe left is one of the visual effects used with the **visual** and **unlock screen with visual effect** commands. (page 363)

Wipe right is one of the visual effects used with the **visual** and **unlock screen with visual effect** commands. (page 363)

Wipe up is one of the visual effects used with the **visual** and **unlock screen with visual effect** commands. (page 363)

Within see **is within**

Word is the chunk of a value delimited by spaces. (page 103)

Words is a modifier used with the **Find** command restricting the search to a perfect match for each of the words in the search string, although the order that they're found in is not considered. (page 247)

Write command copies bytes from any source and stores them in the data fork of a file. (page 367)

Zero is the constant for the value 0. (page 92)

Zoom close is one of the visual effects used with the **visual** and **unlock screen with visual effect** commands. (page 363)

Zoom in is one of the visual effects used with the **visual** and **unlock screen with visual effect** commands. (page 363)

Zoom open is one of the visual effects used with the **visual** and **unlock screen with visual effect** commands. (page 363)

Zoom out is one of the visual effects used with the **visual** and **unlock screen with visual effect** commands. (page 363)

Vocabulary Categories

This appendix divides HyperTalk's command, keyword, function, and property vocabulary words into basic categories. Each word is followed by a pointer to that word's appearance in the major reference section. Some words appear in more than one category.

Not all native vocabulary words appear here. (For example, control structure keywords like **if** and **repeat** are left out.) For an alphabetic list of all words with a brief definition of each, see Appendix E, "Quick Dictionary."

Arithmetic and Trigonometric

Abs (page 377)
Add (page 161)
Annuity (page 379)
Atan (page 380)
Average (page 382)
Compound (page 399)
Cos (page 400)
Divide (page 227)
Exp (page 406)
Exp1 (page 407)
Exp2 (page 408)
Ln (page 421)
Ln1 (page 422)
log2 (page 423)
Max (page 424)
Min (page 429)
Multiply (page 275)
Random (page 452)

Round (page 456)
Sin (page 470)
Sqrt (page 474)
Subtract (page 356)
Tan (page 477)
Trunc (page 486)

Background

CantDelete (page 506)
DontSearch (page 521)
ID (page 548)
Name (page 576)
Number (page 438)
Script (page 599)
ShowPict (page 613)

Button

AutoHilite (page 490)
Bottom (page 497)
BottomRight (page 499)

Close file (page 190)
Close printing (page 193)
Open application (page 277)
Open file (page 280)
Open printing (page 283)
Print card (page 302)
Print document (page 304)
Read (page 318)
Write (page 372)

HyperCard

BlindTyping (page 496)
CantAbort (page 504)
CantPeek (page 511)
DragSpeed (page 526)
Edit (page 235)
EditBkgnd (page 528)
Language (page 550)
LockMessages (page 558)
LockRecent (page 560)
Name (page 579)
NumberFormat (page 585)
PowerKeys (page 592)
Screenrect (page 458)
Suspended (page 620)
TextArrows (page 624)
tool (page 484)
UserLevel (page 639)
UserModify (page 642)
Value (page 487)
Version (page 645)
Wait (page 370)

I/O

Answer file (page 167)
Ask file (page 178)
Dial (page 218)

Picture (page 288)

Keyboard

ArrowKey (page 171)
CommandKey (page 398)
Controlkey (page 195)
EnterInField (page 240)
EnterKey (page 242)
FunctionKey (page 254)
OptionKey (page 444)
ReturnInField (page 325)
ReturnKey (page 328)
ShiftKey (page 469)
Tabkey (page 358)
Type (page 360)

Memory

DiskSpace (page 405)
FreeSize (page 536)
HeapSpace (page 417)
StackSpace (page 475)

Menus

CheckMark (page 514)
CommandChar (page 516)
Create (page 202)
Delete Menu (page 215)
Disable (page 223)
Enable (page 238)
Enabled (page 530)
MenuMessage (page 568)
Menus (page 426)
Name of *Menu* (page 576)
Number (page 583)
Put into menu (page 312)
Reset menuBar (page 322)
TextStyle (page 632)

Sound (page 472)

Stack

CantDelete (page 506)
CantModify (page 508)
Create (page 204)
FreeSize (page 536)
Name (page 579)
Save as (page 329)
Script (page 599)
Size (page 614)
Sort (page 346)
Version (page 645)

Text

CharToNum (page 385)
Length (page 419)
NumToChar (page 440)
Offset (page 442)
TextAlign (page 622)
TextFont (page 625)
TextHeight (page 628)
TextSize (page 630)
TextStyle (page 632)

Time & Date

Convert (page 199)
Date (page 403)
Seconds (page 459)
Ticks (page 480)
Time (page 482)

Value Transfer

Answer (page 163)
Ask (page 174)
Function (page 128)

Get (page 256)
Global (page 132)
Param (page 445)
ParamCount (page 447)
Params (page 449)
Pop (page 297)
Push (page 307)
Put (page 309)
Read (page 318)
Result (page 454)
Return (page 151)
Set (page 336)
Variable Watcher (page 644)
Write (page 372)

Visual

Flash (page 253)
Hide (page 264)
Lock screen (page 270)
LockScreen (page 562)
Picture (page 288)
Show (page 339)
Show cards (page 342)
Show picture (page 344)
Unlock screen (page 363)
Visual (page 367)

Windows

Bottom (page 497)
BottomRight (page 499)
Height (page 539)
Left (page 552)
Location (page 556)
Rectangle (page 593)
Right (page 597)
ScreenRect (page 458)

Appendix G

Changes for 2.0

This appendix, gleaned from the more complete discussion to be found throughout the book, summarizes the major changes that were made in HyperTalk for HyperCard 2.0.

Changes for 2.0 is intended for the scripter already familiar with HyperTalk 1.2.#. For a formal syntactical presentation of all of 2.0 HyperTalk, see Chapter 2.

Some changes and additions were made to the language too late to be included in the main body of this book, or even in this appendix. See Appendix I, "Late Breaking News."

OVERALL CHANGES

HyperTalk was completely rewritten for 2.0. Formerly an interpreted language, HyperTalk is now compiled, considerably increasing its execution speed. (But you'll still have to contend with relatively slow disk access and screen redrawing.)

The language has also been made more flexible. In 1.2.#, HyperTalk had a mechanism called "automatic expansion." It gave broader latitude to the grammar of the language by letting you use certain expressions in certain situations to go beyond what the grammar specified. But 2.0 gives "automatic expansion" throughout the language: HyperTalk now accepts an expression in place of most nonterminals (items that appear in italics) or most sublists (items enclosed in "{" and "}" or "[" and "]").

Unquoted tokens are now allowed everywhere in HyperTalk, letting you use unquoted literals throughout. So the nonterminals *factorOrToken* and *exprOrToken* aren't used anymore.

And the use of the optional "the" is now allowed in more cases — specifically, before an ordinal (the third card), before positionals (the next card), and before the names of windows (the card window).

These new freedoms have a minor cost. In previous versions of HyperTalk, "in" and "of" were lexically equivalent — where you could use one, you could use the other. In HyperCard 2.0, there are two places where they're not equivalent: first, when you use find *expr* in *field*, you can use only "in". And when you refer to properties (as in the **set** command, with expressions such as name of card 1), you can use only "of". These restrictions let the HyperTalk compiler distinguish between such expressions as find name in field 1 and find name of field 1. The HyperTalk interpreter, used in previous versions, could make this kind of distinction using runtime information that isn't available to a compiler.

NEW EDITOR AND DEBUGGER

While version 1.2.# restricted you to editing only one script at a time, HyperTalk 2.0 lets you simultaneously edit as many scripts as you want, up to the limits of your machine's RAM; so cutting and pasting between scripts is quick and easy.

The editor has a number of new features, including full find-and-replace, import-export text (for bringing in scripts from text files), block commenting, and (gasp!) full undo!

All new for 2.0 is an integrated symbolic debugger. You can set checkpoints (stopping places in your code that automatically turn on other sophisticated debugging features), single-step through scripts, watch the flow of messages as well as distinguish between messages that are caught and not caught, and keep track of (as well as manipulate) both local and global variables. See Chapter 2 for the details.

ENVIRONMENTAL CHANGES

HyperTalk gives you better control over the face that your stacks present. For example, you have (nearly) complete control over the menus: you can create and/or delete menus at will, add or take away menu commands (controlled by whatever handlers you want to associate with them), and even associate a command key with each command. (See **put into menu**, **delete**, and **commandChar**, below.)

Your scripts can now control whether dialogs appear or don't appear with commands that create, open, and/or remove cards and stacks. And using the **go** *stack* **in new window** command, you can have open as many stacks at the same time as you want (up to the limits of your machine's RAM).

Styled text lets you control the font, size, and style of chunks of text within a field. For example, you can mix boldface, underlined, and italicized text within the same field, or even have different chunks of text in different fonts.

Several new functions (most notably **clickChunk** and **clickText**, described below) let you create hypertext links far easier than you could in HyperCard 1.2.#.

MESSAGE PASSING AND SENDING

HyperCard 2.0 lets you dynamically extend the message passing path by adding and removing the scripts and resources of up to 10 additional stacks (inserted just before Home). So now you can construct special library scripts that you call or dispose of as appropriate. (TextEdit still limits the size of any script to 30K, putting a cap on the number of handlers you can place in any stack script.) See **stacksInUse** and **start using**, below.

The message sending order has been changed in certain cases. In 1.2.#, the order in which HyperCard sent messages was often counterintuitive. OK, it was stupid. Changes in 2.0 correct this problem in many cases (although the new order might break some old scripts which you'll need to rewrite). See Chapter 11's table of multiple messages.

VOCABULARY ENHANCEMENTS

Many 1.2.# vocabulary words have been enhanced to let HyperTalk take advantage of HyperCard's 2.0 changes. Here's a brief summary of each enhanced vocabulary word showing its added (but not complete) syntax, a brief description of its expanded functionality, and a page reference to complete information.

debug **checkPoint** — an aide to debugging, temporarily halts execution of the handler containing this command and enters the Debugger with this command boxed. (Most people didn't know that the **debug** command existed in 1.2.#.) (page 210)

doMenu *expr* **{, expr} without dialog** — executes certain menu commands (Delete Stack..., Convert Stack..., and Cut Field and Clear Field for backgrounds) without bringing up the usual dialog. (page 229)

get name of [*menu* | *menuItem*] — reflects the names of individual menus or menu items. (page 576)

get number of [menus | *menuItems* | marked cards] — returns the number of menus currently visible on the menu bar (**menus**), number of items in a given menu (**menuItems in** *menu*), or the number of marked cards in the current stack (**marked cards**).

go to *destination* in { a } new window { without dialog } — brings an additional stack to the screen without putting away the currently active stack, optionally preventing any dialog that might appear if the call for the added stack failed. (page 258)

go to {the} [*ordinal*|next|prev] marked card — goes to a card in the current stack whose **marked** property (new in 2.0) has been set to true. (page 567)

open report printing {with [template *expr* | dialog] } — starts the process of printing a report. (page 283)

print marked cards {from *point* to *point*} — (1) prints card(s) whose **marked** property (new in 2.0) has been set to true; and (2) prints the specified area of card(s). (Also see the new **print** command under "New Vocabulary, below.) (page 567)

send *message* to *windowExpr* — for external windows (windows created by XCMDs), sends message to an XCMD that knows what to do with it.

set rect of card {window} — sets the rectangle of the card or card window for the current stack. (page 593)

show marked cards — shows cards in the current stack whose **marked** property (new in 2.0) has been set to true. (page 342)

visual effect [shrink to | stretch from] [bottom | center | top] — prepares new visual effect that executes with next **go** command. (page 367)

NEW VOCABULARY

HyperTalk 2.0 has a host of new native vocabulary words. Here's a summary description of each new command, function, property, and message, with a page reference to complete information.

New Commands

Answer file brings up the Macintosh's Standard GetFile dialog so that you can select the name of a file. Optionally, the script can specify a filter so the names of files of only a particular type (applications, stacks, text files, etc.) are displayed. (page 167)

Ask file brings up the Macintosh's PutFile dialog (the one that lets you name a file) with a string prompt. You can also specify a default name to go in the editable PutFile field. (page 178)

Create menu adds new menus to the menu bar. (page 202)

Create stack creates a new stack without presenting a dialog, optionally using any background of the current stack. (page 204)

Delete menu removes an entire menu, or any single menu item of any menu, from the menu bar. (page 215)

Disable disables a menu or a menu item, preventing a user from working with it. (page 223)

Enable enables a menu or a menu item, allowing a user to work with it. (page 238)

Export paint writes a copy of the current card or background picture to disk under the name you provide. (page 243)

Import paint reads a copy of the paint document stored in the file whose name you provide, and pastes it onto the current card or background. (page 267)

Mark marks the card or cards you specify for some later action (usually display or printing). (page 273)

Palette navigator brings up the new navigation palette. (page 286)

Picture displays a MacPaint image or black and white or color PICT up to 32-bits deep in its own window. (page 288)

Print prints the contents of any field or container, or the value of any expression. (page 299)

Put into menu adds menu items (and, optionally, associated messages) to menus. (page 312)

Reset menuBar restores HyperCard's standard menu bar as appropriate to the current setting of the **userLevel** property. (page 322)

Save as saves a copy of a stack under the name you provide. (page 329)

Start using adds stacks to the message passing path just before the Home stack. (page 351)

Stop using removes a stack previously added to the message passing path by the **start using** command. (page 354)

Unmark sets the **marked** property of one or more cards to false. (page 365)

New Functions

ClickChunk returns the positions of the starting and ending characters of the word or group most recently clicked in a locked field. (page 387)

ClickLine identifies the line most recently clicked in a locked field. (page 391)

ClickText returns the word or group of characters most recently clicked in a locked field. (page 395)

Menus returns a return-separated list of the menu names currently visible in the menu bar. (page 426)

New Properties

CantAbort determines whether pressing Command-period aborts a running script. (page 504)

CantPeek determines whether you can see buttons and fields by pressing Command-option and Command-shift-option, and whether you can open the scripts of buttons and fields by using Command-option-click and Command-shift-option-click. (page 511)

CheckMark determines whether a checkmark (✔) appears to the left of a menu item. (page 514)

CommandChar determines what command character (if any) you can press from the keyboard to execute a specific menu command. (page 516)

DontSearch determines whether the **find** command searches in a given field, card, or background. (page 521)

DontWrap determines whether the text in a given field wraps at that field's right edge, or if it trails off out of sight. (page 523)

Enabled determines whether you can choose a particular menu item, or any item in a given menu. (page 530)

FixedLineHeight reflects whether HyperCard automatically adjusts the spacing above and below lines of text of different sizes (that is, adjusts the leading) in a given field. (page 535)

MarkChar determines what character (if any) appears to the left of a specific menu item. (page 566)

Marked determines whether a card is noted for some possible later action (usually printing or display or further filtering). (page 567)

MenuMessage determines what message, if any, is sent when you choose a particular menu item. (page 568)

MessageWatcher reflects the name of the current message watcher XCMD, HyperCard's facility for tracking messages. (page 571)

ScriptEditor determines the XCMD being used to create and manage the current script editor. (page 602)

Scroll of card window describes the horizontal and vertical scroll of the card within the card window. (page 605)

SharedHilite determines whether a background button, highlighted on one card of a given background, is highlighted on every card of that background. (page 607)

SharedText reflects whether text typed into a background field appears on all cards in that background. (page 608)

StacksInUse reflects what stacks (if any) have been added to the message passing path. (page 615)

Suspended returns true when HyperCard is running in the background (while some other application is running in the foreground), and false when HyperCard is running in the foreground. (page 620)

VariableWatcher determines the current **variable watcher** XCMD, HyperCard's facility for tracking variables. (page 644)

New Messages

ExitField is the message that HyperCard sends when the insertion point is removed from an open field *and the text in that field has not changed*. (page 661)

ResumeStack is the message that HyperCard sends when a previously suspended stack has become active. (page 666)

SuspendStack is the message that HyperCard sends when another stack opens in a new window, or when somebody clicks in the window of another stack already on the screen. (page 666)

Miscellaneous

CmdChar is a synonym for the **commandChar** property (*which see*).

Group is a value for the style of a chunk of text in a field, letting you treat any contiguous run of characters as a single unit. (page 633)

MenuMsg is a synonym for the **menuMessage** property (*which see*).

Appendix H

1.2.# Syntax

This appendix lists the complete syntax of HyperTalk 1.2.#. The syntax symbols used here are the same as those listed for HyperTalk 2.0 at the start of Chapter 3, "Syntax."

Additionally, 1.2.# has the symbol @, the At sign. The At sign (used only in the formal syntax of version 1.2.# described later in this chapter and in Chapter 4 to describe the rules for referring to objects) means that the syntax treats expressions as **expandable** — an expression that yields text in the proper syntactical form is as acceptable as text that already appears in the proper syntactical form. (An expression is any value or any group of values, sources of value, and operators meant to be taken as a single whole.)

For example, the formal syntax for the **click** command is

```
click at [<integer>, <integer>]@
```

The following statement already appears in the proper syntactical form:

```
click at 100, 300
```

The statement

```
click at field 1
```

also works if field 1 contains a value that matches the required syntax for **click** — a pair of integers separated by a comma.

If @ appears before the phrase, HyperTalk tries to evaluate the phrase as an expression before it tries to evaluate the phrase as a **literal** (that is, a group of characters to be taken for their actual face value). This process is used only for stacks.

If @ appears after the phrase (as it does in the example), HyperTalk tries to evaluate the phrase as a literal before it tries to evaluate the phrase as an expression.

FORMAL SYNTAX: 1.2.#

This section describes the One True Syntax for the HyperTalk scripting language on the Macintosh, HyperCard versions through 1.2.#. It shows precisely what's allowed in every construct. It uses the syntax symbols listed in the first section of Chapter 3, "Syntax."

Don't be alarmed

This section presents in a formal way the complete and precise syntax of every vocabulary word. It is valuable both in its own right and as the ultimate resource for settling bets at cocktail parties. It isn't necessary to read or to grasp totally all the information in this section to use HyperTalk well. It is, however, the Final Word.

1.2.# Scripts

```
<script> = <script> <handler> | <handler>

<handler> =
  on <messageKey> <return>
    <stmntList>
  end <messageKey> <return>

<stmntList> = <stmnt> | <stmntList> <stmnt>

<stmnt> = [<messageSend> | <keywordStmnt> | <empty>] <return>

<keywordStmnt> =
  do <expr> |
  exit repeat | exit <messageKey> | exit to HyperCard |
  global <identList> |
  next repeat |
  pass <messageKey> |
  return <expr> |
  send [<expr> | <token>] { to <object> } |
  <ifBlock> | <repeatBlock>
```

```
<ifBlock> =
  if <logical> { <return> } then [<singleThen> | <return> <multiThen>]

<singleThen> = <stmnt> { {<return>} <elseBlock> }

<multiThen> = <stmntList> [ end if | <elseBlock>]

<elseBlock> = else [<stmnt> | <return> <stmntList> end if]

<repeatBlock> =
  repeat {forever | <duration> | <count> | with <identifier> = <range>} <return>
    <stmntList>
  end repeat

<duration> = until <logical> | while <logical>
<count> = { for } <unsigned> { times }
<range> = <integer> { down } to <integer>
```

1.2.# Expressions

```
<expr> = <source> | - <factor> | not <factor> | <expr> <op>
<expr> | ( <expr> ) | <chunk> <factor>


<op> =
  + | - | * | / | & | && | ^ | = | < | > | <> | ≠ |
  <= | >= | ≤ | ≥ | and | or | contains | div | mod |
  is | is not | is in | is not in | is within | is not within

<source> =
  <literal> | <constant> | <simpleContainer> |
  { <adjective> } <function> |
  { <adjective> } <property> of [<object> | <window>]

<literal> = "quoted string"

<constant> =
  down | empty | false | formFeed | lineFeed |
  pi | quote | space | tab | true | up |
  zero | one | two | three | four | five |
  six | seven | eight | nine | ten
```

<adjective> = long | short | abbrev | abbr | abbreviated

<function>=the *<theFunc>* | { the } *<theFunc>* of *<oneFuncArg>* | *<identifier>* (*<funcArgs>*)

<theFunc> =

    abs | annuity | atan | average | charToNum | clickH | clickLoc |
    clickV | commandKey | compound | cos | date | diskSpace | exp |
    exp1 | exp2 | foundChunk | foundField | foundLine | foundText |
    heapSpace | length | ln | ln1 | log2 | max | min | mouse |
    mouseClick | mouseH | mouseLoc | mouseV | number cards |
    numToChar | offset | optionKey | param | paramCount | params |
    random | result | round | screenRect | seconds | selectedChunk |
    selectedField | selectedLine | selectedText | shiftKey | sin |
    sound | sqrt | stackSpace | tan | target | ticks | time | tool |
    trunc | value

Syntax for each individual function appears later in the **Functions** section.

<property> =

    autoHilite | autoTab | blindTyping | botRight | bottom |
    bottomRight | brush | cantDelete | cantModify | centered | cursor |
    dragSpeed | editBkgnd | filled | freeSize | grid | height | highlight |
    highlite | hilight | hilite | icon | id | language | left |
    lineSize | loc | location | lockMessages | lockRecent |
    lockScreen | lockText | multiple | multiSpace | name |
    numberFormat | pattern | polySides | powerKeys | rect | rectangle |
    right | script | scroll | showLines | showName | showPict |
    size | style | textAlign | textArrows | textFont | textHeight |
    textSize | textStyle | top | topLeft | userLevel | userModify |
    version | visible | wideMargins | width

Syntax for each individual property appears at the end of the **Commands** section, in the notes about the **set** command.

1.2.# Objects

<object> =
  [HyperCard | me | { the } target | *<button>* | *<field>* | *<card>* | *<bkgnd>*]@ |
  <stack>

Note: "card field 1" is a field and "card (field 1)" is a card.

```
<button> =
   [button id <unsignedFactor> | button [<factor> | <token>] |
   <ordinal> button] { of <card> }

<field> =
   [field id <unsignedFactor> | field [<factor> | <token>] |
   <ordinal> field] { of <card> }

<part> = <button> | <field>

<ordinal> =
   last | mid | middle | any |
   first | second | third | fourth | fifth |
   sixth | seventh | eigth | ninth | tenth

<card> =
   recent card | back | forth |
   [card id <unsigned> | card [<expr> | <token>] | card <endLine> |
   <ordinal> card | <position> card] { of <bkgnd> }

<position> = this | prev | next

<bkgnd> =
   bkgnd id <unsigned> | bkgnd [<expr> | <token>] | bkgnd
   <endLine> | <ordinal> bkgnd | <position> bkgnd

<stack> = [this stack | stack [<expr> | <line>] | stack
   <endLine>]@ | [@[<expr> | <line>]]
```

1.2.# Containers

```
<simpleContainer> = <variable> | <field> | <messageBox> | { the }
   selection

<container> = <chunk> <simpleContainer> | <simpleContainer>

<messageBox> = { the } msg { box | window }
```

```
<chunk> =
  {[<ordinal> char | char <expr> { to <expr> }] of}
  {[<ordinal> word | word <expr> { to <expr> }] of}
  {[<ordinal> item | item <expr> { to <expr> }] of}
  {[<ordinal> line | line <expr> { to <expr> }] of}
```

1.2.# Commands

Command nonterminals

These nonterminals appear in the **command** syntax (which follows immediately).

```
<dest> =
  [[<card> | <bkgnd>] { of <stack> }]@ | <stack>

<dateItems> =
  <unsigned>,<unsigned>,<unsigned>,<unsigned>,<unsigned>,<unsigned>,
  <unsigned>

<date> =
  <unsigned> | <dateItems>
  <humanDate> { <humanTime> } |
  <humanTime> { <humanDate> }

<dateFormat> = { <adjective> } [seconds | dateItems | date | time]

<dayOfWeek> =
  Sunday | Sun | Monday | Mon | Tuesday | Tue | Wednesday |
  Wed | Thursday | Thu | Friday | Fri | Saturday | Sat

<duration> = until <logical> | while <logical>

<humanDate> =
  { <dayOfWeek> , } <month> <unsigned> , <unsigned> |
  <unsignedFactor> [/ | -] <unsignedFactor> [/ | -] <unsignedFactor>

<humanTime> =
  <unsigned> : <unsigned> { : <unsigned> } { am | pm }
```

```
<month> =
  January | Jan | February | Feb | March | Mar |
  April | Apr | May | June | Jun | July | Jul |
  August | Aug | September | Sep | October | Oct |
  November | Nov | December | Dec

<point> = [<integer> , <integer>]@

<preposition> = before | after | into

<rect> = [<integer> , <integer> , integer> , <integer>]@

<springKeys> = <springKeys> , <springKey> | <springKey>

<springKey> = shiftKey | optionKey | commandKey

<style> =
  [transparent | opaque | rectangle | roundrect |
  shadow | checkBox | radioButton | scrolling]@

<textAlign> = [right | left | center]@

<textStyleList> = <textStyleList> , <textStyle> | <textStyle>

<textStyle> =
  [plain | bold | italic | underline | outline |
  shadow |condense | extend]@

<visEffect> = <visKind> { { very } [slow | slowly | fast] } { to <visSrc> }

<visKind> =
  barn door [open | close] |
  cut | plain | dissolve | venetian blinds | checkerboard |
  iris [open | close] |
  scroll [left | right | up | down] |
  wipe [left | right | up | down] |
  zoom [open | out | close | in ]

<visSrc> = card | black | white | gray | inverse

<window> = [card | pattern | tool] window | <messageBox>
```

1.2.# *Commands*

add
  <*arith*> to <*container*>
answer
  [<*expr*> | <*token*>] {with [<*factor*> | <*token*>] {or [<*factor*> |
  <*token*>] {or [<*factor*> | <*token*>] }}}
arrowkey
  left | right | up | down
ask
  { password } [<*expr*> | <*token*>] { with [<*expr*> | <*line*>] }
beep
  {<*unsigned*>}
choose
  [tool <*unsigned*>]@ |
  [browse | button | field | select | lasso | pencil |
  brush | eraser | line | spray { can } | rect |
  round rect | bucket | oval | curve | text |
  reg poly | poly] tool]@
click
  at <*point*> { with <*springKeys*> }
close
  file [<*expr*> | <*line*>] | printing
controlkey
  <*unsigned*>
convert
  [<*container*> | <*date*>] to <*dateFormat*> { and <*dateFormat*> }
debug
  [<*expr*> | <*line*>]
delete
  [<*chunk*> <*simpleContainer*>]@
dial
  <*expr*> { with modem | with { modem } <*expr*> }
divide
  <*container*> by <*float*>
domenu
  <*expr*> | <*line*>
drag

```
     from <point> to <point> { with <springKeys> }
edit
    { the } script of <object>
enterInField
enterkey
find
    { whole | string | words | word | chars | normal }
    [<expr> | <token>] { in <field> }
functionkey
    <unsigned>
get
    <expr> | { the } <property> { of <object> }
go
    { to } [[<ordinal> | <position>] <endLine> | <dest>]
help
hide
    menuBar | picture of [<object>]@ |
    [ card | bkgnd ] picture | <window> | [<part>]@
lock
    screen
multiply
    <container> by <arith>
open
    printing { with dialog } |
    file [<expr> | <line>] |
    [<expr> | <token>] { with [<expr> | <line>] } |
    <expr> | <line>
play
      stop | [<expr> | <token>] { { tempo <unsigned> } [<expr> |
      <line>] }
pop
    card { <preposition> <container> }
print
    [<expr> | <token>] with [<expr> | <line>] |
    <unsigned> cards | all cards | <card>
push
    <dest>
```

```
put
  [<expr> | <token>] { <preposition> <container> }
read
   from file [<expr> | <token>] [until [<expr> | <token>] | for
   <unsigned>]
reset
  paint
returnInField
returnkey
select
  [{ before | after } [[text of | <chunk> ] [ <field> | <message>]@]@] |
  [<part>]@ | <emptyExpr>
set
  { the } <property> { of [<window> | <object>] } to <propVal>
```
(See notes on set, below.)
```
show
  menuBar | picture of [<object>]@ |
  [ card | bkgnd ] picture |
  [<window> | [<part>]@] { at <point> } |
  { all | <unsigned> } cards
sort
  { ascending | descending }
  { text | numeric | international | dateTime }
    by <expr>
subtract
  <arith> from <container>
tabkey
type
  <expr> { with <springKeys> }
unlock
  screen { with [{ visual { effect }} <visEffect>]@ }
visual
  { effect } <visEffect>
wait
  <duration> | <count> { ticks | tick | seconds | second | sec }
write
  <expr> to file [<expr> | <line>]
```

The following syntax refers only to the **set** command. The general syntax for **set** is:

```
{ the } <property> { of [<window> | <object>] } to <propVal>

<propVal> =
  [<expr> | <line>] | <integer> | <unsigned> | <logical> |
  <point> | <rect> | <style> | <textAlign> | <textStyleList>
```

Set has a different syntax for different groups of properties. The following list shows which nonterminals apply to which properties:

```
[<expr> | <line>]
  name,textFont,icon,script,language,cursor,numberFormat
<integer>
  top,bottom,left,right,width,height
<unsigned>
  textHeight,textSize,lineSize,pattern,brush,polySides,
  multiSpace,userLevel,dragSpeed,scroll
<logical>
  freeSize,showName,lockText,showLines,wideMargins,visible,
  powerKeys,grid,filled,centered,multiple,editBkgnd,hilite,
  lockScreen,lockRecent,autoHilite,blindTyping,lockMessages,
  textArrows,showPict,cantDelete,cantModify,autoTab,userModify
<point>
  loc,topLeft,botRight
<rect>
  rect
<style>
  style
<textAlign>
  textAlign
<textStyleList>
  textStyle
```

1.2.# Functions

Note that *<funcArith>*, *<funcFloat>*, *<funcExpr>*, and *<funcUnsigned>* all take expressions when they're called with parentheses, but they all take factors when they're called with "of".

abs
  <funcArith>
annuity
  <float> , *<float>*
atan
  <funcFloat>
average
  [*<arithList>*]@
chartonum
  <funcExpr>
clickh
clickloc
clickv
commandkey
compound
  <float> , *<float>*
cos
  <funcFloat>
date
diskspace
exp
  <funcFloat>
exp1
  <funcFloat>
exp2
  <funcFloat>
foundChunk
foundField
foundLine
foundText
heapspace
length
  <funcExpr>
ln
  <funcFloat>
ln1
  <funcFloat>

```
log2
   <funcFloat>
max
   [<arithList>]@
min
   [<arithList>]@
mouse
mouseclick
mouseh
mouseloc
mousev
number
   cards { in <bkgnd> } | bkgnds |
   { card | bkgnd } [buttons | fields] |
   [chars | words | items | lines] in <funcExpr> |
   <object>
numToChar
   <funcUnsigned>
offset
   <string> , <string>
optionkey
param
   <funcUnsigned>
paramcount
params
random
   <funcUnsigned>
result
round
   <funcFloat>
screenRect
seconds
selectedChunk
selectedField
selectedLine
selectedText
shiftKey
```

closeBackground
closeCard
closeField
closeStack
deleteBackground
deleteButton
deleteCard
deleteField
deleteStack
idle
mouseDown
mouseEnter
mouseLeave
mouseStillDown
mouseUp

mouseWithin
newBackground
newButton
newCard
newField
newStack
openBackground
openCard
openField
openStack
quit
resume
startup
suspend

Late Breaking News

This apppendix presents changes made to HyperTalk 2.0 so late in its development cycle that they couldn't be included in the main body of this book.

How current is this appendix?

This appendix was finished on May 11, 1990 — the day after HyperCard 2.0 was announced at the Apple Developer's Conference in San Jose, California. As the appendix was being written, book editors hovered over our desk, eager to rip the freshly printed pages from the LaserWriter tray in order to rush them at breakneck speed to the printer, and then to you.

As of that day, this book included descriptions of every feature in 2.0. (It even included descriptions of a couple of features that were still being coded!) It is important to understand, however, that Announce Day and Ship Day are two different days. And the HyperCard Development Team has always been a feisty lot, ignoring minor details like schedules and the blood pressure of product managers. We have no doubt that, on the way to the factory where disks are duplicated before being packaged with manuals, some member of the team was sitting in the back seat with a Macintosh Portable, adding still more features.

Under the circumstances, the first edition of this book is as complete as is humanly possible.

In this appendix, we assume you already understand HyperCard's syntax conventions, and that you're already experienced in the operations of HyperCard's basic vocabulary types (commands, properties, and so on). For details on any of these subjects, see the appropriate chapters.

SCRIPT EDITOR AND DEBUGGER

• Tabs are now treated as white space in handlers.

• In the script editor, option-clicking the close box closes all scripts.

• The script editor maintains a set of global variables. These globals hold values for various script editor settings. Table I-1 shows these globals and what they mean. Note that, at the time of this writing, the global names were still changing; so you'll need to check them to see if they're still as described.

Table I-1:   Script editor globals

Global	Meaning
scriptCaseSens	Case Sensitive box checked?
scriptDebugging	Used internally by script editor to know which window to activate during debugging. Don't touch it.
scriptFindString	Current find string
scriptReplaceString	Current replace string
scriptWholeWord	"Whole Word" button hilited?
scriptWrapAround	Wraparound Search box checked?

• In the Debugger, typing Command-period at a checkpoint or during a trace stops the script.

• Two additional items were added late to the Debugger menu: **Trace into** and **Trace delay**. The new Debugger menu now looks like Figure I-1:

Trace Into (Command-T) continues tracing into handlers called by the current handler. It's the tracing equivalent of the **step into** Debugger command.

Trace Delay... lets you set the delay in ticks that tracing uses before moving on to the next statement. (60 ticks = 1 second). You can set the delay programmatically using the **traceDelay** property.

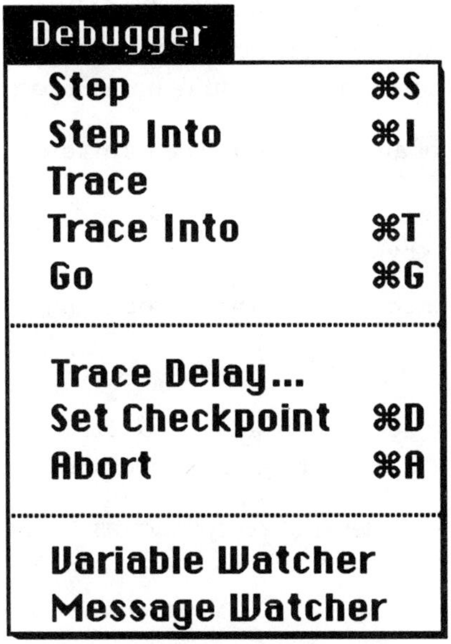

Figure I-1   Debugger menu with added items

OPERATORS

there is — tests for the existence of something. The forms are:

```
there is a{n} <thing>
there is not a{n} <thing>
there is no <thing>
```

```
<thing> = <window> | <menu> | <menuItem> | <file> | <btn> | <fld> |
<cd> | <bg> | <stack>
```

So you can say:

```
if there is not a field "Totals" then makeFieldTotals
if there is no menu "Paste" then create menu "Paste"
if there is a card "Names" then go to card "Fred" else go to card "Martha"
```

This operator is highest on the precedence table (Table 6-5), along with "unary -"
and "not".

"There is" is able to detect the existence of all of HyperCard's menus, even ones that aren't currently in the menu bar. For example, `there is a menu "options"` returns true, even when you're not in a painting tool.

is a — tests the type of an expression. The forms are:

```
<expr> is a{n} <type>
<expr> is not a{n} <type>

<type> = number | integer | point | rect{angle} | date | logical
```

So you can say:

```
if field 5 is an integer then add 1 to field 5
if the Selection is a date then put it into field "Date"
```

This operator has the same level of precedence as "is in" in the precedence table (Table 6-5).

COMMANDS

[hide | show] titleBar — hides or shows the title bar that appears at the top of a card window.

[hide | show] {the} [variable | message] watcher
[hide | show] window ["variable watcher" | "message watcher"]
— hides or shows the named window.

mark cards by finding *findArguments* — marks cards much faster than the standard **mark cards where** syntax. Because it uses the **find** command's hint bits, **mark cards by finding** can skip many cards in a given stack. (**Mark cards where** looks at every card.) So the form

```
mark cards by finding "Fred" in Field 1
```

is much faster than the form

```
mark cards where "Fred" is in field 1
```

You can use all the forms of **find**'s syntax (i.e., by **finding string, by finding whole**, etc.). For details on hint bits, see the **Debug** command in Chapter 8.

reset printing — sets the printing properties back to their defaults. The affected properties and their defaults are listed in Table I-2. For information on each property, see **Properties**, below.

Table I-2: Printing properties and defaults

Property	Default
printTextFont	Geneva
printTextStyle	plain
printTextSize	10
printTextAlign	left
printTextHeight	13
printMargins	0,0,0,0

Hide and Show Groups

There are two new commands for controlling the visibility of grouped text: **show groups** and **hide groups**. The **show groups** command causes all grouped text to be drawn with a two pixel tall gray underline. The **hide groups** command cancels this effect and causes grouped text to be drawn no differently than ungrouped text. These commands affect the drawing of all grouped text in all fields in all stacks until you quit HyperCard.

More Flexible Syntax for Sorting Cards

The syntax for sorting the cards of a stack is more flexible now.

The word "sort" can optionally be followed by "cards" or "stack" or"cards of stack" or "cards of this stack" or "this stack". So you can use forms like the following:

```
sort by field 1
sort this stack by field 1
sort cards of this stack by field 1
sort cards ascending by field 1
sort stack text by field 1
sort cards of stack by field 1
```

These optional words are intended solely to let you make your scripts more readable. They do not have any effect on the operation of the sort command.

Sort Container

The **sort** command now allows you to sort the lines or items of a container:

```
sort lines of field 1
sort items of field 1
sort field 1 — same as sort lines of field 1
sort items of it
```

Of course, sorting a container works with all the same options that sorting cards of a stack does:

```
sort lines of field 1 descending
sort lines of field 1 ascending numeric
sort items of field 1 dateTime
sort it numeric
```

If you don't specify lines or items, the default is lines. If you don't specify ascending or descending, the default is ascending (just as it is for sorting cards). If you don't specify text, numeric, international, or dateTime, the default is text (just as it is for sorting cards).

PROPERTIES

Except where noted, all of the following properties are global. Use the forms

```
get {the} [propertyName | propertyName of windowName ]
set {the} [propertyName | propertyName of windowName ] to value
```

All of these properties revert to their default values (if they exist) when you quit HyperCard.

hideIdle of [window "Message Watcher" | the Message Watcher] — holds a logical value that reflects whether the Message Watcher hides "idle" messages. When this value is true, the box labeled "Hide idle" on the Message Watcher window is checked. The default value is false. For details on the Message Watcher, see Chapter 2.

hideUnused of [window "Message Watcher" | the Message Watcher] — holds a logical value that reflects whether the Message Watcher hides unused messages. The default value is true. When this value is true, the box labeled "Hide unused messages" on the Message Watcher window is checked. For details on the Message Watcher, see Chapter 2.

loc{ation} of window *externalWindowName* — reflects the current location of the named external window. For details on the **location** property, see Chapter 10.

longWindowTitles — holds a logical value reflecting whether the name in the title bar of a card window shows the entire path name (true) or just the name of the current stack (false). An external window can also use this property to show just the name of the file appearing in the window or to show the file's full path name, depending on how the XCMD is written. The default value is false — only the stack (or file) name shows in the title bar.

printMargins — holds a comma-separated list of four numbers that specify the width of margins on a printed page. Used for reports and printed expressions, the four numbers that **printMargins** returns represent respectively the left, top, right, and bottom margins expressed in pixels. 72 pixels equals a margin of one inch. The default value is 0,0,0,0, which means that the smallest possible margin is used (as determined by other settings in your system).

printTextAlign — holds the value left, center, or right, reflecting how text aligns on the printed page of a report or of printed expressions. The default value is left.

printTextFont — reflects the name of font used for printing reports and expressions. The default value is Geneva.

printTextHeight — reflects the vertical space (in pixels) allowed for each line of text in a printed report or page of printed expression(s). (A pixel is about 1/72" high.) The default value is 13

printTextSize — reflects the height of a character in pixels for a printed report or page of printed expression(s). (A pixel is about 1/72" high.) The default value is 10.

printTextStyle — reflects the style of a character in a printed report or page of printed expression(s). The default style is plain.

scriptTextFont — reflects the style of characters for scripts on the display and on the printed page. The default font is Monaco.

scriptTextSize — reflects the height of characters for scripts as they appear on the display and on the printed page. The value represents pixels, each of which is about 1/72" high. The default value is 9.

visible of window *externalWindowName* — reflects whether an external window (including the Message Watcher window) is visible when it's within normally visible boundaries. For details on the **visible** property, see Chapter 10.

FUNCTIONS

number of windows — returns an integer reflecting the count of all existing windows, including ones that aren't visible. The minimum number that this function returns is 8. (Number of windows returns the same result as, but runs faster than, number of items in the windows.)

windows — returns a return-separated list of all existing windows, including built-in palettes, card windows, and external windows, in front-to-back order. The list always includes the following:

Message	Variable Watcher	FatBits
Tool	Message Watcher	<card window name(s)>
Pattern	Scroll	

MESSAGES

commandKeyDown — message sent whenever a command key combination is pressed from the keyboard. Each time a command key combination is pressed, HyperCard passes a single parameter reflecting the character that was typed. Use the following handler (in a card, background, or stack script) to experiment:

```
on commandKeydown whatKey
  put whatKey && charToNum(whatKey)
end commandKeyDown
```

keyDown — message sent whenever a character key is pressed from the keyboard. Each time a key is pressed, HyperCard passes a single parameter reflecting the character that was typed. Use the following handler (in a card, background, or stack script) to experiment:

```
on keydown whatKey
  put whatKey && charToNum(whatKey)
end keyDown
```

EXTERNALS

The following assembly language XFCN is a gift from Bill Atkinson, the father of HyperCard. The function tells you where a string should go in a sorted list (or, if the string is already in the list, where to find it).

You give the function two parameters: a search string plus a multiline expression that holds some sorted values (for example, a field containing an alphabetically sorted list of names). If the search string is in the expression, the function reports the line number that holds the string you're looking for; but if the search string is *not* in the expression, the function reports the line number (reported as a negative number) where the string should be inserted.

```
        CASE    ON
        SEG     'MatchLine'
        INCLUDE 'Traps.a'
        INCLUDE 'PackMacs.a'


MatchLine PROC  EXPORT
;- - - - - - - - - - - - - - - - - - - - - - - - - - - - - -
;
;   XFCN MatchLine(pattern,fieldStr)
;
;   searches for pattern string at start of a line in fieldStr
;   fieldStr input is already sorted alphabetically
;   if pattern is found, then returns the line number,
;   else returns the negative of the line number to insert before
;
;   to build:
;   directory {Boot}
;   asm -w MatchLine.a
;   link -o {boot}TestMatchLine -rt XFCN=0 MatchLine.a.o
;
;   Offsets in an XCmdBlock record:
```

```
;
paramCount        EQU       0
params            EQU       2
returnValue       EQU       66

tempStr           EQU       -256        ;temp string
varsize           EQU       tempStr     ;total locals

         MOVE.L   (SP)+,D0              ;pop return address
         MOVE.L   (SP)+,A1              ;pop cmdBlock Ptr
         MOVE.L   D0,-(SP)              ;push return address
         LINK     A6,#varsize          ;allocate room
         MOVEM.L  A2-A5,-(SP)           ;save registers
         MOVE.L   A1,A5                 ;stash cmdBlock ptr
         MOVE.L   #0,D2                 ;init line number
         CMP.W    #2,paramCount(A5)     ;is paramCount 2 ?
         BNE.S    NOTFOUND              ;oops, return zero
         MOVE.L   params(A5),A2         ;param1 handle = pattern
         MOVE.L   (A2),A2               ;de-reference for srcPtr
         MOVE.L   params+4(A5),A3       ;param2 handle = fieldStr
         MOVE.L   (A3),A3               ;de-reference for dstPtr
         LEA      LCTable,A4            ;point to lowercase table
         MOVEQ    #0,D0                 ;get ready for bytes
         MOVEQ    #0,D1                 ;get ready for bytes
         BRA.S    LINESTRT              ;go to loop start
;
;   skip to start of a line
;
SKIPLINE CMP.B    #13,(A3)+             ;dst char > than return?
         BHI.S    SKIPLINE              ;yes, keep looking
         BEQ.S    LINESTRT              ;branch if line start
         TST.B    -1(A3)                ;was it the terminator?
         BNE.S    SKIPLINE              ;no, reject weird chars
         ADD.L    #1,D2                 ;yes, bump lineCount
         BRA.S    NOTFOUND              ;and quit
;
; now we are at the start of a line, see if pattern matches
```

```
;
LINESTRT ADD.L     #1,D2                  ;increment line number
         MOVE.L    A2,A0                  ;copy srcPtr
         MOVE.L    A3,A1                  ;copy dstPtr
NEXTSRC  MOVE.B    (A0)+,D0               ;get src char
         BEQ.S     FOUND                  ;return true if end of src
         MOVE.B    (A1)+,D1               ;get dst character
         BEQ.S     NOTFOUND               ;not found if dst end
         MOVE.B    0(A4,D0),D0            ;get LC(src)
         CMP.B     0(A4,D1),D0            ;is LC(dst) = LC(src) ?
         BEQ.S     NEXTSRC                ;yes, continue match
         BHI.S     SKIPLINE               ;next line

NOTFOUND NEG.L     D2                     ;return neg num
FOUND    MOVE.L    D2,D0                  ;get the number
         LEA       tempStr(A6),A0         ;point to temp string
         _NumToString                     ;convert to text

         MOVE.L    #16,D0                 ;byteCount
         _NewHandle                        ;allocate a handle
         MOVE.L    A0,returnValue(A5)     ;put in returnValue
         MOVE.L    (A0),A1                ;de-reference handle
         LEA       tempStr(A6),A0         ;point to temp string
         MOVE.B    (A0)+,D1               ;get length byte
         BRA.S     START                  ;to to start of loop
LOOP     MOVE.B    (A0)+,(A1)+            ;copy a character
START    DBRA      D1,LOOP                ;loop all chars
         MOVE.B    #0,(A1)+               ;then zero terminate
         MOVEM.L   (SP)+,A2-A5            ;restore registers
         UNLK      A6                     ;release stack frame
         RTS                              ;return to caller
```

```
;---------------------------
;
;  256 byte lower casing table
;
LCTable   DC.L      $00010203,$04050607,$08090A0B,$0C0D0E0F
          DC.L      $10111213,$14151617,$18191A1B,$1C1D1E1F
          DC.L      $20212223,$24252627,$28292A2B,$2C2D2E2F
          DC.L      $30313233,$34353637,$38393A3B,$3C3D3E3F
          DC.L      $40616263,$64656667,$68696A6B,$6C6D6E6F
          DC.L      $70717273,$74757677,$78797A5B,$5C5D5E5F
          DC.L      $60616263,$64656667,$68696A6B,$6C6D6E6F
          DC.L      $70717273,$74757677,$78797A7B,$7C7D7E7F
          DC.L      $61616365,$6E6F7561,$61616161,$61636565
          DC.L      $65656969,$69696E6F,$6F6F6F6F,$75757575
          DC.L      $A0A1A2A3,$A4A5A6A7,$A8A9AAAB,$ACAD616F
          DC.L      $B0B1B2B3,$B4B5B6B7,$B8B9BA61,$6FBD616F
          DC.L      $C0C1C2C3,$C405C6C7,$C8C9CA61,$616F6F6F
          DC.L      $D0D1D2D3,$D4D5D6D7,$7979DADB,$DCDDDEDF
          DC.L      $E0E1E2E3,$E4616561,$65656969,$69696F6F
          DC.L      $F06F7575,$75F5F6F7,$F8F9FAFB,$FCFDFEFF


          END
```

MISCELLANEOUS

- When you try to launch an application under MultiFinder and the launch fails, the **open** command sets the result. The result will hold "Out of memory." or "Couldn't open that application."

- In visual effects, "fast" is no longer the same as "very fast." "Very fast" means "as fast as the machine can go," while "fast" now means "twice as fast as normal." Of all the speeds, only "very fast" should produce different results on different CPUs.

- To get a return-separated list of all items in a given menu, use *menuName* as an expression:

```
put menu "Utilities" into field "Menu Items"
```

Glossary

This glossary provides a definition for most conceptual terms specific to HyperTalk. For a summary definition of every HyperTalk native vocabulary word, plus a reference to the page where you can find more detailed information, see the Quick Dictionary (Appendix E).

Ampersand — The concatenation operator (&) used to join together two or more strings.

Anomaly — An unusual deviation from some otherwise consistent way of behaving. HyperTalk's way of providing you with an opportunity for growth through adversity. ("We're only doing this for you.")

Argument — Value upon which a function operates.

ASCII — Acronym for American Standard Code for Information Interchange, a system whereby a specific integer represents a text character or special code. See Appendix A for a list of these codes.

Bug — A programming or scripting error. HyperTalk has no bugs; it does, however, have a number of anomalies and heretofore undocumented features.

Caller — That which summons. For example, if Handler A sends the message doSomething (causing the doSomething handler to execute), then Handler A is the caller of the doSomething handler.

Character — Fundamental unit of any source; a single ASCII character.

Chunk — Portion of value. A chunk of any container is itself a container.

Command message — A message that makes HyperCard do something if it gets all the way through the message passing path.

Command — An instruction to HyperCard to do something.

Comment — Any information between the double-dash (--) and the end of a line within any handler, or any text in a script that's not part of a handler. HyperTalk ignores comments; they're strictly for the use of the scripter.

Concatenation — Joining of two string values; process by which two or more strings are joined together through the use of the concatenation operator (&).

Constant — A value that doesn't change (e.g. one, two, etc.); symbolic name representing a value (e.g., pi).

Container — That which holds information supplied either by a scripter or an end-user. HyperTalk's containers are fields, variables, the Selection, the Message box, and chunks of containers.

Control structure — A set of keywords at the top and bottom (and sometimes within the body) of a statement list, which define the order of execution of statements within that list.

CR — Carriage return; shorthand for "press the Return key."

Current — Referring to the card, background, or stack in use now.

Deselect — To unhilite a selection; to remove the insertion point from the Message box or a field.

Dialog — Dialog box; any box (other than the Message box) on the display that solicits and/or presents information, so-called because the user must respond to the box (that is, complete a dialog) before anything else can happen.

Domain — Sphere of influence (e.g, all the cards belonging to a given background are said to be in that background's domain); sphere in which positional numbers operate.

Dynamic path — Message passing path that a message traverses if the current card is different from the card that the handler that sent the message is defined on.

Empty — String of length 0; the null string; holding no value.

Empty script — A script with no code in it.

Error dialog — Dialog from HyperCard indicating a scripting error.

Evaluate — To determine the value of.

Execute — To activate. To execute a handler is to send all the messages in that handler, insofar as the control structures within that handler allow.

Expression — Any value; any group of values, sources of value, and operators meant to be taken as a whole.

External — A vocabulary word not native to HyperTalk but added as a resource through the HyperCard external Interface. HyperCard allows external commands (resource type XCMD) and external functions (resource type XFCN).

Factor — The first fully resolvable portion of an expression.

Feature — Everything this book talks about (except in bug boxes). Also: a bug that the language designer decides not to fix.

File — Named collection of information that resides on a disk.

Formatting — The way that text appears in a script or that numbers appear in a visible container.

Function call — Use of a function to get a value.

Function handler — A user-defined function.

Function — HyperTalk vocabulary word that calculates and returns a value.

Geometric — Adjective applied to an operator that determines whether a point is within the area of a rectangle; the operators **is within** and **is not within.**

Global coordinate — coordinate relative to the screen (as opposed to **local coordinate,** which is relative to the card).

Global variable — Variable whose value is available throughout HyperCard until you quit the program (as opposed to **local variable,** available only in the handler that created it).

Handler — Named group of HyperTalk statements beginning with an **on** or **function** statement and ending with an **end** statement. The handler is the basic HyperTalk structure.

HyperTalk — The object-oriented scripting language that automates HyperCard.

Inheritance path — see **message passing path**

Initialize — To create a variable; to give a variable its first value.

Integer — Whole number; number with no fractional part.

It — Local variable automatically initialized by the **get, answer, ask,** and (sometimes) **convert** commands.

Item — Designator for a chunk whose text is separated by commas.

Iteration — Repetition. Repetition. Repetition.

Keyword — Vocabulary word interpreted directly by HyperTalk. Keywords don't traverse the message passing path.

Layer — Plane of a field or button among all buttons and fields, either background or card, which can be changed with the Bring Closer and Send Farther menu commands; position of a given button among all buttons or fields, relative to the front and reflected in that button's or field's number.

Line continuation character — The character produced by pressing option-Return while a script is open (¬). This character lets you break a single long line into an arbitrary number of shorter segments.

Line — In a script, a single HyperTalk statement comprised of all text from the first non-space character at the left edge of the screen to the first return character (ASCII 13); in a container, the chunk between return characters (or between the start of the container and the first return character, or between the last return character and the final character in the container). The text starts with a comment delimiter (--) or a message name; the rest of the text is either the body of the comment or the parameters to the message name.

Literal — Anything taken at face value; a group of characters to be taken for their actual, as opposed to symbolic, value.

Local coordinate — coordinate relative to the card (as opposed to **global coordinate**, which is relative to the screen).

Local variable — Variable whose existence ceases when the current handler finishes execution (as opposed to **global variable**, whose value is available throughout HyperCard until you quit HyperCard).

Logical — Kind of operation resulting in the value "true" or "false"; kind of operator (**and, or**) used to produce a logical result.

Me — HyperTalk vocabulary word that refers to the object containing the currently running handler.

Message handler — Handler whose statements execute when it catches a message with the same name.

Message — Any statement that traverses the message passing path.

Message passing path — Placement of objects that governs the order in which those objects are given the opportunity to respond to a message. A message passing path can be **static** or **dynamic**.

Native vocabulary word — a HyperTalk word; a word that HyperCard understands.

Non-white character — any printable character except the space character (ASCII 32, created by pressing the space bar).

Null string — String with no characters; the value of the expression ""; empty.

Numeric — Having a value comprised entirely of digits and (optionally) a decimal point and/or a minus sign.

Object — HyperCard unit capable of sending and receiving messages.

Object-oriented — type of computer language in which programming modules are associated with individual objects. In other types of computer language, all modules are part of a single linear program

Operand — An expression upon which an operator performs some action.

Operator — A symbol or word that changes the value of a single operand, or that combines two operands to produce a single result.

Ordinal — The positional constants **first** through **tenth,** plus the special words **any, middle** (or **mid**), or **last.**

Parameter variable — Local variable in a handler that receives the value of a passed parameter.

Parameter — Value that was passed to a handler.

Pass — To transfer from one handler to another when speaking of values or parameters; to put back on the message passing path when speaking of a message.

Path name — see **search path.**

Positional number — An object's position in its domain.

Precedence — Order of execution.

Property — Attribute of an object or window.

Quoted literal — Anything that appears between pairs of double quotation marks (").

Recursion — Condition in which a handler calls itself.

Region — Geometric area expressed in pixels that defines the space of an object.

Relational — Kind of operation in which two values are compared, resulting in the value "true" or "false"; kind of operator ($>$,$<$,$<>$,$\geq$,$\leq$, $=$,$\neq$, etc.) used to compare two values.

Resource — one of two forks that make up every Macintosh file. (The other fork is called the Data fork.) All externals, fonts, sounds, and icons reside in a file's resource fork.

Return — to evaluate an expression and pass its value to the calling function. As a noun, it refers to the Return key.

SANE — Acronym for Standard Apple Numerics Environment, a set of arithmetic routines common to all Apple Computers that guarantee the accuracy of computations.

Script editor — Editor that allows you to construct and modify HyperTalk scripts.

Script — Collection of handlers and comments associated with a particular object.

Search path — Path a program follows to find a particular file. A full search path begins with the name of a disk and includes the names of all folders in nesting order down to the file itself. Each item is separated from its neighbors by a colon (as in "My Hard Disk:HyperCard Stacks:My Creations:The Sought Stack").

Selection — Currently selected text; the insertion point.

Sending order — Order in which HyperCard sends system messages when it sends more than one.

Source — Source of any value (i.e. functions, properties, literals, constants, variables, containers).

Standard file dialog — Dialog from which you choose a file. Standard file dialogs usually list only files that are appropriate for a given operation (e.g., just stacks).

Statement list — Group of statements separated by return characters. Statements outside of control structures are meant to execute in the order listed; statements within control structures operate within the specifications of the keywords that frame that structure.

Statement — Any single valid line of HyperTalk code consisting of a keyword or message name and any accompanying parameters.

Static path — Message passing path that a message traverses while the current card is the card that the handler which sent the message is defined on.

String — Collection of characters.

System message — Message sent by HyperCard to announce that some event has occurred or is about to occur.

Target — Object to which a specific message is first sent.

TextEdit — The simple word processor built into the Macintosh's operating system.

Translator — Filter through which a script is passed before and after it's displayed. It was originally designed to let non-English speaking scripters edit scripts in their native language; but clever hackers are finding new ways to use this feature. (See Chapter 15.)

Unquoted literal — Literal that doesn't appear between pairs of double quotation marks (""").

User-defined message — Message created by user, as opposed to one native to HyperCard.

Variable — User-created invisible container that resides in memory and whose existence ends when a handler stops running (**local variable**) or when you quit HyperCard (**global variable**).

Windoid — The message box, or the Tool or Pattern windows after they've been torn off the menu bar or any palette. Pseudo-window from off-planet.

Word — Chunk of a container delimited by spaces.

WYSIWIG — Acronym for "What you see is what you get," meaning that what you see on the screen is what you get on paper when you print a document.

XCMD — The resource type for, and popular name given to, an external command.

XFCN — The resource type for, and popular name given to, an external function.

Index